# ELIEZER BEN HYRCANUS

THE TRADITION AND THE MAN

PART ONE

# STUDIES IN JUDAISM IN LATE ANTIQUITY

*FROM THE FIRST TO THE SEVENTH CENTURY*

EDITED BY

JACOB NEUSNER

VOLUME THREE

## ELIEZER BEN HYRCANUS
### THE TRADITION AND THE MAN

PART ONE

LEIDEN
E. J. BRILL
1973

# ELIEZER BEN HYRCANUS

## THE TRADITION AND THE MAN

BY

JACOB NEUSNER
Professor of Religious Studies
Brown University

PART ONE

## THE TRADITION

LEIDEN
E. J. BRILL
1973

ISBN 90 04 03753 5



PRINTED IN THE NETHERLANDS

*For Saul Lieberman*
*in homage*

# TABLE OF CONTENTS

## PART ONE


Preface . . . . . . . . . . . . . . . . . . . . . . . . . . xiii
Foreword . . . . . . . . . . . . . . . . . . . . . . . . . xv
List of Abbreviations . . . . . . . . . . . . . . . . . . xvii
Transliterations . . . . . . . . . . . . . . . . . . . . . xviii


## THE TRADITION


I. Introduction . . . . . . . . . . . . . . . . . . . . . 1
i. Locating the Traditions about Eliezer b. Hyrcanus 1
ii. Texts Consulted . . . . . . . . . . . . . . . 14
iii. Purpose of the Comments . . . . . . . . . . . 16

II. The Legal Traditions . . . . . . . . . . . . . . . 18
i. Berakhot . . . . . . . . . . . . . . . . . . . . 18
ii. Pe'ah . . . . . . . . . . . . . . . . . . . . . 34
iii. Demai . . . . . . . . . . . . . . . . . . . . . 36
iv. Kila'im . . . . . . . . . . . . . . . . . . . . 38
v. Shevi'it . . . . . . . . . . . . . . . . . . . . 39
vi. Terumot . . . . . . . . . . . . . . . . . . . . 45
vii. Ma'aserot . . . . . . . . . . . . . . . . . . . 70
viii. Ma'aser Sheni . . . . . . . . . . . . . . . . 72
ix. Ḥallah . . . . . . . . . . . . . . . . . . . . . 76
x. 'Orlah . . . . . . . . . . . . . . . . . . . . . 82
xi. Bikkurim . . . . . . . . . . . . . . . . . . . . 84
xii. Shabbat . . . . . . . . . . . . . . . . . . . . 85
xiii. 'Eruvin . . . . . . . . . . . . . . . . . . . 100
xiv. Pesaḥim . . . . . . . . . . . . . . . . . . . . 117
xv. Sheqalim . . . . . . . . . . . . . . . . . . . . 135
xvi. Yoma, Sukkah, Beṣah . . . . . . . . . . . . . 138
xvii. Rosh HaShanah, Ta'anit, Megillah, Mo'ed Qaṭan, Ḥagigah . . . . . . . . . . . . . . . . . . . . . 154
xviii. Yevamot . . . . . . . . . . . . . . . . . . . 163
xix. Ketuvot . . . . . . . . . . . . . . . . . . . . 181
xx. Nedarim, Nazir, Soṭah . . . . . . . . . . . . . 185
xxi. Giṭṭin, Qiddushin . . . . . . . . . . . . . . 204

xxii. Bava Qamma, Bava Meṣi'a', Bava Batra . . . . . 211
xxiii. Sanhedrin, Makkot, Shavu'ot, 'Avodah Zarah, Horayot . . . . . . . . . . . . . . . . . . . . 217
xxiv. Zevaḥim, Menaḥot . . . . . . . . . . . . . 222
xxv. Ḥullin, Bekhorot, 'Arakhin. . . . . . . . . . . 246
xxvi. Temurah, Keritot, Me'ilah, Tamid . . . . . . . 252
xxvii. Kelim . . . . . . . . . . . . . . . . . . . 276
xxviii. Ohalot, Nega'im . . . . . . . . . . . . . 287
xxix. Parah . . . . . . . . . . . . . . . . . . 302
xxx. Ṭoharot, Miqva'ot . . . . . . . . . . . . . 315
xxxi. Niddah . . . . . . . . . . . . . . . . . 323
xxxii. Makhshirin, Zabim, Yadaim, 'Uqṣin . . . . . . . 330
xxxiii. 'Eduyyot . . . . . . . . . . . . . . . . 337
Appendix to Chapter Two: Legal Pericopae Not Demonstrably Part of the Traditions about Eliezer ben Hyrcanus 346

III. Historical and Biographical Traditions. Wisdom Sayings . 394

IV. Exegetical and Theological Traditions . . . . . . . . 453

PART TWO

List of Abbreviations
Transliterations

## ANALYSIS OF THE TRADITION

V. The Tradition as a Whole . . . . . . . . . . . . . . . . . 1

VI. Forms . . . . . . . . . . . . . . . . . . . . 18
i. The Forms of Eliezer's Tradition . . . . . . . . . . . 18
ii. Forms and Particular Masters. . . . . . . . . . . . 31
iii. History of Forms. . . . . . . . . . . . . . . . 32
iv. Form (C) . . . . . . . . . . . . . . . . . . . 39
v. The Houses and Yoḥanan ben Zakkai and "The Mishnah" before 70 . . . . . . . . . . . . . . . . . . . 44
vi. Eliezer b. Hyrcanus and "The Mishnah" before 70 . . . . . 49
vii. Collections of Traditions . . . . . . . . . . . . . 53
viii. Conclusion . . . . . . . . . . . . . . . . . . 60

VII. Attestations. . . . . . . . . . . . . . . . . . . 63
i. Survey of Attested Pericopae. . . . . . . . . . . . 63
ii. Chains of Traditions . . . . . . . . . . . . . . . 73
iii. Suppressed Traditions. . . . . . . . . . . . . . . 82
iv. Other References to the Formation and Transmission of Eliezer's Traditions. . . . . . . . . . . . . . . . . 85
v. Conclusion . . . . . . . . . . . . . . . . . . . 87

VIII. The Best Traditions . . . . . 92
i. Yavnean Attestations . . . . . 92
ii. The Laws . . . . . 95
iii. Eliezer's Attestations of Houses' Disputes . . . . . 115
iv. Eliezer and the Traditions about pre-70 Masters . . . . . 118
v. Eliezer and the Traditions about Yoḥanan b. Zakkai . . . . 119
vi. Yavnean Chains of Traditions . . . . . 120
vii. Judah b. Ilai's Traditions . . . . . 124
viii. The Earliest Eliezer. . . . . 129

IX. The Better Traditions . . . . . 143
i. The ʿAqiban Eliezer . . . . . 143
ii. The Laws . . . . . 144
iii. The Chains . . . . . 158
iv. The Ushan Eliezer and Yoḥanan b. Zakkai. The Houses . . . 160
v. The Better Traditions . . . . . 167

X. The Fair Traditions . . . . . 170
i. Attestations of the Circle of Judah the Patriarch . . . . . . 170
ii. Pericopae First Attested by Appearance in Mishnah-Tosefta . 172
iii. The Authenticity of Pericopae First Appearing in Mishnah-Tosefta . . . . . 200

XI. Suppressed Traditions . . . . . 205
i. Definition . . . . . 205
ii. The Laws . . . . . 206
iii. Sayings about the Value of Eliezer's Traditions. . . . . . . 219
iv. Conclusion . . . . . 223

XII. The Poor Traditions . . . . . 225
i. Definition and Criteria . . . . . 225
ii. Traditions First Appearing in Tannaitic Exegetical Compilations 226
iii. The Tannaitic Stratum of the *Gemarot* . . . . . 233
iv. Amoraic and Later Contributions to the Traditions about Eliezer . . . . . 236
v. Conclusion . . . . . 243

## THE MAN

XIII. Earlier Views of Eliezer ben Hyrcanus . . . . . 249
i. Introduction . . . . . 249
ii. Compilations of Stories and Sayings. . . . . 250
iii. Special Studies . . . . . 255
iv. Ben Zion Bokser and Louis Finkelstein . . . . . 259
v. Alexander Guttmann . . . . . 263
vi. Yitzhak D. Gilat . . . . . 265
vii. The Eliezer of History and the Eliezer of Biography . . . . . 277

XIV. The Eliezer of History . . . . . 287
i. Introduction . . . . . 287
ii. Origins, Early Life, Education . . . . . 294

iii. Eliezer's Active Career . . . . . . . . . . . . . . . . . . 296
iv. Eliezer's Historical Situation, Pharisaism and Rabbinism . . . 298
v. Eliezer and the Houses . . . . . . . . . . . . . . . . . 307
vi. Eliezer and the Old Law . . . . . . . . . . . . . . . . 310
vii. Eliezer's Own Contribution. . . . . . . . . . . . . . . . 316
viii. The Application of Eliezer's Law. . . . . . . . . . . . . 322
ix. Eliezer's Program for Yavneh . . . . . . . . . . . . . 325
x. Eliezer and the Christians . . . . . . . . . . . . . . . 330

XV. The Eliezer of Tradition . . . . . . . . . . . . . . . . . 335
i. Introduction . . . . . . . . . . . . . . . . . . . . . 335
ii. Origins, Early Life, Education . . . . . . . . . . . . . 343
iii. Eliezer's Active Career . . . . . . . . . . . . . . . . . 346
iv. Eliezer's Historical Situation. Pharisaism and Rabbinism . . . 347
v. Eliezer and the Houses . . . . . . . . . . . . . . . . . 351
vi. Eliezer and the Old Law . . . . . . . . . . . . . . . . 352
vii. Eliezer's Own Contribution . . . . . . . . . . . . . . . 356
viii. The Application of Eliezer's Law. . . . . . . . . . . . . 361
ix. Eliezer's Program for Yavneh . . . . . . . . . . . . . 365
x. Eliezer and the Christians . . . . . . . . . . . . . . . 365
xi. Forms and the Formation of Traditions about Eliezer . . . . 367
xii. The Formation of the *Eliezer + Sages*-Type of Tradition. . . 368
xiii. The Formation of the *Eliezer + Named Master*-Type of Tradition . . . . . . . . . . . . . . . . . . . . . . 371
xiv. The Distribution of Traditions from Identifiable Sources. . . 377
xv. Eliezer and the Tannaim (1): Yavneh . . . . . . . . . . 384
xvi. Eliezer and the Tannaim (2): Usha . . . . . . . . . . . 385
xvii. Conclusion . . . . . . . . . . . . . . . . . . . . . . 386

XVI. Eliezer's Exegeses . . . . . . . . . . . . . . . . . . . . 387
i. Introduction . . . . . . . . . . . . . . . . . . . . . 387
ii. Legal Exegeses. . . . . . . . . . . . . . . . . . . . . 387
iii. Plain *vs.* Fanciful Interpretations . . . . . . . . . . . 392
iv. Techniques of Exegesis . . . . . . . . . . . . . . . . 394
v. Redactional Devices . . . . . . . . . . . . . . . . . . 396
vi. Conclusion . . . . . . . . . . . . . . . . . . . . . . 397

XVII. The Eliezer of Legend . . . . . . . . . . . . . . . . . . . 399
i. Introduction. Eliezer and the Amoraim . . . . . . . . . 399
ii. Origins, Early Life, Education . . . . . . . . . . . . . 403
iii. Eliezer's Active Career. Eliezer and Hillel . . . . . . . . 407
iv. Eliezer's Historical Situation . . . . . . . . . . . . . . 416

Appendix I: G. S. Aleksandrov. *The Role of ʿAqiba in the Bar Kokhba Rebellion.* Translated by Sam Driver . . . . . . . . . . . . . . . . . . 422
Appendix II: *Development of a Legend. Studies on the Traditions Concerning Yoḥanan ben Zakkai*: Corrections, Revisions, and Reconsiderations . . . . . 437

Indices. . . . . . . . . . . . . . . . . . . . . . . . . . . . . 459

# PREFACE

I offer this study in homage to Professor Saul Lieberman, in whose classroom I was privileged to sit between 1958 and 1960, for in my studies about Yoḥanan b. Zakkai, the rabbinic traditions about the Pharisees before 70, and now about Eliezer b. Hyrcanus, scarcely a day has passed without some reference to his *Tosefta Kifshuṭah* and *Tosefet Rishonim*. It is not my place to praise his work, but by dedicating these volumes to him, I hope to pay respect and express gratitude to the man who has given so much. I deem it a privilege and an honor that he has permitted me to do so.

My teacher Morton Smith continues to provide gracious criticism. Conversations and correspondence throughout the composition of this work were a source not only of improvement, but of inspiration. While he bears no responsibility whatever for the limitations of his student, such clarity of thought and of expression as I have been able to achieve is to his credit. If I have been able to formulate and solve significant problems, it was because of his counsel, but, even more, because of his example.

I take pleasure, too, in frequent conversations with Professor Abraham Sachs, whose keen and probing questions show me not only the inadequacy of my conceptions, but the way to reconsider fundamental issues. My dear colleagues, Professor Horst R. Moehring and Ernest S. Frerichs, kindly read and criticized the manuscript at each stage in its development. My students at Brown University have also read the manuscript and provided valuable criticism. Dr. David Goodblatt, Rabbi Baruch Bokser, Rabbi Shamai Kanter, Dr. Robert Goldenberg, Dr. Gary G. Porton, Mr. William Scott Green, Mr. Joel Gereboff, Mr. Charles Primus, all won their teacher's gratitude. Mr. Green generously helped with the proofs.

Brown University paid the formidable costs of typing the manuscript and preparing the indices. Mrs. Marion Craven carefully typed the book in several drafts. Mr. Arthur Woodman prepared the indices. To all I express sincere thanks. To Brown University I am especially grateful for a summer research stipend in 1972. My publisher, E. J. Brill, and its director, Dr. F. C. Wieder, Jr., make possible the presentation of scholarly results in elegant form. Without Brill I could not contemplate such an undertaking as this.

My wife, Suzanne, and our sons, Samuel Aaron, Eli Ephraim, and Noam Mordecai Menahem, share in the pleasure of my work. Now that the newest generation is progressing in its Judaic studies, I may express the hope that in time to come they will read these books and know that, when I was writing them, they made each day a happy one.

The work is completed on my fortieth birthday.

J. N.

Providence, Rhode Island
28 July 1972
17 Av 5732
ערב שבת עקב

# FOREWORD

This work continues the inquiry into the history of the rabbinic tradition in late antiquity begun with *Development of a Legend: Studies on the Traditions Concerning Yoḥanan ben Zakkai* (Leiden, 1970: E. J. Brill. *Studia Post Biblica Volumen Sextum Decimum*), and continued in *The Rabbinic Traditions about the Pharisees before 70. I. The Masters. II. The Houses. III. Conclusions* (Leiden, 1971: E. J. Brill). Its problem is to trace the development of a sample body of rabbinic tradition, to analyze the literary traits of the various sayings and stories, to see whether we can locate characteristic techniques, forms, and tendencies in the formation of various sorts of materials—in all, to develop a form-critical structure and system. At the end are offered some firm conclusions on the historical Eliezer b. Hyrcanus.

Until now students of rabbinic literature have routinely assigned pretty much equal historical value to all sources, without regard to the date of the compilation or collection in which they appear. Exceptions to the rule are episodic, never systematic. Thus a story first occurring in a compilation of midrashim attested at the earliest in the fourteenth century and one first found in Tosefta have generally been given equal weight. Further, it has always been taken for granted that we deal with an essentially consistent, unitary tradition. Therefore all stories must be brought, or forced, into agreement with one another. Differences of viewpoint or of emphasis, where they are even recognized—and this was primarily in the legal, not in the biographical or theological-exegetical materials—have been bypassed or ignored or harmonized. At no point was the question raised, Is it possible that several groups, even in the time of the single master under discussion, had several different opinions about him, not to mention traditions in his name? Just as the texts—e.g., Mishnah, Tosefta—were seen as essentially unitary documents, so the stories and sayings told about, or attributed to, a given authority were taken for granted to be essentially unitary accounts, consistent traditions, from undifferentiated sources or authorities.

In *Development of a Legend* to my knowledge for the first time, I undertook to show by comparison of the forms and versions of all the stories told about one master, that materials found in a document close to his life and times are apt to be historically more reliable than what first occurs in a document attested only long afterward. The traditions about Yoḥanan ben Zakkai are not substantial, however, and while the comparison of the several versions of each story or saying often revealed what seemed to be later emendations, omissions, or additions, yet the total result was limited.

In *The Rabbinic Traditions about the Pharisees before 70* I carried the study much further, first, by pointing out that a saying may be shown to have been known to an authority before its occurrence in a later document. Consideration of such attestations, proposed in *Phar.* III, pp. 180-238, resulted in the division of the rabbinic traditions about the Pharisees into the legal sayings attributed to the Houses, the themes of which often are first attested in Yavneh, and stories about specific, named masters as well as legal materials attributed to them, first known in later times, beginning with the Ushan stratum. It further appeared that the historiographical traditions about the pre-70 Pharisees came to the fore in Ushan times and proved astonishingly pertinent to the theological and political situation of Usha itself.

A second important result was the effort to propose a theory of the history of fixed forms for the formulation and transmission of traditions.

In the present work I have attempted to refine the methods developed in the former studies, both by reconsidering earlier results, and by developing, through the application to new, and more complex materials, the approaches employed in the earlier studies. The traditions about Eliezer b. Hyrcanus proved extremely complicated and demanded the revision and refinement of all former procedures. They represent the first really substantial body of attested materials on an individual master. In quantity they far exceed the whole of the rabbinic traditions about pre-70 masters and are nearly equal to those traditions as well as the ones about the Houses of Shammai and Hillel. In quality they bring us to a quite new situation, in which we have some idea of how traditions were handed on, when and where they were shaped, and what influences affected their formation.

Eliezer b. Hyrcanus stands, along with Joshua b. Ḥananiah, as the first major figure after 70 *in the preserved materials.* From the other early Yavneans, for instance, Ṣaddoq and his son Eleazar, Ṭarfon, as well as those who, beside Eliezer and Joshua, are said to have been disciples of Yoḥanan b. Zakkai—Yosi the Priest, Eleazar b. ʿArakh, and Simeon b. Nathanaʾel,—no important, independent traditions have come down to us. If Gamaliel was a youngster at the outset of the Yavnean period, then he cannot represent the situation in the very beginning. Eliezer's traditions exceed in quantity and in originality those assigned to Joshua; and Joshua's materials stand close, in many respects, to ʿAqiba's. So with Eliezer we begin the study of the foundations of the Yavnean period in the history of Judaism—that is to say, the foundation of rabbinic Judaism as a whole.

My students are undertaking comparable studies of other early and middle Yavneans—Joshua, ʿAqiba, Ishmael, Eleazar b. ʿAzariah, Gamaliel and some minor figures—so that in time we shall have a clear picture of the first stages in the formation of the Yavnean stratum of rabbinic theology and law. When similar studies will have been made of the later, and finally, the last Yavneans, a critical history of the Yavnean period as a whole will become feasible.

It is not my intent, however, to work out further biographical studies at this time. I hope to turn to another aspect of the history of rabbinic Judaism in late antiquity, namely, the study of the history of a corpus of traditions defined by a common theme and independent of a single authority and of a limited historical and geographical setting. That project will require the consideration of a wholly new and different set of methodological problems from those presented by the study of a single historical figure. I intend the present work as a model, for the present, of rabbinic biography. Criticisms from co-workers, particularly of matters of detail and analysis, will be especially welcome as the work proceeds.

References to S. Lieberman, *Tosefta Kifshuṭah* and *Tosefet Rishonim,* are intended to call attention to important discussions of the content of pericopae and their broader implications for the study of Talmudic law. Since these discussions do not directly pertain to the historical and critical problems before us, I have not summarized them. At the same time, it seemed useful to make reference to more extensive treatments of the several pericopae than are given here.

# LIST OF ABBREVIATIONS

Ah. = Ahilot
Ant. = Josephus, *Antiquities*
Ar. = ʿArakhin
ARN = Avot deRabbi Natan
A.Z. = ʿAvodah Zarah
b. = Bavli, Babylonian Talmud
b. = ben
B.B. = Bava Batra
B.M. = Bava Meṣiʿaʾ
B.Q. = Bava Qamma
Ber. = Berakhot
Bes. = Beṣah
Bik. = Bikkurim
Dem. = Demaʾi
*Development* = *Development of a Legend. Studies on the Traditions Concerning Yoḥanan ben Zakkai* (Leiden, 1970)
Ed. = ʿEduyyot
Eruv. = ʿEruvin
Git. = Giṭṭin
Hag. = Ḥagigah
Hal. = Ḥallah
Halivni, *Meqorot* = David Weiss Halivni, *Meqorot uMesorot* (Tel Aviv, 1968)
Hor. = Horayot
Hul. = Ḥullin
Kel. = Kelim
Ker. = Keritot
Kil. = Kilaʾim
M. = Mishnah
M.Q. = Moʿed Qaṭan
M.S. = Maʿaser Sheni
M.T. = Midrash Tannaʾim
Ma. = Maʿaserot
Mak. = Makkot
Maksh = Makshirin
Me. = Meʿilah
Meg. = Megillah
Mekh. = Mekhilta
Men. = Menaḥot
Mid. = Middot
Miq. = Miqvaʾot
Naz. = Nazir
Ned. = Nedarim
Neg. = Negaʿim
Nez. = Nezirot
Nid. = Niddah
*Nusaḥ* = J. N. Epstein, *Introduction to the Text of the Mishnah* (*Mavo leNusaḥ HaMishnah* [Jerusalem, 1964])
Oh. = Ohalot
Orl. = ʿOrlah
Par. = Parah
Pes. = Pesaḥim
*Phar.* = *The Rabbinic Traditions about the Pharisees before 70* (Leiden, 1971), *I. The Masters. II. The Houses. III. Conclusions*
Qid. = Qiddushin
R. = Rabbi
Rabbi = Rabbi Judah the Patriarch
R.H. = Rosh Hashanah
Sanh. = Sanhedrin
Shab. = Shabbat
Shav. = Shavuʿot
Sheq. = Sheqalim
Shev. = Sheviʿit
Sot. = Soṭah
Suk. = Sukkah
Ta. = Taʿanit
*Tan.* = J. N. Epstein, *Introductions to Tannaitic Literature* (*Mevoʾot leSifrut HaTannaʾim* [Jerusalem, 1957])
Tem. = Temurah
Ter. = Terumot
Toh. = Ṭohorot
Tos. = Tosefta
T.Y. = Ṭevul Yom
Uqs. = ʿUqṣin
y. = Yerushalmi, Palestinian Talmud
Y.T. = Yom Ṭov
Yad. = Yadaim
Yev. = Yevamot
Zab. = Zabim
Zer. = Zeraʿim
Zev. = Zevaḥim

# TRANSLITERATIONS

| | | | |
|---|---|---|---|
| א | = ʼ | מ ם | = M |
| ב | = B | נ ן | = N |
| ג | = G | ס | = Ś |
| ד | = D | ע | = ʻ |
| ה | = H | פ | = P |
| ו | = W | צ ץ | = Ṣ |
| ז | = Z | ק | = Q |
| ח | = Ḥ | ר | = R |
| ט | = Ṭ | שׁ | = Š |
| י | = Y | שׂ | = S |
| כ ך | = K | ת | = T |
| ל | = L | | |

# THE TRADITION

CHAPTER ONE

# INTRODUCTION

## i. Locating the Traditions about Eliezer b. Hyrcanus

The traditions about Eliezer b. Hyrcanus occur in a literature which is fundamentally non-historical and non-biographical. Traces of some small, earlier "man-centered" collections can be found, including Eliezer's. But those which told of things the man said or did as such were never very important elements of the tradition or literature. The Mishnah of R. Meir was what he taught, not necessarily his original teachings or teachings original to him, and they certainly were not biographical. But while the literature is primarily concerned with law, and while it presents the law, on the whole, without much regard for individual authorities, the law must have come down through the minds of individuals and been shaped by each of them. It is likely to suppose that each individual's legal opinions were interrelated and formed—if not wholly consistent logically—a sort of system shaped by his tastes, prejudices, ideas, education, and interests. So to understand both history and the development of the law, one has to get at these individual systems, to get behind the impersonal reports of the literature to the historical-biographical reality it presents in discrete form. Here we shall attempt to locate, among those reports, the historical Eliezer b. Hyrcanus, the first important figure in rabbinic Judaism after 70 A.D.

Many Eliezer's lived in the land of Israel after 70 A.D., and not all of them were sons of Hyrcanus. But some of them, such as Eliezer b. Shammuʿa and Eliezer b. Jacob, occasionally entered Tannaitic tradition as *Eliezer*. And then there were the Eleazar's, beginning with Eleazar b. ʿArakh and Eleazar b. ʿAzariah, who produced the abbreviation Rʾ, which, when written out, as often yielded R. Eliezer as R. Eleazar—not to mention the Eliezer's and Eleazar's of the Amoraic stratum! How then to locate teachings indubitably belonging to the traditions about Eliezer b. Hyrcanus? We admittedly cannot locate with any degree of certainty *all* sayings attributed in Talmudic literature to Eliezer b. Hyrcanus, for we do not everywhere know which of many Eliezer's and Eleazar's and R''s is meant. We shall therefore have to suffice with the more modest claim that all traditions cited here are more or less reliably to be assigned to Eliezer b. Hyrcanus. To make such an accurate assignment, I shall offer one of five warrants for supposing a pericope to fall within Eliezer b. Hyrcanus's tradition.[1]

Such warrants will consist, first of an Eliezer's association, within the same pericope, with either a contemporary or a disciple of Eliezer b. Hyrcanus; or, second, of explicit reference by a rabbi to a pericope as belonging to Eliezer *b. Hyrcanus.*

A third warrant for assigning a pericope to our Eliezer is consistency of the legal opinion therein contained with the view of the House of Shammai. The tradition is clear that *sometimes* Eliezer b. Hyrcanus—and no other Eliezer or Eleazar—will rule like, or actually represent, the House of Shammai.

A fourth, most obvious warrant is consistency with opinions or principles already assigned to Eliezer b. Hyrcanus. If we find opinions involving Eliezer and sages, parallel to or consistent with rules stated by Eliezer in association with ʿAqiba or Gamaliel or Joshua, we assume this is the same Eliezer.

Fifth, and very common, if Ilai or Judah b. Ilai cites an Eliezer, we shall suppose that is Eliezer b. Hyrcanus, for the tradition is very firm that Ilai and his son preserve traditions of Eliezer b. Hyrcanus, and we have no reason to suppose they handed on traditions of any other Eliezer. Further, on occasion we shall find a ruling of Judah consistent with a ruling assigned to an Eliezer; where this is clear, I have supposed the Eliezer is ours.

None of these warrants is without its difficulties, and we probably are never on very firm ground in claiming Eliezer b. Hyrcanus is behind an Eliezer-tradition supposed, on these bases, to belong to our Eliezer. In the Appendix to Chapter Two I have further included those legal pericopae in Mishnah-Tosefta which are in the name of Eliezer—or, in some MSS, Eleazar—but not included in the traditions of Eliezer b. Hyrcanus according to our criteria. Other, non-legal sayings in the name of Eliezer/Eleazar have not been catalogued.

[1] Obviously a tradition in the name of an Eliezer which is, in another version, assigned to a specific Eliezer other than ours will not be taken into account. Thus the Eliezer of Mekhilta deR. Ishmael, Pisḥa 15 : 25-30 becomes Eliezer b. Jacob in Tos. Pis. 8 : 18, ed. Lieberman, p. 188, l. 65, so we need not speculate on Eliezer's view about the circumcision of slaves in respect to the partaking of the paschal lamb. In any event the MS readings will hardly support a firm choice of Eliezer b. Hyrcanus.

Obviously, these criteria will exclude materials that possibly belong to our Eliezer. But it is probability, not possibility, that must guide us. I find the MS evidence of some slight help. Where one of the five warrants led me to suppose our Eliezer was at hand, MSS *normally* read Eliezer. Where none of the warrants applies, MSS evidence will have Eleazar as often as Eliezer. This will be clear in a comparison of the evidences in the Appendix to Chapter Two with the pericopae given in Chapter Two.

In addition, an Eliezer called "the Great" or "the Elder" is taken to be ours, though, in all, the title seldom occurs in legal materials, and in the non-legal ones, it sometimes seems given to an Eliezer other than ours, or to be given in one version of a story and omitted in another version of the same story, which clearly seems to be about a different, later Eliezer.

A thorough account of the problem of confusion in readings of Eleazar/Eliezer, including Eleazar b. ʿAzariah, Eleazar b. Shammuʿa, and Eliezer b. Jacob, is given by Y. N. Epstein, *Mavo leNusaḥ HaMishnah* (Jerusalem and Tel Aviv, 1954[2]), Vol. II, pp. 1162-1182. Epstein cites not only MSS evidence, but also allusions to Mishnaic pericopae in the *Gemarot*, in other Talmudic literature, and in the commentaries and novellae of medieval and early modern times. He does not, however, pay much attention to consistencies of opinion from one pericope to another, on which basis I have assigned some ambiguous traditions to Eliezer b. Hyrcanus rather than to one of the other Eliezer's or Eleazar's. I have cited Epstein's reference to each of the Mishnaic passages under consideration, but have not copied his catalogues of readings and MSS evidence.

The following are the legal pericopae in which the masters associated with the named Eliezer are early Yavneans. These pericopae therefore seem to refer to Eliezer b. Hyrcanus:

A. *Eliezer vs. Gamaliel*

| | |
|---|---|
| 1. M. Hal. 4 : 7 | Liability of Syria to tithes. |
| 2. M. Bik. 2 : 6 (Tos. Shev. 4 : 21) | *Etrog* like tree. |

B. *Eliezer, Gamaliel, Sages*

| | |
|---|---|
| 1. M. Ber. 1 : 1 | Recite *Shemaʿ*. |
| 2. M. Git. 1 : 1 | Testimony of messenger re *geṭ*: both gloss anonymous law. |

C. *Houses of Shammai and Hillel + Eliezer*

| | |
|---|---|
| 1. M. Eruv. 1 : 2 | HKŠR MBWY |
| 2. M. Yev. 3 : 1 [Eleazar] | Four brothers married to four sisters. |
| 3. b. Yev. 80a | Eunuch at eighteen or twenty. |
| 4. b. Yev. 89b | Inheriting minor. |
| 5. Tos. Nid. 5 : 6 | |
| 6. M. Nid. 5 : 9 | |
| [7. M. Ed. 5 : 4-5 may be Eleazar] | |
| 8. Tos. Y.T. 1 : 1,3 | Egg born on festival—Eliezer glosses dispute. |

D. *Eliezer + Joshua juxtaposed but not opposed*

| | |
|---|---|
| 1. M. Ber. 1 : 2 | |
| 2. Tos. Ta. 2 : 5 | Fast on Ḥanukkah. |

E. *Eliezer vs. Joshua*

| | |
|---|---|
| 1. b. Ber. 2bA | Eliezer *vs.* Joshua; Meir *vs.* Judah, Ḥanina *vs. Aḥai, re Shema*ʿ. |
| 2. M. Shev. 5 : 3 | Rights of poor to fruits of Sabbatical years, + Tos. Shev. 4 : 3—Eliezer's opinion expanded. |
| 3-11. M. Ter. 4 : 7, 8, 9, 10, 11; Tos. Ter. 5 : 10-12 | Neutralizing Heave-offering—various principles + *ʿAqiba on Eliezer's side.* |
| 12-18. M. Ter. 8 : 1, 2, 3, 8, 9, 10, 11 | Completing an action begun with permission but discovered to be prohibited. |
| 19-20. M. Ter. 11 : 2, Tos. Ter. 9 : 8 | Non-priest drank date-honey etc.—how much to pay back? |
| 21. Tos. Ter. 9 : 9 | Make Heave-offering of grapes into wine, etc. |
| 22. M. Orl. 1 : 7 | Sap of *ʿorlah.* |
| 23. M. Shab. 12 : 4 | Scratching on flesh on Sabbath. (But Tos. Shab. 11 : 15 has *sages.*) |
| 24. M. Shab. 19 : 4 (Tos. Shab. 15 : 10, b. Shab. 137a) | Erred and circumcized on Sabbath when it was not eighth day after birth. |
| 25. Tos. Shab. 1 : 17 | "On that day." |
| 26. M. Eruv. 7 : 10 | *ʿEruv* with loaf *vs.* any kind of food. |
| 27. M. Bes. 1 : 7 | Burning doubtfully unclean Heave-offering of *ḥameṣ* with unclean. |
| 28. M. Pes. 6 : 5 (Tos. Pis. 5 : 4: Simeon) | Slaughter animal appropriate for Passover on Sabbath. |
| 29. Tos. Y.T. 3 : 2 | Animal + its offering in pit on festival. |

| | |
|---|---|
| 30. M. Ta. 1 : 1 | When do they add prayer for rain? |
| 31. y. M.Q. 3 : 5, b. M.Q. 21a | Mourner and *ṭefillin.* |
| 32. y. M.Q. 3 : 5 | When turn over beds as sign of mourning? |
| 33. Tos. Yev. 13 : 3-5 | *Ḥaliṣah* of minor—status of minor's marriage. |
| 34. b. Ket. 52a | Wife who is prohibited to benefit from husband is taken captive—is she ransomed? |
| 35. M. Sot. 1 : 1 | Witnesses required in warning wife. (Yosi b. R. Judah is authority for Eliezer's teaching—Tos. Sot. 1 : 1) |
| 36. M. Sot. 6 : 1 | Evidence that a woman has gone aside. |
| 37. M. Zev. 7 : 4 | Sacrifice *re* Whole-offering of bird. |
| 38. M. Men. 3 : 4 | Residue of meal-offering contracted uncleanness. |
| 39. M. Zev. 8 : 10 | Blood to be sprinkled four times mixed with blood to be sprinkled once. |
| 40. Tos. Men. 4 : 5-6 | Handful of meal *vs.* residue. |
| 41. M. Ar. 6 : 1 (Tos. Ar. 4 : 5 + Houses) | Dedicate goods and owe *Ketuvah.* |
| 42. M. Ker. 4 : 3 | Liability for two sins, without certainty as to which a man did. |
| 43. M. Kel. 14 : 7 | Purifying metal vessels. |
| 44. M. Kel. 17 : 1 | Hole in wooden vessels. |
| 45. M. Kel. 28 : 2 | *Cloth* used for other purposes. |
| 46. M. Oh. 2 : 4 | Stone that seals grave *re* uncleanness by carrying. |
| 47. M. Oh. 8 : 6 + Tos. Ah. 9 : 7 | Jars in house *re* tent. |
| 48. M. Oh. 9 : 15 | Tomb in rock. |
| 49. M. Oh. 12 : 3 | Projecting window-sill. |
| 50. M. Oh. 12 : 8 | Threshhold. |
| 51-52. M. Oh. 14 : 4-5 | Wall-projection. |
| 53. M. Oh. 17 : 2 | Grave-area. |
| 54. M. Par. 5 : 4 | Reed-pipe. |
| 55. M. Par. 9 : 4 | Intention to drink Sin-offering water. |
| 56. M. Par. 10 : 1 | Corpse-uncleanness in heifer-rite. |
| 57. M. Toh. 2 : 2 | Grades of uncleanness. |
| 58. M. Toh. 8 : 7 | Uncleanness on outer parts of vessels. |
| 59. M. Miq. 2 : 7 | Rain water in wine jars. |
| 60. M. Miq. 2 : 8 | Lime pot in cistern. |
| 61. M. Miq. 2 : 10 | Water and mud. |
| 62. M. Nid. 1 : 3 | Types of women who are unclean only from time of menstrual period. |

| | |
|---|---|
| 63. Tos. Nid. 2 : 3 | How long to breast-feed? |
| 64. M. Nid. 4 : 4 | How long have relief? |
| 65. M. Nid. 10 : 3 | *Zab* examined self and was clean on first and seventh day. |
| 66. Tos. Ed. 1 : 10 (M. Toh. 4 : 2) | Weasel and Heave-offering. |
| 67. M. Ed. 6 : 2, 3 (Eliezer *vs.* Joshua and Neḥunya) | Living being/corpse *and* flesh from limb from living being. |

F. *Eliezer vs. ʿAqiba*

| | |
|---|---|
| 1. M. Ber. 4 : 3 B + C | [Following Lieberman]. |
| 2. M. Ber. 5 : 2 | *Re* routine prayer. |
| 3. M. Peʾah 7 : 7 | Field wholly made up of defective clusters. |
| 4. M. Ter. 6 : 6, Tos. Ter. 7 : 9-10 | Repaying Heave-offering. |
| 5. M. Ma. 4 : 6 | Tithe caper bush. |
| 6. M. Hal. 2 : 1 | Produce from Palestine taken abroad *re Ḥallah.* |
| 7. M. Shab. 2 : 3 | Cloth for wick in Sabbaṭh lamp. |
| 8. M. Shab. 19 : 1 | Bringing instruments for circumcision on Sabbath. |
| 9. M. Pes. 6 : 1-2 | Appurtenances of Passover on Sabbath. |
| 10. M. Pes. 9 : 2 | Distant journey. |
| 11. M. Sheq. 8 : 7 | Burning clean and unclean sanctities together [*Re* Houses]. |
| 12. M. Yoma 7 : 3 | When are seven lambs sacrificed? |
| 13. b. Suk. 43a | Appurtenances of *Lulav* [no contrary ruling]. |
| 14. Tos. R.H. 2 : 10 | Biblical warrant for additional service on New Year. |
| 15. M. Yev. 12 : 3 | *Ḥaliṣah* without spitting. |
| 16. M. Naz. 7 : 4 | Blood of corpse renders Nazir unclean—ʿAqiba disagrees with anonymous tradition, which is defended by Eliezer. |
| 17-18. M. Sot. 9 : 3, 9 : 4 | *Re* breaking heifer's neck for unclaimed corpse. |
| 19. M. Sanh. 1 : 4 | Court of twenty-three judges wolf, lion, etc. |
| 20. M. Zev. 8 : 11 | Sin + Guilt-offering alike. |
| 21. M. Ker. 3 : 10 (M. Ker. 4 : 3: Joshua) | Liability for many acts of work in a single category. |
| 22-23. M. Me. 1 : 2-3 | Effect of sprinkling blood on what has gone outside the courtyard. |

(24. See T. 16)

G. *Eliezer vs. Joshua + ʿAqiba*

| | |
|---|---|
| 1. M. Pes. 6 : 2 | M. Pes. 6 : 1 |
| [1A. Tos. Pis. 5 : 1—only ʿAqiba] | |
| 2. M. Sheq. 4 : 7 (Tos. Sheq. 2 : 10) | Property given to Temple [ʿAqiba comments]. |
| 3. M. Yev. 8 : 4 | Joshua's tradition on eunuch explained by Eliezer and ʿAqiba. Joshua b. Batyra cites precedent for ʿAqiba. |
| 4. M. Ned. 10 : 6 | Levir annuls vows. |

H. *Eliezer, Joshua, Ṭarfon, Judah b. Bathyra, ʿAqiba*

1. M. Peʾah 3 : 6

I. *Eliezer vs. Joshua, Gamaliel*

| | |
|---|---|
| 1. M. Shev. 9 : 5 | Three kinds of vegetables pickled in jar—*re* seventh year. |
| 2. M. Yev. 13 : 7 | Levirate status of minor. |
| 3. M. Yev. 16 : 7 | Eliezer + Joshua *vs.* Gamaliel: Remarriage on basis of single witness. |
| 4, 5, 6, 7. M. Ket. 1 : 6, 7, 8, 9 | Gamaliel + Eliezer *vs.* Joshua—*re* woman's testimony on her lack of hymen. |

J. *Eliezer + ʿAqiba vs. Sages + Judah*

| | |
|---|---|
| 1. M. Par. 2 : 5 | White, black hair in heifer. |

K. *Eliezer + ʿAqiba vs. Ishmael*

| | |
|---|---|
| 1. M. Shav. 2 : 5 (Tos. Shav. 1 : 6) | Unawareness. |

L. *Ishmael re Eliezer*

| | |
|---|---|
| 1. Tos. Hal. 1 : 10 | Ishmael approves law *even* if it comes from Eliezer. |

M. *Ilai in name of Eliezer*

| | |
|---|---|
| 1. Tos. Hal. 1 : 6 | Dough-offering from cakes of Thank-offering. |
| 2. M. Eruv. 2 : 6 | Three rulings *re ʿEruv*, carrying in *Kor's* space, Passover bitter-herb. |
| 3. Tos. Suk. 2 : 1 | Ilai visited Eliezer on *Sukkot*. |
| [4. See T. 9] | |

N. *Leazar b. R. Yosah — Yosah b. Durmasqit — Yosah the Galilean — Yoḥanan b. Nuri + Liezer the Great*

| | |
|---|---|
| 1. Tos. Orl. 1 : 8 | *ʿOrlah*-laws do not apply outside of Palestine. |

O. *Eliezer vs. Judah b. Bathyra and Joshua*

| | |
|---|---|
| 1. M. Pes. 3 : 3 | How to give Dough-offering in uncleanness on Passover? |

P. *Eliezer vs. Ṭarfon*

| | |
|---|---|
| 1. M. Qid. 3 : 13 | Purify *mamzerim.* |

Q. *Eliezer vs. Eleazar*

| | |
|---|---|
| 1. M. Tem. 3 : 3 | Substitute of guilt-offering treated like that of Sin-offering. |
| 2. M. Maksh. 6 : 6 | Eliezer *vs.* Eleazar *vs.* Simeon *vs.* Sages, liquids *re Zab.* |

R. *Eliezer vs. Judah b. Bava, ʿAqiba, and Judah b. Ilai [+ Eleazar?]*

1. M. Eruv. 2 : 5-6

S. *Eliezer and Yoḥanan b. Nuri*

1. Tos. Suk. 1 : 9

The following legal pericopae in Mishnah-Tosefta involve *an* Eliezer and "the sages" or have an Eliezer differ from an anonymous rule. While, as noted, it is rare for MSS evidence to supply Eleazar in place of Eliezer when Joshua or ʿAqiba is involved, in many of the following, MSS will give Eleazar nearly as often as Eliezer. Most therefore are given in the Appendix to Chapter Two. Those for which warrant can be found for inclusion in the traditions attributed to Eliezer ben Hyrcanus are in Chapter Two.

T. *Eliezer vs. anonymous rule or sages*

| | |
|---|---|
| 1. M. Ber. 7 : 5 (Tos. Ber. 4 : 3, y. Ber. 6 : 1) | *Re* blessing wine unmixed with water. |
| 2. Tos. Ber. 3 : 11 | *Re* where to recite sanctification on Sabbath-New Moon? |
| 3. M. Pe'ah 4 : 9 | *Pe'ah* for poor man. |
| 4. M. Pe'ah 5 : 2 | Gleanings mixed with standing corn. |
| 5. M. Pe'ah 5 : 4 | Land-owner needs *pe'ah.* |
| 6. M. Dem. 4 : 3 | Designate part of *demai* as Poorman's Tithe. |
| 7. M. Dem. 5 : 9, Tos. Dem. 5 : 22 | Samaritan tithing. |
| 8. M. Dem. 6 : 3 | Priest-share-cropper gets tithes. |

| | |
|---|---|
| [9. Tos. Dem. 1 : 3 | Leʿi in name of Eliezer *re* first fruits] |
| 10. M. Kil. 2 : 10 | Grain sown with vegetables. |
| 11. M. Kil. 3 : 4 | Cucumbers, gourds, beans, in rows. |
| 12. M. Kil. 5 : 3 | Winepress in vineyard (Tos. Kil. 3 : 10: + Eliezer b. Jacob). |
| 13. Tos. Kil. 4 : 4 | Ditch beside light lattice work. |
| 14. M. Kil. 5 : 8 | Thorns in vineyard. |
| 15. M. Kil. 9 : 3 (Tos. Kil. 5 : 18) | Diverse kinds *re* handkerchiefs, etc. |
| [16. M. Shev. 8 : 9, 10 | Hide anointed with oil in Seventh Year; bread of Samaritans. ʿAqiba says this is *not* Eliezer's real opinion.] |
| 17. M. Shev. 9 : 9 | Seventh-Year fruits as gift or inheritance—how disposed of? |
| 18. M. Shev. 10 : 7 = M. Uqs. 3 : 10 | Is beehive immovable property? |
| 19. M. Ter. 2 : 1 (Tos. Ter. 3 : 18) | Clean for unclean Heave-offering. |
| [20. M. Ter. 4 : 5A | Quantity of Heave-offering. Eliezer separate from Ishmael, Ṭarfon, ʿAqiba.] |
| 21. M. Ter. 5 : 2, 4, 56 | Neutralizing Heave-offering; Eliezer = House of Shammai; sages = House of Hillel. |
| 22. M. Ma. 2 : 4, Tos. Ma. 2 : 2 | Produce from which Heave-offering was given before it was stored away. |
| 23. M. Ma. 4 : 3 | Takes olives from press and dips in salt. |
| 24. M. Ma. 4 : 5 | Tithe dill. |
| 25. Tos. Ma. 3 : 7 | Tithe mustard. |
| 26. Tos. M.S. 3 : 16 | Reliability for First, Second Tithe. |
| 27. M. Hal. 1 : 3 | Produce not past a third of growth not liable to Ḥallah. |
| 28. M. Hal. 2 : 4 | Liability to Dough-offering. |
| 29. M. Hal. 2 : 8 | Clean Dough-offering for unclean dough. |
| 30. M. Orl. 2 : 11 | Leaven of unconsecrated food and of Heave-offering. |
| 31. M. Orl. 2 : 7, Tos. Ter. 8 : 15 | Greasing utensils with unclean/clean oil. |
| 32. M. Shab. 1 : 10 | Baking bread Friday afternoon. |
| 33. M. Shab. 6 : 4 | Sword on Sabbath. |
| 34. Tos. Shab. 4 : 6 (*vs.* M. Shab. 6 : 3) | Tiara on Sabbath. |
| 35. Tos. Shab. 4 : 11 (*vs.* M. Shab. 6 : 3) | Spice-box on Sabbath. |
| 36. Tos. Shab. 5 : 12 | Scarf on Sabbath (story). |

| | |
|---|---|
| 37. M. Shab. 10 : 6 (Tos. Shab. 9 : 12, b. Shab. 94b, etc.) | Finger-nails on Sabbath. |
| 38. Tos. Shab. 9 : 13 | Bluing eyes, rouging cheeks, etc., on Sabbath. |
| 39. M. Shab. 13 : 1 (Tos. Shab. 12 : 1, Tos. Y.T. 4 : 4) | Weaving on Sabbath. |
| 40. M. Shab. 17 : 7 (Tos. Shab. 12 : 14) | Window-shutter on Sabbath. |
| 41. M. Shab. 20 : 1 (y. Shab. 20 : 1) | Stretch out filter on Sabbath. |
| 42. M. Shab. 22 : 1 | Honeycombs' liquid exuded on Sabbath. |
| 43. M. Eruv. 3 : 3 | Lost key [Eleazar?]. |
| 44. M. Eruv. 3 : 6 | Are Sabbath and festival separate sanctities or not—*re ʿeruv?* |
| 45. M. Eruv. 7 : 11 | Give money to baker for *ʿeruv.* |
| 46. M. Eruv. 9 : 2 | Breach is neutral [Eleazar?]. |
| 47. M. Pes. 3 : 1 | Women's cosmetics *re* Passover leaven. |
| 48. M. Pes. 5 : 9 | How to hang up and flay Passover on the Sabbath? |
| 49. M. Pes. 6 : 1 | Appurtenances of Passover on Sabbath [*vs.* ʿAqiba, Joshua]. |
| 50. M. Pes. 9 : 4 | *Zab* etc. comes to sanctuary on Passover [Eleazar?]. |
| 51. Tos. Kippurim 2 : 10 | Eliezer's opinion contradicts M. Yoma 4 : 1. |
| 52. Tos. Kippurim 2 : 16 | *vs.* M. Yoma 5 : 3. |
| 53. M. Yoma 5 : 5 | Sprinkling altar (Judah in Eliezer's name: Tos. Kippurim 3 : 1). |
| 54. Tos. Kippurim 3 : 14 | *Re* accidents affecting goat that is sent away. |
| 55. M. Yoma 8 : 11 | Leniencies on Day of Atonement for king, bride, etc. |
| 56. Tos. Kippurim 4 : 3 | Drinking on Day of Atonement. |
| 57. M. Suk. 1 : 11 | Cone-shaped *Sukkah.* |
| 58. M. Suk. 2 : 6 | Meals in *Sukkah.* |
| 59. M. Suk. 4 : 6 | What to say when leaving altar? |
| 60. b. Suk. 27a-b, 31a | *Sukkah*, *Lulav* must be privately owned. |
| 61. M. Bes. 4 : 6 | Woodsplinter as tooth pick. |
| 62. M. Bes. 4 : 7 | Designating produce in Seventh Year. |
| 63. M. R.H. 4 : 1 | *Re* decree of Yoḥanan b. Zakkai. [*Or*: Eleazar] |
| 64. M. Ta. 3 : 9 | If rain came early on fast day. |
| 65. M. Meg. 4 : 10 | Do not read Ezek. 16 : 1 as *Haftarah* |

| | |
|---|---|
| | (Anonymous, contrary rule in Tos. Meg. 4 : 34). |
| 66. M. Meg. 3 : 6 | *ʿAṣṣeret* in relationship to mourning. |
| 67. b. M.Q. 19a | Spin blue thread for fringe on intermediate days of festival. |
| 68. b. M.Q. 10a | Set up millstone on intermediate days of festival. |
| 69. M. Hag. 3 : 8 | Why altars of Temple do not require immersion. |
| 70. M. Yev. 12 : 2 | *Ḥaliṣah* at night, with left foot [Eleazar?]. |
| [71. Tos. Yev. 12 : 11 | M. Yev. 12 : 2—Wooden sandal is valid. Judah has a tradition that Eliezer invalidated it.] |
| 72. Tos. Yev. 12 : 12 | *Ḥaliṣah* of minor invalid. |
| 73. M. Yev. 13 : 2 | *Ḥaliṣah* of minor invalid. |
| 74. M. Yev. 13 : 6 | Levir [Eleazar?]. |
| 75. M. Yev. 13 : 11 | Levirate status of minor [may be Eleazar]. |
| 76. M. Yev. 16 : 2 | Remarriage of widows [may be Eleazar]. |
| 77. Tos. Yev. 11 : 4 | Erroneous marriage—*re* sin-offerings. |
| 78. Tos. Ket. 11 : 4 | *vs.* M. Ket. 11 : 6, rights of minor to *melog.* |
| 79. M. Ned. 4 : 3 | Feed unclean cattle of him who is forbidden by vow to have any benefit. |
| 80. M. Ned. 9 : 1 | Releasing vows. |
| 81. M. Ned. 9 : 2 | Releasing vows. |
| 82. M. Yev. 10 : 5 | Releasing vows of girl past puberty awaiting marriage. |
| 83. M. Yev. 10 : 7 | Releasing vows before they are made. |
| 84. M. Naz. 3 : 3<br>85. M. Naz. 3 : 4<br>86. M. Naz. 3 : 5 | How much does a Nazir lose if he becomes unclean on the last day of his period [Judah is authority for Eliezer's opinion—Tos. Nez. 2 : 12-13]. |
| 87. M. Naz. 6 : 11 | Nazir becomes unclean during sacrifices. |
| 88. M. Naz. 7 : 1 | High priest and Nazir meet neglected corpse. |
| 89. M. Sot. 4 : 3 | One may remain married to sterile woman [may be Eleazar]. |
| 90. M. Sot. 9 : 2 (y. M. Sot. 9 : 2) | Slain man between two cities—both bring heifer. |
| 91. M. Git. 6 : 3<br>92. M. Git. 6 : 4 | When does *Geṭ* take effect *re* Heave-offering [may be Eleazar]. |
| 93. M. Git. 8 : 8 | *Geṭ* and quittance confused. |

| | |
|---|---|
| 94. M. Git. 9 : 1 | Divorce valid for remarriage to anyone except one person. |
| 95. M. Qid. 1 : 9 | Commandments dependent on land observed abroad. [= N. 1] |
| 96. M. Qid. 4 : 3 | Assured stock intermarries [may be Eleazar]. |
| 97. M. Qid. 4 : 13 | Unmarried man may not teach. |
| 98. M. Sanh. 6 : 1A | All who are stoned are hung. |
| 99. M. Sanh. 6 : 1B | Man and woman both hung. |
| 100. Tos. Sanh. 9 : 6 | Man and woman both stoned naked. |
| 101. M. Mak. 3 : 5 | Liability for cutting hair. |
| 102. M. A.Z. 1 : 8 | Make idolatrous ornaments for a fee. |
| 103. M. A.Z. 3 : 9 | Redeem object with funds in a matter of idolatry. |
| 104. M. A.Z. 2 : 7 | *Nasi* brings he-goat. |
| [105. M. Zev. 1 : 1/Tos. Zev. 1 : 11 (*vs.* Joshua) | Guilt-offering must be in its own name (8 : 11: *vs.* ʿAqiba).] |
| [106. M. Zev. 3 : 3/Tos. Zev. 2 : 16—*vs.* Joshua | Slaughter to eat something not eaten—invalid.] |
| 107-110. M. Zev. 8 : 5, 7, 8, 9 | Mixture of acceptable and unacceptable sacrifice—blood, etc. |
| [111. M. Men. 3 : 1 (Tos. Men. 2 : 16—*vs.* Joshua) | Took handful of meal-offering to eat something not usually eaten, etc.] |
| 112. M. Men. 7 : 3 | Bread sanctified if offering blemished. |
| 113. M. Hul. 2 : 7 | Slaughter for gentile. |
| 114. M. Hul. 12 : 2 | Cock-partridge (*re* Deut. 22 : 6-7). |
| 115. M. Bekh. 1 : 5 | Redeem firstling with hybrid. |
| 116. M. Bekh. 1 : 6A = M. Ed. 7 : 1 (*vs.* Ṣaddoq + Joshua) | Redemption-lamb dies. |
| 117. M. Bekh. 1 : 6B | Firstling died. |
| 118. M. Bekh. 4 : 7 | Buy from one who violates law of firstlings. |
| 119. M. Bekh. 5 : 3 | Punish one who blemishes firstling. |
| 120. M. Bekh. 7 : 6 | Dangling warts as blemishes [Eleazar?]. |
| 121. M. Ar. 3 : 2 | Field of inheritance *vs.* purchased field, when redeemed? |
| 122. M. Ar. 6 : 3 | Not take yoke as pledge from farmer. |
| 123. M. Tem. 3 : 1, M. Ed. 7 : 6 (Joshua and Papyas) | Progeny of Peace-offerings not offered as Peace-offerings. |
| 124. M. Tem. 6 : 5 (Tos.: Yosi) | Progeny of *ṭerefah*. |
| 125. M. Ker. 6 : 1 | Suspensive guilt-offering offered any time. |
| 126. M. Kel. 2 : 8 | Comb of water-cooler. |
| 127. M. Kel. 3 : 2 | Measure of hole in lamp. |
| 128. M. Kel. 5 : 10 (M. Ed. 7 : 7: *vs.* Joshua) | Oven of Akhnai. |

| | |
|---|---|
| 129. M. Kel. 8 : 1 (Yoḥanan b. Nuri, Yosi) | Does hive protect from uncleanness in oven? |
| 130. M. Kel. 10 : 1 | Upside-down jar. |
| 131. M. Kel. 11 : 5 | Scorpion-bit. |
| 132. M. Kel. 11 : 8 | Broken necklace. |
| 133. Tos. Kel. B.M. 1 : 9 | Nose-hooklet. |
| 134. M. Kel. 14 : 1 | Hole in metal vessels. |
| 135. Tos. Kel. B.M. 4 : 2 | Hole in leather bottle. |
| 136. M. Kel. 15 : 2 (M. Ed. 7 : 7, Tos. Ed. 3 : 1 = Eliezer *vs.* Joshua and Pappyas) | Baker's shelf affixed to wall. |
| 137. M. Kel. 18 : 9 | Bed. |
| 138. M. Kel. 26 : 2 | Money-pouch. |
| 139. M. Kel. 26 : 4 | Shoe on last. |
| 140. M. Kel. 26 : 5 | Hide for combed wool. |
| 141. M. Kel. 27 : 5 | Child's shirt. |
| 142. M. Kel. 27 : 12 and Simeon *vs.* all | Thrown-out rags. |
| 143. M. Oh. 2 : 2 | Worm from corpse *re* Tent. |
| 144. M. Oh. 2 : 2 | Ashes of cremated corpse *re* Tent. |
| 145. M. Oh. 6 : 1 | Men and vessels as Tent for uncleanness. |
| 146. M. Oh. 6 : 2 (Tos. Ah. 7 : 3) | Corpse-bearers by portico. |
| 147. M. Oh. 17 : 5 | Dirt of grave-area. |
| 148. M. Neg. 6 : 7 | Adds to list of tips not unclean because of raw flesh. |
| 149-150. M. Neg. 7 : 4-5 | Deliberate removal of leprosy-signs. |
| [151. M. Neg. 9 : 3 | Eliezer is asked reason of anonymous Law. Judah b. Batyra answers.] |
| [152. M. Nez. 11 : 7 | Eliezer asked reason of anonymous Law. Judah b. Batyra answers.] |
| 153. M. Nez. 14 : 9 + Ṣimeon | Reuse hyssop. |
| 154. Tos. Neg. 8 : 12 | Reuse hyssop. |
| 155. M. Par. 1 : 1 | Age of heifer. |
| 156. M. Par. 2 : 1A | Pregnant heifer. |
| 157. M. Par. 2 : 1B | Heifer of gentiles. |
| 158. M. Par. 2 : 3 | Heifer that was price of dog, etc. |
| 159-160. M. Par. 4 : 1, 4 : 3 | Intention does not render unfit. |
| 161. Tos. Par. 5 : 9/M. Par. 5 : 7 | Crown of mud holds water in trough. |
| 162. M. Par. 7 : 10 | Unclean guardian of water. |
| 163. Tos. Par. 5 : 9/M. Par. 5 : 7 | Crown of mud serves to collect water. |
| 164-165. M. Par. 9 : 1 | Water or dew falls into flask. |
| 166. M. Par. 9 : 3 | Mouse drank from flask—gloss of sages' rule. |
| 167. M. Par. 9 : 7 | Ashes of heifer mixed with ordinary ashes. |
| 168. M. Par. 10 : 3, M. Ed. 7 : 1 (Tos. Ah. 7 : 11: Joshua) | Uncleanness of jar containing Sin-offering ashes. |

| | |
|---|---|
| 169. M. Par. 11 : 2 | Loosely fastened boards. |
| 170. M. Par. 11 : 7 | Hyssop. |
| 171. M. Toh. 6 : 5 | Contract uncleanness if unsure of contact. |
| 172. Tos. Toh/M. Toh. 6 : 6 | Doubt in private domain. |
| 173. M. Toh. 9 : 3 | Sap from olives. |
| 174. M. Miq. 2 : 4 | Ritual pool. |
| 175. M. Miq. 8 : 1 | Ritual pools of Land of Israel. |
| 176. M. Miq. 9 : 3 | Interposition in ritual pool. |
| 177. M. Nid. 1 : 5 | Who is old woman? |
| 178. M. Nid. 4 : 6 | Woman in hard labor in eighty days of purification. |
| 179. M. Zab. 2 : 2 | Examine *Zab.* |
| 180-181. M. Zab. 5 : 3, 5 : 7 | He who carries carrion, touches flux of *Zab.* |
| 182-183. Tos. Ed. 2 : 7 [=M. Shab. 6 : 1; M. Sanh. 3 : 3] | a) "City of gold" on Sabbath. b) Pigeon-flyer *re* testimony. |

As will be shown, some of the foregoing pericopae are to be included in the traditions about Eliezer b. Hyrcanus. But it cannot be taken for granted that all of them belong to those traditions. As noted, legal pericopae which have been excluded are, for the sake of completeness, discussed in the Appendix to Chapter Two. Perhaps other students of Eliezer b. Hyrcanus may find reason to assign some of them to our Eliezer or to distinguish among their several Eliezer's and Eleazar's. On the other hand, exegetical and historical pericopae not definitively to be assigned to Eliezer b. Hyrcanus have not been reproduced. An important corpus of materials is exegeses attributed to a R. Eliezer, without contrary authority or hint of the context of the exegesis. This corpus also is entirely omitted.

## ii. Texts consulted

1. Mishnah—Ḥanokh Albeq [Albeck], *Šišah Sidré Mishnah* (Tel Aviv-Jerusalem, 1957ff., I-VI).

In the absence of a critical text of the Mishnah, or even of a collation of variant readings occurring in various manuscripts, I consulted the following:

*Mishnah Codex Parma (de Rossi 138)* (Repr. Jerusalem, 1970, I-II) Designated: *Parma.*

*Mishnah ʿIm Perush HaRambam. Defus Rishon, Napoli 1492*, with an introduction by A. M. Haberman (Repr. Jerusalem, 1970, I-II). Designated: *Naples.*

*Faksimile-Ausgabe des Mischna Codex Kaufmann A 50*, published by Georg Beer (Repr. Jerusalem, 1968, I-II). Designated: *Kaufmann.*

W. H. Lowe, *The Mishnah on which the Palestinian Talmud Rests* (Cambridge, 1883). Designated: *Camb.*

*The Mishna Tractates Neziqin Qodashim Teharoth. Codex Jerusalem Heb 4° 1336. A Manuscript Vocalized according to the Yemenite Tradition.* Introduction by Prof. Shelomo Morag (Jerusalem, 1970).

2. Tosefta—Saul Lieberman, *The Tosefta. According to Codex Vienna, with variants from Codex Erfurt, Genizah MSS. and Editio Princeps (Venice, 1521), together with References to Parallel Passages in Talmudic Literature and a Brief Commentary* (N.Y., 1955ff.), for Zeraᶜim, Moᶜed, and Nashim [to date, through Nezirot], and the accompanying commentary, *Tosefta Kifshuṭah. A Comprehensive Commentary on the Tosefta.*

For tractates not published by Lieberman, I followed M. S. Zuckermandel, *Tosephta, based on the Erfurt and Vienna Codices, with parallels and variants* (Repr., Jerusalem, 1963).

3. Babylonian Talmud—I used the standard printed text, and consulted, where available, Raphaelo Rabbinovicz, *Variae Lectiones in Mischnam et in Talmud Babylonicum* (Repr. N.Y., 1960), and, for Giṭṭin, M. S. Feldblum, *Diqduqé Soferim* (N.Y., 1966). I also consulted the following:

*Babylonian Talmud, Codex Munich* (95) (Jerusalem, 1971), Vols. I-III.

*Talmud Bavli. Defus Rishon. Venezia 5280 [Babylonian Talmud. First Edition, Venice, 1520-1523]* (Jerusalem' 1968) Vols. I-XVII.

4. Palestinian Talmud—I used the Gilead reprint (N.Y., 1949) Vols. I-V.

In the absence of a critical text, I consulted the following:

*Talmud Yerushalmi, printed in Venice.* [This is all the bibliographical data printed in the book.]

*Talmud Yerushalmi. Codex Vatican (Vet. Ebr. 133),* (Jerusalem, 1971), with an Introduction by Prof. S. Liberman [Lieberman] ("On the Yerushalmi"). A Page Concordance Index to the Venice edition by Rabbi A. P. Sherry.

*The Palestinian Talmud. Leiden MS. Cod. Scal. 3. A Facsimile of the Original Manuscript.* With Introduction by Saul Lieberman (Jerusalem, 1970) Vols. I-VI.

B. Ratner, *Sefer Ahavat Ṣiyyon Virushalayim* (Vilna, 1901), I. *Berakhot*; II. *Shabbat*; III. *Terumot, Ḥallah*; IV. *Shevi'it*; V. *Kila'im, Ma'aserot*; VI. *Pesaḥim*; VII. *Yoma*; VIII. *Rosh HaShanah, Sukkah*; IX. *Megillah*; X. *Beṣah, Ta'anit.*

For y. Sheq., I followed the text of Abraham Schreiber, *Treatise Sheqalim. With Two Commentaries of Early Rabbinical Authorities (Beginning of the 13th Century). 1) R. Meshullam. 2) A Disciple of R. Samuel b. ben R. Shneur of Evreux. Edited for the First Time from a Unique Manuscript in the Bodleian Library with Explanatory Notes and References* (N.Y., 1954).

Editions and translations of Tannaitic Midrashim, and of the later collections and compilations of Midrashim are specified when cited. Mishnah-Tosefta and Palestinian Talmudic materials are in my own translations. Translations of Babylonian Talmudic passages and of Midrashim are cited in the name of the translator; when no translator is specified, the translation is my own.

### iii. Purpose of the Comments

The comments on the pericopae systematically deal with only three matters. First, an explanation, where called for, of the contents of the pericope is given. Where the meaning is clear and I have nothing to add, I have said nothing. In legal materials explanations are based on Lieberman, and, where Lieberman is unavailable, on Albeq. Second, an observation on the form of the pericope normally will be made. Third, the attestation and context of a pericope are considered: Who refers to it or may supply a hint as to when and where it was known? Appearance in Mishnah-Tosefta is taken as evidence that a pericope had reached its present form by ca. 200-250 A.D. All other historical and form-critical questions are raised in part II.

Pericopae are designated by the following system. The Arabic number indicates merely the order in traditions from a given compilation as cited hereinafter. Thus I.i.50 indicates a pericope from the stratum of Mishnah-Tosefta, cited from Mishnah, fiftieth in our sequence.

| | | |
|---|---|---|
| I.i. | = | Mishnah |
| I.ii. | = | Tosefta |
| II.i. | = | Mekhilta deR. Ishmael |
| II.ii. | = | Mekhilta deR. Simeon b. Yoḥai |
| II.iii. | = | Sifra |

| | | |
|---|---|---|
| II.iv. | = | Sifré |
| II.v. | = | Sifre Zuṭṭa |
| II.vi. | = | Midrash Tanna'im |
| III.i. | = | Traditions signified as Tannaitic in the Palestinian *Gemara* |
| III.ii. | = | Traditions signified as Tannaitic in the Babylonian *Gemara* |
| IV.i. | = | Amoraic Traditions in the Palestinian *Gemara* |
| IV.ii. | = | Amoraic Traditions in the Babylonian *Gemara* |
| V.i. | = | Avot deR. Natan |
| V.ii. | = | Tractate on Mourning (Semaḥot) |
| V.iii. | = | Soferim |
| V.iv. | = | Kallah and Kallah Rabbati |
| V.v. | = | Derekh Ereṣ Rabbah and Derekh Ereṣ Zuṭṭa |
| V.vi. | = | Gerim, Sefer Torah, Tefillin |
| V.vii. | = | Genesis Rabbah |
| V.viii. | = | Leviticus Rabbah |
| V.ix. | = | Pesiqta deR. Kahana and Pesiqta Rabbati |
| V.x. | = | Tanḥuma |
| V.xi. | = | Exodus, Numbers, and Deuteronomy Rabbah |
| V.xii. | = | Other Compilations of Midrashim |

CHAPTER TWO

# LEGAL TRADITIONS

## i. Berakhot

I.i.1.A. From what time do they read the *Shema*ᶜ in the evening?

B. From the hour that the priests enter to eat their Heave-offering.

C. "Until the end of the first watch"—the words of R. Eliezer.

And sages say, "Until midnight."

Rabban Gamaliel says, "Until the morning star rises."

D. *MᶜŚH Š*: his [Gamaliel's] sons came from the banquet house. They said to him, "We have not read the *Shema*ᶜ."

He said to them, "If the morning star has not risen, you are obligated (ḤYYBYN) [Kaufmann, Parma: *Permitted*] to read [it]."

E. And not this only, but in all matters concerning which the sages have said, "Until midnight"—their obligation [persists] until the morning star rises.

Burning the fat and the limbs—their obligation [persists] until the morning star rises. And all which is to be eaten in one day—their obligation [persists] until the morning star rises.

If so, why have the sages said, "Until midnight?" In order to keep a man far from sin.

M. Ber. 1 : 1

I.i.2.A. From what time do they read the *Shema*ᶜ in the morning? From the time that one may distinguish between blue and white.

B. R. Eliezer says, "Between blue and green."

C. [Camb., Parma omit:] *And he completes it* before sunrise.

D. R. Joshua says, "Before the third hour."

E. "For it is the way of princes to arise at the third hour."

F. He who reads thenceforward has not lost, like a man who is reading in the Torah.

M. Ber. 1 : 2 (b. Ber. 25b, y. Ber. 1 : 2)

*Comment*: The dispute of Eliezer, the sages, and Gamaliel pertains only to the second clause, *until.* No party refers to the first part of the answer to the question. *From the hour—Heave-offering* serves equally well—or poorly—to introduce the opinions of all three parties, for parts A and B are complete in themselves. The question is not, *until* when, but *from* when—and that question is answered by B. Part C introduces a new issue. But it begins without a superscription, *Until when do they read the Shema*ʿ *in the evening?*

The same structure is evident in M. Ber. 1 : 2. Part A asks, *From what time,* and *that* question is answered. Eliezer then glosses. Part C completes the pericope: *they read from the time ... until before sunrise.* Then Joshua glosses. Part E extends Joshua's saying by explaining his reasoning, but it clearly is an interpolation, for Joshua's saying is as brief as Eliezer's here, and in M. Ber. 1 : 1 the three opinions are carefully matched: *Until 1. end 2. midnight 3. morning star.* Thus in both instances the form is as follows:

1. Question *From when—*
2. [Anonymous] answer *Until*—[and he completes it...]
3. Yavnean gloss

M. Ber. 1 : 1: Eliezer, sages, Gamaliel
M. Ber. 1 : 2: Eliezer to part A, Joshua to part C.

The present form therefore leads to the supposition that before the Yavnean masters was a segment of a completed code of law, entirely anonymous, of which this segment was subject to discussion. That code would have consisted of the following:

*From when do they read...* evening
From the hour that the priests...
[And he completes it before...]
*From when do they read...* morning
From [the time] that he may distinguish...
*And he completes it before...*

The first *And he completes it before* has been lost. We cannot now guess what the Temple rule would have been. It has been set aside by C. The form left no room for a simple gloss, as in M. Ber. 1 : 2, *And he completes it before... R. Joshua says, Before...*, because a whole set of opinions, not a single gloss, was in hand. So I would guess that the original version had an appropriate conclusion, on the time beyond which one no longer says the *Shema*ʿ. The further, anonymous rules in M. Ber. 1 : 4 and 1 : 5 would evidently form part of the Temple rule. The Houses' pericope (M. Ber. 1 : 3, see *Phar.* II, p. 41) would then represent the first Pharisaic-rabbinic stage of commentary, the early Yavneans' glosses, the second.

Evidently the antecedent code derives from the Temple, for it demarcates time by the priestly service—eating Heave-offering. Then the Yavneans change the imagery, choosing not Temple rites but routine, secular times—first watch, midnight, morning star—which anyone, not merely priests, would understand. But the Temple-imagery recurs in the extended gloss, e.g., burning the fat and the limbs, and is preserved in later strata.

Part D then ignores Eliezer's opinion. It is from a Gamalielite hand, for it harmonizes the sages' opinion with his: the sages really agree with him that it is legitimate to do the various commandments until dawn, but have ruled strictly in order to prevent people from sinning. Therefore Gamaliel and the sages really are in agreement. The counsel Gamaliel gave to his sons was correct—but not under normal circumstances. This leaves Eliezer out; no one bothers to harmonize his opinion, which could have supported the same rationalization. So part D is introduced by a Gamalielite, and part D then harmonizes the sages of C with the story of D. E comes last of all. Before the intrusion of D, it is pointless to say, "and not this only," explicitly referring to the story in D. Standing by itself, moreover, it still depends upon Gamaliel's opinion, therefore probably also upon the story.

The present story obviously would have stood outside of the narrow framework of commentary on the priestly law. The first stage, therefore, would be C, then D and E follow, all within the circle of Gamaliel. On the other hand, we have noticed that named masters before 70, except Ḥananiah Prefect of the Priests and Gamaliel I, normally do not have legal sayings in standard legal form. Their legal opinions come in the form of stories or attributions, which then may be generalized into *Rabbi X says . . .*-form. So it is not out of the question that Gamaliel's original opinion was preserved as the story, D, which yielded the saying in C, followed by equally terse formulations for opinions of Eliezer and the sages, whose stories—if any existed—were simply dropped.

All glosses of the original code are extremely terse—simply completions of the original sentence, therefore depending upon it for context and meaning. Eliezer in M. Ber. 1 : 2B and Joshua in M. Ber. 1 : 2D simply take up the language of M. Ber. 1 : 2 A and C, respectively, and revise its operative clause.

We must ask, finally, whether mnemonic considerations have governed the formulation of pericopae. As for M. Ber. 1 : 1 A and B and M. Ber. 1 : 2 A and C, I see no effort at placing the whole into a single, simple pattern for easy memorization, other than the use of questions and answers. But M. Ber. 1 : 1 C introduces all opinions with the same word, ʿD, and then arranges them in thematically appropriate order: the earliest, middle, and latest time to be specified. The story follows in simple narrative *style*—which is not a disciplined form—but which, as usual, relies on a topic sentence to set the stage, then on dialogue to unfold the story. The long gloss in M. Ber. 1 : 1 E and the shorter one in M. Ber. 1 : 2 E seem to be simple declarative sentences, without mnemonic formulae.

See Epstein, *Tan.*, p. 65.

IV.ii.1.A. From what time do they begin to read the *Shemaʿ* in the evenings?

"From the time that he sanctified the day on the evenings of Sabbaths"—the words of R. Eliezer.

R. Joshua says, "From the time that the priests are purified to eat of their Heave-offering."

B. R. Meir says, "From the time that the priests bathe to eat their Heave-offering [= before twilight]."

R. Judah said to him, "But do the priests not bathe while it is still day? [It must be a later time.]"

C. R. Ḥanina says, "From the time that the poor man enters to eat his crust with salt."

R. Aḥai, and some say R. Aḥa, says, "From the time that most people enter to recline [at table]."

b. Ber. 2b

*Comment*: The pericope is not marked as deriving from Tannaitic authority. It is a singleton, unattested in y. or Tos.; the sequence of times to say the prayer—early to late—matches closely with the sequence of masters. It is difficult to say exactly which Ḥanina and Aḥai/Aḥa are before us, R. Aḥa, among the last Tannaim in the time of R. Judah the Prince, or R. Aḥai [son of R. Josiah; a later second-century Babylonian master]; R. Ḥanina of the time of Gamaliel [so A. Hyman, *Sefer Toledot Tanna'im ve'Amora'im* (London, 1910), II, p. 477] or Ḥanina the nephew of R. Joshua, who settled in Babylonia ca. 100-110 A.D. If the two last names are Babylonians, we would possibly have a *baraita* produced in the later second-century Babylonian schools. But that is a weak conjecture. If, as seems more likely, the Aḥa is Judah the Patriarch's contemporary, then the *baraita* comes, at the very latest, in the beginning of the third century. It represents an effort to string together second- and early third-century sayings according to the model of the Mishnah.

But why then have the Mishnaic forms of the sayings of Eliezer and Joshua not been preserved? Perhaps because several sorts of sayings and traditions were in circulation, which permitted the formulation of still another. Note, for example, the Ushan pericope, now in Tos. Ber. 1 : 1:

> From what time do they read the *Shema'* in the evenings?
>
> "From the time that people enter to eat their bread on the evening of Sabbaths," the words of R. Meir.
>
> And the sages say, "From the time that the priests are proper[ly clean] (ZK'Y) to eat their Heave-offering."
>
> The sign of the matter is the appearance of the stars ...

Meir now is very near Eliezer's opinion—the time is exactly the same, only the formulation is slightly different, for Eliezer speaks of wine, Meir of bread, both on Sabbath evening. The sages and Joshua are virtually the same; the former have ZK'Y for the latter's MṬWHR. Then the rest is out of phase. So it would seem that various opinions were in circulation, to be attributed to the authorities whose names were to be used in the several collections, without reference to what, if anything, had "originally" been stated. The version of b. Ber. 2b therefore presents the most extensive and complicated picture. Its redactor either had traditions different from those in M. and Tos. or artificially created his pericope out of names already used in connection with the same legal materials in M.

and Tos.,—that is, Eliezer, Joshua (but not on precisely the same issue), and Meir—so as to find warrant for Ḥanina's and Aḥai/Aḥai's inclusion as well. Since the Babylonian version is not assigned to Tannaitic authority, we are probably on good ground to follow suit.

It is curious that Tos. has the sages answer the question raised at the outset, *From what time*, with the *sages* now given M. Ber. 1 : 1B, the anonymous opinion of the Mishnah. This we had assigned to the original rule-book.

So the Yavnean version is in the Mishnah, the Ushan version in Tos. The Ushans, uncomfortable with the Yavnean version, which does not answer the question and leaves an anonymous opinion without attribution, evidently improved matters. They now have the opening question answered—by Meir, then the sages—and give the "sages" the unattributed opinion of M. Ber. 1 : 1. Judah the Patriarch preserved the earlier version in his Mishnah.

III.ii.1. R. Eliezer says, "The night is divided into three watches and at each the Holy One blessed be He sits and roars like a lion" etc.

b. Ber. 3a

*Comment*: Eliezer's opinion in M. Ber. 1 : 1 is taken as evidence that there are watches in heaven as on earth. y. Ber. 1 : 1 has Rabbi's view that there are four, but knows nothing of Eliezer's.

II.i.1. R. Eliezer says, "The word 'night' is used here: *And they shall eat the flesh in that night* (Ex. 12 : 8) and the word 'night' is also used there: *For I will go through the land of Egypt in that night.* Just as there, 'night' means not later than midnight, so the word 'night' used here also means only up to midnight."

Mekh. Pisḥa 6 : 40-43 [= 13 : 6-8]
Lauterbach I, p. 46 (b. Ber. 9a)

*Comment*: I do not know why this should be our Eliezer.

II.v.1.A. *And these words shall be upon your heart* (Deut. 6 : 6).

B. "I might say that the whole passage requires the heart's intention. Scripture says, *These*—To here intention is required [Lit.: the commandment of intention]. Henceforward the commandment is merely to read [b.: intention is not necessary]"—the words of R. Eliezer.

C. R. ʿAqiba said to him, "It is not necessary. Lo it says, *Which I command you this day on your heart*, that is to say, the whole passage requires the heart's intention."

Midrash Tannaim to Deut. 6 : 6,
Hoffmann, p. 26 (= b. Ber. 13a)

*Comment*: The issue is whether reciting all of the *Shema*ʿ, or merely the first part, requires intention (*kavanah*). Eliezer holds the latter view, ʿAqiba the former. Meir holds the same view as Eliezer (b. Ber. 13b), but does not cite his opinion.

I.i.3.A. Rabban Gamaliel says, "Every day a man prays eighteen."

R. Joshua says, "The substance (MʿYN) of eighteen."

B. R. ʿAqiba says, "If his prayer is fluent in his mouth, he should pray eighteen; if not, [he should pray] the substance of eighteen."

M. Ber. 4 : 3 [Continued]

*Comment*: Gamaliel supplies a topic-sentence for Joshua; then ʿAqiba stands quite outside the foregoing, takes its substance for granted, and compromises between the conflicting opinions of the earlier masters. *Every day a man prays* serves both Gamaliel and Joshua, and ʿAqiba harmonizes the foregoing opinions. So the difference is *Eighteen vs. MʿYN.* Gamaliel and Joshua take for granted the existence of a structure of Prayer containing eighteen blessings. Eliezer's saying (below) does not refer to MʿYN. He simply requires a "brief prayer," not a fixed text.

The pericope has nothing to do with its setting. Beforehand come rules about the time one should say the Prayer of the morning, then an unrelated rule of Neḥuniah b. Haqqanah, then *Rabban Gamaliel.* M. Ber. 4 : 3 has no relationship to M. Ber. 4 : 1, 2. The redactional connection to M. Ber. 4 : 4, in which Eliezer occurs, is evident in the continuation.

I.i.3.C. R. Eliezer says, "He who makes his prayer routine (QBʿ), his prayer is not supplications."

D. R. Joshua says, "He who walks in a dangerous place prays a brief prayer [Parma, Kaufmann, Naples: *the substance* (MʿYN) *of the eighteen*]. He says, 'Save, O Lord, your people, the remnant of Israel. In every cross-road (PRŠT HʿBWR [Parma and Kaufmann: ṢYBWR]), let their needs be before you. Blessed are you, O Lord, who hears prayer [Parma: *and supplications*).' "

M. Ber. 4 : 4 (b. Ber. 29b)

IV.i.1. R. Eliezer would pray a new prayer every day.

y. Ber. 4 : 4, Gilead, p. 68

*Comment:* Eliezer contrasts routine prayer to the spirit of supplication. His statement is syllogistic—of course if the prayer is routine, it cannot be in the right spirit.

Joshua's saying has nothing to do with Eliezer's. The two are juxtaposed but do not relate to one another. MS evidence adds that the brief prayer should contain a summary of the eighteen, but this is immediately contradicted by the prayer assigned to Joshua, which is not the "substance (MʿYN) of the eighteen benedictions" at all. The phrase is probably inserted from the foregoing (M. Ber. 4 : 3) saying of Joshua. The meaning of PRŠT HʿBWR/ṢYBWR is unclear to me.

As it stands, the masters here form part of nothing more than a random collection of loosely related sayings. The antecedent collection in M. Ber. 4 : 3, however, lists Gamaliel, Joshua, and ʿAqiba, who do have a substantive disagreement. But S. Lieberman (*Tosefta Kifshuṭah Seder Zeraʿim* I, p. 31, to 1.28) points out that M. Ber. 4 : 3 is *completed* by Eliezer's opinion. Since the order of the masters—Gamaliel, Joshua, ʿAqiba, then Eliezer, who normally comes first—evidently seemed unusual to the scribes, they divided Eliezer's opinion from the preceding ones, and joined it to Joshua's. But, Lieberman holds, the correct version must have had the four masters' opinions altogether. Gamaliel holds that one must not change the form of the Eighteen Blessings. Joshua says one may change it by substituting an abbreviated version. ʿAqiba then says if one's prayer is fluent, one must pray the Eighteen. In this matter, Eliezer differs. A man must not make his prayer routine, that is by following a fixed text. Therefore the difference is between Eliezer and ʿAqiba; ʿAqiba's opinion thus introduces and explains Eliezer's.

Following Lieberman, we may observe that no mnemonic considerations seem to have influenced the formulation of ʿAqiba's and Eliezer's opinions, which are morphologically entirely different from one another. ʿAqiba, however, does have a formulation built upon the operative words in Gamaliel's and Joshua's sayings: *Eighteen vs. Abbreviated Eighteen,* then *If—Eighteen*; If *not—Abbreviated Eighteen.* This is a standard means of effecting a compromise between conflicting opinions; one takes the operative language of both opinions and sets them into a new, and neutral morphological framework—both are right, but for different situations.

It is noteworthy that the scribes, according to Lieberman, did exhibit an awareness of commonplace formulae, e.g. the proper order of masters in a sequence of differing opinions. Perhaps mnemonic considerations were likewise not unknown to them. This would further account for splitting Eliezer off from the earlier pericope.

I.ii.1. [If] he was walking in a place of danger and brigands (LSTYN), he prays a brief prayer.

What is a brief prayer?

R. Liezer says, "Your will be done in Heaven above, and give pleasure (NḤT RWḤ) to those that fear you, and do what is good in your eyes. Blessed is he who hears prayer."

Tos. Ber. 3 : 7, Lieberman, p. 13, ls. 28-30

III.ii.2.A. TNW RBNN: He who is walking in a place of bands of wild beasts (GDWDY ḤYH) and brigands (LSTYM) prays a brief prayer.

B. And what is a brief prayer?

R. Eliezer says, "Do your will in heaven above and give pleasure to those that fear you below, and do that which is good in your eyes. Blessed are you, O Lord, who hears prayers."

R. Joshua [Yosi] says, "Hear the cry of your people Israel and quickly do what they ask. Blessed are you, O Lord, who hears prayers."

III.ii.3. Further: R. Eleazar b. R. Ṣaddoq.

b. Ber. 29b

*Comment:* In M. Ber. 4 : 3 (above, p. 23), Joshua alludes to a brief prayer. Here Eliezer's version is given. I am not sure that this is our Eliezer, because in M. Ber. our Eliezer says there should be no fixed text. Here we have no Yavnean juxtaposed to Eliezer. If it is Yosi, then it is an Ushan pericope, and the Eliezer is apt to be one of the Ushans as well.

Lieberman observes (*Tosefta Kifshuṭah Seder Zera'im* I, p. 33), that the Palestinian texts give, "Short prayer, the substance of the eighteen," just as in the textual evidence supplied above. The meaning is that one does not pray the 'substance of the Eighteen blessings,' but a brief précis. Eliezer then differs, holding that the prayer is not merely a brief summary of the Eighteen and does not comprehend the whole.

b. Ber. 29b. B should have Yosi, not Joshua, so Lieberman, following Rabbinovicz, *Diq. Sof.*, p. 153 l. 30. So the Babylonian *baraita* has copied Tos. Ber. 3 : 7, then added an Ushan opinion as well.

| *Tos. Ber. 3 : 7* | *b. Ber. 29b* |
|---|---|
| 1. — | 1. TNW RBNN |
| 2. He was walking in a place of danger and brigands (LSTYN) —prays a brief prayer. | 2. He who was (HMHLK) in a place of *bands of wild beast*[s] and brigands. |
| 3. What is a brief prayer? | 3. " " " |
| 4. R. Liezer says, | 4. Eliezer " " |
| 5. May your will be done in heaven above, and give pleasure (NḤT RWḤ) to those that fear you, and the good in your eyes, do. | 5. Do your will " " " and " " " *below* " " " |
| 6. Blessed is he who hears prayer. | 6. B'Y (= Blessed are you, O Lord) " " |

The *baraita* substitutes the more concrete *beasts* for the general *danger,* thus explaining what the danger consisted of. *Above* is given a counterpart in *below*—a minor, but distinct improvement. The rest is the same, except the Tosefta's (and Palestinian Talmud's) consistent use of Liezer is replaced by the Babylonian Talmud's consistent *E*liezer. Finally, the normal formula for a blessing is spelled out in b., as usual, while in Tos. we have merely the operative words. This could be the work of a later scribe, but it is consistently done in b., while Tos. is spared similar improvements.

IV.i.2. [Re M. Ber. 4 : 4] R. Eliezer would pray a new prayer every day.

R. Abbahu would bless a new blessing every day.

y. Ber. 4 : 4

*Comment*: This comment on M. Ber. 4 : 4 does not allude to Eliezer at all. An Eliezer in contrast to Abbahu probably alludes to Eleazar b. Pedat, Abbahu's student, just as Eliezer and ʿAqiba are juxtaposed. Lieberman has Eleazar. It stands to reason that when Abbahu is juxtaposed to Rʾ it usually must be Eleazar, not Eliezer b. Hyrcanus. For this reason we omit reference to such pericopae.

II.i.2. *And the Lord said unto Moses, "Wherefore criest thou unto Me? Speak unto the children of Israel that they go forward* (Ex. 14 : 15)."

A. R. Joshua says, "The Holy One, blessed be He, said unto Moses, 'Moses, all that Israel has to do is to go forward.' "

B. R. Eliezer says, "The Holy One, blessed be He, said to Moses, 'Moses, My children are in distress, the sea forming a bar and the enemy pursuing, and you stand there reciting long prayers; wherefore criest thou unto Me?' "

C. For R. Eliezer used to say, "There is a time to be brief in prayer and a time to be lengthy."

D. *Heal her now, O God, I beseech Thee* (Num. 12 : 13). This is an instance of being brief.

*And I fell down before the Lord as at the first time*, etc. (Deut. 9 : 18). This is an instance of being lengthy.

Mekh. Beshallaḥ 4 : 1-9, Lauterbach I, p. 216

II.i.3.A. *And he cried unto the Lord* (Ex. 15 : 25). From this you learn that the righteous are not hard to complain to. By the way, you also learn that the prayer of the righteous is short.

B. It happened once that a disciple, in the presence of R. Eliezer, went up to read the service and made his prayers short.

The other disciples remarked to R. Eliezer, "You notice how so-and-so made his prayers short." And they used to say about him, "This one is a scholar who makes short prayers."

But R. Eliezer said to them, "He did not make it shorter than Moses did, as it is said: *Heal her now, O God, I beseech Thee* (Num. 12 : 13)."

C. Again it happened once that a disciple in the presence of R. Eliezer went up to read the service and made his prayers long.

The other disciples remarked to R. Eliezer, "You notice that so-and-so made his prayers long." And they used to say about him, "This one is a scholar who makes long prayer."

But R. Eliezer said to them, "He did not make them longer than Moses did, as it is said, *So I fell down before the Lord the forty days,* etc. (Deut. 9 : 25)."

For R. Eliezer used to say, "There is a time to be brief in prayer and a time to be lengthy."

Mekh. Vayassa 1 : 93-105, Lauterbach II, pp. 91-92

II.ii.1.A. *And the Lord said to Moses, "Why do you cry to me* (Ex. 14 : 15)."

B. R. Joshua says, "Israel has no [choice] but to go forward."

C. R. Eliezer says, "The Holy One blessed be He said to Moses, 'My children are enmeshed in difficulty, and the day is closing, and the enemy is pursuing, and are you standing and making much prayer before me? *Why do you cry to me? Speak to the children of Israel that they go forward.'* "

D. For he would say, "There is a time to be brief and a time to draw out [prayer]."

Mekhilta deR. Simeon b. Yoḥai, p. 57, ls. 4-8

II.iv.1. His disciples asked R. Eliezer, "How long should a man draw out prayer?"

He said to them, "He should not draw it out more than Moses, as it is said, *Oh God, heal her.* There is a time to be brief and a time to draw out [prayer]."

Sifré Num. 105, Friedman, p. 28b

II.ii.2.A. And another story (WŠWB MʿŚH B) A student came before R. Eliezer [to lead prayers] and cut his blessings short.

His disciples said to him, "Rabbi, Have you noticed that so-and-so cut short his blessings? It would be appropriate that the disciples of the sages should speak to him."

He said to them, "He has not abbreviated more than did Moses, who said, *O Lord, heal her* (Num. 12 : 13)."

B. For he would say, "There is a time to abbreviate and a time to draw out [prayer]."

Mekhilta deR. Simeon b. Yoḥai, p. 103, ls. 19-23

III.ii.3.A. TNW RBNN MʿŚH B: A certain disciple went down

before the ark in the presence of R. Eliezer, and was spinning out [the prayer] too much.

His disciples said to him, "Our master, Is this one not long-winded."

He said to them, "Does he spin out [the prayer] more than Moses our master, concerning whom is written, *Forty days and forty nights* (Deut. 9 : 25)."

III.ii.4. ŚWB M'ŚH B: A certain disciple who went down before the ark in the presence of R. Eliezer, and he abbreviated [the prayers] too much. His disciples said to him, "Does this one not abbreviate? Is this one not too short [about it]?"

He said to them, "Does he cut short more than Moses our master, concerning whom it is written, *O Lord, forgive her* (Num. 12 : 13)."

b. Ber. 34a

III.ii.5. *And Moses besought* (YḤL) *the Lord* (Ex. 32 : 11). TNY': R. Eliezer the Great said, "This teaches that Moses stood praying before the Holy One, blessed be He, until an *aḥilu* seized him."

b. Ber. 32a

*Comment*: Warrant for assigning these materials to Eliezer b. Hyrcanus is not strong. It consists of the juxtaposition of the not-closely-related comments of Joshua and Eliezer on Ex. 14 : 15. The masters differ about the explanation of the verse, so it would seem that the Eliezer involved in all sayings about praying briefly or otherwise ought to be Eliezer b. Hyrcanus. The same idea—that there is a time to be brief and a time to be lengthy—takes the form of two stories, which circulate separately. Underlying the several pericopae would be the simple saying, which would then have generated both an exegesis and a story about the two disciples. The legal saying about not making a fixed text for prayers stands by itself, but seems the obvious legal inference to be drawn from the stories, exegeses and sayings.

V.xi.1.A. *Speak unto the children of Israel* (Ex. 14 : 15).

B. R. Eliezer said, "The Holy One, blessed be He, said to Moses, 'There is a time to pray briefly and a time to pray at length. My children are in dire distress, the sea shuts them in and the enemy is pursuing, and you stand here adding prayer on prayer. *Speak unto the children of Israel, that they go forward.*' "

C. R. Joshua said, "God said to Moses, 'All that Israel have to do is to go forward. Therefore, let them go forward! Let their feet step forward from the dry land to the sea, and thou wilt see the miracles which I will perform for them.' "

Ex. R. 21 : 8, trans. S. M. Lehrman, p. 270

III.ii.6.A. TNY᾽: R. Eliezer says, "One should first pray for his own needs and then recite The Prayer, as it is said: *A prayer for the afflicted [himself] when he is overwhelmed, and [then] poureth forth his meditation before the Lord*: (Ps. 102 : 1) and by *'meditation,'* only prayer is meant, as it is said, *And Isaac went out to meditate in the field at the eventide.* (Gen. 24 : 63)."

B. R. Joshua says, "One should first recite The Prayer and then ask for his own needs, as it is said, *I pour out my meditation before Him [then] I declare my [own] affliction before Him* (Ps. 142 : 3)."

b.A.Z. 7b, trans. A. Mishcon, p. 34

*Comment*: The dispute is unknown to Mishnah-Tosefta. Eliezer's opinion is more or less inconsistent with the principle that the Prayer is not fixed at all, so individual needs should be included within its structure.

I.i.4.A. They mention 'the Powers of rain' in "Resurrection of the dead," and ask for rain in the 'Blessing of the Years.'

B. And *Havdalah*—

In 'Favors [man with] knowledge.'

C. R. ʿAqiba says, "He says it as a fourth blessing, by itself."

D. R. Eliezer says, "In 'Thanksgiving.' "

M. Ber. 5 : 2 (y. Ber. 5 : 2, b. Nid. 8a, b. Ber. 29a, 33a-b)

*Comment*: ʿAqiba and Eliezer differ from the anonymous rule in B. No one alludes to A, on which all parties agree. The anonymous opinion (B) is that on Saturday night one says *Havdalah* in the fourth blessing, that beginning with the words 'You favor man with knowledge.' ʿAqiba maintains that the *Havdalah* is said by itself and has its own concluding blessing, "Blessed ... who distinguishes sacred and profane." Then the blessing normally standing at fourth place, 'Favors man with knowledge, is said, now as the fifth. Eliezer says the *Havdalah* is recited in the 'Thanksgiving' prayer, after the normal Eighteen Blessings have been concluded. So ʿAqiba is in disagreement with the anonymous opinion, and Eliezer stands outside the range of that disagreement.

ʿAqiba's saying depends upon B but expands the saying: he says *it.* The simplest structure would be, *And [as to] Havdalah, he says it in 'Favors'... As 'Blessing'... In 'Thanksgiving.'* This was impossible because the opening sentence is a complete thought: *They make mention ... They ask ... And [they say] Havdalah ... They say* thus is understood. But to introduce ʿAqiba's saying, the redactor has had to supply what formerly was understood, so as to separate the dispute from the materials on which all parties stand in agreement. Then Eliezer's saying remains in its brief, "original" form, a single-word-reference to the appropriate place in the service, *In* (B) + *Blessing.*

The two named masters therefore differ with reference to a detail of an already completed pericope, to which their sayings in C + D add a gloss. One must again wonder, therefore, what stood before them, and from what source they derived the rules on which they agreed—in the *very* language now before us?

Perhaps an antecedent code was worked out and handed on to Yavneh; or perhaps Yavneans gave as anonymous law the decisions on which all parties agreed. Here the difference between the two possibilities is a real one. The issue of the anonymous law, A, suggests that someone was working out fundamental issues of liturgy. Perhaps some basic structure of prayer was received at Yavneh, and the Yavnean masters then had to work out and insert some details of the new prayers they proposed to supply—a prayer for rain, *Havdalah*, and so forth. Alternatively, the Yavneans were working out a quite new liturgy, and the antecedent materials on which Eliezer and ʿAqiba comment were the work of their generation alone. I see no grounds for coming to a firm conjecture.

The antecedent rule—One does not stand up to pray except with proper reverence—contains a tradition about the early pious men (*Ḥasidim HaRishonim*). But that tradition interpolates information not essential to the opening rule, and then M. Ber. 5 : 2 begins with language in the same form as M. Ber. 5 : 1, "They do not stand ... They make mention ... They ask ..." M. Ber. 5 : 3 has a quite separate rule, unrelated in substance, and in different sentence-structure, "He who says ... They silence him. He who passes before the ark and errs ..." So the opening paragraphs preserve consistent usage, which changes afterward.

This would seem to indicate that M. Ber. 5 : 1-2 are to be distinguished from M. Ber. 5 : 3ff., and are a separate unit; without the reference to the early pious men, the form would be consistent with M. Ber. 1 : 1, 2: the present participle, in the plural, *From what time do they ...*

Let us assemble all rules that make use of this simple construction:

M. Ber. 1 : 1: From what time do they read the *Shemaʿ* in the evening.

M. Ber. 1 : 2: From what time do they read the *Shemaʿ* in the morning.

[M. Ber. 1 : 3: House of Shammai vs. House of Hillel on proper posture for *Shemaʿ*, interpolated into foregoing]

M. Ber. 1 : 5: They mention the Exodus from Egypt at night. [Drop: Interpolation of Eleazar b. ʿAzariah.]

M. Ber. 2 : 3: Women, slaves, and children are free of the obligation to read *Shemaʿ*.

M. Ber. 1 : 5: They arise to say the Prayer only with reverence.

M. Ber. 5 : 2: They make mention ...

So the pericopae which make use of the present tense participle in the plural pertain to reading the *Shemaʿ* and saying the Prayer. It would then seem that the original "code" alluded to above (p. 19) contained simple rules about saying the *Shemaʿ* and the Prayer in the morning. It has been abbreviated—surely other rules existed—but at the same time richly interpolated by rabbinic rules of various kinds. But none of these is given in the simple plural, present-participial form; whether or not assigned to named masters, *all* make use of forms different from the basic one.

Now let us now look for the same simple construction in the subsequent chapters:

M. Ber. 6 : 1: How do they bless fruit?
1. Fruit from tree
2. Wine.
3. Fruit from earth.
4. Bread.
5. And vegetables (reverts to 3)

M. Ber. 6 : 6: [They were sitting to eat]—Each one blesses for himself.

M. Ber. 7 : 3: How do they invite [for Grace]?
Various cases.

M. Ber. 8 : 6: They do not bless over the light, spice, of gentiles, etc.

In general, where the pericopae diverge from this simple participial structure, they also introduce special cases, exceptions, rules assigned to named masters, and the like. So the present-tense-plural-participial-pericopae supply the following rules: 1. Reciting the *Shemaʿ*; 2. Saying the Prayer; 3. Blessing fruit; 4. Saying Grace after meals—the fundamentals of the ordinary Jew's liturgical life. All other materials differ *both* as to form and as to substance; in the former, all sorts of other constructions *except* this one are used, as to the latter, many kinds of special cases and other sorts of information are supplied.

Are we then able to claim a particular authority for the legal style we have here isolated? I think not. This construction is commonplace. When we consider its chief grammatical characteristic—the use of the present participle in the plural—we find the same construction with reference to the Houses, and in every subsequent stratum. Hence the participial construction, by itself, is merely a technique in the presentation of law (to be sure, a technique absent in Scriptures). But use of that technique cannot have been limited to a single stratum or circle of masters or redactors. What recognition of the technique does permit, however, is the isolation of a stratum within a complex set of pericopae, such as a tractate of Mishnah, and here the picture is clear, as given. Since the earliest Yavneans—Eliezer, Joshua, Gamaliel, and ʿAqiba—attest to the existence, in the exact form before us, of pericopae following the plural-present-tense-participial construction, we may reliably claim that the form of simple rules given in that construction comes before their time. Our results in M. Ber. 1 : 1-2 would suggest that some sort of catechism, or rule book, produced by Temple authorities, but perhaps widely used outside of the Temple, has been taken over by Yavneans and employed as the basic structure for the development of their legal materials, finally redacted as Mishnah tractate Berakhot.

Note b. Ber. 33b: R. Zera-R. Ḥiyya b. Abin-R. Yoḥanan: The law follows R. Eliezer in respect to a festival that follows the Sabbath. y. Ber. 5 : 2, R. Isaac Rabbah in the name of Rabbi: The law follows [as above], etc. Likewise b. Nid. 8a, R. Eleazar says, "The law follows R. Eliezer."

I.ii.2. In services on all [holidays] in which there is no Additional Service, for instance, Ḥanukkah and Purim, in the Morning and Afternoon services one prays the Eighteen Benedictions and says a summary of the event (MʿYN HMWRʾ). If he did not say it, they do not have him go back.

And on all [holidays] on which there is an Additional Service, for example the New Moon and the Intermediate Days of the Festivals, in the Morning and Afternoon services he prays the Eighteen Benedictions, and says the Sanctification of the Day (QDWŠT HYWM) in the Sacrificial Service (ʿBWDH).

R. Liezer says, "In the 'Thanksgiving.'"

Tos. Ber. 3 : 10, Lieberman, p. 15, ls. 47-51 (y. Ber. 7 : 5, b. Shab. 24a)

I.ii.3. [On] Sabbath that coincides with the New Moon and on the intervening days of the festival(s), morning and noon, he prays seven, and says the Sanctification of the Day in the Sacrificial Prayer (ʿBWDH).

R. Liezer says, "In the 'Thanksgiving.'"

Tos. Ber. 3 : 11, Lieberman, p. 15, ls. 52-54 (b. Eruv. 40b, Bes. 17a)

*Comment*: Eliezer is consistent in assigning to the 'Thanksgiving' all additions to the service on the occasion of special events.

III.ii.7. [*Baraita re* the order of Grace after meals.] The Sanctification of the day is mentioned in the middle [of the blessing, 'Who is good and bestows good.']

R. Eliezer says, "If he likes, he can mention it in the consolation, or he can mention it in the blessing of the land, or he can mention it in the benediction which the rabbis instituted in Yavneh [= the fourth, 'Who is good and who does good.']"

And the sages say, "It must be said in the Consolation blessing."

b. Ber. 48b

*Comment*: See Lieberman, *Tosefta Kifshuṭah Seder Zeraʿim* I, p. 40, It is difficult to see how our Eliezer could have referred in the past tense to a blessing made up by the 'rabbis in Yavneh,' of which, one assumes, he was numbered. One gains the impression, however, that the early Yavneans were engaged in arranging various prayers—perhaps adding here and restructuring there—which they had in hand from earlier times.

III.ii.8.A. TNW RBNN: Who is an *ʿam haʾareṣ*?

B. "Whoever does not read the *Shema*ʿ evening and morning," the words of R. Eliezer.

R. Joshua says, "Whoever does not lay *tefillin*."

Ben ʿAzzai says, "Whoever has no *ṣiṣit* on his garment."

C. R. Nathan says, "Whoever has no *mezuzah* on his door."

D. R. Nathan b. R. Joseph says, "Whoever has sons and does not raise them for the study of Torah."

b. Ber. 47b

*Comment*: Note the following, earlier in the same compilation (b. Ber. 47b):

"Who is an *ʿam haʾareṣ*? Anyone who does not eat his secular [unconsecrated] food in ritual cleanness," the words of R. Meir.

The rabbis say, "Whoever does not properly tithe."

The Yavnean opinions stress saying the *Shema*ʿ, *Tefillin*, and *ṣiṣit*, which is consistent both with their focus on the *Shema*ʿ and with Eliezer's sayings about the value of *tefillin*. The Ushans (Meir) distinguish on the basis of tithing/ritual purity, so they asked for what fifty years earlier was done only by Pharisees.

III.ii.9.A. Why should one wipe with the left hand and not with the right?

B. TNYʾ: R. Eliezer says, "Because one eats with it."

R. Joshua says, "Because one writes with it."

R. ʿAqiba says, "Because one points with it to the accents in the scroll."

b. Ber. 62a

V.i.1.A. If one enters a privy, let him turn his face neither to the east nor to the west, but sideways. Nor should he uncover himself standing up, but sitting down. Nor shall a man wipe himself with his right hand, but with his left.

B. Now why was it said that a man should not wipe himself with his right hand, but with his left?

R. Eliezer says, "Because with the right hand the words of the Torah are pointed at."

R. Joshua says, "Because one eats and drinks with it."

ARN Chap. 40, Goldin, p. 168

V.v.1. What is the reason that we do not wipe with the right hand?

R. Eliezer said, "Because one eats with it."

R. Joshua said, "Because one writes with it."

Rabban Gamaliel said, "Because one points with it to the cantillations of the Torah."

Derekh Ereṣ Rabbah 7 : 6, trans. M. Ginsberg, p. 555

*Comment*: b. Ber. 62a has equivalent opinions in the name of Amoraim: "Rava says, 'Because the Torah was given with the right hand'; Rabbah b. b. Ḥana, 'Because it is brought to the mouth ...' R. Naḥman b. Isaac, 'Because one points to the accents in the scroll with it.' " Eliezer has the same opinion as Rabbah b. b. Ḥana, and ʿAqiba is equivalent to Naḥman b. Isaac. ARN then gives Eliezer the opinion of ʿAqiba, and Joshua has Eliezer's opinion. Derekh Ereṣ Rabbah has Eliezer and Joshua as in b. Ber., but gives Gamaliel instead of ʿAqiba. All this is curious. First, if the fourth-century Amoraim had a Tannaitic tradition, then why do they give their own opinions instead of citing the baraita? The other compilations, by contrast, know nothing of the tradition in the Babylonian *Gemara*. But the *Gemara* does have their traditions! On the face of it, it would seem that the final editing of the *Gemara* included traditions unknown to the forth-century Amoraim, but evidently available (assuming ARN comes before the sixth or seventh century) to the Palestinian compilers as Tannaitic teachings.

## ii. Peʾah

I.i.5.A. R. Eliezer says, "Ground of the size of a quarter [*qav*] is liable for *peʾah*."

B. R. Joshua says, "That which produces two *seʾahs*."

C. R. Ṭarfon says, "Six by six *ṭefaḥs*"

D. R. Judah b. Bathyra says, "Sufficient so as to harvest and repeat [the process]."

And the law according to his words.

E. R. ʿAqiba says, "Land of any size is liable for *peʾah*, and for first fruits and to write a *prozbul* on its basis and to buy with it movable property by money, writ, or seizure."

M. Peʾah 3 : 6 (y. Peʾah 3 : 6, 7; y. Peʾah 5 : 2;
b. Qid. 26a, b. B.B. 27b, 150a)

*Comment*: The five masters supply definitions for a fundamental question in respect to the obligation to leave a 'corner of the field'—how big a field is involved?

Eliezer's saying contains language serving all except ʿAqiba, who repeats Eliezer's *Land ... obligated for peʾah*. The others' sayings all take that language for granted. ʿAqiba's saying is considerably longer and more detailed than the others; the introduction of the extraneous issues led to the reformulation of ʿAqiba's KL ŠHWʾ—of any size—into a whole sentence.

Eliezer says land in which one may sow a quarter-*qav* of seed, which is ten and a fifth *amot* by ten and a fifth *amot*, is liable. Joshua measures by the fruitfulness of the land. Ṭarfon's measurement is clear. Judah b. Bathyra's means, If there is in the standing wheat enough twice to fill the hand of the reaper, the piece of land is liable. ʿAqiba selects the smallest possible size of land.

I.i.6.A. A vineyard that was wholly defective clusters (ʿWLLWT)—

B. R. Eliezer says, "[It belongs] to the landowner."

C. R. ʿAqiba says, "To the poor."

D. R. Eliezer said, "*When you gather the grapes of your vineyard, you shall not take the defective clusters* (Deut. 24 : 21). If there has been no grape-gathering, from whence do the defective clusters come?"

E. R. ʿAqiba said to him, "*And from your vineyard you shall not take the defective clusters* (Lev. 19 : 10)—even if the whole consists of defective clusters. If so, why is *When you gather, you shall not take the defective clusters* said? The poor have no right to the defective clusters before the vintage."

M. Peʾah 7 : 7 (Midrash Tannaʾim to Deut. 24 : 2, Hoffmann, p. 162, y. Peʾah 7 : 6)

*Comment*: In the whole field there is not a grapecluster with both shoulder and pendant (M. Peʾah 7 : 4). Eliezer holds the poor therefore have no claim on the field. ʿAqiba says the whole belongs to the poor.

The sayings of both masters complete the topic-sentence: *A vineyard . . . [belongs] to the poor/landowner.* Then we have a debate, in which ʿAqiba has the last word and wins. The order of B-C thus favors Eliezer, but D-E, ʿAqiba.

Eliezer's argument is that Scripture refers to gathering grapes. But since there has been no grape-gathering, the rule of Scripture cannot apply. ʿAqiba's argument is equally close to the plain sense of Scripture—but of a different Scripture. Lev. 19 : 10 is clear that you must not take the defective grapes under any circumstances. But ʿAqiba now has the advantage of dealing also with Deut. 24 : 21. Its meaning is that there is no access for the poor before the vintage—*When* you gather, but *not* before.

This interpretation of the Scripture certainly is close to Eliezer's. Both agree that *When you gather* supplies a definition for the rights of the poor, but Eliezer holds the operative word is *gather*, and ʿAqiba, *when*. What is obviously lacking is Eliezer's interpretation of Lev. 19 : 10. ʿAqiba has not made use of an exegetical device characteristic of the ʿAqiban school and perhaps not held as valid by Eliezer.

Parts A, B, and C therefore seem neutral, but D-E do not.

The question of the pericope is a third-level inquiry, taking for granted that a great many more commonplace situations with respect to the defective-clusters-rules have been covered by legislation. M. Peʾah 7 : 4, defining the grapecluster (leaving out the little problem of the single grape, raised by Judah b. Ilai—who rules in harmony with Eliezer), and M. Peʾah 7 : 6, the Houses on the rules of Grape-gleanings and the defective cluster in the Fourth Year Vineyard, pertain to more basic problems. Hence it looks as if the pericope before us will follow the formulation of M. Pe᾽ah 7 : 4 and 6.

M. Pe᾽ah 7 : 8 deals with a dedication of the vineyard before it can be known which are the defective clusters. This is more difficult to reckon. It would seem a still more remote problem, and Yosi's comment suggests that the problem came up in Usha. But the considerations of the substance of law can never be probative, merely suggestive.

II.iii.1. A vineyard which is entirely made up of defective clusters—

R. Eliezer says, "[It belongs] to the householder."

R. ʿAqiba says, "To the poor . . ."

Sifra Qedoshim Pereq 3 : 1, Weiss, p. 88a

II.iv.2. *When you harvest your vineyard*—

On this basis

R. Eliezer used to say, "A vineyard which is entirely made up of defective clusters belongs to the householder."

R. ʿAqiba says, "To the poor."

Sifré Deut. 285, Finkelstein, p. 302

*Comment*: The Tannaitic *midrashim* simply attach the dispute to the appropriate Scriptures.

II.i.4. *Neither shalt thou favor a poor man in his cause.* Why is this said? Because of this: It says, *Thou shalt not respect the person of the poor nor favor the person of the mighty* (Lev. 19 : 15).

From this I know only these prohibitions in their exact form. But how about reversing them? It says here: *Neither shalt thou favor a poor man in his cause.*

Abba Ḥanin says in the name of R. Eliezer, "Scripture here refers to the gleaning, the forgotten sheaf, and the corner [that one may not favor one poor man over another]."

Mekh. Kaspa 2 : 75-79, Lauterbach III, p. 162.

*Comment*: Eliezer is consistent with the House of Shammai; see *Phar.* II, pp. 55-58.

I.ii.4. Tos. Pe᾽ah 3 : 2; y. Pe᾽ah 6 : 2.

*Comment*: *Phar.* II, pp. 60-3. Here Joshua and Eliezer define a Houses' dispute with respect to the Forgotten Sheaf.

### iii. Demai

I.i.7.A. They give tithe for what [is bought] from an Israelite for what [is bought] from a gentile and *vice versa*; for what [is bought] from an Israelite for what [is bought] from Samaritans (KWTYM), and from what is bought from Samaritans for what is bought from Samaritans.

B. R. Eliezer [Naples, Kaufmann, Parma, Camb.; Eleazar] prohibits [tithing] from what [is bought] from Samaritans for what [is bought] from [other] Samaritans.

M. Dem. 5 : 9

*Comment*: B pertains only to the last clause of A.

I.ii.5. R. Eliezer says, "As to the produce of Samaritans, just as they made the fruits of Israelites *demai* after the majority, [and] they do not tithe from this for this, so they tithe the *demai-* [or, certain WDʾY]) fruits of Samaritans, and they do not tithe from this for this."

Tos. Dem. 5 : 22, Lieberman, p. 92, ls. 94-6

*Comment*: Tos. Dem. 5 : 22 seems to complete the thought of M. Dem. 5 : 9B. Lieberman reads, "So they treated the fruit of Samaritans as *certain[ly un*tithed], after the majority, and they do not tithe this for this." Samaritans do not tithe what they sell, therefore one does not tithe one thing for the other.

The problem before us is whether this is Eliezer or Eleazar [b. ʿAzariah]. MS evidence gives Eleazar. The pertinent passage in y. Dem. 5 : 9 has Leazar. Since Lieberman prints Liezer, I copied the pericope. M. Shev. 8 : 9-10 and y. Shev. 8 : 8 seem to warrant assigning this pericope to our Eliezer. But compare Epstein, *Nusaḥ*, p. 1177, and on the larger problem of Eliezer/Eleazar readings, see pp. 1162-1182. In this instance we shall stand by our warrant to the extent of including the pericope here. But in Parts II and III we cannot make use of it.

I.ii.6.A. The first fruits and the left-over figs in the garden are liable, in the valley are free . . .

B. R. Leʿii says in the name of R. Liezer, "The first fruits are always liable, for they are guarded."

Tos. Dem. 1 : 3, Lieberman, p. 62, ls. 6-8

III.i.1. R. Leʿii said in the name of R. Liezer, "The first fruits—*lo*, they are obligated, because they are *in the presumption of* [being] guarded."

y. Dem. 1 : 1, Gilead, p. 2

*Comment*: Eliezer differs from the antecedent rule with respect to first fruits. The liability is to separate the tithes of *demai*-produce, Tithe, Heave-Offering of Tithe, Poorman's Tithe or Second Tithe. Wild growth is not so obligated (M. Dem. 1 : 1), but what is cultivated is. The y. gloss *re presumption* takes account of the fact that it would hardly pay to hire a guard to protect the crop; hence they are not necessarily "protected," but are in the *presumption* of being protected—a typical quibble. The point is that the landowner *does* take account of them, hence the obligation for Heave-offering and Tithes.

Ilai's Eliezer certainly is ours.

## iv. Kila'im

I.i.8.A. He that keeps thorns in a vineyard—

B. R. Eliezer says, "He has forfeited (QDŠ) [the adjacent vines, on account of mixed seeds in the vineyard]."

C. And sages say, "He has not forfeited (except a thing the like of which they keep.)"

D. Iris, ivy, and fritillary [so Danby for ŠWŠNT HMLK] and all kinds of seeds are not 'mixed seeds' in the vineyard.

M. Kil. 5 : 8 (y. Kil. 1 : 1, 5 : 7)

*Comment*: Here Eliezer and the sages have exactly balanced opinions in the apodosis, QDŠ +/— L'. But the sages' opinion is immediately qualified by a gloss, and this further produces a long explanatory interpolation. The gloss explains the sages' view: since thorns are not usually raised for a useful purpose, they do not fall under the rules of 'mixed seeds.' Eliezer holds that they are fed to cattle, therefore are useful.

Both parties take for granted an unstated generalization, that what is not normally raised will not fall under the rules of 'mixed seeds', for the man must intend some useful purpose in planting, or keeping, the crop before the prohibition of 'mixed seeds' will apply. M. Kil. 3 : 6 has a similar example of that unstated rule, "If a man saw vegetables growing in the vineyard and said, 'When I reach them, I will pick them,' they are not forbidden; 'When I come again, I [then] will pick them,' they are forbidden, even if they have grown only another two-hundredth part." The point is that in allowing the seeds to continue to grow, the man has shown his intention of making use of the product of mixed seeds in a vineyard—a rule that would come before Eliezer's here.

Both Eliezer and the sages thus take for granted that what is decisive is the man's intention—a position consistently taken by the House of Hillel, and consistently rejected by the House of Shammai, which would have ruled, whether or not the crop is made use of, its mere presence—without regard to the man's intention for it—is sufficient to forfeit the adjacent vines. But, while the House of Shammai are represented in M. Kil., they do not raise the issue of intention where it should have been brought up, such as in this case. But Eliezer judges the man's intent by what he has done, not by what he has said. Eliezer therefore is in the position of the House of Shammai, the sages, of Hillel. Interestingly, the pericope follows the usual form for Houses' disputes (*Phar.* II, pp. 1-5). On this basis we tentatively assign the pericope to our Eliezer.

II.iv.3. He who keeps thorns in the vineyard—

R. Eliezer says, "He has sanctified, as it is said, *Which you will sow.*"

And sages say, "*Seed*—excluding him that keeps thorns in the vineyard."

Sifré Deut. 230, Finkelstein, p. 263

*Comment*: Now the dispute is given an exegetical foundation and formulated in Scriptural terms. What the man has done is decisive. Since he keeps the thorns, he wants them—they are "guarded"—and is therefore liable. To the sages, the issue is that the thorns do not fall in the category of useful "seed;" intention is irrelevant.

I.i.9.A. Handkerchiefs, wrappers for Torah-scrolls, and bathtowels do not come under the law of 'diverse kinds.'

B. R. Eliezer [Parma: Leazar] prohibits [= they *do* come under the law of 'diverse kinds'].

M. Kil. 9 : 3

*Comment*: Eliezer's language is inappropriate to the issue; one must know that the 'prohibition' comes if the aforenamed cloths contain a mixture of linen and wool. The issue is whether the cloths constitute garments or not. Eliezer says they do, the antecedent, anonymous rule, that they do not.

See Epstein, *Nusaḥ*, p. 133; *Tan.* pp. 66, 99, 113.

I.ii.7.A. Handkerchiefs and book-wrappers and bath-towels are not subject to the law of 'diverse kinds.'

"R. Liezer prohibits," the words of R. Meir.

B. R. Judah says, "R. Liezer permits, and the sages prohibit."

Tos. Kil. 5 : 18, Lieberman, p. 224, ls. 38-40.

*Comment*: M. Kil. 9 : 3 is Meir's version. Judah has Eliezer in the lenient position, compare M. Ed. 5 : 1. Judah's tradition is adequate warrant to assign the pericope to our Eliezer.

### v. Shevi'it

I.i.10.A. Arum (LWP) which has remained after the Seventh Year—

B. R. Eliezer says, "If the poor have gathered its leaves, they have gathered. And if not, he should come to an agreement (ḤŠBWN) with the poor."

C. R. Joshua says, "If the poor have gathered its leaves, they have gathered. And if not, the poor have no claim (ḤŠBWN) on him."

M. Shev. 5 : 3 (y. Shev. 5 : 2)

*Comment*: The arum was sown in the sixth year and matured in the eighth (the year after the Seventh Year). If the poor have gathered the leaves, it is well and good. If not, what has grown in the Seventh Year belongs to the poor, so the landowner has to give them their share, according to Eliezer. Joshua holds that the poor have no claim in, or therefore after, the Seventh Year. The operative words are as follows:

Eliezer: Y῾ŚH ḤŠBWN ῾M H῾NYYM

Joshua: ᾿YN L῾NYYM ῾LYW ḤŠBWN

The sayings are not closely matched. If we drop the words common to both, together with their auxiliaries, we find Y῾ŚH *vs.* ᾿YN! No effort has been made to set the differing opinions into a syzygous structure, even though the opinions exactly match in substance and could have been adequately rendered through a common verb +/– ᾿YN.

The setting is a ruling about arum; 5 : 2 involves Meir and the sages, "If arum is covered up with earth in the Seventh Year." This immediately yields the problem of 5 : 3—What to do with the result? 5 : 4 has a Houses' dispute on how to dig arum which has remained from the sixth year to the Seventh Year, in logical progression; then 5 : 5, When may arum be gathered after the end of the Seventh Year?—with Judah [b. Ilai]'s opinion. So the subject-matter is fairly coherent, but the masters come from different generations, and the whole cannot have been arranged before Ushan times.

Lieberman notes (*Tosefta Kifshuṭah Seder Zera῾im* II, p. 528) that Eliezer holds the poor alone may eat after the Burning [removal] at the beginning of the Seventh Year. If the arum has sprouted leaves, the poor may then take the leaves in the Seventh Year. The man has not uprooted the arum, but has cut it back. y. Shev. 5 : 2 points out that in M. Shev. 9 : 8, Judah, who says the poor eat after the Burning, follows Eliezer here, and Yosi, who says the rich also do so, follows Joshua.

I.ii.8. Arum which has remained after the Seventh Year—

R. Liezer says, "If it remained [in the ground] three years [after the Seventh Year], he gives the poor a fourth; if it remained two years, he gives the poor a third; one year—he gives the poor half."

Tos. Shev. 4 : 3, Lieberman, p. 179-180, ls. 5-7 (y. Shev. 5 : 2)

*Comment*: The Mishnah specifies that the poor get their share. Tos. tells us what that share consists of, therefore depends upon M. Shev. 5 : 3.

I.ii.9. Tos. Shev. 1 : 5.

*Comment*: See *Phar.* II, pp. 78-79. This is not our Eliezer.

I.i.11. The rose, henna, lotus, and balsam are subject to the law of the Seventh Year and their proceeds are subject to the law of the Seventh Year.

M. Shev. 7 : 6

*Comment*: This rule is consistent with the view of Eliezer, so b. Nid. 8a: R. Pedat said, "Who taught that balsam is a fruit? R. Eliezer." Accordingly, Eliezer stands behind the above.

I.i.12.A. ["An important general rule have they said concerning the Seventh Year: Whatever is gathered solely as food for man may not be used as an emollient [MLGM') for man ... or cattle; and whatever is not solely for food for man may be used as an emollient for man, but not for cattle; and whatever is not solely either for food for man or for food for cattle—if he intended it for food for man and for food for cattle, they place on it the stringent rules regarding man and cattle ..."—[M. Shev. 8 : 1.]

B. A hide which one has anointed with oil of the Seventh Year—

C. R. Eliezer says, "It is to be burned."

D. And sages say, "He should eat [produce of] equal value (Y'KL KNGDW)."

E. They said before R. ʿAqiba, "R. Eliezer used to say, 'A hide which one has anointed with oil of the Seventh Year—it is to be burned.'"

F. He said to them, "Silence. I shall not say to you what R. Eliezer says concerning it."

M. Shev. 8 : 9 (y. Shev. 8 : 8)

I.i.13.A. Further they said before him, "R. Eliezer used to say, 'He who eats the bread of Samaritans is like him who eats the flesh of a pig.'"

B. He said to them, "Silence. I shall not tell you what R. Eliezer says concerning it."

M. Shev. 8 : 10

*Comment*: The general rule is as given in A. R. Eliezer then rules strictly; the punishment is the burning of the whole hide. M. Shev. 8 : 8 has, "Vessels may not be anointed with oil from Seventh Year produce, and if one has done so he must buy and consume produce of equal value." So Eliezer's ruling in C stands in opposition to the earlier, anonymous law, whose ruling then is repeated verbatim in D.

Parts E and F constitute a separate tradition. M. Shev. 8 : 9 and 8 : 10A are similar in structure; F and B are identical. So a single form has been used for two separate laws, concerning which it is stated that Eliezer's real ruling differs from the publicly acknowledged one.

Since M. Shev. 8 : 9 E + F are virtually identical in substance to B + C, one must ask, Which comes first, the story or the generalized rule of law? Clearly, from ʿAqiba's words we may suppose Eliezer is dead; therefore the redactor comes later than Eliezer himself. Further, M. Shev.

8 : 10 has no general rule attributed to Eliezer, only a story which ought to have yielded a standard legal saying. So it does not seem as though Eliezer's opinion in M. Shev. 8 : 10 has produced the appropriate legal structure, and this would suggest that the story-form for his opinion comes before the standard legal saying-form. If so, M. Shev. 8 : 9 E + F come before and produce not only B-C-D, but also M. Shev. 8 : 8, a still more generalized version of the sages' view (D).

M. A. Z. 2 : 6 contains an appropriate saying, without attribution to Eliezer and without allusion to the Samaritans (!): "These things of the gentiles are forbidden, but it is not forbidden to have any benefit at all from them [one may sell, but not consume them]: ... their bread and their oil." This anonymous rule takes for granted that idolators' bread may not be eaten. Eliezer's saying is phrased in such strong language that it invites a contrary view, "And sages say, Permitted." But the issue is not whether idolators' bread is acceptable, but Samaritans', and here the problem is the status of Samaritans, not merely of their bread. We observe in M. Dem. 5 : 9 an equivalent viewpoint on Eliezer's part, though it is uncertain whether in fact that is our Eliezer.

Now one must ask, What has happened to Eliezer's "real" opinion? ʿAqiba claims it is not as represented in M. Shev. 8 : 9C and 10A. Then how did the students know what they claimed to have as a tradition from Eliezer? Presumably someone has taught them an opinion in Eliezer's name, but it cannot be ʿAqiba. Then it is either Eliezer himself, or some other of his disciples—Joshua is out of the question. Now ʿAqiba has a teaching different from that of another of Eliezer's (nameless) disciples.

What was ʿAqiba's teaching? It was either more strict or more lenient that the one now attributed to Eliezer. In M. Shev. 8 : 9 a more strict opinion is simply out of the question—one cannot do more than destroy the hide.

If it then was a more lenient opinion, two possibilities present themselves; first is the opinion now given anonymously in M. Shev. 8 : 8, and to "sages" in 8 : 9; one buys and consumes produce of equal value. Second, he may have a still *more* lenient opinion than the sages. Such an opinion would be that one is not punished for using Seventh Year Oil for anointing hides; that is what the oil is intended for to begin with. So to Eliezer might have been attributed a statement that what is normally used for anointing may be used for anointing in the Seventh Year, as in M. Shev. 8 : 2: "Seventh Year produce is intended for use as food, drink, or unguent; that is to be used as food which is customarily eaten, and that used as drink which is customarily drunk; and that used as unguent which is customarily used for anointing."

Now this is not wholly consistent with 8 : 1: What is customarily gathered for food may not be used for ointment, etc. It is the generalization at the end which is set aside, "Whatsoever is not usually gathered solely as food for man or as food for cattle, yet was intended as food both for man and for cattle, the more stringent rules affecting both man and cattle apply." This leaves room for *cattle* but does not tell us what those rules of cattle are. So M. Shev. 8 : 2—silent on that point—tells us, "That which is used as unguent which is customarily used for anointing" continues to be used for that purpose in the Seventh Year. 8 : 8 applies to vessels, as we saw. Nothing is said about cattle, let alone hides. Eliezer's rule may have been, *As to cattle and hides, what is customarily used for anointing may be used for anointing in the Seventh Year.*

Of these two possibilities, which seems more likely? ʿAqiba threatens to tell the disciples what Eliezer had really said—and ends by saying nothing. So something radically different is to be attributed to him, and this, it would seem, may be the most lenient ruling of all. Likewise with the Samaritans—Eliezer is said to have forbidden eating their bread; in M. Dem. 5 : 9/Tos. Dem. 5 : 22, Eliezer/Eleazar is represented as regarding Samaritan tithing practice as similar to Israelite practice. So why not eat their bread? If ʿAqiba dismisses the disciples' traditions, and those traditions are as stringent as possible, then the alternative traditions ought to have been lenient, perhaps more lenient than other opinions, therefore *Eliezer permits eating Samaritan bread* or some such view, opposite to what the disciples say, ought to be Eliezer's real opinion.

Why does ʿAqiba not say so? In whose interest is it to represent Eliezer as very strict? Why has Eliezer been misrepresented in precisely these matters of law?

IV.i.3.A. What did R. Eliezer say concerning it [the hide, to ʿAqiba, which ʿAqiba would not reveal]?

R. Yosi said, "May the bones of that man moulder."

R. Ḥezeqiah in the name of R. Aḥa said, "It [the hide] is permitted."

B. And further they said before him—

R. Yosi said, "That is to say, it is prohibited to take the daughter of an *ʿam haʾareṣ*."

R. Ḥezeqiah in the name of R. Aḥa said, "R. Eliezer would permit [use of] the leavened products of Samaritans immediately after Passover."

y. Shev. 8 : 8

*Comment*: Ḥezeqiah has it that Eliezer took the lenient position. Yosi's judgment in B is that the *bread* (= cooking) is like the daughter; and the Samaritan is in the same status as the *ʿam haʾareṣ*— so, according to Yosi, Eliezer took a very extreme position. Ḥezeqiah again alleges that Eliezer's view was lenient; the Samaritan is no worse than the gentile, and since gentile leaven is permitted after Passover, the same applies to the Samaritan; but as to bread, it is prohibited.

I.i.14.A. He who pickles three [kinds of] vegetables in a single jar—

B. R. Eliezer says, "They eat according to the first."

C. R. Joshua says, "Even (ʾP) according to the last."

D. Rabban Gamaliel says, "Each whose type has ceased from the field—let him remove its type from the jar."

E. And the law is according to his words.

M. Shev. 9 : 5 (y. Shev. 9 : 4; b. Pes. 52a, 53a)

*Comment*: The rule is: "They may eat Seventh Year produce which they have collected into their houses only so long as like produce is still found free in the fields but not so long as it is still found watched over" (M. Shev. 9 : 4). This is expressed in extremely terse language:

ʾWKLYN ʿL HMPQR
ʾBL Lʾ ʿL HŠMWR

Here too, the operative word is ʾP.

Eliezer: ʾWKLYN ʿL HRʾŠWN
Joshua: ʾP ʿL HʾḤRWN

Gamaliel has a completely separate lemma, out of phase with the others.

Eliezer's point is that when the first species has disappeared from the fields, it cannot be used—and its prohibition extends to the others, even though they are the majority. Joshua takes the opposite extreme: All three are permitted until the last is prohibited. Gamaliel then takes the compromise opinion—each species has its own rule. What disappears in the field must be removed in the house.

II.iii.2.A. He who pickles three pickles in one jar—

B. R. Eliezer says, "When one kind has disappeared (KLH) from the field, the whole jar should be removed."

C. R. Joshua says, "He continues to eat until the last one in it disappears."

D. Rabban Gamaliel says, "When a kind has disappeared from the field, he should remove its kind from the jar."

E. And the law is according to his words.

Sifra Behar Pereq 3 : 4, Weiss, p. 107b

*Comment*: The opinions are fully spelled out, but no different from M. Shev. 9 : 5.

See Epstein, *Nusaḥ*, pp. 687, 951: E is a later interpolation.

I.i.15.A. He who had Seventh Year fruits which came to him as an inheritance or which were given to him as a gift—

B. R. Eliezer says, "Let them be given to those that eat them [= those who eat the produce of the Seventh Year]."

And the sages say, "The sinner is not rewarded. But let them be sold to those that eat them, and their return [in funds] be divided among everyone."

M. Shev. 9 : 9 (y. Shev. 9 : 6)

*Comment*: The fruits ought to have been burned before the advent of the Seventh Year; or they were kept under guard in the Seventh Year and not left as ownerless property. Eliezer's rule is that they should be given to people who eat the prohibited fruit of the Seventh Year (even though those people will be grateful to the giver who has inherited the fruit). But the owner cannot sell them, for the money will then fall under the prohibition of the Seventh Year. The sages object that the people who eat the produce of the Seventh Year should not be permitted to benefit at all. Therefore the food *is* to be sold, and the proceeds given out as freely as Seventh Year produce itself.

The underlying question is the status of the money received as proceeds for the fruit. Eliezer's view is that the money is identical to the fruit—therefore prohibited. The sages agree—therefore the money may be left ownerless.

Eliezer is consistent with the House of Shammai, which hold one may eat produce of the Seventh Year by favor and not by favor (y. Shev. 9 : 6). On this slender basis, we assign the pericope to our Eliezer.

## vi. Terumot

I.i.16.A. They do not give Heave-offering from what is clean for what is unclean, and if they gave Heave-offering, their Heave-offering is Heave-offering. [There intervenes a long interpolation, in which the consequences of this ruling are spelled out in terms of various details.]

B. R. Eliezer says, "They do give Heave-offering from what is clean for what is unclean."

[C. They do not give Heave-offering from unclean for clean (produce).]

M. Ter. 2 : 1 (M. Hal. 2 : 8; y. Ter. 2 : 1)

*Comment*: Warrant for assigning M. Ter. 2 : 1 to Eliezer b. Hyrcanus is in Tos Ter. 3 : 18. Eliezer differs with the anonymous opinion of A. The difference is not substantial, for both agree that, once given, the Heave-offering is valid. The issue is whether, to begin with, one does so. The anonymous ruling (C) proceeds:

> They do not give Heave-offering from the unclean for what is clean. And if he gave Heave-offering—
> Accidentally—His Heave-offering is Heave-offering.
> Intentionally—He has done nothing.
> M. Ter. 2 : 2A

This repeats, and spells out, the position of M. Ter. 2 : 1A. Eliezer is not mentioned; perhaps he would see a distinction between 2 : 1 and 2 : 2, for he agrees one does not give from worse for better produce.

Does Eliezer here gloss a pre-existing rule? Or is his opinion formulated at the same point as the contrary view? It is a strikingly fundamental question. Since the Pharisees for several generations had observed the tithing rules and those of ritual uncleanness, one must wonder how it was that for so long no one had known whether one may give Heave-offering for unclean out of clean produce. M. Hal. 2 : 8 has the following:

> R. Eliezer says, "It [*Ḥallah*] is taken from the clean for the unclean." [There follows a long interpolation, explaining how one does so.]
>
> And sages prohibit.

In the form of M. Hal. 2 : 8, Eliezer differs from his contemporaries. In M. Ter. 2 : 1, he differs from a (pre-existing) anonymous rule. But the difference is about the same principle.

If, as in M. Ber., we isolate rules phrased in plural-present-tense-participles we find the following:

> M. Ter. 1 : 4: They do not give Heave-offering from olives for oil, or grapes for wine; and if they gave Heave-offering, the House of Shammai say, "It may still be deemed Heave-offering for the olives or grapes" (so Danby).
> The House of Hillel say, "Their Heave-offering is not Heave-offering."
>
> M. Ter. 1 : 5: They do not give Heave-offering from Gleanings, Forgotten Sheaf, Corner of the field, ownerless produce, etc.
>
> M. Ter. 1 : 7: They do not give Heave-offering by measure, weight, number, etc.
>
> M. Ter. 1 : 8: They do not give Heave-offering of oil for crushed olives; and if they have done so, the Heave-offering is Heave-offering, but Heave-offering must again be given. (And of these two Heave-offerings, the first renders other produce into which it may fall subject to the law of Heave-offering, etc., but this is not so with the second) [so Danby].

This seems to me decisive evidence that Eliezer differs from a pre-existing law—a law known to the Houses, but which ought to come before them as well.

Eliezer then is the only authority who differs from the fundamental principle spelled out in the list above, carefully restricting Heave-offering to the exact produce for which the Heave-offering is given, and not mixing various forms of the same produce, e.g., olives with oil, for the purpose of giving the Heave-offering. Eliezer alone favors breaking down the rigid principle of separation in giving Heave-offering. One cannot conclude other than that he was breaking new ground. It would further seem not excessive to view Eliezer as the firm *terminus ante quem* for the entire set of ʾYN TWRMYN-rules.

M. Hal. 2 : 8's dispute is 'artificial.' Eliezer's rule has required the inclusion of "the sages," who, in this instance, represent virtually the whole antecedent tradition!

This will further explain the position of Judah [b. Ilai] in his glosses in M. Ter. 2 : 5 and possibly also 2 : 6; there he ignores small distinctions among the produce for all of which Heave-offering is given—a matter of onions.

I.ii.9.A. Tos. Ter. 3 : 16.

*Comment*: See *Phar.* II, pp. 88-89.

I.ii.10.A. R. Liezer says, "They give Heave-offering from what is clean for what is unclean."

B. R. Eliezer said, "M'ŚH W: a fire fell on the threshing floors of Kefar Signa, and they gave Heave-offering from what was clean for what was unclean."

C. They said to him, "Is there proof from there? But they gave Heave-offering from them for them."

D. R. ʾIlai (ʾLʿ ʾYY) says in the name of R. Eliezer, "They give Heave-offering from what is clean for what is unclean, even [y. omits: *even*] in the case of wet (LḤ) [produce] [= y. Ter. 2 : 1, Gilead, p. 19].

E. "How so? He who picked his olives in uncleanness and seeks to give their Heave-offering in cleanness brings a pitcher (MŠPYK) whose funnel is narrower than an egg's [breadth in quantity] and puts it on the mouth of the jar and brings his olives and places them in it, and gives Heave-offering. It so turns out that he gives Heave-offering from what is clean for what is unclean, and from that which is in close neighborhood of those products which are to be redeemed [So Jastrow, II, p. 934A, for MWQP]."

F. They said to him, "Only wine and olives are called 'wet' (LḤ)."

Tos. Ter. 3 : 18, Lieberman, p. 121, ls. 71-77
(M. Ter. 2 : 1; Ilai: y. Ter. 2 : 1, Hal. 2 : 3).

IV.i.4. R. Ṭabi in the name of R. Josiah b. R. Yannai: "The law follows R. Liezer."

R. Yiṣḥaq b. R. Naḥman in the name of R. Hoshaia: "The law follows R. Liezer."

R. Ḥuna, R. Ḥananiah: "The law does not follow R. Liezer."

R. Yosi b. R. Bun, R. Judah in the name of Samuel: "The law does not follow R. Liezer."

y. Ter. 2 : 1, Gilead, p. 19

*Comment*: With reference to Tos. Ter. 3 : 18B, Lieberman calls attention to M. Kel. 5 : 4.

Evidently, Eliezer claims, during the fire they saved unclean grain, and the grain that had already been made into sheaves was rendered unclean. They took clean wheat for Heave-offering. And they took Heave-offering for what was not nearby and from what was clean for what was unclean. The reply is that that is not what happened at all. They took from clean for clean, and not as is alleged in B. In D, Ilai Eliezer's disciple, alleges that one may give Heave-offering from what is wet (therefore unclean)—that is, olives or grapes—for what is clean. The meaning is that dry produce may be given as Heave-offering—thus from clean for unclean produce—*even* if it is not nearby. The sages reply that that is not really 'wet'. The funnel is narrower than an egg's breadth, so only the bottom olive will be unclean and will not render the others unclean. Since the oil that comes out of the olive is joined with the oil of the unclean olives, they are regarded as MWQP, or joined together. In F, the sages reply that dry olives are not joined by the mouth of the pitcher; they will not come through. As to unclean and clean oil and wine, such an arrangement will not do.

I.i.17. [M. Ter. 4 : 3: The proper measure of Heave-offering is one fortieth, one fiftieth, or one sixtieth, for the generous, average, and mean-spirited, respectively, according to the Hillelites. The Shammaites say, One thirtieth, one fortieth, and one fiftieth.]

A. He who would increase in Heave-offering (HMRBH BTRWMH)—

B. R. Eliezer says, "One-tenth, like Heave-offering of the Tithe."

C. More than this, let him designate it Heave-offering of the Tithe for [produce] elsewhere.

D. R. Ishmael says, "One-half unconsecrated produce and one-half Heave-offering."

E. R. Ṭarfon and R. ʿAqiba say, "So long as there remains unconsecrated produce [in any amount]."

M. Ter. 4 : 5 (y. Ter. 4 : 4)

*Comment*: Eliezer's saying is closer to the views of the Houses than are those in D and E, which allow immense portions of the crop to be designated as Heave-offering. The Hillelites allow from 1.6% to 2.5%; the Shammaites, from 2% to 3.3%. Eliezer, going beyond the Shammaite position, permits as much as 10%. Then Ishmael allows up to 50%, and Ṭarfon and ʿAqiba, up to as much as 99%! Clearly, the framework of discussion has changed, if Eliezer says beyond 10% must be devoted to another purpose, and ʿAqiba says one may go as high as virtually the whole amount. Indeed, the real differences are between B and D + E. So far as Eliezer is concerned, anything over 10% is not regarded as Heave-offering at all; the Levite has to render it to the priest (see Albeq, *Seder Zeraʿim*, p. 189).

M. Hal. 1 : 9 is consistent with ʿAqiba and Ṭarfon, "If a man said, let all [the grain in] my threshing-floor be Heave-offering," or "Let all my dough be Dough-offering," his word is void unless he keeps back part of the common produce.

C looks like a development of B's ruling. Obviously it has nothing to do with the Houses or D and E.

See Epstein, *Tan.*, p. 107.

IV.i.5. R. Jeremiah in the name of R. Jacob bar Aḥa in the name of R. Simeon b. Laqish, "R. Eliezer follows the House of Shammai," etc.

y. Ter. 4 : 4, Gilead pp. 41-2

I.i.18.A. R. Eliezer says, "Heave-offering is neutralized [So Danby for ʿWLH] in a hundred and one [parts]."

B. R. Joshua says, "In one hundred and [a bit] more."

C. And this *more* has no [exact] measure . . .

M. Ter. 4 : 7 (y. Ter. 4 : 6; y. Orl. 2 : 1)

I.i.19.A. R. Joshua says, "Black figs neutralize white, and white neutralize black. Large cakes of figs neutralize small, and small neutralize large. Round cakes neutralize square, and square neutralize round."

B. R. Eliezer prohibits.

C. R. ʿAqiba says, "If what fell into [the mixture] is known, they do not neutralize one another. If what fell in is not known, they *do* neutralize one another."

M. Ter. 4 : 8 (y. Ter. 4 : 7)

I.i.20.A. How so? Fifty white figs and fifty black figs—
The black fell in—
The black are prohibited and the white permitted.

B. [If] the white fell in—
The white are prohibited and the black are permitted.

C. If what fell in is not known—
They neutralize one another.

D. And in this instance, R. Eliezer is stringent, and R. Joshua lenient.

M. Ter. 4 : 9 (y. Ter. 4 : 7)

I.i.21.A. And in this R. Eliezer is lenient and R. Joshua strict:

B. In [a case in which] he stuffed a *litra* of dried [Heave-offering] figs into the mouth of a jar, and he does not know which one—

C. R. Eliezer says, "We regard them as if they were separated figs, and the ones on the bottom neutralize those on the top."

D. R. Joshua says, "It will not neutralize, unless one hundred jars are there."

M. Ter. 4 : 10 (b. Bes. 4a, b. Zev. 73a)

I.i.22.A. A *seʾah* of Heave-offering which fell into the mouth of a store-jar, and he skimmed it off—

B. R. Eliezer says, "If in the layer removed were a hundred *seʾahs*, it is neutralized in one hundred and one."

C. And R. Joshua says, "It is not neutralized."

D. A *seʾah* of Heave-offering which fell into the mouth of a store-jar, he should skim it off.

E. If so, why have they said that Heave-offering is neutralized in one hundred and one [parts]?

[That applies only] if it is not known whether they are mixed up, or where it fell [= M. Ter. 4 : 8C].

M. Ter. 4 : 11 (y. Ter. 4 : 8)

*Comment*: While earlier, Eliezer would permit clean Heave-offering to be given for unclean, here he does not allow different colored figs to neutralize one another, so that Heave-offering may be given for the whole. That principle would seem to be inconsistent with the earlier ruling.

*M. Ter. 4 : 7*: If a *qav* of Heave-offering falls into a hundred of unconsecrated produce, the Heave-offering is neutralized; new Heave-offering is given, but the mixture is permitted. Joshua differs on a minute quantity—something less than a *qav* is sufficient. The opinions are unbalanced:

Eliezer: ʾḤD WMʾH

Joshua: MʾH WʿWD

So the difference is ʾḤD *vs.* ʿWD—not a very striking syzygy.

*M. Ter. 4 : 8*: If a fig of Heave-offering—whether white or black—fell into a hundred of unconsecrated produce, of which fifty are white and fifty are black, those two fifties join together to neutralize the fig of Heave-offering, even though if it was a black fig, the white ones are not conceivably forbidden, for among them is no *white* Heave-offering-fig. Joshua permits that the fig be neutralized in this situation. In his opinion Heave-offering is neutralized by a mere majority of unconsecrated food. The sages required a hundred and one. If the whole mixture has that larger quantity, it suffices. And so in the other (unnecessary) examples.

Eliezer prohibits, for the figs which are not in doubt do not join together to neutralize the Heave-offering.

ʿAqiba's position is explained in M. Ter. 4 : 9. If we know for certain that the Heave-offering fig was white (or black), then it will not be neutralized in the mixture of fifty white and fifty black figs. But if not, they do. His position seems to be a compromise—but in fact favors Eliezer. That is, where we know for sure (as in Joshua's case, M. Ter. 4 : 8), then the mixture will not neutralize the Heave-offering. Where we do not know for sure which is which, then *all* are in doubt—and so ʿAqiba stands with Eliezer.

M. Ter. 4 : 9D. therefore accurately refers the dispute of A-C back to Eliezer, for it is Eliezer's position which ʿAqiba has espoused.

*M. Ter. 4 : 10* speaks of a jar in which there are one hundred *litras* of unconsecrated dry figs. The man does not know into which jar he has stuffed the Heave-offering.

Eliezer says one regards the figs in all the jars as if they are not stuck together, but loose. They therefore are all regarded as mixed together and serve to neutralize the *litra* of dried figs of Heave-offering which are on the top of the jar, even though the figs on the bottom in no sense are in doubt as to the prohibition of Heave-offering. Under any circumstances the fig of Heave-offering is on the mouth of the jar. But as to black/white, we *know* the Heave-offering fig is one or the other—so Albeq, *Seder Zera'im*, p. 191.

Joshua says that only if we have a hundred jars is this Heave-offering neutralized by the hundred others. But the ones on the bottom do not mix together with the one(s) on the top and therefore do not neutralize the other—unlike the white/black, where they are mixed together.

The language of the two masters is not matched. Each responds directly to the topic sentence, but only inferentially to the other.

*M. Ter. 4:11* now introduces the case of wheat, a *se'ah* of Heave-offering of which has fallen into the mouth of a store-jar. Then the top layer was skimmed off.

Eliezer rules that if in the removed layer were a hundred *se'ahs*, the *se'ah* of Heave-offering is neutralized in a hundred and one. Joshua says it has not been neutralized. Eliezer thus does not claim that the lower rows of grain are joined to make one hundred *se'ahs.*

Joshua says that since the man is obligated to remove the *se'ah*, it is impossible to claim it will be neutralized. Then part D gives us the basis for the dispute in parts A-B-C: If such a thing happens, you have to skim off the top layer. The reason is that the top layer is regarded as distinguishable from the rest, and it *is* possible to remove it to begin with, so the claim is that the *se'ah* which fell in is the one which is skimmed off. This is everyone's view, for R. Eliezer agrees one must remove the top layer—that is the presupposition of B.

But Eliezer claims that if the top layer contains a hundred *se'ahs*, the Heave-offering is neutralized even in what has been skimmed off! Why must it be skimmed off? Because we do not know where the Heave-offering fell, or even whether it has been mixed up! Thus far according to Albeq and the traditional commentaries he relies upon.

However, let us consider the possibility that we have a composite pericope before us, one element of which is framed in terms of a dispute between Eliezer and Joshua, the other in terms of an anonymous, and unanimous rule:

| *Unanimous* | *Dispute* |
|---|---|
| 1. A *se'ah* of Heave-offering which fell on top of the store-jar | 1. A *se'ah* of Heave-offering which fell on top of the store-jar |
| 2. He should skim it off. | 2. *And he skimmed it off* |
| 3. — — | 3. R. Eliezer says, If in the skim is a hundred *se'ahs*, it is neutralized in a hundred and one. |
| 4. — — | 4. R. Joshua says, It is not neutralized. |

The final question supposedly pertains to both parts:

5. If so, why have they said that
Heave-offering neutralizes in
a hundred and one?

For the unanimous version (D), the meaning is, Why should he have to skim off the top layer at all? And the answer is, one indeed does not have to skim off that layer, if the Heave-offering has been mixed up. Obviously, if one knows where the Heave-offering has fallen, he has no problems.

But the question when directed to parts B and C is strange. Eliezer says it *is* neutralized in a hundred and one. So he should not be asked why he does not say what he has just said. As to Joshua the question is a real question, *but* he *never* said a hundred and one parts will neutralize. For him, it is a hundred and a bit more. Now that may be a quibble, but it seems to me an important one, for Joshua cannot reasonably be asked to answer a question phrased in Eliezer's terms.

Now let us take no. 5 as an indication that something is wrong. If we look at no. 2 we see the problem: *and he skimmed it off* has contaminated A from D. Without it, we have also to remove the opening clause of B, *If in the layer removed were* ... It no longer is pertinent to Eliezer's saying; the *if*-clause has been generated by *he skimmed.* Without the contaminating clause, what do we have?

*A se'ah of Heave-offering which fell into the mouth of a store jar*:
Eliezer: It is neutralized [in a hundred and one] (TʿLH)
Joshua: It is not neutralized (Lʾ TʿLH)

This then is the same case as the foregoing, only in far simpler language. Just as Eliezer says the lower figs neutralize the upper ones, so he says the lower grain neutralizes the upper; and Joshua in both instances says the lower does not neutralize the upper.

The little series of "cases" therefore produces the following rules:

1. Eliezer: One hundred and one.
   Joshua: One hundred and a bit more.
2. Joshua: Black, large, round neutralize white, small, and square.
   Eliezer: No.
   ʿAqiba: If you know what fell into what, they do not [as in Eliezer's rule], but if you do not know, they do neutralize.

(This means we do not know whether black, large, or round has actually fallen into white, small, and square or not—and Joshua's rule is now irrelevant.)

3. Eliezer: Top neutralize bottom—figs, wheat.
   Joshua: Top ones do not neutralize bottom.

As a matter of fact, Eliezer is consistent throughout. Where one really is not sure what has fallen into what, but the species are the same, then one thing *will* neutralize the other. And this then is consistent, in a general way, with Eliezer's position on Heave-offering for unclean from clean produce.

Why then has the glossator (M. Ter. 4 : 9-10) tried to show Eliezer "stringent" as well as "lenient"? I doubt that the glossator stands within the formative process of the pericopae. He simply comments on what he has before him. But in the case of M. Ter. 4 : 8-9, one wonders how closely he has looked, for, from ʿAqiba's viewpoint—and he must be right—there is no dispute between Joshua and Eliezer to begin with. Then the rearrangement of the names allows the more stringent position to come last, the less stringent one first—according to the gloss, Joshua first, Eliezer second, then Eliezer first, and Joshua second. Since in M. Ter. 4 : 10 the opinions are not interchangeable but independent of one another, it was easy enough to rearrange things—if that is what happened. However, since the form calls for (1) Eliezer (2) Joshua throughout, whoever is in the stringent position, it perhaps is M. Ter. 4 : 8A that has been rearranged to put Joshua first—therefore, superficially, in Eliezer's position—until ʿAqiba shows Eliezer's position to be normative, even in M. Ter. 4 : 8A. One obviously could not put 4 : 8B before A. One could, however, have ʿAqiba settle the matter so as to make A = B. My view is that 4 : 8A should have Eliezer to begin with. Joshua should prohibit, and we have no need for ʿAqiba at all.

See Epstein, *Tan.*, p. 92.

IV.i.6. And how is one-out-of-a-hundred [reached]?

R. Eliezer says, "He adds a *seʾah* and raises up [one]."

R. Joshua says, "He adds any amount and raises up."

y. Ter. 4 : 6

*Comment*: The dispute of M. Ter. 4 : 7 now yields instructions on how to effect the viewpoint of each.

IV.i.7. There [Eliezer] says the lower ones neutralize the upper, and here: "If there is in the skim ..."—lo, in the lower (parts), no ...

y. Ter. 4 : 8

*Comment*: The observation pertains to M. Ter. 4 : 11.

I.ii.11.A. "... R. Eliezer says, 'When it is known, it will not neutralize, but when it is not known, it will neutralize.'

"R. Joshua says, 'Whether known or unknown, it will not neutralize' "—the words of R. Meir.

B. R. Judah [says], "R. Eliezer says, 'Whether known or not known, it will not neutralize.'

"R. Joshua says, 'Whether known or not known, it will neutralize.'

"R. ʿAqiba says, 'When known, it will not neutralize, when not known, it will neutralize.' "

Tos. Ter. 5 : 10, Lieberman, p. 133,
ls. 56-60 (y. Ter. 4 : 7)

*Comment*: The reference is to M. Ter. 4 : 8. If the man knows the color of the Heave-offering which has gotten mixed up, we have no mixture, and the unconsecrated food of a different color will not serve to neutralize the lost Heave-offering. Meir's view (A) in reference to Joshua is that if the color *is* known, there can be no neutralization. Judah then gives the position represented in the Mishnah 4 : 8. So the position assigned to Eliezer and Joshua is according to Judah. Meir's tradition had it contrarywise. Judah must be right.

I.ii.12.A. A *litra* of dried figs which he has stuffed into the mouth of a jar and he does not know into which jar he has stuffed it—

Into a large round vessel (KWWRT) and he does not know into which vessel he has stuffed it—

B. "R. Eliezer says, 'We regard the upper ones as if they were separate. If there are one hundred and one *litras*, it is neutralized, and if not, it is not neutralized.'

"R. Joshua says, 'If there are there a hundred mouths [= jars], it is neutralized, and if not, those on top [PWMYN = the mouths] are prohibited and the lower ones (ŠWLYM) are permitted"—the words of R. Meir.

C. R. Judah says, "R. Liezer says, 'If there are there a hundred mouths, it is neutralized, and if not, the mouths [as above] are prohibited, and those on the bottom are permitted.'

"R. Joshua says, 'Even though there are there three hundred mouths [= jars], it is not neutralized.' "

Tos. Ter. 5 : 11, Lieberman, p. 133, ls. 60-67 (y. Ter. 4 : 7; b. Bes. 3b, Zev. 73a)

*Comment*: In B, Eliezer is consistent with M. Ter. 4 : 10, and Joshua likewise, so the Mishnah now follows Meir—but without the *if not* clause; for in M. Ter. 4 : 10 we assume that if there are not a hundred jars, the whole is prohibited.

Judah's view is outside the framework of M. Ter. 4 : 10. The point of Judah's Joshua in C is that we now are in a position of giving Heave-offering by number [count], which is prohibited under all circumstances. Judah has Eliezer in a stringent position, but Joshua's is even more stringent. See Lieberman, *Tosefta Kifshuṭah Seder Zeraʿim*, I, pp. 369-370.

I.i.23.A. A *seʾah* of unclean Heave-offering which fell into a hundred [*seʾahs*] of clean unconsecrated—

B. R. Eliezer says, "It should be raised up and burned—

C. "For I say, 'The *seʾah* which fell is the *seʾah* which has come up.' "

D. And sages say, "It is neutralized (TʿLH) and may be eaten—

E. "Dry, or roast, or kneaded with fruit juice, or it may be divided into lumps [of dough] so that there will not be in a single place as much as an egg's bulk."

M. Ter. 5 : 2 (y. Ter. 5 : 1; y. Shab. 18 : 1, y. Suk. 2 : 8; b. Hul. 22b-23a, b. Tem. 12a; b. Bekh. 22b-23a)

*Comment*: C supplies the reason for B, and E gives details as to the eating process alluded to in D; the basic opinions are balanced:

Eliezer: TRWM TŚRP

Sages: TʿLH TʾKL

following the model of M. Ter. 5 : 4, Eliezer and the sages. As to E, this may well be a contamination from M. Ter. 5 : 3, "A *seʾah* of clean Heave-offering which fell into a hundred of unclean unconsecrated food—it is neutralized and may be eaten dry or roast, etc." And here, Eliezer does not appear.

The case before us concerns unconsecrated food which is dry, thus not susceptible to receive uncleanness. Eliezer says that one must raise up a *seʾah* and give it to a priest, just as with clean Heave-offering which has fallen into a hundred and one times its own quantity of clean unconsecrated food. But the priest burns the Heave-offering he receives, for it is regarded as the unclean Heave-offering which has fallen into the mixture. This is explained in C.

The opinion of the sages is that the Heave-offering that fell in has been neutralized; the new Heave-offering may be eaten, as specified.

The pericope follows in logical sequence upon the foregoing:

M. Ter. 5 : 1: A *seʾah* of unclean Heave-offering which fell into less than a hundred of unconsecrated food, whether unclean or clean—If that *seʾah* was clean ...

M. Ter. 5 : 2: A *seʾah* of unclean Heave-offering which fell into a hundred of clean unconsecrated food ...

M. Ter. 5 : 3: A *seʾah* of clean Heave-offering which fell into a hundred of unclean unconsecrated food ...

M. Ter. 5 : 4: A *seʾah* of unclean Heave-offering which fell into a hundred of clean Heave-offering ...

and so on.

Eliezer and the opposition occur here; then the Houses in 5 : 4, followed by Eliezer's and the sages' ruling just as do the Houses; then Eliezer and the sages in M. Ter. 5 : 5, and 5 : 6. So the whole, as we shall see, is a set of developments of Eliezer's view.

See Epstein, *Nusaḥ*, p. 708.

I.i.24.A. If one *seʾah* of unclean Heave-offering fell into a hundred *seʾahs* of clean Heave-offering—

B. The House of Shammai forbid.

C. And the House of Hillel permit.

D. [Debate.]

E. After they had agreed
F. R. Eliezer says, "It should be taken up and burned."
G. And the sages say, "It is lost through its scantness."
M. Ter. 5 : 4, trans. Danby, p. 58 (y. Ter. 5 : 2)

I.ii.13. Tos. Ter. 6 : 4.

*Comment*: See *Phar.* II, pp. 89-92.

I.i.25.A. A *se'ah* of Heave-offering which fell into a hundred [*se'ahs* of unconsecrated food, and was thereby neutralized], and he raised it up [that is, a new *se'ah* of Heave-offering], and it fell in another place—

B. R. Eliezer says, "It renders it subject to the law of Heave-offering (MDMʿT) like certain Heave-offering. [The new *se'ah* of Heave-offering certainly is Heave-offering]."

C. And sages say, "It renders it subject to the law of Heave-offering (MDMʿT) [so Danby], only if it is in the prescribed proportion."

M. Ter. 5 : 5

I.i.26.A. A *se'ah* of Heave-offering which fell into less than a hundred [*se'ahs* of unconsecrated food], and they were thereby rendered subject to the law of Heave-offering (NDMʿW) [so Danby], and some of the produce mixed with Heave-offering (MDMʿ) fell elsewhere—

B. R. Eliezer says, "It renders subject to the law of Heave-offering (MDMʿT) like certain Heave-offering."

C. And sages say, "That which is subject to the law of doubtful Heave-offering (MDWMʿ) renders subject to the law of doubtful Heave-offering (MDMYʿ) [another quantity of food] only in prescribed proportion (LPY ḤŠBWN).

D. "And what is leavened [with Heave-offering] renders [other dough] leavened [as with Heave-offering] only if it is in prescribed proportion [so Danby]."

And drawn water does not render the immersion pool unfit except in prescribed proportion.

M. Ter. 5 : 6 (y. Ter. 5 : 2; b. Shab. 142a)

*Comment*: M. Ter. 5 : 4, 5, and 6 develop the theme of the *se'ah* of Heave-offering which has been misplaced. 5 : 4 raises the issue of a *se'ah* of unclean Heave-offering that has fallen into a hundred of clean Heave-offering. Eliezer rules an equivalent *se'ah* should be taken up and burned—so it is not neutralized and must be replaced ('for I say, 'The one that fell in is the one which comes up'"). The sages say it has been neutralized, just as in 5 : 2.

M. Ter. 5 : 5 then has the process repeated. A *se'ah* of Heave-offering fell into a hundred of common produce, was lifted out—but then fell elsewhere. Eliezer is consistent in holding the one which fell in was the one which was lifted out, therefore in 5 : 5 the one lifted out has the effect of certain Heave-offering. In this *se'ah* that has been lifted out and fallen elsewhere is only one portion in one-hundred-and-one of Heave-offering—in proportion to the whole pile from which it has been lifted. So one lifts up out of the new *se'ah* from the new pile for the priest *only* that proportion of Heave-offering—one part in one-hundred-and-one.

M. Ter. 5 : 6 then has a *se'ah* of Heave-offering fall into less than a hundred. Now the whole mixture is rendered MDMᶜ—subject to the law of Heave-offering. Then part of that MDMᶜ falls elsewhere. Again, Eliezer consistently rules that this mixture works like a mixture that certainly is Heave-offering. The whole pile of less than a hundred has been subjected to the law of Heave-offering. The sages say, as in 5 : 5, that this is not the case. If a *se'ah* of the mixture that has been rendered subject to the laws of Heave-offering fell into unconsecrated food, it is sufficient to measure a hundred parts of unconsecrated food against a part of the Heave-offering which is found in the *se'ah* of MDWMᶜ. The same rule is then extended in M. Ter. 5 : 6D to parallel situations.

Eliezer's principle remains constant throughout: what has disappeared into a common mixture is what is raised up thereafter. We therefore regard the second *se'ah* of Heave-offering as true Heave-offering in all respects.

The sages persist in preserving differences between what has fallen in and what is raised up. Eliezer's principle would seem a second-order development of the primary rule that one gives Heave-offering from closely-related, but not identical substances—clean for unclean as in M. Ter. 2 : 1. The sages in their philosophy are approximately similar to the anonymous rules in M. Ter. 1 : 3, which emphasize that one preserves the most rigid distinctions among various sorts of similar, but not identical, substances, when giving Heave-offering: one does not give Heave-offering from clean for unclean, from one kind for another, oil for olives, wine for grapes, and the like. The connection between the two sets of disputes is not close, but it cannot be ignored. On this flimsy basis I have included all of these materials in the traditions about our Eliezer.

What sort of literature is represented by M. Ter. 5 : 1-7? It would seem, as observed above, to be a progression of cases, one following from the next, in which consistent rulings are given by the two parties. Unlike M. Ter. 1 : 3, the chapter before us cannot be regarded as the result of Eliezer's glossing of a completed literary unit, even though the literary form—*One se'ah of some sort of Heave-offering which fell into a hundred se'ahs of another mixture—R. Eliezer says ... Sages say ...* is constant. It looks like a single, complex composite of cases, each supplying an example of one principle. But a single case would not have sufficed to illustrate all possibilities of applying that principle, for each of the several cases introduces new considerations, and by showing Eliezer consistent in all, the redactor makes clear that Eliezer's position will not change on account of changing circumstances.

Since it is Eliezer's position which is clarified—he is the sole named authority occurring in all pericopae—the whole would derive from circles in which his opinion was under study. These place Eliezer first throughout, and carefully spell out and gloss his opinions, as much as those of the sages. So they would be masters to whom Eliezer's opinions were important. They therefore ought to be his disciples—if it is not the master himself who stands behind the whole.

Further, since statement of each case takes for granted Eliezer's, and not Joshua's, view of the quantity that will neutralize Heave-offering (M. Ter. 4 : 7), it becomes virtually certain that our Eliezer stands behind the actual formulation of the details of the cases. And the composite of pericopae would then represent a sustained legal essay on the part of Eliezer and his circle. Before such an essay could be undertaken, the basic principles of the neutralization of Heave-offering, such as are represented in M. Ter. 4 : 7-12, had to have been established. Given the minute quantity of produce required for Heave-offering, we should have to regard the problems before us as of interest primarily to legal theoreticians.

On 5 : 5, see Epstein, *Nusaḥ*, p. 270.

I.i.27. [If a man ate Heave-offering in error, instead of giving it to a priest, he must repay its value and an Added Fifth (ḤWMŠ)—M. Ter. 6 : 1]

A. R. Eliezer says, "They pay back from one kind instead of from another kind—

"Provided that he pays back from a better instead of from a worse kind."

B. And R. ʿAqiba says, "They do not pay back except from one kind for its own kind. [Danby: Restitution may be made only from the like kind.]"

C. Therefore if he ate cucumbers grown in the year before the Seventh Year, he must wait for cucumbers grown in the year after the Seventh Year and pay back from them [but may not pay back cucumbers grown in the Seventh Year, which are not liable for Heave-offering. Eliezer says he may pay back from another kind.]

D. From the place [Scripture] on the basis of which R. Eliezer gives a lenient ruling, from that same place R. ʿAqiba gives a stringent ruling:

As it is said, *And he will give to the priest that which is holy* (Lev. 22 : 14)—

"Whatever (KL Š) is appropriate to be holy (R'WY LHYWT [Kaufmann: LHʿŚWT] QWDŠ)"—the words of R. Eliezer.

And R. ʿAqiba says, "*And he will give to the priest that which is holy*—that which he [actually] consumed."

M. Ter. 6 : 6 (y. Ter. 6 : 1, 3)

*Comment*: The pericope lacks a topic sentence. It depends upon M. Ter. 6 : 1. Eliezer's opinion does not supply necessary information for ʿAqiba's. The sayings are independent, but perfectly balanced, except for the glosses *provided*... and *therefore*...

ʿAqiba's example, C, in fact conforms to Eliezer's *provided*, for cucumbers of the sixth year would have hardened, therefore would be worse; and cucumbers of the Seventh Year are not subject to the law of Heave-offering at all, therefore cannot be declared Heave-offering in place of what has gone before. So the two glosses serve to bring the opinions of the masters close together.

The additional clause, D, likewise gives both parties an equally sound Scriptural foundation. Perhaps the ʾT HQDŠ to ʿAqiba is supposed to mean ʾWTW HQDŠ, but if so, this is a mere conceit and does not rely upon the ʿAqiban exegetical devices. So the glossator in all instances has tried to gloss over differences between the masters. The point is Eliezer's view, as noted above, that one may indeed give Heave-offering from one thing for another, somewhat different, thing, only here, the view *is* extreme; from one thing for another—MŠLMYN MMYN ʿL ŠʾYNW MYNW—in contrast to M. Ter. 2 : 4: ʾYN TWRMYN MMYN ʿL ŠʾYNW MYNW! Had TWRMYN replaced MŠLMYN, the real difference would be clear.

I.ii.14.A. R. Liezer says, "They pay back from one kind instead of from another, provided that he pays back from a better instead of from a worse kind.

B. "How so? He ate barley and repays wheat, figs and repays dates—may a blessing come to him."

C. R. ʿAqiba says, "They do not pay back except from one kind for its own kind."

Tos. Ter. 7 : 9 (b. ʿEruv. 29b, Pes. 32a; y. Ter. 6 : 3)

I.ii.15.A. R. Leʿazar [Alt.: Liezer] says, "Just as they pay back from new for old [crops], so they pay back from one kind for another."

Tos. Ter. 7 : 9

I.ii.16.A. He that eats from untithed produce (ṬBL) pays back from Gleanings, Forgotten Sheaf, Corner of the Field, and produce which has not yet reached a third [of its full growth],"—the words of R. Liezer.

B. R. ʿAqiba says, "They do not pay back from them, for they do not pay back from that which has not reached the season [obligation] of tithes."

C. R. Nathan said, "R. Liezer would say, 'Let him wait until the Sabbath is over and go out to the courtyard and complete [it.]"

Tos. Ter. 7 : 10, Lieberman, p. 144, ls. 29-36 (b. Bes. 35a)

*Comment*: Tos. Ter. 7 : 9 explains Eliezer's opinion in M. Ter. 6 : 6. Tos. Ter. 7 : 9 extends it to a matter not mentioned in the Mishnah. Here ʿAqiba agrees, following M. Ter. 6 : 6, *re* cucumbers of the sixth and eighth years.

Tos. Ter. 7 : 10 A + B pertain to M. Ter. 6 : 5: "Restitution may not be made from Gleanings, Forgotten Sheaves, *Pe'ah* of ownerless produce or from First Tithe from which Heave-offering has not been taken or Second Tithe or dedicated produce which has not yet been redeemed ... the words of R. Meir. But the sages permit." Meir evidently follows his teacher, ʿAqiba, and the unnamed sages are in the position of Eliezer. Eliezer's position is that *All which is fitting to be holy* may be used for restitution of Heave-offering.

Tos. Ter. 7 : 10C pertains to M. Ter. 8 : 3, below.

II.iii.3. "How do we know that they do not pay back except from one variety for the same variety?

"Scripture says, *And he will give to the priest that which is holy.*

"Therefore if he ate cucumbers of the sixth year of the Sabbatical cycle, he should wait for the cucumbers of the year after the Sabbatical year and pay back from them," the words of R. ʿAqiba.

R. Eliezer says, "They pay back from one variety for another which is not of the same kind, on condition that he pays back from what is good for what is bad" etc.

Sifra Emor Pereq 6 : 6, Weiss, p. 97b

*Comment*: Eliezer's exegesis is lost by Sifra.

I.i.28.A.1. The woman who was eating of Heave-offering—they came and said to her, "Your husband has died" or "divorced you"—

2. And so, the slave who was eating of Heave-offering, and they came and said to him, "Your master has died" or "sold you to an Israelite" or "given you as a gift" or "freed you"—

3. And so, a priest who was eating of Heave-offering, and it became known that he is the son of a divorce or of a *ḥaluṣah*—

B. R. Eliezer declares [him] liable [for] both the principle and the Added Fifth.

C. And R. Joshua declares exempt.

D. He was standing and offering sacrifices at the altar and it became known that he is the son of a divorcee or of a *ḥaluṣah*—

E. R. Eliezer says, "All the sacrifices that he has offered on the altar are unfit."

F. And R. Joshua declares valid.

G. It became known that he was blemished—his service is unfit.

M. Ter. 8 : 1 (y. Ter. 7 : 2, 8 : 1; b. Pes. 72b, b. Yer. 34a, b. Mak. 11b; Mid. Tan. to Deut. 26 : 3, Hoffmann, p. 171; y. Suk. 2 : 8)

I.i.29.A. And in all cases in which the Heave-offering was in their mouths—

B. R. Eliezer says, "They swallow."

C. R. Joshua says, "They spit out."

D. They said to him, "You have been made unclean" or "The Heave-offering has been made unclean"—

E. R. Eliezer says, "He swallows."

F. And R. Joshua says, "He spits out."

G. "You were unclean" or "The Heave-offering was unclean" or it became known that it was untithed produce, or First Tithe from which Heave-offering had not been taken, or Second Tithe, or dedicated produce that had not been redeemed, or if he tasted the taste of a bedbug in his mouth—lo, he should spit out.

M. Ter. 8 : 2 (y. Ter. 8 : 2)

I.i.30.A. He was eating of a grapecluster and went from the garden to the courtyard—

B. R. Eliezer says, "He finishes."

C. And R. Joshua says, "He does not finish.

D. It got dark on the Sabbath eve—

E. R. Eliezer says, "He finishes."

F. And R. Joshua says, "He does not finish."

M. Ter. 8 : 3 (y. Ter. 8 : 2; y. Ma. 3 : 4, b. Bes. 35a)

*Comment*: As above, we have a composite pericope in which the same general principle is spelled out in a number of situations. A single case here could have yielded all the others. The problem is, What is the rule for someone who has begun doing a deed in the presumption that he is permitted to do so, but, while doing it, discovers he is not permitted to do so? Eliezer consistently rules that what is begun with permission may be completed. Joshua rules contrarywise.

M. Ter. 5 : 2 is tied to M. Ter. 5 : 1 with *And in all cases* (WKLM). The opinions of the masters are closely matched, either using the same word +/— L', or using matched opposites, as BLʿ *vs. PLṬ.*

In M. Ter. 8 : 1 the cases all come down to the same issue: he has lost the right to do so. The larger issue is whether one may complete an action which was permitteed at the outset (y. Ter. 8 : 1). The wife and slave of a priest have the right to Heave-offering. Eliezer requires the restoration both of the quantity of misappropriated Heave-offering and of the penalty of a Fifth in addition. Joshua exempts from the Additional Fifth, for it was accidental, not intentional misappropriation of the holy property.

In 8 : 1B Eliezer has the full statement of the problem. He declares all the sacrifices retroactively invalid; Joshua declares them valid, for the *ḥallal*-priest ought not to sacrifice, but if he does, his sacrifice is valid. Parts E-F are tacked on with no integral relationship with the foregoing, except in principle. Part G brings Joshua over to Eliezer's position.

M. Ter. 8 : 2 then introduces the question, What should the people listed in 8 : 1A do when caught in the act? Eliezer, who held that they must restore both the Heave-offering and the Additional Fifth, permits them to swallow, for they had begun to consume the holy food by right, not against the law. I do not understand the principle underlying Joshua's opinion. Part G now introduces a situation in which the man actually knew in advance that he was unclean, or the Heave-offering was unclean. Everyone agrees he must spit out, for it is no longer an accident—so Albeq, *Seder Zeraʿim*, p. 201. On 8 : 2, W for ʾW, see Epstein, *Nusaḥ*, pp. 1063-4.

The problem of M. Ter. 8 : 3 rests upon the same principle, but involves tithing. Eating at random in the garden does not impose the requirement of tithing. But as soon as the man enters the courtyard, the obligation of tithing applies to the food (M. Ma. 3 : 5). Now even random nibbling without separating tithes is prohibited. Eliezer says he may finish the food without tithing, because he began doing something permitted, therefore may complete the action, just as above. Joshua differs.

As to 8 : 3D, the man was eating at random before the Sabbath, but then it became dark, and the Sabbath's advent is equivalent to entering the courtyard (M. Ma. 4 : 2), so the food now must be tithed. Eliezer is consistent with his former ruling, as is Joshua.

Note also Tos. Ter. 7 : 10C which explains M. Ter. 8 : 3. Eliezer says he should finish. Here, Nathan says he may finish—but only after the Sabbath is over, which leaves Joshua's position identical with Eliezer's: Whatever has been begun with permission may be completed. In y. Ter. 8 : 1 Nathan has still another interpretation of Eliezer's position.

I.i.31.A. A jar of Heave-offering concerning which was born the suspicion of uncleanness (SPQ ṬWMʾH)—

B. R. Eliezer says, "If it was lying in an exposed place (MQWM HTWRPH), he should put it in a hidden place; and if it was uncovered, he should cover it."

C. And R. Joshua says, "If it was lying in a hidden place, he should place it in an exposed place; and if it was covered, he should uncover it."

D. Rabban Gamaliel says, "Let him not do anything new with it [at all]." [Parma + Naples: *KL* DBR]

M. Ter. 8 : 8 (y. Ter. 8 : 4; b. Pes. 15a, 20b, 21a; b. Hul. 33b, b. Bekh. 33b)

I.i.32.A. A jar which was broken in the upper winepress, and the lower one was unclean—

B. R. Eliezer and R. Joshua agree (MWDH) that if he can save from it a fourth in cleanness, he should do so.

C. But if not—

D. R. Eliezer says, "Let it go down and be made unclean, but let him not make it unclean with his own hands."

[E. Joshua is missing.]

M. Ter. 8 : 9 (b. Pes. 15a, 20b, 21a; b. Men. 48a-b; y. Pes. 1 : 8)

I.i.33.A. And so too, a jar of oil which was poured out—

B. R. Eliezer and R. Joshua agree (MWDH) that if he can save from it a quarter in cleanness, he should do so.

C. But if not—

D. R. Eliezer says, "Let it seep down and be swallowed up, but let him not gather it up (YBLʿNH) [Better: YṬMʾNH, as above] with his own hands.

[E. Joshua is missing.]

M. Ter. 8 : 10

I.i.34.A. And on this and on this, R. Joshua said, "This is not the Heave-offering concerning which I am warned not to make it unclean, but [I am warned] merely not to eat. [Danby: "Such Heave-offering is not such whereof I must take heed lest I render it unclean, but lest I eat of it"].

B. "But [that] which you must not make unclean—how is it?" [But what Heave-offering is it which one may not render unclean?]

C. He was going from place to place with loaves of Heave-offering in his hand—

A gentile said to him, "Give me one of them and I shall render it unclean, and if not, I shall make all of them unclean"—

D. R. Eliezer says, "Let him make all of them unclean, but let him not give him [the gentile] one of them that he make it unclean."

E. R. Joshua says, "Let him leave one of them on a rock in front of him."

M. Ter. 8 : 11

*Comment*: The problem of M. Ter. 8 : 1-3, concerning what to do when one assumed he was permitted to use Heave-offering and discovers he is not, now is raised in connection with the Heave-offering itself. What happens when one discovers Heave-offering is not what one thought?

The construction is as tight as formerly: A jar of Heave-offering

1. concerning which was born the suspicion of uncleanness—
2. A jar of Heave-offering wine broken in the upper winepress, over an unclean lower winepress—
3. A jar of Heave-offering oil—

In all instances Eliezer is matched with Joshua, as before. One could have reconstructed the whole from any single instance.

M. Ter. 8 : 8 concerns the basic case. One is not sure whether the jar of Heave-offering is unclean. What to do with the jar? Eliezer says one should put the jar in such a place that it will not be made unclean with a certain uncleanness; even though the matter is in doubt, one must not make things worse by turning doubt into certainty. Joshua says the opposite—using the same words as Eliezer, but conveying the meaning by reversing their order—because he holds that one should indeed turn the doubt into certainty. The jar should be placed in a situation which will lead to its certain uncleanness. Then one may burn, or otherwise dispose of, it, and not keep it, lest things be made still worse by someone's actually drinking the wine.

Eliezer therefore wants to protect the Heave-offering from further uncleanness, while Joshua wants to protect it from being wrongly consumed, therefore to encourage its eventual destruction.

Gamaliel rejects both views and does not compromise between them. He says one should do absolutely nothing; one should not cause further uncleanness, as Joshua suggests, but also should not guard it, as Eliezer holds.

Eliezer and Joshua then agree, in M. Ter. 8 : 9, that if a jar of Heave-offering wine breaks and spills into an unclean vat, the man should save a quarter-*log* of wine in cleanness. Now, Albeq explains, this involves going and looking for a vessel in which to save part of the wine. In the mean-time, the clean Heave-offering wine is going to pour into the unclean, unconsecrated wine and the whole mixture will be completely forbidden (M. Ter. 5 : 1). But in order to save the lower wine, he should *not* make the Heave-offering unclean by receiving it in unclean vessels (Albeq, *Seder Zeraʿim*, p. 203).

This seems to me to read too much into the pericope. If we omit B and C, we find that D adequately deals with the situation laid forth in A: R. Eliezer says the man must do absolutely nothing to add to the uncleanness of the wine—just as in M. Ter. 8 : 8—and therefore should not try to scoop it up in his hands. Joshua's opinion is not given. He obviously would differ. But what instruction would he offer? It is hard to envisage.

B and C are a problem. First, MWDH should be MWDYN/M; but that is minor. The major difficulty is that B tells us what we need not hear in the name of the two masters. Who would not agree that if one can save part of the Heave-offering wine in cleanness, one should do so? All this is tied with D by *But if not*—also superfluous, and for the same reason. So B and C break the well-established form, used throughout M. Ter., in which a statement of a case is given in descriptive form—*A jar which has broken*—without *If*, and followed by Eliezer and Joshua in well-balanced language, sometimes even in syzygies.

The same formal difficulties affect M. Ter. 8 : 10. Now the problem is no different from the foregoing one. Instead of wine, we have oil. But now the jar has not broken; the wine has spilled. Albeq comments that if the jar were broken (as in M. Ter. 8 : 9), Joshua would agree with Eliezer that one does nothing that would add to the uncleanness of the oil. One should not worry about the loss, for Heave-offering-oil which may have been made unclean *may* be used for the lamp. Eliezer's rule is that the oil should be allowed to drip down and be swallowed up, but the man should not try to sponge it up with unclean hands.

M. Ter. 8 : 11 now gives us Joshua's opinion—more or less. He does not say what one should, or should not, do. He simply says that these are not situations where one must prevent uncleanness from affecting Heave-offering. All one must *not* do here is *eat* the Heave-offering. If one can save from it a quarter-*log* in cleanness, for the purpose of eating, one should do so. But if he cannot eat it in a condition of purity, he may indeed render it unclean with his hands.

*How so*? Albeq explains, means, "When are we on guard not to render Heave-offering unclean in a situation in which the Heave-offering may become unclean?" On KYṢD, see Epstein, *Nusaḥ*, p. 1032: it should be omitted.

To this is then tied a separate pericope, C-E. Without B, C would presumably have stood as a separate Mishnah; it simply repeats the principle of the first cases, only now in a dramatic story. The position of Eliezer is that one may do nothing to add to the uncleanness of Heave-offering. Therefore one cannot give the gentile a single loaf to save the rest. What will be will be—the man will not have born responsibility through something he has actually done.

Joshua says one may indeed effect a compromise. One puts down on a rock a single loaf. He thereby has not rendered it unclean. The gentile picks up the loaf. *He* has rendered it unclean. But the bearer has no responsibility for that fact, and, incidentally, has preserved the ritual cleanness of the rest.

In all, Joshua's position seems to me more practical, but less principled. Eliezer is consistent throughout. The pericopae would have been better constructed with opinions from Joshua in M. Ter. 8 : 9 and 8 : 10; something like *Let him save it with any sort of vessel* would not be perfect, but might serve.

I am perplexed by the imperfections of the form, particularly the inclusion of "agreements," the repetition of cases which yield nothing new, the rather complicated saying attributed to Joshua in M. Ter. 8 : 11, which does not take the place of sayings he should have had in 8 : 9 and

8 : 10. I do not see why the dispute could not have been given a general character, in simple language; the proliferation of cases has not produced greater clarity.

IV.ii.2. Rav Judah said in the name of Samuel, and so did Resh Laqish say, and so did R. Naḥman say [in the name of] Rabbah bar Abbuha: "*And lo, I, behold, I have given you the charge of my Heave-offerings* (Num. 18 : 8)—

R. Eliezer reasons (SBR), 'Scripture speaks of two [sorts of] Heave-offerings, one being clean Heave-offering, and one being suspensive Heave-offering [which may or may not be unclean], and the Merciful has said, *Keep charge of it* [not to make it unclean].'

"R. Joshua [says], 'My Heave-offering [singular] is written.'"

b. Bekh. 34a

*Comment*: The third-century Amoraim debate the issue of R. Eliezer's opinion as to whether one follows the traditional reading, including the vowels, or only the written text. Accordingly, Eliezer then is given Scriptural foundation for his position in M. Ter. 8 : 11.

I.i.35.A. [If a non-priest drank in error] date-honey, cider, vinegar from winter-grapes, or any other juices [except wine and oil (M. Ter. 11 : 3)] from Heave-offering fruits—

B. R. Eliezer obligates for the principle and the Added Fifth.

C. And R. Joshua exempts.

D. R. Eliezer declares [the afore-mentioned liquids] capable of becoming unclean, because they are liquids [within the law of liquids capable of rendering produce susceptible to uncleanness].

E. R. Joshua said, "The sages did not list seven liquids [capable of rendering unclean] as [do] those that count up spices [roughly]; but they said, 'Seven [kinds of] liquid render unclean, and all the rest of the liquids are clean [and not capable of rendering susceptible to uncleanness].'"

M. Ter. 11 : 2 (y. Ter. 11 : 2, b. Ber. 38a, b. Hul. 120b)

*Comment*: The rule is that "dates of Heave-offering may not be made into honey, nor apples into cider, nor winter-grapes into vinegar, nor may other fruits be changed from their natural state if they are Heave-offering or Second Tithe, excepting only olives and grapes" (M. Ter. 11 : 2). Before that rule is listed, we have the law about what one should do *if* such juices have been made, and a non-priest has consumed them.

If this is done in error, Eliezer holds one owes the Added Fifth. Joshua says that they are not regarded as liquids, therefore the Added Fifth is not charged (So Albeq, *Seder Zeraʿim*, p. 210).

This is immediately turned into a generalization in D, with the addition of MŠWM MŠQH.

In E Joshua has a full explanation. E should be *R. Joshua declares clean* (insusceptible to uncleanness). But because *Because it is liquid* has been inserted to explain Eliezer's opinion, Joshua's becomes a counter-argument. The sages' list of liquids which render food capable of receiving uncleanness is not approximate, but exact—these and no others. There are only seven such liquids, and all others are clean, including those listed here. Both B and D respond directly to A; D is a better choice than B.

I.ii.17.A. Date-honey—

R. Liezer declares liable for Tithes.

B. R. Nathan said, "R. Liezer agrees that it is free of the liability for tithes.

"But R. Liezer would say that one should not eat from honey before he has taken care of (TQN = given tithes from) the dates.

C. "R. Liezer agrees that if he has taken care of [tithes from] dates here [in Palestine], and he makes honey from them in Aspamia (ʾSPMYʾ), that it is permitted."

D. Date-honey—

R. Liezer declares capable of rendering susceptible of receiving uncleanness as a liquid.

E. R. Nathan said, "R. Liezer agrees that this does not render unclean as a liquid.

"Concerning what did they disagree?

"Concerning the [situation in which] he put water [y.: That water fell] in it—

"For R. Liezer declares capable of rendering susceptible of receiving uncleanness as a liquid.

"And sages say, 'They follow the majority [of the liquid in the mixture].'"

Tos. Ter. 9 : 8, Lieberman, p. 157, ls. 30-35
(y. Ter. 11 : 2; b. Ber. 38a)

I.ii.18.A. "Ḥeave-offering olives which are clean may be made into oil. Unclean may not be made into oil.

"Grapes, whether unclean or clean, may not be made [into wine]"—the words of R. Meir.

B. R. Jacob says in his name, "R. Liezer agrees with R. Joshua concerning clean olives that they should be made [into oil].

"Concerning what did they disagree?

"Concerning unclean olives, for—

"R. Eliezer says, 'They may not be made [into oil.]'

"And R. Joshua says, 'They may be made.'

"And clean grapes may be made, but unclean may not."

C. R. Judah said, "R. Joshua agrees with R. Liezer concerning clean olives and clean grapes, that they may be made [into oil or wine].

"Concerning what did they disagree?

"Concerning the unclean, for—

"R. Liezer says, 'They may not be made.'

"And R. Joshua says, 'They may be made.'"

D. Rabbi said, "R. Liezer and R. Joshua did not disagree concerning clean olives, that they should be made, and concerning unclean grapes, that they should not be made.

"Concerning what did they differ?

"Concerning unclean olives and clean grapes, for—

"R. Eliezer says, 'They may not be made.'

"And R. Joshua says, 'They may be made.'"

Tos. Ter. 9 : 9, Lieberman, pp. 157-8, ls. 35-44 (y. Ter. 11 : 3)

*Comment*: Joshua's position in M. Ter. 11 : 2C is that Heave-offering and Tithe do not have to be given from date-honey; y. explains that if the honey flowed after the dates were rendered obligated to tithing, R. Joshua agrees that it is prohibited to eat the honey, but if before the obligation has affected the dates, the honey is not obligated to tithing at all.

The position of Liezer in Tos Ter. 9 : 8A would evidently concern the liability at all times, and, in B, Nathan then claims Liezer's position is the opposite—along the lines of Joshua's opinion. Nathan holds Liezer regards the honey as free of tithes, but, because it was exuded from untithed produce, it is prohibited. What has come out of something prohibited is prohibited (Lieberman, *Tosefta Kifshuṭah Seder Zeraʿim* I, p. 456).

This would accord with Eliezer's view that, in general, one may ignore distinctions among produce, and give Heave-offering for one thing for another, e.g. clean for unclean. If so, the prohibitions pertaining to one thing likewise would apply to the other. Likewise in M. Ter. 8 : 1-3, if one has started an action legitimately, he may conclude it even though the action has been shown, in the midst of doing it, to be illegitimate. So, contrarywise, what begins in illegitimacy remains illegitimate. Eliezer's position remains consistent throughout.

In y., however, Eliezer is given a completely different tradition:

TNY: R. Nathan says, "Not that R. Liezer declares liable for tithes, but that

R. Liezer says that one should not eat dates until he has given tithe for the honey."

The explanation, Lieberman notes, would then be that honey by itself is free of Tithes, but the dates are liable both for their flesh and for their honey, and so long as he has not tithed the dates—including what is due for the honey—he may not eat the dates. But once the dates are tithed, the honey is permitted.

As to Tos. Ter. 9 : 8A Eliezer differs from M. Maksh. 6 : 4. Nathan's correction of the tradition raises the issue of putting water into the honey. Eliezer holds that if the man has done so, the honey becomes capable of rendering susceptible to uncleanness, and the sages' view is that one judges by what constitutes the greater part of the mixture—if water, then it is unclean, otherwise it is clean. So, according to Nathan, Eliezer does regard date-honey in itself as incapable of rendering something susceptible to uncleanness. Meir elsewhere has the same opinion about water in mixture.

Tos Ter. 9 : 9A represents Meir's opinion as follows: One may not change even olives and grapes from their original condition, except in the case of clean olives, for olive-oil is more valuable than olives; in the case of unclean olives, one still does not permit crushing, lest they be consumed when being crushed; but grapes are more valuable as food than as wine.

M. Ter. 11 : 3 has it that only Heave-offering of olives and grapes may be changed from their natural state, but not Heave-offering of other fruits; and *no* distinction is introduced between unclean and clean olives or grapes.

The saying of Tos. Ter. 9:9B is corrected by Lieberman to *Eliezer and Joshua agree*. Their joint opinion is that both olives and grapes which are clean may be turned into liquids, and unclean grapes may not be made into wine, but they differ with respect to unclean olives. So according to Jacob, Joshua holds they may make oil from grapes and olives. The Mishnah contains no hint of this dispute.

Judah then has another version: Joshua and Eliezer agree on clean olives and clean grapes of Heave-offering, that they *may* be turned into liquids. They differ only with respect to the unclean of both species; they may not be turned into liquids. Judah thus claims Joshua holds that they do make liquids from olives and grapes, whether unclean or clean, and since our Mishnah makes no such distinction, it accords with Judah's opinion.

Judah the Patriarch then claims they agree that clean olives may be made into liquids, and unclean grapes may not, but differ as to unclean olives and clean grapes. Judah the Patriarch therefore agrees with respect to Joshua—you make liquid of olives and grapes. The issue is Eliezer's opinion. Jacob holds they all agree—including Eliezer—that one may make wine from clean grapes. Judah the Patriarch supposes Eliezer thinks that one does not make wine from clean grapes. y. has it that Rabbi holds Eliezer and Joshua agree about clean olives that clean olives may be made into oil, and unclean grapes and unclean olives may not be made into liquid, but differ on clean grapes, with Eliezer prohibiting turning them into wine.

III.ii.10. Does R. ʿAqiba hold that dough which was kneaded with wine, oil, or honey is not fit? WHTNYʾ:

Dough must not be kneaded on Passover with wine, oil, or honey, and if one did knead it—

R. Gamaliel says, "It must be burned immediately."

And sages say, "It may be eaten."

R. ʿAqiba said, "I was staying [on Passover] with R. Eliezer and R. Joshua, and I kneaded dough for them with wine, oil, or honey, and they said nothing to me."

b. Pes. 36a

*Comment*: ʿAqiba's story about his actions with Eliezer and Joshua is taken as testimony that he holds the opinion opposite to that attributed to him. We have no evidence of an apodictic or generalized saying in the name of Eliezer and Joshua on the subject.

y. Pes. 2 : 7 has Eliezer and Joshua in a boat; and now ʿAqiba uses *fruit*-juice.

## vii. Maʿaserot

I.i.36.A. He who takes olives from the press dips [them] one by one in salt and eats. If he salted [them] and set them down before him [self], he is liable [to give the tithes.]

B. R. Eliezer says, "[If] from the clean vat, he is liable, and [if] from the unclean he is free [of liability],

C. "Because he returns what is left over."

M. Ma. 4 : 3 (y. Ma. 4 : 2; b. Bes. 35a)

*Comment*: The rule, M. Ma. 4 : 1, is that if a man pickled, stewed, or salted produce while it is in the field, he is liable for the tithes. The processing of the produce establishes the liability for tithes, even in the field, and salting or pickling is like cooking. But M. Ma. 4 : 3A qualifies this rule, for the man's taking an olive one at a time is not the same thing. If he salted a number of olives, planning to eat them all at once, then he is obligated to tithe, even if he eats them afterward one at a time.

Eliezer now qualifies the foregoing rule. If one takes the olives from a *clean* press and salts and places them before himself, he is liable, for he is not going to return the uneaten portion; the rest have not been made susceptible to receive uncleanness by the oil. Consistent with his position in M. Ter. 11 : 2, Eliezer holds that the liquid renders susceptible to uncleanness; Joshua would differ, except in the case of the seven specified liquids listed in M. Maksh. 6 : 4. So the man has made the olives unclean. Whatever he has put before himself is joined together, and the salting acts, as specified, to render the whole obligated for tithes.

But if the vat was unclean, he can return whatever he does not eat. Therefore whatever he set before himself does not join together; the salting does not render the olives liable; and his eating is random.

I.i.37.A. He that husks barley-husks one by one eats [without tithing]. But if he husked [several grains] and put them in his hand, he is liable.

B. He who rubbed ripe ears of wheat sifts from hand to hand and eats [without tithing]. But if he sifted [them] and collected the grains into his bosom, he is liable.

C. Coriander which he sowed for seed—its plant is exempt. He sowed it for the [sake of] the plant—the seed and the plant are [to be] tithed.

D. R. Eliezer says, "Dill—the seed, plant, and pods are tithed."

E. And sages say, "The seed and plant are tithed, on [in the case of] the pepperwort and eruca [So Danby]."

M. Ma. 4 : 5 (y. Ma. 4 : 4; b. Bekh. 2a; b. A. Z. 7b)

I.i.38.A. Rabban [Naples: Simeon b.] Gamaliel says, "Stalks of fenugreek, mustard, and white beans are liable to tithe."

B. R. Eliezer says, "Caperbush is tithed as to stalks, caperberries, and caper-flowers."

C. R. ʿAqiba says, "Only the caperberries are tithed, because they are fruit."

M. Ma. 4 : 6 (b. Ber. 36a)

*Comment*: M. Ma. 4 : 5D-E present a little dispute on what one tithes of dill. The sages agree that one would tithe the pods. But as to the seed and plant, these are tithed only in the case of the specified species. I suppose the issue is whether one eats the other parts of the plant.

M. Ma. 4 : 6B does not set Eliezer into opposition against Gamaliel. His opinion is consistent with D, and ʿAqiba differs. Only the berries count as food. The form of Eliezer's sayings is:

*Objects*—tithed in respect to [Then: various parts of plant are listed]. The sages now differ as to a minor detail of the former ruling. In 4 : 5E, it is to be the specified type. In M. Ma. 4 : 6C it is as to the part of the plant.

On 4 : 5, see Epstein, *Nusaḥ*, pp. 487, 1177. Epstein prefers *Eliezer*. On 4 : 6, see p. 1199, for Gamaliel/Simeon.

I.ii.19.A. They said before R. Liezer, "Even though he does not return them to this press, lo, he returns them to another press."

B. Coriander—if one planted it for seed and reconsidered concerning it, [wanting] to produce a plant, both the seed and the plant are tithed.

Mustard which he sowed [it] for seed, and he changed his mind concerning it [and also wanted the] plant, both the seed and the plant are tithed.

"They treated its plant [mustard's] [y.: BBT NYYN] leniently"—the words of R. Liezer.

Tos. Ma. 3 : 7, Lieberman, p. 238, ls. 12-15
(M. Ma. 4 : 6; y. Ma. 4 : 6)

*Comment*: A is the reply to Eliezer in M. Ma. 4 : 3—there is no difference between unclean and clean vats, because the man will bring them back to some other vat, if not to the clean one, in the event that the olives are unclean. So the sages agree that if the man returns the uneaten olives, he eats in a random manner. But if they are salted, he cannot return them—so Lieberman.

As to mustard-seed, Eliezer's view is that a lenient rule applies—even if he planted it for the plant, its primary purpose is to produce seed, and one ignores his intention and follows the normal practice. Therefore only the seed is tithed, under all circumstances. See Lieberman, *Tosefta Kifshuṭah Seder Zera'im* II, p. 697-8.

## viii. Ma'aser Sheni

I.ii.20.A. R. Simeon said in the name of R. Liezer, "Saffron is not purchased with the money of Tithe, because it serves no purpose except appearance."

B. R. Judah b. Gaddish said before R. Liezer, "[Those] of the house of father would sell brine (ṢYR) in Jerusalem."

They said, "Who is to say? Perhaps they sold fish with it."

Tos M.S. 1 : 4, Lieberman, pp. 246-7, ls. 47-49 (b. Eruv. 27a)

*Comment*: The money received in exchange for Second Tithe had to be used for the purchase of food to be consumed in Jerusalem. Eliezer's rule is on a minor detail. But the same rule would apply to whatever is used simply for scent or appearance. If, however, something is used as a spice for food, it may be purchased with Tithe-money (Lieberman, *Tosefta Kifshuṭah Seder Zera'im* II, p. 726).

The story of B (with a parallel in b. 'Eruv. 27a, "They would purchase brine for Tithe-money") does not contradict Eliezer's ruling. To be sure, fish-brine may be purchased for Tithe-money, because of the fish-fat mixed in it, even though the fish-taste is not much apparent. It would follow that Eliezer holds one may purchase fish with Tithe-money.

I.ii.21.A. Tos. M.S. 2 : 16 (y. M.S. 3 : 3).

*Comment*: *Phar.* II, pp. 113-116.

I.ii.22.A. "He saw him, that he separated Second Tithe—he is believed as to First Tithe," the words of R. Liezer.

B. And sages say, "He who is believed as to First Tithe is believed as to Second. He who is believed as to Second Tithe is *not* believed as to first."

C. "He separated Heave-offering and First Tithe and Second Tithe and ate them—

"Concerning that particular kind [of produce] he is believed, [but] concerning another kind [of produce] he is not believed," the words of R. Liezer.

D. And sages say, "Even for that particular kind [of produce] he is not believed. He does not have the power to arrange things properly for himself but to come and spoil it [for others]."

Tos. M.S. 3 : 16, Lieberman, p. 261, ls. 53-58 (y. Dem. 4 : 35, y. M.S. 4 : 5; y. Pe'ah 8 : 2)

*Comment*: Eliezer is in accord with the House of Shammai, whose saying immediately precedes:

> The House of Shammai say, "A man separates the First Tithe of *demai* and raises up its Heave-offering and eats it, and does not have to separate Second Tithe."
>
> The House of Hillel say, "He needs to separate Second Tithe, for I say, 'If the Second is raised up, the First is raised up, but if the First is raised up, the Second is not [necessarily] raised up.'"
>
> Tos. M.S. 3 : 15 (*Phar.* II, pp. 116-117)

Eliezer thus stands in the position of the House of Shammai. The sages' view is that the Second Tithe belongs to the man, but he has to take the trouble to eat it in Jerusalem. But First Tithe he merely gives to a Levite, so it is easier to dispose of.

The sages in D hold that the man may give Tithes only for what he eats, but not for what he sells. Therefore he is not relied upon. Eliezer here would seem to take the lenient view.

y. M.S. 4 : 5: Bar Kappara says the House of Shammai is in accord with R. Eliezer.

II.iv.4.A. *And I have not given from it to the dead* (Deut. 26 : 14).

"I have not bought with it a coffin and shrouds for the dead," the words of R. Eliezer.

B. R. ʿAqiba said to him, "If for the corpse, also for the living person it is prohibited. Why does Scripture say, *For the dead?* That I have not exchanged it even for something *clean.*"

Sifré Deut. 303, Finkelstein, p. 322

*Comment*: M. M.S. 5 : 12 has the following:

> *Nor given thereof to the dead*—I have not used anything thereof for a coffin or shrouds for a corpse nor have I given it to other mourners.

Apart from the concluding, italicized clause, this is Eliezer's comment on Deut. 26 : 14. But it is not assigned to him. We have already observed evidence that Eliezer's opinions were either suppressed or given anonymously, not in his name.

See Epstein, *Tan.*, p. 68: Judah b. Ilai, who stands behind Sifra, is the source of Eliezer's law in M. M.S. 5 : 12.

I.ii.23.A. He gave [him] the principle and did not give [him] the Added Fifth—

B. R. Liezer says, "He may eat."

And sages say, "He may not eat."

C. Rabbi [Judah the Patriarch] said, "R. Liezer's opinion appears [preferable] for the Sabbath, and the sages' opinion for ordinary [days]."

D. He who did not designate Heave-offering of *Demai*-produce—

R. Liezer says, "He may eat."

And sages say, "He may not eat."

R. Yosah said, "R. Liezer's opinion is preferable for the Sabbath," etc.

Tos. M.S. 4 : 5-6 (b. B.M. 54a),
Lieberman, p. 263, ls. 16-19

*Comment*: Lieberman drops *him* in A. The man has given the principle of the Second Tithe, but has not given the Fifth (Lev. 27 : 31). May he eat the produce? Eliezer says the Fifth does not present an obstacle to eating the produce that has been redeemed; the sages say it does. Judah the Patriarch rules in Eliezer's favor for the Sabbath; the man may consume the produce on that day. But on the weekday he can just as easily give the Added Fifth, therefore must do so before eating, b. B.M. 54a has the dispute between Eliezer and *Joshua*, and on that basis I have included it here. There the issue is the same. See Lieberman, *Tosefta Kifshuṭah Seder Zeraʿim*, II, p. 768.

I.ii.24. After the Temple was destroyed, the first (R'ŠWN) court (BYT DYN) said nothing about it [fruits of the Fourth-Year Vineyard]. The last ('ḤRWN) court decreed that this should be redeemed near the wall [of Jerusalem].

B. MʿŚH B: R. Eliezer had a vineyard on the side of Kefar Ṭabi east of Lud, and he did not want to redeem it.

His disciples said to him, "Rabbi, since they decreed that this should be redeemed near the wall, you have to redeem it."

R. Eliezer went and harvested and redeemed it.

Tos. M.S. 5 : 15-16, Lieberman, pp. 271-272, ls. 49-54

III.ii.11. TNY': R. Eliezer had [trees of the] Fourth Year [in a] vineyard to the east of Lud near Kefar Ṭabi, and he wished to renounce it for the poor [so as not to have to bring the fruit to Jerusalem].

His disciples said to him, "Master, your colleagues have already voted and permitted it.

Who are 'your colleagues'?

R. Yoḥanan b. Zakkai.

b. Bes. 5a = b. R.H. 31b.

*Comment*: The pertinent Mishnah is M. M.S. 5 : 2:

> Fruit of a Fourth Year Vineyard was taken up to Jerusalem from any place a day's journey in any direction ... When the fruits became too many it was ordained that they might be redeemed even near the wall. And this was the understanding: when they wished the matter might be restored to its former condition.
>
> R. Yosi says, "This was the understanding after the Temple was destroyed, and it was understood that when the Temple would be rebuilt, the matter would be restored to its former condition."

Tos. M.S. 5 : 15A is in accord with R. Yosi, that the decree about redeeming the fruit near the wall of Jerusalem came after the destruction. Eliezer thought it was necessary to bring the grapes to Jerusalem for redemption and did not want to be bothered, so he wanted to declare it ownerless property for use by the poor. The disciples report, in the Babylonian *baraita*, that it is not necessary to do so, because it is possible to redeem it. In Tos. Eliezer wants to leave the grapes as they are so that he will not have to redeem them; the poor can harvest them and bring them to Jerusalem. So Lieberman, *Tosefta Kifshuṭah Seder Zera'im* II, p. 785.

S. Zeitlin, "The Tosefta," *JQR* 57, 1956-7, p. 395, claims "to clarify the seeming contradiction" between Tos. and b.: "It seems that they did not refer to the same orchard of R. Eliezer. The Tosefta refers to the orchard which R. Eliezer had near K'far Tabi, northeast of Lydda, while the Babylonian Talmud refers to an orchard which R. Eliezer had near K'far Tabi southeast of Lydda ..." So the one north of Lydda had to be redeemed, but the one south could not be redeemed "but had to be brought to Jerusalem." Eliezer, further, did not know about Yoḥanan b. Zakkai's and Gamaliel's change of the rule because he had been excommunicated, so Zeitlin. On this basis Zeitlin criticizes Lieberman(!).

## ix. Ḥallah

I.i.39.A. Produce from abroad which entered the Land is liable for Dough-offering.

[Produce] went forth from here to there—

B. R. Eliezer declares liable.

C. And R. ʿAqiba declares exempt.

M. Hal. 2 : 1 (y. Hal. 2 : 1, y. Ma. 5 : 2)

*Comment*: Eliezer and ʿAqiba dispute only about the second clause in the statement of the problem. They agree on the first, which need not antedate them. The form is a standard dispute—*Statement of Problem, Rabbi X.., Rabbi Y...*

The dough prepared in the Land was obligated at the moment of its preparation. y. explains that Eliezer holds, following Num. 15 : 19, this is *Bread of the land*, therefore obligated. ʿAqiba alludes to the same Scripture, *Whither I bring you*— "Since *you* are not in the land, you are not liable." So for the former, the decisive issue is the origin of the *dough*; for the latter, the location of the *person* obligated to give the Dough-offering.

As to A, both evidently agree; the dough was prepared when located in the Land, and so is the man. But what if the produce were already made into dough? Then, when it was actually prepared and became liable for the Dough-offering, it was still abroad, and there should be no obligation.

See Epstein, *Tan.*, pp. 99, 272: This is Meir's version.

II.iv.5.A. *Where I am bringing you*—On this basis you say that fruit from abroad which entered the land is liable for *Ḥallah.*

B. If it went abroad—

R. Eliezer declares liable.

And R. ʿAqiba exempts.

R. Judah says, "Even fruit from abroad which entered the land—

"R. Eliezer declares free of liability, as it is said, *When you will eat of the bread of the land.*"

Sifré Num. 110, Friedman, p. 31a

*Comment*: Our surmise is supported by Judah b. Ilai's tradition. The form is identical to M. Hal. 2 : 1.

I.i.40. [If a man cannot prepare his dough in cleanness, let him prepare portions of one *qav* each—that is, less than the quantity liable for Dough-offering—but let him not prepare it in uncleanness. R. ʿAqiba says, "Let him prepare it in uncleanness, but let him not prepare it in portions of one *qav* each."—M. Hal. 2 : 3.]

A. He who prepares his dough in [portions of] *qavs*, and they came into contact with one another—

B. They are free of liability for the Dough-offering, *until they adhere* [to one another].

C. R. Eliezer says, "Even he who removes [loaves of one *qav* each from the stove] and puts into a basket—the basket joins them for [liability to] Dough-offering [and all the more so in the former case]."

M. Hal. 2 : 4 (y. Hal. 2 : 2; b, Pes. 48b, b. Nid. 8a)

*Comment*: Dough-offering is due from dough of more than a *qav*. The issue then is how and when such *qav*-sized lumps of dough adhere to one another, so as to become a quantity which is liable. The rule of A-B is that the dough must actually adhere, that is, be baked together. This is consistent with M. Hal. 4 : 1, "If two women rolled out two pieces of dough, each of one *qav*, and these touched one another, they are exempt even if they are of the same kind of grain; if they belonged to the same woman, they are liable if like touched like, but not if one touched another kind." Eliezer then gives a stricter rule. They do not have actually to adhere to one another. Even if they do not adhere, they are a single mass if placed in a single basket.

Eliezer's saying is tied to the foregoing with ʾP, *even*, and therefore depends upon A-B for meaning—but not for structure, for Eliezer does *not* repeat the language of A-B. But his *he who removes* is modeled upon *he who makes his dough qavim*; then *he places them in a basket* sets up a condition in opposition to *they touched one another.* No effort has been made to build Eliezer's saying on the substantives of A-B, even though, as noted, it depends upon their rule. Perhaps the reason the sayings are out of balance with one another is that both are developments of what we should have expected: *liable/free* [of liability]. A supplies the topic sentence: *He who prepares... and they came into contact.* B should say, *free* of liability. But B has been glossed with *until they adhere*—which obviously is the point of the question of A. Then Eliezer should say *liable.* But he has a more extreme case: even if the balls of dough do not adhere and, having been baked, could not adhere to one another, they are liable if they are in the same basket. So his ruling goes beyond the one stated in A. In all, the pericope evidently has been developed over a simple one in which the question is answered without complications.

The association with ʿAqiba is warrant for assignment to our Eliezer.

b. Pes. 48b = b. Nid. 8a: Rav Judah in the name of Samuel says the law follows R. Eliezer.

Note also b. Pes. 48b:

R. Eliezer says, "The basket combines them."

R. Joshua says, "The oven combines them."

This seems even better warrant for assigning the pericope to Eliezer b. Hyrcanus's tradition.

On ʾP, see Epstein, *Nusaḥ*, p. 1008. See Epstein, *Tan.*, pp. 271-2.

I.i.41. [The measure prescribed for the Dough-offering is one twenty-fourth part ... If the dough was rendered unclean accidentally or under constraint, the Dough-offering may be one forty-eighth part; but if intentionally it must be one twenty-fourth part ... M. Hal. 2 : 7]

A. R. Eliezer says, "It may be taken from the clean for the unclean.

B. "How so?

"Clean dough and unclean dough—He takes sufficient for the Dough-offering from the dough whose Dough-offering has not been raised up and places [dough] less than about an egg's [size] in the middle, so that he may take from that which is joined together (MWQP)."

C. And sages prohibit.

M. Hal. 2 : 8 (y. Hal. 2 : 3; y. Ter. 2 : 1, Tos. Bik. 1 : 6, Lieberman, p. 287, ls. 17-20; b. Sot. 30a)

*Comment*: Eliezer is consistent with his position with respect to Heave-offering. Heave-offering may be given from clean for unclean produce (but not vice versa, for one cannot give from worse for better produce, and the unclean is of less value). Part C responds to A, and is in a general way consistent with M. Hal. 2 : 7, in distinguishing between unclean and clean dough.

Part B then explains how one may carry out Eliezer's rule in A, therefore is a gloss from a party in agreement with A. Obviously, the sages would prohibit doing things this way. Before one comes to separate from the clean for the unclean dough, he takes from the clean dough the amount of dough required for the Dough-offering for the two quantities of dough. Dough-offering has not yet been taken up from the clean dough, so that he can separate for it Dough-offering in cleanness (if the clean dough is made unclean by touch with unclean dough—so Albeq, *Seder Zera'im*, p. 281). Then he puts less than an egg's bulk in the middle, between the clean and the unclean doughs. The clean will not be made unclean when he brings it near the unclean to separate Dough-offering from it for the unclean dough, for unclean food of less than an egg's quantity does not render unclean. This establishes the two quantities of dough as a single quantity—for they are near one another ["... they must be taken only from what is nearby ...," M. Hal. 1 : 9]. The sages' view is represented in M. Hal. 1 : 9, "They do not take from what is clean instead of from what is unclean."

One wonders why M. Hal. 1 : 9 has not been used as the locus for this dispute. Eliezer's pericope, in which the anonymous opinion of 1 : 9 is made into that of the sages, could as well have been attached as the final paragraph of M. Hal. 1. It could stand as 1 : 10, rather than as the final paragraph of M. Hal. 2—as 2 : 8. I see no close connection with 2 : 7, and there is a very obvious one with 1 : 10. Eliezer uses the same words:

| 1 : 10 | 2 : 8 |
|---|---|
| A. (W) ʾYNN NṬLYN MN HṬHWR ʿL HṬMʾ | NṬLT MN HṬHWR ʿL HṬMʾ |
| B. ʾLʾ MN HMWQP | [KDY ŠYṬL] MN HMWKP |

All that changes in A is the number, from plural to singular; this is on account of the antecedent—Dough-offering *and* Heave-offering in 1 : 9; only Dough-offering occurs in 2 : 8.

As to B, the inclusion of KDY Š in Eliezer's saying seems to me to be pointless—who raised the question of MWQP?—unless the allusion is to the concluding clause of 1 : 10, a rule with which Eliezer perforce agrees! So it would seem that 2 : 8 ought to follow 1 : 9 and serve as the concluding pericope of the foregoing chapter.

Why has it been moved? Perhaps because 2 : 7 alludes to giving unclean Dough-offering and how to give it, within the presumption that clean cannot be given for unclean. Then Eliezer says clean *may* be given for unclean and gives a different set of rules on how to do so.

See Epstein, *Tan.*, pp. 68, 272.

I.ii.25.A. R. Liezer says, "Dough-offering is taken from the clean for the unclean."

B. They said before R. Ishmael, "And is there not So-and-so [= Eliezer!] in the south, and he would teach according to this [A's] instruction?"

C. He said to them, "By the [priestly] garment which father wore and by the plate that he put between his eyes! If I do not [= I shall] teach concerning it to everyone who issues instructions."

D. They said [it] to him in the name of R. Liezer.

E. He said to them, "Even (ʾP) *he* has grounds for his opinion [Lit.: He has what to hang on—YŠ LW BMH YTLH)."

Tos. Hal. 1 : 10, Lieberman, p. 277, ls. 30-33 (b. Pes. 38b)

*Comment*: Immediately preceding is ʿAqiba's rule of M. Hal. 2 : 3. A introduces the story of B-E, but is independent of it, a mere citation of what now occurs in 2 : 8 + ḤLH, as required by the context.

Lieberman explains that in B, the students do not cite Eliezer by name. When Ishmael agrees, then they tell him it is Eliezer. Exactly what are the students supposed to have said in the first place? It ought to be something like A, without reference to Eliezer: "They take *Ḥallah* . . ." The allusion to the south is to Eliezer's residency in Lydda, which means that the story is told in the north. At this time one does *not* cite Eliezer; his principle that clean produce may serve as tithe or offering for unclean is, however, acceptable—but not automatically attributed to him as the authority, which means others held the same view. It no longer was unique to Eliezer. But attributing it to him would do no good. Ishmael also has a teaching—which he, as the son of the old priesthood, is presumed to know from his forefathers—that clean Dough-offering is separated in behalf of unclean dough.

I.i.42.A. Israel[ites] who were sharecroppers for gentiles in Syria—

B. R. Eliezer declares their fruits liable for Tithes and for [observance of the] Seventh Year.

C. And Rabban Gamaliel declares [them] free [of liability.]

D. Rabban Gamaliel says, "Two Dough-offerings [are required] in Syria."

E. And R. Eliezer says, "One Dough-offering."

F. They followed (ʾḤZW) Rabban Gamaliel's lenient ruling and R. Eliezer's lenient ruling.

G. Then they went and followed the opinions of Rabban Gamaliel in both matters.

M. Hal. 4 : 7 (y. Hal. 4 : 4, y. Ma. 5 : 2)

*Comment*: The form of A-C is perfect; Gamaliel's opinion depends upon Eliezer's for the predicate of *declares free*, a commonplace development in the dispute-form. D-E likewise are in good form, but in reversed order. The final gloss, F-G, is unusual.

Syria is partly like Palestine, and partly unlike it. It is liable to tithes, just like the Land of Israel; M. Ma. 5 : 5 lists some lenient rulings. However, those rulings are Ushan—Judah, Simeon b. Gamaliel, then Rabbi:

> If a man bought a field of vegetables in Syria before the tithing season, he is liable to Tithes; but if after the tithing season, he is exempt and may continue to gather the crop himself, after his usual fashion.
>
> R. Judah says, "He may also hire laborers to help gather the crop."
>
> R. Simeon b. Gamaliel says, "This [buying the field before tithing] applies if he had bought the land, but if he had not bought the land, although it was before the tithing season, he is exempt."
>
> Rabbi [Judah the Patriarch] says, "Howbeit he should give tithe according to the proportion [which the crop had grown after he acquired it]."
>
> M. Ma. 5 : 5

Eliezer's rule is strict. The Syrian crop is liable for Tithes and for the observance of the Seventh Year—*just* as if it were the Land of Israel. This must mean that Eliezer regards Syria as part of the biblical inheritance of the people of Israel.

Gamaliel differs; the land belongs to the gentile. The Israelite owns nothing of the land, therefore bears no liability for Tithes and for observance of the Seventh Year. Thus Gamaliel relinquishes the Israelite claim to Syria.

In D-E, the masters' positions are reversed. But the respective opinions are consistent. Gamaliel rules that just as one has to separate two Dough-offerings in the land of which the emigrants from Egypt did not take possession (one for the fire and one for the priest), so too for Syria. Eliezer (coming second) says that the Syrian land is like Israelite land *in all respects,* therefore a single loaf is offered. These opinions depend upon M. Hal. 4 : 8:

> Rabban Gamaliel says, "Three regions are distinguished in what concerns Dough-offering. In the Land of Israel . . . one Dough-offering; from Keziv to the River and to Amanah, two loaves (one for the priest and one for the fire)," etc.

Following Gamaliel's division, we must conclude that giving a single loaf means the land is regarded as Israelite in all respects. So Eliezer's "lenient" ruling in D-E is consistent with his "strict" one in B. Gamaliel is equally consistent.

According to F-G, the original decision was to avoid such consistency. Gamaliel's opinion would be followed in respect to Tithes and the Seventh Year—a considerable advantage, and Eliezer's in respect to Dough-offering, of no great consequence. Then the opinion of Gamaliel is said to have prevailed in all respects, and this meant that Syria was no longer regarded as rightfully Jewish.

y. Hal. 4 : 4: R. Abbahu explains Eliezer's rule.

I.ii.26.A. R. Ilai (ʾLʿ ʾY) said, "I asked R. Joshua, 'Are the cakes of the Thank-offering (ḤḶWT TWDH) and wafers of the Nazirite (RQYQY NZYR) liable for Dough-offering?'

"He said to me, 'Free.'

B. "And when I came and asked R. Liezer, he said to me, 'If he made them for himself, they are free. [If] to sell in the market-place, they are liable.'

C. "And when I came and laid the matters before R. Leazar b. ʿAzariah, he said to me, 'By the covenant! These things were said from Mount Ḥoreb.' "

Tos. Hal. 1 : 6, Lieberman, p. 276
ls. 11-14 (b. Pes. 38b, M. Hal. 1 : 6)

*Comment*: M. Hal. 1 : 6 has the following:

> "The cakes of the Thank-offering and the wafers of the Nazirite are exempt if he made them for his own use, but if to sell in the market they are liable [for Dough-offering]."

M. Hal. 1 : 6 therefore is *exactly* the opinion of Eliezer, incorporating the language of Ilai's question (A) for the topic-sentence. But Eliezer's dispute with Joshua is not mentioned in the Mishnah, nor are we told that the Mishnah is his. b. Pes. 38b gives the following:

> TNYʾ: R. Ilai said, "I asked R. Eliezer, 'What is the law as to a man's fulfilling [his obligation to eat *maṣṣah*] with cakes of the Thank-offering and the wafers of the Nazirite.'
>
> "He said to me, 'I have not heard.'
>
> "I came and asked before R. Joshua.
>
> "He said to me, 'Lo, they have said, 'Cakes of the Thank-offering and the wafers of the Nazirite which he made for himself—a man does not fulfill his

obligation with them; [if he made them] to sell in the market, he does fulfill his obligation with them.'

"And when I came and laid the matters before R. Eliezer, he said to me, 'By the covenant! These are the very words which were said to Moses at Sinai.'"

Here the issue is changed, but the pericope in origin cannot be different from Tos. Hal. 1 : 6, so b. Pes. has a garbled tradition—assuming the *baraita* to begin has not been shaped on the basis of Tos. Hal.

On M. Hal. 1 : 6, see Epstein, *Tan.*, pp. 67, 99; *Nusaḥ*, p. 2.

## x. ʿOrlah

I.i.43.A. R. Eliezer says, "He that curdles [milk] with the sap of *ʿorlah* (ŚRP HʿRLH)—it is prohibited."

B. R. Joshua said, "I heard explicitly that he who curdles with sap of the leaves, with the sap of the roots—it is permitted.

C. "With the sap of the unripe figs—it is prohibited, because they are fruit."

M. Orl. 1 : 7 (y. Orl. 1 : 5;
b. A.Z. 35b, 49a, b. Nid. 8b)

*Comment*: Eliezer's rule is that the curdled milk (cheese) will be forbidden, because of preparation in violation of the *ʿorlah*-law. *ʿOrlah*-fruit cannot be used in any form. Joshua does not differ on the general rule. But the rule applies to *fruit* of *ʿorlah*-trees. The leaves and roots are not fruit. Unripe figs, however, are fruit (C) even before they have ripened.

We do not know what Eliezer would have ruled on the leaves or roots. He specifies only the sap of *ʿorlah*, without specifying fruit, as against roots or leaves. So Joshua supplies to SRP *leaves* and *roots*, filling out Eliezer's rule. But y. understands Eliezer to differ with Joshua, regarding leaves and roots as prohibited just like fruit.

See Epstein, *Nusaḥ*, p. 137.

I.i.44.A. If a leaven of unconsecrated food and [leaven] of Heave-offering fell into dough, there not being enough in either one [separately] in order to leaven the dough, but joined together they do leaven [it]—

B. R. Eliezer says, "I decide according to the last [to fall in]."

C. And sages say, "Whether the prohibited [one] fell in first or last, it never prohibits until enough is in it to leaven [by itself]."

M. Orl. 2 : 11 (y. Orl. 2 : 6; y. A.Z. 5 : 11,
b. Tem. 12a, b. Pes. 26b-27a, b. A.Z. 49b, 73b)

*Comment*: The rule, M. Orl. 2 : 4, is that "whatever is leavened ... with Heave-offering, Orlah-fruit, or Diverse Kinds of the Vineyard is forbidden." Eliezer differs from that rule. If the leaven of Heave-offering fell at the last, thus completing the process of leavening the dough, the dough is prohibited; otherwise it is permitted. The rule in M. Orl. 2 : 8 and 2 : 9 is that if common leaven fell into dough and sufficed to leaven it, and afterward Heave-offering leaven fell in and there was enough to leaven the dough, it is forbidden; likewise, if common leaven fell in and leavened the dough, and afterward Heave-offering leaven fell in and could have leavened the dough, it is forbidden.

So the sages are consistent with the whole antecedent set of rules. With Eliezer holding the opposite, the anonymous rule is again assigned to "the sages." Eliezer's position is clearly the lenient one.

I.i.45.A. Vessels which one has anointed [greased] with unclean oil and then has gone and greased with clean oil; or that one has greased with clean oil and then gone and greased with unclean oil—

B. R. Eliezer says, "I decide [whether the utensil is clean or unclean] by which of them came first."

C. And sages say, "After the last."

M. Orl. 2 : 13 (y. Orl. 2 : 7)

*Comment*: After the unclean oil has dried and the utensils which were made unclean have been mixed with others, the man went and greased them with clean oil, or *vice versa*. Eliezer says that if the first greasing was with unclean oil, the utensils, when used, exude the first oil which they had absorbed, and render others placed among them unclean. The sages have the opposite view.

b. Tem. 12a clearly regards M. Orl. 2 : 11 as the teaching of the same Eliezer who is responsible for M. Ter. 5 : 6, so we may accordingly assign M. Orl. 2 : 11 and 2 : 13 to our Eliezer.

I.ii.27.A. Vessels which one has anointed with unclean oil and gone and anointed with clean oil, or with clean oil and gone and anointed with unclean oil—

B. R. Liezer says, "I come [decide] after the first."

C. And sages say, "After the last."

D. For R. Liezer says, "Let a man anoint his vessels with unclean oil and afterward anoint them with clean oil. When they take out [vessels], they take out only from the first [ones]."

E. And sages say, "Let a man anoint his vessels with clean oil and afterward with unclean. When they take out, they take out only from the last [ones]."

Tos. Ter. 8 : 15, Lieberman, p. 152, ls. 34-39

*Comment*: The issue is how to make use of unclean oil, which is cheaper, for washing dishes. One wants to protect the dishes, that they not remain in uncleanness. Eliezer says to use a little unclean oil first, and afterward clean, for the unclean will drip and dry off, and he will then wash the dish. The sages advise for the opposite. D and E supply reasons for the ruling, and are omitted in M. Orl. M. Orl. 2 : 7A-C and Tos. Ter. 8 : 15A-C are otherwise identical.

I.ii.38. R. Leazar b. R. Yosah said in the name of R. Yosah b. Durmasqit, who said in the name of R. Yosah the Galilean, who said in the name of R. Yoḥanan b. Nuri, who said in the name of R. Liezer the Great, "*ʿOrlah*-laws do not apply outside of the Land."

Tos. Orl. 1 : 8, Lieberman, p. 285, ls. 28-30

*Comment*: The anonymous rule is that what is in doubt as to the *ʿorlah*-laws in Palestine is prohibited, but in Syria and abroad is permitted. R. Judah holds that Syria is part of the prohibited area. Then comes Eliezer's opinion, which stands in opposition to the anonymous opinion, but says nothing about Syria. Presumably he would be the source of Judah's rule; since Eliezer regards Syria as part of Palestine, he would hold that fruit from Syria which is in doubt as to *ʿorlah*-rules is prohibited, just as is the case in Palestine.

### xi. Bikkurim

I.i.46.A. "An *etrog* is like a tree in three aspects, and like a vegetable in one. It is like a tree as to the laws of *ʿorlah*, and Fourth Year, and Seventh Year. And [it is] like a vegetable in one respect, for when it is picked it is to be tithed"—the words of Rabban Gamaliel.

B. R. Eliezer says, "It is like a tree in all respects."

M. Bik. 2 : 6 (y. Bik. 2 : 4; b. Qid. 3a; b. Suk. 39b; y. R.H. 1 : 2, b. R.H. 14b)

*Comment*: The general rule of Gamaliel is that one follows the time that the tree forms fruits (ḤNṬ). If fruits were formed in the third year of the planting of the tree, they are prohibited on account of *ʿorlah*-rules, even though the fruit is picked in the fourth year. If the fruits were formed in the fourth year, they are fourth-year planting, even though picked in the fifth. If they formed fruits in the Seventh Year, and the fruits are picked in the eighth, they are treated like Seventh Year fruit.

But as to tithing, one follows the year in which the fruit is picked. The *etrog*-fruits which are picked in the third year or sixth are liable to Poorman's Tithe, and not to Second Tithe.

Eliezer differs in this regard; they are liable to Second Tithe.

See Epstein, *Nusaḥ*, p. 1177.

I.ii.29.A. MʿŚH B: R. ʿAqiba picked an *etrog* on the first of Shevaṭ and did with it according to the words of the House of Shammai and according to the words of the House of Hillel.

B. R. Yosah b. R. Judah—"According to the words of Rabban Gamaliel and according to the words of R. Liezer."

Tos. Shev. 4 : 21, Lieberman, p. 185, ls. 71-3
(y. Bik. 2 : 4, R.H. 1 : 2, b. Eruv. 7a;
R.H. 14a; Yev. 15a; Suk. 40a)

*Comment*: Lieberman explains the reference to Gamaliel and Eliezer (*Tosefta Kifshuṭah Seder Zeraʿim* II, pp. 545-6). ʿAqiba followed Gamaliel: an *etrog* is to be tithed when it is picked. Therefore if it was picked on the first of Shevaṭ in the third year, according to the House of Shammai (M. R.H. 1 : 1), it is liable to Poorman's Tithe; and to the House of Hillel, to Second Tithe.

ʿAqiba thus followed the stringencies of both Houses and both masters: He separated Second Tithe and redeemed the fruit for money, which he then gave to the poor. As noted above, Eliezer holds that with respect to tithes, one follows the formation of the fruits. Since the *etrog* formed its fruits in the second year, it is liable to Second Tithe.

### xii. Shabbat

III.ii.12. DTNY': R. Eliezer said, "He who kills vermin on the Sabbath is as if he killed a camel."

b. Shab. 12a, 107b

*Comment*: The *baraita* is cited as proof that Eliezer is the authority behind M. Shab. 1 : 3, "One does not search his garments for vermin." Simeon b. Eleazar attributes the law in exactly these words to the House of Shammai. On that warrant I included it here.

III.ii.13. TNY': He who catches a flea on the Sabbath—
R. Eliezer declares [him] liable.
And R. Joshua declares free.

b. Shab. 107b

*Comment*: This is better warrant to assign the above to our Eliezer.

I.i.47.A. [On the eve of the Sabbath] they do not put the bread into the oven at dusk, nor the cake upon the coals, unless there is time that the top [surface] may form a crust while it is still day.

B. R. Eliezer [b., Parma, Cambridge, Naples, Kaufmann: Leazar] says, "So that the bottom [surface only] may form a crust."

M. Shab. 1 : 10 (y. Shab. 1 : 10, b. Shab. 20a)

*Comment*: The pericope follows the model of the Houses' disputes, M. Shab. 1 : 4-8, *Phar.* II, pp. 120-125. In general the House of Hillel is lenient. One may not start work before the Sabbath unless it can be completed before the Sabbath, according to the House of Shammai. The

House of Hillel hold that something may be begun which on the Sabbath will be finished of itself, without the man's assistance.

Eliezer [Eleazar] glosses one item in an anonymous law which follows the form and opinion of the House of Shammai. Had the pericope stood within the Houses' disputes, it would have ended with, *And the House of Hillel permit.* Eliezer does not supply an attestation for the existence of this form for Houses' disputes, for, as is clear, the House of Hillel's opinion is lacking; and we have no attribution to the House of Shammai. That does not mean the form comes after Eliezer, but its peculiar construction—*They do not... unless (KDY Š) ... while it is still day*—certainly was used for his saying, therefore in or before his time.

The problem is that the man may stir up the coals, and therefore, Albeq explains, the House of Hillel here would have to agree that the crust must be formed while it is still light out. But which crust forms first? It would seem that the bottom does, since it is in contact with the coals. That would put Eliezer in the lenient position, therefore with the (imaginary) House of Hillel, for he would allow the work to begin later than would the anonymous [Shammaite] rule.

Eliezer's saying in all respects depends upon the formulation of A. He uses a singular verb (QRM) instead of A's QRMW, because the antecedent of A is PNYH, while his antecedent is THTWN; but his ŠLH indicates that before him is the antecedent PT/ḤRRH/PNYH; this therefore is a simple gloss of an antecedent rule, not an independent saying.

In M. Ter. 8 : 1-3, Eliezer consistently rules that what has started licitly may be completed; Joshua takes the contrary position. Thus a priest at the altar making a sacrifice, who suddenly is discovered to be impaired, has produced an unfit sacrifice, even though at the outset he was regarded as legitimate, so Eliezer. Joshua declares his sacrifices fit. Eliezer's position would accord with that of the House of Hillel, Joshua's with the House of Shammai, so far as the matters are comparable.

See Epstein, *Nusaḥ*, p. 1178 on Eleazar/Eliezer.

I.i.48. [Naught that comes from a tree may be used for lighting (the Sabbath lamp) except flax; and naught that comes from a tree can contract uncleanness by overshadowing except flax.]

A. A wick of cloth that he twisted but did not singe—

B. R. Eliezer [Naples: Eleazar] says, "It is unclean, and they do not light [the Sabbath lamp] with it."

C. R. ʿAqiba says, "It is clean, and they do light the Sabbath lamp with it."

M. Shab. 2 : 3 (y. Shab. 2 : 3, b. Shab. 28b, 29a-b)

*Comment*: The chapter contains laws about the Sabbath lamp, beginning with anonymous rules about what may, and may not, be used as oil.

2 : 3 begins with a generalization, glossed by the dispute of Eliezer and ʿAqiba. The general rule is that flax may be used. What of twisted cloth, made of flax, which has not been marked for use as a wick? Is it like cloth, therefore still able to receive uncleanness? Thus, does mere twisting signify a wick? Eliezer rules strictly, that without singeing, twisting is not sufficient to remove the cloth from the former category. Perhaps the larger issue is how one must signify his intention.

The sayings are carefully balanced. Each element in Eliezer's saying is matched by an opposite one in ʿAqiba's. Note also b. Shab. 28b: Eliezer holds twisting is of no effect; ʿAqiba, that it is effective.

I.i.49.A. A man should not go out [on the Sabbath, from private to public domain] either with a sword, or with a bow, or with a shield, or with a club, or with a spear. And if he went out, he is liable for a sin-offering.

B. R. Eliezer says, "They are adornments for him" [and he is therefore free].

C. And sages say, "They are only for reproach (GNʾY) [and he is therefore liable],

D. "As it is said, *And they shall beat their swords into plowshares and their spears into pruning-hooks. Nation shall not lift up sword against nation, neither shall they learn war any more* (Is. 2 : 4)."

M. Shab. 6 : 4 (y. Shab. 6 : 4; b. Shab. 63a)

*Comment*: The principle is that on the Sabbath one may wear normal clothing, including ornaments; otherwise one is guilty of carrying from the private to the public domain, which is prohibited.

Part A is a general rule. But Eliezer does not give a contrary rule. He simply differs from the foregoing, on the principle that weapons of war are like ornaments. We do not know what consequence he would draw from that fact. Perhaps he would rule that it is prohibited to do so, but if a man did so, he is not liable for a sin-offering (ʾSWR/PṬWR). Or perhaps he would drop the negative rule entirely. Eliezer's comment then provokes C, which gives the theory behind A and is then glossed by the Scripture.

B and C are not integral to A. Indeed, as noted, they do not respond to the legal issues raised in A at all. The decided law is taken for granted in Eliezer's saying; but his saying is tangential to the law. And then the antecedents of C's pronouns are all found in B. So B-C are a unity, tacked on to A but quite irrelevant to it.

Indeed, B-C introduce the issue of whether war-[equipment] is good or bad, which is *not* the issue of A! A simply rules that these are *not* articles of clothing, similar to a woman's bands of wool, forehead band, head-bangles, necklaces, and the like. The issue (6 : 1) is not whether these are ornaments or reproaches, simply whether they are articles of clothing or superfluous. Likewise here, A simply says these are superfluous from the viewpoint of Sabbath-wear. B-C then introduce the issue of whether war is a good thing or not. Surely A comes before, and stands independent of, B-C. Because our Eliezer rules on a similar issue in Tos. Shab. 4 : 6/M. Ed. 2 : 7, I include the pericope in the Eliezer b. Hyrcanus-corpus, though the warrant is not firm.

See Epstein, *Tan.*, p. 288.

III.ii.14. TNY': They said to R. Eliezer, "If they are [really] ornaments for him, why will they cease in the day of the Messiah?"

He said to them, "Because they will be unnecessary [then], as it is said, *Nation will not lift up sword against nation* (Is. 2 : 4)."

b. Shab. 63a

*Comment*: Now Eliezer does not approve of war, but accepts it as a worldly necessity.

I.ii.30.A. R. Liezer says, "A woman goes forth with a 'golden city' [tiara], with a forehead band (ṬWṬPT) and with head-bangles (SRBYṬYN) when they are sewn (TPWRYN)."

Tos. Shab. 4 : 6, Lieberman, pp. 17-18, ls. 18-19 (y. Shab. 6 : 1, b. Shab. 59b, 138a)

*Comment*: The antecedent rule is that a woman should not go forth with a 'golden city,' and if she does so, she is liable for a Sin-offering, according to Meir; and the sages say she should not go forth, but if she does so, she is free of the Sin-offering. Then Eliezer follows, saying that the woman may to begin with go forth with such an ornament.

So the later tradition relies upon the rule that one may not do what Eliezer says one may do. That rule is in M. Shab. 6 : 1: "Nor may she go out with a 'golden city' or a necklace, etc., but if she did so, she is not liable," following the sages. So Eliezer's lenient opinion has been dropped from the Mishnah, which takes for granted the item is prohibited, and rules only on the liability for sin-offering, an issue obviously irrelevant to Eliezer's opinion.

That opinion does occur in M. Ed. 2 : 7:

> Three things did they say before R. ʿAqiba, two in the name of R. Eliezer and one in the name of R. Joshua—
>
> Two in the name of R. Eliezer:
>
> 1. A woman may go forth wearing a 'golden city.'
> 2. And pigeon-racers are not eligible to bear witness ...

Eliezer's ruling therefore circulated in ʿAqiban circles, but was dropped from the Mishnah where it should have appeared. Meir then says the extreme opposite (y. Shab. 6 : 1): "A woman should not wear such a tiara, and if she does, she is liable for a Sin-offering."

As to ṬWṬPT and SRBYṬYN, see Lieberman, *Tosefta Kifshuṭah [III.] Seder Moʿed* [Hereinafter: *Moʿed*] p. 63.

M. Shab. 6 : 5 then follows Eliezer: A woman goes out with forehead band or hair-bangles if they are sewn. So M. Shab. 6 : 1 ignores Eliezer's contrary opinion; 6 : 5 gives Eliezer's opinion, without crediting it to him—a strange state of affairs.

I.ii.31.A. A woman should not go forth to the public way with the key which is on her finger, and if she went forth, lo, such a one is liable [for a sin-offering.]

B. R. Liezer frees [her from the liability] in the case of a spice-box (KWBLT; b.: *Kobelet*; Lieberman: KWKLT = conche].

C. And the sages free [from the liability] in the case of a perfume flask (ṢLWḤYT ŠL PLYYṬYN) when there is perfume in it, etc.

Tos. Shab. 4 : 11, Lieberman, p. 19, ls. 33-35 (b. Shab. 62a, 65a)

*Comment*: M. Shab. 6 : 3 says a woman may not go out with a spice-box, and if she did so, Meir declares her liable for a Sin-offering, and the sages declare her free in the case of a spice-box and a perfume flask, just as here. But the 'sages' are not the Eliezer of B, even though their opinion is the same.

Eliezer is consistent with his earlier leniency. But earlier he said the woman may at the outset wear the ornament, while here he does not differ: she must *not* go forth with a spicebox. But if she does so, she owes no Sin-offering. Eliezer's lenient rulings here are consistently excluded. Rabbi evidently preferred Meir's formulation of the issue, which, following his very strict ruling, has everyone prohibit, but presents a disagreement as to the consequence. Eliezer could not fit into such a scheme—or, rather, his opinion raises questions as to Meir's reason for so strict a judgment.

I.ii.32.A. R. Judah said, "M'ŚH B: Hyrcanus the son of R. Liezer went forth with his scarf (SWDR) to the public domain, but a thread was tied to it on his finger."

B. Sages said, "It was not necessary."

Tos. Shab. 5 : 12, Lieberman, p. 22, ls. 27-29 (b. Shab. 147a)

*Comment*: The thread prevented the scarf from falling off. The sages rule it is not necessary to tie it by a thread. Hyrcanus thought it was necessary for the scarf to appear as a regular garment on his body.

Judah b. Ilai now presents Eliezer's son as following a stricter rule than one would have expected.

I.i.50.A. He who scratches on his flesh—

B. R. Eliezer declares liable for a Sin-offering.

C. And R. Joshua [Venice, 104b: *sages*] declares free [of liability for a Sin-offering.]

M. Shab. 12 : 4 (y. Shab. 12 : 4; b. Shab. 104b-105a)

*Comment*: The antecedent rule is that if a man wrote anything that leaves a lasting mark, he is liable; if he wrote on his skin, he is liable. Then comes the dispute above. Joshua would agree that one should not do so; his PṬR is what we should have expected for the sages in M. Shab. 10 : 6.

The issue is whether a Sin-offering is the punishment for scratching on one's skin. Writing on one's skin produces that punishment. According to Eliezer scratching is no different from writing. Evidently Joshua rules that since there is no lasting mark—the scratch will heal—there is no liability for a Sin-offering.

The dispute is well-balanced, in classic form.

See Epstein, *Nusaḥ*, pp. 1056-7.

I.ii.33.A. He who scratches on his flesh [on the Sabbath]—

B. R. Liezer declares liable.

C. And sages declare exempt.

D. R. Liezer said to them, "And it is not so that Ben Saṭra (Or: Suṭra) only learned (LMD) by this [means]?"

E. They said to him, "And because of one fool shall we declare all the intelligent people liable."

Tos. Shab. 11 : 15, Lieberman, p. 49, ls. 45-47

*Comment*: Scratching on flesh is regarded by Eliezer as writing, for the scratches last. Lieberman prefers SṬR' or SWṬR', and rejects *Stada* [SṬD']. He rejects the identification of Saṭra with Jesus; the passage refers to someone else who brought sorcery from Egypt; he cites J. Brüll who supposes the name SṬR' derives from *sōtēr*.

IV.i.8.A. R. Liezer said to them, "And is it not so that Ben Sṭada (SṬD') brought sorcery from Egypt only by this means [therefore it is writing]?"

B. They said to him, "Because of the fool shall we destroy ('BD) many (KMH) intelligent people.

y. Shab. 12 : 4, Gilead, pp. 139-140

III.ii.15.A. TNY': R. Eliezer said to them, "Did not Ben Sṭada (SṬD') bring out sorcery from Egypt with a scratching which was on his flesh?"

B. They said to him, "He was a fool, and they do not bring proof from the fools."

b. Shab. 104b

*Comment*: On Jesus in Egypt, see *Phar.* I, pp. 83-86, 99-103. According to Lieberman, Eliezer would not supply an attestation of the story that Jesus went to Egypt with Joshua b. Peraḥiah in times of Alexander Jannaeus and Simeon b. Sheṭah, ca. 90 B.C.

I.i.51.A. R. Eliezer says, "He who weaves three threads [on the Sabbath] at the beginning [of the web] or (W) [= and] one on to what is already woven (ʾRYG) is liable [for a Sin-offering]."

B. And sages say, "Whether at the beginning or at the end, the measure [of weaving to render a man liable for 'weaving'] is two threads."

M. Shab. 13 : 1 (y. Kil. 9 : 6; y. Shab. 13 : 1; b. Shab. 104b, 105a; b. Ker. 17a, 19b)

*Comment*: y. takes for granted that this is our Eliezer. Eliezer's rule is that when he begins weaving a garment, he is liable once three threads have been woven together; or if he adds to an already-woven cloth, even one additional thread will produce the same liability. The sages' rule is that two threads under either circumstance produce liability. Evidently, Eliezer takes the lenient position, that the process of weaving must be definitively begun; it takes three to begin it, but to what is already woven, merely adding a single thread has the same effect. The sages make no such distinction.

Another interpretation of the dispute seems warranted. Eliezer says not *or* (ʾW) but *and* (W). It may be, therefore, that he rules one who weaves three onto the beginning of the web *and* one at the end of [the same] web is liable. The sages say whether it is at the beginning or at the end of the same web, two threads determine liability—and the issue is not where the threads are added, but how many. So the difference would pertain to the number of threads it is forbidden to weave, either beginning or end. But none of the parallel versions understands matters this way.

I.ii.34.A. He who weaves two threads on the thick part of the web [So Jastrow, I, p. 260, for GS] and on the border [So Jastrow, I, p. 51, for ʾMRʾ]—lo, such a one is liable.

B. R. Liezer says, "Even one."

Tos. Shab. 12:1, Lieberman, p. 51. ls. 1-2 (b. Shab. 105a)

*Comment*: The sages hold there is no difference between the beginning of the weaving and the end—a man is liable only for two threads, no less.

On M. Shab. 13 : 1, see Epstein, *Nusaḥ*, p. 149; *Tan.*, p. 292.

I.ii.35.A. "He who weaves two knots, whether on holy or ordinary garments; he who writes two letters, whether in sacred or ordinary writings—on the Sabbath is liable for a Sin-offering, and on the festival is flagellated forty [lashes].

B. "He who weaves one knot, whether on holy or ordinary garments; he who writes one letter, whether on holy or profane writings; on the Sabbath is liable for a Sin-offering, and on the festival is smitten forty"—the words of R. Liezer.

C. And sages say, "Whether on the Sabbath or on the festival he is liable only on account of *Shevut.*"

Tos. Y.T. 4 : 4, Lieberman, p. 300, ls. 7-13

*Comment*: The pertinent Mishnah is:

> Any act that is culpable on the Sabbath, whether by virtue of the rules concerning Sabbath rest (*Shevut*) or concerning acts of choice (*Reshut*) or concerning pious duties (*Miṣvah*) is culpable also on a festival-day ...
>
> M. Beṣ. 5:2

In M. Shab. 13:1, above, p. 91. Eliezer says that a person is liable if he weaves three threads at the beginning of the web, or a single one onto a piece of already woven cloth; the sages say the forbidden quantity is two. See Lieberman, *Tosefta Kifshuṭah Seder Mo'ed*, pp. 999-1,000.

I.i.52.A. The window-shutter—

B. R. Eliezer says, "When it is fastened and hung [on the window frame], they close [the window on the Sabbath] with it, but if not, they do not close with it."

C. And sages say, "One way or the other, they close with it [the window on the Sabbath]."

M. Shab. 17 : 7 (y. Shab. 17 : 7,
b. Shab. 125b, 137b, b. Eruv. 44a)

*Comment*: If the window is fastened and suspended, one may use the window shutter. Otherwise one may not, since it is like building on to the house. The sages rule that whether it is fastened or not one may do so, because it is all right to add to a house (tent) in a random way, and one may carry the shutter since it is ready before the Sabbath for that purpose. b. Shab. 138a takes for granted that this is the same Eliezer as in M. Shab. 20 : 1 and Tos. Shab. 4 : 6, so the whole set of traditions is to be assigned to our Eliezer.

I.ii.36.A. The sages agree with R. Liezer that they do not make tents to begin with on the festival, and one need not say, on the Sabbath.

B. Concerning what did they differ?

Concerning those who add, for—

R. Eliezer says, "They do not add [to a building] on the festival, and one need not say, on the Sabbath."

And sages say, "They add on the Sabbath, and one need not say, on the festival."

Tos. Shab. 12 : 14, Lieberman, p. 54, ls. 49-52
(Tos. Suk. 1 : 8, Lieberman, p. 258, ls. 34-35;
b. Shab. 125b, 137b, y. Shab. 20 : 1; b. Eruv. 44a)

*Comment*: According to the sages in the foregoing Mishnah, it is permitted to close and tie the shutter. The Toseftan tradition, if pertinent to the Mishnah before us, explains the reasoning of the respective authorities. According to Eliezer, the unattached and unsuspended shutter cannot be closed, for that would amount to adding to the building, and that is prohibited on both Sabbath and festival days; the sages hold the opposite. But no one holds that one would actually build a house (tent).

I.i.53.A. R. Eliezer says, "If he did not bring an instrument [for circumcision] before the Sabbath, he brings it openly on the Sabbath.

B. "And in [time of] danger, he conceals it in the presence of witnesses."

C. And further did R. Eliezer say, "They cut wood to make coals to make an iron instrument [for circumcision, on the Sabbath]."

D. A general principle did R. ʿAqiba say, "Every kind of work which can be done before the Sabbath does not override the Sabbath, and which cannot be done before the Sabbath does override the Sabbath."

M. Shab. 19 : 1 (y. Shab. 19 : 1, b. Shab. 130a-132a, 136a; b. Eruv. 102b, b. Pes. 69a, y. R.H. 2 : 3; b. Men. 96a [not attributed to ʿAqiba])

*Comment*: Eliezer's rule should follow M. Shab. 19 : 2, which gives the general principle, "They may perform on the Sabbath all things that are needful for circumcision." Eliezer then deals with a detail of that rule—carrying the knife.

By carrying the knife openly, the man shows that it is for the purpose of circumcision, which overrides the Sabbath. This will not accord with ʿAqiba's view that the work cannot be done before the Sabbath, so may be done on the Sabbath; ʿAqiba would rule that one brings the knife in advance. Eliezer's second rule is even more extreme. Certainly one can make the iron tool before the Sabbath. But Eliezer permits the work to be done even on the Sabbath. So the problem is not merely one of defining what can or cannot be done before the Sabbath, with both men in agreement. Eliezer does not say, *if he did not cut wood/make fire*, etc. His rule in C is unequivocal, *They do so and so*, without qualification. The *if*-clause of A may be harmonized with ʿAqiba's rule, but C cannot.

Albeq explains (*Seder Moʿed*, p. 61), that ʿAqiba differs from Eliezer in respect to *all* things needed for the circumcision. Only the actual rite of circumcision overrides the Sabbath, but not preparation for that rite. This would place Eliezer in the lenient position, ʿAqiba in the strict.

B looks like a gloss added after the Bar Kokhba War. We have no evidence of a prohibition of circumcision during Eliezer's lifetime, and B, formally, bears no relationship to Eliezer's saying in A. A formal continuation of Eliezer's saying would have kept the same verb-form for *openly and hidden*, thus *megulleh* should be matched not by *mekhassehu* but by (*uvassakkanah*), *mekhusseh*. ʿL PY ʿDYM is a quibble.

Now as to 19 : 2: the general rule would seem to contradict ʿAqiba, to follow Eliezer, and to generalize Eliezer's principle:

A. R. Eliezer says, They do all the needs of the circumcision on the Sabbath—

B. Excision, tearing, sucking, and putting on a bandage, and cummin.

C. R. ʿAqiba says, Every kind of work which can be done...

The sayings are not closely balanced in form, but in substance they match one another. But then the examples (B) do *not* bear out Eliezer's rule. They impose distinctions which flow only from ʿAqiba's:

If this [cummin] had not been pounded upon the eve of the Sabbath, a man may chew it with his teeth and then apply it.

If the wine and oil had not been mixed on the eve of the Sabbath, each may be applied by itself.

They may not newly make the special bandage, but a rag may be wrapped around the member.

If this had not been prepared on the eve of the Sabbath, one may bring it wrapped around his finger even from another courtyard.

All of these rules accord with ʿAqiba's distinction between what may and may not be done in advance of the Sabbath. And they contradict the opening statement. But so too do the examples given in illustration of that statement. Excision and tearing are not the only "requirements" of the circumcision, so far as Eliezer is concerned. On the contrary, he even permits making a fire to heat coals to forge an iron knife! Excision, tearing, etc. do not illustrate *all the needs* of the circumcision. They so "qualify" *all the needs* as to reverse completely the meaning of the phrase! Now *all the needs* consist of, and specify, the actual act of circumcision, and that alone.

Eliezer's rules in A + C ought to have yielded 19 : 2, and perhaps they did. But then ʿAqiba's principle has generated a gloss that so changes the meaning of 19 : 2 as to render it an illustration of ʿAqiba's principle, instead of a statement of Eliezer's.

I.ii.37.A. R. Liezer says, "Why do they override the Sabbath on account of circumcision? Because they are liable for cutting off on account of [doing] it after [its] time.

"And lo, a *qal veḥomer* argument: If on account of one limb from him [man] they set aside the Sabbath, is not logical that he should set aside the Sabbath on account of his whole [body]! [Thus proving that they set aside the Sabbath in order to save a life.]"

They said to him, "From the place from which you came [= bring proofs, there is the very refutation of your argument]: Just as in your case (LHLN) [one sets aside the Sabbath in a case of] certainty but not doubt [according to Eliezer's reasoning in the following, Tos. Shab.

15 : 10], so here [one sets aside the Sabbath in a case of] certainty and not doubt."

Tos. Shab. 15 : 16, Lieberman, p. 74,
ls. 73-76 (+ ls. 76-80: ʿAqiba's reply)

*Comment*: Liezer's proof follows in a series of arguments about why one should set aside the Sabbath in order to save a life. The question is raised by R. Yosah [b. Ḥalafta], then Liezer, then ʿAqiba, whose proof—from the cult—is not questioned. Yosah alludes to circumcision and the cult, which provokes the other proofs.

Lieberman notes (*Moʿed*, p. 261) that the proof is elsewhere attributed to Eleazar b. ʿAzariah.

III.i.2. TNY: An actual event (MʿŚH) took place, and Rabbi [Judah the Patriarch] taught according to R. Eliezer.

y. Shab. 19 : 1, Gilead, p. 171 (b. Shab. 130b)

III.i.3. TNY in the name of R. Eliezer, "The *Lulav* and all its appurtenances override the Sabbath."

*ibid.*, p. 172 (b. Shab. 131b)

III.i.4. TNY: R. Eliezer says, "Just as slaughtering overrides the Sabbath, so the appurtenances of slaughtering override the Sabbath."

*ibid.*, p. 173

III.ii.16. DTNY': R. Eliezer says, "How do we know that the appurtenances of the two showbreads override the Sabbath? *Bringing* is said with reference to the *ʿomer* (Lev. 23 : 10), and *That come* is said with reference to the two showbreads (Lev. 23 : 17). Just as *That come* which is said with reference to the *ʿomer*—the appurtenances override the Sabbath, so *Bringing* which is said with reference to the showbread [means that] the appurtenances override the Sabbath.

b. Shab. 131a

*Comment*: All of these and other sayings attributed to Eliezer extend his rule from circumcision to the performance on the Sabbath of other commandments.

III.ii.17. R. Eliezer said, "The *shofar* and all its appurtenances override the Sabbath."

b. Shab. 131b

IV.ii.3. R. Isaac said, "There was one town in Palestine where they did according to R. Eliezer, and they died in their proper time, and, moreover, one time the evil kingdom decreed concerning Israel against circumcision, and they did not decree concerning that town."

b. Shab. 130a (b. Eruv. 102b-103a)

IV.ii.4. This is R. Eliezer's reason: Because Scripture says, *And in the eighth day the flesh of his foreskin shall be circumcized* (Lev. 12 : 3)—even on the Sabbath."

b. Shab. 132a

IV.ii.5. In the place of R. Eliezer wood was cut on the Sabbath to make charcoal on which to forge the iron [knife].

b. Shab. 130a (b. Yev. 14a; b. Hul. 116a)

*Comment*: In context, this proves that Eliezer actually carried out his ruling and did not hold it only in theory.

IV.ii.6. R. Zera found R. Assi saying, "R. Simeon b. Laqish in the name of R. Judah the Patriarch [said], 'They once forgot to bring the knife on the eve of the Sabbath so they brought it on the Sabbath'... How could they abandon the opinion of the sages and follow R. Eliezer—a follower of the House of Shammai!"

b. Shab. 130b

I.i.54.A. [He who had two babies, one to circumcize after the Sabbath and one to circumcize on the Sabbath, and forgot and circumcized the one for after the Sabbath on the Sabbath is liable.]

B. [He who had two babies], one to circumcize on the eve of the Sabbath and one to circumcize on the Sabbath and forgot and circumcized the one for the eve of the Sabbath [Friday] on the Sabbath—

C. R. Eliezer declares [him] liable for a Sin-offering.

D. And R. Joshua exempts.

M. Shab. 19 : 4 (y. Shab. 19 : 4; b. Shab. 137a-b; b. Pes. 72a)

*Comment*: In the anonymous case (A) all parties agree the man is liable for a Sin-offering, for he has violated the Sabbath and not carried out the commandment of circumcision on the eighth day, having circumcized the child *before* the eighth day.

In the disputed case (B), Eliezer holds the man has done the same thing. He has circumcized the child on the ninth day, and circumcision not at the proper time—on the eighth day—does not override the Sabbath.

Joshua (D) says that the proper time for the circumcision, if not on the eighth day, is on *any* subsequent day, even on the Sabbath. The man was liable to perform the circumcision on every day after the eighth, therefore the liability is present even on the ninth, which is the Sabbath.

The difference, therefore, is as to the liability for circumcision after the eighth day. Is it such as to permit violating the Sabbath? Eliezer's view is that the obligation is sufficiently diminished so that under any circumstances one should not circumcize on the Sabbath, unless it is the eighth day. Joshua holds that the liability on the eighth day to carry out the circumcision every day thereafter is undiminished.

On M. Shab. 19 : 1, see Epstein, *Nusaḥ*, p. 672; on 19 : 4, pp. 311, 722. On 19 : 1 in Epstein, *Tan.*, see p. 66, 68.

I.ii.38.A. R. Simeon said, "R. Liezer and R. Joshua did not argue about one who had [a child] to circumcize *after* the Sabbath and he circumcized him on the Sabbath, that he *is* liable [to a Sin-offering. So Joshua goes over to Eliezer's position.]

"Concerning what did they disagree?

"Concerning one who had [a child] to circumcize on *Friday* who circumcized him on the sabbath—

"For R. Liezer declares [him] liable for a Sin-offering.

"And R. Joshua declares exempt."

B. R. Liezer said to him, "Do you not agree concerning one who had [a child] to circumcize *after* the Sabbath and who circumcized him on the Sabbath that he is liable, for he changed his [prescribed] time?"

C. R. Joshua said to him, "No, if you spoke concerning him who had [a child] to circumcize after the Sabbath and circumcized him on the Sabbath, that he is liable, for [the reason is that] he was not [subject to the commandment of] 'Rise, circumcize.' But will you say [so] concerning him who had [a child] to circumcize on Friday and who circumcized him on the Sabbath, that he should be liable? For he *is* [subject to the commandment of] 'Arise, circumcize.'"

D. R. Liezer said to him, "The Excess (NWTR = Portions of the sacrifices) will prove the matter, [from the preceding evening it was left over beyond the legal time and bound to be burned. So Jastrow, I, p. 604], for it was subject to the commandment of 'Rise, eat.' But if he ate it the next day, lo, such a one is liable."

E. R. Joshua said to him, "No, if you have said [so] concerning the Excess, which is not [subject to the commandment of] 'Rise, eat' on that very day, will you say so concerning circumcision, concerning which he is *every day* subject [to the commandment of] 'Rise, circumcize'?"

Tos. Shab. 15 : 10, Lieberman, p. 72, ls. 47-56 (A: y. Shab. 19 : 4)

*Comment*: While in M. Shab. 19 : 4, we have two babies, here we have only one. But the principle is not changed; the debate concerns circumcizing on the Sabbath when it is not the eighth day after birth. The obligation persists. But is it so pressing as to override the Sabbath? Both masters recognize that the man has carried out the commandment concerning circumcision—unlike the case in the Mishnah, in which circumcizing the child on the wrong day, a day too early, represents doing no commandment at all.

III.ii.18. TNY': R. Simeon b. Eleazar said, "R. Eliezer and R. Joshua did not disagree concerning one who had two children, one to circumcize on the Sabbath, and one to circumcize after the Sabbath, who forgot and circumcized the one to be done after the Sabbath on the Sabbath, that he is liable.

"Concerning what did they disagree?

"Concerning him who had two infants, one to circumcize on the Friday and one to circumcize on the Sabbath, who forgot and circumcized the one to be done on Friday on the Sabbath, that—

"R. Eliezer declares liable for a Sin-offering.

"And R. Joshua exempts."

b. Shab. 137a

*Comment*: Now we have two infants, but Friday and Saturday, rather than Saturday and Sunday.

III.ii.19. R. Meir: They differed about him who has two infants, one for circumcision after the Sabbath and another for circumcision on the Sabbath, who forgot and circumcized the one to be done after the Sabbath on the Sabbath, etc.

b. Shab. 137a

III.i.5. TNY: R. Simeon said, "R. Liezer and R. Joshua did not differ concerning him who had to circumcize after the Sabbath and circumcized (him) on the Sabbath, that he is liable.

"And concerning what did they differ?

"Concerning him who had to circumcize on Friday and circumcized (him) on the Sabbath, for

"R. Eliezer declares liable for a Sin-offering.

"And R. Joshua exempts."

y. Pes. 6 : 5, Gilead, p. 89
(b. Pes. 72 cites M. Shab. 19 : 4: *Two* infants)

I.i.55.A. R. Eliezer says, "They stretch out the filter on the festival day, and on the Sabbath pour [wine through] one which [already] is stretched out."

B. And sages say, "They do not stretch out the filter on the festival day, and on the Sabbath they do not pour [wine through] one which is [already] stretched out. But on the festival day they [merely] pour [wine through] one which has already been stretched out."

M. Shab. 20 : 1 (y. Shab. 20 : 1; b. Shab. 125b, 137b, 138a)

*Comment*: Eliezer, in the lenient position, holds that stretching out the filter is part of preparation of the food, and one may do so on the festival, even to the extent of making use of the necessary utensils, just as in the case of circumcision. If a filter is stretched out before the Sabbath, one may make use of it, and it is not a case of 'selecting' or 'winnowing' (M. Shab. 7 : 2), which is prohibited, since this is not how winnowing is carried out. But one cannot stretch out the filter on the Sabbath, for it is like spreading a tent, which is prohibited—so Albeq, *Seder Moʿed* p. 63. The sages, consistent with ʿAqiba, here prohibit preparing utensils for preparation of food on the festival, and regard the use of the filter on the Sabbath as equivalent to winnowing. The sayings are in good balance. On the basis of that consistency, I include the pericope in Eliezer b. Hyrcanus's traditions.

See Epstein, *Tan.*, p. 296.

III.i.6. TNY: R. Eliezer and the sages did not differ that they spread out tents at the first instance on the festival.

And concerning what did they differ?

Concerning adding to them—

For R. Eliezer says, "They add on the festival and they do not add on the Sabbath."

And sages say, "They do not add on the festival, and one need not say, On the Sabbath."

y. Shab. 20 : 1, Gilead, p. 180

I.ii.39.A. R. Eliezer says, "On that day they overfilled (GDŠ) the *seʾah*."

B. R. Joshua says, "On that day they made the measure deficient (MḤQ) the *seʾah*, for so long as the measure is full and the man puts [something] into it, in the end it will bring forth from what is in it. [That is, it will spill over; therefore one should not fill the measure to the very top.]"

Tos. Shab. 1 : 17, Lieberman, p. 4, ls. 38-9 (b. Shab. 17a, 153b, y. Shab. 1 : 4)

*Comment*: y. adds:

R. Liezer said to him, "If it were lacking and they filled it, well and good. [It is to be compared to] a vessel which was filled with nuts. [b.: cucumbers and gourds.] So long as you put in it sesame [b.: mustard] seeds, it will take [them]."

R. Joshua said to him, "If it were full and they diminished it, well and

> good. [It is to be compared] to a vessel filled with oil [b.: tub full of honey]. So long as you put water [b.: pomegranates and nuts] in it, it overflows the oil."

The reference is to the antecedent passage, "These are the laws which they said in the upper chamber of Ḥananiah b. Ḥezeqiah b. Garon when they went up to visit him, and they counted and the House of Shammai outnumbered the House of Hillel. Eighteen thing[s] they decreed on that day, and that day was as hard for Israel as the day on which the calf was made" (Tos. Shab. 1 : 16, see *Phar.* II, pp. 127-130).

Eliezer and Joshua allude to the saying. They thus supply an attestation for M. Shab. 1 : 4, "These are among the rulings ... *on that day.*" Eliezer says they filled the measure too much; Joshua says they filled it insufficiently. Both masters agree it was a bad day—so both stand with the House of Hillel.

They hold the decrees were excessive. But what was the excess? Eliezer's saying in y. means that even if the vessel is filled to the top, it can still hold sesame seeds, if not nuts. But they overfilled it. Joshua says one should not fill the measure to the top, lest something spill over. If the measure were filled and they diminished it, well and good.

Both masters therefore know about the rulings *on that day.* But what did they know about them? What was the tradition upon which their comments were made? We have no accurate list of the eighteen things (*Phar.* II, p. 128), and therefore have no way of knowing the 'text' or tradition which provoked these comments. The antecedent illusion is simply to "eighteen things," but nothing in the masters' sayings indicates knowledge of that formulation, apart from the words *on that day.* So what is attested is *on that day*, nothing more.

## xiii. ʿEruvin

I.i.56.A. Rendering an alley-way valid (HKŠR HMBWY)—
The House of Shammai say, "A side-post and cross-beam."
And the House of Hillel say, "A side-post or a cross-beam."
B. R. Eliezer says, "Two side-posts."
C. In the name of R. Ishmael one disciple said before R. ʿAqiba, "The House of Shammai and the House of Hillel did not differ concerning an entry less than four cubits, that it is [valid] either with a side-post or with a cross-beam.
"Concerning what did they differ?
"Concerning [an alley-way] wider than four cubits up to ten, for—
"The House of Shammai say, 'A side-post and a cross-beam.'
"And the House of Hillel say, 'Either a side-post or a cross-beam.'"
D. R. ʿAqiba said, "They differed about both."

M. Eruv. 1 : 2 (y. Eruv. 1 : 2; b. Eruv. 11b-12a, 146, b. Shab. 117a)

*Comment*: The problem is to define "the rules which permit a wider interpretation of the term 'domains' within which it is lawful to move a burden, and to deal with cases when the rule of the 2,000 cubits of a 'Sabbath day's journey' is capable of a less rigid application" (Danby, p. 121, n. 11). Here we have an alley onto which courtyards open from three sides, and the fourth opens into the public road. By constructing a doorway there, the whole is made into a single, private domain, wherein people may carry on the Sabbath.

How to do so? The anonymous rule, M. Eruv. 1 : 1, says in the case of an entry higher than twenty cubits (*amot*) one must diminish the height; if it is wider than ten, one must diminish the width. Then the Houses debate how this is done—a secondary question, taking for granted the opening rule, but not alluding to the language of the opening rule, which is YMʿṬ rather than HKŠR (or some equivalent, e.g., KYṢD MMʿṬYN, *How do they diminish*?) That would suggest the language of the rule of 1 : 1 did not influence the formulation of 1 : 2.

The House of Shammai say one must construct both a side-post and a cross-beam; the House of Hillel say one or the other suffices. The dispute is in standard form and exhibits a commonplace mnemonic pattern in Houses' disputes: *both/and vs. either/or* (W vs. ʾW). Eliezer's opinion depends upon both the statement of the problem in A and the antecedent law (1 : 1); it is identical in form to the Houses' dispute. But Eliezer stands entirely outside the choices laid forth by both Houses, in requiring no cross-beam at all, but two side-posts.

C then ignores B, and goes on to qualify the terms of argument in A; ʿAqiba in D likewise ignores B. So the issue is only whether one requires both a side-post and a cross-beam, or either one, but no party, either ʿAqiban or Ishmaelean, espouses Eliezer's position. The view of the disciple is that the dispute of A pertains to an alley-way between four and ten cubits in width, but anything less than four will suffice, according to both Houses, with the Hillelites' requirement accepted by all. Eliezer does not figure; his proposal of two side-beams is not considered.

It is curious that Eliezer plays no role in C-D. While his view is irrelevant to the definition of the argument of A in C, in the reformulation of the issue of A it surely was pertinent that an opinion of Eliezer had registered on the same dispute. Thus, *The Houses and Eliezer did not differ* would have been called for, had the substance of A-B been before C-D. Either B was absent and only inserted later on, or the Ishmaelean-ʿAqiba circles did know B, but deliberately formulated matters without reference to it. But if ʿAqiba and Ishmael did not know B, then how did Eliezer get into the structure of A-B? It would be reasonable to suppose that available to the redactor of the pericope was an opinion of Eliezer unknown to the ʾAqibans responsible for C-D; in formulation it would be a full sentence, such as in Tos. Judah b. Ilai, who occurs in 1 : 1, through his father Ilai, would be a candidate for the source of Eliezer's saying. But if Judah supplies a *terminus ante quem* for 1 : 1's first clause ("If the cross-beam above the alley-entry is higher than twenty-cubits, it must be made lower. R. Judah says, 'This is not necessary.' "), that does not affect the rest of 1 : 1, let alone 1 : 2. Still, his involvement in the composite pericopae 1 : 1-2 is the sole hint as to how Eliezer's opinion might have been inserted into a structure which then ignores it.

See Epstein, *Nusaḥ*, p. 1064; *Tan.*, pp. 79, 119; Judah b. Ilai is the authority for 1 : 2.

I.ii.40.A. An alley which is shaped like a door, even though wider than ten cubits, does not require diminishing.

B. R. Liezer says, "Rendering an alley-way valid [requires] two side-posts (HKŠR MBWY BLḤYMM)."

C. M'ŚH B: R. Liezer went to Joseph b. Peridah [y.: Yosi b. Yosi b. Perurah; b.: Yosi b. Peridah *his disciple*] to 'Uklin (L'WKLYN; b. + y. 'BLYN) and saw [y.: he showed him; b.: found him sitting] an alley that had only one side-post.

He said to him [b.: My son], "Make for it two" [b.: "Make another side-post"].

He said to him, "Do you say to destroy (STM) it [b.: "Do I need to . . ."; y.: "What . . . to destroy it?]"

He said to him, "Let it be destroyed [b.: And so what?] Why did you spend the Sabbath in such as that [So Lieberman: MH R'YT LŠBWT; y.; WKY MH R'YYH RŠWT LŠBT LBW' LK'N; b.: Omits *Why . . .that.]?"*

Tos. Eruv. 1:2, Lieberman, p. 87, ls. 4-8
(*Ubelin:* M. Tefillin 63a)

*Comment*: B now gives to Eliezer the topic-sentence of M. Eruv. 1 : 2 and drops the Houses entirely. In context Eliezer's saying means that even an alley shaped like a door requires diminishing under any circumstances. B may stand independent of A, however, and may simply repeat his ruling in the Mishnah, as if the Houses' rulings did *not* exist.

I.i.57.A. And R. Judah b. Bava further said, "The garden and the outer area which are (1) [not more than] seventy cubits and two-thirds by seventy cubits and two-thirds (1A) square.

(2) "Surrounded by a wall which is ten handbreadths' high— they carry therein.

(3) "So long as a watchman's hut or dwelling-house is in it [the garden].

(4) "Or that it is near the town."

B. R. Judah says, "Even if there is in it [the garden] only a (3) cistern and pit and cavern, they carry in it."

C. R. 'Aqiba says, "Even if there is in it only one of all these [=3], they carry in it—(1) so long as seventy cubits and two-thirds by seventy cubits and two-thirds are in it."

D. R. Eliezer [y. Parma, Camb.; Leazar; Kaufmann: Eleazar] says, "If its length was greater than its width by even one cubit [= 1A], they do not carry in it."

E. R. Yosi says, "Even if its length was twice its width (1A), they do carry in it."

M. Eruv. 2 : 5 (y. Eruv. 2 : 5, 7; b. Eruv. 23a-b; b. Pes. 39a)

I.i.58.A. R. Ilai (ʾLʿY) said, "I heard from R. Eliezer [Kaufmann: Eleazar], 'And even if it is about a *kor's* space [75,000 square cubits *vs.* (1)].'" [It is permitted to carry in the garden or outer space (QRPP) even if the area is considerably larger, and even if there is no house therein, on account of the walls.]

B. "And so I heard from him, 'Men of a courtyard one of whom forgot and did not prepare an *ʿeruv*—his household is prohibited from bringing in and taking it for him;

"'But for them [the others in the courtyard] it [his house] is permitted.'

C. "And also I heard from him, that they fulfill their obligation on Passover with hart's-tongue (ʿQRBNYM; y.: ʿRQBNYN).

D. "And I besought (ḤZR) among all his disciples, and I sought for myself a colleague [who had the same traditions], but I did not find [any]."

M. Eruv. 2 : 6 (y. Eruv. 2 : 8; b. Eruv. 26b)

*Comment*: This complicated pericope mixes up Ushans with Yavneans, and several distinct rules, as enumerated, are combined in the long sayings attributed to the various masters.

In M. Eruv. 2 : 3 we have an allusion to the general rule under discussion here:

> A. R. Judah says, "[The boards set up around wells so as to establish the wells as a private domain and therefore permitting the wells to be used by cattle on the Sabbath may be removed only] so far as to leave two *seʾahs*' space."
>
> B. They said to him, "They spoke of two *seʾahs*' space only with reference to a garden or an enclosed space [outer space—KRPP] . . ."

The outer space is an enclosure outside a settlement, used for storing wood, but not inhabited. Judah says it is permitted to separate the boards as far as the specified space, that is, an enclosure sufficient to sow two *seʾahs* of grain, equivalent to the size of the courtyard of the tabernacle, a hundred cubits by fifty cubits (Ex. 27 : 18). The sages say that the allusion to two *se'ahs'* space pertains only to the garden or enclosed outer space. These are enclosed not for dwelling, but for storage.

Now in M. Eruv. 2 : 5 A., Judah b. Bava gives the size for such an enclosed space within which it is permitted to carry. He says: 1. it must be not more than 70 2/3 by 70 2/3 cubits; 1A. square. 2. It must be surrounded by a wall ten handbreadth's high. 3. It must contain a hut of some sort. [Or] 4. it must be adjacent to the village. All conditions must be met. The operative ruling, *they carry in it*, is inserted after the first two conditions; then BLBD links the third and fourth.

In B Judah b. Ilai refers only to (3). Thus his saying would match Judah b. Bava's as follows:

> *A garden or enclosure in which there is* a watchman's hut or dwelling—*they carry therein*, the words of Judah b. Bava.
>
> R. Judah says, Even if there is therein only a cistern [pit and cavern] (*A garden* and *they carry therein* are understood).

So the dispute of Judah b. Bava and Judah concerns what must be within the enclosure to signify that it is a single domain. Judah b. Bava requires some sort of dwelling. Judah says merely a well or cistern suffices.

But what about the size of the enclosure? Judah has already agreed that two *se'ahs'* of space are prescribed (2 : 3 = the sages). That is the same amount as 70 2/3 by 70 2/3. So on that question there is no dispute. Then Judah b. Bava's saying has been composed in such a way as to include materials irrelevant to Judah's opinion.

ʿAqiba in C begins in a way consistent with Judah in B. The issue is, *what* must be contained in the field?—not its size, nor the presence of a wall ten handbreadths' high, nor its being a square. Therefore he completes the unit, and his operative ruling is likewise, *they carry therein*:

Judah b. Bava: Watchman's hut or dwelling house
Judah: Cistern, etc.
ʿAqiba: Any of these:

But to ʿAqiba's opening opinion is attached a separate ruling—*they carry therein* + if the field is 70 2/3 by 70 2/3 square. This ruling is identical with Judah b. Bava's, and with Judah's as given earlier—therefore pointless. But other commentaries explain ʿAqiba's "these" to refer to the whole of A-B—measurements and all!

Eliezer's [Eleazar's] ruling in D is pertinent only to that attached clause. He insists the enclosure must be a square, and any deviation from a square renders it unacceptable.

In E Yosi differs from Eliezer [Eleazar]. His *Even if* clause is a development of what we should have expected. He should merely have said, *They do carry*; or he could have said, *If its length was greater than its breadth, they do carry*—thus repeating the operative words of Eliezer [Eleazar]. By saying it is twice the breadth, he adds nothing but an extreme formulation of his position as against Eliezer [Eleazar]—unless he insists upon a rectangle of such proportions, as in the old tabernacle in the wilderness in the time of Moses!

Now D-E raise a question irrelevant to A-B-C, but not entirely so.

Judah b. Bava, Judah, and ʿAqiba all hold the field is to be 70 2/3 by 70 2/3. Eliezer [Eleazar] adds that that is an exact, not approximate measurement, meaning it must be a square. It is that addition that Yosi glosses.

No party alludes to the wall. All take it for granted. As we have observed, the form is extremely complex. Four issues are introduced in M. Eruv. 2 : 5 A, but two of these forthwith are ignored; all parties accept the standard of two *seʾahs.* D-E concern an issue unconsidered by A-C. It is difficult to imagine how Judah b. Bava and Judah b. Ilai can formulate a law in disagreement with their teacher, ʿAqiba, still more difficult to understand Yosi's standing against Eliezer [Eleazar]. We should have expected the disagreement to be formulated among masters of a single generation. That, obviously, is not always the rule. But it would seem more commonplace than an arrangement of two Ushans against a Yavnean, then an Ushan against another Yavnean, teacher of the first.

M. Eruv. 2 : 6A tells us that, if it *is* Eliezer in 2 : 5, then Eliezer gave a completely different rule. Ilai alleges that Eliezer [Eleazar] would accept as a single domain a property much larger than the two *seʾahs.* A *kor's* space is greater than 70 2/3 by 70 2/3; it is 30 *seʾahs*! All then depends upon the walls. Now we have Eliezer standing against, and more liberal than, the whole later tradition [including Eleazar?]. Ilai's language takes for granted the foregoing rulings—but only (1):

| | | | |
|---|---|---|---|
| Judah b. Bava: | 70 2/3 by 70 2/3 | = | two *seʾahs* |
| Judah: | " | " | " |
| ʿAqiba: | " | " | " |
| Eliezer: | *Bet kor* | = | 30 *seʾahs.* |

Ilai's language, *Even a kor's* space, implies the following original formulation for the dispute:

> *The garden, or the outer space, which are 70 2/3 by 70 2/3* (Or: *two seʾahs*) —they carry therein, the words of R. Judah b. Bava/Judah/ʿAqiva.
>
> And R. Eliezer says, Even a *kor's* space.

Obviously, we should prefer to have ʿAqiba as Eliezer's opposition.

Now where do we find a disagreement as to the *size* of the enclosure phrased in such language? Something like it occurs in 2 : 3, as noted, for part B continues:

> The measure of two *seʾahs*' space has been prescribed only in what concerns a garden or an outer area; but in what concerns a cattle-pen or fold or store-yard or court-yard, five or even ten *kors'* space [all the more so, one *kor*!] is permitted.

Eliezer therefore sees no distinction between one sort of enclosed space and another. Judah and "they" agree that two *seʾahs* are prescribed for the garden or the outer area. The sages then add that the other specified areas, all of which have walls, may contain a substantially larger measure of space.

Ilai's Eliezer stands at the extreme on the side of leniency. He does so, obviously, because of the wall. Once a field has a wall, he would agree that, whatever its location, purpose, or contents, it may be of any size. Therefore the Scriptural measure, the size of the tabernacle, is irrelevant.

Now in 2 : 5A, we find a reference to a wall (2), which plays no role in anyone's opinion thereafter. But it *ought* to play a role in Eliezer's opinion, according to Ilai. So Judah b. Bava's formulation of the issue evidently depends upon, and alludes to, an antecedent dispute, concerning the size of a field surrounded by a wall. ʿAqiba says what is decisive is the size—70 2/3 by 70 2/3, plus any sort of house or cistern or whatever.

*If* the opinion in 2 : 5 should be our Eliezer's (and I doubt that it is), how shall we account for it? (If it is Eleazar, what follows is pointless.) Eliezer's original view, that the field may be enormous, is dropped. What remains is the opinion that it must be a perfect square! Perhaps the remnant before us derives from a *kor's space*, which as noted, is 37,500 square cubits, rather than 5,000 square cubits of the two *se'ahs*' space. So the *square*-cubit is taken as the operative issue. Since Eliezer—among others—alluded to *square* cubits, it is taken for granted that he meant a square and not rectangular measure, and Yosi says a rectangular measure is also acceptable. But all the other parties spoke in terms of squares as well. And Ilai's tradition has nothing to do with an *exact* square. So sometime between Ilai and Yosi, Eliezer's original ruling was not only drastically revised—from a *kor* to an (implicit) two *se'ahs*—but it was also rewritten so as to stress the requirement of a *square* field, rather than a rectangular one. Yosi's saying therefore clarifies A-C as well: all parties accept a rectangle, speaking of 'square' only because of the measurements to which allusion was made. Assuming for the moment that 2 : 5D is Eliezer, and that Ilai's tradition is correct, I cannot think of a way more deliberately to falsify not only Eliezer's actual opinion, but also the issue to which his opinion pertained. What had been an extremely lenient ruling was not only made stricter—the *kor* being fropped; but also made to allude to a new issue—the requirement of an *exact square*, no less, no more.

y. Eruv. 2 : 7 has Eliezer in the Mishnah, but its accompanying *baraita* has Eleazar. M. Eruv. 2 : 6B is related to M. Eruv. 6 : 3, as follows:

> If one of them that lived in the courtyard forgot to take part in the ʿ*eruv*, his house is forbidden both to him and to them for taking a burden in or out.
>
> But their houses are permitted both to him and to them.

The topic sentence is identical:

> *The men of a courtyard, one of whom forgot and did not prepare the* ʿ*eruv*—

| *6 : 3* | *Ilai/Eliezer* |
|---|---|
| His house is forbidden both to him and to them for taking in or out. | His house is forbidden *to him* for taking in or out. |
| | *But to them it is permitted* |

The difference is clear. Eliezer rules leniently, so far as he can, in respect to the use of the man's house by others in the courtyard. Eliezer's opinion does not register in M. Eruv. 6 : 3. It was, however, formulated in Ilai's list of three rules—all leniencies.

M. Eruv. 2 : 6C has to do with fulfilling the requirement to consume bitter herbs on Passover. Albeq defines ʿQRBNYM as *colopendrium.* Presumably others say *they do not fulfill.*

Then, in D, Ilai reports that he found no one else who possessed, or would attest to the existence of, these same lenient rulings.

If our interpretation is correct, then Ilai, like ʿAqiba, had a tradition that placed Eliezer's among the lenient rulings. But these rulings have either been suppressed, as in ʿAqiba's testimonies in Terumot, or drastically revised, as possibly in 2 : 5, or ignored, as in 2 : 6B. One must immediately observe that while Ilai's traditions are unique to him, by his own testimony, nonetheless they *are* preserved, right alongside the rulings they contradict or call into question. And Judah b. Ilai here cannot be credited with a role in their preservation. His saying in 2 : 5B is quite unrelated to Eliezer's formulation of the legal issue; he addresses himself to another matter entirely. The redactor of the materials before us clearly has chosen to preserve both the 'official' record and whatever materials he felt relevant to it, even if 'unofficial.' Perhaps the conservatism of the tradents will account for this, as for much else in the way of historically valuable, but clearly subterranean, material. In that case, the reason must be that the final redactor did not know earlier authorities held Eliezer's traditions should not be given place in the official Mishnah; or he differed with those who so decided matters against Eliezer; or the issues that led to Eliezer's sayings' suppression had ceased to be important, so that traditions formerly ignored were permitted to surface. This third reason seems to me most likely. Ilai's list existed right alongside the other, but was preserved in different circles, and only at the last stage in the formation of the Mishnah was it given a place. Still, we have a number of sayings favorable to Eliezer attributed to Judah the Patriarch.

On Eleazar/Eliezer in 2 : 5, see Epstein, *Nusaḥ*, p. 1165; *Tan.*, p. 66. On 2 : 6, see *Tan.*, pp. 187, 300.

I.ii.41. R. Leazar [b.: Eliezer] says, "A garden and an enclosed space which is seventy and two thirds [cubits] by seventy and two thirds [cubits] surrounded by a fence ten handbreadth's high, if its length is twice its width (KŠNYM BRḤBH), they carry therein on the Sabbath. If [twice its breadth by] more than a cubit they do not carry in it on the Sabbath."

Tos. Eruv. 2 : 7, Lieberman, p. 94, ls. 23-26.

I.ii.42. And so would R. Leazar say, "An enclosed space near the village (it is) seventy and two thirds [cubits], even though it is not a square—they carry in it on the Sabbath.

"More than seventy and two thirds, they do not carry in it on the Sabbath."

Tos. Eruv. 2 : 8, Lieberman, p. 94, ls. 26-28

*Comment*: The differences between Judah b. Bava in M. Eruv. 2 : 5 and Leazar here are the absence of ʾMH as the stipulated measure, the specification of a watchman's hut, also absent here, and the detail as to the requirement for the field to be a square.

Tos. Eruv. 2 : 7B is identical with Eliezer's saying in M. Eruv. 2 : 5D. It might seem likely that the tradition should be assigned to Eliezer, rather than to Eleazar, because of Ilai's tradition in M. Eruv. 2 : 6. Accordingly, Ilai had a different tradition for Eliezer. But Lieberman, *Moʿed*, p. 325, n. 34, prefers Eleazar for M. Eruv. 2 : 5, following MSS Kaufmann, Parma, and Tosefta here. If this is Eleazar both here and in M. Eruv. 2 : 5, then, as noted, the foregoing explanation is pointless, for Eleazar had one law, Eliezer another.

Tos. Eruv. 2 : 8 specifies that proximity to the village is decisive; in that case the field does not have to be in the shape of a courtyard [= rectangular].

For further, important discussion, see Lieberman, *Moʿed*, pp. 325-328.

III.ii.20. R. Ilai said in the name of R. Eliezer, "*Arqablin* too [is an herb with which a man discharges his obligation on Passover.] But I went about to all his disciples and sought a companion but did not find one, but when I came before R. Eliezer b. Jacob he agreed with my words."

b. Pes. 39a

I.i.59.A. R. Eliezer says, "A festival next (SMWK) to a Sabbath—whether before or after it—a man prepares two *ʿeruvs* and says, 'The first [day's] *ʿeruv* is on the east and the second [day's] on the west;' [or] 'The first [day's] is on the west and the second on the east;' [or] 'My ʿeruv is on the first, and [for] the second, [mine is] like that of the men of my village;' [or] 'My *ʿeruv* is the second;' and as to the first, [let me be] like the men of my village.'"

B. And sages say, "He makes an *ʿeruv* for one direction or it is no *ʿeruv* at all.

"He prepares an *ʿeruv* for two days, or it is no *ʿeruv* at all.

C. "How should he do it [for the *ʿeruv* to serve for two days, instead of Eliezer's method]? [If] he brings it on the first day, he that brings it on the first day waits over it until nightfall, and takes it and goes his way.

"On the second, he waits over it until nightfall and [then] eats it.

"So it comes out that he is rewarded for his journeying and for his *ʿeruv*. [Danby: For if the *ʿeruv* had been lost the first day, he would, for the second day, have lacked both the *ʿeruv* and the right of journeying beyond the Sabbath limit.]

D. "If it is eaten on the first day, his *ʿeruv* is for the first day, and it is no *ʿeruv* for the second."

E. R. Eliezer said to them, "You [then] agree with me that they [Sabbath and festival] are two [distinct times of] holiness."

M. Eruv. 3 : 6 (y. Eruv. 3 : 7; b. Eruv. 38a-b, 39a)

*Comment*: The problem is how to prepare an *ʿeruv* so that the man may walk beyond the limit on the Sabbath and festival. He wants to go in one direction on one day, and in the opposite on the next. Eliezer holds that before the festival or before the Sabbath he may leave two *ʿeruvs*, one on the east side, the other on the west. Then he specifies, as given in A, which is for which. My first *ʿeruv*, means, the one for the first day; and so the other. Eliezer's principle is that the festival and the Sabbath are two separate 'sanctities'—that is, each one is a holy day by itself. Therefore the man can prepare an *ʿeruv* for one day quite separate from that for the other.

The sages in B say that one prepares a single *ʿeruv* for both days. Either he has that single *ʿeruv*, or he has none. Thus, he prepares an *ʿeruv* for only one direction. Then a new issue is added: "For one *day*, or there is none." What then should he do? He has to move his *ʿeruv* from place to place. Since *one direction/two days* are redundant, Albeq notes, y.'s discussion revises to read, "Either he makes an *ʿeruv* for one direction for two days, or it is not an *ʿeruv* at all." b. explains the Mishnah according to a *baraita*: "Just as for one day they make an *ʿeruv* only for one direction, and not half a day for the east and the other half for the west, so they do not make an *ʿeruv* for two days, one day in the east, the other in the west." But this makes clear what is already obvious.

What then do the sages advise the man to do? If he makes an *ʿeruv* for both days for a single direction, how shall *he* make sure that it is good for the second day? The possibility of moving in a second direction is not raised. If the *ʿeruv* is eaten on the first day, it is no good for the second. So on the festival before the Sabbath he brings the *ʿeruv* for the first day, which is that of the festival, and he waits there until it gets dark, and then the *ʿeruv* has served for the festival. Then he takes it, so it will not be lost, and brings it for the Sabbath and then eats it.

He cannot bring it on the Sabbath from the public domain to his house and does not want to lose it. If the festival falls after the Sabbath, he brings it on the eve of the Sabbath but leaves it there, and on the Sabbath he goes and checks it. If it is still there, the *ʿeruv* is in good order, and he can go beyond the limit on the festival day. So he can go on the Sabbath beyond the normal limit; and he is rewarded in that he eats the *ʿeruv* and he does not lose the normal limit, and he is rewarded in that he eats the *ʿeruv* and does not lose it.

Eliezer then observes that if the *ʿeruv* is eaten on the first day, it is no *ʿeruv* for the second. Therefore the sages agree with him that the festival and the Sabbath are two separate 'sanctities.' Then it *is* possible, on that account, to make an *ʿeruv* in two directions, for if they were only a single sanctity, the *ʿeruv* of the festival, on the first day, would serve also for the second day.

The sages' reason, Albeq adds, is given in b.: they are in doubt about whether the festival and Sabbath are a single sanctity or two sanctities. They therefore rule severely: one can make an *ʿeruv* for both days, for a single direction only, lest they be one sanctity; but if the *ʿeruv* is eaten on the first day, it is no *ʿeruv* for the second, lest they be two sanctities.

This highly developed pericope involves two separate issues. Let us now try to separate them.

In A Eliezer explains how one can make two *ʿeruv* for two days, so he can go in two different directions. He simply sets one in one place, announces its purpose, then goes and sets another in the other place, and announces its purpose. That suffices. The sages differ. In fact the man is permitted to do no such thing. It is *not* possible to go in two directions beyond the Sabbath limits. One can only go in a single direction.

The sages are then given C, which has nothing to do with Eliezer's issue at all. It concerns simply how to make an *ʿeruv* to cover a festival and Sabbath, in succession. Eliezer did not raise that question.

E then makes explicit the implicit difference represented by A-D, namely, whether a festival and a Sabbath are separate entities, or whether they are a single 'sanctity.' But Eliezer's position is unequivocal on that question. The sages have, after all, taken account of the difference between Sabbath and festival, for in C they treat the *ʿeruv* as separate for each day. They therefore admit his principle! But if so, why should they not permit journeys in two different directions on the successive days?

In E, therefore, Eliezer points out the inconsistency of the opposition; they evidently are in agreement with his principle, and therefore should accept his ruling. They are given no good answer. The *gemarot* have to supply them with answers.

What was the law before Eliezer and the sages? Clearly, if Pharisees kept the *ʿeruv*-law as a matter of sectarian observance—they themselves claim the Sadducees did not accept the principle of the *ʿeruv*—then they had not worked out some of the rather fundamental rules in connection with the *ʿeruv*. The issue of whether or not festivals and Sabbaths coming together represent separate 'sanctities' would seem to me to be Eliezer's generation's discovery and once raised, that issue would impose the sorts of specific distinctions debated here.

In M. Eruv. 3 : 7, Judah b. Ilai rules in accord with Eliezer's view, small warrant for assigning the dispute to Eliezer b. Hyrcanus.

See Epstein, *Nusaḥ*, p. 458; *Tan.*, pp. 190, 301, 303.

I.ii.43.A. R. Liezer says, "For a festival next to the Sabbath, whether before or after it, a man makes an *ʿeruv* one day for the north, and on one day for the south; one day for the north, and one day along with the men of that village."

B. R. Liezer agrees that they do not make an *ʿeruv* for half a day to the north and half a day to the south, since they do not divide one day.

C. And sages say, "Just as they do not divide a single day, so they do not divide two days."

D. R. Liezer said to them, "Do you not agree that if one makes an *ʿeruv* with his feet [he walked to the spot, and by his presence there at twilight acquired it as his abode for the next twenty-four hours] on the first day, he must make an ʿeruv with his feet for the second day." [y.: "Do you not agree with me that if he made an *ʿeruv* with a *loaf* on the first day, that he makes an *ʿeruv* with a *loaf* on the second, for if he ate it on the first, it is an *ʿeruv* for the first and not for the second."]

"If his *ʿeruv* is eaten before dark, he does not go forth on its basis on the second day."

E. They said to him, "True."

F. He said to them, "Are they not two days?"

G. They said to him, "Do you not agree that they do not make an *ʿeruv* from one festival day for the Sabbath [alt.: its fellow = next day]?"

H. He said to them, "True."

I. They said to him, "Is it then not one day?"

Tos Eruv. 4(5) : 1, Lieberman, pp. 103-4,
ls. 1-9 (b. Eruv. 38a-b, y. Eruv. 3 : 7)

I.ii.44.A. Sages agree with R. Liezer concerning the two festival days of the New Year that a man makes an *ʿeruv* for one day to the north and for one day to the south, for one day to the north and for one day according to the inhabitants of that town.

B. And R. Yosah prohibits, for the sanctity of them both is one . . . .

Tos. Eruv. 4(5) : 2, Lieberman, p. 104, ls. 13-15

*Comment*: Tos. parts D-I supplies a balanced account of the disagreement.

For a full explanation, see Lieberman, *Moʿed*, pp. 361-365.

I.i.60.A. "They make an *ʿeruv* or a *shittuf* with all [food] except water and salt," the words of R. Eliezer.

B. R. Joshua says, "A loaf is an *ʿeruv*.

C. "Even a baking of one *seʾah* of flour but it is [merely] part [of a loaf]—they do not make an *ʿeruv* with it.

D. "A loaf worth (B) [or K = like the size of] an *issar*, and it is whole, they do make an *ʿeruv* with it."

M. Eruv. 7 : 10 (y. Eruv. 3 : 1, 7 : 10; b. Eruv. 27a-b, 67a-68b, 80a; Joshua: Tos. Eruv. 5 : 5, Lieberman, p. 112, ls. 15-18)

I.i.61.A. "A man gives a *maʿah* to a storekeeper and a baker so as to secure for him an *ʿeruv*," the words of R. Eliezer.

B. And sages say, "His coins have not secured for him [a share in an *ʿeruv*]."

C. And they agree that with any others [except bakers], his coins secured for him [a share in the *ʿeruv*], for they do not make an *ʿeruv* for a man except with his knowledge.

D. R. Judah says, "In what circumstances? In respect to the *ʿeruv* of Sabbath limits, but in respect to the *ʿeruv* of courtyards, they make an *ʿeruv* with or without his knowledge, because they gain an advantage for a man not in his presence [without his knowledge], but they do not obligate a man not in his presence."

M. Eruv. 7 : 11 (y. Eruv. 7 : 10, b. Eruv. 81a-b)

*Comment*: Eliezer's rule in 7 : 10A is given anonymously—as often with Eliezer's lenient rulings, for M. Eruv. 3 : 1 is as follows:

They make an *ʿeruv a shittuf* with all [food] except for water and salt.

That is exactly what is here attributed to Eliezer, and y. Eruv. 3 : 1 says so. Why should his ruling appear both anonymously and also in his name?

A dispute between Eliezer and Joshua is given. Eliezer says anything may be used both for the *ʿeruv* and for the *shittuf*, that is, for making a single domain of a street and courtyards opening into it. Joshua has a contrary, and very strict, opinion, that *only* a whole loaf of bread may be used. Nothing else is acceptable. One could not formulate two more extreme, opposite positions on the question.

C illustrates Joshua's view in B. Even if there is a large quantity of wheat in a baked product, but the produce is not whole but in pieces (PRWSH), it is no *ʿeruv*. But if there is a small quantity of wheat as a whole loaf, it is an acceptable *ʿeruv*. C-D thus represent an extended gloss on B, and not a very fluent one.

M. Eruv. 7 : 11A continues with another lenient ruling of Eliezer in respect to an *ʿeruv*. It is permitted to give a small coin to the baker or the storekeeper. The storekeeper then secures for the man an *ʿeruv* of courtyards. The storekeeper will give some food or bread as a portion in the *ʿeruv* for the courtyards in behalf of the man; the coin acquires the *ʿeruv* for the man.

The sages differ. The coins serve no purpose, for they do not acquire moveables (bread) until the objects are actually taken, and since there is no proper act of acquisition, the portion of the food given by the storekeeper in behalf of the man has not been acquired by the man; and in the case of the *ʿeruv* of courtyards the man must give an *ʿeruv* of his *own* property. But if a man gave coins to anyone other than a baker or storekeeper to acquire food from the baker or storekeeper and to give that food as his *ʿeruv*, it is acceptable, for the man has sent an agent. The latter has actually taken the food for the sender and therefore has acquired the food in his behalf. If the man were to say to the storekeeper to make him an *ʿeruv*, the storekeeper certainly will do the mission and give the *ʿeruv* to someone else to make proper acquisition for the man. But if he said to the storekeeper, "Acquire for me by my coins," acquisition by means of coins alone is not possible—so the sages, according to Albeq.

As to the forms: 7 : 10 A and B do not match. Joshua makes a flat statement, "An *ʿeruv* is . . ." If his saying were to match Eliezer's, it would have had to be, "They do not *make* an *ʿeruv* except with a loaf." 7:11 B alludes to A, but also does not match it. It is brief, a gloss on A.

See Epstein, *Nusaḥ*, pp. 85, 1063, 1160, 1166; *Tan.*, pp. 120, 300, 302.

I.i.62.A. If there was a breach between a courtyard and the public domain [so the status of private domain is lost]—

B. "He that brings from it [the courtyard] to private domain, or from private domain to it [the courtyard] is liable," the words of R. Eliezer [y.: Eleazar; Kaufmann: Meir].

C. And sages say, "From it to the public domain or from the public domain to it [the breached courtyard]—he is free [of liability].

D. "For it is like neutral domain (KRMLYT)."

M. Eruv. 9 : 2 (y. Eruv. 9 : 3; b. Eruv. 94a)

*Comment*: Eliezer [Eleazar] regards the breached courtyard as public property. The sages differ: It is neutral. One need not say that he who brings from this courtyard to private property is free of liability. *Even* if he brings from there to public property, he is free, because it is neutral, neither the one nor the other. It would have been better had the sages ruled on the question introduced by Eliezer [Eleazar]. As it is, their saying sets up a different condition; he speaks of private domain to the breached courtyard, they, public domain.

b. Eruv. 94a: Eliezer holds the sides of the public road are like the public road.

Note also b.B.B. 100a: Judah cites Eliezer in an opinion consistent with this one, so b. Eruv. 94a. See also Epstein, *Nusaḥ*, p. 1166, who is of the same view.

III.ii.21.A. TNW RBNN: How is the order of the Mishnah [to be learned]?

B. Moses learned from the mouth of the Omnipotent. Aaron entered and Moses taught him his lesson. Aaron went out and sat down at Moses' left. Aaron's sons entered and Moses taught them their lesson. They went out and sat down, Eleazar on the right of Moses and Ithamar on the left of Aaron.

C. R. Judah says, "Aaron was on the right of Moses."

D. The elders entered and Moses taught them their lesson. The elders went out and all the people entered, and Moses taught them their lesson.

E. So it came out that Aaron had in hand four [repetitions of the lesson], the sons three, the elders two, and all the people one. Then Moses went out and Aaron repeated to them his lesson (PRQ); Aaron went out and his sons repeated to them their lesson; his sons went out, and the elders repeated to them their lesson. So it came out that everybody heard the lesson four times.

F. On this basis (MK'N),

R. Eliezer said, "It is a man's duty to teach his disciple four times . . ."

F. R. ʿAqiba says, "How do we know that a man must repeat [the teaching] to his disciple until he has learned it . . .?"

b. Eruv. 54b

*Comment*: The story has a firm terminus with Judah b. Ilai's interpolation. A-E illustrate the position of Eliezer. Then in F-G comes the legal dispute between Eliezer and ʿAqiba on how many times a man is obligated to teach a tradition.

See *Phar.* III, pp. 143-179; Epstein, *Tan.*, p. 187.

II.ii.3. *Saying* (Ex. 12 : 1)—R. Eliezer says, "How do we know that according to the order of the speaking (DYBRWT) in the wilderness, was the same in the land of Egypt. It requires no [proof]. It is logical: It says here speaking (DỴBR) and it says speaking (DYBR) in the wilderness (Lev. 11:1). Just as speaking referred to in the wilderness has Aaron hearing and teaching first, so speaking referred to here has Aaron hearing first and repeating first."

Mekhilta de R. Simeon b. Yoḥai, p. 8,
ls. 5-7 (b. Eruv. 54b)

*Comment*: We have no warrant to assign the pericope to our Eliezer. But b. Eruv. has Aaron first, so this saying is congruent.

II.iii.4.A. R. Eliezer says, "(1) They [Nadab and Abihu] became liable for punishment only because they taught law in the presence of Moses their master.

(2) "And whoever teaches law in the presence of his master is liable to death."

B. And (MʿŚH Š) it happened (ʿYRʾ) concerning a certain student who taught before him [Eliezer].

He said to Imma Shalom, his wife, "He will not finish out his Sabbath."

And he died.

C. After the Sabbath the sages came into him. They said to him, "Rabbi, are you a prophet?"

He said to them, "I am not a prophet nor the disciple of a prophet, but thus I have received [as a tradition] from my masters: whoever teaches law in his master's presence is liable to [the] death-[penalty]."

Sifra Shemini Mekhilta deMiluʾim, 2 : 32-3, Weiss, p. 45b
(b. Eruv. 63a: He did not finish out his *year*)

*Comment*: Eliezer's teaching about not teaching law in one's master's presence comes in three forms: an apodictic saying, "Whoever teaches . . . ," an exegesis of the death of Nadab and Abihu, and the story about the disciple. The pericope is in two parts, first (A) exegesis (1) + saying (2), second, story (B) + (C) saying; in both the saying is unchanged.

A persistent theme in Eliezer-stories is the assertion that he never said anything new, but always cited his masters, copying their deeds as well as their words. In some versions the emphasis is on Eliezer's imitating everything Yoḥanan b. Zakkai did. These tend to come later than the sayings and stories in which Eliezer says one must copy the teacher and say nothing he has not said, all the more so not teach in his presence.

It is difficult to say which form of the saying about not teaching in the master's presence comes first. Nor do we know of a particular master or circle to whom such a sentiment was of special benefit. On the contrary, it would characterize the rabbinic movement as a whole, which stressed the disciple's subservience in the master-disciple relationship and held that the only way in which the tradition takes shape is according to what the ancients have said. We find evidence that before 70 similar attitudes characterized Pharisaism; Josephus tells us that the Pharisees were deferential toward their elders. But Josephus comes after 70 and may project backward an attitude important only later on. As noted, the similar allegation with respect to Hillel (*Phar.* I, pp. 304-307) is supplied only in the latest version of stories about his relationship to Shemaʿiah and Abṭalion. I should suppose the method of transmitting teachings from master to disciple imposed the need to emphasize absolute loyalty and subservience to the master, and this method begins in Yavnean circles. But the story's stress that a disciple will die if he does anything in his master's presence suggests a contrary situation.

III.i.6.A. TNY: A disciple who teaches a law in the presence of his master is liable to be put to death.

B. TNY: In the name of R. Eliezer, "Nadab and Abihu died only because they taught [omits: *law*] before Moses their master."

C. MʿŚH B: A disciple taught before R. Eliezer his master.

He said to Imma Shalom, his wife, "He will not survive the week."

And he did not pass the week before he died.

D. His disciples said to him, "Rabbi, are you a prophet?"

He said to them, "I am neither a prophet nor the disciple of a prophet, but this have I received [as a tradition], that every disciple who teaches law in his master's presence is liable to be put to death."

y. Shev. 6 : 1, Gilead, p. 31 = y. Git. 1 : 2, Gilead, p. 10

III.ii.22.A. DTNYʾ: R. Eliezer says, "The sons of Aaron died only because they taught a law in the presence of their master, Moses . . ."

B. R. Eliezer had a disciple who taught a law in his presence. R. Eliezer said to his wife, Imma Shalom, "I shall be surprised if this man will live out the year."

He did not live out the year.

She said to him, "Are you a prophet?"

He said to her, "I am not a prophet nor the son of a prophet, but I have this tradition, 'Whoever gives a legal decision in the presence of his master incurs the penalty of death.'"

C. Rabbah b. b. Ḥana in the name of R. Yoḥanan said, "That disciple was Judah b. Guria, and he was three parasangs distant from him [Eliezer]."

b. Eruv. 63a (b. Yoma 53a)

V.ix.1.A. TNY: In the name of R. Liezer, "Nadab and Abihu died only because they gave instruction in a matter of law before Moses our rabbi.

B. MʿŚH: A disciple gave instruction in a matter of law before R. Liezer, and he said to Imma Shalom his wife, "This [man] will not survive the week before he dies."

And he did not complete the week before he died.

C. His disciples said to him, "Rabbi, are you a prophet?"

D. He said to them, "I am not a prophet nor the son of a prophet but thus I receive as a tradition, that whoever teaches a matter of law before his master is liable for the death-penalty."

TNY R. Liezer: "It is forbidden for a disciple to teach a matter of law before his master until he is distant from him twelve miles, like the camp of Israel."

Pesiqta deR. Kahana ed. Mandelbaum, p. 393, ls. 5-10

II.v.2. *And Moses died there* (Deut. 34 : 3).

R. Eliezer the Great says, "Twelve miles by twelve miles opposite the camp of Israel was the heavenly echo heard, 'Woe, Moses is dead, woe, Moses is dead.'"

Midrash Tannaim to Deut. 34 : 3, Hoffmann, p. 224

III.ii.23. TNY': R. Eliezer the Elder said, "Over an area twelve miles by twelve miles, corresponding to the camp of Israel, an echo proclaimed, *So Moses died there* (Deut. 34 : 5), the great sage of Israel.

b. Sot. 13b, trans. A. Cohen, p. 71

*Comment*: The connection of these sayings to the foregoing is found in Lev. R. 20 : 7, "R. Eleazar taught, 'It is forbidden for a disciple to give a legal decision in the presence of his master until he is twelve miles away from him, the extent of the camp of Israel ..." Eleazar evidently should be the Eliezer of the sayings about not teaching in the presence of the master, and Lev. R. supplies an expansion of his sayings, which then produce the ones about the size of the camp of Israel and then the proclamation of the death of Moses.

### xiv. Pesaḥim

I.i.63. [M. Pes. 1 : 6: R. Ḥanina Prefect of the Priests says, "The priests never refrained from burning flesh that had become unclean from a derived uncleanness [Offspring of Uncleanness] with what had become unclean from a primary uncleanness [Father of Uncleanness], although they thereby added uncleanness to its uncleanness."

R. ʿAqiba added and said, "In all the days of the priests they did not refrain from burning in a lamp rendered unclean by one that had contracted corpse uncleanness (Heave-offering-)oil that was rendered unfit by one that had immersed himself the selfsame day (*Ṭevul-Yom*), although they thereby added uncleanness to its uncleanness."]

A. R. Meir said, "From their words we have learned that they burn clean Heave-offering [that is *ḥameṣ*] with unclean on Passover."

B. R. Yosi said to him, "That is not the inference (MDH)."

C. And R. Eliezer and R. Joshua agree that they burn this by itself and this by itself.

D. Concerning what did they disagree?

E. Concerning [burning together Heave-offering of *ḥameṣ*] that was doubtfully unclean [Lit.: suspended, TLWYH] with (WʿL) what was unclean—

F. For R. Eliezer says, "This is burned by itself, and this by itself."

G. And R. Joshua says, "Both as one are burned together."

M. Pes. 1 : 7 (y. Pes. 1 : 8; b. Pes. 14a, 15a, 20b, 21a; y. Ter. 8 : 4)

*Comment*: While M. Pes. 1 : 6 contains a ruling by Ḥananiah Prefect of the Priests, supplemented by one by ʿAqiba, C-G introduce the names of Eliezer and Joshua. But they were not present in the foregoing rule. We have had no hint they ruled in this issue at all. Announcing their agreement, in C, followed by the reformulation of their agreement in D-E, is virtually certain evidence that some dispute such as the following existed but has been lost, or dropped, from the pericope before us:

*Clean Heave-offering* [that is *ḥameṣ*] *with unclean Heave-offering on Passover—*

Eliezer says, They burn this by itself, and this by itself.

Joshua says, Both as one.

Without such a pericope, what follows in C-G would be incomprehensible

Now who has revised the issue of the topic-sentence? It is not in Ḥanina's rule nor in ʿAqiba's and cannot be read into the rule of either. Meir did not know such a rule, for he seeks to infer it from M. Pes. 1 : 6, which means he had no instruction on the subject. But Yosi has no such pericope, for he rejects Meir's opinion without supplying one of his own (though it would have been: *They do not burn* etc.—that is, Eliezer's). He knows nothing of Eliezer's view, which he would have followed and cited. Yosi merely holds that Meir's logic does not hold. It *is* permitted to make the meat unclean, but it was already unclean to begin with. Part of the Heave-offering, however, is clean. Even though one may not eat it, one may also not make it unclean.

Eliezer is consistent with his view that one may do nothing under any circumstances to render Heave-offering unclean.

Whoever has added C-G cannot be either Meir or Yosi. It would seem reasonably likely that he came afterward, assuming that they were sufficiently central in the formation of Ushan materials to know the bulk of materials that either had come down from Yavneh or were in process of formation. On what basis would he have formulated the dispute before us? It seems to me the generative law is the principle under dispute between Eliezer and Joshua in M. Ter. 8 : 8-11. Eliezer consistently says one must do nothing to render Heave-offering unclean, and Joshua equally consistently rules there are circumstances which permit rendering Heave-offering unclean. One interesting instance exemplifies the principle under debate in C/E. But Joshua is made to agree with Eliezer in C. And in E we are dealing with Heave-offering that may in fact be unclean and Heave-offering that certainly is unclean. While Joshua is willing to allow the two to be mixed together, even here Eliezer remains strict.

In M. Ter. 8 : 8, we have Heave-offering whose uncleanness is in doubt. Eliezer holds it should be protected. Joshua says that it should be allowed certainly to become unclean. Knowing that case, or M. Ter. 8 : 11, one might readily have formulated the argument in this one.

It hardly matters whether the masters "really" disputed about both the case of M. Ter. 8 : 8 and the one before us as well. One would have generated the other. The issues are identical. So perhaps someone who did not have any evidence of Eliezer's and Joshua's opinions on the burning of the clean and unclean Heave-offering of *ḥameṣ* simply on the basis of known disputes made up a quite accurate account of their theoretical opinions on the subject.

b. Pes. 15a says Meir's "from their words" alludes to M. Ter. 8 : 8.

See Epstein, *Tan.*, p. 61: Judah is the authority for this tradition. On *Ḥanina says,* see *Nusaḥ*, p. 1134.

I.ii.45.A. They burn all at once [*ḥameṣ*] Heave-offering of doubtful uncleanness, unclean Heave-offering, and clean Heave-offering"—the words of R. Meir.

B. And sages say, "The doubtful by itself, the clean by itself, and the unclean by itself."

C. R. Simeon said, "R. Liezer and R. Joshua did not disagree concerning the clean and the unclean, that they burn this by itself and that by itself.

D. "Concerning what did they disagree?

"Concerning the doubtfully unclean with the unclean, for—

E. "R. Liezer says, 'This is burned by itself and this by itself.'

F. "And R. Joshua says, 'The two of them [are burned] as one.'"

G. R. Yosah said, "The principle is not like the proof..."

Tos. Pis. 1 : 5, Lieberman, p. 141, ls. 18-22

*Comment*: M. Pes. 1 : 7 parts C-E are now given the appropriate superscription—by Simeon. Simeon and his definition of the dispute are missing in M. Pes. 1 : 7. But M. Pes. 1 : 7 E-G is the same as the above, D-F. Meir in M. Pes. 1 : 7 does not refer to the doubtfully unclean Heave-offering, but if unclean is included, all the more so that which may be clean to begin with.

What is still absent is evidence of the original dispute assigned to Eliezer and Joshua. Simeon seems to have evidence of such a dispute. Lieberman calls attention to Tos. Ter. 7 : 18: "They do not mix doubtful [Heave-offerings] with one another, but they do mix Heave-offering made unclean with a secondary source of uncleanness with Heave-offering made unclean with a primary source of uncleanness." He observes that the dispute of M. Ter. 8 : 8 pertains to the Mishnah before us. See Lieberman, *Mo'ed*, pp. 477-9, for a complete account of the problem.

The Houses dispute the same issue, more or less: Burning clean and unclean meat, Tos. Pis. 1 : 6.

See *Phar.* II, pp. 143-144; also M. Pes. 13 : 1, Epstein, *Tan.*, p. 61.

I.i.64. [M. Pes. 3 : 3: If dough remained in the cracks of a kneading trough and there was an olive's bulk in any one place, it must be removed.]

A. How do they separate Dough-offering in uncleanness on the festival [the fifteenth of Nisan? It cannot be left until the next day, lest it ferment; and it cannot be burned. The dough is unclean. One cannot bake it, for the priest is not permitted to eat it, and whatever cannot be eaten also cannot be baked on a festival. It is also not permitted to burn it, for they do not burn sanctities on the festival. As noted, to leave it overnight is not possible, because of the possibility of fermentation.]

B. R. Eliezer [y. Eruv. 10 : 7: Eleazar] says, "She should not designate it [as Dough-offering] until it is baked."

C. R. Judah b. Bathyra says, "She should put it in cold water."

D. R. Joshua b. Ḥananiah says, "This is not the leaven concerning which people are warned, *Let it not be seen* [Ex. 13 : 7] and *Let it not be found* [Ex. 12 : 19]. But she does separate it [in the normal way] and leave it until the evening, and if it becomes *ḥameṣ*, it becomes *ḥameṣ*."

M. Pes. 3 : 3 (y. Pes. 3 : 3, 6; b. Pes. 46a-b, 48a; y. Eruv. 10 : 14)

*Comment*: Eliezer's solution is to refrain from designating the Dough-offering until after baking. On the festival the housewife may bake the whole thing, for the whole quantity of dough is suitable for eating. After baking the woman designates the Dough-offering and burns it in the evening.

Judah b. Bathyra's solution is to designate the requisite dough as Dough-offering, but then to put it in cold water so that it will not become leavened. This would seem to me the most direct answer to the question, which is not what one should not do ("refrain from designating"), but what one should do.

Joshua supplies the least pertinent answer. He says the problem is no problem. One should not do anything out of the ordinary. The Dough-offering belongs to the priest, not to the householder—Eliezer holds it belongs to the householder (b. Pes. 46b)—and Scripture says no leaven should be seen that is *yours*. So what belongs to someone else is not your problem. Joshua's saying follows the same form as in M. Ter. 8 : 11: "Such Heave-offering is not such whereof I must take heed lest I render it unclean, but lest I eat of it. But what Heave-offering is it which one may not render unclean? . . ."

Eliezer and Joshua stand at opposites. Eliezer says one should not designate the Heave-offering at all; Joshua says one should designate the Heave-offering, but ignores the problem of leaven in the home on Passover! Neither authority thus responds to the question in its own terms.

Formally, the sayings in B, C, and D are quite unrelated to one another, and none is in the same form as the question: *How do they separate* . . . R. Eliezer says, She should not . . . R. Judah b. Bathyra says, She should place . . . Said R. Joshua, This is not . . . . So Joshua comments on the already-completed pericope of Eliezer and Judah b. Bathyra, but, ignoring their answers, goes on to comment on the question of A.

Joshua's saying in D implies that Eliezer has said to him something about Ex. 13 : 7 and Ex. 12 : 19. Perhaps after B, we should have, "R. Joshua says, 'She does it and leaves it until the evening, and if . . .'" The present C is anomalous. Then, "R. Eliezer said to him, 'But if you do so, you transgress Ex. 13 : 7 and Ex. 12 : 19.'" Then: "R. Joshua said to him, 'This is not the leaven . . .'" The discussions of the passage in y. Pes. 3 : 3 and 3 : 6 have Eliezer say to Joshua that he is ignoring the Scriptural laws about *ḥameṣ*.

See Epstein, *Nusaḥ*, p. 1187.

I.ii.46.A. R. Liezer said to R. Joshua, "How do you say that they separate Dough-offering on the festival, and Scripture says, *Seven days leaven will not be found in your house* (Ex. 12 : 19)."

B. R. Joshua said to him, "Lo, it says, *Only what is eaten by every soul* (Ex. 12 : 16)."

C. R. Liezer said to him, "Since (ʿD) the matter is not comparable (ŠQWL), who will decide?" [y. Pes. 3 : 3, y. Eruv. 10 : 4: "They are burned by themselves."]

D. R. Joshua said, "I shall decide. When I do [it] with my own hands, I find myself (NMṢʾTY) transgressing a negative commandment, and lo, it is in my hands [my responsibility]. When I leave it as it is, I find myself transgressing a negative commandment, but it is not in my hands [not my responsibility]."

Tos. Pis. 3 : 7, Lieberman, pp. 152-3, ls. 20-26 (b. Pes. 48a)

I.ii.47.A. What is the measure of the dough (ʿYSH)?

B. R. Ishmael b. R. Yoḥanan b. Beroqah says, "In wheat, up to three *qavs*, and in barley, up to four *qavs* . . ."

C. R. Nathan says in the name of R. Liezer, "The matters are reversed [three for wheat, four for barley]."

Tos. Pis. 3 : 8, Lieberman, p. 153, ls. 29-32

*Comment*: Tos. Pis. 3 : 7 supplies a little debate as a supplement to M. Pes. 3 : 3. R. Eliezer implies the Dough-offering simply is not separated. Joshua says it is done normally. Now Eliezer asks how Joshua can rule as he does. Scripture explicitly prohibits leaven, and the woman is in a situation in which the dough may leaven before it is baked. Scripture states, "No work shall be done on those days, but what every one must eat, that only may be prepared by you." So Joshua points out that preparing food indeed overrides other considerations. But *burning* the [unclean] Dough-offering is explicitly prohibited, for it is not eaten. "When I prepare the Dough-offering, I deliberately disobey the commandment, but when I leave it as it is, I disobey a negative commandment about which I cannot do anything—if it is leavened, it is leavened."

The issue of 3 : 8 is, how much dough can one knead on Passover and keep it from fermenting? b. Pes. 48a has Eleazar.

b. Pes. 48a: Rabbi [Judah the Patriarch] rules the law follows Eliezer; Isaac says it follows the son of Batyra.

I.i.65.A. These things in regard to the Passover override the Sabbath: (1) its slaughtering, and (2) tossing its bloods, and (3) scraping its entrails, and (4) burning its fat.

But (1) roasting it and (2) rinsing its entrails do not override the Sabbath.

B. (3) Carrying it [to the Temple] and (4) bringing it from outside the Sabbath limit and (5) cutting off its wen [from the carcass—compare b. Eruv. 103a] do not override the Sabbath.

C. R. Eliezer says, "They override."

M. Pes. 6 : 1 (y. Pes. 6 : 1, 2; b. Eruv. 103a; b. Pes. 65b, 66a, 68b, 69a-b; b. Men. 95a-b)

I.i.66.A. R. Eliezer said, "[Is it not logical:] If slaughtering, which is [biblically-prohibited] on account of work, overrides the Sabbath, these [aforementioned actions] which are [prohibited] on account of *Shevut* [= rabbinically-prohibited Sabbath-work], ought they not [also] override the Sabbath?"

B. R. Joshua said to him, "The festival will prove the matter, on which they permitted [acts prohibited] on account of [biblically-specified] work but have prohibited on it [acts which are forbidden] on account of *Shevut.*"

C. R. Eliezer said to him, "What is the meaning of this, Joshua? What proof does a voluntary act (RŠWT) [= cooking] afford with respect to a commandment [the Passover]?"

D. R. ʿAqiba answered and said, "Sprinkling [the man made unclean by a corpse, on the third or seventh day] will prove the matter for it is a commandment, and it is [prohibited on the Sabbath] on account of *Shevut*, but does not override the Sabbath. So you, do not be astonished concerning these [aforementioned prohibitions], for, even though they are a commandment, they are [prohibited] on account of *shevut*, and they will *not* override the Sabbath."

E. R. Eliezer said to him, "And concerning it [sprinkling itself] I argue: If slaughtering, which is [prohibited] on account of [biblical-forbidden Sabbath-] work overrides the Sabbath, sprinkling, which is [prohibited on the Sabbath] on account of *Shevut* [alone], is it not logical that it *will* override the Sabbath?"

F. R. ʿAqiba said to him, "Or the opposite: If sprinkling, which is [prohibited on the Sabbath] on account of *Shevut*, does *not* override the Sabbath, slaughtering, which is [prohibited on the Sabbath] on account of [Sabbath] work, is it not logical that it should *not* override the Sabbath?"

G. R. Eliezer said to him, "ʿAqiba, you have uprooted what is written in the Torah: *Between the evenings in its appointed time* [season] (Num. 9 : 3)—whether on weekday or on the Sabbath."

H. He said to him, "Master, bring me an *Appointed time* [season] for these [acts] such as the *Appointed time* for slaughtering."

I. A general principle did R. ʿAqiba say, "Every kind of work which may be done on Friday does not override the Sabbath. But slaughtering, which cannot be done on Friday, does override the Sabbath."

M. Pes. 6 : 2 (y. Pes. 6 : 2, 3; b. A.Z. 46b)

*Comment*: Had the Mishnah been formulated according to Eliezer's view, it would have read simply, "Both slaughtering the Passover and its appurtenances (MKŠYRYN) override the Sabbath"—against ʿAqiba's general rule, just as in M. Shab. 19:1, and as in M. Pes. 6:2I. Eliezer would have held that everything concerned with the Passover sacrifice, both before and afterward, may be done on the Sabbath, and this would include the prohibitions (1) and (2) of M. Pes. 6 : 1A.

Just as Eliezer says the appurtenances of circumcision override the Sabbath (M. Shab. 19 : 1-2), so he rules that every aspect of offering the Passover on the Sabbath, when the fourteenth of Nisan coincides with that day, likewise overrides the Sabbath. The antecedent rule lists four permitted actions, and five forbidden ones. Eliezer's saying in C is simply, "They override." To what does he refer? A consists of two lists, *These things override. But these things do not override*; then B has no topic-sentence, simply a continuation of the list broken by the first *do not override.* Evidently the redactor supposed all parties agree on prohibitions (1) and (2), and Eliezer differs on prohibitions (3), (4), and (5). Prohibitions (1) and (2) are not immediately involved with the sacrifice, rather with use of the animal thereafter; therefore they can wait until the end of the Sabbath. Prohibitions (3), (4), and (5), on the other hand, relate to preparing for the sacrifice One cannot carry it out without bringing the sacrifice to the Temple, etc. So it may be that the redactor is correct in assigning to Eliezer a lenient ruling only with respect to prohibitions 3-5. But Tos. Pis. 5 : 1 explicitly alludes to what is done afterward. The rule of ʿAqiba in M. Shab. 19 : 1 explains the opinion of A-B: "Any act of work that can be done on Friday does not override the Sabbath, but what cannot be done on Friday overrides the Sabbath." Only the actual slaughter and disposition of the carcass (tossing, scraping, burning) are impossible to do except at the proper time on the Sabbath. While we may distinguish, logically, between prohibitions (1) and (2), on the one side, and (3), (4), and (5), on the other, if Eliezer is consistent with his view that one may even cut wood to make charcoal to forge a knife for a Sabbath-circumcision, he probably would rule all five are permitted, as in Tos. Pis. 5 : 1.

The rule on which all parties agree is that the actual slaughter of the Passover does override the Sabbath. That rule is attributed to Hillel (*Phar.* I, pp. 231-235), but without exception or qualification: They asked Hillel, *Does the Passover override the Sabbath?* Accordingly, the issue is the sacrifice, without distinction as to the actions therein involved. Eliezer's position places him closer to that assigned to Hillel than does ʿAqiba's (below).

The pericope attached to the Hillel-story then raises the issue, "What will be the rule for the people who did not bring knives and Passover-offerings to the sanctuary?" This takes for granted that once the sacrifice itself is permitted, *bringing* the sacrifice to the Temple will still pose problems. To Hillel is assigned the answer, "He whose Passover was a lamb hid the knife in its wool, etc., so they brought knives and Passover-sacrifices." That is, the lamb brought the knife. But who brought the lamb? Evidently the man himself did—just as Eliezer rules in respect to "*carrying* it to the Temple and *bringing* it from outside the Sabbath limit." So the presupposition of the question follows the ʿAqiban viewpoint; the answer is Eliezer's—but not really so, for he would have let the people *carry* the knives.

M. Pes. 6 : 2 supplies a complete set of arguments for Eliezer's position, introducing Joshua, then ʿAqiba!—a composite. It looks to me as though we have two separate debates, A-C, Eliezer, Joshua, Eliezer, with Eliezer winning the argument, then D-H, ʿAqiba, Eliezer, ʿAqiba. But the division of the composite is obvious, for ʿAqiba's answer in D responds to Eliezer in A; only the extension of the original argument, *Do not be astonished,* links D to C. I is tacked on last of all, repeated from M. Shab. 19:1-2, or formulated according to the same theory of law. Since ʿAqiba is involved in M. Shab. 19:1-2, it seems that he, and not Joshua, should consistently give the contrary arguments here, as in Tos. Pis. 5:1

In A Eliezer distinguishes between biblically- and rabbinically-prohibited actions in respect to the Sabbath. The former are more serious. Yet slaughtering is biblically-prohibited on the Sabbath (except in the Temple) and is permitted with respect to the Passover-sacrifice. The carrying and bringing of the sacrifice, which are not 'work' in the biblical definition, but are prohibited merely by rabbinical rule, ought all the more to be permitted.

Joshua's reply must then show that the biblical prohibitions of Sabbath work are not invariably more strictly enforced than the rabbinical ones, so that the foregoing argument will not stand up. He points out that some biblically prohibited acts of work are permitted on the festival, while some rabbinically prohibited ones are prohibited. Joshua alludes to the rule in M. Bes. 5 : 2: "Any act culpable on the Sabbath, whether by virtue of rules concerning Sabbath rest (*Shevut*) or concerning acts of choice or concerning duties, is culpable also on a Festival-day... A festival day differs from the Sabbath only in respect to preparing necessary food." Preparing food involves prohibitions ordained in the Scriptures; these are permitted, but other actions, prohibited only by rabbinical rules on account of *Shevut*, are prohibited. Therefore, Joshua argues, the permission of a biblically-prohibited action, such as slaughtering, does not carry in its wake the permission of a rabbinically-prohibited one.

Eliezer in C introduces a further distinction, between a voluntary action (RŠWT) and a commandment. In the latter, one has no choice but to do the deed. But one may or may not do other things. Eating is a voluntary action, not a commandment. But the commandment involved in the Passover-sacrifice requires the violation of acts of Sabbath rest (*Shevut*). So Eliezer's second argument distinguishes preparation of food and sacrifice of the Passover. y. Pes. 6 : 2 supplies Eliezer with a further argument along the same lines. Joshua would say, "The festal offering proves the matter, for they permitted doing 'work' for it but prohibited actions on account of *Shevut*." To this Eliezer would reply, "But punishment for not doing the festal offering properly does not involve cutting off, while punishment for not doing the Passover properly does involve cutting off."

In D ʿAqiba reverts to the main issue introduced in A: Sprinkling the sin-offering water on one made unclean by reason of contact with a corpse on the third day of his becoming unclean (Num. 19:12) will be pertinent. If the seventh day occurs on the Sabbath which is also the eve of Passover, they do not sprinkle the unclean man, even in order that he may carry out the Passover, which is a commandment. Now the sprinkling is prohibited only on account of *Shevut*. Yet it does not override the Sabbath coinciding with Passover.

Strikingly, in this argument, ʿAqiba takes the rule for granted, yet, as we shall see, Eliezer rejects the law on which ʿAqiba's argument is based! This is a strange state of affairs. Normally in a debate all parties agree on the law, but differ as to its implications. A debate generally cannot be constructed between parties who do not agree on fundamental questions of fact.

In E Eliezer argues about ʿAqiba's rule with respect to not sprinkling on the Passover that coincides with the Sabbath. So far as Eliezer is concerned, sprinkling the unclean man so that he can keep the Passover at the proper time is just as much an 'appurtenance' of the commandment as is the actual act of slaughter. If slaughtering is permitted, despite the biblical origin of its prohibition, sprinkling will likewise be permitted. So E refutes the facts, not the argument, of D.

Then, in F, ʿAqiba simply turns the argument around, again on the basis of a different view of the legal facts.

Eliezer introduces a scriptural proof—the same one used by Hillel in Tos. Pis. 4 : 13 (*Phar.* I, p. 231)! Eliezer refers to the use of *Its season* with respect to the Passover (Num. 9:3), without developing the common occurrence into a *heqqesh,* as does Hillel. *Its season* here means that the Passover is carried out fully and completely when it is due, even on the Sabbath. Now to Eliezer this includes everything to do with the slaughtering, as he originally stated. But ʿAqiba's answer limits the probative value of *Its season* to the actual slaughtering. He says, Show me an *Its season* referring to the other actions which you would permit along with the slaughtering.

Then I makes clear the basic issue. Eliezer holds anything connected with the Passover is covered by *Its season*, while ʿAqiba holds only things which cannot be done on the Sabbath are protected by it.

I think it now is clear that the principles of the debate cover all seven items prohibited in 6 : 1A-B. Therefore A is formulated according to the ʿAqiban rule, and Eliezer's position as glossator is an ʿAqiban way of showing the decided law. The distinction between prohibitions (1) and (2), and (3)-(5) is of no consequence so far as the debate is concerned. But since the redactor has made such a distinction with the *do not override*, he has placed Eliezer in the position of agreeing with the ʿAqiban rule in 6 : 2I, contrary to the exact position made evident in 6 : 2A-H.

Where does Hillel fit in? Hillel's position in Tos. Pis. 4:13 is simply that the Passover-sacrifice *does* override the Sabbath. No distinctions are made in what aspects of the sacrifice do, and what do not, override the Sabbath—and this is the position of Eliezer. Only after the general rule is established does ʿAqiba's distinction, between what can and cannot be done other than on the Sabbath, become significant. So Tos. Pis. (*Phar.* I, p. 231-2, that is, the whole of the debate on the general rule) seems to me consistent with Eliezer's position. The proof from *In its season* naturally is not attributed to Eliezer in the Hillel story, but Hillel's explicit use of *In its season* seems consistent with Eliezer's:

> "Another matter: It is said concerning the continual offering, *In its season* (Num. 28 : 2), and it is said concerning the Passover, *In its season* (Num. 9 : 2). Just as the continual offering, concerning which *In its season* is said, overrides the Sabbath, so the Passover, concerning which *In its season* is said, overrides the Sabbath."

Eliezer has a simpler argument based on *In its season*. The simple meaning of the clause is "whether on the weekday or on the Sabbath." Eliezer is not constrained to draw evidence from Num. 28:2, probably because the method of exegesis through *heqqesh* or similar analogical arguments was either unknown to him or unnecessary, I think the former.

It would therefore seem that Eliezer stands closer than does ʿAqiba to Hillel in Tos. Pis. 4 : 13. ʿAqiba inferentially accepts the basic issue confronted by Hillel—whether one slaughters at all. Eliezer's denial of distinctions important to ʿAqiba but absent from the Hillel-story and his use of a central proof assigned to Hillel, seem to me to place Eliezer in the circle of thought attributed to Hillel—if not in the House of Hillel. Or, to put it differently, the stories of Hillel's rise to power, focused as they are upon the issue of Sabbath/Passover, seem to draw upon materials shaped to begin with in the name of, and probably by, Eliezer.

See Epstein, *Nusaḥ*, pp. 309, 427; *Tan.*, pp. 298, 336, 361. On M. Eruv. 10 : 13 in comparison to M. Pes. 6 : 1, see *Tan*, p. 336.

II.v.3.A. R. Eliezer adds four things [which override the Sabbath], "Cutting off the wen (YBLTW), and giving and taking a pledge (MŠKWN), and carrying it from Jerusalem to the Temple mount, and bringing it from outside the boundary."

For R. Joshua would say, "Bringing it from outside the boundary does not override the Sabbath."

B. R. Eliezer says, "It overrides [the Sabbath], from a *qal veḥomer*: If you have permitted slaughtering, which [is prohibited as an act of] work (ML'KH), shall we not permit bringing it, which [is prohibited] because of *Shevut*?"

R. Joshua said to him, "Lo, slaughtering, which takes place on holy convocations in the provinces will prove the matter, for he permitted it on account of work and prohibited it on account of *Shevut*."

C. R. Eliezer said to him, "What is this, Joshua? They do not reason a matter of choice from a matter of obligation, nor a matter of obligation from a matter of choice, but a matter of choice from a matter of choice for a *gezerah shavah*, and a matter of obligation from a matter of obligation for a *gezerah shavah*."

D. R. Joshua stood aside (SLQ) and R. ʿAqiba jumped in.

He said to him, "Lo, he for whom the first sprinkling was done, and the seventh day of his period came on the Sabbath on the eve of Passover: Do you tell him that he should sprinkle so that he may eat the Passover?"

R. Eliezer said to him, "That is the point of my logic (ʿYQR DYNY): If you have permitted slaughtering, which is prohibited on account of an act of work, shall we not permit sprinkling, which is prohibited because of *Shevut?*"

E. R. ʿAqiba said to him, "You deny (KPR) me, and I deny you. If you have prohibited sprinkling, which is on account of *Shevut*, shall we not prohibit slaughtering, which is on account of work?"

R. Eliezer said to him, "ʿAqiba, you cannot ever deny me, for the Torah has said, *In its season*, and *In its season* overrides the Sabbath, *In its season* overrides uncleanness."

He said to him, "Bring me *In its season* for these, in the season for slaughter."

F. A general rule did R. ʿAqiba state: "Every sort of work which can be done on the eve of the Sabbath does not override the Sabbath, and every sort of work which cannot be done on the eve of the Sabbath overrides the Sabbath."

Sifré Zuṭṭa 9:2 Horovitz, pp. 257-58

I. ii.48. Tos. Pis. 4:5-6, Lieberman, pp. 161-162, ls. 33-50.

*Comment*: See below, pp. 224-225.

I.ii.49.A. R. Liezer says, "Just as slaughtering [the Passover] overrides the Sabbath, so the appurtenances of slaughtering [the Passover] will override the Sabbath."

B. A general principle did R. ʿAqiba say, "Every sort of work which can be done on Friday does not override the Sabbath, but which cannot be done on Friday overrides the Sabbath."

C. R. Liezer said to him, "The public offerings will prove the matter, for they are valid [y.: He can do them] after the Sabbath, but they override the Sabbath in their time. What is the difference between the appurtenances of slaughter after slaughter and the appurtenances of slaughter before slaughter?"

D. R. ʿAqiba said, "As to the appurtenances of slaughter after slaughter, indeed the slaughter *has* overridden the Sabbath. But will the appurtenances of slaughter before slaughter override the Sabbath, when indeed the slaughter has not [yet] overridden the Sabbath?"

E. "And further, perhaps a reason for invalidity will happen to it [the sacrifice], and he will be found to have profaned the Sabbath and done nothing [as to the sacrifice]."

Tos. Pis. 5 : 1, Lieberman, pp. 166-7, ls. 1-9
(y. Pes. 6 : 3; b. Pes. 62a; y. Shab. 19 :1)

*Comment*: It clearly is Eliezer's view that one may even bring the knife. So he knows nothing of Hillel's instructions to the people in Tos. Pis. 4:13.

Eliezer's argument in C is that it is possible to complete the process of slaughtering the public sacrifices after the Sabbath, e.g. cleaning out the entrails, or burning the fat. But these are done on the Sabbath. Likewise, things that have to be done in advance of the slaughter may likewise be done on the Sabbath.

ʿAqiba points out that after the slaughter of the public sacrifices has overridden the Sabbath, so may its [later] appurtenances. But will the appurtenances of slaughter override the Sabbath *before* the slaughter itself has done so? Further, he notes, the slaughter may never actually take place in the end. Since the man has begun the commandment, we tell him to complete it, for it is a continuous process up to its conclusion.

III.ii.24. TNY': R. Eliezer said, "A man has nothing else to do on a festival but to eat and drink or to sit and study."

R. Joshua said, "Divide it—half to eating and drinking, half to the school-house."

b. Pes. 68b (Tos. Suk. 2 : 1)

*Comment*: See below, p. 147.

III.ii.25. TNY': R. Eliezer said to him, "'ʿAqiba, you have answered me by 'slaughtering' (ŠḤYṬH)—by slaughtering will be his [your] death."

He said to him, "Master, do not deny me in the hour of argument (DYN). Thus I have received from you: 'Sprinkling is a *Shevut* and does *not* override the Sabbath.'"

b. Pes. 69a

IV.i.9. Thirteen years did R. ʿAqiba serve [study with R. Eliezer]. He entered [debate] with R. Liezer, and he did not recognize him. And this is the beginning of the first reply [ʿAqiba] made before Liezer.

R. Joshua said to him [Eliezer], "Is this not the people whom you have despised. Go now and do battle against him."

y. Pes. 6 : 3, Gilead, p. 83

*Comment*: b. Pes. 69a and y. Pes. 6 : 3 supply a historical setting for the argument. b. Pes. 69a has a poignant exchange, presumably coming from Ushan times, which gives Eliezer the prediction that ʿAqiba will not die a natural death. It also accounts for ʿAqiba's version of the law about sprinkling. ʿAqiba is made to attribute the law to Eliezer himself! Then Eliezer is placed in the position of claiming, in an argument, the exact opposite of what he had taught ʿAqiba. This is incredible.

IV.ii.7. Rav Judah said in the name of Rav, "The law follows R. ʿAqiba."

b. Pes. 69b

*Comment*: The same decision applies to M. Shab. 19 : 1.

I.i.67.A. [As to] the Passover [sacrifice] which he slaughtered not for its own sake [= name—i.e., for a different purpose] on the Sabbath—he is liable on its account for a Sin-offering.

B. And [as to] the rest of all the sacrifices which he slaughtered as a Passover—

If they were not appropriate [for the Passover sacrifice], he is [certainly] liable [for a Sin-offering.]

C. But if they were appropriate [= eligible for the Passover sacrifice]—

D. R. Eliezer [nonetheless] declares liable for a Sin-offering.

E. And R. Joshua exempts.

F. R. Eliezer said, "If [for] the Passover, which is permitted [to be slaughtered on the Sabbath, if done] for its own sake [name—for its own purpose], when he changed its name [slaughtered it for another purpose], he is liable, [then for other] sacrifices which *are* prohibited in their [own] name [even when done for their own purpose], when he changed their name [purpose], is it not logical that he should be liable?"

G. R. Joshua said to him, "No. If you said so concerning the Passover, [the name of] which he changed for something prohibited [= he is culpable because he changed it for something prohibited], will you say so concerning [other] sacrifices, [the name of] which he changed for something permitted?"

H. R. Eliezer said to him, "Public offerings (ʾMWRY ṢYBWR) will prove it, for they are permitted [when slaughtered] in their own name [for their own sake]. But he who slaughters [others] in their own name is liable."

I. R. Joshua said to him, "No, if you said so concerning public offerings, which have a limit (QṢBH), will you say so concerning the Passover, which has no limit?"

J. R. Meir says, "Also he who slaughters for the sake of public offerings is free [of liability.]"

M. Pes. 6 : 5 (b. Zev. 11a; y. Pes. 5 : 4, 6 : 5; b. Pes. 62b, 71b, 72a-b, 73a-b)

*Comment*: The rule of A-B is that if one slaughters on the Sabbath not in order to carry out the commandment concerning the Passover, he is liable. If it was done accidentally, for instance in the assumption that one may slaughter on the Sabbath, or that it is not the Sabbath, the man is liable for a Sin-offering.

What about other sacrifices slaughtered for the sake of Passover on the Sabbath? It they could not have been used for the Passover-sacrifice—e.g. cattle, or females—the man is liable, as before.

But what if they *were* appropriate for the Passover sacrifice? Eliezer says the man is equally liable. He has not only to do the right thing, but also correctly to designate what he is doing, e.g., Passover-sacrifice. Joshua declares the man exempt.

Eliezer's argument in F takes for granted that if one sacrifices a Passover-sacrifice under the wrong designation [= changed the name], he is liable. As to other animal offerings, which cannot be sacrificed in their own name at all, if he changed their name [= designated them correctly], should the slaughterer not be liable? This seems to me simply to repeat what Eliezer has already made clear.

Joshua says the comparison is invalid. If one changed the designation of a Passover-sacrifice to something which is prohibited, that is not the same thing as changing the name of other offerings to that of something which is permitted. The repetition of the original dispute is complete. Each has simply spelled out in detail his original presuppositions.

In H Eliezer introduces a new issue, public sacrifices. These whole-offerings, continual-offerings, and additional offerings are done on the Sabbath. One who slaughters any other sacrifices on the Sabbath for the sake [in the name] of these public sacrifices is liable, even though he changed the name to something permitted on the Sabbath. This is (evidently) granted by Joshua. Joshua then says these are to be distinguished from the Passover, for they have a fixed limit, but the Passover has no fixed limit.

It is noteworthy that Eliezer's argument from the public sacrifices recurs in Hillel's general proofs about slaughtering the Passover on the Sabbath. Hillel repeatedly argues that the continual offering and the Passover-sacrifice both are community sacrifices. Therefore, just as the former overrides the Sabbath, so should the latter. The comparison of the continual offering to the Passover-sacrifice is the foundation of the whole set of Hillel's proofs in Tos. Pisḥa 4 : 13. The answer developed in y. Pes. 6 : 1 is that the continual offering has a fixed limit, but the Passover-offering has no fixed limit, so the two are not comparable—just what Joshua argues here! Once again one gains the impression that Eliezer's proofs have been taken over in Hillel's name; then Eliezer should represent the House of Hillel, and Joshua, the House of Shammai, as in the debate on the oven of ʿAkhnai, pp. 422-427.

Meir's addition is consistent with Joshua's. One who slaughters other offerings for the sake of the public ones is free of liability, just as he who slaughters sacrifices on the Sabbath for the sake of the Passover, is free of liability.

See Epstein, *Tan.*, p. 335; *Nusaḥ*, p. 312.

I.ii.50.A. "As to the fourteenth which coincided with the Sabbath—things which are valid to come as the Passover [sacrifice] and things which are not valid to come as a Passover are one: If he slaughtered them for the sake of the Passover, or slaughtered for the sake of a public Sin-offering, for the sake of the public Whole-offering, or a Passover which he slaughtered on the Sabbath not for its sake [Passover's]—[in all cases] he is not liable"—the words of R. Meir.

B. R. Simeon said, "R. Liezer and R. Joshua did not differ concerning things which are not valid to come as the Passover, which he slaughtered for the sake of Passover, and [concerning] him who slaughters for the sake of a public Sin-offering [or] for the sake of the public Whole-offering, that he *is* liable.

"Concerning what did they differ?

C. "Concerning things which are valid to come as a Passover, which he slaughtered for the sake of Passover—

D. "For R. Liezer declares [him] liable for a Sin-offering.

E. "And R. Joshua exempts [him from the Sin-offering.]"

Tos. Pis. 5 : 4, Lieberman, pp. 167-8, ls. 19-26 (b. Pes. 72b)

*Comment*: C revises the dispute of M. Pes. 6 : 5. There the debate concerned slaughtering animals appropriate for the Passover sacrifice but not slaughtered for the sake of the Passover. Now we are told he has sacrificed animals on the Sabbath which were appropriate for the Passover and he has done so for the sake of Passover—and *still* there is a dispute. Since the man has taken fit lambs and changed their purpose and made them for the Passover, he still is liable.

It is noteworthy that M. Yad. 4 : 2 bypasses the case before us:

> On that day they said, "All animal sacrifices slaughtered under the name of some other offering remain valid, but do not count to their owner ['s credit] (in fulfilment of his obligation) excepting a Passover-offering and a Sin-offering—a Passover-offering in its appointed time and a Sin-offering at any time." R. Eliezer says, "Excepting also the Guilt-offering—a Passover-offering in its appointed time and a Sin-offering and a Guilt-offering at any time."

The issue raised by Eliezer and Joshua is not claimed as pertinent to the on-that-day rule. But on that day "they decreed" the rule now in I.i.67A, and the dispute of Eliezer and Joshua logically follows upon it.

I.i.68. [*If any man . . . shall be unclean . . or be in a journey afar off* (Num. 9 : 9f) and has not kept the first Passover, let him keep the second.

A. What is a distant journey?

C. "From Modi'in and outward, and according to the same measure in every direction," the words of R. 'Aqiba.

D. R. Eliezer says, "From the threshold of the Temple court and beyond."

E. R. Yosi said, "Therefore there is a point over the *Ḥet* in RḤWQH), to indicate, not because it is really distant, but [meaning] from the threshold of the courtyard and beyond."

M. Pes. 9 : 2 (y. Pes. 6 : 3, 9 : 12; b. Pes. 93b)

*Comment*: 'Aqiba and Eliezer gloss a minor detail of the antecedent rule. 'Aqiba supplies a direct and pertinent definition. Eliezer says that a "distant journey" is anything outside of the Temple! That is, if at the time of the Passover sacrifice a man was anywhere outside of the courtyard, for any reason, and he cannot get there, he is regarded as being on a distant journey and is free of the penalty of 'cutting off.' Eliezer's is a still more lenient interpretation. Indeed, he so leniently interprets the rule as to make it inoperative. Anyone not actually in the Temple at the first Passover celebrates the second!

See Epstein, *Nusaḥ*, p. 1261; *Tan.*, pp. 67, 147.

I.ii.51.A. R. ʿAqiba says, "It is said, *Unclean soul* (Num. 9 : 10), and it is said, *A distant way* (Num. 9 : 10). Just as the unclean soul wants to do [it] and cannot, so [the person on] a distant way wants to do it and cannot."

B. R. Liezer says, "It is said, *A distant place* with reference to Tithes, and a *distant place* is said with reference to Passover. Just as the *distant place* said with reference to Tithes alludes to a [place] outside of the place where it is eaten [= Jerusalem], so a *distant place* said with reference to the Passover [means] outside of the place where it is eaten."

Tos. Pis. 8 : 2, Lieberman, p. 183,
ls. 4-8 (b. Pes. 92a, 94)

*Comment*: Tos. supplies an argument for each party. But here Eliezer says the man must be outside of Jerusalem—however far—and not merely outside of the Temple.

II.iv.6.A. *On a distant trip.* I do not know what a distant journey is.

And the sages gave the measure: Whoever was beyond Modiʿim when the Passover was slaughtered—and so for all measures.

R. ʿAqiba says, "It is said here, *Unclean by reason of corpse uncleanness*, and it is said, *A distant journey.* Just as one unclean by reason of corpse uncleanness wants to do it but cannot, so one a distant journey away wants to do it but cannot."

B. R. Eliezer says, "It is said, *Distant from the place* in reference to tithes, and it is said, *Distant from the place*, with reference to the Passover. Just as *Distant from the place* said in connection with tithes means outside of the place where it is eaten, so *Distant from the place* said with reference to the Passover means outside of the place where it is eaten."

"And what is the place where it is eaten? From the gate of Jerusalem inward."

R. Judah says . . .

Sifré Num. 69, Friedman, p. 18a
(Sifré Zuṭṭa, ed. Hoffmann, p. 260)

II.ii.4.A. R. Eliezer says, "Bringing a Passover is said in Egypt and bringing a Passover is said for [future] generations. Just as the Passover brought in Egypt does not come from tithes [so that for future generations should not come from tithes]."

R. ʿAqiba said to him, "Rabbi, do they judge what is possible from what is impossible [there was no tithing in Egypt]? And did they have tithing in Egypt?"

R. Eliezer said to him, "Even what is impossible is an important proof."

R. ʿAqiba went and changed the ground of argument (HḤLYP ʾT HDYN): "In Egypt it is said to bring a Passover, and for future generations it is said to bring a Passover. Just as the Passover to be brought in Egypt comes only from unconsecrated beasts, so the Passover to be brought by future generations comes only from unconsecrated beasts."

Mekhilta deR. Simeon b. Yoḥai, p. 39, ls. 7-14 (b. Men. 82a-b; b. Yev. 46a; another argument about "judging the possible from the impossible" is in Mekh. Nez. 16 : 13-24—parallel is the mode of argument, but on a different subject; also see Sifra Shemini Pereq 10 : 5-6)

*Comment*: In b. Yev. 46a the passage is cited to prove that a possibility may be inferred from an impossibility, against Joshua, and in b. Men. 82a-b for the same purpose against ʿAqiba. But the passage is integral to the law of neither context. Nor do I find a legal setting in M. Pes. to which the passage should be attached.

II.i.5. *But roast with fire*, etc.

"Why is this said? I might have thought what is fit for boiling one may boil, and only what is fit for roasting should one roast. Therefore Scripture says, *But roast with fire; its head with its legs and with the inwards thereof*, i.e., both the inner and the outer parts"—these are the words of R. ʿAqiba.

R. Eliezer says, "It should be barbecued (MQWLS)."

Mekhilta deR. Ishmael Pisḥa 6 : 88-91,
ed. and trans. Lauterbach, I, p. 50

*Comment*: Mekh. deR. Simeon, p. 39, ls. 14-20, gives the same law anonymously, immediately following the foregoing pericope. b. Pes. 74a knows nothing of Eliezer's view on the subject; Tos. Bes. 2 : 15 discusses barbecuing, but makes no reference to Eliezer. Other MSS cited by Lauterbach give Ishmael, or Ṭarfon, who seems to me the best choice.

ii.iv.7.A. *But to the place which the Lord your God will choose . . .*

B. R. Eliezer says, "*In the evening* you sacrifice, *at sunset* you eat, *at the season of your going forth from Egypt*, you burn."

C. R. ʿAqiba says, "*In the evening* you sacrifice, *at sunset* you eat. Until when? Until *the season of your going forth from Egypt*."

Sifré Deut. 133, Finkelstein, p. 190
(Midrash Tannaim, ed. Hoffmann, p. 92)

*Comment*: Finkelstein does not regard the pericope as integral to Sifré.

III.ii.26.A. *There you shall sacrifice the Passover-offering at evening, at the going down of the sun, at the season that you came forth from Egypt* (Deut. 16 : 6).

B. R. Eliezer says, "*At evening*—you sacrifice; *at sunset*—you eat; and *at the season that you came out of Egypt*—you burn the remainder."

R. Joshua says, "*At evening*—you sacrifice; *at sunset*—you eat. And how long do you continue to eat? Until the *season that you came out of Egypt*."

b. Ber. 9a, trans. Maurice Simon, p. 47

*Comment*: Eliezer says one may eat the Passover at sunset, but at midnight one burns the remainder; and ʿAqiba or Joshua says one may eat it until midnight. M. Pes. 5 : 1 says the Passover offering is made after the afternoon Tamid. y. Pes. 5 : 1 has the exegesis in the name of R. Jeremiah: In the evening you sacrifice, at sunset you eat, at the season of your going forth from the land of Egypt you roast (ṢWLH).

## xv. Sheqalim

I.i.69.A. He who sanctifies his goods [property to the Temple], and there were among them cattle valid for the altar, males and females—

B. R. Eliezer says, "The males will be sold to those that need whole-offerings, and the females will be sold to those that need peace-offerings, and their proceeds and the rest of the property will fall for the upkeep of the House [Temple fund]."

C. R. Joshua says, "The males themselves will be sacrificed as whole-offerings, and the females will be sold to those that need peace-offerings. And he will bring with their proceeds whole offerings. And the rest of the property will fall for the upkeep of the House."

D. R. ʿAqiba says, "I see [prefer] the opinion of R. Eliezer to the opinion of R. Joshua, for R. Eliezer applied his rule equally [So Danby, p. 156, for HŠWH ʾT MDTW], and R. Joshua made distinction[s] (ḤLQ)."

E. R. Papyas said, "I heard [traditions] according to the opinions of them both, that he that sanctifies explicitly [is adjudged] according to the opinion of R. Eliezer, and he that sanctifies plain (STM) [Danby: without terms] [is adjudged] according to the opinion of R. Joshua."

M. Sheq. 4 : 7 (y. Sheq. 4 : 4; b. Zev. 103a, b. Tem. 20a, 31b; Sifra Vayiqra Parashah 5 : 4, Weiss, p. 7b).

*Comment*: The issue is whether the man's act of sanctifying his property has intended for those animals in the donation appropriate to the altar to be sacrificed on it.

Eliezer holds that the males fit for the altar are to be sold to someone who requires them for that purpose, and the females, not fit for the altar, will be sold and the funds added to the Temple treasury. Eliezer's view is that while both sanctified animals and property normally are meant for the treasury (M. Tem. 7 : 1), whatever is suitable for the altar is sold and redeemed only for the needs of the altar, so Albeq, *Seder Mo'ed*, p. 198.

Joshua says that whatever is fitting for the altar was intended by the man for the altar itself, therefore the animals themselves are sacrificed.

The form of the dispute is perfect. After the topic-sentence, the two opinions are given in careful balance, each element matched in the opposite statement.

'Aqiba's comment supplies a firm *terminus* for the form and substance of the foregoing. He says that Eliezer has been consistent. Nothing goes to the altar. Everything is sold. Joshua has the males sacrificed, but the females sold.

Then Papyas claims to have traditions according to each, meaning he has conflicting, anonymous rulings on the same subject. Eliezer is consistent with ruling about him who sanctifies explicitly for the Temple fund. Joshua is consistent with one about him who is not explicit. In that case, it is taken for granted that what is good for the altar is to go there. Note also M. Sheq. 4 : 8:

> He who sanctifies property and there were in it things appropriate for the altar—wines, olives, oils, birds—
>
> R. Eleazar [Eliezer] says, "They will be sold for the needs of that particular offering, and he will bring with their proceeds birds, and the rest of the property falls to the upkeep of the House."

Eleazar [Eliezer] is not wholly consistent with Eliezer in the foregoing, for the aforementioned items are not used for the Temple, but for the altar. Lieberman prefers *Eliezer.*

See Epstein, *Nusaḥ*, p. 1134; *Tan.*, p. 344.

I.ii.52.A. He who sanctifies his goods [to the Temple] and there were among them cattle valid for the altar, males and females—

B. R. Liezer says, "The males will be sold to those that need whole-offerings (ZBḤY 'WLWT), and the females will be sold to those that need peace-offerings, and their proceeds will fall with the rest of the property for the upkeep of the House."

C. R. Joshua says, "The males themselves will be offered as whole-offerings, and the females will be sold for the needs of peace-offerings, and he will bring with their proceeds whole-offerings."

D. R. Yosah and R. Simeon say, "The words of R. Liezer are the same as (HN HN) the words of R. Joshua, and the words of R. Joshua are the same as the words of R. Liezer."

Tos. Sheq. 2 : 10, Lieberman, p. 209, ls. 45-50

*Comment*: The only difference between Tos. Sheq. B and C and M. Sheq. is the absence, in the final clause of Joshua's saying here, of *and the rest of the property will fall for the upkeep of the House.* Otherwise the two versions are identical. But while in M. Sheq. ʿAqiba sees important differences in the two opinions, here Yosah and Simeon allege there are none!

Lieberman explains (*Moʿed*, p. 686), that the reference of D is to M. Sheq. 4 : 8, the opinion of Eliezer (not Eleazar). There, Eliezer says the property is sold for the particular offering, and not for the upkeep of the House, and on *this* matter, the masters comment that Eliezer now is in agreement with Joshua, that what can be used for the altar is so used, and not merely for the upkeep of the House. But Eliezer evidently will agree that things which cannot be redeemed are used for the purchase of whole-offerings. So A-C before us are simply copied from M. Sheq. 4 : 7, but M. Sheq. 4 : 8, to which D alludes, is missing.

See Epstein, *Tan.*, p. 344.

I.i.70.A. R. Eliezer says, "What has contracted uncleanness from a primary source of uncleanness, whether inside [the Temple Court] or outside it, must be burned outside, and what has contracted uncleanness from a derived uncleanness, whether inside or outside, must be burned inside."

B. R. ʿAqiba says, "Where it contracted uncleanness, there should it be burned."

M. Sheq. 8 : 7 (y. Sheq. 8 : 3)

I.ii.53.

Tos. Sheq. 3 : 16, Lieberman,
pp. 216-217, ls. 46-53

II.iii.5.

Sifra Ṣav Pereq 8 : 7, ed. Weiss, p. 33a

*Comment*: See *Phar.* II, pp. 100-105, 148-149.

## xvi. Yoma, Sukkah, Beṣah

I.ii.54. [He shook the urn and took up the two lots. On one was written, 'For the Lord,' and on the other, 'For Azazel.' The prefect was on his right and the chief of the father's house on the left. If the lot bearing the Name came up in the right hand, the Prefect would say to him, 'My lord, High Priest, raise your right hand.' If it came up in the left, the chief of the father's house would say to him, 'My lord, High Priest, raise thy left hand.—M. Yoma 4 : 1].

A. R. Judah said in the name of R. Eliezer, "The Prefect and the High Priest stretch out their two rights as one [b: put their hand into the urn]. If in the right hand of the High Priest it came up, the Prefect says to him, 'My lord, High Priest, raise your right hand.' If in the right hand of the Prefect it came up, the head of the house of the father says to him, 'Prefect, say your word (DBR M'YLK; b.: MYLK) [= A sin-offering unto the Lord']."' [Lieberman gives DBR M'YLK —'Announce concerning what is in your hand.']

Tos. Kippurim 2 : 10, Lieberman, p. 235, ls. 84-87 (b. Yoma 39a)

*Comment*: Judah b. Ilai's tradition from Eliezer does not occur in M. Yoma 4 : 1, to which it is pertinent. According to Eliezer, both the high priest and the prefect take lots, one for each, in the right hand. Then the ritual proceeds, without participation of the head of the father's house. So the prefect plays as important a role in the rite as does the High Priest—a view rejected by Judah the Patriarch. See Lieberman, *Mo'ed*, p. 767.

I.ii.55. [And so would he (the high priest when sprinkling the blood) count: "One, one and one, one and two, one and three, one and four, one and five, one and six, one and seven."—M. Yoma 5 : 3].

A. R. Judah said in the name of R. Liezer, "Thus he used to count: 'One, one and one, two and one, three and one, four and one, five and one, six and one, seven and one.'"

Tos. Kippurim 2 : 16, Lieberman, p. 239, ls. 131-133

*Comment*: Tos. again has a different version, in Eliezer's name, in place of the (anonymous) Mishnah's. Since Eliezer differs from the tradition contained in the Mishnah, it looks as though the composition of a record of the Temple rite on the Day of Atonement was underway at Yavneh. Eliezer's view of things was excluded from that composition.

At issue, Lieberman explains, is counting the sprinklings. The sprinkling in the upward stroke was counted by itself, and the sprinkling below began a new enumeration. So that the priest would not err, he counted the upward sprinkling with each downward sprinkling. Eliezer's tradition, given by Judah, is that they counted the detail first (two and twenty, three and twenty). Here too they would count "three and one," rather than "one and three." See *Mo'ed*, pp. 774-5.

I.i.71.A. *And he went out to the altar which is before the Lord* (Lev. 16 : 18)—this is the golden altar.

B. He began to sprinkle downward (MḤṬ' WYWRD)—from where does he begin? From the northeast horn (corner), north-west, south-west, south-east.

C. The place from which he begins sprinkling on the outer altar, there he would complete the sprinkling of the inner altar.

D. R. Eliezer says, "In his place did he stand and sprinkle."

E. And on all of them he would place [sprinkle—NWTN] from bottom to top, except for this [sprinkling on the corner] which was before him, on which he would place [sprinkle] from top to bottom."

M. Yoma 5 : 5 (y. Yoma 5 : 5, 6; b. Yoma 58b)

*Comment*: Eliezer glosses a detail of the account of the cult on the Day of Atonement. Other glosses in the name of masters follow the same form, an anonymous statement of the law, in the past tense, interrupted by the gloss, *Rabbi X says...*

The goat was slaughtered, the blood caught in a basin, and then the priest would sprinkle the blood (M. Yoma 5 : 4). The anonymous rule in A-C has it that the high priest would sprinkle from one corner, then move to the next, circumambulating the altar. Eliezer in D holds the priest would stand in one place, not moving from corner to corner. He stood in the north-east corner and from there sprinkled all four, for the golden altar was only one cubit square.

E is not necessarily a continuation of Eliezer's sayings. It completes C as much as D.

See Epstein, Nusaḥ, p. 141; *Tan.*, p. 68.

I.ii.56.A. On all of them he places [sprinkles the blood] from below to above, except on this, which was before him, which he used to sprinkle from above to below.

B. R. Judah [y.: omits *Judah*] said in the name of R. Liezer, "In his place he would stand and sprinkle (MḤṬ'), and on all of them he places [sprinkles] from below to above [y.: *Above to below*], except for this one which was before him, diagonally opposite ('LKSWN) on which he would sprinkle from above to below [y. *Below to above*]."

Tos. Kippurim 3 : 1, Lieberman, p. 240,
ls. 5-8 (y. Yoma 5 : 5, b. Yoma 58b-59a)

*Comment*: b. Yoma 59a has, "...which he made from above downward *to prevent his garments from becoming sullied.*" Judah supplies warrant for assigning M. Yoma 5 : 5 to our Eliezer.

II.iii.6. *And he will sprinkle on the horns of the altar, beginning from the north-east* etc.

R. Judah says in the name of R. Eliezer, "He stands in his place and sprinkles on all of them (etc.)."

Sifra Aḥaré Mot Pereq 4 : 10, Weiss, p. 81b (b. Yoma 59b, Zev. 40a, 52b)

I.ii.57.A. They asked R. Liezer, "Lo, if the goat that is sent forth fell ill, what is the law as to his [the one who was to lead the goat away, M. Yoma 6:3] carrying it away?" [y. has this as second question: "If that which is sent out fell ill . . ."]

B. He said to them, "He can carry others." [y. "He can carry you and me."]

C. [y.: Starts here] "The one who sends him forth [y.: ŠLYḤ] fell ill—what is the law as to sending it forth with the hand of another?" [y. omits *what . . . another.*]

D. He said to them, "Thus may you and I be in peace." [y.: "Thus may you be in peace."]

E. "He pushed it [the goat down the hill] and it did not die—what is the law as to his going down after it and killing it?"

F. He said to them, "So may be the enemies of the Omnipresent [y.: Heaven]." [b.: *Thus may the enemies of the Lord perish* (Judges 5 : 31).] [y.: *Not that he wanted to put them off, but he would not say to them things he had not heard.*]

G. And sages say, "He fell ill—he carries it [y.: *on an ass*]. [If] the one who sends him forth fell ill, they send it [the goat] with another; he pushed it and it did not die—he goes down after it and kills it."

Tos. Kippurim 3 : 14, Lieberman, pp. 245, ls. 61-65 (y. Yoma 6 : 3)

*Comment*: The little dialogue between "them" and Eliezer deals with the law in M. Yoma 6 : 3ff., about leading away the Scapegoat. The answers of Eliezer are indirect, evasive. The explanation of his answers is still more difficult because of the varying textual evidences of what those answers actually consisted. See Lieberman, *Mo'ed*, p. 796, for a full survey of the several readings and explanations.

III.ii.27. They asked R. Eliezer, "[If] it [the scapegoat] fell ill, what is the law as to his carrying it on his shoulder?"

B. He said to them, "He can carry you and me."

C. "The one who sends it forth fell ill—what is the law as to sending it forth with someone else?"

D. He said to them, "May you and I be in peace."

E. "He pushed it and it did not die—what is the law as to his going down after him and killing it?"

F. He said to them, "*Thus may all your enemies perish, O Lord* (Judges 5 : 31)."

G. And sages say, "[If it] fell ill, he carries it on his shoulder. If the one who sends it forth fell ill, they send it forth with another. If he pushed it and it did not die, he goes down after it and kills it."

H. They asked R. Eliezer, "So and so—what is his [lot] as to the world to come?"

I. He said to them, "Have you asked me only as to such-and-such [a man, and no one else]?"

J. "What is the law as to a shepherd's saving the lamb from the lion?"

K. He said to them, "Have you asked me only in reference to the lamb?"

L. "What is to the law as to saving the shepherd from the lion?"

M. He said to them, "Have you only asked me as to the shepherd?"

N. "The *Mamzer*—what is his law as to inheriting?"

O. "What is his law as to Levirate marriage?"

P. "What in respect to whitewashing his house?"

Q. "May one whitewash his grave?"

R. Not because he put them off with words, but because he never said a thing which he had not heard from his master.

S. A wise woman asked R. Eliezer, "Since with respect to the sin of the Golden Calf, they [all Israel] were equal, why were they not equal as to the penalty of death?"

T. He answered, "The only wisdom of a woman is in respect to the distaff. Thus also does Scripture say, *And all the women that were wise-hearted did spin with their hands* (Ex. 335 : 25)."

b. Yoma 66b

*Comment*: As usual, the *baraita*-stratum contains considerable additions to Tos.'s version of a tradition. Part R is an important interpolation.

III.ii.28.A. TNW RBNN: M'ŚH B: R. Eliezer spent the Sabbath in Upper Galilee.

They asked him for thirty decisions in the laws of *Sukkah*. Of twelve he said, "I heard them." Of eighteen he said, "I have not heard." [Here intervenes a gloss of R. Yosi b. R. Judah.]

They said to him, "Are all your words only [reproductions of what you have] heard?"

He said to them, "You forced me to say something which I have not heard from my masters.

B. "During all my life no man was earlier than I in the school. I never slept or dozed in the school. I never left a person in the school when I went out. I never uttered profane speech. I never said a thing which I did not hear from my master."

C. They said concerning R. Yoḥanan b. Zakkai . . .

D. And so did his disciple Eliezer conduct himself after him.

b. Suk. 28a

*Comment*: The pericope is in four parts. First comes the story about Eliezer's visit to Galilee. He publicly says he has not heard a law. He is asked, Do you state only what you have heard? He says that is the case.

B then takes a separate saying and ties it to the foregoing. The last clause, *I never said a thing which I did not hear*, is the connection to the foregoing.

In C we have a separate set of allegations concerning Yoḥanan b. Zakkai, *Development*, p. 90. In that list are all the traits attributed to Eliezer, as well as expansions of those traits and entirely new ones. Then D ties C to the foregoing.

See *Development*, p. 90, 216, 219, and *Phar.* I, pp. 206-208. It would seem that A stood separately, and only later on was made to serve as a narrative setting for B-D.

I.i.72. [Then the High Priest came (to the court of the women) to read. If he wanted to read in linen garments, he read (in them), and if not, he read in his white vestment.—M. Yoma 7 : 1.]

A. If he reads in linen garment, he [then] sanctified his hands and feet, took [it] off, descended, bathed, went up, and dried off.

They brought to him the golden vestments, and he put [them] on, sanctified his hands and his feet, and went forth and prepared his ram and the ram of the people—

B. —"And the seven unblemished lambs a year old"—the words of R. Eliezer.

C. R. ʿAqiba says, "With the Continual Sacrifice of the morning they were offered."

D. "And the bullock for the whole-offering and the he-goat that is offered outside were offered with the afternoon Daily Whole-offering."

M. Yoma 7 : 3 (y. Yoma 7 : 2,
y. Nazir 7 : 1; b. Yoma 70a-b)

*Comment*: B and C + D interrupt the account. Eliezer evidently adds "and . . . old," and his gloss is glossed by ʿAqiba. Both sayings begin with *says*, as if we had independent legal sayings, not glosses.

The issue is when the seven lambs were offered. ʿAqiba holds they were offered with the morning continual sacrifice (Tamid) referred to in M. Yoma 3 : 4. Eliezer's view is that they came as additional offerings, after the rams (Num. 29 : 8), following the order in which they are referred to in Scripture.

Lieberman observes (*Moʿed*, p. 804) that D is a continuation of C, all part of ʿAqiba's position.

See Epstein, *Nusaḥ*, pp. 79, 381; *Tan.*, pp. 66, 87.

I.ii.58.A. R. Liezer says, "This was the order of the offerings [which] they would offer: The bullock for the whole-offering and the he-goat which was prepared outside were offered up with the continual offering of the morning, and afterward the bullock and the he-goat which was made inside, and afterward his ram and the ram of the people, and afterward the seven unblemished lambs [a year old]."

B. R. ʿAqiba says, "The bullock for the whole-offering and the seven unblemished lambs were offered up with the continual offering of the morning, as it is said, *Beside the burned-offering of the morning which is for a continual burned-offering* (Num. 28 : 23), and afterward the bullock and the goat which was prepared inside, and afterward the goat which was prepared outside, as it is said, [*One he-goat for a sin-offering*] *beside the sin-offering of atonement and the continual whole-offering and its meal and their drinks* (Num. 29 : 11) and afterward his ram and the ram of the people."

C. R. Judah says in the name of R. Liezer, "One is offered with the morning continual offering and six are offered with the continual offering of twilight."

Tos. Kippurim 3 : 19, Lieberman, pp. 247-248, ls. 85-93
(Sifra Aḥaré Mot 6 : 5, y. Yoma 7 : 2, b. Yoma 70b)

*Comment*: Eliezer's view is that the Scriptures imply that they place together the additional offerings and the continual offering, but, because of the fatigue of the high priest, they postpone the seven lambs until after the service inside the court. ʿAqiba notes that Scripture lists together all the additional offerings with the continual offering, excepting the goat of the additional service (not to mention the sin-offering of atonement), implying that the goat has already been prepared inside. Judah then adds that one lamb of the additional service was offered with the continual offering in the morning, to keep together the additional offerings with the continual offering, except the ram of the people, prepared with the high priests' ram.

Lieberman explains (*Moʿed*, p. 804) that here Eliezer divides the additional offerings. The priest offers, with the morning continual offering, the bullock whole-offering and the goat that is prepared outside, and afterward he carries out the service of the Day of Atonement, and afterward come his ram and that of the people and the seven lambs. ʿAqiba then says D—the additional offerings come with the morning continual offering, except the goat, etc.

Let us now compare the several versions of the law:

| *M. Yoma 7 : 3* | *Tos.: Eliezer* | *Tos.: ʿAqiba* |
|---|---|---|
| 1. And he went out and offered his ram and the ram of the people. | 1. They offered the bullock for the whole-offering, then the goat made outside, with the morning continual offering; then the bullock, the goat prepared outside, then *his ram and the ram of the people, then the seven perfect lambs* [Italics = Mishnah nos. 1 + 2] | 1. They offered the bullock for the whole-offering *and the seven perfect lambs with the morning continual offering...* Then the bullock and the goat made inside; then the goat prepared outside... then his ram and the ram of the people... |
| 2. Eliezer: And the seven perfect lambs a year old [+ ʿAqiba: They were offered with the morning continual offering. Accordingly, ʿAqiba's Mishnah would read simply:] | | |
| 3. ...*ram of the people* and the goat that was made outside were offered with the afternoon continual whole-offering. | | |

M. Yoma 7 : 3 thus does not contain reference to all of the sacrifices, the time of whose offering is at issue between Eliezer and ʿAqiba. It bypasses *bullock for the whole-offering, goat made inside* (as does Eliezer). One cannot differ from Lieberman that no. 3 is a continuation of ʿAqiba's opinion. But the real problem is, How has the Mishnah been formulated? Evidently, Judah the Patriarch has supplied an introductory clause, no. 1, quite neutral on the points at issue, then taken only *part* of Eliezer's opinion as represented in Tos., and as noted, the bulk of ʿAqiba's.

Note also y. Yoma 7 : 2, R. Huna in the name of R. Joseph, "R. Liezer is in accord with the House of Shammai."

I.ii.59. [He who drinks a mouthful (MLʾ LWGMYW) is liable.—M. Yoma 8 : 2]

A. R. Leazar [Liezer] says, "He who drinks a mouthful (MLʾ LWGMYW) is liable."

Tos. Kippurim 4 : 3, Lieberman, p. 250, 1. 16
(b. Yoma 80a; y. Yoma 8 : 2)

*Comment*: See Lieberman, *Moʿed*, pp. 815-816; *Phar.* II, pp. 149-150.

I.i.73.A. He who makes his *Sukkah* like a cone-shaped hut or who leaned it up against the wall—

B. R. Eliezer declares [it] unfit, *because it has no roof.*

C. And sages declare fit.

D. A large reed-mat (MḤṢLT QNYM)—[If] he made it for lying, it (1) receives uncleanness, and they (2) do not use it for *Sukkah*-roofing (ʾYN MSKKYN BH). [If] for *Sukkah*-roofing (LSKWK), they (2) use it for *Sukkah*-roofing and it (1) does not receive uncleanness.

E. R. Eliezer [Kaufmann, Camb., Parma: Leazar] says, "It is all the same whether big or small: [If] he made it for lying, it receives uncleanness and they do not use it for *Sukkah*-roofing. [If] for *Sukkah*-roofing, they use it for *Sukkah*-roofing and it does not receive uncleanness."

M. Suk. 1 : 11 (y. Suk. 1 : 12;
b. Suk. 7b, 16a, 19b, 20a)

*Comment*: The form is a standard dispute, with a statement of the topic or problem, followed by the appropriate rulings. The order 1,2, 2,1 is determined by the *if*-clause.

Eliezer's saying (B) is glossed, in italics, but the gloss—perhaps by Nathan—makes evident what was already clear, namely, the issue is what to do with a *Sukkah* which has no roof.

The second dispute is equally well-balanced. Eliezer's saying exactly matches the foregoing, except for his topic sentence—*it is all the same*—which tells us that the dispute concerns a large or a small reed-mat. According to the sages, the rules pertain to a large one only. But a small one is normally used for lying and therefore will receive uncleanness and will not be used for *Sukkah*-roofing (the latter is a consequence of the former, M. Suk. 1 : 4). Eliezer therefore is prepared to distinguish not according to size, but according to the purpose for which the mat was made. The sages take for granted a small one will never serve a purpose other than lying. Eliezer is in the lenient position in D-E.

b. Suk. 16a has Eliezer prohibiting both the large and the small, without qualification—both serve for lying.

See Epstein, *Nusaḥ*, p. 1105; *Tan.*, pp. 66, 170: This is the teaching of Nathan.

III.ii.29: TNYʾ: A large reed-matting may be used for *Sukkah*-roofing.

R. Eliezer says, "If it does not receive uncleanness, it may be used."

b. Suk. 20a

*Comment*: The *baraita* now has Eliezer's rule on the large alone—consistent with M. Suk. 1 : 11. This looks like a brief summary of the Mishnah.

I.ii.60.A. He who makes his *Sukkah* like a cone-shaped hut or leaned it against the wall—

B. R. Liezer agrees that if there is in its roof [as much as a] handbreadth (y.: PWTḤ ṬPḤ), or [if] it was (y.: *placed on stones*) a handbreadth above the earth, it is acceptable.

Tos. Suk. 1 : 10, Lieberman, pp. 258-9, ls. 30-32 (y. Suk. 1 : 12, b. Suk. 19b)

*Comment*: Tos. accords with the gloss of M. Suk. 1 : 11, because *it has no roof.* But if it has any sort of roof, it *is* acceptable. If it was raised above the earth, it is a tent, the *Sukkah*-covering serving as a roof.

b. Suk. 19b has: "R. Eliezer agrees that if he raised it off the ground a handbreadth or separated it from the wall a handbreadth, it is acceptable." Also, a separate *baraita* has: "R. Nathan says, R. Eliezer invalidates it *because it has no roof.*" This is the sole warrant for including the tradition here.

I.ii.61.A. Sages agree with R. Liezer that they do not make tents to begin with on the festival, and one need not say, on the Sabbath.

B. For sages say, "They add on the Sabbath, and one need not say, on the festival."

Tos. Suk. 1 : 8, Lieberman, p. 258, ls. 22-24

*Comment*: See above, Tos. Shab. 12 : 14, p. 92.

I.ii.62.A. MʿŚH B: R. Eliezer was sitting (b.: *passed the Sabbath*) in the *Sukkah* of Yoḥanan b. Ilai (ʾLʿY) in Caesarea, and the sun came into the *Sukkah*.

B. He [Yoḥanan] said to him, "What is the law as to spreading a cloth (SDYN) over it?"

C. He said to him, "You have no tribe in Israel that did not bring forth a prophet (b.: Judge)."

D. The sun reached the middle of the *Sukkah*.

E. He said to him, "What is the law as to spreading over it a cloth?"

F. He said to him, "You have no tribe that did not bring forth a judge (b.: Prophet)."

"The tribe of Judah and Benjamin brought forth kings according to the instruction of prophets."

G. The sun reached R. Liezer's feet. He [b.: Yoḥanan] took the cloth and spreak it over the *Sukkah*, and R. Liezer stretched out

(HPŠYL) [b.: tied up his coat, threw it over his back] his feet and went away. [b.: "Not in order to evade, but because he never said anything which he had not heard from his master."]

Tos. Suk. 1 : 9, Lieberman, p. 258, ls. 24-30 (b. Suk. 27b)

*Comment*: Eliezer prohibits adding to the tent on the festival, but perhaps, Yoḥanan thought, it is permitted here, because the cloth is not removed from the status of clothing, so this is not adding to the tent at all. Eliezer as usual did not answer the question directly, but he indicated his displeasure by changing the subject. When Yoḥanan, misinterpreting Eliezer's opinion, actually covered the *Sukkah*, Eliezer simply left. His opinion is that it is prohibited to add to the tent on the Sabbath and on the festival days. Evidently the legal rule was formulated on the basis of the story; Yoḥanan obviously heard no such law. b. misses the point.

I.ii.63.A. M'ŚH B: R. Ilai went to R. Liezer to Lud. He said to him, "What is this, Ilai [y. omits]? Are you not among those who rest (ŠWBTY) on the festival? Did they not say, It is no praise of a man [y.: TLMYDY ḤKMYM] to leave his house on the festival, as it is said, *You will rejoice in your festival* (Deut. 16 : 14)."

Tos. Suk. 2 : 1, Lieberman, p. 260, ls. 2-4 (y. Suk. 2 : 5; b. Suk. 27b)

*Comment*: The antecedent law is cited verbatim: It is no praise of a man to leave his house on the festival. Eliezer criticizes Ilai for visiting him on the festival, rather than remaining at home with his family. It is curious that the following stories have Eliezer say a man must spend the whole day in study with his master or at home, preferably the former, while Joshua says one spends part here, part there.

III.ii.30.A. TNW RBNN M'ŚH B: R. Eliezer was once sitting and expounding the whole day [of the festival] on festival laws.

The first group left. He said, "These are people of butts (PṬSYN)."

The second group. He said, "These are people of casks."

The third—he said, "These are people of pitchers."

The fourth—he said, "These are the people of the curse."

He cast his eyes at his disciples and their faces began to turn pale.

He said to them, "My sons, not of you did I say this, but of those who went out, who put aside eternal life and occupy themselves with temporal life."

B. When they were taking their leave he said to them, "*Go your way, eat the fat and drink the sweet and send portions to him for whom nothing is prepared, for this day is holy unto our Lord. Neither be ye grieved, for the joy of the Lord is your stronghold* (Neh. 8 : 10)."

C. But the enjoyment of the festival is a religious duty?

R. Eliezer is consistent, for he said, "Rejoicing on the festival is optional."

D. For it was taught (TNY'): R. Eliezer says, "On a festival a man has [nothing to do] except either eat and drink, or sit and learn."

R. Joshua says, "Divide it: half for the Lord and half for yourselves."

b. Bes. 15b

*Comment*: The dispute of D is warrant to assign the story of A to Eliezer. Variant readings give Eleazar. But the story illustrates the position of Eliezer in the apodictic law.

No story tells us what Joshua would have done. Eliezer's view is that one may either study the law or eat and drink, and the right thing is to study. Therefore when disciples left for their families, Eliezer insulted, and finally cursed them in the presence of the remaining students. He had then to assure his disciples he did not mean them, so evidently the story-teller assumed that in addition to the disciples ordinary folk came to study with the master on the festival. On that account Eliezer had to assure the disciples it was all right for them to go home; but this would soften his position about doing one thing or the other, but not both. So B seems to be an interpolation, inconsistent with A but consistent with Joshua in D!

III.i.7. TNY in the name of R. Liezer, "He who did not make his *Sukkah* on the eve of the festival should not make it on the festival."

y. Suk. 2 : 7 (b. Suk. 9a, 27b)

III.i.8. TNY: Just as they clear out the *Sukkah* because of rain, so [they do it] because of heat (ŠRḆ) or flies.

Rabban Gamaliel enters and leaves all right.

R. Liezer enters and leaves all right.

y. Suk. 2 : 10

*Comment*: That is, the rabbis would come back when the rain had stopped. They thus hold one must stay in the *Sukkah* as much as possible.

III.ii.31.A. TNY': R. Eliezer says, "They do not go forth from *Sukkah* to *Sukkah*, and they do not make a *Sukkah* on the intermediate days of the festival."

B. And sages say, "They go forth from *Sukkah* to *Sukkah*, and they do make a *Sukkah* on the intermediate days of the festival."

C. And they are of one mind (ŠWYN) that if it falls down, he goes and builds it again on the intermediate days of the festival.

b. Suk. 27a-b

III.ii.32.A. TNYʾ: R. Eliezer says, "Just as a man does not carry out his obligation on the first day of the festival with the *Lulav* of his fellow ... so a man does not carry out his obligation with his *Sukkah* on the festival of *Sukkot.*"

B. And sages say, "Even though they have said, 'A man does not carry out his obligation on the first day of the festival with the *Lulav* of his fellow,' he does carry out his obligation with the *Sukkah* of his fellow."

b. Suk. 27b

*Comment*: These traditions are not known to Mishnah-Tosefta. The form is standard. Both sayings contain glosses, omitted here, supplying appropriate proof-texts. In b. Suk. 27a-b A, Eliezer goes over to the sages' position. y. Suk. 2 : 7 has only the first rule, not its revision. The rule behind b. Suk. 27b concerns *Lulav*; both parties then explain its relationship to *Sukkah*.

II.iv.8.A. R. Eliezer says, "Just as a man does not fulfill his obligation on the first day of the Festival with his fellow's *Lulav*, so he does not fulfill his obligation on the first day of the Festival with the *Sukkah* of his fellow, as it says, *You will make for yourself.*"

B. And sages say, "With his fellow's *Lulav* he does not fulfill his obligation, as it says, *And you will take for yourself* for each one. But he *does* fulfill his obligation with the *Sukkah* of his fellow, as it says, *Every resident in Israel will dwell in Sukkot*—all Israel may dwell in a single *Sukkah.*"

Sifré Deut. 140, Finkelstein, p. 194

III.ii.33. TNW RBNN: In the case of a stolen *Sukkah* or one made by placing *Sukkah*-roofing over a public road—

R. Eliezer declares them invalid.

And the sages declare them valid.

b. Suk. 31a

*Comment*: Eliezer is consistent in requiring private ownership for the objects used to fulfill all the obligations of *Sukkot.*

III.ii.34. TNYʾ: The *Lulav* and all its appurtenances override the Sabbath, the words of R. Eliezer.

b. Suk. 43a

*Comment*: ʿAqiba should be represented here by a negative opinion.

I.ii.64.A. An egg born on the festival—

B. Others said in the name of R. Liezer [y.: Leazar], "Both it and the hen [lit.: its mother] may be eaten.

Tos. Y.T. 1 : 1, Lieberman, p. 279, ls. 1-2 (y. Bes. 1 : 1, b. Bes. 4a)

*Comment*: In M. Bes. 1 : 1 we find the following:

> An egg laid on a festival day—
> The House of Shammai say, "It may be eaten."
> And the House of Hillel say, "It may not be eaten."

Eliezer gives the reason for the position taken by the House of Shammai. The egg may be eaten, even though the man did not intend to do so before the festival, because on the preceding day the hen was ready for the slaughter, and the egg may be eaten on account of the hen's being ready for consumption. The authority of this teaching therefore assigns Liezer to the House of Shammai. Lieberman (*Mo'ed*, pp. 911-913) observes that the pericope before us should stand as the conclusion to M. Bes. 1 : 1. The assumption of Meir, who is the authority for the pericope before us, Lieberman explains, is that the average hen is ready for slaughter. R. Ba, in y., holds the contrary. b. Bes. 4a has, "The egg, the hen, the chicken and its shell may be eaten."

See *Phar.* II, pp. 158ff.

I.ii.65.A. [An egg the greater part of which came forth on the eve of the festival, even though it was completed on the festival, lo, this is permitted.] [If] it was born on the Sabbath, it may be eaten on the festival. [If it was born] on the festival, it may eaten on the Sabbath.

B. R. Judah says in the name of R. Liezer, "The dispute is still in its place."

Tos. Y.T. 1-3, Lieberman, p. 279, ls. 5-7 (b. Bes. 4a)

*Comment*: b. Bes. 4a has:

> If it is laid on a Sabbath, it may be eaten on a festival; on a festival, it may be eaten on a Sabbath.
>
> R. Judah says in the name of R. Eliezer, "The dispute still continues, for the House of Shammai say, 'It may be eaten,' and the House of Hillel say, 'It may not be eaten.'"

Eliezer holds that the Sabbath and festival are two separate sanctities, above, p. 108ff. Therefore something from one is prohibited for the other. But here A sees them as separate sanctities. Eliezer thus takes the opposite of the position assigned to him on that question. One who held they are a single sanctity certainly would prohibit the egg. Judah has Eliezer in the position of the House of Hillel, so Lieberman, *Mo'ed*, p. 917.

II.i.6.A. *Bake that which ye will bake.*

R. Joshua says, "If one liked it baked, it would become baked for him; if one liked it cooked, it would become cooked for him."

B. R. Eleazar of Modiʿim says, "If one liked to eat something baked, he could taste in the manna the taste of any kind of baked things in the world; if one liked to eat something cooked, he could taste in it the taste of any dish in the world."

C. R. Eliezer says, "Adding to what is already baked, you may bake; adding to what is already cooked, you may cook. How so? In the case of a holiday falling on the day preceding the Sabbath—hence can you prove that one is not permitted to bake or to cook on it for the Sabbath unless one has previously performed the ceremony of *ʿeruv*? It is said, *Bake that which ye will bake*—only when adding to what has previously been baked, you may bake, and only when adding to what has previously been cooked, you may cook."

Mekh. Vayassa 5 : 41-50, Lauterbach II, p. 118
(b. Bes. 15b, y. Bes. 2 : 1)

III.ii.35. *Bake that which you will bake, and boil that which you will boil* (Ex. 16 : 23). From this R. Eliezer says, "You may bake only [in dependence on] what is already baked and boil only in dependence on what is already boiled."

Herein the sages found biblical support for *ʿeruv tavshilin.*

[*y. adds*: R. Joshua says, "They bake and boil [in dependence] on what is already boiled."]

b. Bes. 15b (y. Bes. 2 : 1)

*Comment*: M. Bes. 2 : 1 says, "A man may prepare a dish on the eve of the festival and rely upon it to prepare food for the Sabbath." Eliezer supplies an exegetical foundation for that rule. In Mekh. his saying, C, is separate and distinct from the exegeses attributed to Joshua and Eleazar. They relate to *manna.* Eliezer interprets the verse as evidence that in the case of a festival coming before the Sabbath, one may prepare an *ʿeruv* to cover both days. In b. Bes. this point is made explicit.

I.i.74.A. R. Eliezer says, "A man takes a wood-splinter (QYSM) (Lieberman omits) from that which is before him [on the ground, and not prepared for that purpose, on the festival] with which to pick his teeth. And he heaps up from [that which is in] the courtyard and kindles [a fire]. For all which is in the courtyard is [regarded as] ready [from before the festival, and may be used on the festival]."

B. And sages say, "He heaps up [only] from that which is before him and kindles [a fire]."

M. Bes. 4 : 6 (y. Bes. 1 : 4, 4 : 6; b. Bes. 33a-b)

I.i.75.A. (They do not produce fire either out of wood or out of stones or out of dirt or out of water, nor do they heat white-hot the tiles to roast thereon.)

B. And further did R. Eliezer say, "A man stands by the rear court (MQṢH) on the eve of the Sabbath in the Seventh Year and says, 'From here I shall eat tomorrow.'"

C. And sages say, "Only if he marks it out and says, 'From here to here.'"

M. Bes. 4 : 7 (y. Bes. 1 : 4, 4 : 7;
b. Bes. 38a-b, 34a-b, 35a-b; y. Ma. 1 : 4)

*Comment*: In M. Bes. 4 : 6A, Eliezer rules leniently, that on the festival a man may make use of a splinter with which to pick his teeth, even though the wood was not set aside for that purpose on the preceding day. Likewise, he may gather wood from the whole courtyard.

The sages do not allude to the first issue. In the second they say he takes only what is before him in the house, but not from the courtyard. What is in the house has been made ready before the festival, but not what is in the courtyard.

M. Bes. 4 : 7A is an interpolation in the repertoire of Eliezer's rulings. It is not pertinent, but because the foregoing has dealt with making fire with wood, it has been introduced here.

In B, Eliezer's saying is introduced with the past tense, *said*, rather than the usual *says*, because of its position in the list of his rulings. Eliezer refers to the rear court, which is explained (Albeq, *Seder Mo'ed*, p. 298), as a place where fruit is spread out for drying. In the Seventh Year, tithes are not required from the fruit. One is permitted to eat them on the Sabbath if he prepared them before the Sabbath. The preparation involved, according to Eliezer, is the designation, "From here (in general) I shall take food tomorrow." The sages say that the designation must be specific. The man has to signify the place and state its limits.

Eliezer is consistent with the view of the House of Hillel, the sages, with the House of Shammai, in M. Bes. 1 : 3 (as is noted by y. Bes. 1 : 4, 4 : 7):

> The House of Shammai say, "A man may not take pigeons for slaughtering on a festival day, unless he stirred them up [handled] them the day before."
>
> And the House of Hillel say, "He need only go up and say, 'This one and this one I shall take.'"

Here, like the House of Hillel, Eliezer says the man merely states his intention. The House of Shammai and the sages require a specific act of designation, in the former case, handling the pigeons, in the latter, marking the place.

The sayings in 4 : 6 are not properly matched. But the second clause of Eliezer matches the saying of the sages:

Eliezer: WMGBB MN HḤṢR WMDLYQ (ŠKL MH ŠBḤṢR MWKN HW' is a gloss)

Sages: MGBB MŠLPNYW WMDLYQ.

This makes all the more striking the omission of a matching opinion about the toothpicks. In 4 : 7 the sages' opinion depends upon Eliezer's for context and meaning; *Only if he*... takes for granted the whole of his saying.

See Epstein, *Nusaḥ*. pp. 113, 1012, 1181; *Tan.*, pp. 93, 302, 359-60. Tan., p. 359: The authority is Simeon.

I.ii.66.A. R. Liezer says, "A man takes a splinter with which to pick his teeth."

And sages say, "He should take only from the cattle-crib and only on condition that he may not cut it off (QṬM) in order to pick his teeth with it."

C. If he cut it off (QṬM) on the Sabbath, he is liable for a Sin-offering; on the festival, he is flagellated forty [lashes].

D. R. Liezer says, "He sweeps up the courtyard and kindles [a fire with the chips]."

E. "Only that he should not make piles (ṢBWRYN)." [y.: Eliezer says he *may* do so.]

F. And R. Simeon permits, for the whole courtyard is ready (MWKN).

Tos. Y.T. 3 : 18, Lieberman, p. 298,
ls. 61-65 (y. Bes. 4 : 6; b. Bes. 33b)

*Comment*: Now B supplies the sages' opinion, missing in 4 : 6A, on the toothpick. The man may make use of a piece of straw from the cattle-crib, for whatever is ready for eating may be used for any purpose. But the wood may be carried only for adding to a fire.

Part C carries forward *and solely that he may not cut off.* b. Bes. 53b has it as follows:

> And they are of one mind that he may not cut off a piece and if he did cut off to pick his teeth or to open a door with it—
>
> "If he did it unwittingly on a Sabbath, he is liable to a Sin-offering, and if he did it deliberately on a festival, he is liable to receive forty lashes," this is the opinion of R. Eliezer.
>
> But the sages say, "Both the one and the other are forbidden only as *Shevut.*"

Accordingly, the final clause in the sages' opinion as given in B is assigned to both parties. But Tos. clearly assigns *and solely*, etc., to the sages. So they prohibit cutting the straw off for a tooth-pick.

Part D is the same as 4 : 6A, without the gloss, *for all*... But then it is qualified. Eliezer says the man cannot sweep up the chips into piles. Simeon permits doing so. So Eliezer's position in 4 : 6A is clarified; one *may* sweep, but not into little heaps. But the gloss of Simeon is assigned to Eliezer in the Mishnaic parallel.

See Lieberman, *Tosefta Kifshuṭah Seder Mo*ʿ*ed*, pp. 989-991. He points out that neither the Babylonian nor the Palestinian Talmud's tradition on this point is consistent with Tos. b. omits reference to Eliezer, and y. concludes that Eliezer says one *may* make the chips into heaps. None of the early commentators paid attention to Tos.

I.ii.67. It [the animal] and its offspring which fell into the pit—

A. R. Liezer says, "He raises the first on condition of slaughtering it and slaughtered it, and the second he feeds in its place, so that it will not die."

B. R. Joshua says, "He raises the first in order to slaughter it but does not slaughter it, and uses subtlety [in not slaughtering the first] (MʿRYM) and raises the second." [y. adds: *Even though he did not in advance plan to slaughter one of them, it is permitted.* b. adds: *And he may slaughter whichever he wants.*]

Tos. Y.T. 3 : 2, Lieberman, p. 293, ls. 1-10
(y. Bes. 3 : 4, b. Bes. 37a; b. Shab. 117b, 124a, y. Pes. 3 : 3)

*Comment*: The pertinent Mishnah is M. Bes. 3 : 4:

> If a firstling [which may be slaughtered outside the Temple only if it is blemished] fell into a pit [on the festival]—
>
> R. Judah says, "Let a skilled person go down and look at it. If it has incurred a blemish, let him bring it up and slaughter it; otherwise it may not be slaughtered."
>
> R. Simeon says, "In that its blemish was not perceived on the day before, it cannot count as what is set in unreadiness."

Judah therefore holds that if there was no blemish, it is not regarded as in readiness for slaughter from the preceding day and therefore may not be slaughtered.

But the rule about an ordinary beast which fell into a pit is not given; we do not know whether it is permitted to raise it up to slaughter it, or even *not* to slaughter it (in the latter instance, out of kindness to animals). The same issue is before us. One cannot slaughter the animal and its offspring on the same day. One of the animals is not available for slaughter at all. Eliezer says· one raises up the one that may be slaughtered. The other is to be left. Joshua says one raises both—the first for slaughter, but then the slaughter does not take place, and afterward, the second is raised up. But even Joshua permits raising up only in order to slaughter.

See Lieberman, *Seder Moʿed*, p. 965.

## xvii. Rosh Hashanah, Taʿanit, Megillah, Moʿed Qaṭan, Ḥagigah.

I.ii.68.A. R. Judah says R. Liezer says, "*A solemn rest* (Lev. 23 : 24) means (ʾWMR) the sanctification of the day. *A memorial*—these are the Memorial verses (*Zikhronot*, in the Additional Service of the New Year). [*Proclaimed with the blast of*] *trumpets*—these are the

*Shofar*-verses. *A holy convocation*—sanctify it [by not working]."

B. R. ʿAqiba said to him, "Why should we not say, *A solemn rest—Shevut* [a solemn rest means one should abstain from work], for lo, it touches on resting first of all. But *A memorial*—these are the Memorial verses. *Trumpets*—These are the *Shofar*-verses. *A holy convocation*—These [refer to] the Sanctification of the day."

Tos. R.H. 2 : 10, Lieberman, pp. 315-316, ls. 39-44
(Sifra Emor Parashah 11 : 1, Weiss, p. 101b)

III.ii.36.A. Our rabbis taught: Whence do we learn that we are to say Kingship, Remembrance and *Shofar* [verses]?

B. R. Eliezer says, "Because it is written, *A solemn rest, a memorial proclaimed with the blast of trumpets, a holy convocation* (Lev. 23 : 24). *A solemn rest*—this indicates the sanctification of the day. *A memorial*—this indicates Remembrance verses. *Proclaimed with the blast of horns*—this indicates Shofar verses. *A holy convocation*—sanctify it by [abstaining from] the doing of work."

C. Said R. ʿAqiba to him, "Why should we not interpret *a solemn rest* to apply to the abstention from work, seeing that the text placed this first? No, [we should interpret thus]: *A solemn rest*; sanctify it by [abstaining from] the doing of work. *A memorial*; this indicates the remembrance verses. *Proclaimed with the blowing of horns*: this indicates *shofar*-verses. *A holy convocation*: this indicates the sanctification of the day."

b. R.H. 32a, trans. M. Simon, p. 154

*Comment*: The *baraita* in b. R.H. 32a omits reference to Judah as the authority of Eliezer's saying. It also supplies a full citation of the Scripture under discussion by Eliezer and ʿAqiba. Eliezer says that the 'solemn rest' refers to the sanctification of the day, see Lieberman, *Seder Moʿed*, p. 1051, n. 50.

I.i.76.A. From what time [in the year] do they make mention of the 'powers of rain' [adding the prayer, 'He restores the wind and brings down rain,' to the Eighteen Benedictions]?

B. R. Eliezer says, "From the first festival day of the Festival (ḤG) [of *Sukkot*]."

C. R. Joshua says, "From the last festival day of the Festival."

D. R. Joshua said to him, "Since rains are nothing but a sign of curse on the festival, why does he mention [them before the end]?"

E. R. Eliezer said to him, "Also (ʾP) I did not say to *beseech*, but to *mention*, 'He restores the wind and brings down rain' in its season [when the rain is wanted]." [y.: "*In its season it is as beloved as the resurrection of the dead.*"]

F. He said to him, "If so, he should always mention [it, through the whole year]."

M. Ta. 1 : 1 (y. Ta. 1 : 1, b. Ta. 2a-b, 4a-b)

*Comment*: The relationship of the prayer for rain to the festival of *Sukkot* is conceded by all parties. Rains generally start at that time, and the cult is directed toward effecting them. Since on the festival of *Sukkot* Heaven decides on the rains of the coming year (M. R.H. 1 : 2), Eliezer says the appropriate prayer on *Sukkot* is introduced into the Eighteen Benedictions. Joshua points out that one does not want rain before the end of the festival—for the people are supposed to be living in the *Sukkah*—and therefore it should be mentioned at the end. Eliezer's reply is that one does not say, "Give dew and rain," added to the ninth benediction later on, but rather, the specified remembrance, which asks for rain *in its season*—but not now. In that case, Joshua replies, why should it not be said all the time? That is a good reply, but it begs the question. The debate is not impressive; the differences between the two parties are not clarified, and such underlying principles as may inhere in their respective positions do not emerge.

See Epstein, *Nusaḥ*, pp. 251, 715.

III.i.9. TNY: R. Liezer says, "From the time of taking the *Lulav.*" R. Joshua says, "From the time of putting it down."

y. Ta. 1 : 1 (b. Ta. 2b)

*Comment*: This corresponds to the answer of R. Abbahu, What was Eliezer's basis? He says Eliezer deduced the rule from an analogy to the *Lulav.*

I.i.77. [If] they fasted and rains fell before dawn, they should not complete [the fast through the whole day]; after dawn, they should complete [the fast.]

B. R. Eliezer says, "Before noon—they should not complete [it]. After noon—they should complete [it]."

C. MʿŠH Š: They decreed a fast in Lydda, and rain fell before noon. R. Ṭarfon said to them, "Go and eat and drink and celebrate a holiday."

They went and ate and drank and celebrated a holiday. They came in the afternoon and read the Great Hallel.

M. Ta. 3 : 9 (y. Ta. 3 : 11, b. Ta. 19a)

*Comment*: The anonymous rule takes *dawn* as the dividing point, Eliezer takes *noon.* B depends upon A for context and meaning; Eliezer supplies a different operative clause for it, *noon* instead of *dawn.*

Ṭarfon's story depends upon Eliezer's rule, in specifying noon rather than dawn. It tells us that the local authority in Eliezer's town, presumably after Eliezer's death, followed his rule.

See Epstein, *Nusaḥ*, p. 972.

I.ii.69.A. MʿŚH W: They decreed a fast on *Ḥanukkah* in Lud.

B. They told it to R. Liezer, and he got a haircut [b.: washed]; to R. Joshua, and he washed [b.: got a haircut].

C. R. Joshua said to them, "Go and fast in atonement for having fasted [on *Ḥanukkah*]."

Tos. Ta. 2 : 5, Lieberman, p. 331, ls. 36-38
(b. R.H. 18b; y. Ta. 2 : 12; Told by Yoḥanan:
y. Meg. 1 : 4; y. Ned. 8 : 1)

*Comment*: Eliezer and Joshua say one does not fast on *Ḥanukkah*, and if one began such a fast, he must stop even in the middle. The story is pertinent to the following:

> They do not decree a public fast on the first day of the month or during *Ḥanukkah* or at Purim.
>
> "But if they had begun, they may not interrupt the fast"—the words of Rabban Gamaliel.
>
> M. Ta. 2 : 10

Eliezer's and Joshua's opinions would be, *They do interrupt*. Their view is not formulated as an apodictic law, rather only in the story before us.

III.ii.37.A. TNW RBNN MʿŚH B: R. Eliezer ordained thirteen fasts upon the community and no rain fell. In the end, as the people began to depart [from the synagogue], he exclaimed, "Have you prepared graves for yourselves?" Thereupon the people sobbed loudly and rain fell.

B. ŠWB MʿŚH B: R. Eliezer stepped down before the Ark and recited the twenty-four benedictions [for fast days] and his prayer was not answered. R. ʿAqiba stepped down after him and exclaimed, "Our Father, our King, we have no King but Thee, our Father, our King, for Thy sake have mercy upon us." And rain fell.

C. The rabbis present suspected [R. Eliezer], whereupon an echo went forth and said, "[The prayer of] this man [R. ʿAqiba was answered] not because he is greater than the other man, but because he is ever forbearing and the other is not (MʿBYR ʿL MDWTYW)."

b. Ta. 25b, trans. J. Rabbinowitz, p. 132

*Comment*: A is to be assigned to Eliezer b. Hyrcanus because of B. A is neutral. Eliezer advised the people that they did not pray with the proper urgency; when they did, it rained. B is a similar story, but now,

*Eliezer*'s prayers, not the people's, are not answered, ʿAqiba's prayers are answered instead. C then explains matters—as if it were not clear—that ʿAqiba was of greater spiritual worth than Eliezer, because Eliezer is not forbearing (following Rabbinowitz's translation of ʿBR ʿL MDWT). The story then is ʿAqiban and sets the master's merits below those of the disciple.

Note also b. Ta. 2b, references to M. Ta. 1 : 1 by Judah b. Ilai and Rabbi [Judah the Patriarch], thus an Ushan attestation. I am not sure whether the sayings attributed to ʿAqiba and Judah b. Batyra attest the pericope to Yavnean times, in its present form.

I.i.78. (If a man buried his dead three days before the Feast [of *Sukkot*], the rule of seven [days' mourning] is annulled for him. For they have said, "The Sabbath is included [in the first seven days], but does not interrupt [the seven days], while the festivals interrupt and are not included."—M. M.Q. 3 : 5).

A. R. Eliezer says, "Since the Temple has been destroyed, *ʿAṣṣeret* [*Shavuʿot*] is like the Sabbath."

B. Rabban Gamaliel says, "The New Year and the Day of Atonement are like the festivals."

C. And sages say, "Not according to the words of this one, and not according to the words of that one [is the law], but *ʿAṣṣeret* is like the festivals, and the New Year and the Day of Atonement are like the Sabbath."

M. M.Q. 3 : 6 (y. M.Q. 3 : 6, b. M.Q. 19a, 24a)

*Comment*: Eliezer's and Gamaliel's sayings take for granted the preceding rule in its present formulation; once it is established that something is "like the Sabbath," the meaning and law follow naturally.

According to Eliezer, *ʿAṣṣeret* counts in the 'seven' and the 'thirty' but does not interrupt—that is, it is added to the total. But in Temple times, when a person who did not bring his offerings on the festival could bring them all six days after *Shavuot* as after all the other festivals (M. Hag. 2 : 4), *ʿAṣṣeret* was regarded as similar to the other festivals, which interrupt but are not included.

Gamaliel does not differ from Eliezer's rule; he has another.

Then the sages reject both—nothing has changed, so far as *ʿAṣṣeret* is concerned, in consequence of the destruction of the Temple.

III.ii.38. (R. Judah says, "A person may write [the Scriptural sections for] the *tefillin* or *mezuzot* for himself and may spin on his thigh the blue-wool for his fringe.—M. M.Q. 3 : 4).

A. TNW RBNN: "A person may spin on his thigh the blue thread for his fringe, but not do so with a stone [as a spindle-whorl]"—the words of R. Eliezer.

B. But sages say, "Even with a stone."

C. R. Judah says in his name, "With a stone, but not with a spindle. But the sages say, 'Either with a stone or with a spindle.'"

b. M.Q. 19a

*Comment*: Judah's tradition on the Mishnah derives from, or is attributed to, Eliezer in A, but without the qualification as to not using a stone. But this seems implied by reference in the Mishnah to *his thigh*. That surely excludes the sages' stone. Then Judah in C contradicts Judah in M. M.Q. 3 : 4.

III.i.10. [Mishnah: He whose dead (still) lies before him (unburied) is free (of the obligation of) saying the *Shemaᶜ* and of the *tefillin*.]

TNY: *And of the tefillin.*

A. "A mourner on the first day does not put on *tefillin*. On the second day he does put on *tefillin*. But if new faces [comforters] come, he removes them, for all seven days"—the words of R. Eliezer.

R. Joshua says, "On the first and on the second day, he does not put on *tefillin*. On the third day, he does put on *tefillin*, but if new faces come, he does not remove them."

B. R. Zeᶜira, R. Jeremiah in the name of Rav [stated], "The law follows R. Eliezer as to putting on [*tefillin*] and R. Joshua as to removing them."

C. From what time do they overturn the beds?

"From when the corpse has gone forth from the door of the courtyard," the words of R. Eliezer.

R. Joshua says, "From when the boulder [grave-stone] has sealed [the grave]."

D. And when R. Gamaliel (R"G) died, after [his corpse] had gone forth from the gate of the courtyard, R. Eliezer said to his disciples, "Overturn the beds."

And then the boulder had sealed [the grave], R. Joshua said, "Overturn the beds."

They said to him, "You [Alt.: *we*] have already overturned them according to the authority of the elder."

y. Ber. 3 : 1, Gil'ead, pp. 42, 43 (b. M.Q. 27a, y. M.Q. 3 : 5)

*Comment*: What is interesting for biographical purposes is C-D. Here, a generalized law in C is then shown in D to have been carried out by the respective masters in accord with their own views. Eliezer instructed his disciples to overturn the beds as soon as the corpse passed out of the courtyard. It is noteworthy that Joshua is given no disciples. He simply tells Eliezer's what to do, and they reply that they have done what their master told them—the authority (ʿL PY) of the elder has been carried out. So Joshua is represented as subordinate to Eliezer, who is not older in years, but the Elder in authority.

According to the story, Eliezer survived Gamaliel; other stories make clear that Joshua outlived Eliezer. If we had a usable date for the death of Gamaliel, we might be able to propose a chronology for other Yavneans. Elsewhere, Eliezer's curse is credited with the death of Gamaliel, below pp. 423-424.

IV.i.10. "A mourner on the first day [of his mourning-period] does not place [put on] *Tefillin*. On the second day, he puts on *Tefillin*. If new faces came [to comfort him], he takes them off all seven [days]"—the words of R. Liezer.

B. R. Joshua says, "On the first and on the second day he does not put on *Tefillin*. On the third day he puts on *Tefillin*. If new faces come, he does not take them off."

y. M.Q. 3 : 5 (y. Ber. 3 : 1; M. Semaḥot 6 : 3,
trans. Zlotnick, p. 48; Gen. R. 100 : 7)

*Comment*: Before burial, the mourner is free of the obligation of wearing *Tefillin* (M. Ber. 3 : 1). The rule for the days after burial is given above.

IV.i.11.A. From what time do they turn over the beds?

B. "After the corpse has gone forth from the gate of the courtyard"—the words of R. Liezer.

C. And R. Joshua says, "When the stone has closed [the tomb]."

D. And when Rabban Gamaliel [b. adds: *the Elder*] died, after they had gone from the gate of the courtyard, R. Liezer said to *his* disciples, [b.: *to them*], "Turn over the [b.: *your*] beds."

And then the stone had closed [the tomb], R. Joshua said to *the* disciples, "Turn over the beds."

E. They said to him, "We have already turned them over at the instructions of the elder."

y. M.Q. 3 : 5 (b. M.Q. 27a, y. Ber. 3 : 1;
M. Semaḥot 11 : 19, trans. Zlotnick, p. 80; b. Ket. 4b)

III.ii.39.A. TNW RBNN: "The mourner on the three first days [of the seven] is prohibited from putting on *Tefillin*. From the third day following—including the third day—it is permitted to put on *Tefillin* and if new faces come he does not remove them"—the words of R. Eliezer.

B. R. Joshua says, "The mourner on the first two days is

prohibited from putting on *Tefillin.* From the second—and the second is included—he is permitted to put on *Tefillin*, and if new faces come, he removes them."

b. M.Q. 21a

*Comment*: The Babylonian tradition differs from the Palestinian one. In y. M.Q. Eliezer regards the first two days as different from the rest; but the man takes off the *Tefillin* if new comforters arrive. Here he puts them on from the third day, but does *not* remove them—the position of Joshua in y. M.Q.! Then Joshua takes Eliezer's position as to removing the *Tefillin* if new people come.

y. Ber. 3 : 1: R. Zeʿirah, R. Jeremiah in the name of Rav: "The law is according to R. Eliezer in putting on, and R. Joshua in taking off." The same tradition is in y. M.Q. 3 : 1.

III.i.11. TNY MʿŚH Š: The serving-maid of R. Eliezer died, and his disciples came to console him, but he would not receive [them]. He went before them to the court, and they followed after him; to the house, and they followed after him.

He said to them, "I thought that you would be scalded in luke-warm water, but you are not scalded even in boiling water. And have they not said, 'They do not receive consolation for slaves because slaves are like cattle.' If for other free beasts they do not receive consolation, all the more so for slaves. One says to him whose slave or ox dies, 'May the Omnipresent replace your loss.'"

y. Ber. 2 : 8, Gilead, p. 39

*Comment*: We do not know for certain that this is our Eliezer.

The pericope illustrates the apodictic teaching, also assigned to Gamaliel, that one does not receive consolation for slaves, followed by a story that Gamaliel *did* receive consolation on the death of Ṭabi his slave. The story may illustrate the contrary principle through the behavior of Eliezer, Gamaliel's contemporary. However, that is slender evidence on the basis of which to assign the story to Eliezer b. Hyrcanus.

The saying, cited verbatim in both stories, must come before Gamaliel or in his time, since both he and Eliezer are represented as having taught it, evidently not as a private instruction but as a citation of an existing rule of mourning.

III.ii.40.A. TNW RBNN: For male and female slaves, no row [of comforters] is formed, nor is the blessing of mourners said, nor is condolence offered.

B. MʿŚH W: The female slave of R. Eliezer died. His disciples came to console him.

When he saw them, he went up to the upper room, and they went up after him. He went into the anteroom (ʾNPLYWN), and they went in after him. He went into the dining room. They went in after him.

He said to them, "It seemed to me that you would be scalded with warm water. Now, you are not scalded even with the hottest.

C. "Did I not teach you, 'As to male and female slaves—they do not stand over them in a row, and they do not say on their account the blessing of mourners or the condolences of mourners. But what do they say concerning them? Just what they say to a man on account of his ox and his ass which have died: 'May the Omnipresent replace your loss.' So they say to him concerning his male and female slave, 'The Omnipresent may replace your loss.'"

b. Ber. 16b

V.ii.1.A. One does not receive condolences for slaves. It happened that when Rabbi Eliezer's maidservant died, his disciples came to comfort him. He withdrew into the courtyard, but they followed him. He then went into the house. Again they followed him.

"I thought you would be scalded by tepid water," said he to them, "but even boiling water does not seem to burn you. Have I not taught you that one does not receive condolences for slaves, because slaves are regarded as the same as cattle?"

B. When Rabbi Gamaliel's slave, Ṭabi, died, the Sage accepted condolences for him.

Mourning (Semaḥot) 1 : 10, trans. Dov Zlotnick, p. 32

II.iii.7. "*His clothing will be rent* (PRWMYM)—it will be torn (QRWʿYM). *And his head will be PRWʿ*—to grow loose"—the words of R. Eliezer.

R. ʿAqiba says, "*Shall be* is said with reference to his head, and *shall be* is said in reference to his clothing. Just as *shall be* said in reference to the clothing refers to things which are outside of his body, so *shall be* said in reference to his head refers to things external to his body."

Sifra Tazriʿa Pereq 12 : 6, Weiss, p. 67b

III.ii.41.A. Should a leper wear *Tefillin*? Come and hear:

B. "*And the leper [in whom the plague is, his clothes shall be rent and the hair of his head shall be loose* (Lev. 13 : 45)]—to include the high priest. *His clothes shall be torn*—that they should be rent (PRWMYM/MQWRʿYM). *And his head will be loose—Loose* refers only to growing the hair"—the words of R. Eliezer.

R. ʿAqiba says, "*Shall be* is said in connection with the head of the leper, and *shall be* is said in reference to the leper's garment. Just as *shall be* said in reference to the clothing refers to something external to his body, so *shall be* in reference to the head is something external to his body."

b. M.Q. 15a

*Comment*: The exegetical dispute is taken, in b. M.Q. 15a, to mean that the leper should not wear *tefillin*. The context is a discussion of the mourner's wearing *tefillin*; then the leper is introduced.

IV.ii.8. (An oven stove or mill may be set up during the festival [week]. R. Judah says, "A pair of millstones is not to be compressed for the first time [in the festival week.]"—M. M.Q. 1 : 9.)

A. "They set up an oven, stove and mill in the festival-week, on condition that he should not complete their preparation"—the words of R. Eliezer.

B. And sages say, "He may even finish."

C. R. Judah says in his name, "They set up the new, and an old [mill] may be compressed."

D. And some say, "They do not press at all."

b. M.Q. 10a

*Comment*: The Mishnah omits Eliezer's condition about not completing the work. It therefore is a teaching of the sages of b. M.Q. Judah's tradition in the Mishnah differs from that attributed by him to Eliezer.

III.ii.42.A. TNW RBNN: "If one overturned the couch [as an act of mourning] three days before the festival, he does not overturn it afterward," the words of R. Eliezer.

And sages say, "Even if he had done so only one day or even one hour."

R. Simeon b. Eleazar said, "These are the opinions of the House of Shammai and of the House of Hillel, for the House of Shammai say, 'For three days,' and the House of Hillel say, 'Even for one day.'"

b. M.Q. 20a (M. Semaḥot 7 : 1; b. Meg. 26a)

*Comment*: See *Phar.* II, pp. 182-183. But y. Meg. 3 : 1 has Eliezer b. R. Ṣaddoq.

## xviii. YEVAMOT

III.ii.43. b. Yev. 80a, = M. Nid. 5 : 1, *re* Houses on what evidence shows one is a eunuch at eighteen or twenty. Eliezer rules in the same pericope. See *Phar.* II, p. 301. Warrant for including the pericope in Eliezer b. Hyrcanus's tradition is in M. Yev. 13 : 6-7, below, p. 172.

I.i.79.A. R. Joshua said, "I heard that the eunuch submits to *ḥaliṣah* and that they [his brothers] submit to *ḥaliṣah* from his wife; and [I heard another tradition that] the eunuch does *not* submit to *ḥaliṣah* and that [his brothers] do *not* submit to *ḥaliṣah* from his wife. And I have no explanation."

B. R. ʿAqiba said, "I shall explain. He who was made a eunuch by man submits to *ḥaliṣah* and [his brothers] submit to *ḥaliṣah* by his wife, because he had a time [in which he was] fitting (ŠʿT HKŠR) [Danby: "There was a time when he was potent"].

"But one who was made a eunuch by the sun [by nature] does not submit to *ḥaliṣah* and [his brothers] do not submit to *ḥaliṣah* by his wife, because he did not have a time [in which he was] fitting."

C. R. Eliezer says, "Not so, but the eunuch [sterilized by] the sun submits to *ḥaliṣah* and [his brothers] submit to *ḥaliṣah* by his wife, because he has a remedy.

"But one made a eunuch by man does not submit to *ḥaliṣah* and [his brothers] do not submit to *ḥaliṣah* by his wife, because he has no remedy."

D. R. Joshua b. Batyra gave testimony concerning Ben Megusat who lived in Jerusalem, a eunuch [made by] man, and they contracted Levirate marriage with his wife"—to back up the words [opinion] of R. ʿAqiba.

M. Yev. 8 : 4 (y. Yev. 8 : 4,
b. Yev. 79b, 80a; b. Bekh. 42b)

*Comment*: Joshua has contradictory traditions on the Levirate rules pertaining to the eunuch. Eliezer and ʿAqiba attempt to sort them out. Both introduce the same distinction, between the sources of the man's sterilization—man *vs.* nature. They then differ as to the consequence of each. They supply reasons for their rulings, so they evidently had no firm tradition, but had to rely upon logic to explain the contradictory traditions.

Joshua's traditions consisted of *eunuch—ḤLṢ —+/- —not.* ʿAqiba then assigned the *eunuch + ḤLṢ* to the eunuch made by man, and the *eunuch + ḤLṢ + not* to the eunuch made by nature. Eliezer held the opposite. The *because*-clauses are in rough mnemonic balance: *because + he has/had +* the operative words: ŠʿT HKŠR *vs.* RPWʾH. The opinions are fully articulated; on the surface neither depends for context and meaning on the other, but, as is clear, giving a reason is superfluous except in the presence of an opposing opinion and alternative reason.

Joshua b. Batyra's precedent cannot have been known to Joshua, for if it had, he would not have turned to Eliezer and ʿAqiba. The precedent makes clear that the Jerusalemite, who was a eunuch made by man, entered Levirate marriage, therefore would have submitted to *ḥaliṣah*. The gloss, *to back up ʿAqiba*, makes obvious what already is self-evident. The form of Joshua b. Batyra's precedent is ʿL (concerning), plus the subject and necessary adjectives, then the verb; precedents frequently come in the MʿŚH B form; if we substituted MʿŚH B for ʿL, we should have to make no further changes in the subject or predicate of the sentence. On the form of precedents in Houses-materials, see *Phar.* III, pp. 28-30.

III.ii.44. R. Eliezer says, "A eunuch by the sun submits to *ḥaliṣah* and his wife performs *ḥaliṣah* because such as he are healed in Alexandria, Egypt.

b. Yev. 80a

*Comment*: This expands the *remedy*-clause. On M. Yev. 8 : 4 see Epstein, *Nusaḥ*, p. 384; *Tan.*, p. 429.

I.i.80. (The rite of *ḥaliṣah* must be performed before three judges (DYNYN), even though the three are laymen (HDWYṬWT). If the woman performed *ḥaliṣah* with a shoe, it is valid; with a felt sock, it is not valid; with a sandal that has a heel piece, it is valid; with one that has no heel piece, it is not valid. [If the straps of the sandal were fastened] below the knee, her *ḥaliṣah* is valid; above the knee, it is not valid—M. Yev. 12 : 1.)

A. If she performed *ḥaliṣah* with a shoe that did not belong to the brother-in-law, or with a wooden sandal, or with a left-foot-shoe worn on the right foot, her *ḥaliṣah* is valid. If she performed it with a shoe that was too large for him, but such that he could walk in it, or with a shoe that was too small for him but such that it covered the greater part of his foot, her *ḥaliṣah* is valid.

B. She performed *ḥaliṣah* at night—her *ḥaliṣah* is valid.

C. And R. Eliezer [b.: Eleazar] declares invalid.

D. [If she performed *ḥaliṣah*] with the left foot, her *ḥaliṣah* is invalid.

E. And R. Eliezer [b.: Eleazar] declares it valid.

M. Yev. 12 : 2 (y. Yev. 12 : 2; b. Yev. 104a)

I.i.81.A. If she drew off the shoe and spat but did not pronounce the prescribed words (QRʾ), her *ḥaliṣah* is valid. If she pronounced the words and spat but did not draw off the shoe, her *ḥaliṣah* is invalid.

B. [If] she drew off the shoe and read [pronounced the words] but did not spit—

C. R. Eliezer says, "Her *ḥaliṣah* is invalid."

D. R. ʿAqiba says, "Her *ḥaliṣah* is valid."

E. R. Eliezer said, "*Thus it will be done* (Y'ŚH) (Deut. 25 : 9)—everything which is a deed (M'ŚH) [if not done] impairs [the effectiveness of the ceremony]."

F. R. ʿAqiba said to him, "From there [do you bring] proof? *Thus will be done to the man* (Deut. 25 : 9)—every thing which is a deed in respect to the man [impairs the ceremony, but spitting is a deed in respect to the woman.]"

M. Yev. 12 : 3 (y. Yev. 12 : 3, b. Yev. 104a-b, 105a)

*Comment*: In M. Yev. 12 : 2 we have an anonymous list of *ḥaliṣah*-rules. Eliezer glosses a minor detail of the list. If the *ḥaliṣah*-ceremony took place at night, it is invalid, for, Eliezer holds, *ḥaliṣah* is a matter of court-action, and courts are in session only by day (M. Sanh. 4 : 1). The anonymous rule evidently is based on the supposition that it is not a court-affair—despite the opening statement that the ceremony is performed before three judges. The gloss then changes that rule, even though they are three ordinary people—HDYWṬWT, rather than DYNYN! So the anonymous rule begins consistent with Eliezer's position, but then has been changed by *even though*, and Eliezer's view is left a private matter, rather than normative.

D holds that if the *ḥaliṣah* ceremony is performed with the left foot, it is invalid. Scripture states that the woman removes his sandal from his foot and spits before him, without specifying which foot is involved. The anonymous list of rules required the right foot; Eliezer found no Scriptural warrant for that rule. Eliezer in both instances therefore depends upon Scripture for the definition of the way the rite is to be carried on.

Scripture refers (Deut. 25 : 9) to the *elders*, understood by Eliezer to mean the judges; the glossator as well as the authority behind B evidently did not interpret elders specifically to mean *judges.* Likewise Scripture says in *in the eyes of*, which ought to mean only in daytime.

M. Yev. 12 : 3A continues the foregoing list, following its simple form: she performed *ḥaliṣah* in such and such a way, but she did not . . . . At issue between ʿAqiba and Eliezer is the act of spitting. Eliezer, as earlier, closely follows Scripture in its plain sense. The law is that the woman must spit. She did not spit. Therefore the act is invalid. ʿAqiba says that the act remains valid. Eliezer points out that Scripture explicitly requires spitting. ʿAqiba's exegesis depends upon *to the man* as an exclusionary clause: to the man *and not to the woman.* The spitting is done by the woman, therefore its omission will not impair the effectiveness of the rite. What action would impair the rite? If the sandal were not removed from the man's foot, the rite would be ineffective. But the spitting, which has nothing to do with the man himself, does not impair it.

On M. Yev. 12 : 2-3, see Epstein, *Nusaḥ*, pp. 195, 258, 1064 n. 3; and *Tan.*, p. 99.

I.ii.70. R. Judah said, "If R. Liezer saw a wooden sandal of the present time, he would say concerning it, 'Lo it is like an [acceptable] sandal in every respect.'"

Tos. Yev. 12 : 11, Lieberman, p. 43, ls. 47-8 (y. Yev. 12 : 2)

*Comment*: M. Yev. 12 : 2 specifically states that a wooden sandal is valid, but this presumably is only after the fact. Evidently Judah had a tradition in Eliezer's name that held it either was never valid, or was valid only after the fact, probably the latter. But that tradition is not alluded to in M. Yev. 12 : 2.

II.iv.9.A. If she read but did not spit—

R. Eliezer says, "Her *ḥaliṣah* is invalid."

And R. ʿAqiba says, "Her *ḥaliṣah* is valid."

B. *Thus shall be done*—

R. Eliezer said, "*Thus shall be done*—in a matter which involves action the ceremony is spoiled."

R. ʿAqiba said to him, "Is there proof from there? *Thus shall be done to the man*—something involving the man [but not the woman] may spoil the ceremony."

Sifré Deut. 291, Finkelstein, p. 310 (b. Men. 82a, b. Nid. 37b, Midrash Tannaim to Deut. 25 : 9, Hoffmann, p. 167)

*Comment*: Sifré Deut. cites the law, A, and the exegesis, joining the two with the citation of the relevant Scripture.

I.i.82. (The House of Hillel said to the House of Shammai, "She exercises the right of refusal [if a girl was a minor and was given in marriage by her mother or brothers, she may abjure the contract before two witnesses and be set free without the need of a bill of divorce] and [while] she is a minor, even four or five times." The House of Shammai said to them, "The daughters of Israel are not ownerless property. But she exercises the right of refusal [once] and waits until she comes of age, and she exercises the right of refusal and remarries."—M. Yev. 13 : 1.)

A. Who is the minor who must exercise the right of refusal?

Any girl whose mother and brothers gave her in marriage with her consent. If they gave her in marriage not with her consent (DʿT), she does not have to exercise the right of refusal [in a court of law].

R. Ḥanina b. Anṭignos says, "Every female child who cannot guard her betrothal gift does not need to exercise the right of refusal."

B. R. Eliezer says, "The deed of a female child is nothing. But she is like one who has been seduced.

C. "The daughter of an Israelite married to a priest should not eat Heave-offering. The daughter of a priest married to an Israelite [continues to] eat Heave-offering." [Neither is regarded as married.]

M. Yev. 13 : 2 (y. Yev. 13 : 2, b. Yev. 89b, 107b, 108a)

*Comment*: Eliezer stands entirely outside the foregoing range of arguments. He holds that, if a minor's mother or brothers have given her in marriage, she is not regarded as married at all but merely as seduced. He then would require no rite of refusal, and accordingly the issues separating the Houses are false, so far as a minor (QṬNH) is concerned. So the antecedent rules, A, with its gloss by Ḥanina, are rejected by Eliezer.

The question, Who is the minor who must exercise the right of refusal? is meaningless to Eliezer. No minor exercises the right of refusal. Eliezer's opinion, however, has been phrased within the setting of A, rather than as an independent opinion. The question presupposes the answer and the position of A. Without the question, Who is the minor? we should have simply:

> Every [minor] whose mother and brothers gave her in marriage (*with her consent*) requires the rite of refusal.
>
> R. Eliezer says, "The minor (QṬNH) does not exercise [or: does not require] the rite of refusal."

The marriage *without consent* does not enter the picture, for all parties agree no rite of refusal will be required. Here, therefore, whatever language was originally used in the formulation of Eliezer's opinion cannot be before us.

Part C spells out what is obvious in B. Since the girl is not regarded as married, she does not change in status in respect to the priesthood. If she was the daughter of a priest married to an Israelite, she still has not lost the right to eat Heave-offering, and contrarywise. C, or something like it, will be introduced wherever the subject is the status of a marriage. The party who holds a marriage invalid will say C, and the party who holds a marriage valid will say the opposite. But it is a perfectly obvious inference, and spelling it out is not required, except by glossators.

See Epstein, *Nusaḥ*, p. 1164.

I.ii.71.A. She who exercises the right of refusal has no *Ketuvah.* If he gave her a *Geṭ*, she has a *Ketuvah* [marriage-contract].

B. R. Liezer says, "The deed of a female minor is nothing. He has no right to what she may find or to the work of her hands, or to annul her vows, nor does he inherit her, nor does he become unclean for her [if he is a priest, should she die], nor is she like his wife in any respect, but only that she goes out from him [y.: *But she requires from him . . .*] with the rite of refusal."

C. R. Joshua says, "He has the right to what she may find and to the work of her hands, to annul her vows; and he inherits her and becomes unclean for her, and lo, she is like his wife in every respect, only that she goes forth from him with the rite of refusal."

D. R. Ishmael [b. drops Ishmael] said, "I have reviewed all the logic of the sages, and I have not found anyone whose logic is consistent in respect to minor girls, except for R. Liezer [y.: *But that he said she requires from him a rite of refusal*]. And I prefer the words of R. Liezer to the words of R. Joshua, for R. Liezer is consistent (HŠWH ʾT MDTW), and R. Joshua is inconsistent (ḤLQ)."

E. She who exercises the rite of refusal against a man, and he brought her back to him [self] and died—she either performs *ḥaliṣah* or enters Levirate marriage. [If] he divorced her and brought her back to him and died, she either performs *ḥaliṣah* or enters Levirate marriage.

F. R. Liezer says, "She performs *ḥaliṣah* but does not enter Levirate marriage, because she was prohibited to him for one hour."

G. Sages agree with R. Liezer in the case of a minor whose father gave her in marriage and was then divorced but was brought back to him [the original husband], who then died, that she performs *ḥaliṣah* and does not enter Levirate marriage, because she was prohibited to him for one hour. For the divorce was a complete divorce, but the remarriage was not a complete remarriage.

H. Under what circumstances? When he divorced her as a minor and brought her back as a minor, but if he divorced her as a minor and brought her back when she had come of age, or divorced her as a minor and brought her back as a minor but she came of age while married to him, and he died, she either performs *ḥaliṣah* or enters Levirate marriage.

I. R. Liezer says, "She performs *ḥaliṣah* but does not enter Levirate marriage, because she was prohibited to him for one hour."

Tos. Yev. 13 : 3-5, Lieberman, pp. 46, ls. 11-24 (y. Yev. 13 : 2, b. Yev. 108a)

*Comment*: Eliezer in Tos. Yev. 13 : 3-5 B is consistent with the brief expression of his view in M. Yev. 13 : 2. There he states that the deed of the minor is nothing. Here he spells out the consequences of that dictum.

In E-F, we have the case of M. Yev. 13 : 6 (below); there Eliezer says she is prohibited to the Levir. Here he says she should perform *ḥaliṣah*. The reason is as given here in F. The sages of G are in the same position as in M. Yev. 13 : 6. In Tos. Yev. 13 : 3-5I Eliezer is consistent with his opinion in M. Yev. 13 : 6 as well. I looks like a repetition of F.

In b. Yev. 108a, Rav Judah in the name of Samuel says D, and adds, "For R. Eliezer gave her the status of one who walks with him in the courtyard and arises from his bosom and washes and in the evening eats Heave-offering." That is, she is in no way a wife. Likewise, the preference for Eliezer's opinion is given in the name of Judah the Patriarch.

See Lieberman, *Tosefta Kifshuṭah Seder Nashim*, pp. 154-157.

III.ii.45. TNY': R. Eliezer said, "A priest shall not marry a minor."

b. Yev. 61b

*Comment*: He must have a taintless marriage, and the legal status of a minor's marriage is dubious.

I.ii.72. "A minor who performed the ceremony of *ḥaliṣah* must [again] perform the ceremony of *ḥaliṣah* when she comes of age. If she has not [as an adult] performed *ḥaliṣah*, her [first] *ḥaliṣah* is invalid," the words of R. Liezer.

B. And sages say, "If she did not perform [a second] *ḥaliṣah*, her [first] *ḥaliṣah* is acceptable."

Tos. Yev. 12 : 12, Lieberman, p. 43, ls. 53-55

*Comment*: M. Yev. 12 : 4 has:

> If a girl, still a minor, performed *ḥaliṣah*, she must perform *ḥaliṣah* when she comes of age. And if she does not do so, her [first] *ḥaliṣah* is invalid.

Tos. Yev. thus attributes that law, in the same words, to Eliezer. b. Yev. 61b supplies the *baraita*: "A minor enters Levirate marriage, but does not undergo the rite of *ḥaliṣah*," the words of R. Eliezer.

Lieberman points out (*Tosefta Kifshuṭah Nashim*, p. 136) that all the Palestinian versions of M. Yev. 12 : 4 have her *ḥaliṣah* is *valid*—therefore *not* according to Eliezer. Then Tos. has a contradictory view for Eliezer, consistent with M. Yev. 13 : 2B. M. Yev. 12 : 4 therefore has not suppressed Eliezer's name.

IV.i.12.A. R. Abbahu said, "M'ŚH B The mother of R. Liezer was nagging him to marry the daughter of his sister.

"And he would say to her [the girl], 'My daughter, go, marry. My daughter, go, marry.'

B. "She finally said to him, 'Lo, I am a handmaiden to you, to wash the feet of the servants of my lord.'

C. "Even so, when he married her, he did not recognize her until she brought two hairs [as evidence she had come of age.]"

y. Yev. 13 : 2, Gilead, p. 141

*Comment*: Abbahu's story illustrates Eliezer's view that the marriage of a minor counts for nothing. He therefore carried out his mother's wishes but also refrained from treating the niece as his bride until she had come of age. This is the sort of story that would follow the formulation of an apodictic law. Whether Abbahu had heard or made it up for himself we do not know, but since he comes late in the formation of the traditions about Eliezer, it stands to reason that the story depends upon the antecedent law, already well known in Mishnah-Tosefta, and combines that law with the theme of the sages' respect for their mothers and fathers.

III.ii.46. WHTNY': From what time does a man inherit his minor wife?

The House of Shammai say, "When she reaches full height [= puberty]."

And the House of Hillel say, "When she enters the marriage-canopy."

R. Eliezer says, "When she has intercourse."

Then he inherits her and makes himself unclean for her [if she dies and he is a priest], and she eats Heave-offering.

b. Yev. 89b

*Comment*: The anonymous *Gemara* immediately raises the question, "But R. Eliezer said the act of a minor has no legal force?" Then the text is changed, "Read: *After she has grown up and* [connubial] *intercourse has taken place*."

V.i.2.A. Lo, there was [the case of] Rabbi Eliezer the Great . . .

Now he raised his sister's daughter for thirteen years, and she slept with him in the same bed until the signs of her puberty appeared. Then he said to her, "Go now and be wedded to a man."

Said she, "Is not thy handmaid a servant to wash the feet of thy disciples?"

"My child," he declared, "I am already an old man. Go now and be wedded to a young man thine own age."

"Have I not already told thee," she insisted, "is not thy handmaid a servant to wash the feet of thy disciples?"

When he heard what she said, asking her permission he betrothed her and came to her.

ARN Chap. 16, trans. Goldin, pp. 84-85

*Comment*: ARN has lost y. Yev. 13 : 2A. Eliezer's mother is dropped, so too is 13 : 2C. Instead, ARN supplies a dialogue between Eliezer and the niece.

I.i.83.A. He who divorces [his] wife and remarries her—she is permitted to the Levir [= to marry her deceased husband's brother].

B. And R. Eliezer [b., y., Parma, Naples, Kaufmann: Leazar] prohibits.

C. And so too, he who divorces the orphan-girl [his wife was an orphan], and remarries her—she is permitted to the Levir.

D. And R. Eliezer [y.: Leazar] prohibits.

E. A minor whose father has given her in marriage and was then divorced is like an orphan in her father's lifetime [she is not within his control, and he cannot give her in betrothal]. If he remarried her, all agree [Naples: Sages agree with R. Eliezer] she is prohibited to the Levir. [M. in y. Yev. adds: *because her divorce was complete, but not her return.*]

M. Yev. 13 : 6 (y. Yev. 13 : 6, b. Yev. 109a; y. Yev. 3 : 1, b. Yev. 41a, b. Ket. 73a-b, 74a)

I.i.84.A. If two brothers were married to two sisters that were minors and orphans, and the husband of one of them died, she is exempt [from Levirate marriage] by virtue of being the sister of his wife.

So too, with two sisters that were deaf-mutes, if one was of age and the other a minor, and the husband of the minor died, she is exempt [from Levirate marriage] by virtue of being the sister of his wife.

B. If the husband of her that was of age died—

C. R. Eliezer [Parma: Leazar] says, "They instruct the minor to exercise the right of refusal against him."

D. Rabban Gamaliel says, "If she exercised the right of refusal against him, she has exercised it [= it is valid].

"But if not, she should wait until she is of age, and then the other is exempt [from Levirate marriage] by virtue of being the sister of his wife."

E. R. Joshua says, "Woe to him because of his wife [who has died], and woe to him because of the wife of his brother [also lost to him]. He divorces his wife with a *Geṭ*, and the wife of his brother with *ḥaliṣah*."

M. Yev. 13 : 7 (y. Yev. 13 : 7, b. Yev. 28a, 109a; b. Nid. 8a)

IV.ii.9. Rav Judah in the name of Samuel said, "The law follows R. Eliezer."

b. Yev. 110a (b. Nid. 8a): also Eleazar)

*Comment*: The case of M. Yev. 13 : 6A pertains to a woman who, while divorced, has ceased for a time to be subject to the Levir [deceased husband's brother.] The anonymous rule is that even though she has once ceased to be subject to the Levir, she has once again become subject to him and therefore may enter Levirate marriage. Eliezer holds that once freed of Levirate obligation, she never again is subject to it. This is the view of the House of Hillel in M. Yev. 3 : 1, according to Eliezer's formulation of the rule in B. Once the surviving wives for a time have been prohibited to the surviving brother, because of having been prohibited to the Levir, she remains so for all time. Now M. Yev. 3 : 1A—the anonymous rule—becomes both the House of Hillel's and Eliezer's. M. Yev. 13 : 6A then is consistent with the position of the House of Shammai.

In 13 : 6C the minor is divorced and remarried. Is her status different from that of an adult woman in the same circumstance? C is consistent with A; she is no different. And Eliezer agrees! The rulings are consistent with M. Yev. 13 : 1. The minor may exercise the right of refusal, therefore *not* consistent with Eliezer's position in M. Yev. 13 : 2. The minor is like one who has been seduced. If so, here too he should rule that she is like one who has been seduced, and therefore neither the marriage nor the divorce was effective. But then, in remarrying the minor, the man has not subjected her to Levirate marriage in the case of his death, and therefore Eliezer really is consistent in ruling that she is prohibited to the Levir. The ruling, however, is for a reason different from that prevailing in 13 : 6A-B. The whole set of rulings is to be assigned to our Eliezer.

In 13 : 6E Eliezer remains consistent, but the rule of the anonymous sages changes. According to the sages, the girl now is no different from any orphan. Her divorce is valid, but the remarriage is not, for she is in the status of an orphaned minor. The marriage cannot wholly overcome the valid divorce, and she therefore is not subject to the Levir by reason of the remarriage. So the sages come over to Eliezer's position, but their reason still is not the same as his. He regards her as never having been married to begin with, while they regard the first marriage as valid, but the second as insufficiently valid to overcome the intervening divorce.

M. Yev. 13 : 7A introduces the complication of a marriage of two brothers to two minor sisters who are orphans. All parties agree in 13 : 6E that a minor who is married and then divorced and then remarried is prohibited to the Levir. Now we have two such minor-sisters married to two brothers. If one of the brothers died, his wife is free of Levirate obligation, because of her sister. Even though she is married in a lesser degree—her marriage is accepted not biblically but by rabbinic rule—she is free of the Levirate obligation and from *ḥaliṣah*, just like an adult. The same rule applies to the deaf-mute for the same reason. Then comes the case of an adult and a minor sister married to two brothers. The marriage-connection of the latter is on a less firm basis than that of the former. If the husband of the minor dies, she is free of the Levirate obligation. B introduces a disputed case. The husband of the adult dies. What is the status of his wife? Does she now enter Levirate marriage with the husband of the minor? Or is she free of the obligation by reason of 'sister of the wife'?

In C, Eliezer says the minor is to exercise the right of refusal against her husband, and then the husband of the minor enters Levirate marriage with the surviving wife, who is of age. Eliezer holds that the marriage-connection of the minor is on a less firm basis than the (former) connection of the adult-sister. Therefore the minor is told to reject the marriage, and her sister takes her place in a Levirate connection.

Gamaliel says she may exercise right of refusal, in which case the minor's husband takes the adult-sister as his Levirate wife. But if not, then the minor must wait until she comes of age, when her marriage will be fully in effect. At that point the woman awaiting Levirate connection goes free, on account of 'sister of the wife.' So the man may remain married to the minor. Eliezer would force the couple to separate. The difference between Gamaliel and Eliezer is the strength of the Levir's marriage tie. As noted, Eliezer says the Levir's marriage tie to his minor wife is not so strong as to free him from connection with his brother's deceased brother's wife. He may therefore no longer remain with his minor wife.

Joshua then introduces a still stricter ruling. The surviving brother loses all. Joshua agrees with Eliezer: the minor wife now is forbidden to him, so he must divorce her because of the force of her sister's connection through the requirement of impending Levirate marriage. But Joshua says we do *not* instruct the minor to exercise the right of refusal. The man must undergo the *ḥaliṣah* ceremony with his deceased brother's wife, who is of age.

I find Eliezer's position somewhat curious, for he has earlier ruled that there is no marriage-connection in the case of a minor, and her deed means nothing. She needs not exercise the right of refusal. Yet here Eliezer says the right of refusal must be exercised, hence there is a marriage connection.

M. Yev. 13 : 7C, D, and E are all formulated as an answer to B, but only C constitutes a direct instruction. D responds to C. Gamaliel could have completed B with *she should—sister of his wife.* The intervening phrase ties his saying to C. E likewise responds to the foregoing: Joshua's opinion completes B with *he divorces—with ḥaliṣah.*"

See Epstein, *Nusaḥ*, pp. 307, 968, 1163-4.

IV.i.13. R. Ḥaggai said before R. Ze<sup></sup>ira, Menaḥem in the name of R. Yoḥanan: "The law is according to R. Eliezer," etc.

y. Yev. 13 : 7

I.i.85.A. If one [of the deceased husband's widows] was adult and one a minor, and the deceased husband's brother had Levirate connection with the adult and then had connection with the minor, or his brother had connection with the minor, he has not rendered the adult ineligible.

B. If the surviving brother had Levirate connection with the minor and then went and entered Levirate connection with the adult, or his brother had Levirate connection with the adult—he has rendered the minor ineligible.

C. R. Eliezer [Kaufmann, Parma, Naples: Eleazar] says, "They instruct the minor to exercise the right of refusal against him."

M. Yev. 13 : 11

*Comment*: In A the surviving brother had Levirate connection with the adult and therefore acquired her as a Levirate wife. Therefore the connection is a valid one, and the adult is not ineligible to continue in the Levirate marriage. But if the first connection was with the minor and the second with the adult, the minor is ineligible to remain in the Levirate marriage. Consistent with his position in M. Yev. 13 : 7, Eliezer in this situation has the minor exercise the right of refusal, so that the Levirate marriage of the adult sister can remain in force. The case is no different from M. Yev. 13 : 7, except for the example. 13 : 7 has deaf-mutes, and 13 : 11 does not. But otherwise, what has changed?

| *13 : 7* | *13 : 11* |
|---|---|
| *The husband of the adult died* | *The Levir came first to the minor, then to the adult* |

In fact, the situation is identical. In both instances, the problem is the relationship of the Levir to the adult sister, in a situation in which the minor sister has a Levirate tie. In 13 : 7 the Levirate connection is between the minor sister and the husband of the adult sister; 13 : 11 has a different narrative but posits the same situation and the same legal problem. In this case we should expect rulings from Joshua and Gamaliel.

See Epstein, *Nusaḥ*, p. 1164.

I.ii.73.A. A minor goes out with a *Geṭ* and an adult goes out with *Geṭ* and *ḥaliṣah.*

B. R. Liezer [Leazar] says, "In all of them, they teach the minor to exercise the right of refusal against him."

Tos. Yev. 13 : 7, Lieberman, p. 48, ls. 44-5

*Comment*: The pericope is a supplement to M. Yev. 13 : 11. Lieberman shows it should be Leazar, and the correct reading in M. Yev. 13 : 11 also is Eleazar, not Eliezer.

I.i.86.A. Two sisters-in-law [wives of two brothers]—this one says, "My husband died," and this one says, "My husband died"—each is prohibited [to marry others] on account of the husband of the other [for each is subject to the Levirate connection with the husband of her sister, and he may yet be alive; even though his wife says he has died, she is not believed to such a degree as to permit her sister to marry others.]

B. This one has witnesses [to the husband's death] but this one has no witnesses—the one who has witnesses is forbidden [to marry others], but the one who has no witnesses is permitted [for the death of the first is well attested].

C. This one has children and the other does not—the one who has children is permitted [to remarry], and the one who has no children is forbidden.

D. They entered Levirate connection, and the Levirs died—the widows are forbidden to remarry.

E. R. Eliezer [Parma, Kaufmann: Eleazar] says, "Since they were permitted to the Levirs [who now have died], they are permitted to any man [for marriage]."

M. Yev. 16 : 2

*Comment*: The view of D is that each wife is prohibited to marry because of the husband of the other, who is her Levir, lest he be alive and able to enter Levirate connection, just as was the situation before the Levirate connection.

Eliezer [Eleazar] says that since the women were permitted to enter Levirate marriage with the first Levirs, in the assumption that their husbands have died, they now are permitted to marry anyone, in the same assumption. So again, once free of the Levirate connection, Eliezer [Eleazar] holds, a woman remains free. Here the Levirate connection has been served.

Lieberman, *Tosefta Kifshuṭah Seder Nashim*, p. 173, points out most MSS have Eleazar. See also Epstein, *Nusaḥ*, p. 1165.

I.ii.74.A. The woman who went abroad with her husband and came [home] and said, "My husband has died"—she is permitted [to remarry] but her co-wife is prohibited.

B. R. Liezer [Leazar] says, "Since she is permitted, so too is her co-wife."

C. They entered Levirate marriage and the Levirs died, they are prohibited from remarrying.

D. R. Eliezer says, "Since they [once] were permitted to the Levirs, they were [remain] permitted to any man."

Tos. Yev. 14 : 3, Lieberman, p. 51, ls. 22-25

*Comment*: C-D is in M. Yev. 16 : 2D-E.

I.i.87.A. R. ʿAqiba said, "When I went down to Nehardea to ordain a leap-year, R. Nehemiah of Bet Deli met me and said to me, 'I have heard that in the land of Israel, the sages, excepting R. Judah b. Baba, do not allow a woman to marry again on the evidence of one witness.'

"I answered, 'It is so.'

"He said to me, 'Tell them in my name . . . I have received a tradition from Rabban Gamaliel the Elder that they allow a woman to marry again on the evidence of one witness.'

"And when I came and told the matter before Rabban Gamaliel, he rejoiced at my words and said, 'We have now found a fellow for R. Judah b. Baba.'"

Whereupon Rabban Gamaliel remembered that certain men were killed at Tel Arza, and Rabban Gamaliel the Elder allowed their wives to marry again on the evidence of one witness.

B. And the rule was established to allow a woman to marry again on the evidence of one witness [who testifies what he has heard] from [another witness] or from a slave or from a woman or from a bondwoman.

C. R. Eliezer and R. Joshua say, "They do not allow a woman to marry on the evidence of one witness."

D. R. ʿAqiba says, "[They do] not [allow a woman to remarry] on the evidence of a woman or on the evidence of relatives."

E. They said to him, "Once certain Levites went to Ṣoar, city of palms, and one of them fell sick by the way, and they brought him to an inn. When they returned there, they asked the hostess, 'Where is our companion?' She answered, 'He died and I buried him.' And they allowed his wife to marry again."

F. They said to R. ʿAqiba, "And should not a priest's wife be [deemed as trustworthy] as the hostess of an inn?"

G. He said to them, "Only when the mistress of an inn could be deemed trustworthy. For in this case the mistress of the inn brought out to them his staff and his bag and the scroll of the Torah that belonged to him."

M. Yev. 16 : 7 (y. Yev. 16 : 8; b. Yev. 120a)

*Comment*: The sages who do not allow a woman to marry again on the evidence of one witness include Eliezer and Joshua. When Gamaliel the Elder's tradition is reported by ʿAqiba, Judah b. Baba's teacher, to Gamaliel of Yavneh, he is glad. He, like Judah b. Baba, holds the view contrary to Eliezer's and Joshua's. Then ʿAqiba is introduced in a separate pericope, unrelated to the foregoing. So in an apodictic legal pericope, we should have had the following:

"They allow a woman to marry again on the evidence of one witness"—the words of Rabban Gamaliel.

R. Eliezer and R. Joshua say, "They do *not* allow a woman to marry on the evidence of one witness."

Such a pericope ought to have been produced by the story before us.

Eliezer's and Joshua's saying would fit such an apodictic formulation. See Epstein, *Tan.*, p. 442.

I.ii.75.A. They asked R. Liezer, "A mamzer—may he inherit?" He said to them, "May he perform *ḥaliṣah*."

B. "May he perform *ḥaliṣah*?"

He said to them, "May he inherit?"

C. "May he inherit?"

He said to them, "May one plaster his house?"

D. [*Should be*: "May one plaster his house?"]

He said to them, "May one plaster his grave?"

E. "May one plaster his grave?"

He said to them, "May one raise dogs?"

F. "May one raise dogs?"

He said to them, "May one raise pigs?"

G. "May one raise pigs?"

He said, "May one raise roosters?"

H. "May one raise roosters?"

He said to them, "May one raise small cattle?"

I. "May one raise small cattle?"

He said to them, "May one save the shepherd from the wolf?"

J. "May one save the shepherd from the wolf?"

He said to them, "It seems you have asked me only concerning the (KBŚH) lamb?"

K. And as regards the lamb, "May one save [it]?"

He said to them, "It seems you have asked only about the shepherd."

L. "So-and-so, what is he as to [does he enter] the world to come? So and so, what is he as to the world to come?"

He said to them, "It seems that you have asked only about so-and-so."

M. "And so-and-so, what is he [= his status] as to the world to come?"

N. R. Liezer was not putting them off, but he never said anything which he had not heard.

Tos. Yev. 3, Lieberman, p. 9, ls. 18-29

*Comment*: See above, p. 146, and Lieberman, *Tosefta Kifshuṭah Seder Nashim*, pp. 22-24. The story is a supplement to M. Yev. 2 : 5, with reference to a *mamzer's* Levirate status. The question of A is whether the *mamzer* performs *ḥaliṣah*; b. Yoma 66b has, "Does he enter Levirate marriage?" Then Eliezer asks about whether he inherits—dismissing the earlier question. As to E-F, see b. B.Q. 8a.

IV.i.14. They asked R. Eliezer, "The eleventh generation of a *mamzer*—what is the law?"

He said to them, "Bring me the third generation and I shall declare him clean (ṬHR)."

y. Yev. 8 : 3, Gilead, p. 98 = y. Qid. 4 : 2, Gilead, p. 86 (b. Yev. 78b: Female-*mamzer*)

*Comment*: Compare M. Qid. 3 : 13, below, p. 209. This saying does not contradict that opinion. But I am not sure this is our Eliezer.

I.ii.76.A. The woman whose husband went abroad. They came and told her, "Your husband has died," and the court instructed her to remarry. She went and married. [If it is the case of] a widow to high priest, a divorce or woman who has undergone the ceremony of *ḥaliṣah* to an ordinary priest—

B. "She is liable for an offering for each act of intercourse," the words of R. Liezer.

C. And sages say, "One sacrifice for all."

D. Sages agree with R. Liezer that if she married five men, she is liable to bring an offering for each [man].

Tos. Yev. 11 : 4, Lieberman, pp. 34-5, ls. 14-18 (b. Yev. 34a)

*Comment*: The pericope supplements M. Yev. 10 : 2:

> If a woman's husband had gone abroad, and she was told, "Your husband has died"—If she married with the consent of the court [and her first husband returned], the marriage is annulled, and she is not liable to a sin-offering.
> But if without the consent of the court, the marriage is annulled, and she is liable for a sin-offering.

Eliezer requires an offering for each act of intercourse. The sages say one covers all. Neither party holds *no* offering is required.

III.ii.47.A. TNY᾽: R. Eliezer said, "How do we know that an uncircumcized [priest] may not eat Heave-offering? *A sojourner and a hired servant* (Ex. 12 : 45) are referred to in regard to the Passover, and *A sojourner and a hired servant* (Lev. 22 : 10) are referred to in regard to Heave-offering. As the Passover, concerning which *A sojourner and a hired servant* are mentioned, is forbidden to the uncircumcized [Ex. 12 : 48], the same is so with respect to Heave-offering."

B. R. ʿAqiba said, "It is unnecessary. Since it was said *Whosoever* (Lev. 22 : 4), the uncircumcized also is included."

b. Yev. 70a (b. Men. 17b)

*Comment*: The dispute is whether an exegesis is required for Eliezer's proposition. Both masters agree on the law. See the important discussion of David Weiss Halivni, *Meqorot uMesorot* (Tel Aviv, 1968), pp. 78-80.

III.ii.48.A. TNW RBNN: If a proselyte was circumcized but had not performed the ritual bath—

R. Eliezer says, "Lo, he is a proper proselyte, for we find that our forefathers were circumcized but had not performed the ritual bath."

If he performed the ritual bath but had not been circumcized—

R. Joshua says, "Lo, he is a proper proselyte, for so we find that the mothers had performed ritual ablution but had not been circumcized."

And sages say, "Whether he had performed the ritual bath but had not been circumcized, or *vice versa*, he is not a proper proselyte, unless he has been circumcized and also performed the ritual bath."

b. Yev. 46a (b. Yev. 71a; y. Qid. 3 : 12; M. Gerim 60a; Eliezer *vs.* ʿAqiba)

*Comment*: The rules of admitting a proselyte evidently were not settled by early Yavnean times.

See Halivni, *Meqorot uMesorot*, pp. 53-5.

II.iv.10. *And you will bring her to your house and shave her head and she will prepare her nails* (Deut. 21 : 12)—

R. Eliezer says, "She should cut them off."

R. ʿAqiba says, "She should let them grow."

R. Eliezer said, "It says, *And doing* concerning the head, and it says *doing* concerning the nails. Just as *doing* concerning the head means *removing*, so *doing* said concerning the nails means *removing*."

R. ʿAqiba says, "*Doing* is said concerning the head, and *doing* is said concerning the nails. Just as *doing* said concerning the head means disfigurement (NYWWL), so doing said concerning the nails means disfigurement."

Sifré Deut. 212, pp. 245-246 (M. Semaḥot 7 : 13)

II.iv.11. *And she will weep for her father and her mother a month of days* (Deut. 21 : 12)—

"*Her father and her mother*—literally," the words of R. Eliezer.

R. ʿAqiba says, "*Her mother and her father* mean only idolatry, as it is said (Jer. 2 : 27), *Saying to wood, you are my father*."

Sifré Deut. 213, Finkelstein, p. 246

III.ii.49. TNW RBNN: *And she shall shave her head and do her nails* (Deut. 21 : 12).

R. ʿAqiba said, "She shall let them grow."

R. Eliezer said, "An act was mentioned in respect to the head and also in respect to the nails. As disfigurement is the purpose of the former, so is disfigurement the purpose of the latter."

III.ii.50. Our rabbis taught, *And bewail her father and mother* (Deut. 21 : 15).

R. Eliezer said, "Her father means her real father, and her mother likewise."

R. ʿAqiba said, "*Her father and her mother* refer to idolatry, for so Scripture says, *Who say to a stock, Thou art my father* (Jer. 2 : 27)."

b. Yev. 48a-b

III.ii.51. TNYʾ: *Therefore shall a man leave his father and his mother* (Gen. 2 : 24).

R. Eliezer said, "*His father* means his father's sister, *his mother*, his mother's sister."

R. ʿAqiba said, "*His father* means his father's wife, *his mother* is literally meant, *And he shall cleave*, but not to a male; *to his wife*, but not to his neighbor's wife, *and they shall be as one flesh*, applying to those that can become one flesh, thus excluding cattle and beasts, which cannot become one flesh with man."

b. Sanh. 58a, trans. H. Freedman, p. 395

*Comment*: The disputes of Eliezer and ʿAqiba in the first instance concern the interpretation of Scripture, but here they have legal consequences. The same principle of interpretation is authority for both masters, the *heqqesh*. In Sifré Deut. 213 and b. Sanh. 58a on the other hand, the problem is whether Scripture is to be interpreted according to its literal meaning. b. Sanh. has Eliezer forbidding relationships with the father's and mother's sisters. ʿAqiba says the Scripture prohibits the father's wife and the mother (if the father has more than one wife)—thus ʿAqiba is in the literal position.

## xix. Ketuvot

I.i.88.A. He who marries the woman and did not find in her tokens of virginity [Deut. 22 : 14]—

B. She says, "After you betrothed me, I was raped, and your field was laid waste."

C. And the other says, "Not so, but before I betrothed you [it happened], and my purchase was an erroneous purchase."

D. Rabban Gamaliel and R. Eliezer say, "She is believed."

E. R. Joshua says, "We do not rely on her word [Lit.: Not from her mouth do we live], but lo, this one is in the presumption of having been subject to intercourse (BʿWLH) before she was betrothed, and she deceived him, unless she will bring proof for her claim (DBRYH)."

M. Ket. 1 : 6 (y. Ket. 1 : 6, b. Ket. 12b, 16a)

I.i.89.A. She claims, "I am injured by [a piece of] wood [Danby: "It was through accident"], and he says, "Not so, but you have been trampled by man"—

B. Rabban Gamaliel and R. Eliezer say, "She is believed."

C. And R. Joshua says, "We do not rely on her word, but lo, such a one is in the presumption of having been trampled by a man, unless she will bring proof for her claim."

M. Ket. 1 : 7 (y. Ket. 1 : 7, b. Ket. 11b, 13a)

I.i.90.A. They saw her speaking with one [man] in the market. They said to her, "What is the character of this man?"

B. [She replies], "He is so-and-so, and a priest"—

C. Rabban Gamaliel and R. Eliezer [Naples: Eleazar] say, "She is believed [therefore may marry a priest]."

D. And R. Joshua says, "We do not rely on her word, but lo, such a one is in the presumption of having been subject to intercourse by a *Netin* or a *Mamzer*, unless she will bring proof of her claim."

M. Ket. 1 : 8 (y. Ket. 1 : 8, b. Ket. 13a)

I.i.91.A. She was pregnant. They said to her, "What is the nature of this embryo?"

B. "He is from so-and-so, and he is a priest."

C. Rabban Gamaliel and R. Eliezer say, "She is believed."

D. R. Joshua says, "We do not rely on her words. But lo, such a one is in the presumption of having been made pregnant by a *Netin* or a *Mamzer*, unless she will bring proof for her claim."

M. Ket. 1 : 9 (y. Ket. 1 : 9; b. Ket. 12b, 13a, 16a; b. Qid. 74a)

III.ii.52. If they saw her go in with someone into a secret place or a ruin, and they said to her, "What sort of person is he," [and she said], "He is a priest and the son of my father's brother..." [The rest as above.]

b. Ket. 13a-b

*Comment*: This little collection of rulings on several examples of the same problem follows a disciplined form: (1) statement of the situation; (2) ruling of Gamaliel and Eliezer ("She is believed"); (3) ruling of Joshua ("She is not believed"—developed into "She is in the presumption that... until she brings proof"). The statement of the problem in M. Ket. 1 : 7, 8, and 9, depends upon 1 : 6A, so the collection is a unity. All that changes is the claim of the woman. In all instances the rulings could have been spelled out from the first example. The practical consequence is the payment of the *Ketuvah*. Gamaliel and Eliezer consistently rule the *Ketuvah* must be paid. Joshua rules the contrary; he who makes a claim against his fellow must bring proof before the claim is paid. The issue of 1 : 8 and 1 : 9 is whether the woman, then the child, may marry into the priesthood. Intercourse with a *Netin* or a *Mamzer* means she cannot. See Halivni, *Meqorot uMesorot*, pp. 143-146.

I.ii.77.A. She was pregnant, [and] they said to her, "What is the nature of this embryo?"

B. "From so-and-so, and he is a priest."

C. Rabban Gamaliel and R. Liezer say, "She is believed, for this is testimony which a woman is fitting [to give]."

D. R. Joshua says, "She is not believed."

E. R. Joshua said to them, "Do you not agree concerning the woman taken captive by gentiles, who has witnesses that she was taken captive, and she says, 'I am clean,' that she is not believed? [Likewise here, there is adequate testimony that the woman has had intercourse.]"

F. They said to him, "No, if you [pl.] have said so concerning the woman taken captive who has witnesses [that she was taken captive], will you say so concerning this one, who has no witnesses [that she has had intercourse with someone who renders her unfit for the priesthood]?"

G. He said to them, "And what evidence is greater than this, for lo, her belly is between her teeth!"

H. They said to him, "Because gentiles are suspected (ḤŠWD) concerning forbidden sexual relations."

I. He said to them, "There is no custodian as to forbidden sexual relations."

J. "In what circumstances? In respect to testimony concerning [the woman about] herself. But as to the child, all agree he is a *shetuqi* [= of unknown parentage.]"

Tos. Ket. 1 : 6, Lieberman, p. 59, ls. 41-48 (b. Ket. 13b)

*Comment*: M. Ket. 1 : 9 is supplemented here. The principle is that a woman is believed about what she says concerning herself when there are no witnesses. She could have claimed she was not taken captive, but admits it, while denying she has been raped. Having admitted what she could have denied, she is believed about what she does deny. Joshua in G points out there is ample evidence that the woman has had intercourse, so we have no grounds to take her word as to the character of the father. Gamaliel and Eliezer in H point out that if a woman is taken captive, it can be taken for granted that she has been raped, since gentiles normally do things like that. So the cases are no different.

In I Joshua replies in the presupposition that a woman just as commonly is indifferent to the origins of the seducer. If she has committed lewdness, she presumably has not been concerned, so we assume it was with someone who renders her unfit.

See Lieberman, *Tosefta Kifshuṭah Seder Nashim*, pp. 196-7.

Note also b. Ket. 12b: Rav Judah + Samuel: The law follows Gamaliel, etc.

I.ii.78.A. R. Liezer says, "An orphan has the right to worn-out articles [= indemnity for the loss on her *melog*-property]."

B. R. Judah says in the name of R. Liezer, "The orphan has the right to usufruct [increase on her *melog*-property]."

Tos. Ket. 11 : 4, Lieberman, p. 94, ls. 24-5 (b. Ket. 101a)

*Comment*: M. Ket. 11 : 6 has: "A minor [Lieberman: *Orphan*] who exercised the right of refusal ... is not entitled to the *Ketuvah*, or to the right to usufruct [benefits of her *melog*-property] or to maintenance, or to her worn-out articles [= indemnity]."

Eliezer holds that the orphan *has* such a right. Her deeds are of no consequence. She was never really subject to the marriage [*Qiddushin*]. Therefore the orphan has the right to her original property intact. But of course she has no right to the *Ketuvah* or to *maintenance*. Eliezer is consistent here and therefore differs from M. Ket. 11 : 6.

III.ii.53. He who forbids his wife by a vow [from enjoying benefit from him], and she is taken captive [among the gentiles]—

B. R. Eliezer says, "He redeems her and gives to her her *Ketuvah*."

R. Joshua says, "He gives to her her *Ketuvah* and does not redeem [her]."

R. Nathan says ...

b. Ket. 52a

*Comment*: According to Eliezer, the husband now pays the ransom, then divorces her. The *Ketuvah* itself obligates him to ransom her, consistent with M. Ket. 4 : 8. Nathan provides a valid *terminus*; he says he asked Symmachus about Joshua's opinion.

IV.ii.10. "During the twenty-four months [of nursing a child] one may thresh within and winnow without"—the words of R. Eliezer.

Others said to him, "Such actions are only like the practice of Er and Onan."

b. Yev. 34b

III.i.11. TNY᾽: "The infant goes on nursing for twenty-four months. Thereafter it is like suckling an abomination," the words of R. Eliezer.

R. Joshua says, "He continues nursing even four or five years. But if he separates, they do not bring him back [to the breast]."

y. Ket. 5 : 6, Gilead, p. 72 (b. Ket. 60a)

*Comment*: Compare *Phar.* II, pp. 207-208, 227.

## xx. Nedarim, Nazir, Soṭah

I.i.92.A. R. Eliezer says, "They open for a man [the way to release him from his vow] with reference to the honor of his father and mother."

B. And sages prohibit.

C. R. Ṣaddoq said, "Before they open for a man with reference to his father's and mother's honor, let them open for with reference to the honor of the Omnipresent. If so, there [could be] no vows!"

D. And sages agree with R. Eliezer regarding a matter between himself and his father or mother that they open to him with reference to the honor of his father and mother.

M. Ned. 9 : 1 (y. Ned. 9 : 1; b. Ned. 64a-b)

I.i.93.A. And further did R. Eliezer say, "They open with reference to what happens (BNWLD) [Danby: "By reason of what befalls unexpectedly"]."

B. And sages prohibit.

C. How so?

D. [If he said] "*Qonam* that I shall not enjoy benefit from so-and-so," and he [the other] is made a scribe, or he was marrying off his son in the near future, and he [the vower then] said, "Had I known that he would be made a scribe, or that he would marry off his son in the near future, I should not have vowed," [they release him from his vow].

E. [If he said] "*Qonam* that I shall not enter this house," and it was made a synagogue, [and he then] said, "If I had known that it would be made into a synagogue, I should not have vowed"—

F. R. Eliezer releases [him from the vow] (MTYR).

G. And sages declare it binding ('WSRYN).

M. Ned. 9 : 2 (y. Ned. 9 : 2;
b. Ned. 64a-b, b. Naz. 32b)

*Comment*: A vow may be released if it can be shown that it was made under a false presupposition. The sage may declare the vow released as though it had not been made. He seeks an "opening" of the vow so as to release the man from its effect. Eliezer in both cases rules very leniently. In M. Ned. 9 : 1 he says that honor of father and mother is sufficient grounds for releasing a man from his vow. One cannot vow in such a way as to dishonor them. The sage says (Albeq, *Seder Nashim*, p. 174), "If you had known that you would bring your father and mother into shame, would you have vowed?"

Since it is regarded as a dishonor to Heaven to make vows, Ṣaddoq observes that on that basis no vow will ever be binding—which, perhaps, was Eliezer's intention. The saying is a clear interpolation. The sages' saying fully balances Eliezer's.

The sages, to be sure, agree that a man cannot be held to a vow in a matter which specifically pertains to the father and mother. For instance, if he declared by vow that his father or mother will not benefit from his property or that he will not speak with them, one may say to him, "Had you known that you are liable to honor them, would you have vowed?" If he says no, he is released from the vow.

M. Ned. 9 : 2 presents Eliezer in a similarly lenient position. Now he says one may release a vow by reference to what takes place thereafter, and the two examples make perfectly clear that so far as Eliezer is concerned, a man might merely claim, "Had I known, I should not have vowed." The cases of D and E are formulated from the viewpoint of both Eliezer and the sages; there is no disagreement on the definition of the dispute.

See Epstein, *Tan.*, pp. 302, 377.

IV.i.15. R. Simon in the name of R. Joshua b. Levi [said], "R. Eliezer learned from Moses, for the Holy One blessed be He opened [a vow] for him with reference to what happens . . ."

y. Ned. 9 : 2 (b. Ned. 64b: R. Ḥisda)

III.ii.54. [The laws concerning the dissolution of vows hover in the air and have no basis [lit.: nothing to rest on]—M. Hag. 1 : 1.]

A. TNY': R. Eliezer says, "They have a basis [lit.: something to rest on], for it is said, *When one shall clearly utter* [a vow] (Lev. 27 : 2, Num. 6 : 2), *When one shall clearly utter* [a vow] (Lev. 27 : 2, Num. 6 : 2)—two times: one [refers to] an utterance to bind, the other to an utterance to dissolve."

B. R. Joshua says, "They have a basis [lit.: something to rest on], for it is said, *Wherefore I swore in my wrath* (Ps. 95 : 11). I swore in my wrath, but I retracted."

b. Hag. 10a

*Comment*: Other such proofs come from Isaac and Ḥananiah nephew of R. Joshua. y. Ned. 9 : 2 gives Joshua's proof, B, to Eliezer.

I.i.94.A. A woman past puberty [BWGRT = a girl twelve years six months and one day old, whose father no longer annuls her vows], and one [a woman betrothed] that had waited twelve months, and a widow thirty days [from when the betrother has sought to complete the marriage]—

B. R. Eliezer says, "Since her husband is [now] liable for her maintenance, he may annul [her vows]."

C. And sages say, "The husband does not annul [them] until she enters his domain (RŠWT)."

M. Ned. 10 : 5 (y. Ned. 10 : 4, b, Ned. 70b, 73b; b. Ket. 57b)

I.i.95.A. She who awaits Levirate marriage, whether there was one brother-in-law or two—

B. R. Eliezer [y.: Eleazar] says, "He [the Levir] may annul [her vows]."

C. R. Joshua says, "[He may do so if there is] one [brother-in-law] but *not* when there are two."

D. R. ʿAqiba says, "Not by one and not by two."

E. R. Eliezer said, "If he may annul the vows of a woman whom he has acquired for himself, may he not annul the vows of a woman whom Heaven has acquired for him?"

F. R. ʿAqiba said to him, "No, if you have said so concerning a woman whom he has acquired for himself, in whom others have no right, will you say so of a woman whom Heaven has acquired for him, in whom others [other Levirs] do have a right?"

G. R. Joshua said to him, "ʿAqiba, your words [pertain] to two Levirs. What will you answer concerning one Levir?"

H. He said to him, "The deceased husband's widow is not so completely bound to the Levir as is the betrothed woman to her man."

M. Ned. (y. Ned. b. Ned. 74a-b, b. Yev. 29b)

I.i.96.A. He who says to his wife, "All the vows which you will vow from now until I return from such-and-such a place, lo, they are confirmed"—he has said nothing.

B. "Lo, they are released"—

C. R. Eliezer says, "It is released."

D. And sages say, "It is not released."

E. R. Eliezer said, "If he released vows which have already had the force of a prohibition [the husband annuls his wife's vows which have already been in force before he revoked them], can he not [in advance] release vows which have *not* had the force of a prohibition?"

F. They said to him, "Lo, it says, *Her husband will confirm it and her husband will annul it* (Num. 30 : 14). What comes into the category of confirmation comes into the category of annulling. If it has not come into the category of confirmation, it has not come into the category of annulling [and since the husband cannot confirm the vows, as in A, he cannot annul them in advance either]."

M. Ned. 10 : 7 (y. Ned. 10 : 7, b. Ned. 72b, 75a-b; b. Naz. 12)

II.iv.12.A. *And he will annul her vows—the vows which are [already] upon her he may annul* but not vows which are [not yet] upon her.

B. For R. Eliezer says, "He may annul. And logic," etc. [= M. Ned. 10 : 7E].

Sifré Num. 153, Friedman, p. 57b

*Comment*: The three cases listed in M. Ned. 10 : 5A have in common the fact that the prospective husband is liable for the girl's support (M. Ket. 5 : 2). Eliezer holds the prospective husband is now in a position to annul the vows as well. The sages rule he cannot do so until he has completed the marriage-process (M. Ket. 4 : 5). Eliezer thus seeks to extend the possibilities of annulling the vows.

Eliezer in 10 : 6 likewise rules that the Levir(s) may annul the vows of the deceased husband's wife while she is awaiting Levirate marriage to one of them, even before the Levirate marriage has taken place. Joshua says one Levir may do so, but not both. Eliezer compares the woman to one who has been betrothed. Just as he argued above that the prospective husband with the girl's father may annul vows, he now argues, so may the prospective Levirate-husband. The former is liable to support her. b. Ned. 74a says Eliezer is consistent with the House of Shammai that a declaration (M'MR) acquires. Here there has been a declaration of betrothal on the part of one of the Levirs.

ʿAqiba then argues that a Levir (of two or more) has not got exclusive right to the woman, while the prospective husband does have exclusive right to her. So the cases cannot be compared, and the same rights do not pertain. Joshua then points out that ʿAqiba has supported his own, but has not refuted Joshua's, position, for Joshua holds a single Levir may do so, and in this instance, others have *no* right to the woman.

ʿAqiba's reply is that the two still are not similar, for the right of the Levir is not so complete as the right of the prospective groom. One who has intercourse with her is not liable to the death penalty, but one who has intercourse with a betrothed woman is liable to the death penalty.

M. Ned. 10 : 7 has another lenient ruling of Eliezer. In this case all parties agree that one cannot prospectively confirm vows. Eliezer however holds that one can prospectively annul them. Eliezer argues that if the husband can annul vows which have already come into force, he ought to be able to annul those which have yet to come into force. The sages say that the right to annul depends upon the right to confirm, and if, as all agree, he cannot confirm vows in advance, he also cannot annul them in advance.

It would have been better to have the dispute of B-D before the agreement represented by A, but the setting—confirming, then annulling, as in Scripture—evidently prevented it.

See Epstein, *Nusaḥ*, pp. 529, 973, 1168. Epstein prefers Eleazar for 10 : 5. See also Halivni, *Meqorot uMesorot*, pp. 335-339.

IV.ii.11. Rabbah said, "R. Eliezer and the first Mishnah taught the same thing [with reference to b. Ket. 57a]."

b. Ket. 73b

IV.ii.12. R. Eliezer agrees with the House of Shammai that the M'MR completely acquires [the Hillelites require cohabitation].

b. Ket. 74a

*Comment*: Note also b. Naz. 62a: TNY': "Annulment of vows has no foundation [is without Scriptural support]. R. Eliezer says, 'It has support, for twice Scripture says, *When a man shall clearly utter* (Lev. 27 : 2, Num. 6 : 2), meaning, one to signify a distinct binding expression, and one a distinctness [to open the way] to annulment.' "

I.ii.79.A. She who awaits Levirate marriage, whether one or two Levirs—

B. R. Liezer says, "He may annul [her vows]."

C. R. Joshua says, "[If she is waiting] for one, and not for two [is it permitted to annul her vows]."

D. R. ʿAqiba says, "Not for one and not for two."

E. R. Leazar [Should be: *Liezer*] said, "If when a woman, in whom I have no part [y.: right (RŠWT)] until she comes to my possession, is completed for me [the relationship is complete], a woman in whom I have a part [y.; right] *before* she comes into my possession, when she comes into my position, is it not logical that she should be completely mine?"

F. R. ʿAqiba said to him, "No, if you have said so concerning a woman in whom I [y.: you] have no part before she comes into my [y.: your] possession, but when she comes into my possession, is completely mine, for just as I [beforehand] have no part in her, so others have no part in ḥer, will you say so concerning a woman in whom I *have* a part before she comes into my possession, and when she comes into my possession, she is completely mine? For just as I have a part in her, so others have a part in her."

G. R. Joshua said to him, "ʿAqiba, your words [apply] to two Levirs. What will you reply concerning one Levir?"

H. He said to him, "Just as you have not distinguished for us between [y. adds: *her who waits for*] one Levir and between two Levirs, between one who bespoke her and one who did not bespeak her (ʿŚH BH MʾMR = make a 'word'), so with reference to vows and oaths you should not make [such] distinctions." [y.: He said to him, "True."]

I. He said to him, "Would that you were in the time of Leazar b. ʿArakh [y.: Who said, The 'word' does not effect complete possession and agrees that he does not annul her vows until she enters his possession] and had answered such an answer!"

J. R. Liezer [Lieberman: *He*, meaning ʿAqiba; b.: *They said to R. Eliezer*] said to him, "A ritual pool (MQWH) will prove the point, for it raises up unclean things from their uncleanness, but does not save clean things from becoming unclean."

K. R. Liezer went and argued differently: "If in a situation in which he does not annul his own vows [after making them], lo, he [still] annuls his *own* vows before he vows, a situation in which he may annul the vows of his wife *after* she vows, is it not logical that he may annul the vows of his wife *before* she vows?"

L. They said to him, "But as to his annulling his own vows before he vows, if he wants to confirm, he confirms them. Will he annul the vows of his wife before she vows, for if he wants to confirm them, he cannot do so?"

M. "Another matter: *Her husband will confirm it and her husband will release it.* Whatever can be confirmed can be released, but whatever cannot be confirmed cannot be released."

Tos. Ned. 6 : 5, Lieberman, pp. 118-119,
ls. 23-41 (y. Ned. 10 : 6; part J: y. Ned. 10 : 7;
b. Ned. 75a = E, F; 75b = K)

*Comment*: Parts A-I supplement M. Ned. 10 : 6, and parts J-M supplement M. Ned. 10 : 7.

Parts A-D are identical to M. Ned. 10 : 6. Both Talmuds explain Eliezer's position in respect to the Levirs: one of them bespoke her (ʿŚH MʾMR). Eliezer holds that the Levir may then annul the vows, in association with the father.

Eliezer holds that a 'declaration' (MʾMR) completely acquires the woman, which is consistent with the view of the House of Shammai. The House of Hillel say only cohabitation effects the right to annul her vows, so b. Ned. 74a.

Joshua says if there is another Levir, beside the one who has bespoken the deceased husband's sister, then neither one can annul her vows. While the superficial sense of the Mishnah is that we are speaking of the two Levirs, either one of whom may annul the vows, it states, *he may annul*, not *they may annul*. Joshua says if she is waiting for one, he may annul the vow, but not for two.

b. Ned. 74a explains: R. Eliezer rules . . . that a declaration *completely* acquires the deceased brother's wife. But R. Joshua says that that applies only to one Levir, but not to two, "for can there be such a case that, though when his brother comes, he can prohibit her to him by cohabitation or divorce, yet he first can annul!"

Eliezer's argument in E is that if a man can annul his betrothed's vows, although before she has come into his possession he has no rights over her, he surely can annul the vows of the deceased husband's wife, in whom he has rights even before the Levirate marriage has taken place. He can, after all, prevent her from marrying anyone else. In F ʿAqiba points out that likewise no one else has any rights over the woman who becomes betrothed *until* her betrothal, so Eliezer's Levir has no special status. But others have a portion in the deceased husband's wife—the other Levir! Lieberman does not comment on this element. I am not clear on what right others have in the woman *after* the Levirate marriage.

In H, ʿAqiba then replies to Joshua's case, in which a single Levir may annul the vows. He says that there is no distinguishing between one or two Levirs. Even if there is only one Levir who has bespoken to woman, the person who has intercourse with her is not liable to the death penalty. Lieberman prefers the reply in M. Ned. 10 : 6: The deceased brother's wife is not completely in the possession of the Levir, but the betrothed woman *is* completely in the possession of her husband-to-be.

In I, Joshua says that Eleazar b. ʿArakh was of the view that the act of bespeaking (M'MR) acquires completely, even to free the co-wife. He might have accepted the answer in regard to annulling the vows of the woman awaiting Levirate marriage after the bespeaking (M'MR). He was of the view that as to annulling the vows, she is completely his wife, so he may annul vows, so Lieberman, *Tosefta Kifshuṭah Seder Nashim*, p. 485.

The argument with reference to annulling a wife's vows in advance (M. Ned. 10:7) begins in J. Lieberman says it is ʿAqiba's argument. Just as the ritual pool can annul uncleanness, but not prevent it, so the husband can annul vows after they are made, but not in advance. The answer is to the argument of Eliezer that if he can annul vows which have already been in force, he should be able to annul those which have not yet come into force. Then: "The ritual pool will prove otherwise . . ."

In K Eliezer argues that a man cannot annul his own vows after he has uttered them, but he *can* annul his own vows in advance. He should be able to annul his wife's vows in advance, since he also can annul them after she has uttered them. A man annuls his own vows in advance, according to M. Ned. 3 : 1, by saying, "Let no vow that I vow hereafter be binding." The answer in L is a good one. Even though a man may annul his own vows in advance, he may also confirm them. But—Eliezer has already agreed—he cannot confirm his wife's vows in advance.

M then repeats what is already in the Mishnah.

On Leazar b. ʿArakh, see Halivni, *Meqorot uMesorot*, pp. 338-339.

IV.ii.13. R. Eliezer said to them, "If defiled seeds are rendered clean by being sown in the soil, how much more so if sown and rooted!"

b. Ned. 76a

*Comment*: Likewise if a vow can be annulled when in force, surely annulment can prevent its enforceability.

I.i.97.A. He who said, "Lo, I am a Nazir," and became unclean on the thirtieth day loses (SWTR) the whole [preceding thirty days, and begins his vow again].

B. R. Eliezer says, "He loses only seven days."

C. [If he said] "Lo, I am a Nazir thirty days," and became unclean on the thirtieth day—he loses the whole.

M. Naz. 3 : 3 (y. Naz. 3 : 3, b. Naz. 6b, 16a-b)

I.i.98.A. [If he said] "Lo, I am a Nazir a hundred days[s]," and is made unclean on the hundredth day—he loses all.

B. R. Eliezer says, "He loses only thirty [days]."

C. [If] he is made unclean on the hundred and first day, he loses thirty days.

D. R. Eliezer says, "He loses only seven."

M. Naz. 3 : 4 (y. Naz. 3 : 4; b. Naz. 6b, 16a-b)

I.i.99.A. He who made the vow of a Nazir while in a graveyard—even if he was there thirty days, these do not count for him from the number [of days of the vow], nor does he bring an offering for uncleanness [contracted during his Nazirite period].

B. [If] he went out and came back, they count for him from the number [of days of the vow], and he does bring an offering for uncleanness.

C. R. Eliezer says, "Not [if he contracted uncleanness] on the same day [as he went forth from the graveyard], for it is written, *But the former days shall be void* (Num. 6 : 12)—only when he has 'former days' [may he bring the offering for uncleanness]."

M. Naz. 3 : 5 (y. Naz. 3 : 5; b. Naz. 16b;
Sifré Zuṭṭa 6 : 12, Horovitz, p. 243-244)

*Comment*: Num. 6 : 9-12 holds that if a Nazir is made unclean by contact with a corpse, the Nazir shaves his head and brings an offering and loses the time he has already observed his vow. The rule of M. Naz. 3 : 1 is that one who says, "Lo, I am a Nazir," shaves on the thirty-first day, but if he does so on the thirtieth, he has fulfilled his obligation. If, however, he specifies *thirty* days, he has not fulfilled his obligation if he shaves on the thirtieth.

How much time does he lose? A holds that if he is unclean on the thirtieth day—and the ordinary Nazirite vow is for thirty days (M. Naz. 1 : 3)—he loses the entire period, for Scripture says, *The former days shall be void.* Eliezer rules more leniently. The man loses only seven days, because he was fit to bring his offerings on the thirtieth day. He shaves his head on the seventh day of his uncleanness (M. Naz. 6 : 6), and he counts seven days to grow a new crop of hair, and shaves the clean growth (6 : 7), so he loses from the days already observed of the Nazirite vow only seven days—so Albeq, *Seder Nashim*, p. 201. These are, to be sure, in addition to the seven unclean—fourteen in all.

In C Eliezer agrees that the man loses the whole period, since on the thirtieth day he was not fit to bring his Nazirite sacrifices.

Eliezer is consistent in M. Naz. 3 : 4. If the man is made unclean on the hundredth day, he is not fit to bring his offerings. But Eliezer holds that since the man was made unclean on the day on which his Nazirite vow was complete, he does not lose more than thirty days, even though he was not fit to bring his sacrifices—a more lenient ruling than the foregoing. Eliezer therefore imposes a new Nazirite period, but not a whole hundred days. If the man is made unclean on the hundred-first day, when he indeed is fit to bring his sacrifices (or, if he was made unclean on the thirty-first day of a Nazirite vow of unspecified length), he loses thirty days according to the anonymous authority, and seven according to Eliezer. Eliezer here repeats his ruling in M. Naz. 3 : 3B, and for the same reason.

The one who made a vow while in a graveyard and does not leave the graveyard has not yet begun to observe his vow; therefore he does not bring an uncleanness-sacrifice. The days he spends in the graveyard do not count toward the completion of his vow. But if he went out and came back, the days he observed after he went out from the graveyard count toward the fulfillment of his vow. If he goes back before completing the vow, he does bring a sacrifice and loses the days he was outside of the graveyard. Eliezer rules that if the man was made unclean on the day on which he began to observe the days of his Nazirite vow, he does not lose that day and does not bring an offering because Scripture speaks of *days*, meaning more than one, to be lost—not a single day.

See Epstein, *Tan.*, pp. 66, 68, 121, 387-8; Halivni, *Meqorot uMesorot*, pp. 374-377, an important discussion.

I.ii.80.A. He who said, "Lo, I am a Nazir [for an unspecified period of time]," and contracts uncleanness on the thirtieth day loses the whole [period already observed]."

B. R. Judah says in the name of R. Liezer, "He loses only seven [days]."

C. [If he said], "Lo, I am a Nazir for thirty days," and contracts uncleanness on the thirtieth day, he loses the whole.

D. [If he said], "Lo, I am a Nazir for a hundred day[s]," and he contracts uncleanness on the hundredth day, he loses the whole.

E. R. Judah says in the name of R. Liezer, "He has lost only thirty [days]."

F. He who contracts uncleanness on the hundred-first day loses thirty.

G. R. Judah says in the name of R. Liezer, "He loses only seven."

H. This is the general rule that R. Judah said in the name of R. Liezer: "Whoever contracts on uncleanness on the day on which he is [*not*] fit to bring a sacrifice and does have to count (SPR) loses thirty days. And whoever contracts uncleanness on the day on which he is [Delete: *not*] fit to bring the sacrifice and does [not] have to count loses only seven days, excluding only the days of his uncleanness."

Tos. Nez. 2 : 12-13, Lieberman, p. 129, ls. 32-40

*Comment*: Judah is not cited in M. Naz. 3 : 3 as the tradent of Eliezer's teaching. Lieberman explains B: The Nazir counts seven clean days *after* the seven days in observance of his uncleanness. H should read following Lieberman, *Tosefta Kifshuṭah Seder Nashim*, p. 523), "Whoever contracts uncleanness on a day on which he is not fit to bring a sacrifice and has to count loses all" (= C). He who does not have to count loses thirty days (= E). And whoever contracts uncleanness on a day on which he is fit to bring the sacrifice and does not have to count has lost only seven days (= G) etc.

Thus if the man contracts uncleanness before the Nazir-sacrifices come due and has to count [more days of Naziriteship], he loses the antecedent period of Naziriteship which he has already observed. But if he contracts uncleanness on the day on which he may bring his sacrifice and has to count no more days, he loses only seven days, that is, as in B and G. The man observes the period of uncleanness and then seven clean days for the Hair-offering.

I.ii.81.A. "[A Nazir] who contracts uncleanness on his seventh day [of his period of purifying after the sprinkling for a former uncleanness] and went and contracted uncleanness on the eighth [Should be as in B: *seventh*] day [of the subsequent period, etc.] brings a sacrifice for each [contracting of uncleanness]," the words of R. Liezer.

B. R. Simeon says, "One sacrifice for all, until he brings his Guilt-offering [at the conclusion of the Nazirite period]."

Tos. Nez. 4 : 8, ed. Lieberman, p. 139,
ls. 40-43 (b. Naz. 18b, 19a-b, 20a, 54a)

*Comment*: If a Nazir contracted uncleanness on the seventh day after he has already begun to count the days of his Naziriteship in cleanness, he is liable for another sacrifice. See Lieberman, *Tosefta Kifshuṭah Seder Nashim*, pp. 551-553.

III.ii.55. Our rabbis taught: "If [a Nazirite] contracts uncleanness on the seventh day [of purification] and again contracts uncleanness on the seventh day following, he is required to offer only one sacrifice. If he contracts uncleanness on the eighth day and then again on the eighth day, he has to offer a sacrifice for each. He begins to reckon [the new period of Naziriteship] immediately"—the words of R. Eliezer.

B. But sages say, "He is required to offer only one sacrifice for all, so long as he has not yet offered Sin-offering."

b. Naz. 18b

*Comment*: This *baraita* follows the *eighth*-day reading in Tos. Ner. 4 : 8.

III.ii.56. TNY' NMY HKY: R. Judah says in the name of R. Eliezer, "Scripture says, *And this is the law of the Nazirite* [*on the day when the days of his separation are fulfilled* (Num. 6 : 13)]—the Torah says that if he contracts uncleanness on the day of his fulfillment, he is given the law of a Nazirite."

b. Naz. 20a

*Comment*: That is, he owes a new sacrifice for each such uncleanness.

IV.ii.14. R. Eliezer holds that [uncleanness contracted] after the fulfillment [of the period] renders void only seven days.

b. Naz. 16b

*Comment*: See M. Naz. 3 : 3.

I.i.100.A. He [the Nazir] in whose behalf the blood of one of the offerings was tossed [against the altar], and who [suddenly] contracted uncleanness—

B. R. Eliezer says, "He loses all [the offerings]."

C. And sages say, "Let him bring the rest of his offerings when [lit.: *and*] he will be clean."

D. They said to him, "M'ŚH B Miriam the Palmyrean in whose behalf the blood of one of the offerings was tossed, when they came and said to her concerning her daughter that she was in danger [of dying], and she went and found that she had died—

E. "Sages said, 'Let her bring the rest of her offerings [and] then she will be clean.'"

M. Naz. 6 : 11 (y. Naz. 6 : 11,
b. Naz. 14b, 47a, 63a)

*Comment*: The Nazir, at the conclusion of his Naziriteship, brings a male lamb, ewe lamb, and ram, which the priest offers (Num. 6 : 13ff). Here the sacrifice has begun and the blood of one of them was tossed, but then the Nazirite was made unclean (as in D). According to Eliezer he loses all the sacrifices, even the one whose blood has already been tossed, since the three offerings must be brought together, and not in segments. The sages credit the man with the sacrifice brought before he became unclean. They cite a precedent. E uses exactly the language of C, except for the feminine.

In M. Naz. 8 : 1 Joshua takes for granted one cannot bring his offerings piecemeal. He therefore knows the rule here attributed to Eliezer and agrees with it, against Ben Zoma. But Eliezer is not cited. Still, that is warrant for assigning the pericope to our Eliezer.

See Epstein, *Nusaḥ*, pp. 479, 1152; *Tan.*, pp. 66, 384.

I.ii.82.A. [A Nazir] on whose behalf the blood of one of the sacrifices has been tossed, who then contracts uncleanness—

B. R. Liezer says, "He loses all [the sacrifices already offered]."

C. And sages say, "Let him bring the rest of his sacrifice[s] [when he has become] clean, because his hair was sanctified by the blood." [After one of the sacrifice's blood has been sprinkled, his hair has been sanctified, and his Naziriteship has been completed.]

D. MʿŚH B: In behalf of Miriam the Palmyrean the blood of one of the sacrifices was tossed, and they came and they told her concerning the daughter, that she was in danger, and she went and found that she had died, and she became unclean on account of her [burial].

Sages said, "Let her bring the rest of her sacrifice [when she becomes] clean, because the hair has been sanctified by the blood."

Tos. Nez. 4 : 9-10, Lieberman, p. 140, ls. 53-57 (b. Naz. 28a, b. Shav. 28a: Eliezer says, "Shaving is a bar to drinking wine"; 39b; 46a: the whole rite must be completed)

*Comment*: Tos. adds the reason for the sages' opinion. When is the man ready to be shaved in completion of his Naziriteship? Scripture says that *after* the offerings, "The Nazirite shall shave his consecrated head at the door of the tent of meeting and shall take the hair from his consecrated head and put it on the fire ..." (Num. 6 : 18).

Eliezer holds that so long as all the sacrifices have not been offered, the Nazir is not ready to be shaved. If he is made unclean before the final one, the sacrifices which are already offered are as if they were offered during the period of his vow and are unfit. So long as the hair is on his head, he remains a Nazir. The sages' view is that the sprinkling of the blood of the first sacrifice marks the end of his Naziriteship Therefore when he becomes clean, he brings the rest of the offerings which he owes.

II.iv.13. *All the days of his Naziriteship* (Num. 6 : 4)—to make the days after his Naziriteship like the days in the midst of his Naziriteship, until the bringing of the sacrifice. For I might [say] he should not be liable except before he completes his Naziriteship. Scripture says, *And after that the Nazir will drink wine* (Num. 6 : 20)—"after *all* the [required] deeds," the words of R. Eliezer.

Sifré Num. 24, Friedman, p. 8b

*Comment*: Sifré supplies an appropriate exegesis for Eliezer's position.

I.i.101.A. A high priest and a Nazir do not make themselves unclean [by contact with the corpse of] their relatives [Lev. 21 : 11, Num. 6 : 7], but they make themselves unclean for a neglected corpse [MT MṢWH, Lev. 21 : 1].

B. [If] they were walking [together] on the way and found a neglected corpse—

C. R. Eliezer says, "The high priest should make himself unclean [in burying it] but the Nazir should not make himself unclean."

D. And sages say, "The Nazir should make himself unclean, but the high priest should not make himself unclean."

E. R. Eliezer said to them, "The priest should make himself unclean, for he does not bring a sacrifice on account of his uncleanness, but the Nazir should not make himself unclean, for he brings a sacrifice on account of his uncleanness."

F. They said to him, "Let the Nazir become unclean, for his sanctity is not a perpetual sanctity, but let not the priest make himself unclean, for his sanctity is a perpetual sanctity (QDŠT ʿWLM)."

M. Naz. 7 : 1 (y. Naz. 7 : 1; b. Naz. 47a;
M. Semaḥot 4 : 17, trans. Zlotnick, p. 44)

*Comment*: The issues are clearly set forth in the debate. Parts B-F elaborate A.

Since the high priest and the Nazir both make themselves unclean to bury a neglected corpse, the question naturally arises, If the two are together, which one does it? The theoretical question produces a carefully balanced, legal dispute in standard form. The only difference between C and D is the placing of the *not*; between E and F, the *for*-clauses.

Eliezer reasons that the Nazir should be saved the need to bring his uncleanness-sacrifice. The sages' view is that the sanctity of the high priest is a higher sanctity, for it lasts forever. That is why they drop *high* in F, since the high priest's sanctity in this perspective is no different from that of an ordinary priest; and in E Eliezer's *high* priest becomes a priest, presumably by analogy.

IV.i.15. R. Abin said . . . , "We have learned, 'The sages agree with R. Eliezer concerning a high priest and a Nazir that the Nazir should contract uncleanness and not the high priest, and R. Eliezer agrees with the sages . . . that the Nazir should contract uncleanness and not the high priest . . .'"

y. Naz. 7 : 1, Gilead, p. 68

*Comment*: I do not understand Abin's tradition.

IV.i.16. R. Huna in the name of R. Joseph, "The teaching of R. Eliezer is according to the House of Shammai, for the House of Shammai say, 'That which is continual and that which is holy—that which is continual comes first' [b. Ber. 51b]. R. Eliezer says, 'That which is continual and that which is holy—that which is continual comes first.'"

y. Naz. 7 : 1, Gilead, p. 68

*Comment*: See *Phar.* II, pp. 50-52. Here is warrant for assigning the pericope to our Eliezer.

I.i.102. (Because of these uncleannesses must the Nazirite cut off his hair: [Uncleanness contracted from] a corpse, or an olive's bulk of the flesh of a corpse . . . or a half-*log* of blood, or a half-*qav* of bones . . . whether [the uncleanness is contracted] from contact, or carrying, or overshadowing . . . Because of these a Nazirite must cut off his hair and be sprinkled on the third and seventh day; and it makes the preceding days of no effect; and he may not begin to count anew until he has become clean and brought his offerings—M. Naz. 7 : 2.)

A. R. ʿAqiba said, "I reasoned before R. Eliezer [as follows]: If a barleycorn's bulk of bone, which does not render a man unclean by overshadowing, causes the Nazir to shave on account of [his] touching and carrying [it], a quarter-*log* of blood, which does render a man unclean by overshadowing, ought logically to cause the Nazir to shave on account of [his] touching or carrying [it]."

B. "He said to me, 'What is this ʿAqiba! They do not reason here from a *qal veḥomer*.'

C. "And when I came and laid the matters out before R. Joshua, he said to me, 'Well have you spoken. But thus have they stated [the] law.'"

M. Naz. 7 : 4 (y. Naz. 7 : 4; b. Naz. 53a; 56b-57a; b. Pes. 81b)

*Comment*: ʿAqiba alludes to an anomaly in the law in M. Naz. 7 : 2. A barleycorn's bulk of bone is less effective in causing uncleanness than a quarter-*log* of blood. Yet the former does cause sufficient uncleanness to render the Nazir unclean, and the latter does not. Logically the quarter-*log* of blood should effect uncleanness. Yet M. Naz. 7 : 2 specifies a half-*log* of blood, not a quarter. Eliezer says that in such matters the *qal veḥomer* argument is inappropriate. Joshua tells ʿAqiba the same thing.

See Epstein, *Tan.*, pp. 81, 504, n. 30, 508; *Nusaḥ*, pp. 1136, 1168; Halivni, *Meqorot uMesorot*, pp. 422-3, an important discussion.

I.ii.83.A. R. Liezer says, "At first were the elders divided. Some say, 'A quarter-*log* of blood, and a quarter-*qav* of bones, and some say, 'Half-a-*qav* of bones and half-a-*log* of blood [b.: (are required) *for everything*].'

"The court which was after them said, 'A quarter-*log* of blood and a quarter-*qav* of bones as to Heave-offering and holy things [meats—these are burned if they come into contact with that quantity of blood or bones], and half-a-*qav* of bones and half-a-*log* of blood with reference to a Nazir and to [coming to] the sanctuary. [b. *baraita* has: Half-a-*qav* of bones/blood is for everything, a quarter-*qav* of bones/blood (is sufficient to render unclean) Heave-offering and sacred meats, but not in the case of a Nazirite or one preparing the paschal lamb.]"

Tos. Naz. 5 : 1, Lieberman, p. 141, ls. 5-9 (b. Naz. 52a, 53a)

*Comment*: See Lieberman, *Tosefta Kifshuṭah Nashim*, p. 557; Halivni, *Meqorot uMesorot*, pp. 419-422, for b. Naz. 52a.

I.i.103.A. He who warns [is jealous of] his wife (QN') [warns her not to go to a private place with a certain man]—

B. R. Eliezer says, "He warns her before two [witnesses] and makes her drink [the water of bitterness, Num. 5 : 18] before [on the evidence of] one [witness] or before [on the evidence of] himself."

C. R. Joshua says, "He warns her before two [witnesses] and causes her to drink on the evidence of two [witnesses]."

M. Sot. 1 : 1 (y. Sot. 1 : 1, 6 : 3; b. Sot. 2a-b; b. Sanh. 88a)

*Comment*: Eliezer and Joshua debate the evidence required for administering the 'water of bitterness' mentioned in Num. 5 : 14. According to Eliezer two witnesses must testify that the jealous husband warned her in their presence; otherwise she is not considered to have been warned, and she is not prohibited to the husband if she should go secretly with the named man, and he cannot make her drink the bitter water. If one witness or the husband himself testified that she indeed has gone secretly with the man, she must undergo the rite. Joshua regards the whole as subject to the normal laws of testimony; two witnesses are required for each stage in the process. M. Sot. 1 : 2 is formulated according to 1 : 1C:

> How does he warn her?
>
> If he said to her before two witnesses, "Speak not with such a one," and she spoke with him, she may still consort with her husband, and she may eat of Heave-offering.
>
> If she went aside with him in secret and remained with him long enough to suffer defilement, she may not consort with her husband, and she may not eat of Heave-offering.
>
> If her husband died [childless] she must perform *ḥaliṣah* and may not contract Levirate marriage.

See Halivni, *Meqorot uMesorot*, pp. 435-6.

I.ii.84. R. Yosi b. R. Judah says in the name of R. Eliezer, "He who warns his wife [does so] on the evidence of one witness or on his own evidence, and he causes her to drink on the evidence of two."

B. They answered the opinion of R. Yosi b. R. Judah, "The matter has no limit."

Tos. Sot. 1 : 1, Zuckermandel, p. 293, 1.1 (b. Sot. 2b)

I.ii.85.A. How much time is involved in intercourse, concerning which period of time witnesses must give testimony? Enough time for coition (HʿRʾH). And how much is [required for] coition?

B. R. Eliezer says [b.: Ishmael], "As much as walking around a palm tree (ḤZRT HDQL)." [Alt.: "For a date-palm to rebound," so A. Cohen].

C. R. Joshua says [b.: Eliezer], "Enough to mix a cup of wine."

D. Ben ʿAzzai says [b.: Joshua], "Enough time to drink it."

E. R. ʿAqiba says, [b.: Ben ʿAzzai], "Enough time to roast an egg." [b.: ʿAqiba, "Enough time to swallow it."]

F. R. Judah b. Batyra says, "Enough time to swallow three eggs, one after the other."

G. R. Eleazar b. ʿAzariah [b.: Jeremiah; y.: Pinḥas] says, "Enough time for a weaver to tie a knot (HGRDY NYMʾ)."

H. Ḥanan b. Menaḥem [b.: Pinḥas; y.: Minyamin] says, "Enough time for her to put out her hand to take a loaf from the basket..." [b.: "hand to her mouth to remove a chip of wood"].

Tos. Sot. 1 : 2, Zuckermandel, p. 293, ls. 6-9 (b. Sot. 44a; y. Sot. 1 : 2 = Tos. Sot. with minor changes)

*Comment*: Yosi has reversed the position of Eliezer.

IV.i.17. R. Leazar b. R. Yosi said before R. Yasa, "R. Liezer follows the House of Shammai, and R. Joshua, the House of Ḥillel."

y. Sot. 1 : 1, Gilead, p. 1

*Comment*: The reference is to M. Git. 9 : 10, *Phar.* II, pp. 37, 232.

II.iv.14.A. *And she is secreted with him* (Num. 5 : 13)—We have not heard the measure of 'being in secret with him' so that she should be unclean. Being in secret sufficient to become unclean is [one of the following:]

"Sufficient to walk around the palm tree," the words of R. Ishmael.

R. Eliezer says, "Enough to mix the cup."

R. Joshua says, "Enough to drink it."

Ben ʿAzzai says, "Enough to bake an egg."

R. ʿAqiba says, "Enough to swallow it."

R. Judah b. Bathyra says, "Enough to swallow three eggs one after another."

Sifré Num. 7, Friedman, p. 4a (Num. R. 9 : 10)

I.i.104.A. Hardly has she finished drinking before her face turns yellow and her eyes bulge and her veins swell, and they say, 'Take her away! take her away!—so that the Temple court not be made unclean.

But if she had any merit, this holds her punishment in suspense.

B. There is merit which suspends one year, there is merit which suspends two years, there is merit which suspends for three years.

C. On this basis—

Ben ʿAzzai says, "A man is obligated to teach his daughter Torah, that if she should drink [the bitter waters], she will know that the merit suspends for her." [If the process does not work immediately, it will work in time to come.]

D. R. Eliezer says, "Whoever teaches his daughter Torah is as if he teaches her lechery (TPLWT)."

E. R. Joshua says, "A woman prefers a *qav* [of sustenance] and lechery [sexual relations] to nine *qavs* [of sustenance] and abstinence [from sexual relations]."

M. Sot. 3 : 4 (b. Sot. 20a, 21b; y. Sot. 3 : 4)

*Comment*: C, D, E, and F are tacked on to the law of A. D and E are independent sayings. Once the question of merit's suspending the working of the water is raised, the issue of how the woman has acquired merit will be discussed. This produces Ben ʿAzzai's comment, that a man should teach his daughter Torah, so that if she should have to drink the bitter water, she will know that it will work eventually, if not right away.

Eliezer differs—for the same reason. If the daughter *has* merit, she will not fear the rite and therefore will be tempted.

Joshua says a woman would rather have a small amount of food but TPLWT, which must mean sexual relations, rather than a large living, but celibacy. Joshua's saying does not address the issues raised by Ben ʿAzzai's and Eliezer's, but is included because of the general consistency with the foregoing. The disagreement of C-D is not formulated in matching expressions. Ben ʿAzzai says a man is obligated to teach —Eliezer responds with a saying pertinent in substance, but not in form.

On TPLWT, see Epstein, *Nusaḥ*, p. 669; also *Tan.*, pp. 407-408.

I.i.105.A. One who warned his wife and she went aside in secret—

B. "Even if he heard from a bird flying by, he divorces her and gives the *Ketuvah*," the words of R. Eliezer.

C. R. Joshua says, "Until [Cambridge adds: ʾP] the women who spin their yarn by moonlight gossip about her."

M. Sot. 6 : 1 (y. Sot. 6 : 1; b. Sot. 31a)

*Comment*: Eliezer says the husband is obligated to divorce his wife, once she has been put on notice, on the basis of the flimsiest evidence. Joshua says the evidence of gossips is required—that is, slightly better than the former. Both are more or less consistent with their positions in M. Sot. 1 : 1. But on the basis of such evidence the woman does not lose her *Ketuvah*, nor does she drink.

See Epstein, *Nusaḥ*, pp. 84, 1161; *Tan.*, p. 411.

I.i.106. (*If one be found slain in the land lying in the field, and it is not known who slew him, then the elders and judges shall come forth and they shall measure the distance to the cities which are around him that is slain; and the elders of the city which is nearest the slain man shall take a heifer . . . and break the heifer's neck . . .* Deut. 21 : 1ff.)

A. "[If] he is found exactly between two cities, both of them bring two heifers," the words of R. Eliezer [Camb.: Leazar].

M. Sot. 9 : 2 (y. Sot. 9 : 2; b. Sot. 45b; Tos. Neg. 1 : 13)

I.i.107.A. "If his head is found in one place and his body in another place, they bring the head to the body," the words of R. Eliezer.

B. R. ʿAqiba says, "The body to the head."

M. Sot. 9 : 3 (y. Sot. 9 : 4; b. Sot. 45b)

I.i.108.A. From where do they measure?

B. R. Eliezer says, "From his navel [y. adds: The place where the embryo is found]."

C. R. ʿAqiba says, "From his nose [y. adds: The place of recognition]."

D. R. Eliezer b. Jacob says, "From the place where he was wounded—from the neck."

M. Sot. 9 : 4 (y. Sot. 9 : 3, b. Sot. 45b; b. Sanh. 88a; Mid. Tan. to Deut. 21 : 2, Hoffmann, pp. 123-4)

II.iv.15. "If they find the corpse's head in one place and the body in another, they bring the head to the body," the opinion of R. Eliezer.

R. ʿAqiba says, "The body to the head."

Sifré Deut. 205, Finkelstein, p. 241

II.iv.16. "If the corpse is found between two towns, both bring heifers," the words of R. Eliezer.

And sages say, "One town brings, but two do not bring two heifers."

Sifré Deut. 206, Finkelstein, p. 241 (b. Bekh. 18a)

II.iv.17. *The heifer of the herd—*

R. Eliezer says, "A heifer a year old and a red heifer two years old," etc. [see below, M. Par., p. 302].

Sifré Deut. 206, Finkelstein, p. 242

*Comment*: Eliezer's ruling comes without opposition in M. Sot. 9 : 2. He supplies a minor detail of what to do if the body is exactly between two towns. Do they each bring a heifer, or do they share in the cost of a single one? He holds they each bring one. y.'s version of M. Sot. 9 : 2 adds: "And sages say, 'One city brings a heifer (ʿGLH ʿRWPH), and two cities do not bring two heifers.'"

The little tractate continues in M. Sot. 9 : 3. Eliezer and ʿAqiba then differ as to the mode of measuring from a decapitated body, and in 9 : 4 they specify the point on the body where the measurement begins.

See Epstein, *Tan.*, pp. 173, 406.

II.v.4. *And he will cause the woman to drink*—against her wishes.

R. Eliezer says, "They beat her with the width of a sword and torment her (MʿRʿRYN), and they make her drink against her wishes."

R. ʿAqiba said to him, "We [thereby] shall know whether she is clean, if she said, 'I am unclean,' or if she said, 'I am clean.' When do they *force* her to drink? Once the Divine Name has been erased."

Sifré Zuṭṭa 24, Horovitz, p. 236

(Compare b. Sot. 19b, which omits Eliezer)

IV.i.18. [R. Joshua said in the name of] R. Liezer, "It is an obligation (ḤWBH)."

R. Joshua said, "It is optional (RŠWT)."

R. Leazar b. R. Yosi said before R. Yasa, "That of R. Liezer follows the House of Shammai, and that of R. Joshua follows the House of Hillel" etc.

y. Sot. 1 : 1, Gilead, p. 1

V.xi.2. *And he be jealous of his wife* (Num. 5 : 14).

R. Eliezer says, "It is his duty to do so."

And R. Joshua says, "It is optional."

R. Eliezer b. R. Yosi observed in the presence of R. Yosi, "R. Eliezer's view accords with that of the House of Shammai, while R. Joshua's view accords with that of the House of Hillel. R. Eliezer's with that of the House of Shammai, for the House of Shammai hold that a man may not divorce his wife unless he has found her to have committed an act of immorality. If he has found unseemly things in her, he cannot divorce her, since he has not found her to have acted immorally; neither can he retain her, because he has found unseemly things in her. Owing to these considerations R. Eliezer says it is the husband's *duty* to warn her.

"R. Joshua, however, follows the House of Hillel, for the latter say she can be divorced even if she has spoilt his broth, and for this reason he maintains that the warning is optional; if he wishes to warn her, he may do so; if he wishes to divorce her, he may do so."

Num. R. 9 : 30, trans. J. J. Slotki, p. 299

*Comment*: Eliezer's and Joshua's comment on Num. 5 : 14 consists of the single words, ḤWBH/RŠWT.

### xxi Giṭṭin, Qiddushin

I.i.109.A. He [an agent] who brings a *Geṭ from abroad* must say, "In my presence it was written, and in my presence it was sealed."

B. Rabban Gamaliel says, "Also he who brings [it] from HaReqem and from HaḤeger."

C. R. Eliezer [b: Eleazar] says, "Even from Kefar Ludim to Lud."

D. And sages say, "One does not have to say, 'In my presence it was written, and in my presence it was sealed,' except for him who brings [it] from abroad, and for him who takes it [abroad] (HMWLYK)."

M. Git. 1 : 1 (y. Git. 1 : 1, 2; b. Git. 4a)

*Comment*: Gamaliel and Eliezer (probably not Eleazar because of *Lud*) gloss the italicized words in A. Otherwise A was known to them, and they accepted its rule that the bearer must attest direct knowledge of the preparation of the *Geṭ*.

Gamaliel holds that if one brings the *Geṭ* from Reqem, on the eastern frontier of Palestine, and from Ḥeger, evidently on the south, he must make such a declaration, that is, not only from abroad (MDYNT HYM), but from nearby lands. Eliezer rules the declaration must be made even within Palestine, from a nearby village. So Eliezer and Gamaliel differ from A's *abroad*.

Then the sages in D differ from B-C, repeating the rule of A and taking into account the opinions of B-C. D has not generated A, but must depend on it.

*And him who takes it abroad* then is tacked on; no one has alluded to that matter.

In M. Git. 1 : 2, Judah refers to Reqem, therefore he knew 1 : 1 in its present form. But he has Ashqelon instead of Ḥeger and adds a northern locale.

See Epstein, *Nusaḥ*, p. 1108; Halivni, *Meqorot uMesorot*, pp. 481-485.

I.i.110.A. He who divorces his wife and says to her, "Lo, you are permitted to any man, except for so-and-so"—

B. R. Eliezer permits.

C. And sages prohibit.

D. What should he do? He should take it from her and give it to her again and say, "Lo, you are free to marry any man."

But if he had written [the condition in the *Geṭ*], even if he erased it, the *Geṭ* remains invalid.

M. Git. 9 : 1 (y. Git. 9 : 1; b. Git. 82a-b, 83a-b, 84a, 86a)

*Comment*: Eliezer regards the conditional *Geṭ* as valid. The wife may marry anyone except the specified man and is regarded as fully divorced. The sages say that she is not divorced, since the husband has limited the force of the *Geṭ*, which now does not permit her to marry anyone at all. D then depends upon, and takes for granted the correctness of the rule of, C.

See Halivni, *Meqorot uMesorot*, pp. 604-606.

III.ii.57. TNY': R. Yosi b. R. Judah said, "R. Eliezer and the sages did not differ concerning him who divorced his wife and said to her, 'Lo, you are free [to marry] every man except for so-and-so,' that she is not divorced.

"Concerning what [case] did they differ?

"Concerning him who divorces his wife and said to her, 'Lo, you are free to any man, on condition that you not marry so-and-so.' for—

"R. Eliezer [declares her] free for any man except that man.

"And sages prohibit."

b. Git. 82a-b

I.ii.86.A. He who divorces his wife and said to her, "Lo, you are permitted to any man except for so-and-so."

B. R. Eliezer permits her to marry any man except for that man.

C. And R. Eliezer agrees that if she remarried another and was widowed or divorced, she [then] is permitted to marry that one to whom she had been prohibited [by the exclusionary clause].

D. And after the death of R. Eliezer, four elders came together to reply to his opinions, R. Ṭarfon, R. Yosi the Galilean, R. Eleazar b. ʿAzariah, and R. ʿAqiba. [y. + b. add: R. Joshua said to them, "Are you not answering the lion after death?"]

E. R. Ṭarfon said, "If she went and married his brother [of the one forbidden to her], and he died without issue, how is she going to enter Levirate marriage? Does it not result that he makes a [contractural] condition against [b.: *Uproot*] what is written in the Torah, and whoever makes a condition against what is written in the Torah—his condition is invalid.

"Thus we [Sifré: you] have learned that this is not 'cutting off.'"

F. R. Yosi the Galilean said, "Where have we found a forbidden connection (ʿRWH) in the Torah permitted to one [man] and prohibited to [another] one.

"But she who is permitted to one is permitted to every man, and who is prohibited to one is prohibited to every man. Thus we have learned that this is not a 'cutting off.'"

G. R. Eleazar b. ʿAzariah says, "Cutting off—a thing [document] which cuts [the tie] between her and between him. [b.: *Thus you have learned that this is not a 'cutting off'*]."

R. Yosi the Galilean said, "I prefer the words of R. Eleazar."[y. omits. b. has a separate *baraita*.]

R. Simeon b. Eleazar says, "If she went and married another, and he divorced her and said to her, 'Lo, you are permitted to every man'—how does this one permit what the other had prohibited? Thus we have learned that this is not a 'cutting off.'" [b. omits here, adds afterward, so b. Git. 83b. Sifré omits.]

R. ʿAqiba said [Sifré: *says*], "Lo, if the one to whom she was prohibited was a priest, and the one who divorced her died—does it not come out that to him [that priest] she is a widow, but to [b.: *everyone*—omits:] all his brothers, the priests, she is a divorcee!

"Another matter [Sifré begins here]: And with whom did the Torah deal more stringently? Divorcées or widows? Divorcées are dealt with more stringently than widows. Now the divorcée, who is more stringently treated, is not prohibited from the one who is prohibited, but a widow, who is less stringently dealt with—is it not logical that she should be prohibited from him to whom she is permitted? [b.: There then follows an argument *a fortiori*: Seeing that she would have been forbidden to the priest as a divorcée, though this involves only a minor (transgression), should she not all the more as a married woman, which is much more serious, be forbidden to all men? From this you learn that this is no 'cutting off.']

"Another matter: [b. starts ʿAqiba here], She went and married another [b. From the market], and he had children from her and died [b.: She was widowed or divorced], when she returns to this one to whom she is [originally] prohibited, does it not come out that [b.: The *Geṭ* is void] the children of the first are *mamzerim*? Thus you have learned that this is not a cutting off."

[b. adds Joshua as in D.]

[b.: Rava said, "All these objections can be countered, except that of R. Eleazar b. ʿAzariah, in which there is no flaw." TNY NMY HKY: R. Yosi said, "I prefer the argument of R. Eleazar b. ʿAzariah."]

Tos. Git. 9 : 1-5, Zuckermandel, pp. 333-4, ls. 15-30, 1-3 (y. Git. 9 : 1, b. Git. 83a-b; Sifré Deut. 269, ed. Finkelstein, p. 289)

*Comment*: Deut. 24 : 1 speaks of a "book of cutting off," meaning a divorce-document which effects a "cutting off" or complete separation is required (b. Git. 21b).

C is necessary for the arguments of Ṭarfon and ʿAqiba that follow, which take for granted the inoperability of the clause after the first remarriage. Eleazar b. ʿAzariah's and Yosi's arguments stand without reference to complications after the first remarriage. So C looks like an ʿAqiban interpolation.

The four surviving rabbis offer arguments against Eliezer's position that a conditional clause in a *Geṭ* is acceptable. Ṭarfon points out the possibility that the *Geṭ* contains a clause potentially contrary to Torah-law, for the husband cannot establish conditions which might make it impossible for the divorced wife to carry out the commandment concerning Levirate marriage. Yosi simply says that the divorce has to be complete. One cannot divorce for everyone, but remain married in respect to one man. Eleazar b. ʿAzariah has essentially the same argument, but his is phrased in exegetical terms. ʿAqiba, like Ṭarfon, points out a possible anomaly in the situation. If the woman is prohibited from marrying a priest, and then the one who divorced her died, to that priest she now is not regarded as a divorcée— if she were a divorcée, she could not marry him—but only as a widow. So she cannot marry any priest except that one who was prohibited to her under the terms of the divorce. The *qal veḥomer* spells out the anomaly.

Then comes a weightier argument. If later on she remarries and has children, and then the second husband dies, she may then marry the one prohibited in terms of the original divorce (as specified in C). But this act retroactively renders the children of the second marriage *mamzerim,* for their mother at the time of their birth was not legally divorced.

Eleazar b. ʿAzariah's argument, based on exegesis, is selected by Rava and by Yosi. b.'s *baraita,* assigning the saying to Yosi b. Ḥalafta, is probably better than Tos., which gives it to Yosi the Galilean, who is a party to the discussion.

Tos.'s text is satisfactory, because of the inclusion of the later Simeon b. Eleazar. y. interpolates Amoraic comments. b. has straightened things out.

II.i.7.A. *He shall send him out free.* I might understand this to mean that the master must write him a writ of emancipation. But it says, "For his eye's sake."

B. R. Eliezer says, "Here *sending out* is spoken of and there (Deut. 24 : 1) *sending out* is spoken of. Just as the *sending out* spoken of there means by a writ, so also the *sending out* spoken of here means by a writ."

Mekh. Neziqin 9 : 29-30, Lauterbach III, pp. 71-72 = 9 : 53ff., III, p. 73 (y. Git. 4 : 4, b. Git. 42b, b. Qid. 24b)

*Comment*: Eliezer's opinion is given in b. Git. 42b in the setting of those of Meir, Ṭarfon, and ʿAqiba. This *may* be our Eliezer. But b. Git. knows nothing of his *heqqesh.* In Mekh., Ishmael follows, on a separate matter.

III.ii.58. TNYʾ: [*To sell her to a foreign people he shall have no power] seeing that he has dealt deceitfully with her* (BBGDW BH) (Ex. 21 : 8)—"Once he spread his cloak (BGD) over her, he can no longer sell her," the words of R. ʿAqiba.

R. Eliezer says, "Seeing that he has dealt deceitfully with her—having dealt deceitfully with her, he cannot sell her [again]."

b. Qid. 18b (b. Bekh. 34a)

*Comment*: ʿAqiba interprets *deceitfully* as *cloak* (BBDGW/BGD), while Eliezer follows the ordinary meaning of the Scripture.

I.i.111.A. Every commandment which depends upon the land is observed only in the Land [of Israel], and which does not depend upon the land is observed in the Land [of Israel] and abroad, except (ḤWS MN) for ʿ*orlah* and mixed seeds (KLʾYM).

B. R. Eliezer [b.: Eleazar] says, "Also except for (ʾP MN) the [law of] new [produce]."

M. Qid. 1 : 9 (y. Qid. 1 : 8 reverses order of A; b. Qid. 73a; Sifré Deut. 59, Finkelstein, p. 125; Midrash Tannaim to Deut. 12 : 1, ed. Hoffmann, p. 47)

*Comment*: Commandments pertaining to agriculture, such as Heave-offerings and tithes, are observed only in Palestine. Those which pertain to ordinary daily life, such as the Sabbath, are observed everywhere. The specified exceptions have to do with ʿ*orlah*-fruit and produce grown from mixed seeds (Lev. 19 : 19, 23), taboos which apply abroad as well.

Eliezer's saying is formulated as a gloss on the foregoing; ʾP(MN) depends upon ḤWS(MN). He holds that the prohibition against eating new grain before the offering of the ʿ*omer* (Lev. 23 : 14), even though this too is an obligation pertaining to land, applies abroad as well as in Palestine.

It is difficult to find an exegetical basis for the exceptions. Lev. 19 includes reference to *Peʾah*, the forgotten sheaves, as well as mixed seeds, ʿ*orlah* fruit, and the like.

III.ii.59. R. Yoḥanan b. Nuri in the name of R. Eliezer the Great, "There is no ʿ*orlah* in the diaspora."

b. Qid. 39a = Tos. Orl. 1 : 8 (p. 83)

*Comment*: Accordingly, Eliezer would exclude ʿ*orlah* in A, and ʾP is dropped. This is warrant for assigning the foregoing to our Eliezer. But Yoḥanan knows nothing about Eliezer on the new-produce-taboo; if he had, he should have said ʾP or included ḤDŠ. ʿAqiba and Ishmael comment on the same problem, b. Qid. 37a.

See Epstein, *Nusaḥ*, pp. 342, 535; *Tan.*, p. 178: The authority is Eliezer b. R. Yosi.

I.i.112.A. R. Ṭarfon says, "*Mamzers* can be purified [from their *mamzerut*, so that their children will not be *mamzers*.]

B. "How so? A *mamzer* who married a female slave—the off-spring is a slave. [If] he frees him, it comes out that the son is a free man."

C. R. Eliezer says, "Lo, this one is [remains merely] a *mamzer*-slave."

M. Qid. 3:13 (y. Qid. 3:13; b. Qid. 69a; b. Yev. 85b)

*Comment*: According to Ṭarfon the offspring of the marriage of a *mamzer* and a female slave is not regarded as a *mamzer*. Ṭarfon has drawn the consequences of the antecedent law (M. Qid. 3 : 12) and also holds a *mamzer* may marry a slave.

If the betrothal was valid and no transgression befell [by reason of the marriage], the standing of the offspring follows that of the male parent. Such is the case when a woman that is the daughter of a priest, a Levite, or an Israelite, is married to a priest, Levite, or Israelite.

If the betrothal was valid but transgression befell [by reason of the marriage], the standing of the offspring follows that of the blemished party. Such is the case when a widow is married to a High Priest, or a divorced woman or one that has performed *ḥaliṣah* is married to a common priest, or a *mamzer* or a *Netinah* is married to an Israelite, or the daughter of an Israelite to a *mamzer* or a *Netin*.

If her betrothal to this man was not valid, but her betrothal with others would be valid, the offspring is a *mamzer*.

Such is the case when a man has connection with any of the forbidden degrees prescribed in the Torah.

If her betrothal with this man was not valid, and her betrothal with others would also not be valid, the offspring is of her own standing [e.g. Ṭarfon's case]. This is the case when the offspring is by a slave-woman or a gentile woman.

Ṭarfon relying upon the final clause, holds that the slave-woman cannot become validly betrothed to anyone. Therefore the offspring follows the standing of the mother. Eliezer does not accept the foregoing rule, for he says that the status of *mamzer* is not overcome through such a marriage. But we have no general rule according to which he gives his specific decision.

See Epstein, *Nusaḥ*, pp. 1136, 1167.

I.ii.87. [*Do not profane your daughter by making her a harlot*] *lest the land fall into harlotry* [*and the land become full of wickedness*] (Lev. 19 : 29).

B. What is harlotry?

C. R. Eliezer [Eleazar] says, "This is the unattached man who has intercourse with the unattached woman not for the sake of marriage."

D. R. Eliezer [Eleazar] said, "How do we know that he is punished before the Omnipresent like one who has intercourse with a woman and her mother? Here [Lev. 19 : 29] *harlotry* is said: *A man who takes a woman and her mother—it is harlotry* (Lev. 20 : 14)."

Tos. Qid. 1 : 4, Zuckermandel, p. 335 ls. 2-4

*Comment*: See Lieberman, *Tosefet Rishonim*, II, p. 82, for *Eleazar*.

III.ii.60. TNY': *Do not profane thy daughter to cause her to be a whore* (Lev. 19 : 29). R. Eliezer says, "This refers to marrying one's [young] daughter to an old man."

R. ʿAqiba says, "This refers to the delay in marrying off a daughter who is already a *bogeret.*"

b. Sanh. 76a, trans. H. Freedman, pp. 516-517

III.ii.61.A. TNY': "*Zonah* [Lev. 21 : 7, a priest cannot marry a harlot] is what the name suggests [= a faithless wife],"—the words of R. Eliezer.

B. R. ʿAqiba says, "A *zonah* is a prostitute."

b. Yev. 61b

III.ii.62. R. Eliezer [Eleazar] said, "An unmarried man who had intercourse with an unmarried woman without matrimonial intent renders her a *zonah.*"

b. Yev. 61b (b. Sanh. 51a)

*Comment*: ʿAqiba would seem to provide a small warrant assigning the several sayings to our Eliezer.

### xxii. Bava Qamma, Bava Meṣiʿa', Bava Baṭra

I.i.113.A. If a man lit a fire within his own [property], how far may it spread [for him to be accountable for the damage it causes within that area]?

B. R. Eleazar b. ʿAzariah says, "They regard it as if it is in the middle of a *bet kor* of land."

C. R. Eliezer says, "Sixteen cubits [in every direction], like the public road."

D. R. ʿAqiba says, "Fifty cubits."

E. R. Simeon says, "*The one who makes the fire will certainly pay* (Ex. 22 : 5)—all goes according to the fire."

M. B.Q. 6 : 4 (y. B.Q. 6 : 6, b. B.Q. 61a-b; Mekh. Nez. 14 : 37-42)

*Comment*: Eleazar b. ʿAzariah says one regards the fire as if it were set in the middle of a square field the size of a *bet kor*, 274 cubits by 274 cubits (75,000 square cubits), so in every direction are 137 cubits. If the fire passes that measure, the man is free of liability. Eliezer and ʿAqiba give measurements for that same distance; their sayings depend upon Eleazar's, and the pericope is a unity. Simeon says all depends upon the size of the fire.

The pericope follows a series of laws on the subject of culpability for damages caused by fire. All are anonymous. The Yavnean problem is introduced by the following: "If it [the fire] passed over a fence four cubits high or over a public way or a river, he that caused it is not culpable." Albeq explains the principle: It is not common for a fire to spread such distances. Then comes A, which applies the foregoing to private domain.

On Simeon, see Epstein, *Nusaḥ*, p. 1136.

I.ii.88.A. He who kindles a fire in his own property, how far may the fire spread spread?

B. R. Eliezer says, "Sixteen cubits, like the public road; when there is wind, thirty cubits."

C. R. Judah says, "Thirty cubits; when there is wind, fifty cubits."

D. R. ʿAqiba says, "Fifty cubits; when there is wind, three hundred [y.: *one hundred*] cubits."

Tos. B.Q. 6 : 22, Zuckermandel,
p. 356, ls. 18-21 (y. B.Q. 6 : 6)

*Comment*: Tos. introduces a windy day, drops Eleazar b. ʿAzariah, and introduces Judah [b. Ilai]. The opinions of Eliezer and ʿAqiba remain as in M. B.Q. 6 : 4.

III.i.12. TNY | : "*And the owner of the ox shall be clear* (NQY) (Ex. 21 : 28)—clear of paying half the ransom (KWPR)"—the words of R. Eliezer.

R. ʿAqiba said to him, "Rabbi, Is he not first (MWQDM) for stoning, [which is] stringent? [Therefore no ransom is required, and why produce an exegesis to prove the obvious?]"

He said to him, "I spoke only of the case where he [the ox] intended to kill the ox and killed the man [where he is not put to death]."

y. B.Q. 4 : 5, Gilead, p. 40

III.ii.63A. TNW RBNN: *But the owner of the ox shall be clear* (Ex. 21 : 28)—"Clear from paying half the ransom (*kofer*) [in the case of an animal not used to do damage (TM)]"—the words of R. Eliezer.

B. R. ʿAqiba said to him, "Since [any actual liability in the case of the] ox itself is not paid except out of its body, [why cannot the owner say to the plaintiff] 'Bring it to court and be reimbursed out of it'?"

C. R. Eliezer said to him, "Am I such in your eyes that my exposition (DYNY) [should be taken to refer to a case of an ox] liable [to be stoned to] death?

"My exposition referred only to one who killed a human being in the presence of one witness or in the presence of the owner [when the ox is not stoned to death]."

D. TNY' 'YDK: R. Eliezer said to him, "'Aqiba, Am I such in your eyes that my exposition [refers to an ox] liable [to be stoned] to death? My exposition [referred] only to one who had been intending to kill [another] beast and by accident killed a man ... [when he is not liable to the death penalty]."

b. B.Q. 41b-42a

*Comment*: M. B.Q. 4 : 5 reads: "If an ox gores a man and he dies, the *mu'ad* pays the *kofer*, and the *Tam* is clear of the *kofer*, and both [kinds of ox] are liable to be put to death." Eliezer's exegesis has the owner free of liability for the ransom in the case of the *tam*; accordingly, he (along with 'Aqiba) stands behind, or agrees with, M. B.Q. 4 : 5. 'Aqiba says that since the ox is put to death and its carcass cannot be used, there can be no payment in the case of a *tam*; the exegesis is purposeless. Eliezer replies that he speaks of a case in which the ox is not stoned, or of an accidental killing, in which the ox is put to death. The exegesis serves that situation.

I.ii.89. R. Eliezer [b.: the Great] says, "He who raises dogs is like him who raises pigs."

Tos. B.Q. 8 : 17, Zuckermandel,
p. 362, ls. 31-2 (b. B.Q. 83a)

*Comment*: Now we have an affirmative formulation of Eliezer's saying, above Tos. Yev. 2 : 4, p. 178. Tos. B.B. 1 : 9, Zuckermandel, p. 398, l. 31 has, "R. Eleazar says, "He who raises bees (DBWRYM) is like him who raises dogs."

III.ii.64. TNY': R. Eliezer said, "*An eye for an eye* (Ex. 21 : 24)—means literally an eye [is removed]."

b. B.Q. 84a

*Comment*: Eliezer stands against the exegetes who understand the Scripture to require a money-payment in the value of an eye. This is not necessarily our Eliezer.

I.ii.90.A. "He who acquires the property of the proselyte—if he walked in it [the land], whether its length or its width, lo, he has acquired the place where he walked," the words of R. Eliezer.

And sages say, "The two of them did not acquire until the time that they established possession."

Tos. B.B. 2 : 11, Zuckermandel, p. 400,
ls. 22-25 (b. B.B. 100a; y. Qid. 1 : 3, 5;
M. Gerim 3 : 9; Gen. R. 41 : 10)

*Comment*: Eliezer here holds one acquires property by walking in it. b. B.B. 100a says this teaching is consistent with that of the Eliezer mentioned in b. Eruv. 94a (above, p. 113) so this would seem to be our Eliezer; but the argument is circular—perhaps neither is ours. This should, in fact, *not* be our Eliezer, in the light of M. B.B. 9 : 7, where Eliezer is clear on the matter of acquiring real estate!

I.i.114.A. He who apportions his goods by his word—

B. R. Eliezer says, "Whether [he is] healthy or dying—property for which there is security [= real estate] [So Danby, p. 379, for NKSYM ŠYŠ LHN ʾḤRYWT] is acquired by money, writ, or by usucaption [= the buyer does some kind of work on the land].

"And those [movables] which do not have security are acquired only by usucaption."

C. They said to him, "MʿŚH B The mother of the sons of Rokhel was sick, and she said, 'Give my veil to my daughter,' and it was worth twelve hundred *denars*. And she died and they carried out her words."

D. He said to them, "May their mother bury the sons of Rokhel."

E. And sages [Alt.: R. Eliezer says] say, "On the Sabbath, his words are carried out, because he cannot write, but not on the weekday."

F. R. Joshua says, "[If] they said so concerning the Sabbath [that he may assign property without acquisition], how much the more so on the weekday."

M. B.B. 9 : 7 (y. B.B. 9 : 7, b. B.B. 156a-b)

*Comment*: Eliezer's rule is that a verbal will is of no effect. He then distinguishes between real estate (secured property) and movables (other property). The former is acquired in one of the three ways listed, the latter only by usucaption. The sages cite a precedent in which movables were acquired other than by usucaption, for, in the case of a dying person, acquisition is not required. So the sages' opinion should have been something like, "In health, by acquisition; and at the point of death, not by acquisition," etc.

Eliezer rejects the precedent by claiming that the sages were especially strict with the sons of Rokhel, and therefore they had to give up the veil even without the proper act of acquisition on the part of the daughter.

Then in E we gave a distinction between the Sabbath and weekdays, in which sages [or Eliezer] say that on the Sabbath no act of acquisition is required. Joshua replies that since it is possible on a Sabbath to acquire, even though no act of acquisition or deed normally is done, likewise this must be possible on the weekdays.

See Epstein, *Nusaḥ*, pp. 134, 1143, 1160, 1179; *Tan.*, pp. 66, 236.

I.ii.91.A.1. He who was dying and divided his goods orally, whether on the weekday or on the Sabbath, the words of the dead are to be done. But a healthy person—[they are not acquired] until he will make acquisition with money, a document, or usucaption.

2. R. Eliezer says, "Real estate is acquired with money and with a document and with usucaption, and movables are acquired only by money."

B. R. Eliezer said, "MʿŚH B A Meronite was in Jerusalem, and he had many movables and wanted to give them as a gift. They said to him, 'You cannot, for you have no land.' [y.: *You have no remedy but to buy land.*] He went and bought a stone near Jerusalem.

"He said, 'Its northern [*part*] [y.: *half*] is of [= belongs to] this one, and with it a hundred sheep and a hundred jars of wine are given to so-and-so.'

'Its southern corner [y.: *half*] is for this one, and with it a hundred sheep and a hundred jars of wine are given to so-and-so. [y. omits:] 'Its eastern corner is of this one, and with it a hundred sheep and a hundred jars of wine are given to so-and-so.'

"And the [y.: *matter came to*] sages confirmed his words."

[y. omits:] Under what circumstances? On a weekday, but not on the Sabbath is it done; but if he did it, it is done.

R. Joshua says, "They spoke of the Sabbath, all the more so of a weekday."

Tos. B.B. 10 : 12, Zuckermandel, p. 412, ls. 24-34
(y. B.B. 9 : 7; b. B.B. 156b-157a)

*Comment*: Now Eliezer has a precedent for his opinion.

III.ii.65.A. TNYʾ: R. Eliezer said to the sages, "Once there was a man of Meron in Jerusalem who had much movable property, which he wanted to give as a gift. They said to him that there is no means [of doing so] unless he transferred possession [to the donees] by land [transferred to them at the same time].

"He bought a rocky piece of land near Jerusalem and said, 'Its northern side is for so-and-so, together with it a hundred sheep and a hundred casks.'

"And when he died, the sages confirmed his instructions."

B. They said to him, "Is there proof from there? The Meronite was in good health [but if he had been dying, oral instructions alone would have sufficed]."

b. B.B. 156b

III.ii.66.A. TNYʾ: R. Meir says, "R. Eliezer said, 'On a week day his [verbal] instructions are legally valid because he is able to write, but not on the Sabbath.' R. Joshua said, 'They said this in respect to a weekday, and how much the more so in the case of the Sabbath ...'"

III.ii.67. R. Judah said, "R. Eliezer said, 'On the Sabbath his instructions are legally valid, because he is unable to write, but not on a weekday.' R. Joshua said, 'If they said this in respect to the Sabbath, how much the more so in the case of a weekday ...'"

b. B.B. 157a

*Comment*: The Mishnah follows R. Judah's version.

The course of the discussions of the various traditions permits me to propose that several distinct issues have been combined in the pericopae just reviewed.

First, is a verbal will of legal effect? Eliezer says it is of no legal effect. Whether well or sick, the man can do nothing. So property for which there is security must be acquired in the normal way, and movables likewise. Then the precedent in M. B.B. 9 : 7B is cited to indicate to the contrary, that the verbal will (of a dying person) is of effect. Eliezer rejects the precedent.

Then the issue is revised in E-F, and the problem is introduced, What of the Sabbath (as above, p. 74, in respect to tithing)? Eliezer, or the sages, is now made to say that a verbal will is acceptable on the Sabbath, but not on a weekday—so his former position is rejected, and a new one, consistent with an established principle enunciated by Eliezer, is introduced. Joshua then reaffirms the original proposition: Under all circumstances a verbal will is acceptable.

So the primary issue must be as given in M. B.B. 9 : 7B, and M. B.B. 9 : 7A is an inappropriate superscription for B, because it ignores what Eliezer is actually going to say, namely, that one may under no circumstances apportion his goods by his word. But A does serve for E-F, and not merely in a general way.

If we drop the connecting word, *and*, we have

> He who apportions his good by his word—
>
> Sages/Eliezer say[s], On the Sabbath, his words are carried out, but not on the weekday.
>
> Joshua says, Both on the Sabbath and on the weekday, his words are carried out.

Now, why should Eliezer agree that one may effect the will on the Sabbath? If the man is well, there is no reason for such a concession. Clearly, the reason must be that the man is sick. So the distinction between Sabbath/weekday carries in its wake the issue of whether the man is well or sick. The contrary is not necessarily the case. If so, B's *whether he is healthy or dying* is irrelevant where it stands, but it is pertinent to E-F. The primary issue should be as represented in B, in which case B has been doctored after the completion of the revisions represented by E-F.

Eliezer's original saying should be simply that a verbal will is not possible; then he should be made to say it is acceptable for the Sabbath, but not otherwise, and this will produce F for Joshua. But the considerable development of B—with a distinction between real estate and movables—is beside the point. This is shown by C. The point of the precedent is simply that a verbal will has been carried out, not that the veil has been (from Eliezer's viewpoint, improperly) acquired. That matter is never introduced. We do not have Eliezer's original opinion.

Yet, perhaps his original words were irrelevant to the issue at hand. B may be those original words, and they may pertain to another question entirely, namely, differing ways of acquiring real estate and movables. The whole complex has been placed in a new setting, with the addition of *whether healthy or dying*—the only words pertinent to the new redactional framework, and irrelevant to the distinction between real estate and movables. In that case the best formulation of Eleazar's ruling is Tos. B.B. 10 : 12A2 which makes no reference to health or sickness, Sabbath or weekday—or to a verbal will! Then in B Eliezer is supplied with a precedent for his opinion, confirming the supposition that the issue of Eliezer's saying is the principle of how one acquires a gift, not the problem of a verbal will at all. Tos. strikingly ignores the redactional and legal issues of M. M.'s clauses E-F are central to Meir's and Judah's formulation of the problem, and the Mishnaic version ought to begin with them—particularly, with Judah—and Tos. should in this case provide an accurate account of the original issue addressed by Eliezer.

## xxiii. Sanhedrin, Makkot, Shavuʿot, ʿAvodah Zarah, Horayot

I.i.115.A. The wolf, the lion, the bear, the panther, the leopard, and the snake are judged for capital crimes (MYTTN) by a court of twenty-three.

B. R. Eliezer says, "Whoever comes first to kill him [without a court action] has acquired merit."

C. R. ʿAqiba says, "They are judged for capital crimes by a court of twenty-three."

M. Sanh. 1 : 4 (y. Sanh. 1 : 2; b. Sanh. 2a, 15b)

*Comment*: The antecedent law rules that as the owner of an ox is put to death by a court of twenty-three, so too is the ox. The anonymous rule in A, repeated by ʿAqiba in C, with *they* for the list of animals, extends the same law to the other beasts. Eliezer says they are *not* given a court trial; he is not consistent with his position in M. B.Q. 1 : 4. It would seem that B glosses A, and C glosses by repeating A. If B-C come before A, they have not been matched; B depends upon A for its meaning. Does this mean that ʿAqiba knew A and simply cited it? Or was ʿAqiba's formulation of the law taken up and made into A?

b. Sanh. 15b says ʿAqiba differs with A in respect to the snake.

I.ii.92.A. An ox which killed—it is all the same for an ox that killed and for other beasts and cattle [b. omits:] and birds that killed—they [all] are judged for a capital crime (MYTTN) by a court of twenty-three [judges].

B. R. Eliezer says, "The ox that killed is judged for his capital crime by a court of twenty-three. But the rest of the cattle, beasts, and birds which killed—whoever comes first to kill them acquires merit in Heaven, as it is said, *And you will kill the woman and the ox*, and it says, *And the ox you will kill* (Lev. 20 : 16)."

Tos. Sanh. 3 : 1, Zuckermandel, p. 418, ls. 7-10 (b. Sanh. 15b)

*Comment*: Now we have Eliezer's view phrased as a general rule, not in respect only to the aforementioned beasts alone. He holds only the ox is judged by a regular court. Other animals are simply slaughtered as rapidly as possible.

II.ii.5. R. Eliezer says, "The ox that kills is put to death by the decision of a court of twenty-three, and as to other cattle and wild beasts and birds that killed—whoever kills them first acquires merit in Heaven."

Mekhilta deR. Simeon b. Yoḥai, p. 181, ls. 6-7

I.i.116.A. "All those who are stoned to death are hung," the words of R. Eliezer.

B. And sages say, "Only the blasphemer and idolator are hung."

C. "They hang the man with his face to the people, and the woman with her face to the tree," the words of R. Eliezer.

D. And sages say, "The man is hung, and the woman is not hung."

E. R. Eliezer said to them, "Did not Simeon b. Sheṭaḥ hang women in Ashqelon?"

F. They said to him, "He hung eighty women, and they do not judge two on one day." [y. adds: *But the hour required it.*]

M. Sanh. 6 : 4 (y. Sanh. 6 : 6, b. Sanh. 45b, 46a)

*Comment*: A-B are straightforward. Deut. 21 : 22 says that they hang a person on a tree. Deut. 21 : 23 says, *For hanging is a curse of God.* Eliezer holds that as the one who curses God—the blasphemer—is stoned and hung, so *all* who are stoned are to be hung. The sages say the reference is specific: the blasphemer *alone.*

But in C Eliezer does not rule on the issue raised by D. The sages say women are not hung. Eliezer does not say women are hung. He takes that for granted and rules that they are hung *facing the tree.* His saying is not appropriate to D. But the *precedent* of E is appropriate: the issue is hanging women, not which way to hang their bodies. If E were matched with C, it would have had something about Simeon's hanging the women with their faces to the tree. F is incomplete; it should add that the times required extreme action, but in normal times one would not hang women, as in y.

See *Phar.* I, pp. 90-93; Epstein, *Nusaḥ*, p. 1261; *Tan.*, pp. 155, 418.

III.ii.68. TNW RBNN: "*And if he be put to death, then you shall hang him on a tree* (Deut. 21 : 22). I might think that all who are put to death are to be hanged. Scripture states, *For he is hanged because of a curse of God.* Just as the blasphemer is stoned, so all who are stoned [are hanged]"—the words of R. Eliezer.

And sages say, "Just as the blasphemer denied the fundamental principle, so all who deny the fundamental principle [are hung, but no others]."

b. Sanh. 45b

I.ii.93.A. "At a distance of four cubits from the place of stoning, they would take off the clothes of the man and cover for him a section (PRQ) in front, and the woman, the section (PRQ) in front and behind, because the woman is wholly erotic (ʿRWWH)"—the words of R. Judah, which he said in the name of R. Eliezer.

B. And sages say, "The man is stoned naked, and the woman is not stoned naked."

Tos. Sanh. 9 : 6, Zuckermandel, p. 429, ls. 15-18

II.iv.18. *And when a man is subject to the death penalty and is put to death*—

The man is hung and the woman is not hung.

R. Eliezer says, "Also the woman is hung."

R. Eliezer said to them, "And did not Simeon b. Sheṭaḥ hang women in Ashqelon?"

They said to him, "He hung eighty women, and they do not judge two [to death] on one day. But the hour required teaching others by that means."

Sifré Deut. 221, Finkelstein, p. 253

II.iv.19. R. Eliezer says, "Just as the blasphemer is special in that he is stoned, and he is hung, so all who are stoned are hung."

Sifré Deut. 221, Finkelstein, p. 254
(Mid. Tan. to Deut. 21 : 22, ed. Hoffmann, p. 132)

*Comment*: The disagreement is now extended to stoning, but the principle is the same. And the phrasing of Eliezer's saying is just as inappropriate. It takes for granted that a woman is stoned *naked* and explains just how this is done. But the sages' comment makes it clear that the issue is not *how* it is done, but whether it is done at all, just as in M. It would seem that Judah has developed Eliezer's opinion, which ought to have been, *Both a man and a woman are stoned naked*, into a description of the procedure for so doing.

Judah provides both warrant for assigning the whole set to our Eliezer and an Ushan attestation.

I.i.117. (If a man contracted uncleanness in the Temple court and the uncleanness was forgotten by him, though he was aware that he was in the Temple; or if the Temple was forgotten by him, though he was aware of his uncleanness; or if both were forgotten by him, and he prostrated himself or stayed long enough to prostrate himself; or if he went out by the longer way, he is liable [to a Rising and Falling Offering]. But if by the shorter way, he is free.—M. Shav. 2 : 3).

A. R. Eliezer says, "*The creeping thing ... and it is forgotten* (NʿLM) *by him* (Lev. 5 : 2)—For unawareness of the creeping thing he is liable, but he is not liable for unawareness of the Temple."

B. R. ʿAqiba says, "*And it is forgotten by him and he is unclean*—He is liable for unawareness of the uncleanness, and he is not liable for unawareness of the Temple."

C. R. Ishmael says, "*And it is forgotten, and it is forgotten*—two times, to make him liable both on account of unawareness of uncleanness and on account of unawareness of the sanctuary."

M. Shav. 2 : 5 (y. Shav. 2 : 1, 2 : 5; b. Nid. 28b;
b. Shav. 14b, 18b-19a; b. Hor. 5a;
Sifra Vayiqra Pereq 12 : 7, Weiss, p. 23a)

*Comment*: Scripture says, *Or if any one touches an unclean thing ... and it is hidden from him and he has become unclean, he shall be guilty. Or if he touches human uncleanness ... and he is hidden from him, when he comes to know it, he shall be guilty* (Lev. 5 : 2-3). If the man knew he was unclean and then it was forgotten by him, he is liable for an offering if he ate holy food or entered the Temple.

Eliezer and ʿAqiba hold the man is not liable for unawareness that he is in the Temple in an unclean state. Eliezer's proof derives from Lev. 5 : 2. Scripture refers to uncleanness on account of the creeping thing, of which the man is unaware, but not to the Temple. ʿAqiba alludes to the concluding part of the same Scripture.

Ishmael says Scripture refers to two *unawarenesses*, one for the uncleanness, one for the Temple. M. Shav. 2 : 3 therefore accords with Ishmael's exegesis.

See Epstein, *Nusaḥ*, p. 360.

I.ii.94.A. One contracted uncleanness in the court [of the Temple] and the uncleanness was forgotten by him; [or] he remembered the sanctuary and the sanctuary was forgotten by him; [if] he remembered the uncleanness, and this and this were forgotten by him, and he prostrated himself or remained long enough to prostrate himself, or he talked with his fellow long enough to prostrate himself, or he entered the additional part of the courtyard and remained long enough for a prostration—

B. —"He is liable for each one," the words of R. Ishmael. For R. Ishmael would expound, "*And it was forgotten by him, and it was forgotten by him*—two times, to make him liable for the unawareness of uncleanness and for the unawareness of the sanctuary."

C. R. Eliezer and R. ʿAqiba say, "He is liable only for the unawareness of the uncleanness alone."

Tos. Shav. 1 : 6, Zuckermandel, p. 447, ls. 8-13

*Comment*: Now Eliezer and ʿAqiba are given the same opinion and no exegesis at all. For M. Shav. their sayings give different exegeses. Ishmael's opinion is attached to the appropriate rule, which now is assigned to him by name.

IV.ii.15. R. Sheshet would change the words of R. Eliezer for those of R. ʿAqiba and *vice versa*.

b. Shav. 19a

*Comment*: The confusion was on account of their saying the same law, only in slightly different exegeses.

III.ii.69. "If a man lends his neighbor on a pledge and the pledge was lost, he swears, and takes his money"—the words of R. Eliezer.

R. ʿAqiba says, "He may say to him, 'Did you not lend me because of the pledge? Since the pledge is lost, your money is lost.'"

b. Shav. 43b (b. B.M. 81b)

II.iv.20. [When a man vows a vow to the Lord or swears an oath to bind himself by a pledge] *he shall not break his word [according to all that shall proceed out of his mouth* (Num. 30 : 2).]

A. R. Eliezer says, "To make the utterance (HBṬ'H) like an oath."

B. R. ʿAqiba says, "*According to all that proceeds out of his mouth*" [that is, the Scripture itself suffices to make that point, without further exegesis].

Sifré Num. 153, Friedman, p. 56a (Horovitz, p. 200)

II.iv.21. R. Eliezer says, "How do we know that he who cuts down the *asherah* is liable to uproot it? Scripture says, *And you will blot out their name* (Deut. 12 : 3)."

R. ʿAqiba said to him, "Why do I need [a proof]? And has it not already been said, *You will surely blot them out.* Why does Scripture say, *And you will blot out their name*? To change their name."

Sifré Deut. 61, Finkelstein, p. 127
(Tos. A.Z. 6 : 4; y. A.Z. 3 : 8; b. A.Z. 45b;
Mid. Tan. to Deut. 12 : 4, Hoffmann, p. 48)

*Comment*: The law is not at issue.

## xxiv. Zevaḥim, Menaḥot

I.i.118.A. All sacrifices which were sacrificed not for their own name [Danby, p. 468: "Under the name of some other offering"] are fit, although (ʾLʾ Š) they do not go to the credit of their owner for fulfilling an obligation, except for the Passover and the Sin-offering.

B. The Passover at its appointed time and a Sin-offering at any time [are subject to this rule—that is, they are unfit when offered not in their own name].

C. R. Eliezer says, "Also the Guilt-offering [is invalid]."

D. The Passover in its appointed time, the Sin-offering and Guilt-offering at all times [are subject to this rule].

E. R. Eliezer said, "The Sin-offering comes on account of sin and the Guilt-offering comes on account of sin. Just as the Sin-offering is unfit [when offered] not for its own name ["if slaughtered under some other name"], so the Guilt-offering is unfit [when offered] not for its own name."

M. Zev. 1 : 1 (b. Zev. 2a, 5a, 10a, 115a;
b. Men. 28a; compare Sifra Vayiqra Parashah 11 : 9;
Weiss p. 25b; y. Pes. 3 : 3)

*Comment*: Eliezer's gloss of the antecedent rule in C produces a reformulation of the rule in D. Then in E we have a statement of Eliezer's reasoning. So A-B stands by itself. The development of A in B/D cannot come much before Eliezer. It looks as though the rule antecedent to Eliezer consisted of A, up to the *except*-clause. Then the *except*-clause produces B, which repeats it, adding only what is obvious. Eliezer then revises B and, as noted, D spells out Eliezer's opinion in a general rule, and E further supplies the reason for his opinion. The complex pericope looks like what would have emerged from Eliezer's school, if the school had in hand a rule-book to be studied and glossed.

*Fit* here means that the blood may be thrown on the altar, the parts to be burned, and the flesh that is to be eaten may be eaten. But the owner has to offer another sacrifice. As to the Passover, if it is slaughtered under some other designation, it is not valid on the 14th of Nisan.

M. Zev. 1 : 3 develops the rule on the Passover.

See Epstein, *Nusaḥ*, p. 569; *Tan.*, p. 424.

I.ii.95.A. R. Joshua says, "All the sacrifices which were sacrificed not for their name are valid—but they do not go on the owner's credit—except for the Passover and the Sin-offering, the Passover in its season and the Sin-offering at all times."

B. R. Eliezer says, "Also [except] the Guilt-offering, [as well as] the Passover in its season, and the Sin-offering at all times."

C. R. Eliezer says, "A Sin-offering comes on account of sin, and the Guilt-offering comes on account of guilt. Just as the Sin-offering is invalid [when] not [offered] for its name, so the Guilt-offering is invalid when not offered for its name."

D. R. Joshua said to him, "No. If you have said so concerning the Sin-offering, its blood is sprinkled above [the line]. If therefore he slaughtered it not for its name, it is invalid. But will you say so concerning the Guilt-offering, whose blood is sprinkled below [the line]. If he slaughtered it not for its name, it *is* valid."

E. R. Eliezer said to him, "The Passover will prove [my case], for its blood is sprinkled below the line, and if he slaughtered it not for its name, it is invalid. So I bring the Guilt-offering, whose blood is sprinkled below the line. If he slaughtered it not for its name, it is invalid."

F. R. Joshua said to him, "No, if you have said so concerning the Passover, which has a fixed time, if he slaughtered it not for its name, it is invalid. [But] will you say so concerning the Guilt-offering, which has no fixed time. If he slaughtered it not for its name, it is valid."

G. R. Eliezer said to him, "The Sin-offering will prove the matter, for it has no fixed time, and if he slaughtered it not for its name, it is invalid. So I bring the Guilt-offering, which has no fixed time. If he slaughtered it not for its name, it should be unfit."

H. R. Joshua said to him, "I am moving in a circle (ḤZR ḤLYLH)."

I. R. Eliezer says, "*It is a Sin-offering* (Lev. 5 : 9). *It is a Guilt-offering* (Lev. 5 : 19)—just as the Sin-offering is invalid when offered not for its own name, so the Guilt-offering is unfit when not for its own name."

J. R. Joshua said to him, "In connection with the Sin-offering, it says, *And he will slaughter it as a Sin-offering* (Lev. 4 : 24)—that its slaughter should be for the name [sake] of Sin-offering. In connection with the Passover it says, *And it is a Passover-offering* (ZBḤ PSḤ) *to the Lord* (Ex. 12 : 27)—that its slaughtering should be for the name of the Passover.

"But in connection with the Guilt-offering, it does not say, *It is a Guilt-offering*. But in the time of burning the [forbidden] fat, it itself, even though he did not burn the [its] fat, is valid."

Tos. Zev. 1 : 1, Zuckermandel, p. 479, ls. 1-17 (b. Zev. 8b, 10a-b)

*Comment*: M. Zev. 1 : 1A now is credited to Joshua. Eliezer's argument M. Zev. 1 : 1E is presented as part of a long exchange with Joshua. Tos. Zev. 1 : 1C repeats M. Zev. 1 : 1E, except for "on account of *guilt*." Then comes an answer of Joshua: the Sin-offering and Guilt-offering are to be distinguished. The blood of the former is sprinkled above the red line on the altar; of the latter, below it. Eliezer then points to the Passover, whose blood is sprinkled below, and which, if slaughtered not for its own name, is invalid. Joshua has to distinguish the Passover from the Guilt-offering. The former has a fixed time. Eliezer then introduces the Sin-offering—that is, he returns to his original argument. And Joshua points out that fact. Then comes Eliezer's Scriptural argument, tacked on with *says*. Joshua points out that the Scriptural arguments cut both ways. This is a separate pericope, developed in support of C.

b. Zev. 10a-b develops J, the argument based on Lev. 4 : 24 and Ex. 12 : 27.

I.ii.96.A. They slaughtered other(s) [sacrifices] for its name as a Passover offering on the fourteenth [of Nisan]—

B. R. Liezer declares invalid.

C. And R. Joshua declares valid.

D. R. Joshua said, "If on the rest of the days of the year, when it is not valid [if slaughtered] in its own name, yet others [slaughtered] in its name are valid [= M. Zev. 1 : 1], on the fourteenth [of Nisan], when it *is* valid in its own name, is it not logical that others [slaughtered] in its name should [also] be valid?"

E. R. Liezer said to him, "If it is valid [when slaughtered] during the rest of the year in the name of another sacrifice, though it is not valid [if slaughtered] then in its own name, is it not logical that it should be valid [when slaughtered] on the fourteenth in its own name and for the name of other(s) [sacrifices]. And so do you say? [Is this your argument?]

"On what account are others valid when sacrificed in its [the Passover's] name on the rest of the days of the year? Because it is indeed valid [when sacrificed] for the sake of others. Shall the others be valid in *its* name on the fourteenth, on which the Passover is not valid [if slaughtered] for the name of others. [Then] it is not logical that others should be valid for its name."

F. R. Joshua said to him, "If so, you diminish the strength of the Passover-offering and increase the strength of peace-offerings." [H. Freedman, *Zebaḥim*, explains (p. 55, n. 4) that at the proper season for Peace-offerings—during the rest of the year—the Passover, if slaughtered as a Peace-offering, is fit. But at the season of the Passover (14th of Nisan) a Peace-offering slaughtered in the name of a Passover is unfit. Freedman says, "Weaken and strengthen mean to weaken and strengthen the necessity for slaughtering these sacrifices for nought but their own sake."]

G. R. Liezer went and brought another argument: "We find that a Passover-remainder comes as a Peace-offering, but a Peace-offering-remainder does not come as a Passover-offering. Now if the Passover-offering, whose remainder comes as a Peace-offering, is unfit if one slaughters it in its season as a Peace-offering, is it not logical that the Peace-offering should be unfit if slaughtered in the name of a Passover-offering on the fourteenth, seeing that its remainder does not come as a Passover-offering?"

H. R. Joshua said to him, "We find that a Sin-offering-remainder comes as a Burned-offering, but a Whole-offering remainder does *not* come as a Sin-offering. Now, if the Sin-offering is unfit when slaughtered as a Whole-offering, though its remainder comes as a Whole-offering, is it not logical that a Whole-offering slaughtered as a Sin-offering is unfit, seeing that its remainder does *not* come as a Sin-offering?"

I. R. Liezer said to him, "No, if you speak of a Sin-offering, the reason [that a Whole-offering slaughtered in its name is fit] is that it [the Sin-offering] is fit [when slaughtered] in its own name throughout the year.

"Will you say the same of a Passover-offering which is fit [when slaughtered] in its own name *only* in its season? Since it itself is unfit [when slaughtered] in its own name [during the rest of the year], it is logical that others slaughtered in its name [during the rest of the year] are unfit."

Tos. Pisḥa 4 : 5-6, Lieberman,
pp. 161-162, ls. 33-50 (b. Zev. 11a-b)

II.iii.8. *A fire-offering.* R. Eliezer says, "A fire-offering for the sake of fire-offerings."

Sifra Ṣav Parashah 4 : 4, Weiss, p. 33b

II.iii.9. R. Eleazar said, "A Sin-offering comes on account of sin and a Guilt-offering comes on account of a sin. Just as a Sin-offering is invalid when sacrificed not for its name, so a Guilt-offering is invalid when sacrificed not for its name."

Sifra Ṣav Parashah 4 : 6, Weiss, p. 33b (b. Zev. 10a)

*Comment*: Sifra repeats M. Zev. 1 : 1E.

I.i.119.A. [If] he slaughters the sacrifice to eat something which is not usually eaten, to offer up something which is not usually offered up [outside the proper time or place]—it is valid.

B. R. Eliezer declares invalid.

C. To eat something which is usually eaten, to offer up something which is usually offered up—less than an olive's bulk, it is valid.

D. To eat about half an olive's bulk, and to offer up about half an olive's bulk, it is valid, for eating and offering up do not join together [to form the forbidden quantity].

M. Zev. 3 : 3 (b. Zev. 28a, 29b, 31b, 35a)

*Comment*: The law is given in M. Zev. 2 : 3:

This is the general rule: If anyone slaughtered or received or conveyed or tossed the blood intending to eat a thing that usually is eaten or to burn a thing that is usually burned outside its proper *place*, the offering is invalid, but punishment by Extirpation is not incurred [by eating].

But if [he intended to do so] outside the proper *time*, the offering becomes Refuse (PGWL) and punishment by Extirpation is incurred [by eating it], provided that what renders [the offering] permissible [= sprinkling the blood] is offered according to its prescribed rite.

M. Zev. 3 : 3A now deals with a situation in which a man intended to eat what is not usually eaten or to burn what is not usually burned. The issue is, Is he subject to the same rule? The issue depends upon M. Zev. 2 : 3. Eliezer holds that the slaughter is invalid. Nothing is said as to Extirpation.

b. Zev. 28a observes that Eliezer rules one may *intend* with effect for human consumption what is meant for the altar and *vice versa*.

See Epstein, *Tan.*, p. 189.

I.ii.97.A. He who slaughters the sacrifice to eat its parts [which have burned on the altar] and to offer its flesh [which is to be eaten], to eat something which is not ordinarily eaten, and to offer up something which is not ordinarily offered up—it is valid. And R. Judah declares invalid.

B. Rabbi said, "R. Eliezer declares invalid, and R. Joshua declares valid."

Tos. Zev. 2 : 16, Zuckermandel, p. 483, (b. Men. 17b)

*Comment*: The story continues, about Rabbi's teaching to Issi the

Babylonian the tradition (B) in the name of Eliezer and Joshua (ls. 4-15). Issi reports to Rabbi that Judah [b. Ilai] told them it was invalid. Judah the Patriarch says to him, "Judah is the disciple of Ilai and Ilai is the disciple of R. Eliezer. Therefore he teaches the Mishnah of R. Eliezer." This accounts for Issi's tradition about Judah's teaching that it is invalid. For the Mishnah, Rabbi has given Joshua's opinion anonymously, then has dropped Judah and replaced him with Eliezer.

b. Men. 17b has: "TNY'—If one slaughtered an animal-offering, planning to drink its blood [which is usually consumed by the altar] on the next day, or to burn its flesh on the next day [flesh usually was eaten by the man], or to eat the sacrificial portions on the next day, the offering is valid. R. Eliezer declares it invalid. If he intended to leave some of the blood for the next day, R. Judah declares it invalid. R. Eleazar said, 'Even in this case, R. Eliezer declares it to be invalid, and the sages declare it to be valid.'"

II.iii.10. *And if it is eaten on the third day, it will not be pleasing* (Lev. 7 : 18).

R. Eliezer said, "Incline your ear to hear, that one who slaughters his offering in order to eat it on the third day, lo, this comes into the category of *not-being-pleasing.*"

R. ʿAqiba said, "I hear that if he will eat from the flesh of his peace-offerings on the third day, it will not be pleasing. If he ate from it on the third day it will be invalid. But it is not possible to say that once it has been rendered valid, it will again be made invalid. So we find concerning a *Zab* and a *Zabah* and a woman who watches from day to day in the presumption of cleanness, and when they saw [a sign of uncleanness], they have lost [the clean days]. So this, which was in the presumption of being permitted, if he ate from it on the third day, should it be unfit? Scripture says, *He who offers*—when it is offered, it is made unfit, but it is *not* made unfit on the third day."

Sifra Ṣav Parashah 8 : 1, Weiss, p. 36a (b. Zev. 29a)

III.ii.70. TNW RBNN: *And if any of the flesh of the sacrifice of his peace-offerings be at all eaten* [*on the third day*].

R. Eliezer said, "Incline your ear to hear. Scripture speaks of one who intends to eat his sacrifice on the third day."

"Yet perhaps this is not the case, but rather, it speaks of one who actually eats the sacrifice on the third day? You can answer: After it has become fit, shall it then become unfit?" [Surely not. It was fit when sacrificed, and cannot be made unfit because he eats it three days later.]

R. ʿAqiba said to him, "Lo, we find that a *Zab* and a *Zabah* and a woman who watches etc. are presumed to be clean, but if they have a discharge they lose [the earlier days]. You too need not be surprised that after the sacrifice has become unfit, it becomes unfit to him."

He [ʿAqiba] said to him, "Lo, it says, *He who sacrifices*—it becomes unfit at the offering, but not on the third day ..."

b. Zev. 29a

*Comment*: Sifra and the Babylonian *baraita* supply an argument between Eliezer and ʿAqiba about whether one may retrospectively render the offering unfit. Tos. Zev. has Joshua in a position consistent with ʿAqiba's; M. Zev. 3 : 3A has ʿAqiba's position without his name. But the argument here pertains to the exegesis of Scriptures, rather than to the generalized legal point of M. Zev.

See below, M. Me. 1 : 2, pp. 268-273.

I.i.120. (The Sin-offering of a bird is valid if offered [properly] below [the red line], after the manner of a Sin-offering, and under the name of a Sin-offering. It is invalid if offered [improperly] after the manner of a Sin-offering and under the name of a Whole-offering; or after the manner of a Whole-offering and under the name of a Sin-offering; or after the manner of a Whole-offering and under the name of a Whole-offering—M. Zev. 7 : 1).

(The whole-offering of a bird is valid if it is offered above, after the manner of a Whole-offering, and under the name of a Whole-offering ... But it becomes invalid if it is offered after the manner of a Sin-offering and under the name of a Whole-offering, or after the manner of a Sin-offering and under the name of a Sin-offering.—M. Zev. 7 : 2).

([Even if invalid] none of them conveys uncleanness and the law of sacrilege still applies to them, except the Sin-offering of a bird offered below after the manner of a Sin-offering and under the name of a Sin-offering [to which the law of sacrilege does not apply].—M. Zev. 7 : 3).

A. The Whole-offering of a bird that was offered below [the red line, though it should be offered above, as in 7 : 2], after the manner of the Sin-offering and for the sake of the Sin-offering—

B. R. Eliezer says, "It is subject to the law of sacrilege [Lev. 5 : 15] (MWʿLYN BH)."

C. R. Joshua says, "It is not subject to the law of sacrilege."

D. R. Eliezer said, "If a Sin-offering, which is not subject to the law of sacrilege, when he changed its name [did it not under the name of Sin-offering], is subject to the law of sacrilege, the Whole-offering, which *is* subject to the law of sacrilege, when he changed its name, is it not logical that it should [still] be subject to the law of sacrilege?"

E. R. Joshua said to him, "No. If you have said so concerning the Sin-offering [the reason is that] when he changed its name to the name of the Whole-offering, he has changed its name to that of something which *is* subject to the law of sacrilege. But will you say so of a Whole-offering, whose name he changed to the name of a Sin-offering? For thus he has changed its name to that of something which is *not* subject to the law of sacrilege."

F. R. Eliezer said to him, "Lo, Most Holy Things (QDŠY QDŠYM) which he slaughtered in the south [side of the altar instead of on the north, 5 : 1] and slaughtered for the sake of Lesser Holy Things [after their blood has been poured out; the law of sacrilege applies only to their sacrificial portions, but not to the flesh, which is for the priests] will prove the matter. For he has changed their name for something to which the law of sacrilege does not apply. But the law of sacrilege still does apply to them.

"So you, do not be astonished concerning the Whole-offering, for even though he changed its name to that of something to which the law of sacrilege does not apply, the law of sacrilege will [continue to] apply to it."

G. R. Joshua said to him, "If you have said so concerning Most Holy Things which he slaughtered in the south and slaughtered for the sake of Lesser Holy Things, he has [at least] changed their name for [that of] a thing which is both forbidden and permitted. [The sacrificial portions of Lesser Holy Things are forbidden under the law of sacrilege, but the flesh is permitted.] But will you say so concerning the Whole-offering, the name of which he changed to that of something which is wholly permitted? [The Sin-offering of a bird has no sacrificial portions—4 : 4.]"

M. Zev. 7 : 4 (b. Zev. 66b, 67a)

*Comment*: The problem of A is set by M. Zev. 7 : 3. There we find that the law of sacrilege applies to the Sin-offering of a bird offered properly—below the line and in its own name. Then the question is raised, What about the Whole-offering of a bird offered for the sake of, and in the manner of, the Sin-offering, but below, rather than above the line as is required? Does the law of the Sin-offering apply, which therefore makes it subject to sacrilege? Eliezer holds it is no different from other Whole-offerings of birds. It remains in its own status; M. Me. 2 : 2 explicitly states, "The law of sacrilege applies to the Whole-offering of a bird so soon as it has been dedicated." Joshua says that it enters the category of Sin-offering, to which the law of sacrilege does not apply.

Eliezer argues in D that the Sin-offering, when offered as a Whole-offering, becomes subject to the law of sacrilege like a Whole-offering (7 : 3—invalid, but the law of sacrilege still applies). Likewise the Whole-offering should *remain* subject to the law of sacrilege. Joshua quite reasonably replies that the Sin-offering when given the name of Whole-offering has been subjected to the laws of something which is under the law of sacrilege. But when you change the name of the Whole-offering to that of Sin-offering, you have given it the name of something which is not subject to the law of sacrilege.

In effect D and E simply restate the positions of B and C. Eliezer holds that changing the name of the Whole-offering is of no effect. Joshua says changing the name of the Whole-offering subjects the sacrifice to the laws of that to which the name has been changed.

It is now Eliezer's task to show that the law of sacrilege will remain valid for something subject to the law of sacrilege in its own status when it enters another status to which the law does not apply. This will be Most Holy Things slaughtered in the wrong place and for the wrong purpose. When the priest slaughtered them in the south and for the sake of Lesser Holy Things, he has slaughtered them for that to which the laws of sacrilege do not apply, but the law of sacrilege continues to apply to the Most Holy Things. Likewise the same rule will apply to the Whole-offering of the bird.

Joshua now has to show that the Most Holy Things are a special case, which can prove nothing about the Whole-offering of the bird. He points out that the Most Holy Things retain something of their former stringency. The Lesser Holy Things are subject both to prohibition and to permission; the sacrificial portions are forbidden under the law of sacrilege, but the flesh is permitted. But the Whole-offering of the bird has been given a name of something which is *wholly* permitted. So the cases are not comparable. The continued application of the law of sacrilege in the case of Most Holy Things offered as Lesser Holy Things is on account of the continued prohibition of the sacrificial portions. But the Whole-offering of the bird has no sacrificial portions. Therefore the cases are not similar, and the law of sacrilege will not apply.

The debate ends with both parties having fully spelled out their reasoning. The special case has now been wholly worked out, and all possibilities for logic to decide the case have been given. The form is perfect: statement of the legal problem, rulings of the respective parties, then a debate, first giving the rulings along with the reasons therefor, second, giving the reasons for rejecting the rulings on the part of the opposing parties.

I.ii.98.A. A Whole-offering of a bird which he made above [the line], [in the] rite of [the] Sin-offering, for the sake of a Sin-offering—

R. Eliezer says, "The law of sacrilege applies to it."

R. Joshua says, "The law of sacrilege does not apply to it."

B. R. Eliezer said, "The Sin-offering, to which the law of sacrifice does not apply [when it is offered] for its own name, when he changed its name, is it not logical that the law of sacrilege should apply to it?"

R. Joshua said to him, "No. If you have said so concerning the Sin-offering, whose name he changed for the name of a Whole-offering, [in this case] he changed its name for the name of something to which the law of sacrifice *does* apply. Will you say so concerning the Whole-offering whose name he changed for the name of a Sin-offering? For thus he changed its name to that of something to which the law of sacrilege does *not* apply."

C. R. Eliezer said to him, "Lo, he who slaughters Most Holy Things on the north [of the altar] for the sake of Peace-offerings will prove the matter. For lo, he changed its name for that of something to which the law of sacrilege does not apply, but the law of sacrilege applies to them. Do not be astonished that even though he changed its name for something to which the law of sacrilege does not apply, the law of sacrilege should apply to it."

R. Joshua said to him, "No. If you have said so concerning him who slaughters Most Holy Things on the north [part of the altar] for the sake of Peace-offerings, even though he changed their name, he did not change their [proper] place. Will you say so concerning this one, for he both changed its name and changed its place?"

D. R. Eliezer said to him, "Lo, he who slaughters the Whole-offering of an ox in the south for the sake of the Guilt-offering will prove the matter. For he changed its name, and he changed its place, and the law of sacrilege does apply to it. So you, do not be astonished that even though he changed its name and changed its place, the law of sacrilege applies to it."

R. Joshua said to him, "No. If you have said so concerning him who slaughters the Whole-offering of an ox in the south for the sake of a Guilt-offering, even though he changed its name and changed its place, he did not change its rite. And he changed it for a thing to which the law of sacrilege applies in part. Will you say so concerning this one, whose name he changed, and whose place he changed, and whose rite he changed? And he changed it for a thing to which the law of sacrilege does not apply [even] in part."

Tos. Zev. 7 : 16-20, Zuckermandel, p. 490,
ls. 19-236 (b. Zev. 67a)

III.ii.71.A. TNY': R. Eliezer said to R. Joshua, "A Guilt-offering which he slaughtered on the north for the sake of Peace-offerings will prove it, for he changed its name, and the law of sacrilege applies to it. You too, do not be astonished at the Whole-offering, which, even though he changed its name, is subject to the law of sacrilege."

B. R. Joshua said to him, "No. If you have said so concerning the Guilt-offering, of which, if he changed its name, he did not change its place, will you say so concerning the Whole-offering, whose name and place he changed?"

C. He said to him, "The Guilt-offering which he slaughtered in the south for the sake of Peace-offerings will prove it. For he changed its name and its place, and the law of sacrilege does apply. You too, do not be surprised concerning the Whole-offering, for, even though he changed its name and its place, the law of sacrilege applies."

D. R. Joshua said to him, "No. If you have said so concerning the Guilt-offering whose name and place he changed, he did not change its rite (MʿŚYW). Will you say so concerning the Whole-offering whose name and place and rite he changed?"

E. Thereupon he was silent.

b. Zev. 67a

*Comment*: Here Joshua is allowed to win the argument. E is a typical addition in a *baraita*.

I.i.121. (If animal-offerings were confused with sin-offerings that had been left to die or with an ox to be stoned, though it be one among ten thousand, all must be left to die.—M. Zev. 8 : 1).

(If consecrated beasts were confused with other consecrated beasts belonging to the like kind of offering, each may be offered in behalf of any of the owners. But if consecrated beasts were confused with other consecrated beasts belonging to a different kind of offering, they must be left to pasture until they suffer a blemish.—M. Zev. 8 : 2).

(If a Guilt-offering was confused with a Peace-offering, they must be left to pasture until they suffer a blemish.—M. Zev. 8 : 3).

A. The limbs of a Sin-offering which were mixed up with the limbs of a Whole-offering—

B. R. Eliezer [Naples: Eleazar] says, "Let him put [them] above [the altar-fires], and I regard (RWʾH) the flesh of the Sin-offering above [the altar-fire] as if it were wood." [The limbs of the Sin-offering normally are eaten by the priests and prohibited to be burned (So Albeq, *Seder Qodashim*, p. 34). The limbs of the Whole-offering are offered on the altar. Now all are to be burned on the altar. The former are not regarded as other than wood.]

C. And sages say, "Let their appearance be disfigured (TʿBR ṢWRTN), and let it go out to the place of burning [where invalid offerings are destroyed]." [Let them be kept overnight and burned like *Notar.* M. Sheq. 7 : 3 says, "If flesh was found in the Temple court in the form of entire limbs, it is deemed to belong to a Whole-offering; if in cut-up pieces, to a Sin-offering . . . Its appearance must be spoiled and it must be taken away to the place of burning."]

M. Zev. 8 : 4 (b. Zev. 76b, 77a, b. Men. 48a)

*Comment*: The issue is where the limbs are to be burned. Eliezer holds that everything enters the category of the Whole-offering and is burned on the altar-fire; but the Sin-offering-limbs are regarded as mere wood. The sages say that the whole enters the category of unfit or invalid flesh of sacrifices, burned outside the cult.

In general, Eliezer will assign to a higher category of sanctity a mixture of sacrifices or of the blood of sacrifices of lower and higher sanctity, while the sages will assign such a mixture to the status of sanctity of the lowest contained within it.

III.ii.72. TNYʾ: R. Eliezer said, "*For a sweet savor* (Lev. 2 : 12)—you may not take it up on the altar, but you may take it up for fuel."

b. Zev. 76b-77a (b. Men. 106b; b. Yoma 47b, b. Sot. 23a)

*Comment*: Eliezer is given an exegesis in support of his opinion.

I.ii.99.A. R. Judah said, "Sages agree with R. Eliezer concerning the limbs of sacrifices (ZBḤYM) which were mixed up with the limbs of the Whole-offering, that they should be offered up."

B. R. Eliezer agrees with the sages about those that were mixed up with the ox that has committed bestiality, or the ox against which bestiality was committed [and other prohibited items], that the appearance should be disfigured, and they should go out to the place of burning.

C. "Concerning what did they differ? Concerning a mixture of the limbs of a blemished animal and perfect animal (TMYM), for R. Eliezer says, 'They should be offered up, and I regard the things of the blemished [animal] mixed with the unblemished [animal] as if they were pieces of wood.'

"And sages say, 'Let their appearance be disfigured, and let them be taken out to the place of burning.'"

Tos. Zev. 8 : 15, Zuckermandel, p. 492, ls. 1-6 (b. Zev. 77a)

*Comment*: Judah [b. Ilai] assigns the disagreement to a different, and finer case.

I.i.122.A. Limbs [of Whole-offering, which were valid and mixed up with] limbs of blemished animals [that were brought for sacrifice, but cannot be sacrificed because of a blemish]—

B. R. Eliezer [Camb., Kaufmann: Leazar] says, "If the head of one of them [the blemished beasts] was [accidentally] sacrificed, all of the heads may [then] be sacrificed. [If] the leg of one of them [had been sacrificed], the legs of all of them may be sacrificed."

C. And sages say, "Even if all of them were sacrificed except one of them, let it go forth to the place of burning."

M. Zev. 8 : 5 (b. Zev. 74a, 77b; b. Pes. 34b, b. Yoma 64a; b. Sot. 23a, *re* Lev. 2 : 12)

I.i.123. ([If] blood was mixed with water, and it still had the appearance of blood, [it remains] valid [for the prescribed sprinklings on the altar]. If it was mixed with wine, the wine is regarded as water [and the mixture is valid]. If it was mixed with the blood of a beast [that was unconsecrated] or of a wild animal, it [the blood of the unconsecrated beast] is regarded as water. R. Judah says, "Blood cannot render other blood invalid."—M. Zev. 8 : 6).

A. [If] it [the blood of a valid sacrifice] was mixed with the blood of unfit sacrifices, let it be poured out into the gutter.

If the blood exuded [after death], let it be poured out into the gutter [for it is prohibited to sprinkle the blood of unfit sacrifice on the altar].

B. R. Eliezer [Parma, Camb., Kaufmann: Eleazar] declares it [the exuded blood] valid.

C. If [the priest] had not given thought (NMLK) [as to whether the blood was suitable for sprinkling], it is valid. [We regard the blood of the invalid sacrifices as water, and if the blood looked like blood, it is valid for sprinkling, as above].

M. Zev. 8 : 7 (b. Zev. 77b-78b; b. Yoma 47b, 64a)

I.i.124.A. Blood of unblemished offerings [if mixed with] the blood of blemished offerings—

B. Let it be poured out into the gutter.

C. A bowl with bowls [if bowls containing the one kind of blood were confused with bowls containing the other kind]—

D. R. Eliezer [Parma, Kaufmann: Leazar] says, "[If] one bowl was offered, all the bowls will be offered."

E. And sages say, "Even if all of them were offered except for one of them, let it [that remaining one] be spilled into the gutter."

M. Zev. 8 : 8 (b. Zev. 79b-80a-b; b. R.H. 28b)

I.i.125.A. [If] blood [that is to be sprinkled below was mixed with [blood] that was to be sprinkled above [the red line]—

B. R. Eliezer says, "Let it be sprinkled above. And I regard the [blood to be] sprinkled below [which was sprinkled] above as if it was water. And he goes and sprinkles below [as well]."

C. And sages say, "Let it [all] be poured out into the gutter."

D. But if the priest had not given thought [as to whether the blood was suitable for sprinkling], it is valid.

M. Zev. 8 : 9

I.i.126.A. If blood that should be sprinkled once was mixed up with other blood that should be sprinkled once, each is sprinkled once [as normally is the case].

B. If what should be sprinkled four times was mixed up with what should be sprinkled four times, each is sprinkled four times.

C. If what should be sprinkled four times was mixed up with what should be sprinkled once—

D. R. Eliezer says, "Let each be sprinkled four times."

E. R. Joshua says, "Let each be sprinkled once."

F. R. Eliezer said to him, "Lo, he transgresses, *You shall not diminish [take] from it* (Deut. 12 : 32)."

G. R. Joshua said to him, "Lo, he transgresses, *You shall not add* [*thereto*, so the sprinkling itself suffices]."

H. R. Eliezer said to him, "*You shall not add* is said only in reference to the act itself. [The sprinkling itself suffices; to sprinkle the one blood three times again does not transgress against *adding*, since it can be regarded as water.]"

I. R. Joshua said to him, "The law *You shall not diminish* applies only to the act in itself [therefore there is no need to sprinkle more than once]."

J. And further did R. Joshua say, "When you sprinkled, you transgressed *You shall not add*, and also you perform an act [of transgression] with your own hand. But when you did not sprinkle, you transgressed *You shall not diminish*, but you did not do a deed with your own hand."

M. Zev. 8 : 10 (y. Eruv. 10 : 14, b. Eruv. 100a, y. Pes. 3 : 3, b. R.H. 28b; Mid. Tan. to Deut. 13 : 1, Hoffmann, p. 63)

I.i.127.A. If blood that was to be sprinkled inside [= sin-offering] was mixed up with blood that was to be sprinkled outside, it should be poured out into the gutter.

B. If he sprinkled outside and [had not given thought and] then went and sprinkled inside, it is valid. If he sprinkled inside and then went and sprinkled outside—

C. R. ʿAqiba declares it invalid.

D. And the sages declare it valid.

E. For R. ʿAqiba used to say, "Any blood [that should have been sprinkled outside] that is brought inside the sanctuary to make atonement is invalid."

F. And sages say, "[That applies] to the Sin-offering alone."

G. R. Eliezer says, "Also [to] the Guilt-offering, as it is said, "*As is the Sin-offering, so is the Guilt-offering* (Lev. 7 : 7)."

M. Zev. 8 : 11 (b. Zev. 10b, 81b, 82a; Sifra Ṣav Pereq 8 : 1, Weiss, p. 33a)

I.i.128. (If the blood of a Sin-offering was received in two bowls, [and] one of them went outside [the Temple court], that which remains inside is [still] valid. If one of them entered inside [the Temple court], R. Yosi the Galilean declares the one outside still valid; and sages declare it invalid. R. Yosi the Galilean said, "If in the case where intention renders invalid [as when there is intention to sprinkle the blood] outside [the Temple court], this does not alter in the like fashion or render invalid the blood that remains, must we not infer, in the case where intention does not render invalid, as when there is intention to sprinkle blood inside the sanctuary, that we must not treat that which remains in like fashion as that which enters in.")

A. "If it was taken inside to make atonement, even if it has not made atonement [been sprinkled], it becomes invalid"—the words of R. Eliezer [Parma, Kaufmann: Leazar].

B. R. Simeon says, "[It does not become invalid] until it makes atonement." [After it is sprinkled within, it becomes invalid for sprinkling on the outer altar.]

C. R. Judah says, "If it was taken inside by error, it is invalid."

M. Zev. 8 : 12 (b. Zev. 82a, 83a)

*Comment*: In M. Zev. 8 : 5 the mixture is of Whole-offering limbs which were valid and of Whole-offering limbs which were blemished. Eliezer says that if by accident the head of one of them is offered, all may be offered, for we say that the one which was offered is that of the blemished animal, and everything else is valid. This is consistent with his view in M. Ter. 5 : 2: "For I say, the *se'ah* which fell in is the one which is lifted out." The sages hold the exact opposite. Whatever happens, even if only one remains unsacrificed, we assume that very one is the head of the unblemished offering.

M. Zev. 8 : 7B deals with a detail of A. The sages rule that if the blood mixed with exuded blood, which cannot be sprinkled (M. Zev. 3 : 1), it is to be poured out into the gutter. Eliezer differs as to the exuded blood.

When bowls of unfit blood are mixed with bowls of valid blood (M. Zev. 8 : 8C-E), Eliezer says that if one bowl is offered, the rest may be offered, for we assume the one which was accidentally offered was the invalid one, and the rest are acceptable, as in 8 : 5. The sages are consistent with their earlier ruling.

In M. Zev. 8 : 9 Eliezer takes a similarly lenient position. Here, blood of sacrifices to be sprinkled below the red line was mixed up with blood of sacrifices to be sprinkled above it, that is, with the blood of the Sin-offering, which has to be sprinkled above the red line. Eliezer says one sprinkles above the red line and does the required four sprinklings for the Sin-offering. Then the priest goes and sprinkles below, according to the rules about sprinkling below, and the sprinkling below is credited also for the pouring out of the excess blood of the Sin-offering, to be poured out below. The sages reject the rule; the whole thing is poured out.

But, as in M. Zev. 8 : 7, if the priest did not give thought to whether what he was doing with the blood was valid, the sages agree it is valid. The invalid sprinkling is as of water.

In M. Zev. 8 : 10 we have a parallel case. Now the problem is a mixture of bloods to be sprinkled once (such as the blood of a firstling with the blood of a tithe). This is treated in an ordinary way—one sprinkling is made. Likewise if a mixture of blood which was to be sprinkled four times was made with other such blood—for instance, the blood of a Whole-offering mixed with the blood of a Guilt-offering—the same rule applies.

Now the issue is, What happens when blood which is to be sprinkled four times is mixed with blood which is to be sprinkled only one time? Eliezer says that one sprinkles four times, and we regard the excess sprinklings of the blood which was to be sprinkled only once as if it were merely a sprinkling of water, of no consequence, just as in M. Zev. 8 : 9. Joshua says the mixture is sprinkled only once.

The Scriptural proof serving each is Deut. 12 : 32: *Everything that I command you, you shall be careful to do: you shall not add to it or take away from it.* Obviously, each opinion has an appropriate clause in the Scripture. Citing it is a formality.

Eliezer argues that *not adding* applies to the act itself. If the priest sprinkles only once from blood which is to be sprinkled four times, he has transgressed *not diminishing* from what is required. If the blood is by itself, not mixed with other, then he obviously should not add to the number of sprinklings. Here, where there is a mixture, whatever *is* sprinkled that should *not* be sprinkled is regarded as water, as above. Joshua argues the opposite. He is given a further argument, familiar from M. Ter. 8 : 11, that if the man actually *does* the extra sprinkling, he violates the law against *not adding* by his action. But if he merely refrains from doing the sprinklings, to be sure he violates not diminishing, but not by something he actually has done.

M. Zev. 8 : 11A has a parallel problem, but Eliezer does not participate in solving it. He is put in the position of glossing the sages' ruling, F, by adding the Guilt-offering to their list, consistent with his view in M. Zev. 1 : 1. But Eliezer already has ruled that if blood to be sprinkled above the red line was mixed with blood that was to be sprinkled below the red line, the sprinkling may take place both above and below the line. That involved the Sin-offering. Here too, therefore, he should be in agreement with the sages, as opposed to ʿAqiba, in C-D, and he should not agree with the sages in F at all; he should say ʿAqiba's rule is invalid even with respect to the Sin-offering. So evidently either M. Zev. 8 : 9 has a ruling which Eliezer would not apply here—and I see no difference between the cases, other than the switch from *above/below* to *inside/outside*. Or 8 : 11B is out of place, copied from M. Zev. 1 : 1, where it does belong. So while G accurately portrays Eliezer's opinion as to the equivalence of Guilt- and Sin-offering, it evidently does not give his opinion on the issue at hand but stands as an independent gloss.

M. Zev. 8 : 12 stands outside of the foregoing range of issues. Eliezer holds that if the priest brought the blood from outside to inside intending to sprinkle it, even if he did not sprinkle it, he has rendered the blood outside unfit—consistent with the sages, who say that if one of the bowls was brought inside, both bowls are unfit. Intention is decisive, whether or not the blood was actually sprinkled. Yosi would hold that what remains outside remains valid. If this interpretation is correct, then the dispute of Yosi [b. Ḥalafta] and the sages follows the same principles as that of Eliezer and Simeon, but the fact that Eliezer's and Simeon's pertains to a detail has caused it to be placed after the later masters' dispute.

See Epstein, *Nusaḥ*, p. 1169.

I.ii.100.A. If the blood was mixed up with the blood of invalid animals, it should be poured out into the gutter.

B. Or with the blood that exuded.

C. They say to him that he should not sprinkle, and if he sprinkled, we regard it as if it is wine with water. If its appearance was annulled, it is invalid; and if not, it is acceptable.

D. R. Eliezer declares valid in the case of the exuded blood.

Tos. Zev. 8 : 19,
Zuckermandel, p. 492, ls. 11-13

*Comment*: See above M. Zev. 8 : 7; and Lieberman, *Tosefet Rishonim*, II, p. 210.

I.ii.101A. One bowl in a hundred bowls—

B. R. Eliezer says, "If he offered one bowl, let all the bowls be offered."

C. And sages say, "Even if he offered all except for one, it should be poured out into the gutter."

D. R. Judah said, "R. Eliezer and sages did not differ concerning the blood of a Whole-offering which was mixed up with the blood of sacrifices (ZBḤYM), that it should be offered.

"Or concerning [a mixture of] the blood of [various prohibited animals], that it should be poured out into the gutter.

E. "Concerning what did they differ?

F. "Concerning a case in which the mixture was of blood of a blemished animal with that of a perfect one, for—

G. "R. Eliezer says, 'They should offer it, and I regard the blood of the blemished animal among the perfect one's [blood] as if it is water.'

"And sages say, 'Let it be poured out into the gutter.'"

Tos. Zev. 8 : 20, Zuckermandel, p. 492, ls. 18ff. (b. Zev. 81a)

*Comment*: See Tos. Zev. 8 : 15. Now Judah the Patriarch has given F, Judah b. Ilai's version, M. Zev. 8 : 8A, as the unanimous opinion, and rejected Judah's view of the difference, in 8 : 8C.

I.ii.102.A. If the blood that was to be sprinkled below was mixed with blood to be sprinkled above—

B. R. Eliezer says, "Let it be sprinkled above."

C. And sages say, "Let it be poured out into the gutter."

D. He sprinkled it below and did not pay attention—

E. R. Eliezer says, "Let it sprinkled above."

F. And sages say, "Let him pour it out into the gutter, and the blood sprinkled below counts for his credit."

G. If he sprinkled it above and did not take note of it, both agree that he should go and sprinkle below, and these do not count for his credit.

Tos. Zev. 8 : 21, Zuckermandel, p. 492, ls. 22-25

*Comment*: See M. Zev. 8 : 9. Tos. Zev. 8 : 21B is the same as 8 : 9D, and therefore the latter represents Eliezer's opinion.

I.ii.103.A. Blood that was to be sprinkled with a single sprinkling which was mixed up with blood that was to be sprinkled with one sprinkling—let them be sprinkled with one sprinkling, etc.

B. If blood to be sprinkled four times was mixed with blood to be sprinkled one time—

C. R. Eliezer says, "Let it be sprinkled four times."

D. R. Joshua says, "Let it be sprinkled one time."

E. R. Eliezer said, "Lo, he transgresses *You shall not diminish.*"

F. R. Joshua said, "Lo, he transgresses *You shall not add.*"

G. R. Eliezer said, "*You shall not add* is only said concerning [the act] by itself, but you add to it when it is involved with other [actions]."

H. R. Joshua said, "*You shall not diminish* is said only concerning [the act] by itself, but you diminish from it when it is involved with other [actions]."

I. R. Eliezer said, "The matter is still suspended. Who will decide?"

J. R. Joshua said to him, "I shall decide. When I do it with my own hand, I am found transgressing against a negative commandment, but lo, it is in my hands. When I leave it as it is, I am found transgressing a negative commandment, but it is *not* in my own hands."

Tos. Zev. 8 : 23, Zuckermandel, p. 492, ls. 30-39

*Comment*: See M. Zev. 8 : 10. See also Tos. Pes. 2 : 7, Zuckermandel, p. 158, 1. 26.

I.ii.104.A. Blood that was to be sprinkled inside which was mixed with blood that was to be sprinkled outside is to be poured out into the gutter ... except for a Sin-offering for a Sin-offering whose blood was brought inside is invalid.

B. R. Eliezer says, "Also the Guilt-offering, as it is said, *Like the Sin-offering ... like the Guilt-offering* (Lev. 7 : 7)."

Tos. Zev. 8 : 24, Zuckermandel, p. 492, l. 39, p. 493, ls. 1-3

*Comment*: See M. Zev. 8 : 11B.

[I.i.129. M. Zev. 13 : 5-6. Parma, Camb., and Naples give [E]leazar; we have no warrant for assigning the pericope to our Eliezer.]

I.i.130.A. He who took a handful of meal-offering in order to eat a thing which is not ordinarily eaten, or to offer up a thing which is not ordinarily offered up—[the handful] remains valid.

B. R. Eliezer declares [it] invalid.

C. To eat something which is ordinarily eaten, to offer up something which is ordinarily offered up—less than an olive's bulk [leaves the meal-offering] valid; to offer up as much as an olive's bulk—valid, for eating and offering up do not join [to form a forbidden quantity].

M. Men. 3 : 1 (b. Men. 12b, 17a-b, 18a)

*Comment*: Eliezer is consistent with his position in M. Zev. 3 : 3 = Tos. Zev. 2 : 16. If a man intended to eat something not ordinarily eaten, planning to do so outside of the proper time or the proper place, he has not rendered the meal-offering unfit. Eliezer holds that he has done so.

b. Men. 17a-b has R. Yoḥanan's explanation of Eliezer's view.

See Epstein, *Nusaḥ*, p. 1170, n. 1; *Tan*., p. 190.

I.ii.105.A. He who takes a handful of the meal-offering in order to eat the handful [which is offered] and to offer up the remainder [which is eaten], to eat something which is not ordinarily eaten and to offer something which is not ordinarily offered up, [the handful of meal] is valid.

B. And R. Judah declares it invalid.

C. To leave the handful and its remainder for the next day or to take them outside [of the courtyard], it is valid.

D. And R. Judah declares [it] invalid.

E. R. Eleazar says, "R. Eliezer declares invalid, and R. Joshua declares valid."

F. R. Judah said to him, "Now if he left the handful for the next day, he does not render it invalid. And sages say, 'This and this are valid.' So you have nothing which renders unfit except the intention concerning taking the handful and offering it up alone."

Tos. Men. 2 : 16, Zuckermandel, p. 515, ls. 4-9

*Comment*: Judah follows Eliezer, and Tos. now assigns the sages' opinion to Joshua.

I.i.131.A. [If] the residue [of the meal-offering] contracted uncleanness or was burned or was lost [before the meal-offering was offered up]—

B. According to the rule (MDH) of R. Eliezer, it is valid, and according to the rule of R. Joshua, it is invalid.

M. Men. 3 : 4 (b. Men. 26a;
y. Pes. 7 : 5, b. Men. 9a)

*Comment*: The reference is to Tos. Zev. 4 : 1-2, b. Pes. 77a. If blood was sprinkled on an offering whose flesh became unclean or was lost, the offering is still regarded as valid. Eliezer says the blood is fit even if there is no flesh. Joshua says if there is no flesh, the blood is unacceptable, and *vice versa*. Likewise here, if the residue was lost, it is still valid to offer up the handful of meal-offering, according to Eliezer. Evidently no tradition explicitly assigning such a position to Eliezer and Joshua existed, but the reasoning of the tradents led them to invent it.

See Epstein, *Tan*., p. 175.

I.ii.106.A. The handful of meal-offering which was mixed up with the remainder, lo, this should not be offered. And if it was offered, it is valid.

B. R. Eliezer says, "It should be offered."

C. If it was mixed up with the remainder of another handful of meal-offering or with meal-offering which has not been taken up by a handful (NQMṢH), lo, this should not be offered, and if it is offered, it is valid.

R. Eliezer says, "It should be offered."

Tos. Men. 4 : 2, Zuckermandel, p. 516, ls. 6-9

I.ii.107.A. R. Yosi said, "I prefer the opinion of R. Eliezer, who said, 'If there is no handful of meal, there is no residue, even though there is no residue, there is a handful of meal,' over the opinion of R. Joshua, who said, 'If there is no handful of meal, there is no residue; if there is no residue, there is no handful of meal.'"

Tos. Men. 4 : 5, Zuckermandel, p. 516, ls. 15-18

I.ii.108.A. If the handful of meal contracted uncleanness or was rendered invalid or went outside the hangings, the residue's appearance (ṢWRTN) is disfigured, and it goes out to the place of burning.

If the residue contracts uncleanness or is rendered unfit or goes outside of the hangings—

R. Eliezer says, "He may offer up the handful of meal."

And R. Joshua says, "He may not offer up the handful of meal."

And if he offered it up, whether accidentally R. Joshua agrees that it is acceptable.

Tos. Men. 4 : 6, Zuckermandel, p. 516, ls. 18-20 (b. Men. 9a-b, 12a)

*Comment*: As in M. Zevaḥim, so here Eliezer rules leniently in the case of a mixture of suitable and unsuitable holy things. He presumably will rule that the handful which is taken out of the mixture described in Tos. Men. 4 : 2 is the originally valid handful of meal-offering, not the residue.

In Tos. Men. 4 : 5-6, Eliezer holds that the handful of meal is not rendered unfit if the residue is rendered unfit, while Joshua says that if the one is unfit, so is the other. This is along the lines of their argument in Tos. Zev. 4 : 1, Zuckermandel, p. 484, ls. 30ff. Yosi supplies a *terminus ante quem* for the dispute. Presumably in a well-ordered text, his opinion would have followed the statement of the dispute. Perhaps it was his opinion, based upon a generalized, but unformulated tradition, which generated the dispute that follows it.

I.i.132.A. If a man slaughtered the Thank-offering within [the Temple court], and the Bread-offering thereof was outside the wall, the bread is not made holy. If he slaughtered it before [the loaves] had formed a crust in the oven, or even if all but one had formed a crust, the bread is not made holy. If he slaughtered it [intending an act] outside the proper time or proper place, the bread is made holy. He slaughtered it, and it was found to be *ṭerefah*, the bread is not made holy.

B. He slaughtered it, and it was found to be blemished (BʿLT MWM)—

C. R. Eliezer says, "[The bread] has been sanctified."

D. And sages say, "[The bread] has not been sanctified.

M. Men. 7 : 3 (b. Men. 78b, 79a; b. Pes. 77a-b)

*Comment*: The Thank-offering can make the bread with it (Lev. 7 : 13) to become refuse (*piggul*), so M. Men. 2 : 3. Now we have a series of definitions of when the bread-offering is made holy—therefore made refuse or unfit. The dispute concerns the blemished offering. Eliezer holds that the bread has been made holy, consistent with ʿAqiba's view in M. Zev. 9 : 3. Since the blemished offering is valid according to ʿAqiba, its accompanying bread-offering also will be regarded as sanctified.

I.ii.109.A. If he slaughtered it, and it was found out to be *ṭerefah*, the bread has not been sanctified.

B. "He slaughtered it, and it was found to be blemished—

C. "R. Eliezer says, 'It was sanctified.' "

D. "R. Joshua says, 'It was not sanctified' "—the words of R. Meir.

E. R. Judah says, "R. Eliezer and R. Joshua did not differ concerning a case in which he slaughtered it (1) outside of its time, that the bread *has* been sanctified; or concerning a case in which he slaughtered it and it was found to be (2) blemished, that the bread has *not* been sanctified [= Meir's Joshua].

F. "Concerning what did they disagree?

G. "Concerning a case in which he slaughtered it [intending to eat it] outside of its proper place—

"For R. Eliezer says, 'It [the bread] has been sanctified.'

"And R. Joshua says, 'It has not been sanctified.'

H. "R. Eliezer said to him, 'Do you not agree that if he slaughtered it [intending to eat it] outside of its proper time, the bread has been sanctified? Also when he slaughtered it [intending to eat it] outside of its proper place, the bread should be sanctified.'

I. "R. Joshua said to him, 'Do you not agree that if he slaughtered it, and it was found to be blemished, that the bread has not been sanctified. Also if he slaughtered it [intending to eat it] outside of its proper place, the bread should not be sanctified.'

J. "R. Eliezer said to him, 'You compare it to a blemished animal, and I compare it to [slaughter intending to eat it] outside of its proper time. Let us see to what it is similar? If it is similar to a blemish, let us learn it [= reason] from the blemished animal, and if it is similar to [slaughter intending to eat it] outside of the proper time, let us learn it [= reason] from [slaughter intending to eat it] outside of its proper time.'

K. "R. Eliezer says, 'Slaughter [intending to eat it] outside of the proper time is rendered invalid by intention, and slaughter [intending to eat it] outside of the proper place is rendered invalid by intention. But let not the blemished sacrifice prove the matter, for it is not rendered invalid by intention, but by actual deed [physical blemish].'

L. "R. Joshua says, 'A blemished animal is invalid, and 'Cutting off' does not apply to it, and slaughter [intending to eat] outside of the proper place is invalid, and 'Cutting off' does not apply. But let not slaughter [intending to eat] outside of the proper time prove the matter, for the law of refuse applies to it, and they *are* liable on its account to the law of 'Cutting off.'"

[b. adds: "R. Eliezer was silent."]

Tos. Men. 8 : 19, Zuckermandel, p. 524, ls. 18-34 (b. Men. 78b-79a)

*Comment*: The Mishnah is Meir's. But Judah evidently had received a quite different tradition.

III.ii.73. The father of R. Jeremiah b. Abba taught (TNY):

"If the two loaves were taken out [of the sanctuary] between the slaughtering [of the two lambs] and the sprinkling of their blood, and then [the priest] sprinkled the blood of the lambs [and at the same time expressed the intention of eating the flesh] outside the prescribed time—

"R. Eliezer says, 'The bread is not subject to the law of refuse.'

"And R. ʿAqiba says, 'The bread is subject to the law of refuse.'"

b. Men. 47a-b

*Comment*: This is parallel to Judah's excluded case, E1. Eliezer says it has not been sanctified, ʿAqiba that it has. Eliezer here is inconsistent with E1.

IV.ii.16. R. Eliezer says, "It is not necessary. Lo, it says, *You will count for yourself* (Deut. 16 : 9). The counting [of the days from Passover to Pentecost] depends upon the court [for they know how to interpret *the morrow after the Sabbath* as the morrow after the festival]. Accordingly the Sabbath of creation cannot be intended, which any one is able to count."

B. R. Joshua says, "The Torah has said, *Count days and sanctify the month, count days and sanctify Pentecost.* Just as in regard to the month there is something distinctive at the commencement of the counting [= the New Moon], so with the Pentecost there is something distinctive at the commencement [of the counting, namely, Passover—but not Sunday] . . ."

R. Ishmael says, "The Torah has said, *Bring the ʿomer on Passover and the two showbreads on Pentecost.* Just as the latter are offered on the festival at the beginning of the festival, so the former is offered on the festival and at the beginning of the festival."

R. Judah b. Batyra says, "*Sabbath* is said below [Lev. 23 : 16] and above [Lev. 23 : 11]. Just as in the former case the beginning of the festival is near [the Sabbath], so in the latter case the festival is near the [*ʿomer*]."

b. Men. 65b (Compare trans. Eli Cashdan, pp. 385-7; b. Men. 82b; b. Yev. 46a)

*Comment*: The above tradition is attached to a story about Yoḥanan b. Zakkai and the Sadducees, disputing the date of Pentecost (*Development*, pp. 153-154). Immediately following is a tradition, marked TNW RBNN, in which Yosi b. Judah, Judah b. Batyra, Yosi, and Simeon b. Eleazar debate the same issue, and Judah b. Batyra has the same exegesis as is given to Eliezer here, while Yosi has the exegesis of Judah b. Batyra here. Eliezer's saying, moreover, begins with *it is not necessary*, which takes for granted some sort of antecedent proof, if not the one in the Yoḥanan b. Zakkai-pericope. On the whole the Amoraic tradition seems curious. The pericope involving Eliezer, Joshua, Ishmael, and Judah b. Batyra is not given a Tannaitic superscription, while the following one has TNW RBNN, and I see no reason to differ from the redactors responsible for the superscription. The tradition before us would seem to be pseudepigraphic.

See Epstein, *Nusaḥ*, p. 1186.

III.ii.74. *And if you bring a meal-offering of first fruits* (Lev. 2 : 14) refers to the meal-offering of the *ʿomer.*

Of what was it offered? Of barley.

You say barley, but perhaps it was of wheat?

R. Eliezer says, "*Aviv* is said with reference to [the events in] Egypt, and *Aviv* is said with reference to the [future] generations. Just as that referred to in Egypt meant barley, so *Aviv* mentioned in regard to [future] generations means barley."

And R. ʿAqiba says, "We find the individual may bring what is required of him from barley, and the community brings which is required of it from wheat and from barley. If you say that the *ʿomer* was offered of wheat, we have not found a case in which the community brings what is required of it from barley..." etc.

b. Men. 68b

II.iii.11. From what does it [the *ʿomer*] come?

From barley.

Or perhaps it comes from wheat?

R. Eliezer said, "*Aviv* is said here, and *Aviv* is said in reference to Egypt. Just as *Aviv* said in reference to Egypt means that barley is brought in the *ʿomer*, so too here the requirement is barley.

[R. ʿAqiba offers a different proof for the same proposition, as above.]

Sifra Vayiqra Parashah 13 : 4, Weiss, p. 12b (b. Men. 68b)

*Comment*: Eliezer and ʿAqiba bring alternative proofs for the same proposition, that the *ʿomer* is composed of barley.

## xxv. Ḥullin, Bekhorot, ʿArakhin

I.i.133.A. He who slaughters the dying animal—

B. Rabban [Kaufmann, Camb., Naples omit: Simeon b.] Gamaliel says, "[It is not valid] unless it can jerk a fore-leg and a hind-leg."

C. R. Eliezer says, "It is sufficient if [the blood] spurts forth (ZNQH)."

D. R. Simeon says, "Also he who slaughters at night, and [if] the next day he arose (KŠKM) and found the walls [of the neck] filled with blood, it is valid for it [the blood] has spurted."

And [this is] according to the ruling (MDH) of R. Eliezer.

E. And sages say, "[It is not valid] until it jerks a fore-leg or a hind-leg or until it can wag its tail—

F. "Whether a small or a large beast."

M. Hul. 2 : 6 (b. Hul. 37a, 38a)

*Comment*: If the animal cannot jerk a leg, it is assumed that it died before the slaughter was completed. Eliezer says it is sufficient if the blood spurts at the point of slaughter. Simeon adds that evidence that the blood *has* spurted is accepted. The ruling of the sages in E repeats

[Simeon b.] Gamaliel in B, but adds to the movement of the fore-leg and the hind-leg the possibility of the animal's moving the tail as a vital sign. Without Eliezer, E would have sufficed with, *Also (ʾP) move the tail.* Since the sages' saying is fully articulated, the pericope is a unity: Gamaliel followed by, and in disagreement with, Eliezer. Simeon adds a ruling in accord with Eliezer's logic. Then the sages repeat Gamaliel's ruling, with their addition in accord with his ruling.

See Epstein, *Nusaḥ*, p. 1202.

I.ii.110. R. Simeon says in the name of R. Eliezer, "He who slaughters at night and in the morning arose (ʿMD) and found the walls [of the neck] filled with blood, it is valid, in the knowledge that it spurted."

Tos. Hul. 2 : 11, Zuckermandel, p. 502, ls. 24-5

*Comment*: M. Hul. 2 : 6D is now given in Eliezer's name, rather than as a logical extension of his earlier ruling.

I.i.134.A. (The law to *let the dam go* [Deut. 22 : 6-7] does not apply to the unclean bird. An unclean bird sitting on the eggs of a clean bird or a clean bird sitting on the eggs of an unclean bird is not subject to the law of sending forth [the dam].)

B. A cock-partridge (QWRʾ ZKR) [Jer. 17 : 11, the partridge sits on an egg which he has not laid]—

C. R. Eliezer declares liable.

D. And sages declare free [of liability to send the bird forth when taking the eggs].

M. Hul. 12 : 2 (b. Hul. 138b, 140b;
Mid. Tan. to Deut. 22 : 7, Hoffmann, pp. 135-6;
Sifré Deut. 228, Finkelstein, p. 260)

*Comment*: The cock-partridge sits on the eggs like the dam. Eliezer rules that since that is the case, it must not be taken with the eggs, for it functions like the dam. The sages differ.

Note also b. Hul. 79b: *It and its young* applies to a hybrid and a *koy*. R. Eliezer says, "To a hybrid, the offspring of a goat, and a ewe, but not to a *koy*." Also b. Hul. 132a: The law of the shoulder, two cheeks, and the maw applies to a hybrid and a *koy*. R. Eliezer says, "To a hybrid, the offspring of a goat and a ewe is subject; the offspring of a he-goat and a hind is exempt."

M. Bekh. 1 : 5-6 has Eliezer consistent with b. Hul. 79b, a flimsy warrant to include the *koy*-rulings, and by inference, M. Hul. 12 : 2, in his tradition.

See Epstein, *Nusaḥ*, p. 1170, n. 1.

I.i.135.A. They do not redeem [a Firstling] with a calf, a wild animal, an animal that has been slaughtered, a *ṭerefah*-animal, or with a hybrid, [produced by a ram and a she-goat, for instance] or a *koy*.

B. R. Eliezer [Kaufmann, Parma, Camb., Naples: Leazar] permits [redemption of a Firstling with] a hybrid, because it is a lamb, and forbids with a *koy*, beecause it is a doubt as to whether it is a cattle or a wild beast] [M. Hul. 6 : 1].

C. If he gave it [the firstling of an ass] to the priest, he [the priest] cannot keep it until he sets apart a lamb in its place.

M. Bekh. 1 : 5 (b. Bekh. 12a-b)

I.i.136.A. He who separates the redemption [lamb] for the firstling of an ass and it died—

B. R. Eliezer says, "They are liable for its responsibility (ḤYB—'HRYWT), as [they are answerable for] the five *selas* for [redemption] of the son."

C. And sages say, "They are not liable for its responsibility, [as they are not answerable for] the redemption [money] of Second Tithe."

D. R. Joshua and R. Ṣaddoq gave testimony concerning the redemption [lamb] for the firstling of an ass that died, that the priest can claim nothing.

E. The firstling of an ass died—

F. R. Eliezer says, "It should be buried [it is holy], and the owner may enjoy the benefit of the lamb [which he had set apart to redeem it.]"

G. And sages say, "It need not be buried, and the lamb [which had been set apart for its redemption still] belongs to the priest.

M. Bekh. 1 : 6 (y. Ter. 6 : 1; b. Bekh. 12b, 13a)

*Comment*: Scripture says, *And every firstling of an ass you shall redeem with a lamb* (Ex. 13 : 13). This may be a lamb from the sheep or goats, male or female, large or small, perfect or blemished, so M. Bekh. 1 : 4. M. Bekh. 1 : 5 then raises the issue of other animals which may or may not be used for redemption of a firstling. One may not use a calf, even though it may be as small as a lamb, or a wild animal, which does not fall into the category of 'lamb,' or a slaughtered lamb or a *ṭerefah*-one (which is alive), or what is cross-bred or a *koy*, which is a species of wild sheep, or a cross between a goat and a gazelle (Danby, p. 794).

Eliezer permits use of a cross-bred animal, for instance an offspring of a sheep and a goat, because it falls into the category of 'lamb.' But he forbids the *koy*—as stated in A—because one is in doubt whether it is a wild beast or a cow. Eliezer's saying thus glosses A, repeating two of its elements and giving reasons for his respective rulings with, and against, A, in each of them. A ought therefore to have been before Eliezer when his saying was formulated.

M. Bekh. 1 : 6 phrases the issue as a problem, A, to which B and C then respond. If the lamb set apart for redeeming the firstling of an ass dies before being given to the priest, what does one do? The owner is liable to give the priest another lamb, according to Eliezer. The sages say that one is not liable to separate another lamb. The former uses the analogy of the money set aside for the redemption of the first-born, for which the father remains responsible should the coins be lost. The latter refer to the Redemption-money of Second Tithe. If it is lost, the owner is not responsible. He does not have to go up to Jerusalem and spend other funds.

D then supplies an opinion of Joshua and Ṣaddoq in support of C, but in a different form. They *testify* concerning the same problem, but their operative language is different from that used in B-C. It is no longer ḤYB B'ḤRYWT, but rather, "The priest has nothing here."

E raises the logically related problem: What does one do if the firstling of the ass itself should die? What to do with the corpse? And what to do with the lamb set aside for its redemption? Both parties in F-G rule on both problems. Eliezer says the corpse is to be buried as if it were holy, not redeemed. Since the owner is liable for the redemption-lamb, it now belongs to him. The sages say the owner need not bury the corpse, but the lamb belongs to the priest, for once it was separated, it is his, and the firstling has already been redeemed by it. F-G spells out the consequences of the rulings in B-C.

The form of 1 : 6 is standard, excluding the interpolation of D, with a statement of the problem, followed by rulings of Eliezer, and with the sages' responding to, and depending upon the language of, the statement of the problem.

Note b. Bekh. 7a, Joshua *vs.* Eliezer *re* Deut. 14 : 4.

See Epstein, *Tan.*, p. 439, on 1 : 6; *Nusaḥ*, p. 1170, on 1 : 5, and p. 646, on 1 : 6. For 1 : 5, Epstein prefers Eleazar.

I.i.137.A. "He that slit the ear of a firstling—lo, this [firstling] may never be slaughtered," the words of R. Eliezer.

B. And sages say, "When some other blemish is born [in the firstling], he may slaughter it on that account."

M. Bekh. 5 : 3 (b. Bekh. 34a-b)

*Comment*: The difference is whether the man who blemished the firstling will be fined so that he may never again make use of the firstling. Eliezer says the man is fined. The sages say that when some other, legitimate blemish appears, the animal may be slaughtered.

The pericope is followed by a story about a quaestor who deliberately made a blemish on a blemished firstling; the sages permitted the animal, and the man went and did the same with others, so the sages declared it forbidden. This is followed by a general rule: "If it is done intentionally by its owner, in order to make it permissible to slaughter the firstling, it is forbidden; but if the blemish is not made deliberately, the firstling is permitted."

M. Neg. 7 : 5 supplies ample warrant for assigning this pericope to our Eliezer, according to b. Bekh. 34a-b, which takes for granted the same Eliezer stands behind both laws and shows Eliezer does not contradict himself.

See Epstein, *Nusaḥ*, p. 187.

I.i.138.A. He who dedicated his goods and was still liable for his wife's *Ketuvah*—

B. R. Eliezer says, "When he divorces her, let him make her vow to yield [no] benefit [to him]."

C. R. Joshua says, "It is not necessary."

D. Similarly, Rabban Simeon b. Gamaliel said, "If a man was guarantor for a woman's *Ketuvah* and her husband divorced her, the husband must vow to derive no further benefit from her, lest he make a conspiracy against the property of the guarantor and take back his wife again."

M. Ar. 6 : 1 (b. Ar. 23a)

*Comment*: The man has given his property to the Temple, but at the same time has a liability for the wife's *Ketuvah.* He causes her to take a vow not to give benefit to him. Then she collects the *Ketuvah* from the sanctuary. The suspicion is that he divorces her so that she can collect her *Ketuvah* from the sanctuary, and afterward he may remarry her; hence the Temple would have been defrauded, so Albeq, *ad loc.* Joshua says it is not necessary to make her take such an oath.

Simeon b. Gamaliel follows Eliezer's reasoning in the case of a man who serves as a pledge for a woman's *Ketuvah*, if her husband cannot pay it. If the husband divorces the woman and cannot pay the *Ketuvah*, she collects from the guarantor. To do so, the husband makes the wife vow not to derive benefit, lest the two have conspired against the property of the man who made the pledge.

b. Ar. 23a explains that the issue of M. Ar. 6 : 1 is whether a man will engage in a conspiracy against the sanctuary.

I.ii.111. He who dedicated his goods and planned to divorce his wife—

B. R. Eliezer says, "Let him cause her to vow [against deriving] benefit, and collect her *Ketuvah* from the sanctuary, and if he wants to remarry her, he may remarry her."

C. R. Joshua says, "If he wants to remarry her, he may not remarry her."

D. The House of Hillel say, "If he wants to remarry her, he may not remarry her."

E. R. Eliezer rules according to the House of Shammai and R. Joshua rules according to the House of Hillel.

Tos. Ar. 4 : 5, Zuckermandel, p. 547, ls. 9-12

*Comment*: Lieberman, *Tosefet Rishonim*, II, p. 279, says the text should be understood to mean that the man vows that he will not derive benefit from the *sanctuary*—not from his wife—for Eliezer holds a man cannot free himself from a vow to the sanctuary. If on that account he divorces his wife intentionally, so as to recover his goods, he is forced to vow against benefitting from her property. Then there is no worry about remarrying, and he may indeed remarry, a question on which M. Ar. 6 : 1 is silent.

Joshua thinks that a man *may* seek absolution from a vow in respect to what he has sanctified. Therefore if he regrets his gift, he can hope to get it back. But then Joshua considers the possibility that the wife may incite him to divorce her with the idea of remarrying him, and she will then recover her *Ketuvah*. Therefore Joshua says they may not remarry.

Lieberman restores the clause as to the Houses: R. Eleazar b. R. Simeon says, "The House of Shammai say, 'If he wants to remarry her, he may do so.'" The House of Hillel is as given. And then comes the allusion to the Houses' parallels with the masters. The difference between the Houses is that the House of Shammai rule a dedication to the Temple done in error remains dedicated; and the House of Hillel hold the contrary. Therefore the man takes an oath against benefitting from his property, which is irrevocably given to the sanctuary. But they may remarry, since the sanctuary's property is protected. The House of Hillel say he *can* hope to recover the property on the claim that it was dedicated in error; therefore he may *not* remarry.

I.i.139.A. Although they have said, 'Pledges must be taken from them that are bound by a vow of Valuation,' they leave him sustenance for thirty days, and clothing for a year, and a bed and bedding, shoes and *tefillin*—for himself, but not for his wife and children.

If he was a craftsman, they give him two tools of his craft of every kind.

If he was a carpenter, they leave him two axes and two saws.

B. R. Eliezer says, "If he was a farmer, they give him his yoke [of oxen]; [if he was] an assdriver, they give him his ass."

M. Ar. 6 : 3 (b. Ar. 18a, 23b, 24a)

*Comment*: When a man vows his own value, he is expected to pay according to the ability of him that vows (M. Ar. 4 : 1). M. Ar. 5 : 6 states, "Pledges must be taken from them that are bound by a vow of Valuation, but not from them that are liable to Sin-offerings or Guilt-offerings." So M. Ar. 6 : 3 glosses the foregoing, and Eliezer adds to that gloss and in its spirit, specifying further examples of the sorts of things which are not taken as pledge from a man who has vowed his own value. This is more or less consistent with Eliezer's view in M. Ar. 8 : 4.

See Epstein, *Nusaḥ*, p. 1171.

I.ii.112.A. Even though they have said, 'Pledges must be taken from them that are bound by a vow of Valuation,' they give him food for thirty days, clothing for a year...

B. R. Eliezer says, "If he was a farmer, they give him his yoke."

C. R. Eliezer says, "An ass-driver, they give him two asses."

Tos. Ar. 4 : 6, Zuckermandel, p. 547, ls. 15-19

*Comment*: On the second *R. Eliezer says*, see Lieberman, *Tosefet Rishonim* II, p. 280. It should be deleted.

I.i.140.A. "A man may dedicate (ḤRM) part of his flock and part of his herd, some of his Canaanite man-servants and some of his [Canaanite] maid-servants. But if he has declared all of them to be dedicated (ḤRM), they are not dedicated"—the words of R. Eliezer [Naples, Parma: Eleazar].

B. R. Eleazar b. ʿAzariah said, "Now if to the Highest men may not devote all of their property, how much the more so then must men not squander their goods."

M. Ar. 8 : 4 (b. Ar. 28a)

*Comment*: Eliezer speaks of the things devoted (declared *Ḥerem*) referred to in Lev. 27 : 28. These cannot be sold or redeemed. They remain holy. If a man has not left to himself any part of a certain type of goods, then the whole gift is of no effect. Scripture speaks *Of all that he has.* Eliezer interprets this as an exclusion: *Of all*, but not *all* (b. Ar. 28a.)

See Epstein, *Nusaḥ*, p. 1171.

I.ii.113. (*That a man devotes to the Lord, of anything that he has, whether of man or of beast or of his inherited field.*)

A. R. Eliezer says, "*Of a man*, and not all the man, *of a beast* and not all the beasts, *of an inherited field*, and not the whole inherited field. Therefore if he dedicated all of them, they are not devoted (ḤRM)."

Tos. Ar. 4 : 24, Zuckermandel, p. 548, ls. 29-30

### xxvi. Temurah, Keritot, Meʿilah, Tamid

I.i.141. (All may substitute another beast in place of that which they had first assigned for an offering. Not that one has the right to make such a substitute, but if he has done so, it is substituted [the second animal for the first], and he incurs the forty stripes.—M. Tem. 1 : 1).

A. These are the sacrifices whose progeny and their substitutes are like (KYWṢ') them [Danby, p. 557: "Of these animal-offerings, what is born from them and what is substituted for them may be offered as the like kind of offering"].

B. The progeny of the Peace-offering, and their substitute, and their progeny, and the progeny's progeny, without limit—lo, these are like Peace-offerings, and require laying on of hands, and drink-offerings, and waving of the breast and thigh [which must be given to the priests].

C. R. Eliezer says, "The progeny of Peace-offerings may not be offered as Peace-offerings."

D. And sages say, "It may be brought."

E. R. Simeon said, "They did not differ concerning the progeny of the progeny of Peace-offerings, and concerning the progeny of the progeny of the substitute, that they should not be brought.

F. "Concerning what did they differ?

"Concerning the progeny [itself]—

"For R. Eliezer says, 'It may not be brought.'"

"And sages say, 'It may be brought.'"

G. R. Joshua and R. Pappyas gave testimony concerning the progeny of Peace-offerings that it *may* be brought as Peace-offerings [as in 1 : 1].

H. R. Pappyas said, "I testify that we had a heifer that was offered as a Peace-offering. We ate it at Passover, and we ate its progeny as Peace-offerings on the Festival [of Sukkot]."

M. Tem. 3 : 1 (b. Tem. 18a-b)

*Comment*: A opens as if it will supply an extensive list, but then ends with the first item, Peace-offerings. Then B presents a fully articulated law, with all the details as to what is required for the progeny of the Peace-offering and their substitute, etc. C has Eliezer reject the rule of B. D duplicates B. One or the other ought to be redundant. Either the law should read as does B, or B should be dropped and the dispute should be contained in C-D alone.

In E Simeon clarifies what has already been made perfectly clear in C: Eliezer and the sages differ about the progeny of Peace-offerings, and not merely about the next generation(s). Before Simeon ought to have been a dispute which had Eliezer rule on the progeny of the progeny of Peace-offerings and of the substitute, with Eliezer saying they should not be brought, the sages, that they should—this is the point of B. Then Simeon had B, followed by *Eliezer: offered*, and *sages: not offered.* C's formulation of Eliezer's position is in accord with Simeon in F.

C gives a general report that Joshua and Pappyas agree with the sages, and in H we have the actual language attributed to Pappyas.

See Epstein, *Nusaḥ*, p. 419; *Tan.*, pp. 151, 440, 457.

I.i.142.A. He who separates a female beast as a Whole-offering and it bore a male, it [the male] is left to pasture until it suffers a blemish, and then it will be sold, and he will bring with its price a Whole-offering.

R. Eliezer [Parma, Camb., Naples: Leazar] says, "It itself is offered as a Whole-offering."

B. He who separates a female beast for a Guilt-offering, it is left to pasture until it is blemished, and it is to be sold, and he will bring with its price a Guilt-offering.

And if he had brought his Guilt-offering, the price will fall to the Temple as a Freewill-offering.

R. Simeon says, "It is sold immediately, before it is blemished."

C. The substitute of a Guilt-offering, the progeny of its substitute, its young and its progeny's progeny, without limit, must be left to pasture until they are blemished. Then they are sold, and their price will fall [to the Temple] as a Freewill-offering.

D. R. Eliezer says, "They must be left to die."

E. And R. Eleazar [Camb.: Joshua] says, "Let him bring with their price Whole-offerings."

F. A Guilt-offering whose owner died, or whose owner has done atonement, is left to pasture until it is blemished, and it will be sold, and its price will fall for a Freewill-offering.

G. R. Eliezer says, "It will die."

H. R. Eleazar [Camb.: Joshua] says, "He will bring with its price a Whole-offering."

M. Tem. 3 : 3 (b. Tem. 16b, 18b, 19a, 20b; b. Pes. 73a, b. Shav. 12a; b. Mak. 12a)

*Comment*: Eliezer's rulings pertain to the Guilt-offering. He holds that the substitute for a Guilt-offering is treated like that of the Sin-offering—just as he treats the Guilt- and Sin-offerings as identical in other circumstances (above, p. 222), for M. Tem. 2 : 2 states:

> The Sin-offerings of the individual whose owner has [otherwise] already made atonement are left to die, but those of the congregation are not left to die. R. Judah says, "They are left to die."

The same applies to the substitute of the Guilt-offering, and in F Eliezer says the same of the Guilt-offering whose owner has died, just as Judah [b. Ilai] rules in the case of the Sin-offering whose owner has already atoned.

The form of C-H has the statement of a rule, followed by Eliezer's and Eleazar's dissenting opinions, rejecting the rule entirely. A standard superscription would have been: *The substitute of a Guilt-offering*... followed by: *R. Eliezer*... *R. Eleazar*... *Sages say: They are left to pasture*...

See Epstein, *Nusaḥ*, pp. 1171-1172.

I.i.143.A. All beasts which may not be offered on the altar—their progeny are permitted.

B. The progeny of a *ṭerefah*—

C. R. Eliezer [Parma: Leazar] says, "It should not be offered on the altar."

D. And sages say, "It may be offered."

E. R. Ḥanina b. Anṭignos says, "A valid beast that has suckled from a *ṭerefah* is invalid for the altar."

M. Tem. 6 : 5 (b. Tem. 30b, b. Hul. 58a: *vs.* Joshua)

*Comment*: The *ṭerefah* falls within the rule of A; D then repeats A. Eliezer holds that the rule of A has an exception in the progeny of the *ṭerefah*.

b. Tem. 30b has Eleazar; 31a has Eliezer.

See Epstein, *Nusaḥ*, p. 232.

I.ii.114. (Beasts that may not be offered on the altar render others forbidden ... e.g., beasts that had committed or suffered an unnatural crime, or one that had been set apart or that had been worshipped or that was the hire of a harlot or the price of a dog or that was cross-bred or that was *ṭerefah* ... M. Tem. 6 : 1).

A. R. Yosi says, "They substitute for a beast that has committed or suffered an unnatural crime, and for one that had been set apart, and for one that has been worshipped, and for a harlot's hire, and for the price of a dog, and for hybrid, and for *ṭerefah*, and for the fetus born of caesarean section."

B. R. Eliezer says, "The hybrid and the *ṭerefah* and the fetus born by caesarean section and the *ṭumṭum* [with hidden genitals] and the androgynous animal are not sanctified and do not sanctify [other animals, therefore are not substituted and do not effect an exchange]."

Tos. Tem. 1 : 9, Zuckermandel, p. 551, ls. 39-40, p. 552, ls. 1-2 (b. Tem. 11a, 17a; b. Yev. 84a, b. Bekh. 42a; b. Tem. 16b: Eleazar)

*Comment*: Eliezer's rule in M. Tem. 3 : 3 deals only with the progeny of a *ṭerefah*. Now we have a full list of animals the progeny of which would enter the same category.

b. Tem. 17a has Eliezer.

I.i.144.A. R. ʿAqiba said, "I asked R. Eliezer, 'He who does many [individual] acts of work of a single type of work (MʿYN ML'KH 'ḤT) in one period of forgetfulness (BHʿLM 'ḤD), what is it [the rule]? Is he liable for one [Sin-offering] for all of them, or for one for each and every [individual] act?'

B. "He said to me, 'He is liable for each and every a one, from a *qal veḥomer*: If [one who has sexual relations with] the menstrual woman, to which many classes (TWṢ'WT HRBH) and many [ways of] sins (ḤṬ'WT HRBH) do not apply, is liable for each and every act, [for] the Sabbath, to which many classes and many [ways of] sins do apply, is it not logical that he should be liable for each and every one?'

C. "I said to him, 'No. If you have said so concerning a menstrual woman, to whom two prohibitions ('ZHRWT) apply—for he is prohibited from [having sexual relations with] the menstrual woman, and the menstrual woman is prohibited [from having sexual relations with] him, will you say so concerning the Sabbath, to which only one prohibition applies?'

D. "He said to me, 'He that has sexual relations with [menstruous] minors will prove the matter, for only one prohibition [that against his not having intercourse with a menstruous woman] applies to them, and he is liable for each and every act [of intercourse].'

E. "I said to him, 'No. If you have said so concerning him who has sexual relations with minors, with whom though [no prohibition] now applies, it will apply afterward, will you say so concerning the Sabbath, which he has no right [to profane] now or afterward?'

F. "He said to me, 'He that has sexual relations with the beast will prove the matter.'

G. "I said to him, 'The cattle is like the Sabbath.'"

M. Ker. 3 : 10 (b. Ker. 16a-b, 17a-b; y. Shab. 7 : 1)

III.ii.75.A. TNW RBNN: If one had intercourse [inadvertently with one of the prohibited relations], and then again, and then again—

B. "He is liable for each act," the words of R. Eliezer.

C. And sages say, "He is liable only once."

D. The sages agree with R. Eliezer that if a man had intercourse at the same time with each of his five menstruous wives, he is liable

for each act, since he caused them to be liable for separate offerings.
b. Ker. 15a

*Comment*: The setting—M. Ker. 3 : 7ff.—is a set of first-person sayings of ʿAqiba. In M. Ker. 3 : 7 he asks Gamaliel and Joshua a similar sort of question: If a man had connection with his sister and his father's sister and his mother's sister during one period of forgetfulness, is he liable for a Sin-offering for each, or for all in one Sin-offering?

M. Ker. 3 : 8 has him ask them whether a member of a beast hanging loose conveys uncleanness like a member from a living being.

In M. Ker. 3 : 9 he asks, "If a man slaughtered five animal-offerings outside the Temple court during one spell of forgetfulness, is he liable for one offering for all, or for one for each of them?"

Then comes the Sabbath-question—essentially the same question using different details. They reply with what they have heard. In M. Ker. 3 : 7: "We have heard no tradition about this, but we have heard a tradition that if a man had connexion during one spell of forgetfulness with his wives that were menstruants, he is liable for each one of them." In M. Ker. 3 : 9, Joshua says, "I have heard a tradition about one who, during one spell of forgetfulness, ate of one animal-offering out of five dishes, that he is culpable on each count under the law of sacrilege."

The question of M. Ker. 3 : 10A concerns one type of work in one period of forgetfulness. If the man did many kinds of work, not of a single kind, he certainly would be liable for each one or for each Sabbath. Eliezer replies like Joshua: the man is liable for each. He, however, has no tradition, but a logical argument, based on sexual relations with the menstrual woman. A person is liable for each act of sexual relations with a menstrual woman. He should be liable for each act of breaking the Sabbath. There are not many kinds of sin in respect to the former; the only prohibition has to do with the act of sex. Yet as M. Ker. 3 : 7 makes clear—and takes for granted—one is liable for each such act. Likewise here, where there are many sorts of acts of work which are prohibited, a similar liability should pertain. Therefore 3 : 10B depends upon the same fact as is given in M. Ker. 3 : 7, the tradition that one is liable for each act of sexual relations with the menstrual woman.

ʿAqiba does not argue with Joshua in M. Ker. 3 : 7, so he is expected to accept the same answer here. But he rejects the answer, showing that sexual relations and Sabbath-violation are not comparable. In the former case two prohibitions are involved, one applying to the man, the other to the woman. So ʿAqiba turns the matter upside down. Each woman mentioned in M. Ker. 3 : 7 is liable for having sexual relations with the man. He therefore is liable for having sexual relations with each woman.

In D Eliezer introduces the case of a man who has sexual relations with five minors who are in their menstrual period, but who are not liable for their sexual relations. Now only one party is involved in the Sin-offering—the man himself, not the girls—yet he is liable for each one. ʿAqiba rejects this argument, for, even though now the individual minors are not liable, when they grow up, they will be liable. So there is the potentiality of two prohibitions. But in the case of the Sabbath, there is no such potentiality.

F-G introduce an unarticulated argument, now concerning sexual relations with a number of beasts. They are subject to no prohibitions, but the man is liable for each one. This should complete Eliezer's case. But ʿAqiba begs the question: "I am asking as much in the case of the cattle as of the Sabbath, whether the man is liable for each cattle's sexual relationship." So what is taken for fact by Eliezer is turned into a question by ʿAqiba, and the original issue stands.

Apart from the introductory words, *I said to him . . . he said to me*, the debate is standard.

See Epstein, *Nusaḥ*, pp. 59, 220.

II.iii.12. R. ʿAqiba said, "I asked R. Eleazar, 'He who does many acts of work of a single type of work on many Sabbaths in one spell of forgetfulness, what is the law? Is he liable for each one [Sin-offering] for all of them, or one for each?'

"He said to me, 'He is liable for each one, from a *qal veḥomer*: If the menstruating woman, who does not produce many results and many Sin-offerings, is liable [for each act of intercourse], the Sabbath, which [has] many results and many Sin-offerings, is it not logical that he should be liable for each one?'

"I said to him, 'No. If you have said so concerning the menstruating woman, to whom apply two prohibitions, for he is prohibited against having intercourse with the menstruating woman, and the menstruating woman is prohibited against him, will you say so concerning the Sabbath, to which only a single prohibition applies?'

"He said to me, 'He that has intercourse with minors will prove the matter, for there applies to them only a single prohibition [his], and he is liable for each.'

"I said to him, 'No, if you have said so concerning him who has intercourse with minors, the fact is that even though there is no [prohibition] applying to them now, there will be in the future. Will you say so concerning the Sabbath, which has none either now or in the future?'

"He said to me, 'He that has intercourse with the beast will prove the matter.'

"I said to him, 'The beast is like the Sabbath.'"

Sifra Vayiqra Pereq 1 : 13, Weiss, p. 16b

I.i.145. (Just as a man is liable only to one Sin-offering if, during one period of forgetfulness, he ate forbidden fat, and again ate forbidden fat, so too when the transgression is not known of a certainty, he brings only one [Suspensive] Guilt-offering. If there was certainty, he brings only one [Suspensive] Guilt-offering. If there was knowledge in the meantime, just as he must bring one Sin-offering for each act, so too he must bring one Suspensive Guilt-offering for each act. Just as a man is liable on each count if he ate fat and blood and Remnant and Refuse during one period of forgetfulness, so too if the transgression was not known of a certainty, he must bring a Suspensive Guilt-offering for each act.—M. Ker. 4 : 2A).

A. There was forbidden fat and Remnant before him. He ate one of them and it is not known which one of them he ate—

B. His wife, who was in her menstrual period, and his sister were with him in the house, and he accidentally [had intercourse] with one of them, and it is not known with which one of them he accidentally [had intercourse] [!]—

C. Sabbath and the Day of Atonement, and he did work at sundown, and it is not known on which of them he worked—

D. R. Eliezer declares him liable for a Sin-offering.

E. And R. Joshua declares him free [of liability].

F. R. Yosi said, "They did not dispute concerning him who works at sundown, that he is free of liability, for I say, 'He did part of the work on one day and part on the next.'

G. "And concerning what did they dispute?

H. "Concerning his doing the work in the midst of the day, but it is not known whether he did it on the Sabbath or whether he did it on the Day of Atonement—

"Or concerning the one who did it, and it is not known what kind of work he did—

I. "R. Eliezer declares [him] liable for a Sin-offering.

J. "And R. Joshua declares [him] free."

K. R. Judah said, "R. Joshua would also declare him free of a Suspensive Guilt-offering."

M. Ker. 4 : 2 (b. Ker. 19a-b, 20a;
y. Shab. 7 : 1, 13 : 1, b. Shavu. 18b-19a)

I.i.146.A. R. Simeon Shezuri and R. Simeon say, "They did not dispute concerning whether he was liable through a transgression falling within one class [Danby, p. 509, for DBR SHWʾ MŠWM ŠM ʾḤD, ŠHWʾ ḤYB).

B. "Concerning what did they dispute?

C. "Concerning something which is [prohibited] on account of two names [Danby: "A transgression falling within two classes," e.g. whether he sowed or reaped, or whether he reaped wheat or barley]—

D. "For Eliezer declares liable for a Sin-offering.

E. "And R. Joshua exempts."

F. R. Judah says, "Even if he intended to gather figs and he gathered grapes, grapes and he gathered figs; black and he gathered white; white and he gathered black—

G. "R. Eliezer declares him liable for a Sin-offering.

H. "And R. Joshua declares him exempt."

I. R. Judah said, "I am surprised if R. Joshua would exempt him in such a case. If so, why is it written, *In which he has sinned* [Lev. 3 : 17, 7 : 26, 17 : 10, 14, 19 : 26, Deut. 12 : 16, 23, 15 : 23]?

J. "To exclude him that had occupied himself [otherwise, and unintentionally committed transgression]."

M. Ker. 4 : 3 (y. Shab. 10 : 4)

*Comment*: While A, B, and C relate to three parallel problems, Yosi's tradition concerns only C. Presumably one can rework the details of A and B to conform to the revision of Yosi in C. The three cases involve the same problem, namely, the liability for an offering where one is not wholly certain what sin has actually been committed.

Eliezer holds that a Sin-offering is required, since the man has certainly sinned.

Joshua says that Scripture (Lev. 4 : 23) speaks of actually knowing that one has sinned. Until one actually knows in what way he has sinned—e.g. with forbidden fat or with Remnant, with the menstrual wife or with the sister, on the Sabbath or on the Day of Atonement—even though the man has certainly done some sin, we do not hold him liable for the Sin-offering. Yosi's revision concerns the Sabbath/Day of Atonement. One is not liable for violating the Sabbath or the Day of Atonement unless a complete act of work has been done. If only part of it is done on one day, and part on the next, he is free of liability, even according to Eliezer. Therefore in H Yosi revises the issue. The man completed the work on one of the two days, but he does not know on which day he did the work. Or, a gloss adds, one does not know exactly what work he did. Eliezer and Joshua take the same positions as before. Judah extends the range of Joshua's ruling; the man does not bring even a Suspensive Guilt-offering. Yosi's improvement of C in H does not change the facts of the case or the issue at hand. But Judah's ruling is important. We know that the man has certainly sinned, but we are not sure of the *type* of sin; the Suspensive Guilt-offering applies only where we are in doubt *that* the man has sinned. So it too is irrelevant to the case.

M. Ker. 4 : 3 has another Ushan revision, this time Simeon Shezuri's and Simeon's. They hold that both sides agree that if the sin was on account of a single prohibition—for instance, if he gathered (LQṬ) on the Sabbath by accident and did not know what it was that he had gathered—the man is liable. So they would differ from Yosi in H, above, for doing work on one day or on the other is subject to a single prohibition. Now, the two Simeons aver, the dispute concerns liability for doing something prohibited because of two different prohibitions,—that is, the examples ignored by Yosi in 4 : 2A and B. There, the man is liable under separate laws, one against forbidden fat, the other against Remnant; one against having sexual relations with the menstrual wife, the other against having sexual relations with a close relative. Those cases, ignored or rejected by Yosi ("R. Yosi said, 'They did not differ concerning . . .'"), are regarded by the Simeon's as the point at issue, that is, a much grosser definition of the dispute, now about violating two separate laws.

Judah in 4 : 3F differs from the Simeon's. He says that if it is not clear precisely what a man has done—even within the violation of a single prohibition—then Joshua regards him as free of liability. Thus one who has gathered on the Sabbath accidentally is not liable according to Joshua, if he intended one kind and gathered another, even dates *vs.* grapes, or even two different kinds of dates. Eliezer's position will not change. But Joshua's has been revised and his view of the range of liability still further reduced.

In I Judah then expresses surprise that Joshua would hold such a position. He raises a question which should be asked by Eliezer: Why does Scripture say, *In which he has sinned*? What now can be included under such a narrow definition as Joshua's? J is either a continuation of Joshua's saying or a gloss supplied to answer his question. Scripture refers to a man who had not the slightest intention of doing a sin, for instance, if he intended to raise up on the Sabbath something not attached to the ground, but uprooted something attached to the ground. In that case, the offering is required. But if he intended to do a prohibited action, even though he did not intend to do the particular action which he actually did, he is going to be free of liability.

Note y. Shab. 7 : 1—TNY: R. Eliezer the Great says, "An adult taken captive by gentiles is liable for each sin," etc. Also y. Shab. 14 : 3: "He wrote one letter on this Sabbath and one on the next—R. Eliezer declares liable; R. Joshua exempts." This is an extreme formulation of the issue.

See Epstein, *Nusaḥ*, p. 1138, 1193.

I.ii.115. A leper (MṢWRʿ) that was afflicted (NTNGʿ) and again was afflicted and again was afflicted brings one sacrifice for all.

B. "He brought his nails and was [again] afflicted, he brings a sacrifice for each and every one," the words of R. Eliezer.

And sages say, "One sacrifice for all, until he brings his Sin-offering."

Tos. Ker. 1 : 14, Zuckermandel, p. 562, ls. 5-7

*Comment*: See Tos. Neg. 9 : 7, and especially Tos. Nez. 4 : 8, Lieberman, p. 139, ls. 40-44, above, p. 196.

The issue now is what marks the end of period of affliction. Eliezer holds it is the nail-clipping, the sages, the Sin-offering. If the period has ended, all parties agree that further sacrifices will have to be brought.

I.ii.116. His wife and his sister: he had sexual relations with one of them, and it is not known with which one—

B. Two women, one menstruous, one not menstruous: he had sexual relations with one of them and it is not known with which one—

C. Forbidden fat and Remnant were before him; he ate one of them, and it is not known of which one he ate—

D. Sabbath and the Day of Atonement: he did work on one of them, and it is not known on which of them he did work—

E. R. Eliezer declares him liable for a Sin-offering.

F. And R. Joshua exempts.

G. R. Eliezer says, "*His sin which he sinned* (Lev. 4 : 23)—a sin of any kind."

H. R. Joshua said to him, "*If it is known to him his sin which he sinned*—when his sin is made known to him [he is liable]."

I. R. Yosi said, "Even though R. Joshua declares him exempt from the Sin-offering, he would declare him liable to the Suspensive-Guilt-offering."

J. R. Judah says, "R. Eliezer declares liable for a Sin-offering, and R. Joshua declares exempt."

K. R. Simeon says, "R. Eliezer declares liable for a Sin-offering, and R. Joshua for a Suspensive Guilt-offering."

L. R. Judah said to him, "It is not in this case that R. Joshua declares liable for a Suspensive Guilt-offering, but where there is a doubt as to whether or not he has sinned. But this one, who certainly *has* sinned, how [on what basis] will he bring a Suspensive Guilt-offering?"

M. R. Simeon said to him, "But of this very case Scripture spoke, *And he did not know, and he was guilty, and he will bear his sin, and he will bring an unblemished ram from the flock* (Lev. 5 : 17-18)."

N. R. Judah said, "R. Eliezer and R. Joshua did not differ concerning him who intended to do a certain work and did something like it.

O. "How so? His wife and his sister: he intended to have sexual relations with this one and had sexual relations with the other—

P. His two wives, one was menstruous and the other not; he intended to have sexual relations with one and had sexual relations with the other—

Q. "Figs and grapes were before him: he intended to gather figs and gathered grapes; grapes and he gathered figs; black and he gathered white; white and he gathered black—

"R. Eliezer declares liable for a Sin-offering.

"And R. Joshua frees him."

R. R. Judah said, "R. Joshua declared him free even from a Suspensive Guilt-offering."

S. And R. Simeon Shezuri and R. Simeon say, "They did not differ concerning something [prohibited] on account of two categories, for R. Eliezer declared him liable for a Sin-offering, and R. Joshua exempts [him.]

T. "The Day of Atonement that coincided with Friday; he did work at sundown—

"R. Eliezer declares him liable for a Sin-offering.

"And R. Joshua exempts."

U. R. Yosi said, "I do not see the opinion of R. Eliezer in this case. For I say, '[If] he wrote two letters, one on the Sabbath and one on the Day of Atonement, he is free of liability, for the two days do not join together for the purpose [of completing] a single act of work.'"

V. They said to him, "Smiting on the anvil will prove the matter."

W. He said to them, "Raising up the [hammer] was on the Sabbath, and bringing it down was on the Day of Atonement." [Lieberman, *Tosefet Rishonim*, II, p. 295, supplies the following, from b. Ker. 19b: TNY', R. Yosi said, "R. Eliezer and R. Joshua did not debate concerning one who does work at sundown, that he is free of liability, for I say that the raising up was while it was still day, and the setting down was the next day (after sundown)."]

X. If he worked on the Day of Atonement, whether before it or after it, he is free of a Suspensive Guilt-offering, for the whole Day [of Atonement] does atonement. If he did work on the sundown of the Sabbath, whether before or after it, he is liable.

Tos. Ker. 2 : 12-15, Zuckermandel, p. 564, ls. 9-32 (Writing two letters: y. Shab. 7 : 1, b. Ker. 17a, 19b; b. Shab. 104b, 105a; Intercourse with menstruous wife: b. Ker. 17a—Simeon b. Eleazar)

*Comment*: The cases of A and B differ from those in the Mishnah (= C-D), for here it is not known whether or not the man has actually sinned at all. Eliezer still holds the man liable, for if the offering is not for this sin, it will be for some other. Joshua exempts the man from a Sin-offering until he knows precisely what he has done to incur the liability.

Yosi then claims that Joshua would impose liability for a Suspensive Guilt-offering, in the supposition that he may have done something wrong. In K Simeon espouses the same viewpoint, explicitly attributing to Joshua the view that a Suspensive Guilt-offering *is* required of the man.

In L Judah replies that Joshua, in a case where a man has certainly sinned (as in C and D), will not require a Suspensive Guilt-offering. But in A-B, acccording to Judah, he will, for it is not known whether the man has done a sin or not. In M Simeon then claims that it is the one who has done some sin, but does not know which one, that Scripture has required to bring the Suspensive Sin-offering.

Then in N-Q Judah returns to the case set forth in C-D, where a man intended a sin, but is not sure which sin he has actually committed. In S the two Simeon's take the opposite extreme. Eliezer and Joshua agree that a man who did something prohibited on account of two categories, according to Joshua, is free from a Sin-offering—again as in C-D.

I.ii.117.A. A piece of forbidden fat which was Refuse and a piece of Remnant: he ate one of them, and he does not know which one of them he ate—he brings two Suspensive Guilt-offerings.

B. R. Eliezer says, "He brings a Sin-offering and a Suspensive Guilt-offering."

C. [If] he ate the second, he brings three Sin-offerings...

D. A piece of Refuse and a piece of Remnant: he ate one of them, and it is not known which of them he ate—

E. R. Eliezer declares liable for a Sin-offering.

F. And R. Joshua exempts...

G. A piece of forbidden fat of Refuse and a piece of forbidden fat of Remnant: he ate one of them, and it is not known which of them he ate—

H. He brings a Sin-offering and a Suspensive Guilt-offering. And, according to the words of R. Eliezer, he brings two Sin-offerings...

I. A piece of holy forbidden fat of Refuse and a piece of Remnant: he ate one of them, and it is not known which of them he ate—

J. He brings a Sin-offering and a Suspensive Guilt-offering.

K. And, according to the words of R. ʿAqiba, he brings a Sin-offering and two Suspensive Guilt-offerings.

L. And according to the words of R. Eleazar [Eliezer] he brings three Sin-offerings . . .

Tos. Ker. 3 : 5-8, Zuckermandel, p. 565, ls. 23-35

III.ii.76. TNY': R. Eliezer said, "In any event [he has sinned.] If it was the forbidden fat that he ate, he is liable; if it was the Remnant, he is liable; if it was his menstrous wife, he is liable, if his sister, he is liable; if it was the Sabbath when he did the work, he is liable, if the Day of Atonement, he is liable."

R. Joshua said to him, "It says, *Wherein he has sinned*—it must be known to him wherein he sinned."

b. Ker. 19a

II.iii.13. *In which he has sinned*—

A. R. Judah says: "His menstruating wife and his sister were in the house with him. He erred in respect to one of them, and it is not known with which one he erred—

"The Sabbath and the Day of Atonement—he did work at sunset on one of them, and it is not known on which one of them he did it—

"Forbidden fat and Remnant are before him, and he ate one of them, and it is not known which of them he ate—

"R. Eliezer declares liable for a Sin-offering.

"And R. Joshua exempts.

B. "R. Eliezer said to him, 'What do you prefer? His wife is menstruating. If he had intercourse [with her], he is liable. If he had intercourse with his sister, he is liable. If he profaned the Sabbath, he is liable. If he profaned the Day of Atonement, he is liable. If he ate forbidden fat, he is liable; Remnant—he is liable.'

"R. Joshua said to him, '*In which he sinned* teaches that he is not liable until his sin is known to him.'"

C. R. Yosi said, "They did not dispute concerning him who does various acts of work, that he is free of liability, for I say, 'Part of it he did today, part the next day.'

"Concerning what did they differ?

"Concerning him who does it in the midst of a single day and does not know whether he did it on the Sabbath or on the Day of Atonement.

"Or concerning him who did work and does not know what sort of work he did.

"R. Eliezer declares liable for a Sin-offering, and R. Joshua declares free of liability."

D. R. Judah said, "R. Joshua would declare free of liability even for a Suspensive Guilt-offering."

E. R. Ishmael and R. Simeon Shezuri say(s), "They did not dispute concerning something which is in a single category, that he *is* liable.

"Concerning what did they dispute?

"Concerning something which is prohibited on two categories.

"For R. Eliezer declares liable for a Sin-offering.

"And R. Joshua exempts."

F. And R. Judah says, "Even on account of something which is prohibited in a single category did R. Joshua declare exempt," etc.

Sifra Vayiqra Pereq 7 : 26-31, Weiss, p. 20a-b
(= Sifra Vayiqra Parashah 12 : 4, Weiss, p. 26b)

*Comment*: The cases before us involve eating forbidden fat which was Refuse and forbidden fat which was Remnant, as in M. Ker. 4 : 2A. So the man is liable for two sins, but he is not sure which is which. According to A, he therefore brings two Suspensive Guilt-offerings. Eliezer rules one is surely subject to a Sin-offering (as in 4 : 2A + D). The other is a Suspensive Guilt-offering. M. Ker. 5 : 5 has the following:

> If there was a piece of unconsecrated [and permitted] fat and a piece of forbidden fat, and a man ate one of them, and it is not known which of them he ate, he must bring a Suspensive Guilt-offering.

But here, as noted, *both* pieces are prohibited. A pertinent Mishnah is M. Ker. 5 : 6:

> If there was a piece of forbidden fat and a piece of permitted but consecrated fat, and a man ate one of them, and it is not known which of them he ate, he must bring a Suspensive Guilt-offering.
>
> If he ate the second also, he must bring a Sin-offering and an Unconditional Guilt-offering.
>
> If one person ate the one, and another came and ate the other, they must each bring a Suspensive Guilt-offering.
>
> R. Simeon says, "They together bring one Sin-offering and one Guilt-offering."
>
> R. Yosi says, "Two cannot together bring one Sin-offering and one Guilt-offering."

Both pieces were prohibited. According to Tos. Ker. 3 : 5-8 he brings two Suspensive Guilt-offerings. Eliezer holds he brings one Sin-offering and one Suspensive Guilt-offering. So Tos. Ker. 3 : 5-8 would seem to stand outside of the rulings of M. Ker. 5 : 6. In M. Ker. 5 : 7, we have the following:

> If there was a piece of forbidden fat and a piece of consecrated fat, and a man ate one of them, and it is not known which of them he ate, he must bring a Sin-offering.
>
> R. ʿAqiba says, "He must bring a Suspensive Guilt-offering."
>
> If he ate the second also, he must bring two Sin-offerings and an Unconditional Guilt-offering.

M. Ker. 5 : 8 is as follows:

> If there was a piece of fat and a piece of Remnant-fat, and a man ate one of them, etc., he must bring a Sin-offering and a Suspensive Guilt-offering. If he ate the second also, he must bring three Sin-offerings.

None of the cases in the Mishnah deals with the problems before us.

As to Eliezer's and Joshua's dispute in D-E, this would follow the view of M. Ker. 4 : 2A-E. Joshua will exempt the man from a Sin-offering, even where it is known that he certainly has sinned, until one is certain precisely which sin one has committed.

I.i.147.A. He that brings a Suspensive Guilt-offering, and it becomes known to him that he has not sinned—

B. If [it became known] before it was slaughtered—

"It [the sacrificial animal] should go forth and pasture in the flock," the words of R. Meir.

C. And sages say, "It pastures until it is blemished, then it is sold, and the price falls to the Freewill-offering."

D. R. Eliezer says, "Let it be offered, for if it does not come on account of this sin, lo, it will come on account of another sin."

M. Ker. 6 : 1A (b. Ker. 23b, 24b; b. Men. 102b, b. Hul. 41b; Sifra Vayiqra Pereq 21 : 4, Weiss, p. 27a)

I.i.148.A. R. Eliezer says, "A man may volunteer a Suspensive Guilt-offering every day and at every hour he wants, and it is called 'The Guilt-offering of the Pious.'"

B. They said concerning Bava ben Buṭi that he would volunteer a Suspensive Guilt-offering every day except the one after the Day of Atonement...

C. And sages say, "They do not bring a Suspensive Guilt-offering except for a matter which, if one did it deliberately, he is liable to Extirpation, and if in error, to a Sin-offering."

M. Ker. 6 : 3 (b. Ker. 18a, 25a-b)

I.ii.118.A. R. Eliezer says, "A man may volunteer a Suspensive Guilt-offering every day and whenever he wants. It was called the 'Guilt-offering of the pious.'"

B. They said concerning Bava b. Buṭa that he would volunteer a Suspensive Guilt-offering every day... [etc.]

C. And sages say, "They bring a Suspensive Guilt-offering only for a matter whose intentional commission is subject to Extirpation and whose accidental commission is liable for a Sin-offering."

Tos. Ker. 4 : 4, Zuckermandel, p. 566, ls. 10-14

*Comment*: In M. Ker. 6 : 1A, Eliezer stands outside of the range of opinions in B-C. In his opinion the Suspensive Guilt-offering serves for *some* sin, if not the one for which it will originally have been brought.

Meir and the sages differ. Their problem is what to do with the useless Suspensive Guilt-offering, in the presumption that it will *not* be offered at all. Eliezer is consistent with his position in M. Ker. 4 : 2-3, for according to Judah, Joshua would free the man from the Suspensive Guilt-offering if we are not sure of the type of sin a man has done, even though we know he certainly has sinned. Then Eliezer would hold that the man must bring the Suspensive Guilt-offering if we know a man has sinned, even though we are not sure exactly what he has done.

M. Ker. 6 : 3A and C further articulate the dispute between Eliezer and "sages," represented in 6 : 1 by Meir and his "sages." Eliezer says one may volunteer a Suspensive Guilt-offering any time. The sages say one may bring such an offering only under the specified conditions. M. Ker. 1 : 2 defines those circumstances: "If in these things he transgressed wantonly, he is liable to Extirpation, and if in error, to a Sin-offering; and if it was in doubt whether he had committed a transgression, he is liable to a Suspensive Guilt-offering . . ."

M. Ker. 6 : 3B is an interpolation. It makes use of the language of Eliezer, "A man volunteers . . . every day . . . Baba b. Buṭi would volunteer . . . every day." The contrary instruction excluded only the 11th of Tishri, the day after the Day of Atonement. The Day of Atonement has covered matters of doubt, and on the very next day one cannot conceive such further doubtful sins exist. The interpolation breaks up what is otherwise a legal dispute in classic dispute-form.

See Epstein, *Nusaḥ*, p. 297; *Tan.*, p. 107; *Phar.* I, pp. 389-391.

I.ii.119.A. They are five Guilt-offerings: the Guilt-offering for theft [Lev. 5 : 21], the Guilt-offering for Sacrilege [Lev. 5 : 15], the Guilt-offering of the designated bond-maid (ŠPḤH ḤRWPH [Lev. 19 : 20]), the Guilt-offering of the Nazir [Num. 6 : 12], and the Guilt-0ffering of the Leper [Lev. 14 : 12].

B. R. Eliezer says, "The Suspensive Guilt-offering."

Tos. Ker. 1 : 19, Zuckermandel, p. 562,
ls. 30-32 (b. Ker. 25b)

*Comment*: The five effect complete atonement. The sixth does not, so b. Ker. 25b.

I.i.149.A. The flesh of Most Holy Things which went out [of the courtyard] before the sprinkling of the blood—

B. R. Eliezer says, "The law of sacrilege applies to it (MWʿLYN BH), but they are not liable on its account because of [transgression of the laws of] Refuse, Remnant, or uncleanness [Remnant = sacrifice that remains after the time for eating it. Refuse = an offering which a man slaughtered intending to eat things not usually eaten or to burn outside of its proper place, so M. Zev. 2 : 3]."

C. R. ʿAqiba says, "The law of sacrilege does not apply to it, but they are liable on its account because of [transgression of the laws of] Refuse, Remnant, or uncleanness."

D. R. ʿAqiba said, "Lo, he that separates a Sin-offering which was lost and separated another in its place, and afterward the first was found, and lo, both of them are standing [to be slaughtered], and he slaughtered both and received the blood of both in separate bowls, but sprinkled the blood of only one of them—is it not so that just as its blood [that of one beast] exempts its [own] flesh, so it exempts the flesh of its fellow?

"Now if [sprinkling] its blood exempted the flesh of its fellow from the law of sacrilege, it is logical that it should exempt its [own] flesh [from the law of sacrilege]."

M. Me. 1 : 2 (b. Me. 6b; b. Men. 47b-48a)

I.i.150.A. The sacrificial portions of the Less Holy Things (ʾMWRY QDŠYM QLYM) which went forth before the sprinkling of the blood—

B. R. Eliezer says, "The law of sacrilege does not apply to them, and they are not liable on their account because of [transgression of the law of] Refuse, Remnant, and uncleanness."

C. R. ʿAqiba says, "The law of sacrilege applies to them, and they are liable on their account because of [transgression of the law of] Refuse, Remnant, and uncleanness."

M. Me. 1 : 3 (b. Me. 6b; b. Zev. 89b-90a)

I.ii.120.A. The flesh of Most Holy Things which went out before the sprinkling of the blood, and the blood was sprinkled for it—

B. R. Eliezer says, "The law of sacrilege applies to it, and they are not liable on its account because of [violation of the law of] Refuse, Remnant, and uncleanness."

Tos. Me. 1 : 4, Zuckermandel, p. 557 ls. 5-8

I.ii.121.A. The sacrificial portions of the Less Holy Things which went out before the sprinkling of the blood, and the blood was sprinkled in their behalf—

B. R. Eliezer says, "The law of sacrilege does not apply to them, and they are not liable on their account because of [transgression of the laws of] Refuse, Remnant, and uncleanness."

C. R. ʿAqiba says, "The frontlet propitiates for what goes forth. The law of sacrilege applies to them, and they are liable on their account because of [transgression of the laws of] Refuse, Remnant, and uncleanness."

Tos. Me. 1 : 6, Zuckermandel, p. 557, ls. 15-18

*Comment: The frontlet propitiates* is added, an explanation of ʿAqiba's position. Nothing else changes.

I.ii.122.A. He took the handful of meal in silence, the residue went forth outside of the hangings, and he offered up the handful of meal in silence—

R. Eliezer says, "Lo, this is as it was. The law of sacrilege applies to the residue, and they are not liable on its account because of Remnant and uncleanness."

R. ʿAqiba says, "The frontlet propitiated for what goes forth, and there is nothing in the residue, but they are liable on their account because of Remnant and uncleanness."

Tos. Men. 4 : 10, Zuckermandel, p. 516, ls. 30-33

I.ii.123.A. He took a handful of meal in silence, and the residue went outside the hangings, and he offered the handful of meal outside of its proper time; or he took the handful of meal outside of its proper time, and the residue went outside of the hangings, and he offered up the handful of meal in silence; or he took the handful of meal outside of its proper time, and the residue went outside of the hangings, and he offered up the handful of meal outside of its proper time—

B. R. Eliezer says, "Lo, this is as it was. The law of sacrilege applies to the residue, and they are not liable on its account of the law of Refuse."

C. R. ʿAqiba says, "If the frontlet propitiated for what has gone forth, until then the law of sacrilege applies to the residue, and they are liable on its account because of the law of Refuse."

D. If the residue contracted uncleanness, and he offered up the handful of meal outside of its time, all agree that to that extent the law of sacrilege applies to the residue, and they are liable on account of the law of Refuse, for the frontlet propitiates for what is unclean, and it does not propitiate either for what stays overnight or for what goes outside [of the hangings].

E. The two showbreads which went outside of the hangings, and the blood of their sheep (KBŚYM) was sprinkled outside of its proper time—

F. R. Eliezer says, "They are not liable in respect to this bread on account of the law of Refuse."

G. R. ʿAqiba says, "They are liable in respect to this bread on account of the law of Refuse."

Tos. Men. 4 : 14-15, Zuckermandel, p. 517, ls. 3-12

I.ii.129.A. He slaughtered in silence and the flesh went beyond the hangings, and he sprinkled the blood in silence—

B. R. Eliezer says, "Lo, it [the meat] is like a corpse, for the law of sacrilege applies to the flesh of Most Holy Things, and the law of sacrilege does not apply to the pieces of Less Holy Things [= M. Me. 1 : 3], and they are not obligated on their account because of Remnant and uncleanness..."

C. R. ʿAqiba says, "The frontlet propitiates concerning what goes out. The law of sacrilege does not apply to the flesh of Most Holy Things. But it does apply to pieces of Less Holy Things, and they are liable on their account for Remnant and uncleanness."

D. The meat contracted uncleanness, and he sprinkled the blood in silence—

All agree that the law of sacrilege does not apply to the flesh of the Most Holy Things.

But it does apply to the pieces of the Less Holy Things, and they are liable on their account because of Remainder and because of uncleanness, for the frontlet propitiates for what is unclean but not for what is kept overnight or goes outside.

Tos. Zev. 4 : 5, Zuckermandel, p. 485, ls. 15-21 (b. Me. 3b, 4b)

I.ii.125.A. He slaughtered in silence and the flesh went outside the hangings, and he sprinkled the blood outside of its time; or he slaughtered outside of its time, and the flesh went outside the hangings, and he sprinkled the blood in silence; or he slaughtered outside of its time, and the flesh went outside of the hangings, and he sprinkled the blood in silence; or he slaughtered outside of the proper time and the flesh went outside the hangings, and he sprinkled the blood outside of its time—

B. R. Eliezer says, "Lo, this is as it was. The law of sacrilege applies to the flesh of Most Holy Things and does not apply to the pieces of Less Holy Things, and they are not liable on their account because the law of Refuse."

C. R. ʿAqiba says, "The frontlet is appeased by what goes forth to that extent (ʿD'N). The law of sacrilege applies to the flesh of Most Holy Things, and the law of sacrilege does not apply to pieces of Less

Holy Things, but they are [Lieberman, *Tosefet Rishonim*, II, p. 206: *not*] liable on their account because of the law of Refuse."

Tos. Zev. 4 : 8, Zuckermandel, p. 485, ls. 27-34

III.ii.77.A. TNW RBNN: *And if any of the flesh of the sacrifice of his Peace-offerings be at all eaten on the third day* (Lev. 7 : 18).

B. R. Eliezer said, "Incline your ear to hear: Scripture speaks of one who intends to eat his sacrifice on the third day—or perhaps it speaks only of one who [actually] eats his scrifice on the third day? You may say, 'After it has become fit, shall it then become unfit?' [No! If it was sacrificed with the proper intention and was fit, it cannot become unfit merely because he eats it on the third day]."

C. R. ʿAqiba said to him, "Lo, we find that a *Zab* and a *Zabah* and a woman who 'watches from day to day' are presumed clean, yet a discharge undoes [their cleanness]. So do not be astonished concerning this one, which, although it *was* acceptable, [now] goes and becomes invalidated."

D. He [ʿAqiba] said to him, "Lo, it says, *He that offers*—in the hour of the offering it may be invalidated, but it is not invalidated [later, namely] on the third day. Or yet perhaps it is not so, but it says *Him who offers*—meaning the *priest* who offers it. When it says *it*, Scripture speaks of the *sacrifice*, not of the priest . . ."

b. Zev. 29a

*Comment*: The dispute between Eliezer and ʿAqiba follows the general rule (M. Me. 1 : 1) of Joshua: Whatever was once permitted to the priests is not subject to the law of sacrilege, and what was not once permitted to the priests *is* subject to the law of sacrilege. In the former category is specified meat which has been kept overnight (after the sprinkling of the blood), thus Remnant, or meat which has become unclean, or meat which has been taken outside of the Temple hangings. What has not been permitted to the priests is something which was slaughtered outside of the proper time or outside of the proper place, or whose blood unfit priests have received and sprinkled.

Now, in 1 : 2, the issue is whether the flesh of Most Holy Things taken out before the sprinkling of the blood has been permitted to the priests. Eliezer holds that it has *not* been permitted to the priests, therefore the law of sacrilege applies, but the other specified rules do not. The blood without the meat is ineffectual (p. 274). ʿAqiba holds it *has* been permitted to the priests, therefore the law of sacrilege does not apply, but the other specified rules do. ʿAqiba agrees with Joshua that the blood without the meat *is* effectual.

In the opinion of Eliezer, if the flesh of the Most Holy Things has been taken outside of the court and rendered unfit, and afterward the blood has been sprinkled, the law of sacrilege applies, for the sprinkling of the blood does not work for meat which has been taken out, to release it from the law of sacrilege. The priests have never had a right to it. This is consistent with the ruling in Tos. Zev., p. 274, that if there is no blood, there is no meat. The law of Refuse applies if the priest intended, when he made the sacrifice, to sprinkle the blood or to burn the sacrificial parts or to eat the flesh outside of the proper time. If he ate of the flesh which was taken out, he is not liable for Extirpation on account of consuming Refuse, because the sprinkling of the blood has not taken effect. Likewise if the meat is made unclean or if it was unclean and the priest ate it, he is not liable. According to ʿAqiba—following Joshua—the sprinkling *has* taken effect. Therefore the law of sacrilege does not apply, but the other liabilities hold.

ʿAqiba is given an argument, but Eliezer has no counter-argument. His argument in D has to do with two Sin-offerings awaiting sacrifice for a single sin. Even though the second one has not been sacrificed, the blood of the first exempts its flesh *and* the flesh of its fellow from the law of sacrilege. Even though the second's blood has not been sprinkled, it cannot be offered. If the sprinkling of the blood serves to release the unfit flesh of the fellow-offering from the law of sacrilege, it should likewise exempt its own flesh from the law of sacrilege—even though the flesh has been recorded invalid by its going forth from the court, so Albeq, *Seder Qodashim*, p. 274.

In M. Me. 1 : 3 we have the same debate, this time concerning the sacrificial portions of the Less Holy Things which went forth before the sprinkling. These are the fats which are offered on the altar. The law of sacrilege applies to them only after the sprinkling. Eliezer is consistent in holding that, just as the sprinkling does not serve to release the flesh of Most Holy Things which went forth from the court *from* the law of sacrilege, likewise it does not serve to subject the sacrificial portions of the Less Sanctities *to* the law of sacrilege. ʿAqiba is equally consistent. The sprinkling has released from the laws of sacrilege what went out. So it will subject to the law of sacrilege what is only subjected after the sprinkling. Me. 1 : 3 could have been omitted, since it merely repeats the issue of M. Me. 1 : 2.

See Epstein, *Tan.*, p. 457, n. 2.

III.ii.78. TNYʾ: R. Simeon said, "When I went to Kefar Pagi an old man met me and asked me, 'Does R. ʿAqiba indeed hold that sprinkling is of effect in the case of an offering that was taken out? . . .'"

b. Me. 7a

*Comment*: Simeon's saying supplies an Ushan attestation for the foregoing pericope.

I.ii.126.A. R. Eliezer says, "If there is no blood, there is no flesh, but even though there is no flesh, there is blood."

R. Joshua says, "If there is no blood there is no flesh, if there is no flesh, there is no blood.

How so?

B. If the blood contracts uncleanness or is poured out or went out beyond the hangings, the flesh's appearance is changed [disfigured], and it goes forth to the place of burning.

C. If the flesh is made unclean or is rendered invalid or goes out beyond the hangings [curtains]—

R. Eliezer says, "He should sprinkle the blood."

R. Joshua says, "He should not sprinkle the blood."

D. If he sprinkled the blood, whether accidentally or intentionally R. Joshua agrees that it is accepted [= the head-plate propitiates].

E. R. Joshua says, "Lo, it says, *And you will make your offerings, the flesh and the blood* (Deut. 12 : 27)—If there is no blood, there is no flesh, if there is no flesh, there is no blood.

F. R. Eliezer said to him, "Lo, it says, *And the blood of your sacrifices will be poured out on the altar of the Lord your God* (Deut. 12 : 27).—Even though there is no flesh. And how do I interpret *the flesh and the blood* (Deut. 12 : 27)? It relates flesh to blood: Just as blood is with [requires] sprinkling, so the flesh is with sprinkling [the meat is thrown on the altar]. One might suppose he should sprinkle and pile up (RBG, not DWBQ)—Scripture says, *And the priest will arrange them* (Lev. 1 : 12)—he sprinkles and arranges, and he does not sprinkle and pile up."

Tos. Zev. 4 : 1-2, Zuckermandel, p. 484, ls. 30-34, p. 485, ls. 1-5 (b. Zev. 29b, 89b-90a, 104a, b. Pes. 77a; b. Men. 9a, 26a)

*Comment*: On DBQ-RBG, see Lieberman, *Tosefet Rishonim* II, p. 205.

The pertinent Mishnah is M. Zev. 2 : 3:

> This is the general rule: If any man slaughtered or received, conveyed or tossed the blood intending to eat a thing that is usually eaten or to burn a thing that is usually burned outside its proper *place*, the offering is invalid, but punishment by Cutting Off is not incurred.
>
> But if outside its proper *time*, the offering becomes Refuse and the punishment by Cutting Off is incurred—provided that what renders the offering permissible is offered according to its prescribed rite.

Now what renders the sacrificial portions permissible to be burned on the altar and the flesh to be consumed by the priest or owner is the proper sprinkling (tossing) of the blood. M. Zev. 2 : 4 then continues:

How is 'what renders the offering permissible' offered according to its prescribed rite?

If he had slaughtered [= *flesh*] in silence, but had received, conveyed, and tossed the *blood* [while intending an act] outside the proper time; or if he had slaughtered outside the proper time but had received, conveyed and tossed the blood in silence; or if he had slaughtered, and received, conveyed, and tossed the blood [while intending an act] outside the proper time, such is a case where 'what renders the offering permissible' is offered according to its prescribed rite [= it becomes Refuse, etc.].

Accordingly, if the slaughter is acceptable, but the blood-rite is not acceptable, or if the slaughter is not acceptable, but the blood rite is acceptable, the offering is permissible. This is in accord with Joshua, who says if there is no blood, there is no flesh, and *vice versa.* If the blood-rite is not acceptable, the meat-rite is equally unacceptable, and *vice versa.* According to Eliezer if the blood-rite is not acceptable, the flesh-rite is likewise not. But if the flesh-rite is not acceptable, the blood-rite still is carried out.

A spells out the disagreement, without an antecedent statement of the problem. *How so?* then serves to introduce the abstract statement. Both parties agree on the blood. If the blood-rite is not properly done, the flesh is to be burned. But they differ as to a case in which the flesh is made unclean. Eliezer says, the blood nonetheless *is* to be sprinkled. Joshua says the one depends on the other, as before.

E then supplies an exegetical argument, in which the pertinent Scriptures are expounded. Joshua sees the flesh equivalent to the blood, repeating his original opinion. Eliezer interprets the Scripture differently.

II.iv.22. *And you will make your offerings, the flesh and the blood.*

R. Joshua says, "If there is no blood, there is no flesh, and if there is no flesh, there is no blood."

R. Eliezer says, "*And the blood of your sacrifices will be poured out*—even though there is no flesh. Then how do I explain *And you will make your offerings, the flesh and the blood?* Scripture relates flesh to blood. Just as blood is with sprinkling, so the flesh is with sprinkling. One might say he should stand from a distance and sprinkle. Scripture says, *And the priest will arrange them* (Lev. 1 : 2)—he stands near by and arranges them on the altar."

Sifré Deut. 75, Finkelstein, p. 143, (Tos. Zev. 4 : 1, Tos. Pes. 6 : 3, Sifra Nedavah 4 : 12, b. Pes. 77a, b. Zev. 104a; Mid. Tan. to Deut. 12 : 26, Hoffmann, p. 54, Mid. Tan. to Deut. 12 : 15, Hoffmann, p. 60)

III.ii.79. TNY': R. Yosi said, "I agree with the words of R. Eliezer in respect to meal-offerings and [animal] sacrifices, and with the words of R. Joshua in respect to [animal] sacrifices and meal-offerings."

b. Pes. 77a

*Comment*: Yosi provides a firm Ushan attestation for the whole complex of materials.

## xxvii. KELIM

I.i.151.A. A torch is unclean. And the reservoir of a lamp receives uncleanness from [an uncleanness within] its air [space].

B. The comb [shaped filter] of the water-cooler—

C. R. Eliezer [Naples: Eleazar] declares clean.

D. And sages declare unclean.

M. Kel. 2 : 8

*Comment*: The form is standard: Statement of problem, then the opposed opinions of Eliezer, sages.

The ṢRṢWR is a bottle covered by a web of pottery, and around the web are teeth like the teeth of a comb, so Albeq, *Seder Ṭoharot*, p. 27. If uncleanness enters the air-space of the comb, Eliezer declares it ineffective to transmit uncleanness to the cooler, because the air-space of a comb is not regarded as a receptacle.

Tos. Ed. 2 : 1 is ample warrant for assigning this pericope to our Eliezer.

See Epstein, *Nusaḥ*, p. 1173.

I.ii.127.A. The comb-shaped filter of the water-cooler—

B. R. Eliezer says, "It is not unclean as to its air-space."

C. And sages say, "It is unclean as to its air-space."

Tos. Kel. B.Q. 2 : 8, Zuckermandel, p. 571, ls. 11-12

*Comment*: Tos. explicitly defines the dispute in respect to the air-space of the comb.

I.i.152.A. "In a jar the measure of the hole [that renders the vessel clean] is such that a dried fig [will fall through]," the words of R. Simeon.

B. R. Judah says, "A walnut."

C. R. Meir says, "Olives."

D. In a stewpan or cooking-pot the measure is an olive; in a cruse or ewer the measure is such that oil will drip through; in a water-cooler the measure is such that water will flow through.

E. R. Simeon says, "For all three, [the measure is such that] seeds [will fall through]."

F. A lamp—its measure [the size of the hole must be sufficient for] oil [to flow through].

G. R. Eliezer says, "A small *peruṭah* [coin] [must be able to drop through.]"

M. Kel. 3 : 2

*Comment*: Eliezer's pericope stands apart from the foregoing. A lamp of pottery will contain oil and a wick. Eliezer holds that if it will release a small coin, it is incapable of receiving uncleanness.

M. Kel. 14 : 1 is warrant for assigning this pericope to our Eliezer. But see Epstein, *Nusaḥ*, p. 1173; *Tan.*, p. 133.

II.iii.14. (A baking oven becomes susceptible to uncleanness after its manufacture is complete. What counts as the completion of its manufacture? When it has been heated to a degree sufficient to bake spongy cakes. R. Judah says, "When a new oven has been heated to a degree sufficient to bake spongy cakes in an old oven" [which requires less heat than a new one].—Kel. 5 : 1).

A. "An oven—I understand (ŠWMʿ) [the law to refer to an oven] whether it is new or old [= whether or not it has been heated up]. And it is logical (DYN HWʾ). An earthenware vessel is capable of receiving uncleanness and an oven is capable of receiving uncleanness. Just as an earthenware vessel [becomes susceptible to uncleanness] when its manufacture is completed [*without being heated up*], so an oven [should become unclean] when its manufacture is completed [without being heated up]"—the words of R. Eliezer.

B. R. ʿAqiba said to him, "And do they decide that which is impossible from that which is possible?"

[May one draw an analogy from one rule to another, when in one instance an alternative is possible, and in the other, no alternative is possible? An earthenware vessel *can* be used without being heated first, but ovens cannot. Therefore, to draw an analogy for the rule regarding ovens from that regarding earthenware is to deduce a rule concerning the impossible from that concerning the possible, so Professor Louis Finkelstein, personal letter, November 19, 1971.]

C. R. Eliezer said to him, "Also that which is [im]possible is important proof."

D. R. ʿAqiba went and changed the terms of argument: "An earthenware vessel is susceptible to uncleanness, and an earthenware oven is susceptible to uncleanness. Just as an earthenware vessel [becomes unclean] once its manufacture has been completed [by heating in] an oven, so an earthenware oven [becomes unclean] when its manufacture has been completed [by heating in] an oven."

Sifra Shemini Pereq 10 : 5-6, Weiss p. 55b (M. Kel. 5 : 1)

*Comment*: The dispute of Eliezer and ʿAqiba comes before M. Kel. 5 : 1, which defines the extent to which the oven has to be heated, that is, according to ʿAqiba. There the difference between Judah and the anonymous rule takes for granted that the oven has to be heated at all, against Eliezer, whose opinion does not register in M. Kel. 5 : 1.

The reply of ʿAqiba in B is as explained by Professor Finkelstein. He further comments on ʿAqiba in D as follows: Now ʿAqiba formulates the analogy as he thought it should have been formulated in the first place. He disagrees with Eliezer not only in rejecting Eliezer's basing a rule regarding the impossible on that regarding the possible, but he also disagrees with Eliezer regarding the rule for earthenware in general.

Eliezer holds that earthenware containers are subject to impurity as soon as they are sufficiently dry to hold material, even if they are not heated at all. ʿAqiba requires that they too should be completed by being put into a furnace. Therefore, he argues, just as other earthenware vessels are subject to defilement only if they have been completed through heating, so an oven is subject to defilement only if it has been heated. Then, at the end of 10 : 6, the disciples of ʿAqiba accept his decision that an oven becomes subject to defilement only after it has been heated. They disagree concerning the extent to which a new oven needs to be heated to satisfy ʿAqiba's requirement.

Finkelstein therefore reads in B, "Do they judge that which is *im*possible from that which is possible", rather than, "Do they judge that which is possible from that which is impossible", and I have followed his correction of the text in my translation. Elsewhere, however, the contrary is correct.

I.i.153.A. If it [the oven] was cut up into rings (ḤWLYWT), and he put sand between each ring—

B. R. Eliezer declares clean.

C. And sages declare unclean.

D. This is the oven of ʿAkhnai [Parma, Kaufmann, Camb.: ḤKYNYY].

E. As for the cauldrons of the Arabs, which are hollows dug in the ground and plastered with clay, if the plastering can stand of itself, it is susceptible to uncleanness; otherwise it is not susceptible. Such was the oven of Ben Dinai.

M. Kel. 5 : 10 (b. Ber. 19a, b. B.M. 59b [below, pp. 422-427])

*Comment*: M. Kel. 5 : 8 states:

"If [the oven] was cut up breadthwise into rings, so that each is less than four handbreadths high, it becomes clean. If it was again set up and plastered over with clay, it becomes susceptible to uncleanness."

The oven before us has been cut into rings and then set up with sand. Eliezer declares it clean, because the sand intervenes between the rings and does not join them together. The sages declare it capable of receiving uncleanness, because the plastering over the sand joins the rings.

D alludes to the famous dispute in b. B.M. 59b. It looks like a gloss. See Epstein, *Tan.*, pp. 132, 466.

I.i.154.A. The oven which was divided by boards or hangings—[If] an insect was found in one place, the whole is unclean.

B. If there is an insect within a bee-hive that was broken-down and patched with straw hung down within the air of the oven, the oven is unclean.

The insect was within the oven—the food which is in it [the beehive] is unclean.

C. R. Eliezer declares it clean.

D. R. Eliezer [Naples: Eleazar] said, "If it saves [things within it from uncleanness caused] by the corpse, which is stringent, will it not save [from uncleanness contracted from] an earthenware vessel?"

E. They said to him, "If it saved from the more stringent matter of corpse [uncleanness], [the reason is] that they divide tents [Danby, p. 614: "Partitions afford protection in a 'Tent.'"]. Will it save in the lenient matter of [uncleanness contracted from] an earthenware vessel, for they do *not* divide earthenware vessels ["respecting which partitions afford no protection"]."

M. Kel. 8 : 1 (b. Zev. 3a;
Sifra Shemini Parashah 7 : 10, Weiss, p. 54a)

*Comment*: Eliezer rules that if the creeping thing is found within the oven, the food in the beehive is clean. The sages hold that the hive does not serve as a divider. Eliezer says that the hive stuffed with straw will serve as protection. Eliezer then argues that the beehive in the tent of a corpse will preserve what is in it from uncleanness (M. Oh. 9 : 3) even though the corpse is a severe source of uncleanness. It also ought to save from the creeping thing. The sages answer that a divider will serve to save from uncleanness in tents (M. Oh. 15 : 4), but the divider will not serve in an earthenware vessel to save from uncleanness—as stated in A, which Eliezer presumably accepts. So Eliezer has not got much of an argument here.

See Epstein, *Tan.*, pp. 212, 462.

I.ii.128.A. A beehive that was broken down and patched with straw and hung into the air-space of an oven—if a creeping thing is in it, the oven is unclean.

B. The creeping thing is in the oven—the food which is in it [the bee-hive] is unclean.

C. And R. Eliezer declares it to be clean.

D. R. Eliezer said, "From a *qal veḥomer*: If it saves [from uncleanness] caused by [being within] the Tent of a corpse, which is severe, will it not save from [uncleanness contracted] from an earthenware vessel, which is lenient?"

E. R. Yoḥanan b. Nuri said, "I said (NMTY) to R. Eliezer, 'If (tents) [dividers afford protection] in the Tent of the corpse, [the reason is] that they divide Tents. Will tents save tents in the Tent of the creeping thing, for they do not divide an earthenware vessel?'"

F. R. Yosi said, "I said to R. Yoḥanan b. Nuri, 'I should be surprised if R. Eliezer accepted your answer. But [this is] the answer to his words: 'If tents save from tents in the Tent of the corpse, [the reason is that] he makes a handbreadth by a handbreadth with a handbreadth's height in a clean house [M. Oh. 3 : 7]. Will tents save in the case of a creeping thing, for if he makes a handbreadth by a handbreadth in an earthenware vessel, it is unclean [affords no protection].'"

G. Rabbi said, "The answer of R. Yosi is the same as the answer of R. Yoḥanan b. Nuri."

Tos. Kel. B.M. 6 : 4, Zuckermandel, p. 575, ls. 15-24

*Comment*: Rabbi has attributed M. Kel. 8 : 1E to "them" and given the essential argument, that a division in a Tent will afford protection from corpse-uncleanness, but a division in an earthenware vessel will not serve to afford protection from uncleanness."

M. Oh. 3 : 7 alluded to in F is as follows: "A space one handbreadth square and one handbreadth high in the form of a cube serves both to give passage to the uncleanness and to afford a screen against uncleanness."

I.i.155.A. [If] metal vessels have been broken because of their uncleanness, how large must they be [so that they still remain susceptible to uncleanness or retain their old uncleanness]?

B. A bucket must still be of a size such that it can draw water; a boiler, such that water can still be heated in it; a kettle, such that it can hold *selas*; a cauldron, such that it can hold jugs; jugs, such that they can hold *perutaḥs*; wine-measures and oil-measures, such that they can still measure oil and wine.

C. R. Eliezer says, "In all of them, [such that they can hold] *perutaḥs*."

D. R. ʿAqiba says, "Any vessel that lacks trimming [to make it of use] is susceptible to uncleanness, but what needs polishing is not susceptible."

M. Kel. 14 : 1 (b. Shab. 96a *re* perforated pot)

*Comment*: Eliezer is consistent with his earlier ruling, M. Kel. 3 : 2, where the required measure is a small *peruṭah*. If it holds that quantity, it is still a vessel, even though one cannot use it because it is broken.

D is irrelevant to the foregoing.

See Epstein, *Nusaḥ*, p. 1173.

I.ii.129. Wine- and oil-measures, their size [so that they still remain susceptible to uncleanness, if broken] is [such that they can still pass] liquids.

B. And R. Eliezer says, "*Peruṭahs.*"

C. A leather bottle (NWD)—liquids.

D. R. Eliezer says, "*Peruṭahs.*"

Tos. Kel. B.M. 4 : 2, Zuckermandel, p. 582, ls. 18-19

*Comment*: For the reading of C-D, Lieberman, *Tosefet Rishonim*, p. 45. In M. Kel. 14 : 1, Eliezer's ruling pertained to the whole of the foregoing list; now it is limited to the last item. Without *in all of them* M. and Tos. would have the same ruling. Tos then adds leather-bottles; M. deals explicitly with metalware.

I.i.156.A. "Metal vessels may become unclean and be made clean when broken," the words of R. Eliezer.

B. R. Joshua says, "They can be made clean only when whole."

C. (How so?) "[If] he sprinkled on them, and they were broken on the same day and recast and sprinkled again on the same day, then they are clean," the words of R. Eliezer.

D. R. Joshua says, "Sprinkling [is effective] only on the third and seventh days. [They may not be sprinkled earlier than the third day, for the first sprinkling, and the seventh, for the second.]"

M. Kel. 14 : 7

*Comment*: Broken vessels lying in the Tent of a corpse may be rendered clean. The vessel is made unclean by the Tent. One may sprinkle on them when they are broken. So, according to A, Eliezer holds they can be purified.

But the "example" of C specifies that it can be done even on the same day, so the issue is no longer whether broken vessels can be made clean—as in A-B—but whether the whole can be done on one day. In C Eliezer says they can be sprinkled, recast, and resprinkled, and become clean. So Eliezer holds that after breaking, the man does not have to wait four days between sprinklings. The breaking of the vessels suffices to purify them. For another explanation, see Albeq, *Seder Ṭoharot*, p. 522. See Epstein, *Nusaḥ*, p. 1036, *re how so.*

I.ii.130.A. R. Eliezer says, "A metal vessel which was made unclean and broken and repaired—he sprinkled on it on the same day and should repeat on it on the fourth day.

"And [as to a metal vessel] which was made unclean, and he [the owner] sprinkled on it, and it was [*then*] broken, and he repaired it, he should repeat [the sprinkling] on that very same day."

B. R. Joshua says, "Sprinkling cannot take place less than on the third and seventh day [of uncleanness]."

R. Nathan says, "R. Eliezer says, 'A metal vessel which was unclean and broken and repaired, and he sprinkled on it, and it was broken and repaired—he should repeat [the sprinkling] on it on the same day."

"R. Joshua says, 'Sprinkling is not less than on the third and seventh days.'"

Tos. Kel. B.M. 4 : 14, Zuckermandel, p. 583, ls. 9-13

*Comment*: Tos. treats M. Kel. 14 : 7C-D as a separate dispute, so C, *how so*, is to be deleted.

I.i.157.A. The baking boards of bakers are unclean; of householders—clean.

B. If they were colored red or saffron, they are susceptible.

C. The baker's shelf which he fixed to the wall—

D. R. Eliezer declares clean.

E. And sages declare unclean.

F. The baker's frame is susceptible to uncleanness, etc.

M. Kel. 15 : 2 (b. B.B. 66a)

*Comment*: Warrant for assigning the passage to our Eliezer is in M. Ed. 7 : 7. The board is used for leavening the dough. Eliezer regards it as fixed to the ground, consistent with the rule of M. Kel. 11 : 2, whatever is fixed to the ground is clean. The sages say it is unclean, since it remains a vessel unto itself even though it has been fastened, consistent with ʿAqiba in M. Kel. 20 : 4, so Albeq, Ṭoharot, p. 69.

See Epstein, *Tan.*, pp. 66, 434, 440, 466, 468, 483.

I.i.158.A. All [wooden] vessels of householders [that are broken because of their uncleanness become clean if the holes therein are] such size that pomegranates [will drop through them.]

B. R. Eliezer [Naples: Eleazar] says, "[It depends] on what they are (BMH ŠHN)." [If objects are kept in it, the whole must be big enough to allow such objects to drop through; and if the objects are small, holes corresponding to their size suffice to render the vessel clean, so I. W. Slotki, *Kelim, Translated into English with Notes* (London, repr. 1948), p. 81, n. 4.]

C. Gardeners' vegetable baskets [become clean if the holes in them are of] the size of bundles of vegetables; baskets of house holders—the size of bundles of straw; those of bathkeepers—bundles of shavings.

D. R. Joshua says, "[The size that renders a vessel clean] in the case of all of these is that of pomegranates."

M. Kel. 17 : 1

*Comment*: C illustrates the opinion of Eliezer in B. Then D repeats the rule in A, so Joshua extends the rule of A to all the enumerated vessels, that is, to all wooden vessels.

I.i.159.A. "A bed contracts uncleanness [only] when [all its parts are] bound together (ḤBYLH), and is rendered clean again only when [all its parts are] bound together"—the words of R. Eliezer.

B. And sages say, "It becomes unclean in pieces and becomes clean in pieces."

M. Kel. 18 : 9

*Comment*: A bed contracts uncleanness when not divided into parts. When bound together, if one part becomes unclean, the whole becomes unclean. When one dips into a ritual pool a whole bed, part of which has become unclean, the bed becomes clean. The other parts do not intervene between it and the water—so Eliezer.

The sages say that since each part becomes unclean by itself, if one is unclean, the rest are not made unclean. But each part requires dipping in the ritual pool by itself: Dipping the whole together is unsatisfactory, because the parts will intervene between the unclean part and the water. See Albeq, *Seder Ṭoharot*, p. 85.

I.ii.131.A. "A bed contracts uncleanness when bound together and is rendered clean when bound together," the words of R. Eliezer.

B. And sages say, "It contracts uncleanness in parts and is rendered clean in parts."

C. How so? A leg of a bedstead which was taken off with the long side and with the short side—

D. "R. Eliezer says, 'Lo, this is a connection, and if he dipped it [in the ritual pool], it does not intervene [between the water and the uncleanness, so the whole is purified].'

E. "And sages say, 'It is not a connection, and if he dipped it, lo, this does intervene,"—the words of R. Simeon.

F. Rabbi [Judah the Patriarch] says, "R. Eliezer says, 'A bed is purified when bound together only when it is whole.'"

Tos. Kel. B.M. 8 : 8, Zuckermandel, p. 587, ls. 29-34

*Comment*: Lieberman, *Tosefet Rishonim*, III, p. 61, explains that the argument of Eliezer and the sages in M. Kel. 18 : 9 concerns the effect of a connector for uncleanness in the event that only one piece of the bed has become unclean, and in respect to a connector if the owner dipped both parts of the bed into a ritual pool.

[I.i.160. M. Kel. 23 : 1 states: "If a ball, a shoe-last, an amulet, or a phylactery (contracted corpse-uncleanness and) were torn, he that touches them becomes unclean; but if he touched what was within them, he remains clean." Goldin, ARN, p. 196, n. 9, commenting on Eliezer's death scene, in ARN and b. Sanh. 68b (pp. 410-416), explains, "According to Rabbi Eliezer, what is within objects like a cushion, etc., is regarded as part of the subject as a whole; if, therefore, something of corpse-uncleanness came into contact with the outer covering or container, even though it were torn open, the whole object becomes unclean, including what is within. This seems to be the first point R. Eliezer is making (for a contrary view, see M. Kel. 23 : 1). In line with his reasoning, R. Eliezer then insists that in order to be made clean, the whole object is to be immersed as it is, i.e. we do not consider the contents as constituting an interposing element... preventing the water of the immersion pool from purifying the object as a whole." Accordingly, M. Kel. 23 : 1 is formulated in opposition to the opinion of Eliezer, but his contrary opinion is *not* included. The pertinent passage in Tos. Kel. B.B. 2 : 6, Zuckermandel, p. 592, ls. 13-15, is as follows: "The ball, the shoe-last, the amulet, and the *tefillin*, and the round cushion (KST ʿGWLH) which were torn—if they hold what is in them, they are unclean. R. Joshua b. Qorḥa says in the name of R. Eliezer [*sic*] b. ʿAzariah, 'He immerses them as they are.' " So no tradition attributed to Eliezer in a legal, apodictic saying preserves his rule, but Eliezer b. ʿAzariah seems to have it in Tos.]

I.i.161.A. A money pouch (ṢRWR HMʿWT)—
B. R. Eliezer declares unclean.
C. And sages declare clean.

M. Kel. 26 : 2

*Comment*: The issue is whether it is a bag. Eliezer holds that it is, therefore it can receive uncleanness. The disagreement is as to the properties of the pouch, not as to the law. Since the pouch is continually opened, it is not regarded by the sages as a valid receptacle.

See Epstein, *Tan.*, pp. 114, 436.

I.ii.132.A. R. Nathan said, "R. Eliezer and the sages did not differ concerning the money-bag (ṢRWR MʿWT), that it is clean.

B. "Concerning what did they differ?

C. "Concerning the bag for pearls, for

D. "R. Eliezer declares it susceptible of uncleanness, and sages declare it clean."

Tos. Kel. B.B. 4 : 3, Zuckermandel, p. 593, ls. 38-40

*Comment*: M. Kel. 26 : 2 reads, "A pearl-pouch *is* susceptible to uncleanness. A money pouch ..." Nathan evidently had the dispute after pearl-pouch, and had both parties agree that the money-pouch was clean—that is, the sages' position in M. Kel. 26 : 2.

I.i.162.A. The shoe that is [still] on the last—

B. R. Eliezer declares clean.

C. And sages declare unclean.

M. Kel. 26 : 4 (b. Shab. 141b, y. Bes. 1 : 12)

*Comment*: The work on the shoe is not completed until the cobbler takes it off the last, therefore the shoe is not yet subject to uncleanness, so Eliezer.

See Epstein, *Tan.*, pp. 133, 466.

I.ii.133.A. A shoe on the last—

B. R. Eliezer declares clean.

C. And sages declare unclean.

D. R. Simeon Shezuri said, "R. Eliezer and the sages did not differ concerning the shoe on the last, that it is clean [since it is unfinished].

E. "Concerning what did they dispute?

F. "Concerning [the situation in which] he took it off the last, for R. Eliezer declares unclean, and the sages declare clean, because the woman ties it and puts it back on the last."

Tos. Kel. B.B. 4 : 7, Zuckermandel, p. 594, ls. 9-12

III.ii.80. TNYʾ: R. Judah in the name of R. Eliezer: If it is loose, it is permitted [to remove it on the Sabbath, since it is finished].

b. Shab. 141b

*Comment*: The issue now centers on whether the shoe is regarded as finished if it is removed and returned to the last. The sages say the work now is still not yet finished. Tos. Ed. 2 : 1 and b. Shab. 141b provide strong warrant to assign the whole to our Eliezer.

I.i.163.A. If a piece of cloth three handbreadths square was torn and put on a stool, and the flesh of him that sits on it touches the stool, it is not susceptible to uncleanness; but if it does not touch the stool, it is susceptible. If from a piece of cloth three handbreadths square one thread was worn away, or if a knot was found in it, or if two threads ran alongside each other, it is not susceptible to uncleanness. If a piece of stuff three finger-breadths square was thrown on the dungheap, it is not susceptible to uncleanness. If it was brought back again, it becomes susceptible.

B. Throwing it away always renders it insusceptible to uncleanness, and bringing it back renders it again susceptible, except only purple or fine crimson stuff [which remain unclean when thrown out].

C. R. Eliezer says, "Also the new patch of new cloth is like them."

D. R. Simeon says, "They all become clean [if thrown out...]"

M. Kel. 27 : 12 (y. Shab. 2 : 3)

*Comment*: According to Eliezer a piece of new cloth is like purple and crimson cloth. It retains value; throwing it away will not effect its purification. M. Kel. 28 : 2 is warrant for assigning 27 : 12 to our Eliezer.

I.i.164.A. "[A piece of cloth] less than three by three which he used to block up [a hole in] the bath house, or [to hold and] empty out a cooking pot, or to wipe mill stones, whether kept ready [for that purpose] or not kept ready is unclean"—the words of R. Eliezer.

B. R. Joshua says, "Whether kept ready or not kept ready [for such purposes], it is clean."

C. R. ʿAqiba says, "When kept ready [for that purpose], it is unclean; when not kept ready [for that purpose], it is clean."

M. Kel. 28 : 2 (y. Shab. 2 : 3, b. Shab. 29a, 39a)

*Comment*: Eliezer holds that whether the small cloth is kept for the purpose listed, or whether it is not used specifically for such a purpose, since it has not been thrown out (27 : 12), it is still made use of, and it can receive uncleanness.

Joshua says that the cloth is not used for clothing. It is merely a rag, as if it were thrown out. Therefore it is clean. ʿAqiba then distinguishes between what is set aside for a particular purpose, which is not a rag, and what is lying around and used for one thing or another, which is like a rag thrown into the garbage.

See Epstein, *Tan.*, pp. 92, 107.

Tos. Kel. B.B. 6 : 8, Zuckermandel, p. 596, gives the above as Judah's version of the dispute, against Meir's view that Eliezer distinguishes between what is kept ready, which is unclean, and what is not kept ready, which is clean. Judah's view of Joshua's opinion is the same as Meir's and

ʿAqiba's ruling appears as above. Accordingly, Meir's view is that Eliezer and ʿAqiba have the same opinion; this is curious, and raises the question of why Meir has not given Eliezer's opinion to ʿAqiba to begin with. The likely answer is that ʿAqiba's view was not known in ʿAqiba's name to Meir, so C above and the ʿAqiba-element in Tos. should be added by another hand.

## xxviii. Ohalot, Negaʿim

I.i.165.A. (These render unclean in the Tent [by overshadowing]: the corpse, or an olive's bulk [of the flesh] of a corpse, or an olive's bulk of corpse-dregs, or a ladleful of corpse-mould, or the backbone, or the skull, or any [severed] member of a corpse or any [severed] member from a living man that still bears its proper flesh, or a quarter [-*qav*] from the larger bones or the great number of the bones, and the greater part of a corpse, or the greater number of its bones, even if they are less than a quarter [-*qav*], are unclean. — M. Oh. 2 : 1).

A. A quarter [-*log*] of blood, or a quarter [-*log*] of mingled blood from one corpse.

B. R. ʿAqiba says, "From two corpses."

C. The blood of a new-born child all of which has flowed out —

D. R. ʿAqiba says, "Any quantity."

E. And sages say, "A quarter[-*log*]."

F. An olive's bulk of worm (RMH) [from a corpse], whether live or dead —

G. R. Eliezer declares [it] unclean, like its flesh [that of the corpse].

H. And sages declare clean.

I. The ash of cremated [corpses] —

J. R. Eliezer says, "Its measure is a quarter[-*qav*].

K. And sages declare [it] clean.

M. Oh. 2 : 2 (b. Nid. 28b)

*Comment*: Eliezer adds to the glosses of the antecedent list, along with ʿAqiba. He holds that the specified quantity of worms render unclean in a Tent. Likewise, the ashes of a cremated corpse in the quantity of a quarter-*qav* — the same quantity as applies to the bones in M. Oh. 2 : 1 — will render unclean in a Tent. So Eliezer regards the ashes as equivalent to the bones. In both cases, the sages declare clean — that is, these substances do not render unclean in a Tent and are not regarded as equivalent to a corpse.

See Abraham Goldberg, *Massekhet Ohalot* (Jerusalem, 1956), p. 16; Epstein, *Nusaḥ*, p. 1055.

I.i.166.A. The stone that seals a grave (GWLL) and its buttressing stone (DWPQ) render unclean by contact and in the Tent [Num. 19 : 16] and do not render unclean by carrying.

B. R. Eliezer says, "They render unclean by carrying."

C. R. Joshua says, "If there is under them the dust of graves, they render unclean by carrying, and if not, they do not render unclean by carrying."

D. What is the buttressing stone? That which the sealing-stone rests on. But the buttressing stone for the buttressing stone is clean.

M. Oh. 2 : 4 (Sifré Zuṭṭa, Horovitz, p. 5a, l. 18; 19; 16, Horovitz, p. 313)

*Comment*: Eliezer holds that the sealing-stone and its buttress will render unclean not only by contact and in the Tent but also by carrying. Joshua says that if grave-dust is underneath them, they will convey uncleanness by carrying. So three positions on the question are before us. M. Oh. 2 : 2 has, "A ladleful and more of grave-dust is unclean, but R. Simeon declares it clean." Joshua therefore regards the grave-dust as unclean. A evidently holds it either is clean or does not matter. Eliezer regards its presence as irrelevant.

Goldberg, p. 19, observes that Joshua's reason is consistent with M. Oh. 2 : 2. See also Epstein, *Tan.*, pp. 140, 168.

I.ii.134.A. The sealing-stone and its buttressing stone render unclean by contact and in the Tent and do not render unclean by carrying.

B. R. Eliezer says, "They render unclean in carrying.

C. "If they render unclean by contact, which is less stringent, will they not render unclean, by carrying, which is more stringent?"

D. R. ʿAqiba said to him, "If they render unclean in contact, which is abundant (MRWBH), will they render unclean by carrying, which is uncommon [MWʿṬ)?"

E. R. Eliezer said to him, "What is this, ʿAqiba? Is not the uncleanness of the Tent less [frequent] than either of them. [For it applies only to the corpse, but carrying applies to the *Zab*.] And lo, they both render unclean in [the Tent]. And if they render unclean in the Tent, which is uncommon [inconsiderable], will they not render unclean in carrying, which is abundant?"

F. R. ʿAqiba departed and R. Joshua lept forward. He said to him, "More abundant is the uncleanness of the Tent than the uncleanness of carrying! For he that overshadows the corpse in the *Sukkah* is unclean, but he that moves it [the *Sukkah*] is clean, and if he makes his *Sukkah* over the door of a grave, one that overshadows it is unclean, but he that moves it is clean."

Tos. Ahilot 3 : 7, Zuckermandel, p. 600, ls. 6-13
(Sifré Zuṭṭa 19 : 16, Horovitz, p. 312)

*Comment*: Eliezer's *qal veḥomer* in C is based on the fact that touching the corpse produces no uncleanness of the clothes, but carrying the corpse renders the clothes unclean. So Lieberman, *Tosefet Rishonim*, III, p. 100.

ʿAqiba's reply in D is that *contact* with the source of uncleanness happens abundantly (MRWBH), for instance, touching creeping things, having emissions, and touching Sin-water not sufficient for sprinkling, all of which render unclean by contact and not by carrying (M. Kel. 1 : 1). But contact by carrying is less frequent (MWʿṬ), so the stones should not render unclean by that means.

In E Eliezer turns the argument against ʿAqiba. Uncleanness because of the Tent is least common of the three, but the stones render unclean in the Tent. If they render unclean in the Tent, which is infrequent, will they not render unclean through carrying, which is commonplace?

Joshua's argument is that Tent-uncleanness is *more* commonplace than the uncleanness of carrying. He gives as the example overshadowing a corpse in a *Sukkah* [= where a *Sukkah* is over the corpse], which renders unclean. But moving it is not a source of uncleanness. If one makes his *Sukkah* over a grave, he who overshadows or touches the *Sukkah* is unclean, but he who moves it remains clean. So ʿAqiba's facts after all are correct, according to Joshua's argument, and therefore ʿAqiba's reasoning is supported by Joshua.

In Tos. Ahilot 3 : 8, Simeon carries the argument forward; Eliezer does not recur.

I.i.167.A. Men and vessels serve as Tents for uncleanness, but not for cleanness. [Man and vessels can serve as Tents in such a way as to give passage to uncleanness, but not in such a way as to protect what is above them from uncleanness that is below them, as can clean vessels together with the walls of the Tent.]

B. How so? Four carrying the bier (NRBD or NRWWD)—If there was uncleanness under it, the vessels which are on it are unclean. If there was uncleanness on top of it, the vessels under it are unclean.

C. R. Eliezer declares clean.

M. Oh. 6 : 1

*Comment*: If the four men are clean, Eliezer declares the vessels in both cases clean. According to the anonymous rule the vessels on top of the bier are unclean, for the bier does not intervene, since it is carried by men. Likewise those underneath will be unclean, for the same reason. The uncleanness goes down and makes all unclean, and the bier thus serves as a Tent but does not protect from uncleanness. According to Eliezer, a bier carried by men is capable of intervening between the uncleanness and what is underneath or above it. Eliezer does not reject A, but he does reject the example of A in B. Compare M. Oh. 16 : 1, see Goldberg, p. 45.

I.ii.135.A. Four who were carrying the bier, [or stone (NDBK)], and the staves were not thick as an ox-goad:

If uncleanness was underneath it, vessels which are on top of it are unclean. If uncleanness was on top of it, the vessels which are underneath it are unclean.

B. R. Eliezer declares [them] clean.

C. And so R. Eliezer would say, "If an olive's bulk of a corpse in the mouth of the raven overshadowed the bier, men and vessels which are under it are clean.

"If it overshadowed the oven and new mill-stones, they are clean."

D. If it was set on four vessels, even vessels of dung, stone, or earth, and they are not a handbreadth, if uncleanness was under it, the vessels which are on it are unclean. If uncleanness was on top of it, vessels which are under it are unclean.

E. It was set on four chairs placed on four stones and they are not a handbreadth in height, if uncleanness was under it, the vessels which are on it are unclean. If uncleanness was on top of it, vessels which are under it are unclean.

F. And R. Eliezer declares [them] clean.

Tos. Ahilot 7 : 1, Zuckermandel, p. 603, ls. 32-39, p. 604, ls. 1-2

*Comment*: On the NDBK, see Lieberman, *Tosefet Rishonim*, p. 111. He points out that the reference to the thickness of the staves is on account of Eliezer's position. If they are as thick as an ox-goad, the bearers will be unclean, according to Eliezer as well as according to the sages.

As to the raven (C), the additional point is that, while in the Mishnah, Eliezer declares clean when the uncleanness is not opposite the vessels—whether above or below, in that case, even though the plank (stone) were not there, they would *still* be clean. The sages hold they would be unclean even when not directly opposite (under, above) the uncleanness. The case of the raven flying by now shows that the bier serves as a Tent in every respect, both to overshadow and to intervene.

I.ii.136. R. Judah says in the name of R. Eliezer, "Even though the door is open, the house is clean, because the lock is unclean."

Tos. Ahilot 7 : 3, Zuckermandel, p. 604, ls. 6-7

*Comment*: The pertinent Mishnah is 6 : 2:

> If corpse-bearers passed through the portico [before a house], and someone shut the door and locked it with the key, if the door was able to stand of itself [without the key], what is in the house remains clean. But if it could not stand of itself, what is in the house becomes unclean.

Eliezer rules that the door need not be closed at all. See Lieberman, *Tosefet Rishonim*, III, p. 113. Goldberg, p. 45: But if the lock were unclean, the house would be unclean, consistent with 6 : 1A.

I.ii.137. (If two jars, each containing a half-olive's bulk [of a corpse] and each having a tightly stopped-up cover, were lying in a house, they are clean, but the house is unclean. If one of them was opened, it and the house are unclean, but the other remains clean. And the like applies to two chambers that open into a house. Thus: If a half olive's bulk was in each, and they were shut up, the house, i.e., the room into which the two cells opened, is unclean, since the uncleanness must in the end go out through it.—M. Oh. 8 : 6, and Danby, p. 661, n. 1.)

A. R. Judah said, "I say one thing and they said one thing.

B. "I say to them, 'R. Eliezer agrees with R. Joshua concerning two jars which are open into a house, that the house is unclean.

C. "Concerning what did they [Eliezer and Joshua] differ? "Concerning two rooms of a house, for R. Eliezer declares unclean, and R. Joshua declares clean.

D. "And they said to me, 'R. Joshua agrees with R. Eliezer concerning two rooms open to the house, that the house is clean.

E. "Concerning what did they differ?

F. "Concerning two jars—

G. " 'R. Eliezer declares unclean, and R. Joshua declares clean.'"

Tos. Ahilot 9 : 7, Zuckermandel, p. 606, ls. 31-35

*Comment*: The pertinent Mishnah, M. Oh. 8 : 6, contains no hint of a dispute between Eliezer and Joshua. But the authority for it is Judah in the name of Eliezer (Goldberg, p. 66). According to Judah, Eliezer and Joshua differ concerning two rooms in a house. The "others" have them differ as to two jars. In both cases, the Mishnah explicitly declares the house unclean, following Eliezer. See Lieberman, *Tosefet Rishonim*, pp. 122-123.

I.i.168.A. A tomb which is wide on top and narrow on the bottom, and the corpse was within it—

B. He who touches from below is clean; from above, is unclean.

C. If it was wide on the top and narrow on the bottom—

D. He who touches it on any spot is unclean.

E. It was equal [top and bottom]—

F. "He touches on it on any spot is unclean"—the words of R. Eliezer.

G. R. Joshua says, "[He that touches the rock] more than a handbreadth below [the lid] is clean; he that touches it less than a handbreadth below [the lid] is unclean."

H. If it was made in the form of a clothes-chest, what touches it anywhere becomes unclean; if it was made in the form of a case (GLWSQWS), he that touches it anywhere, excepting at the place where it opens, is clean.

M. Oh. 9 : 15

*Comment*: The tomb was carved out of rock. The rock was cut away, so that the structure is above the ground. "Broad below and narrow above" means that the movable lid over the cavity containing the corpse was narrower than the rock mass below it, so Danby, p. 663, n. 2. In that case, he who touches the rock below is clean, but if he touches it above, he is unclean. Only that portion of the rock directly below the covering stone is regarded as unclean, parallel to the buttressing stone (M. Oh. 2 : 4). The rest of the tomb is part of the earth and insusceptible to uncleanness. The uncleanness of the lid goes perpendicularly up and down, so Danby, p. 663, n. 3. If the tomb is wider on the top than on the bottom, the top serves as a Tent for the whole, and the uncleanness is diffused throughout.

The dispute affects the tomb which is equally wide, top and bottom. Eliezer says that in that case touching it anywhere makes a person unclean. The uncleanness is diffused throughout as before. Joshua says that what is more than a handbreadth below is clean, less than a handbreadth below is unclean. Only the one handbreadth of rock immediately below the lid is regarded as belonging to the tomb. The rest is part of the earth. Albeq observes that the corpse evidently was lying a handbreadth below the lid. But Tos. Ah. 10 : 8D supplies a different reason.

The dispute of Eliezer and Joshua depends on the antecedent laws both for language and for law. E, which introduces their dispute, depends upon A + C.

See Goldberg, pp. 74-75.

I.ii.138.A. One which was made like a case (DLYSQS)—he that touches on it from any place is clean.

B. He that touches on its Š<sup></sup>WH—

C. R. Eliezer declares unclean.

D. And R. Joshua says, "From a handbreadth and upward is

unclean, and from a handbreadth and downward is clean, for they do not raise offerings above the ground a handbreadth."

Tos. Ahilot 10 : 8, Zuckermandel, p. 607, ls. 38-39

*Commment*: See Lieberman, *Tosefet Rishonim*, p. 125. On GL-WSQWM, etc., see Eric M. Meyers, *Jewish Ossuaries*: *Reburial and Rebirth* (Rome, 1971), p. 55.

I.i.169.A. A projecting window-sill (BṬḤ) [or, a bath-tub fixed to the ground over which a board is laid so that it projects from the two ends but not at the sides] does not convey uncleanness. [If cvershadowed by a corpse on the outside, it does not bring the uncleanness into the house].

B. If there was a projection (ZYZ) on it [above the window] [and the uncleanness was under the projection]—

C. R. Eliezer says, "It does not [Camb. omits *not*] bring the uncleanness [into the house]."

D. R. Joshua says, "We regard the projecting window-sill as if it were not [present], and the projection which is above it brings in the uncleanness."

M. Oh. 12 : 3

*Comment*: The issue is whether the projecting window-sill serves as protection against uncleanness. In itself it will not bring uncleanness into the house. But what if above it projects something else? Does it then intervene or not? Eliezer holds that it does intervene, so the uncleanness above the projection will not be introduced into the house via the projecting window-sill. Joshua says that it does not intervene. Joshua's saying is somewhat developed; a simpler form would be simply, "It does bring ..." Joshua explains that ruling in the opening part of D; of the *We regard*-clause is an interpolation.

See Goldberg, p. 91, on BṬḤ.

I.ii.139.A. And R. Eliezer agrees concerning the projecting window-sill (ʾBṬ) which he made in the first place, that it does bring uncleanness [into the house.]

Tos. Ahilot 13 : 3, Zuckermandel, p. 610, ls. 19-20

*Comment*: See Lieberman, *Tosefet Rishonim*, III, p. 132. Goldberg, p. 91, explains Eliezer's view. If the projection was made together with the BṬḤ, it brings uncleanness to what is under it.

I.i.170.A. An olive's bulk of the corpse cleaved to the [outer side of the door-jamb] of the threshold—

B. R. Eliezer declares the house unclean.

C. R. Joshua declares it clean.

D. If it lay below the threshold, [the thickness of the threshold] is deemed to be divided into halves [and only if the uncleanness lay below the inner half is the house unclean].

E. If it cleaved to the lintel, the house is unclean. R. Yosi declares it clean.

F. If it lay within the house and anyone touched the lintel [under the outer half], he becomes unclean.

G. [If] he touched the threshold—

H. R. Eliezer declares him unclean.

I. R. Joshua says, "[If] he touched a part of the outer side of the threshold from a handbreadth and downward, he is clean; from a handbreadth and upward, he is unclean."

M. Oh. 12 : 8

*Comment*: D, E, and F interrupt the pericope of Eliezer and Joshua, which deals with the situation of a suitable quantity of corpse's cleaving to the threshold. The house is unclean, according to Eliezer, and so too, he who touches the threshold will be unclean. The threshold is no different from the house. Joshua says that the house is clean.

As to the situation of the person who touches the threshold, it depends on where he touched it. If he touched a part of the outer side of the threshold less than a handbreadth from the ground, he is clean; higher than that, he is unclean, just as in 9 : 15. Below a handbreadth, the man has touched the house, above it, he has not, as earlier.

See Goldberg, p. 94; Epstein, *Tan.*, p. 191.

I.ii.140.A. An olive's bulk of the corpse cleaved onto the [outer side of the door-jamb] of the threshold—

B. R. Eliezer declares the house unclean.

C. And R. Joshua declares [it] clean.

D. "If it lay below the threshold, [the thickness of the threshold is deemed to be divided into halves] to make the house unclean,"—the words of R. Jacob.

E. R. Simeon said, "R. Eliezer and R. Joshua did not differ about that which was placed under the threshold, that the house is clean.

"Concerning what did they dispute?

"Concerning that which cleaved on to the threshold, for R. Eliezer declares the house unclean, and R. Joshua declares it clean."

Tos. Ahilot 13 : 10, Zuckermandel, p. 611, ls. 9-13

*Comment*: Simeon has Eliezer and Joshua agree on D, in disagreement with Jacob. M. Oh. 12 : 8D has an anonymous opinion, that if the uncleanness lay below the inner half, the house is unclean, as in Jacob's opinion here. Now the dispute of Simeon is the same as A. That must mean that he had a version which would have had them differ as to uncleanness below the threshold, and presumably Eliezer would have declared the house unclean, Joshua, clean. M. Oh. 12 : 8D solves the problem by dividing the threshold, so both are right; Simeon has both parties take up Joshua's position.

I.i.171.A. A wall projection (ZYZ) [one handbreadth deep] surrounds the whole house and extends ('WKL) at the door three fingerbreadths—

B. [If] there was uncleanness in the house, the vessels which are under it are unclean.

C. If there was uncleanness under it [the projection]—

D. R. Eliezer declares the house unclean.

E. R. Joshua declares it clean.

M. Oh. 14 : 4

I.i.172.A. Two wall-projections, one above the other, each a handbreadth deep, with a space between them [of] a handbreadth wide—

B. [If] uncleanness is under them—

C. [What is] under them is unclean.

D. Between them—

E. [What is] between them is unclean.

F. On top of them—

G. What is above it up to the sky is unclean.

H. The upper one was projecting over the lower one a handbreadth—

I. [If there was] uncleanness underneath them or between them, [what is] underneath or between them is unclean.

J. On top of them—directly above it upward is unclean.

K. The upper one projected above the lower one less than a handbreadth—

L. Uncleanness underneath them—

M. [What is] underneath them and between them is unclean.

N. [Uncleanness] between them or under the overhanging part—

O. R. Eliezer says, "Underneath them and between them it is unclean."

P. R. Joshua says, "Between them and underneath the overhanging part it is unclean, but underneath them it is clean."

M. Oh. 14 : 5

*Comment*: The handbreadth is four fingerbreadths, so the wall-projection above the door is less than that which surrounds the rest of the house. Uncleanness in the house will render everything under the wall-projection unclean, for uncleanness exudes from within (M. Oh. 3 : 7). If the uncleanness is under the projection, Eliezer declares the whole house unclean. Even though the projection is not a handbreadth out from the door, since it goes around the house, it is regarded by Eliezer as part of the house and brings the uncleanness into the house through the door. Joshua holds that uncleanness exudes from, but does not enter, the house. The house remains clean, because by the door is not a handbreadth-width. Joshua is consistent with M. Oh. 14 : 2:

> A wall-projection above a doorway gives passage to the uncleanness if it is a handbreadth in depth.

Eliezer takes account of the rest of the projection; Joshua does not. 14 : 2 leaves that question open, since it refers only to the doorway.

M. Oh. 14 : 5A-J has two wall projections of equal width, a handbreadth. Here there is no disagreement. They will seal uncleanness between them, if it is within; above them, if it is above; and below them, if it is below. The problem comes when the upper projection exceeds the lower. Then, if uncleanness is between them or under the overhanging part, Eliezer says they do not intervene, and what is underneath is unclean. They join together to form the Tent. Joshua says that what is underneath the overhang is unclean, but what is underneath the lower projection remains clean. They do not join together to form a Tent. At issue therefore is whether the lower projection intervenes. Joshua holds that the upper projection which sticks out even less than a handbreadth does bring uncleanness underneath the lower projection. He is not consistent with his position in M. Oh. 14 : 4, less than a handbreadth's projection will not bring uncleanness into the house. But see Goldberg, pp. 105-107.

I.ii.141.A. The funeral cortege (QWBRY HMT) that was passing in the public way—

B. "Their Tent joins with the Tent of the window [in the nearby house] to make the house unclean," the words of R. Eliezer.

C. R. Joshua says, "They do not raise up what is lower to complete one Tent with another."

Tos. Ahilot 13 : 12, Zuckermandel, p. 611, ls. 16-18

*Comment*: The Tent of the bier joins with the Tent formed by the wall-projections. If above the window projects a half-handbreadth, it joins with the Tent of the bier to bring the uncleanness into the house. Eliezer therefore says one raises the lower Tent to the upper to convey uncleanness into the house. Joshua differs. See Lieberman, *Tosefet Rishonim*, III, p. 135. The issue is as in M. Oh. 14 : 5 N, O, P.

I.i.173.A. If a man was ploughing and struck against a rock or a wall, or if he shook off the soil from the plough, thus far only is the field accounted a grave-area.

B. R. Eliezer says, "A grave-area may make a grave-area." [Camb. omits.]

C. R. Joshua says, "Sometimes it makes, and some times it does not make [a grave-area]."

D. "How so? He ploughed a half furrow and then returned and ploughed a half-furrow, and then ploughed to the side—this is accounted a grave-area.

"But if the ploughed a whole furrow and then ploughed from that point onwards, beyond this [first furrow] is not counted as a grave-area."

M. Oh. 17 : 2 (b. Tem. 126;
compare Sifré Zuṭṭa 19 : 16,
Horovitz, p. 313)

*Comment*: The rule (M. Oh. 17 : 1) is that if a man ploughed up a grave, the field is regarded as a grave-area. A priest is warned against going therein. How is the space measured? A furrow's length, one hundred square cubits, a space of four *se'ahs* will be the grave-area.

The issue of B-C is whether one grave-area can generate another. If a new furrow is begun anywhere within the hundred cubits of the grave-area, the whole of the hundred cubits from that beginning is accounted by Eliezer as a grave-area, so Danby, p. 673, n. 11. Joshua says that this is sometimes the case, and sometimes not. If he ploughed half a furrow and went back to the beginning and ploughed from that point to the side, the new furrow is a new grave-area. But if he completed a whole furrow and then continued, the continuation is not a grave-area.

See Goldberg, p. 124: Eliezer follows the House of Hillel.

I.i.174.A. Dirt of a grave area and dirt from abroad which came [mixed] in vegetables join together to make up the bulk equal to the seal of packing-bags [that suffices to convey uncleanness]," the words of R. Eliezer.

B. And sages say, "[It conveys uncleanness] only if in one place was a bulk equal to the seal of packing-bags."

M. Oh. 17 : 5

*Comment*: If among the collections of dirt there is enough to supply the mud-seal which was used to seal packings bags, large sacks used for shipments, the dirt is unclean. Eliezer says the two sorts of dirt will join together for that purpose. The sages say a sufficient quantity must be found in a single type of dirt.

See Goldberg, p. 126-7, MRṢPYN = *marsupion*. Ṭarfon, Tos. Kel. B.M. 7 : 1, rules that a far smaller amount of dirt will make up the required quantity for uncleanness.

See Epstein, *Tan.*, p. 67.

I.ii.142.A. R. Judah said, "R. Eliezer and the sages did not differ concerning the dirt that comes from the grave-area that comes from vegetables, that it is clean until there is in one place sufficient dirt for the seal of packing-bags.

B. "Concerning what did they differ?

C. "Concerning dirt which comes from abroad in vegetables, for R. Eliezer says, 'It joins [with the other].'

"And sages say, 'It does not join with the others, until there is in one place sufficient for the seal of letters.' "

Tos. Ahilot 17 : 6, Zuckermandel, p. 615, ls. 21-26

*Comment*: The rule of the sages is that when there is enough dirt in one place for the seal of letters, then it joins to the measure of dirt used for the seal of packing bags, but less than this does not join together.

Judah's saying is pertinent to the concluding element in M. Oh. 17 : 5, "R. Judah said, 'Letters once came from beyond the sea to the Sons of the High Priests, and there was on them about a *se'ah* or two *se'ahs* of seals, yet the sages were not scrupulous about them as regards uncleanness [since none was alone as large as a packing-bag seal]."

According to M. Oh. 17 : 5, Eliezer holds dirt of the grave-area and dirt from abroad are joined together. The sages say it does not join together. In A Judah claims Eliezer agrees with the sages. But what they agree on is that dirt from the grave-area that comes on vegetables is clean until it reaches the specified quantity—and that is not the issue in M. Oh. 17 : 5. They differ as to dirt from abroad that comes on vegetables. The sages now require a sufficient amount of dirt *to seal letters*—an issue absent in 17 : 5 A + B, but only introduced in Judah's saying that concern for uncleanness will begin when there is enough to seal letters. See Goldberg, p. 127, for a good explanation of Judah's saying.

I.i.175.A. If a man plucked out the tokens of uncleanness or cauterized quick flesh, he transgresses a negative commandment [Deut. 24 : 8: *Take heed in an attack of leprosy to be very careful to do according to all that the Levitical priests shall direct you].*

B. And as to the question of cleanness: [If he did so] before he came before the priest, he is clean. If after his decision, he is unclean.

C. R. ʿAqiba said, "I asked Rabban Gamaliel and R. Joshua, while going to Gadvad (*sic*) [Camb.: NDBT], 'What would be the law if he did so during the period of his being shut up?' They said to me, 'We have not heard. But we *have* heard, 'Before he came to the priest, he is clean, after his decision, he is unclean.' I began to bring proofs for them."

D. It is all the same whether one is standing before the priest or is in the midst of his being shut up—he is clean until the priest shall declare him unclean.

E. When does he become clean [again, after the case alluded to in B, where the man removed the signs of uncleanness after the priest's decision, and so became unclean]?

F. R. Eliezer says, "After another sign of leprosy will be born in him, and he has become clean again after it."

G. And sages say, "Only after it has spread over his whole body, or until the bright spot grows smaller than a split bean."

M. Neg. 7 : 4 (Sifra Tazriʿa Negaʿim Pereq 2 : 1)

I.i.176.A. He who had a bright spot on him which was cut off is clean.

B. If he intentionally cut it off—

C. R. Eliezer says, "[He becomes clean again] after another leprosy sign will be born in him, and he has become clean again after it."

D. And sages say, "After it has spread over his whole [body]."

M. Neg. 7 : 5 (b. Bekh. 34a-b, *re* M. Bekh. 5 : 3)

*Comment*: C interrupts the pericope, which goes from B to D and is answered by D. ʿAqiba's saying supplies a valuable *terminus ante quem* for B, which must come in its present formulation before the time of Joshua and Gamaliel.

Eliezer then deals with a problem logically consequent upon, and produced by, B-D, namely, when does a man who has deliberately removed the signs of leprosy become clean, if he did so after the priest's decision and so has been declared unclean? Eliezer says that after a new spot of leprosy appears and the man is healed from that one, then he is healed from the first as well. The sages hold that after leprosy breaks out over his whole body, he is clean. But even if he had not removed the signs of uncleanness, he would have been unclean by this means (M. Neg. 8 : 3). Their other possibility is that the leprosy will begin to disappear. The difference between F and G is not in principle.

M. Neg. 7 : 5 has the same problem. The sages do not refer to the bright spot, because the man has cut off the bright spot.

I.ii.143.A. He cut it off intentionally—

B. R. Eliezer says, "When another leprosy-sign is born in him, and he is purified from it [then he is purified from the one he deliberately cut off]."

C. And sages say, "He never can be purified."

D. R. Judah said, "R. Eliezer and sages did not differ concerning him who cut it off and cut off with it living flesh, that such a one can never be purified.

"Or concerning him who cut if off and left from it any amount [of the leprosy], that if it spread over his whole body, lo, he is clean.

"Concerning what did they differ?

"Concerning him who cut it off [as] dead [flesh], for—

"R. Eliezer says, 'He has no purification until another leprosy-sign is born in him, and he is purified from it.'

"And sages say, 'If it spread a little, he is unclean; if it spread over his whole [body], he is clean.' "

Tos. Neg. 3 : 5, Zuckermandel, p. 621, ls. 13-18

*Comment*: The opinion of the sages in C is not represented in the Mishnaic parallel. Eliezer's view is unchanged. Then Judah in D has the two parties agree on the sages' opinion about cutting off living flesh—an issue not raised at all in M. Neg. 7 : 4-5. Leaving any amount is treated as a normal matter. If he cut it off dead, Eliezer's opinion is as in the Mishnah. The sages' opinion is identical. *If it spread a little—unclean* ignores the issue, which is, how does he become *clean* again?

I.i.177.A. They asked R. Eliezer [Kaufmann: Eleazar], "He into whose hand a bright spot the size of a *sela* arose, and its place [becomes] the scar of the boil (Lev. 13 : 23) [that is, the scar covers the bright spot—what is the law?"]

B. He said to them, "Let him be shut up."

C. They said to him, "Why? [Signs of uncleanness cannot arise there.] It is not fit for growing white hair, and there can be no spreading there, and raw flesh does not render it unclean."

D. He said to them, "Perhaps it will contract and spread again."

E. They said to him, "But is its place not the size of a bean?" [Danby, p. 687: "But does not the question, why should it be shut up, still stand, even if the scar contracts, and its place is but the space of a split bean? " For it is *not* unclean, and Eliezer has in any case not distinguished one size from another.]

F. He said to them, "I have not heard."

G. R. Judah b. Batyra said to him, "May I teach concerning it? "

H. He said to him, "If to support the words of sages, yes."

I. He said to him, "Perhaps there will be born in him another boil outside it and spread *into* it."

J. He said to him, "You are a great sage, for you have confirmed the words of sages."

M. Neg. 9 : 3 (Sifra Tazriʿa Negaʿim Pereq 6 : 7, Weiss, p. 64b; Sifra Tazriʿa Negaʿim Pereq 12 : 10, Weiss, p. 68a)

*Comment*: Since the palm of the hand does not grow hair, and the boil or the raw flesh will not spread—as is stated in M. Neg. 9 : 2, "A boil and a burning cannot be included together [to make up the space of a bean that would render the man unclean; a spreading from one to the other, from them to the skin of the flesh, or from the skin of the flesh to them, does not count as a spreading"—why should the man be shut up? Raw flesh will not render unclean, for M. Neg. 9 : 1 explicitly states, "A boil or burning can be certified unclean within one week and by two tokens, white hair or spreading." And here there is no spreading. Eliezer admits he has a tradition, but he has not heard a reason concerning it.

Judah b. Batyra supplies a reason for shutting the man up. A boil can spread into a boil, even though, as noted, a boil and a burning do not spread into one another. For this reason, the man into whose hand a bright spot the size of a *sela* arose, and in whom the spot becomes the scar of the boil, is shut up.

The pericope takes account of M. Neg. 9 : 3, though the sages cited do not quote the exact language.

I.i.178.A. In a summer garment that has colored and white checks, they [leprosy-signs] spread from one [colored check] to the other.

B. They asked R. Eliezer, "Lo, it [the white color] is on one check only?"

C. He said to them, "I have not heard."

D. R. Judah b. Batyra said to him, "May I teach concerning it?"

E. He said to him, "If to confirm the words of sages, yes."

F. He said to him, "Perhaps it will remain unchanged on it for two weeks, and what remains unchanged in garments for two weeks is unclean." [Lev. 13 : 55: *And the priest shall examine the diseased thing after it has been washed* (a week after the first appearance). *And if the diseased spot has not changed color, though the disease has not spread, it is unclean*.]

G. He said to him, "You are a great sage, for you have confirmed the words of sages."

M. Neg. 11 : 7 (Sifra Tazriʿa Negaʿim Pereq 13 : 2, Weiss, p. 68a; 16 : 9, Weiss, p. 69b)

*Comment*: The rule of A is that if there is a leprosy-sign on a white square and it spreads to a colored one, the whole garment is unclean, even though colored garments do not become unclean by reason of leprosy-signs. The question to Eliezer concerns the antecedent rule. The white square stands by itself. How should the spreading to a colored square make it unclean (so Albeq, *Seder Ṭoharot*, p. 234)? Eliezer answers that he does not know the reason for the rule of A.

Judah b. Batyra says that the argument is *not* unclean because of the spreading. But if the unclean leprosy-sign remains apparent for two weeks and the white square is unclean, all the colored squares are linked to it, and the whole is regarded as unclean. The meaning, then, of *spread from one to the other* is that the uncleanness will affect the colored squares when the white are unclean. Albeq says the language *perhaps it will remain* does not belong.

So the original interpretation of the question, B, is based upon a false understanding of A. Judah has to clarify the meaning of the antecedent rule, which had been handed down without explanatory information.

See Epstein, *Nusaḥ*, p. 1078.

## XXIX. Parah

I.i.179.A. R. Eliezer says, "The heifer (ʿGLH) [whose neck is broken—Deut. 21 : 1ff.] should be in her [first] year, and the red heifer (PRH) should be two years old."

B. And sages say, "The heifer should be two years old, and the red heifer three or four years old."

M. Par. 1 : 1 (Pesiqta Rabbati 14, Braude, pp. 260-1, pp. 289-290; Sifré Num. 123; Pesiqta de R. Kahana, Mandelbaum, p. 73, Is. 2-3)

*Comment*: Eliezer regards a heifer (ʿGLH) as a cow in the first year of life; afterward it is called *parah*. Deut. 21 : 3, which refers to the heifer (ʿGLH) whose neck is to be broken, must therefore refer to one within the first year. But the red heifer is acceptable in the second. The sages' view is that ʿGLH applies to a heifer up to the second year. The red heifer must be three or four, no less, no more—so Albeq, *Seder Ṭoharot*, p. 257. See Epstein, *Tan.*, p. 317.

V.x.1. R. Aḥa in the name of R. Yosi b. R. Ḥanina said, "When Moses went up to the firmament, he heard the sound of the Holy One, blessed be he, sitting and occupied in the section [of the Torah] dealing with the Red Heifer, and saying the law in the name of the responsible authority: R. Eliezer says, 'A heifer a year old and a red heifer two years old.'

"Moses said, 'Lord of the world, Are not [all] those [creatures] above and below yours? And do you say the law in the name of mortal man?'

"He said to him, 'One righteous man is destined to arise in my world, and to begin the section about the Red Heifer first: R. Eliezer says, ʿA heifer a year old, and a red heifer two years old.'

"He [Moses] said before him [God], 'Lord of the world, May it be your will that he comes from my loins.'

"He said to him, 'By your life! He is from your loins, as it is said,

*The name of one* [of Moses' sons] *is Eliezer* (Ex. 18 : 4). The name of that special one is Eliezer.' "

Midrash Tanḥuma Ḥuqat 24, Buber, II, pp. 59a-b

*Comment*: Aḥa's story about Moses in Heaven depends upon knowledge of M. Par. and on the fact that Moses's son is named Eliezer. On this basis some suppose Eliezer was a Levite (!).

V.xi.3. R. Aḥa in the name of R. Ḥanina said, "When Moses ascended into heaven, he heard the voice of the Holy One, blessed be He, as He sat studying the section dealing with the red heifer, and quoting the law in the name of its author. Thus: R. Eliezer says, 'The broken-necked calf must be a year old while the red heifer must be two years.'

"Said Moses to Him, 'Sovereign of the worlds! May it please Thee that this scholar shall issue from my loins!'

"Said He to him, 'By your life! He will come out of your loins!' Hence it is written, *And the name of the one was Eliezer* (Ex. 18 : 4), as much as to say: the name of that gifted one."

Num. R. 19 : 7, trans. J. J. Slotki, p. 757

I.i.180.A. R. Eliezer says, "The red heifer for the Sin-offering [rite] that was pregnant is valid."

B. And sages declare invalid.

C. R. Eliezer says, "It is not purchased from the gentiles."

D. And sages declare valid [= It is purchased; *or* permit.]

M. Par. 2 : 1 (y. A.Z. 2 : 1;
b. A.Z. 23a1, 46b Sifré Zuṭṭa 19 : 2)

I.i.181.A. [A heifer] born of Caesarean section (YWṢ' DWPN), or the hire of a harlot, or the price of a dog is invalid.

B. R. Eliezer [Parma, Kaufmann, Camb.: Eleazar] declares valid, as it is said, *You shall not bring the hire of a harlot or the price of a dog into the House of the Lord your God* (Deut. 23 : 19)—but this [sacrifice] does not come to the House.

M. Par. 2 : 3 (Sifré Deut. 261)

I.i.182.A. If there were on it [the red heifer] two black hairs, or white, in a single hole (GM'), it is invalid.

B. R. Judah says, "Even in a single hollow (KWS)."

C. If they were in two hollows that were adjacent, it is invalid.

D. R. ʿAqiba says, "Even four, even five, and they are scattered, he should pluck them [out—and it will be valid]."

E. R. Eliezer says, "Even fifty."

F. R. Joshua b. Batyra says, "Even one in her head and one in her tail [make her] invalid.

M. Par. 2 : 5 (Sifré Zuṭṭa 19 : 2)

*Comment*: The several pericopae supply laws as to the selection of the red heifer.

Eliezer regards the embryo as part of the body of the heifer. Merely because a male has had relations with her, she has not been made invalid (M. Par. 2 : 4). The sages regard them as two heifers.

Since the heifer cannot be permitted to be used for work, one cannot purchase it from gentiles, who might have done some work with it, so Eliezer. The sages say that it is assumed to be valid.

In M. Par. 2 : 3 the issue is the exegesis of Deut. 23 : 19, which alludes to unfit animals specifically in respect to the Temple. Since the heifer-sacrifice does not come to the Temple, that law does not apply to it. But Eliezer agrees that the heifer born not in the natural way is unfit (M. Bekh. 7 : 7).

In M. Par. 2 : 5 the issue is the presence of black or white hairs on the red heifer. Part A says that if two black hairs grow in a single hole, they render the heifer invalid, since it is not completely red. But if they grew in separate holes, it would be valid. Judah uses KWS instead of GWMʾ, but refers to the same thing, so Albeq, *Seder Ṭoharot*, p. 261. If the hairs were in two separate holes opposite one another, so that the hair grows as one, they render the heifer unfit. ʿAqiba and Eliezer then say that so long as the hairs are scattered, these hairs may be plucked out. The animal then is valid. Joshua b. Batyra has the exact opposite opinion.

See Epstein, *Tan*., pp. 68, 235; *Nusaḥ*, pp. 1174, 1028, 1063.

I.ii.144.A. R. Eliezer says, "It is not purchased from the gentiles."

B. They said to him, "MʿŚH W: They purchased it from among the gentiles in Sidon, and it [the cow] was called Doma."

Tos. Par. 2 : 1, Zuckermandel, p. 630, ls. 7-8

*Comment*: Instead of an abstract rule, the sages are given a precedent. Lieberman notes that here the name Doma applies to the heifer. b. A.Z. 24a has "Doma was *his* name," so *Tosefet Rishonim*, III, pp. 211-212. See below, p. 450, on Doma's honoring his father.

I.ii.145.A. [A heifer which was] the hire of a harlot or the price of a dog is invalid.

B. R. Eliezer declares it valid, as it is said, "*You will not bring the hire of a harlot or the price of a dog into the House of the Lord your God*"—this is not a coming to the House.

Tos. Par. 2 : 2B, Zuckermandel, p. 630, ls. 11-13

*Comment*: There is no change from M. Par. 2 : 3, but the topic sentence, A, makes clear what was already clear in the Mishnah, that Eliezer's ruling does not pertain to the heifer born of a Caesarean section.

I.i.183.A. [If] the heifer at the Sin-offering was slaughtered not for its own name [Danby, p. 701: "Under some other name"], or he received and sprinkled [its blood] not for its own name, or for its own name and not for its own name, or not for its own name and for its own name—it is unfit.

B. R. Eliezer [Camb., Naples, Parma, Kaufmann: Eleazar] declares it fit.

C. [If it was slaughtered by a priest] with unwashed hands and feet, it is unfit.

D. R. Eliezer [Camb., Naples, Parma, Kaufmann: Eleazar] declares it fit.

E. [If it was slaughtered] not by the High Priest, it is unfit.

F. R. Judah declares it fit.

M. Par. 4 : 1

I.i.184.A. [If] it was burned not with wood, or with any sort of wood [but that which is required, which according to M. Par. 3 : 8, is cedar, spruce, pine, fig-tree]—even with straw and stubble—it is valid.

B. [If] he flayed and cut it up, it is valid.

C. He slaughtered it in order to eat of its flesh and to drink of its blood, it is (valid) [Alt.: *Invalid*].

D. R. Eliezer [Parma, Camb.: Eleazar] says, "The intention does not render invalid in the Red Heifer sacrifice."

M. Par. 4 : 3

*Comment*: The ruling of Eliezer in M. Par. 4 : 1 is explained in M. Par. 4 : 3: Intention here is not affective. The intention of the officiating priest carries no weight. In M. Zev. 2 : 1 the rule is that if the priest's hands and feet are not washed, the offering is invalid. Here Eliezer holds the same rule does not apply, consistent with his view that the rites of the Red Heifer sacrifice are not subject to the same rules as those of the sanctuary.

M. Par. 4 : 3 then makes explicit Eliezer's position, that the wrong intention does not matter.

The form is standard for Eliezer's legal pericopae: a general statement of a law followed by a contrary view of Eliezer. As it stands, 4 : 3D breaks the pattern, for here Eliezer does not differ from C. However, Albeq observes that MSS evidences for C have, *invalid*, which certainly is preferable from a formal viewpoint.

See Epstein, *Nusaḥ*, pp. 210, 189, 1174.

I.i.185.A. A reed pipe that was cut [freshly from the ground] for [holding the water or ashes of] the Sin-offering—

B. R. Eliezer says, "He should immerse it immediately."

C. R. Joshua says, "He should render it unclean and immerse it."

M. Par. 5 : 4 (b. Hag. 23a)

*Comment*: M. Kel. 17 : 7 rules, "A reed-pipe which was cut in order to hold anything remains insusceptible to uncleanness until all the pith has been taken away." The heifer-ashes were mixed with water in a stone trough; they were kept in the reed-pipe and then deposited in the water. Eliezer holds that the priest should forthwith immerse the pipe after it is cut for the sake of the Sin-offering water. Joshua says that it should be rendered unclean and then immersed so that it will enter the status of *Ṭevul-Yom*, that which has been immersed and awaits the setting of the sun to complete its process of purification. This is in accord with the law of the Red Heifer, which was to be prepared by one who has immersed and awaits sunset to complete his rite of purification, as in M. Par. 3 : 7:

> There was a place of immersion there, and they first rendered unclean the priest that burns the Red Heifer, [who would then immerse, and enter the status of him that awaits sunset for the completion of his rite of purification, for the Pharisees held that the rite was to be done by the *Ṭevul Yom* [—he that has immersed on the day and awaits the sunset], because of the Sadducees, that they should not be able to say, "It must be performed only by them on whom the sun has set" [someone *wholly* clean from a ritual viewpoint].

Joshua's and Eliezer's dispute thus extends to the appurtenances of the rite. Eliezer holds that that consideration does not affect the reed-pipe, which is ritually clean when cut. Joshua says it does and presumably would require other appurtenances, where appropriate, to be in the like ritual status.

I.ii.146.A. A reed pipe that was cut [freshly from the ground] for [holding the water or ashes of] the Sin-offering—

B. R. Eliezer says, "He should make it unclean, and does not need to immerse it [*sic*]."

C. R. Joshua says, "He should make it unclean and should immerse it."

Tos. Par. 5 : 6, Zuckermandel, p. 634, ls. 29-30

*Comment*: Eliezer's position is now completely revised. He says the reed should be used in a state of uncleanness! Joshua's position is the same as above. This is impossible. Lieberman, *Tosefet Rishonim*, III, p. 233, corrects the text, "He should immerse it, and does not need to make it unclean." So Tos. has a slight variation on the wording of Eliezer's saying in M. Par. 5 : 4B.

I.ii.147. R. Judah says in the name of R. Eliezer, "If he made for it a crown of mud so that the water will go there, whether it is taken with it or not taken with it, it is valid."

Tos. Par. 5 : 9, Zuckermandel, p. 635, ls. 7-8

*Comment*: The pertinent Mishnah is M. Par. 5 : 7:

> A trough hewn in the rock—they may not gather the water into it or mix the ashes therein...
>
> If there was a hole in it below, and this was stopped up by rags, the water therein is invalid [for mixing the ashes] since it is not wholly enclosed by the vessel...
>
> If the vessel was crowned with a brim of clay and water reached it, it [such of the water as reaches the clay brim] is invalid; but if the brim was firm enough for the vessel to be moved therewith, the water is valid.

Eliezer regards the water as valid no matter the state of the brim.

Living water is required for the heifer-rite. The Mishnah states that a crown of mud is invalid if used in collecting the water into the trough hewn in the rock. Eliezer says it is valid. The water is not regarded as though it was gathered of itself, but since the man made a crown for the trough so that the water would go into the trough and not flow out on the ground, the water is regarded in the Mishnah as having been drawn by man; see Lieberman, *Tosefet Rishonim*, III, p. 235.

I.i.186.A. He that gives his water to one that is unclean—the water is unfit; to one that was clean—it is fit.

B. R. Eliezer [Parma, Kaufmann: Eleazar] says, "Even [if he gave it] to one that was unclean, it is fit, if [meanwhile] the owner did no act of work."

M. Par. 7 : 10

*Comment*: The context is a set of details concerning work which will render water unfit when done between the drawing of the water and its use in the rite. There can be no interruption by other work done between filling the vessel with water and the mixing of the ashes.

A says one who gives his water to an unclean person to watch for him renders the water unfit, for an unclean person cannot keep the water and protect it from uncleanness. One may give it to a clean person to watch, and then the owner is free to do work, since the water is not now within the guardianship of the clean person.

Eliezer says that one may give it to an unclean person, because the water remains within the right of the owner. If the owner did some other work before the sanctification of the water, *he* therefore renders the water unclean. But if he gave it to a clean person, the owner may work, for the water now is fully under the control of the clean guard, who is permitted to touch it, unlike the unclean guard—so Albeq, *Seder Ṭoharot*, p. 276.

I.ii.148.A. R. Eliezer says, "He who hands over his water to one who is unclean, and the owner [of the water] did work—[the water] is unfit."

B. R. Judah says in his name, "If the unclean person did work, [the water] is valid, because it is in the possession of the owner. If the owner did work, it is unfit, since it is in the possession of an unclean person."

Tos. Par. 7 : 7, Zuckermandel, p. 636, l. 39, p. 637, ls. 1-2

*Comment*: A is the same as Eliezer's ruling in M. Par. 7 : 10. Then Judah adds the consistent rule that the unclean guard who did work will *not* render the water invalid, for obvious reasons.

See Epstein, *Tan.*, p. 68.

I.i.187.A. A flask [containing the ashes of the red heifer mixed with water and ready for sprinkling] into which fell any amount of water—

B. R. Eliezer says, "Let him sprinkle two sprinklings."

C. And sages declare unfit.

D. If dew fell into it—

E. R. Eliezer says, "Let him leave it in the sun and the dew evaporates."

F. And sages declare unfit.

M. Par. 9 : 1 (b. Zev. 80b)

I.i.188.A. If cattle or wild animals drank from it, it becomes invalid. All birds [that drank from it] render it unfit, except for the dove, since it sucks up water.

B. All creeping things do not render it unfit, except for the weasel, since it laps up the water.

C. Rabban Gamaliel says, "Also the snake, since it vomits."

D. R. Eliezer [Kaufmann: Leazar] says, "Also the mouse."

M. Par. 9 : 3 (Compare 11 : 1)

I.i.189.A. He that intends concerning Sin-offering-water to drink it—

B. R. Eliezer says, "He has rendered it unfit."

C. R. Joshua says, "When he will turn up [the flask, to drink from it]."

D. R. Yosi says, "Under what circumstances? With water which has not been sanctified.

"But with water that has been sanctified—

E. "R. Eliezer says, 'When he will turn up [the flask, etc.]'

F. "R. Joshua says, 'When he [actually] drinks.'

G. "But if he poured it into his throat [and his mouth did not touch the flask], it is valid."

M. Par. 9 : 4

I.i.190.A. Ashes that were valid which were mixed up with ashes from the stove—we follow the greater in quantity as to declaring them unclean; but they do not sanctify water with it [even though the majority are valid ashes].

B. R. Eliezer says, "They sanctify with the whole [since valid ashes will be contained in the mixture]."

M. Par. 9 : 7

*Comment*: Eliezer in general follows his theory that when something unfit accidentally falls into something fit, the unfit substance is removable ("For I say, the *se'ah* which came up is the one that fell in"). In M. Par. 9 : 1, he therefore holds that if a flask which is ready for sprinkling has received any amount of water which is not sanctified, the man should make two sprinklings, for certainly in those two sprinklings will be holy water. But if he makes one sprinkling, it is possible that it is entirely made up of water which is not holy. As to dew, Eliezer holds the dew will evaporate from the water. In both cases the sages hold, to the contrary, that the whole has been made unfit.

The problem in M. Par. 9 : 3 is that the various animals slobber into the water and so render it unfit. Eliezer here only glosses the antecedent list. The mouse's drinking will also render the water unfit; it too presumably vomits, as Gamaliel says of the snake, or slobbers. M. Par. 11 : 1 omits Eliezer.

M. Par. 9 : 4 concerns the force of intention in respect to the Sin-offering waters. Eliezer holds that intention renders unfit! The man does not actually have to drink the water to spoil it. Joshua holds to the contrary.

In M. Par. 4 : 3, Eliezer holds that intention will not render unfit the sacrifice of the Red Heifer. Evidently he would distinguish between the actual sacrifice and the water mixed with the ashes of the sacrifice.

Yosi supplies a different definition of the problem of 9 : 4 A. He says the issue of A concerns water which has not yet been sanctified. There Eliezer holds mere intention to drink the water will render it unfit. But in respect to water which has already been sanctified, that is, into which the ashes have been placed, the intention alone will not render the mixture unfit, for the mixture has already been sanctified. Then, only when the man actually tips the vessel to his mouth is the mixture rendered unfit.

Joshua holds only when he actually drinks does he do so, and then because the spit in his mouth will mix with the water. Therefore G spells out the consequence of Joshua's position in F. It will not affect Eliezer's view, for to pour the water into one's throat, he has to turn up the flask.

In M. Par. 9 : 7 the sages rule that if the majority of the mixture of ashes is made up of heifer-ashes, then the mixture renders unclean with contact and carrying. But it cannot be used for sanctification. Eliezer says one may sanctify with the whole mixture, because the whole mixture certainly contains the valid ash—consistent with M. Par. 9 : 1.

I.ii.149.A. [If] dew fell on it during the night—

B. R. Eliezer says, "Let him leave it in the sun and the dew will evaporate."

C. And sages say, "The dew evaporates only from fruit."

Tos. Par. 9 : 3, Zuckermandel, p. 638, ls. 5-6

*Comment*: Now we have the sages' reason for their ruling in M. Par. 9 : 1F.

I.ii.150. Rabbi [Judah the Patriarch] said, "If [we rule] according to the words of R. Eliezer, then sprinkling of any amount is valid."

Tos. Par. 9 : 5, Zuckermandel, p. 638, l. 9

*Comment*: See M. Par. 9 : 1.

I.ii.151. R. Yosi said, "And are not the words of R. Eliezer in respect to the red-heifer rite only to rule leniently, for R. Eliezer says, 'When he will turn up [the flask, to drink it, it is invalid], and R. Joshua says, 'When he will drink, because of the liquid of his mouth [it is invalid], and if he poured it into his throat, it is valid."

Tos. Par. 9 : 6, Zuckermandel, p. 638, ls. 14-16

*Comment*: Yosi claims Eliezer rules leniently, and consistently so. Therefore according to Eliezer, intention cannot render the water invalid, except when the water is not yet sanctified.

But as to M. Par. 9 : 4 B, Yosi claims that this is not a valid tradition for Eliezer, because it places him into a position more strict than is consistent with other such rulings, as we have already observed. That accounts for Yosi's redefinition of the problem.

See Lieberman, *Tosefet Rishonim*, III, p. 246.

I.i.191.A. All which is susceptible to be made unclean by *midras*-uncleanness, whether it is unclean or whether it is clean, is regarded as [unclean with] *maddaf*-uncleanness for [them that occupy themselves with] the Sin-offering water. And also to man [does this rule apply.]

B. All which is susceptible to become unclean on account of corpse-uncleanness, whether unclean or clean—

C. R. Eliezer says, "[It is] not [regarded as unclean with] *maddaf*-uncleanness."

D. R. Joshua says, "[It is regarded as unclean with] *maddaf*-uncleanness."

E. And sages say, "If unclean, it is regarded as unclean with *maddaf*-uncleanness. If clean, it is not regarded as unclean with *maddaf*-uncleanness.

M. Par. 10 : 1

I.i.192.A. The jar (QLL) containing the [ashes of the] Sin-offering which touched a [dead] creeping thing is clean.

B. He put it on top of it [= if the jar was set above the creeping thing]—

C. R. Eliezer declares it clean.

D. And sages declare it unclean.

E. If the jar touched unclean foodstuffs or liquids or the Holy Scriptures, it remains clean.

If it was put above them, R. Yosi declares it clean, but the sages declare it unclean.

M. Par. 10 : 3 = M. Ed. 7 : 5

*Comment*: *Maddaf*-uncleanness denotes uncleanness from slight or indirect contact. Danby, p. 794, states, "It denotes the degree of uncleanness conveyed by those enumerated in Lev. 15 : 2, 25." [Lev. 15 : 2: *When any man has a discharge from his body, his discharge is unclean*; 15 : 25: *If a woman has a discharge of blood for many days not at the time of her impurity... all the days of the discharge she will continue in uncleanness.*] Thus, the *Zab* and the *Zabah* are at issue. The *Zab* and the *Zabah* convey uncleanness to what lies above them, though they do not actually touch it. This derived uncleanness will render food and liquid unclean.

*Midras*-uncleanness is uncleanness derived from pressure or treading. Danby, p. 795, explains:, "It denotes the degree of uncleanness suffered by an object which any of those enumerated in Lev. 12 : 2, 15 : 2, 25, sits, lies, or rides upon or leans against. [Lev. 12 : 2: *If a woman bears a male child, she shall be unclean seven days... On the eighth day the flesh of his foreskin shall be circumcized. Then she shall continue for thirty-three days in the blood of her purifying; she shall not touch any hallowed thing, nor come into the sanctuary, until the days of her purifying are completed. But if she bears a female child, she shall be unclean two weeks... and continue in the blood of her purifying for sixty-six days.*] Any object which is fit to sit, lie, or ride upon, and which is usually sat, lain, or ridden upon... is deemed to be susceptible to *midras*-uncleanness."

M. Par. 10 : 1 holds that whatever can be made unclean by the tread of the *Zab*—that is, a vessel which is for lying and sitting—is regarded as unclean for the one who prepares Sin-offering water, as if it is already unclean with *maddaf*-uncleanness. Whether the vessel is unclean or clean, it renders unclean him who is clean in regard to Sin-offering water, for even the slightest uncleanness like the most severe uncleanness renders unclean for Sin-offering waters. This is consistent with M. Hag. 2 : 7: "For them that occupy themselves with the Sin-offering water, the clothes of them that eat Hallowed Things count as suffering *midras*-uncleanness." That is, if they can become unclean on account of *midras*-uncleanness, they are unclean on account of *maddaf*-uncleanness. They therefore render unclean the Sin-offering water even by carrying or by moving it, *as if* they were unclean because of *midras*-uncleanness. The rule also applies to man. That is, a man who is clean, but is not purified so far as Sin-offering water is concerned, is regarded as suffering *maddaf*-uncleanness, and renders the Sin-offering water unclean if he carries or moves it.

The issue to which Eliezer addresses himself concerns what is susceptible to uncleanness because of contact with the corpse. M. Kel. 24 lists vessels which are susceptible to *midras*-uncleanness, to corpse-uncleanness, and to no uncleanness at all. Eliezer holds that what is susceptible to uncleanness because of contact with the corpse is not regarded as unclean with *maddaf*-uncleanness. This means that he will not render the Sin-offering water unclean by carrying or moving it. Joshua holds that he is so regarded. The sages' rule supplies a compromise. If a vessel is made unclean by corpse-uncleanness, it is regarded as suffering *maddaf*-uncleanness, and renders the Sin-offering unclean by carrying and contact. If clean, it is not regarded as suffering *madaf*-uncleanness—unlike the rule in A—and therefore will not render the Sin-offering unclean by carrying and moving, but, to be sure, contact will render the Sin-offering water unclean. The sages' saying ignores the qualification in B, *whether unclean or clean*. They effect a compromise by rephrasing the problem and introducing a distinction explicitly rejected at the outset.

Eliezer's position, therefore, is to make a clearcut distinction between what is susceptible to corpse-uncleanness and what is susceptible to *midras*-uncleanness. The latter is regarded as unclean by reason of *maddaf*-uncleanness. The former is regarded as *not* unclean by reason of *maddaf*-uncleanness. Joshua says that what is susceptible to corpse-uncleanness is no different from what is susceptible to *midras*-uncleanness.

The problem of M. Par. 10 : 3 involves a jar which is not susceptible to uncleanness, for it is made of stone (M. Par. 3 : 2). If the jar touches a creeping thing, it is regarded as clean. If the jar was placed on top of the creeping thing, Eliezer declares the ashes within the jar to be clean. The sages say they are unclean. Since the jar is insusceptible to uncleanness, the ashes within it are in a safely-clean place, so Eliezer. Sages rule that the ashes are made unclean, for now the ashes are *not* in a clean place—they are now on top of the creeping thing, and Num. 19 : 9 states, "And he will place it outside of the camp, in a *clean* place."

The creeping thing is a primary source of uncleanness. The case 10 : 3. A involves secondary sources of uncleanness. Here the sages will regard the ashes as clean, for the unclean things listed in E are not Scripturally unclean, but made so only by scribes' ordinance. Yosi carries the sages' rule of D to its logical conclusion; the ashes here also will be unclean. On 10 : 3, see Epstein, *Tan.*, p. 440.

I.ii.152.A. A jar containing the ashes of the Sin-offering which he placed on top of the creeping thing—

B. R. Eliezer declares clean.

C. And sages declare unclean.

D. Under what circumstances? If he takes the creeping thing away, and the jar would move. But if he can take away the creeping thing, and the jar will stand in its place, even though a corpse or carrion were touching on it on the back, it is clean.

Tos. Par. 10 : 5, Zuckermandel, p. 639 ls. 8-11

*Comment*: Since Scriptural law is that one who *moves* a corpse is unclean, one has to suppose that in Tos. Par. 10 : 4 Eliezer is dealing with a quantity *less* than that ordinarily subject to uncleanness. Otherwise his saying contradicts Scriptural law, which is not likely. Tos. Par. 10 : 5 deals with the problem of M. Par. 10 : 3. The jar is set above a creeping thing. Eliezer rules it is clean, just as in the Mishnah. But as to D, we have to be dealing with less than an olive's bulk of corpse, because if it is more than that quantity, the jar overshadows the corpse and is unclean on that account, so Lieberman, *Tosefet Rishonim*, III, pp. 239, 249.

A. "Whoever is susceptible of becoming unclean by reason of corpse-uncleanness, even though he is actually unclean, is not unclean by reason of *maddaf*-uncleannes, and whoever is not unclean by reason of *maddaf*-uncleanness in respect to Heave-offering is not unclean by reason of *maddaf*-uncleanness with respect to the Sin-offering[water], and they [the sages] did not innovate in regard to uncleanness with respect to the Sin-offering[water]," the words of R. Eliezer.

B. R. Eliezer said, "(MʿŚH B) Shemaʿiah of Kefar ʿOtnai who had in his hand a jar full of Sin-offering water, and he pushed on a door, to which was suspended a key unclean by reason of corpse-uncleanness. And he came and asked Rabban Yoḥanan ben Zakkai, who said to him, 'Shemaʿiah, Go and sprinkle your waters' [for they are not unclean]."

C. And R. Joshua says, "Even if he is clean, he is subject to *maddaf*-uncleanness."

Tos. Par. 10 : 2 (Zuckermandel, p. 638, 1s. 30-35)

*Comment*: Compare M. Hag. 2 : 2 and b. Hag. 23b, and Lieberman, *Tosefet Rishonim*, III, p. 247. The story, B, provides proof for Eliezer's opinion in A. Joshua, C, responds to the opening assertion of A.

I.ii.153.A. [One who is clean for the Sin-offering rite who] moved the creeping thing, the corpse, and the emission [of a *Zab*]—

B. R. Eliezer declares clean.

C. And R. Joshua declares unclean.

Tos. Par. 10 : 4, Zuckermandel, p. 639, ls. 7-8

I.ii.154.A. "If the jar containing the ashes of Sin-offering was placed in the window, and there is in its place a cubic handbreadth, if there is not a handbreadth between its mouth and the lintel (SQWP), lo, this saves [from uncleanness], and otherwise it does not save"—the words of R. Eliezer.

B. And R. Joshua says, "It saves only when there is inward from it an empty space of a handbreadth."

Tos. Ahilot 7 : 11, Zuckermandel, p. 605, ls. 2-4

*Comment*: Lieberman, *Tosefet Rishonim*, III, p. 115, explains that Joshua requires that the jar be in a clean place, even though the jar has not been made unclean, and R. Eliezer declares it clean. The rule here illustrates M. Par. 10 : 3.

I.i.193. (Any condition of doubt regarded as clean when it concerns Heave-offering is also regarded as clean when it concerns the Sin-offering water. Any condition in which the decision is left in suspense when it concerns Heave-offering [M. Ter. 8 : 8, M. Toh. 4 : 5], in like condition the Sin-offering water must be poured out. If acts that must be done in cleanness were done after sprinkling by such Sin-offering water, their validity must be left in suspense.)

A. Wooden lattice work is clean in what concerns Hallowed Things or Heave-offering or the Sin-offering water.

B. R. Eliezer [Parma: Leazar] says, "Loosely fastened boards (RʿDWT) are unclean in what concerns the Sin-offering water."

M. Par. 11 : 2

*Comment*: The issues of A and B concern what can contract *midras*-uncleanness or corpse-uncleanness. Wooden lattice-work cannot count as vessels and cannot contract *midras*- or corpse-uncleanness. Eliezer then rules on loosely fastened boards. These may be used to sit or lie upon, therefore they are susceptible to *midras*-uncleanness, and thus, even when clean, are regarded as subject to *maddaf*-uncleanness, so far as the cleanness required for Sin-offering water is concerned, so Danby, p. 710, n. 6.

Albeq, *Seder Ṭoharot*, p. 286, says that the loosened boards (RʿDWT) are the same as the wooden lattice-work (RPPWT), so Eliezer differs from the foregoing rule. Then, he says that the lattice-work is unclean in respect to Sin-offering water, but will not be unclean in respect to

Hallowed Things or Heave-offering as in M. Toh. 10 : 1, which is warrant for including this pericope in our Eliezer's corpus.

See Epstein, *Tan.*, p. 235; *Nusaḥ*, pp. 2, 1078, 1174.

I.ii.155.A. They did not dispute concerning law, but concerning language, for R. Eliezer says, "They burn on their account Heave-offering, but they are not liable on their account for uncleanness in respect to the sanctuary."

Tos. Par. 11 : 8, Zuckermandel, p. 640, ls. 5-6.

I.i.194. (Any kind of hyssop that is given a special name is invalid; but hyssop simply so called is valid; Greek hyssop, stibium hyssop, Roman hyssop, or wild hyssop is invalid; if it is unclean Heave-offering, it is invalid; and even if it is clean Heave-offering, it should not be used for sprinkling, but if they sprinkled with it, it is valid.)

A. They do not sprinkle with the young shoots or with the berries [of the hyssop].

B. They are not liable because of the young shoots in regard to coming to the sanctuary.

C. R. Eliezer [Camb., Parma, Kaufmann, Eleazar] says, "Also, not for the berries."

M. Par. 11 : 7

*Comment*: The point of B is that, while they are not to sprinkle with the young shoots or berries, if they sprinkled with the young shoots, it is an acceptable sprinkling, and one who enters the Temple relying on purification of that sort is not liable for a Sin-offering. Eliezer says the same is so for the berries, an unimportant gloss, making clear that B does not distinguish between shoots and berries. Both are in the same category: not to be done, but if done, acceptable.

See Epstein, *Tan.*, p. 234; *Nusaḥ*, p. 1029.

## xxx. Ṭoharot, Miqva'ot

I.i.195.A. R. Eliezer [Camb.: Leazar] says, "He who eats food [unclean in a] first-grade [uncleanness is unclean at a] first [level of uncleanness]; [if it was food of a] second-[grade uncleanness, he becomes unclean at a] second [level of uncleanness]; food of a third-[grade of uncleanness makes him subject to a] third [level of uncleanness]."

B. R. Joshua says, "He who eats food [unclean in a] first-, and food unclean in a second-[grade of uncleanness is unclean at the] second [level of uncleanness]; of a third [-grade of uncleanness is unclean] at the second level for Holy Things, but not at a second [-grade] for Heave-offering."

C. [These rules apply to] unconsecrated food which was kept in cleanness for Heave-offering.

M. Toh. 2 : 2 (y. Hag. 3 : 2; b. Sot. 30a, b. Shab. 14a, b. Hul. 33b)

*Comment*: The following are pertinent to the above:

1. First-grade uncleanness in common food is unclean and renders Heave-offering unclean. Second-grade uncleanness renders Heave-offering invalid, but not unclean; while common food suffering third-grade uncleanness may be consumed in pottage containing Heave-offering.—M. Toh. 2 : 3.

2. First-grade uncleanness and second-grade uncleanness and second-grade uncleanness in Heave-offering are unclean and render Hallowed Things unclean; third-grade uncleanness renders Hallowed Things invalid but not unclean...—M. Toh. 2 : 4.

3. First-, second-, and third-grades of uncleanness in Hallowed Things are unclean and render Hallowed Things unclean...—M. Toh. 2 : 5.

4. Second-grade uncleanness in common food renders unclean liquid that is a common food and renders invalid foods that are Heave-offering. Third-grade uncleanness in Heave-offering renders unclean liquid pertaining to Hallowed Things and renders invalid food pertaining to Hallowed Things if it was kept in cleanness proper to Hallowed Things...—M. Toh. 2 : 6.

Eliezer says that the sages decreed that he who eats unclean food is made unclean (M. Zab. 5 : 12) at the food's level of uncleanness. Thus he who eats food unclean in the first-grade of uncleanness renders Heave-offering unclean, etc., as in M. Toh. 2 : 3ff., which spells out the consequences of Eliezer's and Joshua's dispute.

Joshua holds that whether a person eats first- or second-degree-unclean food, he is made unclean in the second degree. He thus will render Heave-offering unfit.

Albeq explains, *Seder Ṭoharot*, p. 304, that a second-grade uncleanness makes something unclean in the second degree, by means of liquids. The second-grade uncleanness makes liquids unclean in the first degree, and they render unclean other food, so that the food enters the second degree of uncleanness. But we do not find that a first-degree-uncleanness ever renders something else unclean in the first degree. He who eats food unclean in the third degree becomes unclean in the second degree so far as holy things are concerned. But as to Heave-offering, he is not unclean in the second, but only in the third degree. The ruling as to the third degree pertains not only to Heave-offering, but also to unconsecrated food, so Albeq.

I.ii.156.A. R. Joshua said to R. Eliezer, "Where have we found an uncleanness in the Torah which renders [something else] unclean like itself [that is—in the same degree of uncleanness], that you say [first-grade uncleanness] should make [that which it rendered unclean, unclean in the] first[-degree]?"

B. He said to him, "You also have said that it [second-degree uncleanness] renders liquid unclean [so as to be able to render [unclean in the] first [degree], and the liquids [then] render food unclean [such as to] render [unclean] in the second degree. But we have not found a first[-degree-uncleanness] which is able [to] render [unclean in the] first[-degree] anywhere."

Tos. Toh. 2 : 1, Zuckermandel,
p. 662, ls. 6-9 (b. Hul. 34a)

*Comment*: The debate explains Joshua's position, ignores Eliezer's. Some readings reverse the names, in which case they would have to reverse the positions in M. Toh. 2 : 2 as well. Normally, as we have seen, when Eliezer and Joshua appear together, the order is Eliezer, then Joshua.

I.i.196.A. He entered a valley in the rainy season, and there was uncleanness in such-and-such a field, and he said, "I went into that place, but I do not know whether or not I entered that field"—

B. R. Eliezer [Parma, Kaufmann: Leazar] declares [him] clean.

C. And sages declare [him] unclean.

M. Toh. 6 : 5 (b. Pes. 10a: R';
b. A.Z. 9a, 70a-b, b. B.B. 55b, b. A.Z. 70a)

*Comment*: Eliezer says that if there is doubt that the man went into the unclean place, he is clean, even though there are no fences around the place. Since the fields nonetheless are separate from one another, the condition of doubt is regarded as cleanness, in conformity with M. Toh. 6 : 4:

> "When you can multiply doubts and doubts about doubts, if it concerns private property, the condition is regarded as unclean, but if about public, it is regarded as clean."

In a situation in which there is no doubt that uncleanness was present, but there *is* doubt that the man had entered the place, Eliezer says that the man is clean. If there is doubt whether the man had touched what was unclean, he is regarded as unclean. Eliezer in 6 : 5 is consistent.

Some texts give Eleazar. Tos., below, and b. B.B. 55b-56a give Eliezer. See Epstein, *Nusaḥ*, p. 1174.

I.ii.157.A. One who entered a valley in the rainy season and there was uncleanness in such-and-such a field—

B. They said before R. Eliezer, "Lo, it [the field], belongs to a private party [and in accord with M. Toh. 6 : 4, we should rule he is unclean]?"

C. R. Marinus explained in his name, "Which ever [field] has a name for itself [is a private field, but otherwise, it is not]."

Tos. Toh. 7 : 7, Zuckermandel, p. 667, ls. 49-40

*Comment*: The foregoing situation is clarified. A private field has to be known by its own name. In b. B.B. 56a, R. Papa explains, "If for instance people call it, 'The field of so-and-so's well.' "

I.ii.158. (A condition of doubt concerning a private domain is accounted unclean unless a man can say, 'I did not touch.' A condition of doubt concerning the public domain is accounted clean unless a man can say, 'I did touch.' ... Paths that lead only (HMPWLŠYN) towards cisterns, pits, caverns, and winepresses are accounted private domain in what concerns [the laws of the] Sabbath and public domain in what concerns [the laws of] uncleanness.—M. Toh. 6 : 6).

A. R. Eliezer says, "When they are open (MPWLŠYN) [= a thoroughfare, as in M. Eruv. 9 : 4], they are regarded as a public way for both. When they are not open they are regarded as a private domain for the Sabbath and public domain for uncleanness."

Tos. Toh. 7 : 9, Zuckermandel, p. 668, ls. 3-6

*Comment*: Eliezer qualifies the foregoing Mishnah. I have followed Lieberman on the reading of Eliezer's saying, see *Tosefet Rishonim*, IV, p. 78. Judah in M. Eruv. 9 : 4 is consistent with Eliezer's position here. On this flimsy basis I have assigned the whole to our Eliezer.

I.i.197.A. The outer parts of vessels which were made unclean by liquids—

B. R. Eliezer says, "They make liquids unclean, but they do not render food invalid."

C. R. Joshua says, "They make liquids unclean, and they *do* render food invalid."

D. Simeon the brother of ʿAzaryah says, "Neither thus nor so. But liquids which were made unclean by the outer parts of vessels render unclean [at] one [remove] and render invalid [at] one [remove].

"Lo, this one says, 'What renders you unclean [namely, outer parts of vessels] does not render me unclean, but *you* have rendered me unclean.' "

M. Toh. 8 : 7

*Comment*: The uncleanness is slight. The outside of the cup is unclean, but the inside is clean (M. Kel. 25 : 6). But the outsides render other liquids unclean. Eliezer holds they do not make food unclean, and Joshua says they do make food—that is, Heave-offering—invalid.

Simeon has a completely different tradition. According to him the issue is the effect of uncleanness contracted *from* outer parts of vessels. The vessels were unclean and made liquid unclean, thus the result of the process of A-B-C is that outer parts made unclean by liquids make unclean other liquids with which they come into contact. According to Simeon the liquid made unclean by the backside of vessels is a first-grade source of uncleanness. It renders Heave-offering food unclean and makes it a second-grade source of uncleanness. And the second-grade source of uncleanness renders other Heave-offering invalid.

According to Eliezer's rule the food which is made unclean by the liquid says to the liquid, 'The thing which made you unclean could not make me unclean. For the outer parts of the vessel which made you unclean could not have made me unclean,' for they are not able to render food invalid, according to Eliezer (M. Par. 8 : 2-7). We do not know what could be said according to Joshua, for in this instance the liquid *can* make Heave-offering invalid.

I.ii.159.A. The outer sides of vessels which were made unclean by liquids—

B. R. Eliezer said, "They render liquids unclean, but do not render [Heave-offering] food invalid."

And the law is according to his words.

C. R. Joshua says, "They render liquids unclean and render [Heave-offering] food invalid.

D. "And it is a *qal veḥomer*: If a *Ṭevul-Yom*, who does not render unclean liquid [of] unconsecrated [food], does render invalid Heave-offering food, the outer side of vessels, which do render liquid [of] unconsecrated [food] invalid, is it not logical that it should render unfit Heave-offering foods?"

E. Simeon the brother of ʿAzaryiaʾ says, "The matters are reversed. If a *Ṭevul-Yom* renders invalid Heave-offering food, but does not render unclean unconsecrated liquid, the outer sides of vessels, which do not render invalid Heave-offering food, logically ought *not* to render unclean unconsecrated liquid."

Tos. Ṭevul Yom 1 : 8, Zuckermandel,
pp. 684, ls. 34-38, 685, ls. 1-3

*Comment*: The *Ṭevul-Yom* is one who is in a diminished state of uncleanness. He has immersed himself and awaits only the sunset to complete his purification. That is the basis of Joshua's argument. Simeon then turns the whole around, in opposition to both Eliezer and Joshua in respect to rendering liquids unclean; his argument is based upon Eliezer's rule that the outer sides of the vessels will not render Heave-offering food invalid. Obviously, he has nothing to say with respect to Joshua's view. Yosi (1 : 9) attests the foregoing.

I.i.198. (From what time do olives become susceptible to uncleanness? After they exude moisture that comes out of them... Rabban Gamaliel says, "After preparation is finished [as soon as a batch of olives is harvested and ready for the oil-press]." And the sages agree with his words.—M. Toh. 9 : 1)

A. When their work is finished, lo, they are ready (MWKŠRYN) to receive uncleanness.

B. If unclean liquids fell on them, [Add: *they become unclean*].

C. The sap that comes forth from them—

D. R. Eliezer declares clean.

E. And sages declare unclean.

F. R. Simeon [Camb.: Ishmael] said, "They did not dispute concerning the sap that exudes from the olives, that it is clean.

"Concerning what did they dispute?

"Concerning what exudes from the [oil] vat, for—

"R. Eliezer declares clean.

"And sages declare unclean."

M. Toh. 9 : 3 (y. Ter. 11 : 2)

*Comment*: The sap that exudes after the work is completed is insusceptible according to Eliezer, because the sap is not like a liquid. Eliezer rejects A as well, that is, Gamaliel's opinion. The sages say the liquid is susceptible to uncleanness. Simeon rejects this definition of the dispute. All parties agree on Eliezer's position. The dispute pertains to what exudes from the vat where the olives are pressed.

Note also *Phar.* II, pp. 289-290; Epstein, *Nusaḥ*, p. 1175, n. 2.

I.i.199.A. R. Eliezer says, "A quarter [-*log*] of drawn water at the outset renders the ritual pool invalid, and three *logs* on the surface [of a pool of valid rain water that lacks forty *se'ahs* render the ritual pool invalid]."

B. And sages say, "Whether at the outset or at the end, its measure [to render the pool unfit through drawn water] is three *logs*."

M. Miq. 2 : 4

*Comment*: The immersion pool requires forty *se'ahs* of water at a depth in which the whole body can be covered. The water cannot be drawn—that is, taken from water that has been standing in a vessel—but must be taken from a river or a spring or rain-water that flows directly into the pool [Danby, p. 732, n. 5].

Eliezer's rule is that if the pool contains a quarter-*log* at the outset, which then is supplemented by forty *se'ahs* of valid rain-water, the pool is invalid. If three *logs* are added to a pool of valid rain water that lacks any of the required forty *se'ahs*, they also will render the pool invalid. The sages rule that three *logs*, whether at the outset of filling the pool, or added to a pool lacking the forty *se'ahs*, will render the pool unfit. They are consistent with M. Ed. 1 : 3, Hillel says one *hin*, Shammai says nine *qavs* and Shemaʿiah and Abṭalion say three *logs* render the immersion pool unfit. (Four *logs* are one *qav*, 3 *qavs* are one *hin*, see *Phar.* I, p. 156.) So Eliezer's tradition about distinguishing *when* the drawn water was added is rejected by the sages, who supply the opinion attributed in M. Ed. 1 : 3 to Shemaʿiah and Abṭalion but who know nothing of the attribution to Shemaʿiah and Abṭalion.

Warrant for assigning this pericope to our Eliezer is in M. Miq. 2 : 7, where the Eliezer there is consistent with the Eliezer here.

I.ii.160.A. A vessel (GSṬR') resting on the ground of the cistern of a press into which rain fell, and which filled [with water]—lo, it is unfit [to serve as a ritual pool] because it is [water] produced by [collected in] vessels [and therefore the water is regarded as drawn water.]

B. R. Eliezer declares valid, for the drawn water does not render the ritual pool invalid until it falls into it.

Tos. Miq. 3 : 1, Zuckermandel, p. 655, ls. 8-10

*Comment*: Since the cistern of the press does not hold the water, all the water is kept in by the vessel, and therefore the water is regarded as drawn water. Eliezer says that the water was not drawn water when it was falling into the cistern, therefore it is a valid immersion-pool, see Lieberman, *Tosefet Rishonim*, IV, p. 10.

I.i.201.A. He who leaves [empty] wine-jars on the roof to dry them out, and they were filled with water [by the rains]—

B. R. Eliezer says, "If it is the rainy season, if there is [in it] as little water as in the cistern, it may be broken [so the water will flow into the pool, and the water is valid and not drawn water], and if not, it may not be broken."

C. R. Joshua says, "One way or the other, it may be broken or turned upside down, but he may not [directly] empty [it into the pool]."

M. Miq. 2 : 7

*Comment*: If the jar is filled with water, it certainly will be rain water. If the ritual pool contains a little valid water and is not completely dried up, the water may be added to the pool by breaking the jars. Eliezer says that even a quarter[-*log*] of drawn water at the outset will render the pool invalid; here too, if the water of the jar *starts* the pool, since it appears to be drawn, it renders the pool unfit.

Joshua rejects that distinction—therefore is consistent with the sages of M. Miq. 2 : 4—and says that in any case the water may be used, either by breaking the jar, or by turning it upside down so the water will flow into the cistern. But one may not raise up the jar and empty it into the pool, for by emptying the water he makes it drawn water; the water of the pool cannot be poured into it by the hand of man.

The pericope is a development of M. Miq. 2 : 4. The operative distinction is the same: the amount of water remaining in the cistern.

See Epstein, *Tan.*, p. 147.

I.i.202.A. "The plasterer who forgot his [lime-]pot (ʿṢYṢ) in the cistern, and it was filled with water—

B. "If the water floated over it in any amount, it may be broken, and if not, it may not be broken"—the words of R. Eliezer.

C. And R. Joshua says, "One way or the other it may be broken."

M. Miq. 2 : 8

*Comment*: Eliezer says that if the water of the pool has entered the pot and made it overflow, then the water is regarded as if it is still in the pool, and the pot may be broken, for its water is valid. But otherwise the water in the pot is regarded as drawn water and will render the pool unfit, for the pot has been filled at the intent of the plasterer. Joshua, as earlier, rejects this distinction.

I.i.202.D. An immersion-pool which has in it forty *seʾahs* of water and mud—

E. R. Eliezer says, "They immerse in the water, and do not immerse in the mud."

F. R. Joshua says, "In the water and in the mud."

G. In what kind of mud do they immerse? In mud over which the water floats.

H. If the water was on one side, R. Joshua agrees that they immerse in the water, and they do not immerse in the mud.

I. Of what kind of mud did they speak?

"Such that a reed will sink into it of itself," the words of R. Meir.

R. Judah says, "Such that the measuring rod will not stand there of itself."

J. Abba Eleazar b. Dolai (DWLʿʾY) says, "Such that a plummet will sink there."

K. R. Eliezer says, "That which will go into the narrow neck of a jar."

L. Rabbi Simeon says, "That which will go into the spout of a water-skin."

M. R. Eliezer b. R. Ṣadoq says, "Such as can be measured in a *log*-[measure]."

M. Miq. 2 : 10

*Comment*: The mud may complete the forty *se'ahs* (M. Miq. 7 : 1). But Eliezer says one should immerse in the water. Joshua says that if the mud may complete the required measure, it may also serve for immersion. G–H qualify Joshua's rule in F. He rules in such a case when the two are mixed together, but if they are separated, then obviously one will immerse in the water.

I-M then define the sort of mud which can complete the forty *se'ahs.* I has Meir and Judah answer the question, and then follow opinions attributed to others, responding not to the opinions of Meir and Judah but to the opening question. Since Eliezer says one cannot immerse in the mud, he should not care what kind of mud is under discussion.

See Epstein, *Nusaḥ*, p. 1175.

## xxxi. Niddah

I.i.203. (Shammai says, "For all women it is enough for them [that they be deemed unclean only from] their time [of suffering a flow.]" Hillel says, "[A woman is deemed to have been unclean] from [the previous] examination to [the present] examination..." But the sages say, "It is not according to the opinion of either, but [she is deemed to have been unclean] during the preceding twenty-four hours if this is less than [the time] from [the previous] examination to [the present] examination, or else from [the previous] examination to [the present] examination, if this is less than twenty-four hours."—M. Nid. 1 : 1)

A. R. Eliezer says, "Four [types of] women—Enough for them is their time (Š'TN) [of suffering a flow]: the virgin, the pregnant woman, the nursing mother, and the old woman."

B. R. Joshua said, "I have heard only the virgin."

C. But the law is according to R. Eliezer.

M. Nid. 1 : 3 (y. Nid. 1 : 2; b. Nid. 3a: Rabbi refers to Eliezer's ruling; 6a-b, 7a-b)

I.i.204.A. Who is the old woman? Whoever has passed three periods [without suffering a flow] about the time of her old age [menopause].

B. R. Eliezer [Parma, y.: Leazar] says, "Every woman for whom three periods have passed [without menstruating]—enough for her is her time."

C. R. Yosi says, "A pregnant woman and a nursing mother for whom three periods have passed [without menstruation]—enough for them is their time."

M. Nid. 1 : 5 (y. Nid. 1 : 4, b. Nid. 7a-b, 8a-b, 9b, 10b; b. Eruv. 46a; y. Yev. 5 : 6, b. Ket. 60a)

*Comment*: Since the four women mentioned by Eliezer in 1 : 3 do not usually have an irregular menstrual flow, it is sufficient for them to be regarded as unclean only from the time that they actually do suffer a flow. This is both contrary to the rule of the House of Shammai and also consistent with that rule in its selection of language; *time* (Šʿ H), not *examination*, to which no one alludes.

Eliezer knows nothing about the rule of the House of Shammai, unless his saying is construed as a gloss on, and qualification of, that rule.

Joshua has a similar tradition, but his speaks of only the virgin, thus:
Shammai: *All* women—their time is sufficient.
Eliezer: Four women.
Joshua: One woman.

Behind all three traditions is DYN ŠʿTN, and each master supplies the appropriate protasis.

M. Nid. 1 : 5 then glosses Eliezer's rule in 1 : 3. An old woman is a woman who, around the time of menopause, misses three periods. Eliezer drops the reference to menopause. The rule will apply to anyone who is irregular to that extent.

Yosi then glosses M. Nid. 1 : 3 without reference to M. Nid. 1 : 5A + B. See Epstein, *Nusaḥ*, p. 1176; *Phar.* I, pp. 303-307.

I.ii.161.A. R. Eliezer says, "Four [kinds of] women—enough for them is their period: The virgin, the pregnant woman, the nursing mother, and the old lady."

B. R. Joshua said, "I heard only the virgin."

C. R. Eliezer said to him, "They do not say to one who has not seen the New Moon, 'Let him come and give testimony', but they do say so to him who has seen it. You have not heard, and we have heard. You have heard one, and we have heard four."

D. All the days of R. Eliezer the people would behave according to his words. (y.: *All the days . . . the law was according to R. Joshua.*) After R. Eliezer died, R. Joshua restored matters to their former condition. (y.: *After he died, R. Joshua applied the law according to R. Liezer.*)

E. But the law is according to R. Eliezer.

Tos. Nid. 1 : 5, Zuckermandel, p. 641, ls. 32-36 (y. Nid. 1 : 2; Qoh. R. 12 : 11 : 1)

*Comment*: Eliezer rejects Joshua's tradition, M. Nid. 1 : 3B, saying he too has a tradition.

See Lieberman, *Tosefet Rishonim*, III, p. 257.

III.ii.81.A. TNY': R. Eliezer said to R. Joshua, "You have not heard, but I have heard; you have heard only one tradition, but I have heard many. People do not ask him who has not seen the New Moon to give testimony, but only him who has seen it."

B. While R. Eliezer was alive, people followed the ruling of R. Joshua, but after R. Eliezer died, R. Joshua restored the thing to its old state [Eliezer's rule].

C. Why did he not follow R. Eliezer during his lifetime?

Because R. Eliezer was a disciple of Shammai, and he felt that if they acted in agreement with his ruling in one matter, they would do so in other matters...

b. Nid. 7b

III.ii.82. TNY': R. Eliezer said to the sages, "M'ŚH B: A young woman at Haitalu had her menstrual flow interrupted for three periods, and when the matter came to the sages, they said it sufficed for her to reckon her uncleanness from the time she observed the flow."

They said to him, "A time of emergency is no proof."

b. Nid. 9b

IV.ii.17. Rav Judah in the name of Samuel said, "The law is in accord with R. Eliezer in four cases."

b. Nid. 7b

*Comment*: The cases are M. Nid. 1 : 3, M. Nid. 4 : 4, M. Nid. 10 : 3, and M. Toh. 8 : 7.

III.ii.83. TNW RBNN: M'ŚH B: Rabbi ruled in agreement with R. Eliezer, and after he reminded himself, he said, "R. Eliezer is worthy to be ruled upon in any emergency."

b. Nid. 9b (b. Eruv. 46a)

I.ii.162. "A child continues to suckle for twenty-four months. Afterward, he is like one who sucks from an abominable thing (ŠQṢ)," the words of R. Eliezer.

And R. Joshua says, "A child continues to suck even five years. But if he stops and then goes back after twenty-four months, lo, this is one who sucks from an abominable thing."

Tos. Nid. 2 : 3, Zuckermandel, p. 642, ls. 28-30
(y. Ket. 5 : 6, Nid. 1 : 4; b. Ket. 60a)

*Comment*: See above, p. 184, and Lieberman, *Tosefet Rishonim*, III, pp. 258-9.

I.ii.163. R. Eliezer says one of the strict rulings of the House of Shammai and the strict rulings of the House of Hillel, etc.

Tos. Nid. 5 : 6, Zuckermandel, p. 645, ls. 32-36, p. 646, ls. 1-4

*Comment*: See *Phar.* II, pp. 306-308.

I.ii.164.A. All those who are examined are examined only by women.

B. Thus R. Eliezer would give them over to his wife [for examination.]

C. And R. Ishmael would give them to his mother.

Tos. Nid. 6 : 8, Zuckermandel, p. 647, ls. 32-33 (b. Nid. 48b)

*Comment*: Lieberman, *Tosefet Rishonim*, III, p. 274, gives Joshua in C.

I.i.205.A. She who was in hard labor (HMQŠH) [whatever blood that flows is regarded as unclean as] menstrual blood (NDH). [She that was in hard labor and sees blood is regarded as a menstrual woman, but *not* as a Zabah.]

B. She was in hard labor three days out of eleven [the period of time between periods; a flow during these eleven days is regarded as a flux, Lev. 15 : 25]—

C. "If she had relief [from her pains] for twenty-four hours and then gave birth, this is one who gives birth while she had a flux (BZWB)"—the words of R. Eliezer [Kaufmann: Eleazar].

D. R. Joshua says, "[She must have had relief for a whole] night and a [whole] day, like the night of the Sabbath and its day, for she may have had relief from the pain but not from the blood."

M. Nid. 4 : 4 (y. Nid. 4 : 4, b. Nid. 7b, 36b, 37b, b. Sanh. 87b; b. Eruv. 46a; b. Naz. 65a)

I.i.206.A. She who is in hard labor during the eighty [days of purifying] of the female [child],—all the blood that she sees is clean, until the baby comes out.

B. And R. Eliezer declares her unclean.

C. They said to R. Eliezer, "Now in a place where [the law] dealt stringently, with the blood discharged without travail (DM HŠPY), [the law] dealt leniently, with the blood of travail (DM HQŠY), [then] in a place in which [the law] dealt leniently, with the blood discharged without travail [she is clean through the eighty days], should we not deal leniently with the blood discharged *with* travail?"

D. He said to them, "It is enough if the inferred law is as strict as that from which it is inferred. In what respect did [the law] deal leniently with her? With the uncleanness from flux. But she is still unclean with the uncleanness of the menstruant."

M. Nid. 4 : 6; (y. Nid. 4 : 6; b. Nid. 7b, 38b; y. Meg. 1 : 8; Sifra Tazriʿa Pereq 2 : 4, Weiss, p. 58b)

*Comment*: M. Nid. 4 : 4 begins with the rule that a woman who is in hard labor and sees a spot of blood is regarded as a menstruant. But she is not regarded as a *Zabah*, even if she should be in hard labor and see blood three days running in the days of flux, that is, in the eleven days between menstrual periods. During that time the blood produced by hard travail does not make her a *Zabah*. If it did, she would have to count seven clean days like her who gives birth as a *Zabah*. A Zabah, as noted above, is described in Lev. 15 : 25: *When a woman has a discharge of blood for many days, not at the time of her impurity, or if she has a discharge beyond the time of her impurity, all the days of the discharge she shall continue in uncleanness; as in the days of her impurity [= seven] she shall be unclean.*

B then introduces the case of the woman who was in hard labor three days out of the eleven between periods ("not at the time of her impurity"). If she has relief from the labor pains and then gives birth, she is in the category of one who gives birth while a *Zabah*, because the blood is shown—by the cessation of the labor pains—to be blood not of labor pains on account of the birth, but of the *Zabah*.

Joshua (D) then says that if she had rest from the pains for a whole night and the following day, she is regarded as one who gives birth while a *Zabah*. But if she had rest for twenty-four hours, for instance from noon to noon, this is not regarded as a rest, for the blood came from the birth, and she is not a woman who gives birth while a *Zabah*. The difference between Eliezer and Joshua therefore pertains to the period of relief which will signify the end of the blood that might be due to labor; the one says twenty-four hours, however they come, and the other says twenty-four hours, *only night then day*.

M. Nid. 4 : 6 then introduces a related problem: a woman has given birth to a girl. Lev. 12 : 2ff. says that when a woman bears a male child, she is unclean for seven days. On the eighth day is the circumcision. Then: *She shall continue for thirty-three days in the blood of her purifying. She shall not touch any hallowed thing nor come to the sanctuary until the days of her purifying are completed. But if she bears a female child, then she shall be unclean two weeks, as in her menstruation, and she shall continue in the blood of her purifying for sixty-six days.*

What has happened, therefore, is that after twenty-four days of the birth of the female child, the woman immersed herself and had intercourse and become pregnant, but then suffered a miscarriage. If she is in hard labor in that time, whatever blood she suffers is clean, until the embryo comes out, so the sages. The blood is regarded as the *blood of her purifying*, and not as menstrual blood or a flux.

Eliezer rules that the blood is unclean. It is on account of the embryo and not on account of the 'blood of purifying.' It is the blood of hard labor, and this is unclean like menstrual blood, as in M. Nid. 4 : 4.

The sages then point out that with reference to the blood discharged without travail, that is, blood discharged three days during a flux, which marks the woman as one who has given birth during a flux, the law deals leniently. If a woman saw blood during labor at such a time, she is not one who gives birth as a *Zabah*, as stated explicitly in M. Nid. 4 : 4. Now, in respect to the days of her purifying, when whatever blood she sees is regarded as clean, should the rule not be that the blood consequent upon the miscarriage is regarded as no other than blood of purifying, and clean?

The point of the argument is that blood seen during the eleven days between periods could be flux but is treated as blood of the labor, unless the conditions specified by Eliezer and Joshua in M. Nid. 4 : 4 should pertain. So there Scripture could have dealt stringently and could have regarded it as blood of flux, but instead regarded it as blood of labor. Now here blood which she sees normally is regarded as blood of her purifying. Should the rule in A not apply, that whatever blood comes during the eighty days is clean, until the embryo comes out?

Eliezer answers with a cliché, DYW LB' MN HDYN LHYWT KNDWN. This is a standard phrase, attributed also to Ṭarfon in M. B.Q. 2 : 5 and elsewhere. To be sure, Scripture dealt leniently with the woman who sees blood during labor. In that event she is regarded as unclean. The leniency is that she is unclean like a menstrual woman, not like a *Zabah*. Nonetheless she *is* unclean. So here too she is unclean.

Another way of phrasing the argument would be, "No, if you have said so concerning the woman in the days of her purifying, who, if she sees blood, is entirely clean, will you say so concerning the woman who gives birth in hard labor, who, if she sees blood, is surely unclean [as a menstruant, if not as a *Zabah*]." So *dayyo* is simply a development of an established mode of argument and not a new logical rule.

Eliezer thus ignores the fact that the woman of whom we speak is within the eighty days of purifying; the sages ignore the fact that the blood referred to in M. Nid. 4 : 4, on which they build their argument, necessarily produces an uncleanness, so there is no valid basis for the *qal veḥomer* such as they propose.

I.i.207.A. "If a woman twenty years old has not grown two hairs, she must bring proof that she is twenty years old; she is reckoned sterile and she may not perform *ḥaliṣah*, nor contract Levirate marriage.

"If a man twenty years old has not grown two hairs, he must bring proof that he is twenty years old. He is regarded as a eunuch. He does not submit to *ḥaliṣah* nor contract Levirate marriage"—the words of the House of Hillel.

B. The House of Shammai say, "In either case this applies when at the age of eighteen."

C. R. Eliezer [Naples: Eleazar] says, "For a male the rule is according to the House of Hillel, and for a female it is according to the House of Shammai, for the growth of a woman is more speedy than that of a man."

M. Nid. 5 : 9, trans. Danby, p. 751
(b. Nid. 47b, 48a; b. Yev. 80a)

*Comment*: See *Phar.* II p. 301; Epstein, *Nuṣah*, p. 1176; and above, p. 163.

I.i.208.A. A *Zab* and a *Zabah* [A man or a woman that had a flux] who examined themselves on the first day and found themselves to be clean, and on the seventh day and found themselves to be clean, and the rest of the intervening days they did not examine themselves—

B. R. Eliezer says, "Lo, they are in the presumption of being clean."

C. R. Joshua says, "They have only the first and seventh day [as days of cleanness and must count an additional five days of cleanness]."

D. R. ʿAqiba says, "They have only the seventh day alone [as a day of cleanness and must count six more consecutive clean days]."

M. Nid. 10 : 3 (b. Nid. 7b, 68b; Sifra Meṣoraʿ
Zabim Pereq 5 : 4, Weiss, p. 77a)

*Comment*: Eliezer grants the *Zab* or the *Zabah* the whole period on the presumption that nothing was emitted on the intervening days, so the required seven clean days have passed. Joshua grants them only the two days on which they actually examined themselves—a compromise position. But since the seven days are to be consecutive, it is an illogical compromise: either the intervening days were all clean, in which case Joshua should agree with Eliezer; or they were all in the presumption of uncleanness, and then only the seventh day will count toward the required seven clean days, as ʿAqiba says.

I.ii.165.A. R. Eliezer said to R. Joshua, "How do you say that the first day and the seventh day are clean, but the intervening ones are unclean?"

B. He said to him, "But you also agree concerning one who counts with interruptions (MSWRGYN) in the case of a Nazir who sits on *Sekhakh* (b.: *Who walked under overshadowing branches or mural projections* [under which was a corpse]); and concerning the one who sees a flux in the days of their counting, that they count with interruptions (MSWRGYN)."

C. R. Yosi and R. Simeon say, "The words of R. Eliezer are preferable to the words of R. Joshua, and the words of R. ʿAqiba are best of all, but the law is according to the words of R. Eliezer."

Tos. Nid. 9 : 13, Zuckermandel, p. 65, ls. 19-23 (b. Nid. 68b, 69a-b)

III.ii.84. TNY': R. Eliezer said to R. Joshua, "According to your view [that the first and seventh days are counted], you are counting with interruptions, but did not the Torah state, *After that she shall be clean* (Lev. 15 : 28)—meaning, after all of them, so that no uncleanness may intervene between them."

R. Joshua said to him, "Do you not agree that a *Zab* who saw an emission of semen or a Nazirite who walked under overshadowing branches or mural projections counts with interruptions, though the Torah has said, *But the former days shall be void* (Num. 6 : 12)."

b. Nid. 68b

### xxxii. Makhshirin, Zabim, Yadaim, ʿUqṣin

I.i.209.A. These [liquids] render unclean and render susceptible to uncleanness: The flux of a *Zab*, his spit, his semen, his urine, and a quarter-*log* [of blood] from a corpse, and the blood of a menstruant.

B. R. Eliezer says, "His [the *Zab's*] semen does not render susceptible to uncleanness."

C. R. Eleazar b. ʿAzariah says, "The blood of a menstruant does not render susceptible to uncleanness."

D. R. Simeon says, "The blood from a corpse does not render susceptible to uncleanness."

M. Maksh. 6 : 6

*Comment*: Unclean liquids simultaneously render susceptible to uncleanness and render unclean, so M. Maksh. 1 : 1: "Unclean liquids convey uncleanness whether their presence is acceptable or not." The list comes before B, C, and D, and each of the named masters then drops an item from it, agreeing, then, only on the flux, spit, and urine of the *Zab*.

See Epstein, *Tan.*, p. 209.

I.ii.166.A. Tos. Makhsh. 1 : 4, Zuckermandel, p. 673, ls. 28-31.

*Comment*: See *Phar.* II, pp. 314-316.

I.i.210.A. Whatever carries, or is carried upon, that which is used for lying [by a *Zab*] is clean, except for man.

Whatever carries or is carried on carrion (NBLH) is clean, except for him that moves it.

B. R. Eliezer [Camb., Parma, Kaufmann: Eleazar] says, "Also [except for] him that carried it."

C. Whatever carries or is carried on a corpse is clean, except for what overshadows it, or a man when he moves it.

M. Zab. 5 : 3

I.i.211.A. One who touches the flux of the *Zab*, his spit, his semen, and his urine, and the blood of a menstruant renders unclean at [the first] two [grades of uncleanness] and renders [Heave-offering] invalid at one [the third remove]. If he was separated [from the uncleanness] he [still] renders unclean at the first [grade of uncleanness and renders Heave-offering] invalid at one [a second remove].

B. It is all the same for one who touches and one who moves.

C. R. Eliezer [Camb., Parma, Kaufmann: Eleazar] says, "Also one who carries."

M. Zab. 5 : 7

*Comment*: The rule in M. Zab. 5 : 1 is that "whoever touches a *Zab* or is touched by him or moves the *Zab* or is moved by the *Zab* renders unclean food and liquid and vessels that can be made clean by immersing [of wood or metal]."

M. Zab. 5 : 3 then gives a general rule, which is glossed by Eliezer: Whoever carries that which a *Zab* may lie on but who has not actually touched it, or who is carried on top of that on which a *Zab* lies is clean, except for a man. A man who carries or is carried on top of it and did not touch it or shift it is unclean.

Eliezer enters the second clause in the general rule. Whoever carries or is carried on carrion is clean, except for the one who shifts the carrion—even without touching it. Eliezer says that the one who *carries* the carrion is also unclean. He would then revise the *Whoever carries or is carried*-clause, which conforms to the pattern of A, to read, *Whoever is carried... clean*, and accordingly, there would be no reference at all to the carrier; or the carrier would be referred to in the *except*-clause. M. Kel. 1 : 2 states that one who carries carrion is unclean: "They convey uncleanness to him that carries them, so that he too conveys uncleanness to garments by contact..." So the general rule of 5 : 3. A contradicts that of M. Kel. 1 : 2; alternately, M. Kel. 1 : 2 is formulated according to Eliezer's view. But Eliezer makes no appearance in that chapter.

M. Zab. 5 : 7. A is qualified by B, which adds *one who moves*, and this is qualified by Eliezer in C, *also one who carries.* The rule in M. Zab. 5 : 6-7 is that one who touches (etc.) renders unclean like a primary source of uncleanness; he therefore makes unconsecrated food that he touches unclean in the second grade of uncleanness, and this will render Heave-offering invalid. When he separates from the source of uncleanness, he renders unfit like that which is unfit in the first grade, that is, renders unconsecrated food unclean in the second degree, and this will render Heave-offering invalid, as above, M. Toh., p. 315.

See Epstein, *Nusaḥ*, pp. 565, 1176; *Tan*., p. 64.

I.ii.167.A. His semen [of the *Zab*]—

B. R. Eliezer says, "It does not render unclean in carrying."

C. And sages say, "It does render unclean in carrying, for it is not possible to [find] semen without urine."

Tos. Zab. 5 : 2, Zuckermandel, p. 679, ls. 31-3 (b. Naz. 66a: Joshua instead of sages; M. Maksh. 6 : 6; b. B.Q. 25a)

*Comment*: See Lieberman, *Tosefet Rishonim*, IV, p. 136. On the basis of b. Naz. we assign the whole set to our Eliezer.

I.i.212.A. On that day they said—

B. All the sacrifices which were slaughtered not for their own name are valid, though they do not go to their owner's credit for [meeting their] obligation, except for the Passover and the Sin-offering, the Passover in its appointed time, and the Sin-offering at all time.

C. R. Eliezer says, "Also the Guilt-offering."

M. Yad. 4 : 2

*Comment*: For the law, see above, M. Zev. 1 : 1. Here we have a narrative framework, but the text of the legal pericope has not been tampered with. See Epstein, *Tan*., pp. 125, 424-5.

I.i.23.A. On that day they said, "What of Ammon and Moab in the Seventh Year?"

R. Ṭarfon decreed, "[They must give] Poorman's Tithe."

And R. Eleazar b. ʿAzariah decreed, "[They must give] Second Tithe."

R. Ishmael said to him, "Eleazar b. ʿAzariah, thou must bring forth proof since thou givest the more stringent ruling; for every one that would give a more stringent ruling must bring forth proof."

R. Eleazar b. ʿAzariah said to him, "Ishmael my brother, it is not I that have changed the order of the years. Ṭarfon, my brother, has changed it, and he must bring forth proof."

R. Ṭarfon answered, "Egypt is outside the Land [of Israel] and Ammon and Moab are outside the Land [of Israel]; therefore as in Egypt Poorman's Tithe must be given in the Seventh Year, so in

Ammon and Moab Poorman's Tithe must be given in the Seventh Year."

R. Eleazar b. ʿAzariah answered, "Babylon is outside the Land [of Israel], and Ammon and Moab are outside the Land [of Israel]; therefore as in Babylon Second Tithe must be given in the Seventh Year, so in Ammon and Moab Second Tithe must be given in the Seventh Year."

R. Ṭarfon said, "On Egypt, because it is near, have they imposed Poorman's Tithe, that the poor of Israel might be stayed thereby in the Seventh Year; so, too, on Ammon and Moab, which are near, have they imposed Poorman's Tithe, that the poor of Israel might be staved thereby in the Seventh Year."

R. Eleazar b. ʿAzariah answered, "Lo, thou art as one that would bestow on them worldly gain, yet thou art but as one that would suffer souls to perish; thou wouldest rob the heavens so that they send down neither dew nor rain, for it is written, *Will a man rob God? yet ye rob me. But ye say, Wherein have we robbed thee? In tithes and heave offerings* (Malachi 3 : 8)."

R. Joshua said, "Lo, I am as one that will answer on behalf of Ṭarfon my brother, but not according to the subject of his words. [The rule touching] Egypt is a new work, and [the rule touching] Babylon is an old work, and the argument before us is a new work; let us argue concerning a new work from a new work, but let us not argue concerning a new work from an old work. [The rule touching] Egypt is the work of the elders; but [the rule touching] Babylon is the work of the Prophets, and the issue before us is the work of the elders; let us argue concerning a work of the elders from a work of the elders, but let us not argue concerning a work of the elders from a work of the Prophets."

B. They voted and decided that Ammon and Moab should give Poorman's Tithe in the Seventh Year.

C. And when R. Yosi the son of the Damascene (DRMSQYT) came to R. Eliezer in Lydda, he said to him, "What new thing did you have in the House of Study today?"

D. He said to him, "They voted and decided that Ammon and Moab must give Poorman's Tithe in the Seventh Year."

E. R. Eliezer wept and said, "*The secret of the Lord is with them that fear him, and he will show them this covenant* (Ps. 25 : 14). Go and tell them, 'Be not anxious by reason of your voting, for I have received a tradition from Rabban Yoḥanan b. Zakkai, who heard it from his teacher, and his teacher from his teacher, as a *Halakhah* given to Moses from Sinai, that Ammon and Moab give Poorman's Tithe in the Seventh Year.' "

M. Yad. 4 : 3, trans. Danby, pp. 782-783 (b. Hag. 3b)

*Comment*: C-E is attached to the antecedent pericope, but is independent of it. Eliezer's materials are excluded from *on-that day* collection, but, as noted in M. Yad. 4 : 2 (p. 332), the *on-that-day* superscription is attached to an Eliezer-pericope, leaving the impression that Eliezer was absent from the consistory that deposed Gamaliel, but that his traditions were accepted at that consistory.

The story of Yosi's report to Eliezer concludes with the citation, as a law received from Yoḥanan b. Zakkai, and by him from his master (RBW) back to Sinai, with *A law given to Moses at Sinai* interpolated in exactly the language adopted at Yavneh! See *Development*, pp. 69, 202.

I.ii.168.A. R. Yosi b. Durmusqit said, "I was with the first elders when they were coming from Yavneh to Lud. And I came and found R. Eliezer, who was sitting in the stall of the bakers in Lud.

B. "He said, 'What new thing did you have in the house of study today?'

"I said to him, 'We are your students and drink from your waters.'

"He said to me, 'Even so, what new thing?'

"I told to him the laws and the responses in voting (BMYNYN), and when I came to this one, his eyes welled with tears.

C. "He said, '*The secret of the Lord is to those that fear him and he will show them his covenant* (Ps. 25 : 14), and it says, *For the Lord God will not do anything without revealing his secret to his servants the prophets* (Amos 3 : 2).

" 'Tell them, Do not doubt your vote. I have a tradition from Rabban Yoḥanan b. Zakkai, who received it as a tradition from the pairs, and the pairs from the prophets, and the prophets from Moses, as a law to Moses at Sinai, that Ammon and Moab give Poorman's Tithe in the Seventh Year.' "

Tos. Yad. 2 : 16, Zuckermandel, p. 683, ls. 18-26 (b. Hag. 3b)

*Comment*: See Lieberman, *Tosefet Rishonim* IV, pp. 157-8. The consistory is dropped, but C is identical in both versions, therefore is independent, possibly also prior. While M. has a long account of *on that day*, Tos. knows only a routine encounter, with a cliché of courtesy (B) to introduce the operative saying.

Note also b. Yev. 16a, where Dosa b. Harkinas says to Joshua, Eleazar b. ʿAzariah, and ʿAqiba, "I call heaven and earth to witness that upon this mortar (MDWKH) the prophet Haggai sat and taught three things: (1) A daughter's rival is forbidden; (2) Ammon and Moab give Poorman's Tithe in Seventh Year; (3) Proselytes are accepted from the Cordyenians and Tarmodites [Palmyrenes]."

This ruling is identical in content and wording, but the story-teller in b. Yev. 16a knows nothing about the other "historical" setting in which it is cited. Eliezer is not involved, nor does anyone know that Yoḥanan b. Zakkai has said the same thing. The tradition therefore comes down in two quite different settings, unrelated to one another (unless there is some connection between Hyrcanus and Harkinas—HRQNWS/HRKYNS—and I see none). The ruling itself, because of its substance, must come after 70. But that does not help us in finding a *terminus ante quem* for either of the "historical" settings assigned to it—the deposition of Gamaliel and the vote of the consistory, a tradition received by Yoḥanan b. Zakkai from Moses, or a teaching of Haggai the prophet. None seems to me more credible than the others. In any event the law cannot be assigned to Eliezer.

It is curious that Eliezer will accept Eleazar's reasoning. For Eleazar takes for granted that the Babylonian Jews have to give tithes at all, while Eliezer holds—in a very-well attested tradition—that the agricultural rules do not apply abroad. But in another aspect, Eliezer will agree with the rejection of Ṭarfon's reasoning, for if Ammon and Moab are outside of the Land of Israel, then they are rightly compared to Egypt. The dispute about the status of Syria makes this point perfectly clear. If Eliezer regards Ammon and Moab as outside of the land of Israel, they therefore will not have to give any tithes at all, and the issue is simply irrelevant. Consequently, Eliezer is represented as regarding Ammon and Moab as no different from the Land of Israel.

Just as he is supposed to regard Syria as Jewish, so he holds Ammon and Moab are Jewish—and he further represents Yoḥanan b. Zakkai as laying claim in behalf of the Jews to considerable gentile territories. These facts render all the more puzzling the allegation that Joshua, Eleazar, and ʿAqiba know nothing either about Yoḥanan's opinion or about Eliezer's agreement with it. The story in M. Yad. therefore looks spurious, and its object, to make Yoḥanan and Eliezer into crypto-Zealots, seems still more likely to contradict the truth. The story is in the same stratum as the one about the Jews' claim to Syria and forms part of a larger effort to claim Eliezer as a pro-war, pro-Zealot, anti-Roman authority—and to claim Yoḥanan in the bargain!

I.i.214.A. A beehive—

B. R. Eliezer says, "Lo, it is like immovable property:

1. "And they write a *prozbul* on it[s security].

2. "And it does not receive uncleanness [while it remains] in its place.

3. "And he who scrapes honey from it on the Sabbath is liable."

C. And sages say, "It is not like immovable property:

1. "And they do not write the *prozbul* on it[s security];

2. "And it receives uncleanness in its place;

3. "And he who scrapes honey from it on the Sabbath is exempt [from punishment]."

M. Shev. 10 : 7 [= M. Uqs. 3 : 10]
(y. Shev. 10 : 3; b. B.B. 65b, 80a-b)

*Comment*: B.1,2,3 and C.1,2,3 spell out what is implicit in B and C and therefore look like extended glosses, making explicit what is already obvious. *And* is awkwardly used as a joining-word. So the issue is phrased in QRQʿ +/— ʾYN. The setting is laws of the *prozbul*; 10 : 3 relates the origins of the *prozbul*; 10 : 4 gives the formula; 10 : 5 and 10 : 6 deal with details of writing the *prozbul.* 10 : 6 says that a *prozbul* may only be written for a loan secured by immovable property. Then the issue of the bee-hive is raised, because of the reference to *prozbul.*

In M. ʿUqs. 3 : 10 the pericope is part of a small collection on bee-hives (3 : 10) and honeycombs (3 : 11)—with no more integral connection to the setting there than here.

Before redaction, the pericope stood by itself, beginning with Bee-hive—QRQʿ +/— ʾYN, then with the consequences spelled out (1,2,3), finally in completed form, set wherever it might (appropriately) go.

I.i.215.A. A beehive—

B. R. Eliezer says, "Lo, it is like immovable property (QRQʿ). And they write a *Prozbul* on its basis, and it does not receive uncleanness [when standing] in its place, and he that collects honey from it on the Sabbath is liable for a Sin-offering."

C. And sages say, "It is not like immovable property, and they do not write a *Prozbul* on its basis, and it does receive uncleanness [when standing] in its place, and he that collects honey from it on the Sabbath is free of liability."

M. Uqs. 3 : 10

I.ii.169.A. R. Judah said, "R. Eliezer and sages did not differ concerning honey-combs, that they do not receive uncleanness in their spread-out parts (BʾBYHN)...

B. "Concerning what did they differ? Concerning the Sabbath and the Seventh Year, for—

C. "R. Eliezer says, 'Lo, it is like immovable property.'

D. "And sages so, 'Lo, it is like a vessel.'

E. "But if it was covered with mud, all agree that it is like immovable property for every purpose..."

Tos. Uqs. 3 : 15, Zuckermandel, p. 689,
ls. 32-3, p. 690, ls. 1-3

*Comment*: See Lieberman, *Tosefet Rishonim*, IV, p. 189. Accordingly, Judah removes reference to uncleanness, leaving the issue of collecting honey on the Sabbath and writing a *Prozbul* on the basis of the beehive. Judah is sufficient warrant for assigning these materials to our Eliezer.
See Epstein, *Tan.*, p. 99.

### xxxiii. ʿEduyyot

I.ii.170.A. The law always is according to the opinion of the majority.

B. The opinion of the individual is mentioned among the majority only to render it invalid.

C. R. Judah says, "The opinion of the individual is mentioned among the majority only because, perhaps the time may require it, and they may rely on it" [so one may follow Eliezer's law if necessary].

D. And sages say, "The words of the individual are mentioned only among the majority only because, since this one says unclean, and this one says clean, this one said unclean according to the words of R. Eliezer.

"They [may] say to him, 'According to the words of R. Eliezer have you heard [and your tradition therefore is invalid]'."

Tos. Ed. 1 : 4, Zuckermandel, p. 455, ls. 6-9

*Comment*: M. Ed. 1 : 6 attributes the end of D to Judah:

> R. Judah said, "If so, why do they record the opinion of the individual against that of the majority when it does not prevail? That if one shall say, 'I have received such a tradition,' another may answer, 'You heard it only as the opinion of such-a-one.' "

Now Tos. supplies *Eliezer* in place of *such-a-one*. Judah the Patriarch evidently substituted for Eliezer's name an anonymous authority. Lieberman observes (*Tosefet Rishonim*, II, p. 181 [and *Tosefta Kifshuṭah Seder Zeraʿim ad loc.*]) that Tos. Hal. 1 : 10 (Zuckermandel, p. 98, l. 10) has "Is not *so-and-so* in the south, and he would teach this teaching," and *so-and-so* is then identified as Eliezer. Judah's explanation preserves the possibility of following *so-and-so* = Eliezer. The sages take for granted one will not do so. The story about Rabbi (b. Nid., p. 325) is in accord with Judah's view.

I.i.216.A. Three things did they say before R. ʿAqiba, two in the name of R. Eliezer and one in the name of R. Joshua.

B. Two in the name of R. Eliezer:

C. (1) "A woman may go out [on the Sabbath] wearing a 'golden city'.

D. (2) "And pigeon-flyers are not eligible to bear witness."

E. And one in the name of R. Joshua: "If a weasel had a [dead] creeping thing in its mouth, and it passed over loaves of Heave-offering and it is in doubt whether [the creeping thing] touched them or did not touch them, their condition of doubt is deemed clean."

M. Ed. 2 : 7, trans. Danby, p. 426 (y. R.H. 1 : 7; Witness: y. Sanh. 3 : 5, y. Shavu. 7 : 4)

*Comment*: See M. Shab. 6 : 1 and M. Sanh. 3 : 3. Neither includes a reference to Eliezer. M. Shab. 6 : 1 says a woman may not go out with the 'golden city'; M. Sanh. 3 : 3 says pigeon-flyers may not bear witness, as is here attributed to Eliezer. As to E, see M. Toh. 4 : 2, where Eliezer does not occur. M. R.H. 1 : 7 likewise omits Eliezer, but y. R.H. 1 : 7 says it is his teaching.

See Epstein, *Tan*., pp. 433, 451 n. 43, 288.

I.ii.171.A. Three things they said before R. ʿAqiba, two in the name of R. Eliezer, and one in the name of R. Joshua, and he [ʿAqiba] did not say to them either prohibited or permitted, valid or invalid, unclean or clean.

B. Two in the name of R. Eliezer:

C. A woman: what is the law as to her going out with a 'city of gold.' And [ʿAqiba) did not say concerning her either prohibited or permitted.

C. R. Eliezer permits, and sages prohibit.

D. Those who fly pigeons—are they permitted to testify?

E. He did not say to them either valid or invalid.

F. And R. Eliezer declares valid, and the sages declare invalid.

G. One in the name of R. Joshua:

H. The creeping thing in the mouth of the weasel, and the weasel is walking on top of loaves of Heave-offering, but it is in doubt whether it touched or did not touch them—

I. R. Eliezer declares clean

J. And R. Joshua declare unclean

K. And sages say, "What is certainly unclean is in doubt as to whether it is clean."

Tos. Ed. 1 : 10, Zuckermandel, p. 456, ls. 1-9

*Comment*: For H-K, see M. Toh. 4 : 2. Tos. spells out B-C and D-F as fully articulated legal pericopae, rather than merely citing Eliezer's opinion as in M. Ed. 2 : 7. M. Toh. 4 : 2 is consistent with Eliezer in H-K.

I.ii.172.A. Four things does R. Eliezer declare clean and the sages unclean:

B. (1) The comb of the cooler—

C. R. Eliezer says, "It does not render unclean as to its air-space."

D. And sages say, "It renders unclean as to its air-space."

E. (2) The shelf of the bakers which they fixed with a nail, joined with a joist (MRYŠ) or with a beam (QWRH)—

F. R. Eliezer declares clean.

G. And sages declare unclean.

H. (3) A shoe on the last—

I. R. Eliezer declares clean.

J. And sages declare unclean.

K. (4) He slices it into rings [the oven] and puts sand between each ring—

L. R. Eliezer declares clean.

M. And sages declare unclean.

N. And it was called the 'Oven of ʿAkhnai,' concerning which disputes multiplied in Israel.

Tos. Ed. 2 : 1, Zuckermandel, p. 457, ls. 4-8

I.ii.173.A. Twenty-four lenient rulings of the House of Shammai and stringent rulings of the House of Hillel:

B. An egg born on the festival—

C. Others say in the name of R. Eliezer, "It may be eaten, both it and its mother."

Tos. Ed. 2 : 2, Zuckermandel, p. 457, ls. 9-11, Tos. Ed. 2 : 1

*Comment*: 2 : 1, B-D = M. Kel. 2 : 8; E-G = M. Kel. 15 : 2; H-J = M. Kel. 26 : 4; K-M = M. Kel. 5 : 10. Tos. Ed. 2 : 2 = Tos. Y.T. 1 : 1, Zuckermandel, p. 200, 1. 27.

I.ii.174. R. Eliezer says, "Two rulings of the lenient rulings of the House of Shammai and the strict rulings of the House of Hillel," etc.

Tos. Ed. 2 : 8, Zuckermandel, p. 458, ls. 16ff.

*Comment*: See *Phar.* II, pp. 342-343.

I.ii.175.A. R. Joshua and R. Pappyas testified concerning the shelf of the bakers which they fastened with a joist (MRYŠ) or with a beam, or that they fixed a nail, that it is unclean.

B. And R. Eliezer declares it clean.

C. And if he did not fix it sufficiently, all agree that it is unclean.

Tos. Ed. 3 : 1, Zuckermandel, p. 459, ls. 12-13

*Comment*: Now the *sages* of Tos. Ed. 2 : 1 = M. Kel. 15 : 2 are Joshua and Pappyas.

I.i.217.A. R. Joshua and R. Neḥunya b. Elinatan of Kefar HaBavli testified [sing.] concerning a limb from a corpse [even less than an olive's bulk, if it is a complete limb] that it is unclean.

B. [For] R. Eliezer says, "They spoke only about a limb from a living being [M. Oh. 1 : 7]."

C. They said to him, "Is it not a *qal veḥomer*: A limb which separates from the living being, which is clean, is unclean, A limb which separates from a corpse, which is unclean, will it not be unclean?"

D. He said to them, "They spoke only about a limb from a living being."

E. "Another matter: The uncleanness of living beings is greater than the uncleanness of corpses, for the living being renders that on which he lies and sits capable of rendering man and clothing unclean, and he also conveys *maddaf*-uncleanness to what is above him, so that they convey uncleanness to food and liquids, an uncleanness the corpse does not convey."

M. Ed. 6 : 2

*Comment*: The issue is whether less than the prescribed quantity of bone renders unclean in a tent. The tradition cited by Joshua and Neḥunya is that the limb of a corpse renders unclean. Eliezer's saying is joined by Š, which has no place here.

His reply is that the tradition concerns only the smaller than prescribed quantity of a limb from a living person, that it renders unclean. In C we have a *qal veḥomer*, which Eliezer does not reject in D. He simply repeats his saying in B. Then in E he supplies a refutation for the *qal veḥomer*, namely: What is regarded as a lesser source of uncleanness in C is in fact the greater source of uncleanness. Either D or E is superfluous, probably D. Eliezer's proof is that the uncleanness produced by the living being is greater than that produced by a corpse, for there are more forms of uncleanness produced by the former than the latter; for instance, the *Zab* (M. Zab 4 : 6) produces greater and more stringent uncleanness than the corpse, which renders unclean only the vessel which touches it, as in M. Oh. 1 : 2.

I.i.218.A. An olive's bulk of flesh which separates from a limb from a living being—

B. R. Eliezer declares unclean [in a Tent, as if it were from a corpse].

C. And R. Joshua and R. Neḥunya declare clean.

D. A bone about a barleycorn in bulk which separates from a limb from a living being—

E. R. Neḥunya declares unclean [in contact and carrying, like that from a corpse].

F. And R. Eliezer and R. Joshua declare [it] clean.

G. They said to R. Eliezer, "On what basis do you declare unclean an olive's bulk of flesh which separates from a limb from a living being?"

H. He said to them, "We find that a limb from a living being is like a whole corpse. Just as an olive's bulk of flesh which separates from it [the corpse] is unclean, so an olive's bulk of flesh which separates from the limb of a living being should be unclean."

I. They said to him, "No. If you have declared unclean an olive's bulk of flesh which separates from the corpse, the reason is that you have declared unclean a bone as much as a barleycorn which separates from it. But will you declare unclean an olive's bulk of flesh which separates from the limb of a living being, when you have declared clean a bone as much as a barleycorn which separates from him?" [Eliezer's inconsistency defeats him.]

J. They said to R. Neḥunya, "Why do you declare unclean the bone a barleycorn in bulk which separates from a limb from a living being?"

K. He said to them, "We have found that a limb from a living being is like a whole corpse. Now if a bone the size of a barley corn which separates from a corpse is unclean, so the bone the size of a barleycorn which separates from a living being should be unclean."

L. They said to him, "No. If you have declared unclean the bone a barleycorn in size which separates from a corpse, you have also declared unclean flesh an olive's bulk which separates from him. But will you declare unclean a bone a barleycorn's size which separates from a limb from a living being, when you have declared clean an olive's bulk of flesh which separates from him?" [Likewise, Neḥunya is inconsistent.]

M. They said to R. Eliezer, "For what reason did you divide your rules? Either declare unclean in both cases or declare clean in both cases."

N. He said to them, "Greater is the uncleanness of flesh than the uncleanness of bones, for flesh[-uncleanness] applies both to corpses and to creeping things, which is not the case with bones.

"Moreover, a limb which has the appropriate amount of flesh renders unclean through contact, carrying, and in a Tent; if it lacks flesh, it is [still] unclean; if it lacks bone, it is clean." [= Which depends on which?]

O. They said to R. Neḥunya, "Why have you divided your rules? Either declare unclean in both cases, or declare clean in both cases."

P. He said to them, "Greater is the uncleanness of bones than the uncleanness of flesh, for flesh which separates from the living being is clean, but a bone which separates from him which is as it was created [in its natural state] is unclean.

Q. "Another matter: An olives' bulk of flesh renders unclean in contact and in carrying and in the Tent, and the greater part of the bones render unclean in touching, carrying and Tent. If the flesh is lacking, it is clean. If the greater part of the bones is lacking, even though it is clean so far as Tent is concerned, it renders unclean through contact and carrying.

R. "Another matter: All flesh of the corpse which is less than an olive's bulk is clean. The greater part of the corpse's bulk and members, although they are not a quarter[-*qav*], is unclean."

S. They said to R. Joshua, "On what basis did you declare clean in both cases?"

T. He said to them, "No, if you have said so concerning the corpse, to which apply the terms 'greater part,' 'quarter,' and 'corpse-dust' (RB RBʿ RQB), will you say so concerning the living being, to which do not apply the terms 'greater part,' 'quarter,' and 'corpse dust'? "

M. Ed. 6 : 3 (b. Hul. 129b)

*Comment*: This elegant pericope supplies a full account of the reasoning of three parties, with three sets of opinions, ending with Joshua's explanation for his view. Since Joshua is not contradicted, the presumption is that he wins the argument.

M. Ed. 6 : 2 dealt with the uncleanness of a limb from a living being, which Eliezer regards as unclean, and the limb from a corpse, which Joshua and Neḥunya say is clean. In M. Ed. 6 : 3 we have two rules, on an olive's bulk of flesh from a limb from a living being. Here both parties are consistent with the foregoing. The limb is unclean, so is the flesh, according to Eliezer; and Joshua and Neḥunya rule as they do before. Then comes a bone from the limb of a living being. Now Neḥunya and Eliezer change positions. Eliezer says it is clean, Neḥunya says it is unclean, though the limb is unclean according to Eliezer, and clean according to Neḥunya. Joshua remains consistent. He says that whatever comes from the limb is clean, just as he says the limb itself is clean.

Each party is then asked, Why do you declare unclean? Why do you declare clean? How do you distinguish one from the other?

Eliezer compares the limb from a living being to a whole corpse. Just as a bit of flesh which separates from a corpse is unclean, so will the flesh separated from a limb from a living being be unclean. They reply that Eliezer is not consistent. He has declared unclean an olive's bulk of flesh which separates from a corpse and likewise of bone. But he has also declared clean a piece of bone which separates from a living being. He should not be inconsistent in respect to the flesh. The question therefore underlines the alleged inconsistency of Eliezer's rulings. The same is the case with Neḥunya in J-K-L.

M then introduces a new question for Eliezer and Neḥunya. Each now is asked the basis for his inconsistency. Eliezer says that the uncleanness of flesh is greater than that of bones. Therefore in B he says the flesh is unclean, but in F he says the bone is clean. Flesh-uncleanness pertains to corpses and creeping things. A limb with flesh renders unclean. A limb without flesh is unclean. But a limb without bone is clean, so flesh is more susceptible to uncleanness than bone.

In O-P-Q-R Neḥunya is supplied with three answers. First, he states that bones are more unclean than flesh. Flesh that separates from a living being is clean (as in C); bone is unclean (as in E). To this point Neḥunya has simply repeated his original ruling. Then, in Q, he points out that if flesh is lacking, what remains is clean. But if the bones are lacking in the requisite quantity, they *still* render unclean in contact and carrying, for a bone as much as a barleycorn's bulk will render unclean in those respects. Further, less than the requisite quantity of flesh is clean. But less than the requisite quantity (quarter-*qav*) of bones is still unclean, if the larger parts of the bulk and number of the bones of the corpse are present.

Finally, Joshua is asked his reason. He says that the corpse is different from the living creature, therefore what is separated from a limb of a living creature, whether flesh or bone, is clean. He alludes to three key-words, *greater part*, meaning, the greater part of the bones of a corpse render unclean; a *quarter-qav*, a quarter-*qav* of bones even *not* the greater part of the corpse will render unclean; and *corpse-dust*, which renders unclean. None of these applies to the limb of the living being.

The pericope is beautifully balanced. Each party gets to give his reasons for his rulings, and no one is refuted, except by other parties to the argument.

I.ii.176.A. An olive's bulk of flesh which separates from a limb from a living being—

B. R. Eliezer declares unclean.

C. Rabbi [Judah the Patriarch] said, "They answered R. Eliezer three replies:

D. "No, if you have said so concerning the corpse, to which apply the rules RWB RWBʿ HQB [Should be: RQB, as in M. Ed. 6 : 3], will you say so concerning the limb from the living being, to which do not apply RWB RWBʿ and RQB?"

E. "Another matter: What depends on what? Does the limb

depend on the flesh, or does the flesh depend on the limb? The flesh depends on the limb. Is it possible that the flesh renders unclean with contact, carrying, and in a Tent, and the limb should be clean?"

F. R. Simeon said, "I should be astonished if R. Eliezer declared it unclean [in all circumstances]. He declared it unclean only when there is on the limb the appropriate amount of flesh, so that both should render unclean in contact and in carrying and in a Tent."

G. A bone about the size of a barleycorn which separates from a limb from a living being—

H. R. Neḥunya declares it unclean.

J. They answered R. Neḥunya three replies, etc.

Tos. Ed. 2 : 10, Zuckermandel, p. 458, ls. 27-32, p. 459, ls. 1-9

*Comment*: We have only two replies to Eliezer. D is Joshua's, E is similar to M. Ed. 6 : 3 N. In M. Ed. 6 : 2-3 we do not have three replies. Each authority is dealt with separately.

I.ii.177.A. An olive's bulk of flesh taken from the limb of a living person—

B. R. Eliezer declares unclean.

C. They answered him three answers.

D. "No. If you have said so concerning the corpse, on which there is the greater part of a quarter[-*qav*] of rottenness (RQB), will you say so concerning a limb from a living man, on which there is not the greater part of a quarter[-*qav*] of rottenness?

E. "Another matter: What depends on what? Does the limb depend on the flesh, or does the flesh depend on the limb? The flesh depends on the limb. Is it possible that the flesh will make unclean by contact and carrying in a Tent, and yet the limb will be clean?"

F. R. Simeon said, "I should be astonished if R. Eliezer declared it unclean [under all circumstances]. He declared it unclean only when there is on the limb sufficient flesh so that both should render unclean in contact and carrying and in a Tent."

Tos. Ahilot 2 : 7, Zuckermandel, p. 599, ls. 9-15

*Comment*: See M. Ed. 6 : 2-3, Tos. Ed. 2 : 10, Zuckermandel, p. 458, 1 : 28ff. The passage here supplements M. Oh. 2 : 6, in which Eliezer does not occur.

I.i.219.A. R. Joshua and R. Ṣaddoq testified that:

B. If the redemption[-lamb] for the firstborn of an ass died, the priest has no more claim therein.

C. R. Eliezer says, "The owner is still answerable for it, as [in like case he is answerable for] the five *selas*, [the redemption price] for a [firstborn] son."

D. But the sages say, "He is not answerable for it as [in like case he is not answerable for] the redemption price of Second Tithe."

M. Ed. 7 : 1

*Comment*: See M. Bekh. 1 : 6, p. 248; Epstein, *Tan.*, p. 439.

I.i.220. R. Joshua and R. Yaqqim of Haddar testified that:
If the jar containing [the ashes of] the Sin-offering was set on top of a creeping thing, it became unclean, whereas R. Eliezer declared it clean.

M. Ed. 7 : 5

*Comment*: See M. Par. 10 : 3, p. 311; Epstein, *Tan.*, p. 440

I.i.221.A. R. Joshua and R. Pappyas testified that the young of a Peace-offering could be offered as a Peace-offering, whereas R. Eliezer says, "The young of a Peace-offering may not be offered as a Peace-offering." But the sages say, "It may be so offered."

B. R. Pappyas said, "I testify that we had a heifer that was a Peace-offering; we consumed it at Passover and we consumed its young as a Peace-offering at the following feast [of Pentecost]."

M. Ed. 7 : 6

*Comment*: See M. Tem. 3 : 1, p. 253.

I.i.211.A. They testified that the baking-boards of bakers are susceptible to uncleanness, whereas R. Eliezer declared them insusceptible.

B. They testified that if a baking-oven was cut up into rings and sand put between each ring, it still remains susceptible to uncleanness, whereas R. Eliezer declared it insusceptible.

M. Ed. 7 : 7 (M. Ed. 7 : 1, 5-7; I follow trans. Danby, pp. 434-435; b. Meg. 10b)

*Comment*: A: See M. Kel. 15 : 2, p. 282. B: M. Kel. 5 : 10, p. 278. See Epstein, *Tan.*, pp. 66, 434, 466, 481.
N.B. M. Ed. 8 : 6 is discussed below, p. 398.

[I.i.223. M. Ed. 8 : 4 is cited by Eliezer, Sifra Shemini Parashah 8 : 5, Weiss, p. 55a. See *Phar.* I, pp. 61-2, 70-71, 80-81. On 8 : 4 see also Epstein, *Tan.*, pp. 505-6; *Nusaḥ*, pp. 181, 1153. Note also b. Nid. 18b-19a.]

APPENDIX TO CHAPTER TWO

# LEGAL PERICOPAE NOT DEMONSTRABLY PART OF THE TRADITIONS ABOUT ELIEZER BEN HYRCANUS

The following pericopae, chiefly in Mishnah-Tosefta, cannot be either reliably assigned to, or decisively excluded from, the traditions about Eliezer b. Hyrcanus. Those in which an Eliezer disputes a matter of law with Simeon or Judah, however, are apt not to be our Eliezer's, for Simeon is, in ʿAqiban sources, normally taken to be Simeon b. Yoḥai, and Judah is generally Judah b. Ilai, both Ushan masters; Judah in addition would normally stand with, not opposed to, our Eliezer. Nonetheless, I see sufficient ambiguity to record the pericopae here.

I.i.224. "They do not bless the wine until he places in it water," the words of R. Eliezer.

And the sages say, "They bless."

M. Ber. 7 : 5

*Comment*: The clause appears at the end of a Mishnaic pericope to which it is irrelevant. It stands wholly by itself. The issue is whether the undiluted wine is regarded as wine, that is, before it is properly prepared with water. Eliezer holds it gets no special blessing. The sages differ. The presupposition then is that the undiluted wine is not blessed at all. But, as we shall see, other versions take for granted some blessing is said but have Eliezer and the sages differ on precisely which blessing is to be used. Hence the Tos. + y + b.-versions all narrow the range of difference. In another (Ushan) form, it would have been:

> "R. Eliezer and the sages did not differ as to whether they bless. All agree they do bless. Concerning what did they differ? Concerning how they bless for
>
> "R. Eliezer says, 'They say, Creator of the fruit of the tree.'
>
> "And sages say, 'Creator of the fruit of the vine.' "

Facing this form, or something like it, we should have supposed the Mishnaic version comes before the Tos. + y. + b.-versions. Hence we had best regard the one before us as the beginning of the matter.

I.ii.128.A. "Fresh wine (YYN ḤY)—they bless over it, 'Creator of the fruit of the tree,' and they wash hands with it.

B. "And if he mixed in it water, they bless over it, 'Creator of the fruit of the vine,' and do not wash hands with it,"—the words of R. Eliezer.

C. And the sages say, "In either case, they bless over it, 'Creator of the fruit of the vine,' and they do not wash hands with it."

Tos. Ber. 4 : 3, Lieberman,
p. 18, l. 5-p. 19, l. 8 (b. Ber. 50b)

III.i.13.A. "Wine—when it is in its original state (BZMN ŠHWʾ KMWT ŠHWʾ), one says over it, '... Who creates the fruit of the tree,' and they do *not* wash hands with it. When it is mixed, one says over it, '... Creator of the fruit of the vine' and they do wash hands with it,"— the words of R. Eliezer.

B. And sages say, "Whether in its original state (ḤY) or mixed, they say over it, '... Creator of the fruit of the vine' and wash hands with it."

y. Ber. 6 : 1, Repr. Gilead, p. 83

B. "They do not bless the wine until he puts wine in it,"—the words of R. Eliezer.

And sages say, "They bless."

y. Ber. 7 : 5, Repr. Gilead, p. 110

III.ii.85.A. TNW RBNN: "Wine—Before he placed into it water, they do not bless over it, '... Creator of the fruit of the vine,' but, '... Creator of the fruit of the tree,' and they wash hands with it. When he has placed into it water, they bless over it '... Creator of the fruit of the vine,' and they do not wash hands with it,"—the words of R. Eliezer.

B. And sages say, "In one case or the other, they bless over it, '... Creator of the fruit of the vine,' and they do not wash hands with it."

b. Ber. 50b

*Comment*: In the Mishnah Eliezer's opinion omits reference to washing the hands. Eliezer holds that until the wine is mixed with water, it is not blessed at all. However, Tos., y., and b. all introduce new issues:

| *M. Ber. 7 : 5* | *Tos. Ber. 4 : 3* | *y. Ber. 6 : 1* | *b. Ber. 50b* |
|---|---|---|---|
| 1. They do not bless wine until he places into it water, the words of R. Eliezer. | 1. YYN ḤY—they *bless* over it Creator of the fruit of the tree | 1. YYN-BZMN ŠHWʾ KMWT ŠHWʾ He says " " " [= Tos.] | 1. YYN—Before he placed in it water, they do not bless over it Creator of the fruit of the wine but Creator of the fruit of the tree |
| 2. — — | 2. and they wash with it the hands | 2. " " *not* " " | 2. and they *wash* " " " |

| | | | |
|---|---|---|---|
| 3. — — | 3. And if he placed within it water they bless over it Creator of the fruit of the vine, and they do not wash hands with it—the words of R. Eliezer | 3. BZMN SHW' MZWG *he says* over it " " " | 3. After he has placed into it water, they bless over it " " " |
| 4. And sages say, They bless. | 4. In either case they bless over it Creator of the fruit of the vine and they do not wash with it the hands. | 4. BYN HY BYN MZWG they say over it " " " and they *do wash* " " " | 4. " " " [= Tos.] |

The minor differences between Tos. and y. are in word-choice—*say vs. bless.* The major differences come in no. 2: *Do they wash?* b. follows Tos. in all important respects; the changes in word-choices are minor and characteristic. But y. holds one washes, where Tos. holds one does *not* wash, and this is an important difference. All versions, moreover, ignore the Mishnah, which excludes the detail as to whether or not one washes hands with the wine. The Mishnah's version certainly is preferable, since the normal rule is that one does not waste liquid-foods in ritual-washings.

I.i.225.A. He who has gathered the *pe'ah* and said, "Lo this is for so-and-so, a poor man [Parma omits: ʿNY]"—

B. R. Eliezer says, "He was acquired it for him."

C. And sages say, "Let him give it to the poor man that is found first."

M. Pe'ah 4 : 9 (b. Git. 12a; b. B.M. 96)

*Comment*: Eliezer's saying completes the statement of the case. The sages do not complete the statement, but respond to Eliezer's saying instead: *He has not acquired ... but let him ...* In other words, one simply cannot set aside *pe'ah* for a particular man. Without B the sages could have said simply, "Has not done a thing (L' ʿŚH KLWM)" or some such. But it is equally possible that once Eliezer introduced his opinion, it was necessary to revise the completed sentence of A; B thus requires the formulation of C in its present form, instead of our projected conclusion.

This raises the question, was A originally a complete rule, or did Eliezer formulate A in order to complete it as he does in B? From C we can derive no help, for obvious reasons. M. Pe'ah 5 : 2 supplies a useful model. There the introductory statement of the problem, A, is followed by the completion of the sentence in B. Then in C Eliezer, in the position of the sages here, questions the whole of the foregoing ruling. So 4 : 9 A ought to have been followed by a completion of the opening statement in B. Eliezer's saying in B has taken the place of whatever was in that opening rule. If the whole were to have been assigned to Eliezer, it would have read, '*He who has gathered ... to him,*" *the words of R. Eliezer.* It looks as if Eliezer's saying has forced the dropping of an antecedent rule, which has then been reinstated in the opinion of the "sages"—who then are in the position of the lost opening rule. It therefore seems as though Eliezer here is in the position of commenting upon, and revising, a pre-existing statement of law.

One might argue that here Eliezer is consistent with the view of the House of Shammai that one may make use of tithes for the poor—in the Seventh Year—both by favor and not by favor. Here likewise one may show favor to a particular poor man. But since I cannot find in the *Gemarot* evidence that the matter was interpreted in this way, I am not certain Eliezer's opinion actually accords with, or even is relevant to, that of the House of Shammai; therefore the pericope cannot be demonstrated to belong to our Eliezer.

I.i.226.A. An ear of corn belonging to the Gleanings which was mixed up with the standing wheat—

B. He tithes one sheaf of wheat and gives [it] to him [the poor man].

C. R. Eliezer said, "But how shall this poor man exchange something which has not come into his possession? But he [the owner] gives possession to the poor man for the whole heap, and then tithes a sheaf of wheat and gives [it] to him."

M. Pe'ah 5 : 2 (y. Pe'ah 5 : 2)

*Comment*: As noted, Eliezer here comments on a completed rule. The problem is how to tithe the property of the poor man. One must give him properly tithed food. The poor man's original ear of corn would have been free of the obligation of tithing, so the one replacing it must be equally free of further obligation. But, Eliezer observes, the poor man has not yet made acquisition of the ear that was in the possession of the landowner. One cannot—according to the sages of M. Pe'ah 4 : 9—set aside an ear of corn for a particular poor man. So Eliezer takes the occasion to point out the inconsistency in the anonymous rule. The poor man cannot exchange the Gleanings for a particular sheaf. One then gives him the whole heap in which the gleanings are found, as a gift on condition that he return it. The appropriate sheaf then comes into the possession of the poor man. The poor man *then* acquires the sheaf and is able to exchange it (so Albeq, *Seder Zera'im*, p. 53).

Certainly, Eliezer's saying takes for granted the existence of the antecedent rule, A. Eliezer has not revised A-B. He could have done so, by dropping B and substituting C, *He gives*... Eliezer has formulated his rule in consonance with the language of the foregoing adding only *He gives possession—heap*, then repeating the entire antecedent language. It therefore seems that A-B were before Eliezer in their present form.

I.i.227.A. "A landowner that was going from place to place and needs [Parma and Kaufmann: *he takes*] to take Gleanings, the Forgotten Sheaf, or *Pe'ah*, or Poorman's Tithe—he may take. And when he returns to his home, he makes it up [to the poor]"—the words of R. Eliezer.

And the sages say, "He was poor at that hour."

M. Pe'ah 5 : 4

*Comment*: According to Eliezer, the landowner has to return to the poor, who normally would have been entitled to the produce, what he has taken, thus the poor of that particular village. The sages comment not on the rule, but on the philosophy behind it. A simpler, more salient saying would have been, *He does not make it up.* That form is taken for granted, then explained, "He does not make it up because..." Therefore the sages know and comment on Eliezer's rule. But what came before Eliezer? It would seem no rule at all existed, hence Eliezer had to formulate one out of whole cloth. What style has he selected? He has preferred an imperfect/perfect construction, *who was going—he will take—when he will return—he will pay back*—all in the form of a story, rather than a descriptive rule, telling how things are done in general.

I.ii.179. Abba Yosah b. Dostai said in the name of R. Liezer, "If he wanted, he may place before them [the poor] a third, and leave two thirds to his relatives."

Tos. Pe'ah 4 : 2

*Comment*: M. Pe'ah 8 : 6 says that if a man wants to keep something back for his poor relatives, he should take away half and give half to the poor. Eliezer allows a greater portion for the kinsfolk. I am not sure this is our Eliezer. Abba Yosi b. Dostai is an Ushan, and this may be one of the Ushan Eliezer's.

I.i.228.A. R. Eliezer [y.: Eleazar] says, "A man does not have to designate part of *demai*-produce as Poorman's Tithe."

B. And sages say, "He designates [it] but does not have to separate [it.]"

M. Dem. 4 : 3 (y. Dem. 4 : 3, b. Ned. 84a-b)

*Comment*: Ordinary folk are supposed not to give Tithes, but normally to give Heave-offering, which is of a high degree of sanctity and involves merely a grain of wheat. *Demai*, or doubtful produce, purchased from common people, is therefore assumed to be appropriately prepared as to Heave-offering, but not as to other tithes. Therefore the *ḥaver*, or Pharisaic fellow, separates the Heave-offering of the Tithe, that is, the priest's portion of the First Tithe and Second Tithe in the first, second, fourth, and fifth years of the Sabbatical cycle; he designates, but does not give, First Tithe, or, in the third and sixth years of the cycle, Poorman's Tithe, for the Levite or poor man has to prove that that obligation has not yet been met. These rules are attributed to Yoḥanan the High Priest (*Phar.* I, pp. 160-161; M. M.S. 5 : 15).

Eliezer now rules that one does not have to designate the Poorman's

Tithe at all, because the ordinary folk normally separate it, but then keep it for themselves. So the purchaser of *demai* does not have to separate Poorman's Tithe. The sages differ; it must be designated, but need not be given, for it is up to the poor man to prove that he should receive what has not already been given.

The pericope is part of a loosely-strung-together list of rules; the antecedent and following ones have nothing to do with Poorman's Tithe, though 4 : 4 deals with designating Heave-Offering of Tithe of *demai* and Poorman's Tithe of what has certainly been tithed in regard to the Sabbath—at best thematically related. Eliezer's rule therefore has been placed without much regard for the setting.

The sages' saying, B, depends upon A; without A we do not know that B is talking about designating Poorman's Tithe. A is a complete saying, fully comprehensible in itself and requiring no superscription or explanatory glosses. It is a standard legal saying, producing, through B, a little dispute.

I.i.229.A. A priest and a Levite who leased a field from an Israelite—

Just as they [the owner and the sharecroppers] divide the profane produce (ḤLYN), so they divide the Heave-offering.

B. R. Eliezer [Parma: R. ʾLYʿ] says, "(Also) the Tithes are theirs, for it was on this account that they came."

M. Dem. 6 : 3 (y. Dem. 6 : 2, 6 : 4)

*Comment*: The pericope is part of a series of laws on sharecropping property and paying the required agricultural offerings from the produce thereof. If a man hired the field from an Israelite, gentile, or Samaritan, he divides the produce in their presence but is not responsible for tithing their part of the crop. If he hired it from a gentile, he sets aside Tithes and then makes payment. Then comes the above case. The anonymous rule is that the owner and the priest or Levite share in the Heave-offering. It is given to any priest the owner likes. Eliezer holds, however, that the tithes belong to the priest or Levite, who reckoned the tithes, which normally are theirs, as part of the return on the property.

*Heave-offering* here comprehends all tithes, in contradistinction to profane produce. Then Eliezer differs not only with respect to Tithes. The priest keeps back *all* the Heave-offering, the Levite all the tithe. *Tithes* thus includes Heave-offering (so Albeq, *Seder Zeraʿim*, p. 87). *Also/even* is out of place.

In this instance, the anonymous ruling and Eliezer's both serve to complete the topic-sentence—*Priest or Levite that leased a field from an Israelite*, (A). *Just as they*... or (B). *The Tithes are*... The sayings, however, do not match. The anonymous one alludes to Heave-offering, meaning all offerings, and Eliezer refers to Tithes, meaning the same. So Eliezer's saying has been formulated without reference to A, the language of which is ignored in his saying; but the substance of A ought to have been known to him, at least as an alternative way of deciding the matter.

We observe no mnemonic patterns in Eliezer's Mishnaic sayings. He either formulates independent sayings, or glosses antecedent ones, or, as here, differs from an antecedent rule without indicating knowledge of its language. But in no instance have we located in his traditions a consistent disciplined mnemonic pattern. And in this case we do not even know that Eliezer saw the antecedent rule at all, therefore cannot claim it comes before Eliezer.

On 'P, Epstein, *Nusaḥ*, pp. 1007-1008.

I.i.230.A. Grain [may be sown alongside] vegetables or vegetables alongside grain [only if there intervenes] a quarter-*qav*'s [space].

B. R. Eliezer says, "Vegetables [may be sown] alongside grain [only if there intervenes] six *ṭefaḥs*."

M. Kil. 2 : 10 (y. Kil. 2 : 8)

*Comment*: Eliezer differs from the foregoing anonymous rule:

| | 1 | 2 | 3 |
|---|---|---|---|
| A. | TBW'H BYRQ, | YRQ BTBW'H— | BYT RB' |
| B. | — | YRQ BTBW'H— | ŠŠH ṬPḤYM |

So the difference pertains only to the last clause. Eliezer presumably sees a difference between wheat sown among vegetables, and vegetables sown among wheat, while the master of (A) does not make such a distinction. Had Eliezer's saying stood independent of A, it would have repeated A1, but it still would have represented a comment on the antecedent law, which deals with similar issues. So Eliezer here makes a minor alteration of an existing law.

See Epstein, *Nusaḥ*, p. 1177.

I.i.231.A. 1. He who plants two rows of cucumbers, two rows of gourds, two rows of Egyptian beans—permitted.

2. A row of cucumbers, a row of gourds, a row of Egyptian beans—prohibited.

B. A row of cucumbers, a row of gourds, a row of Egyptian beans, and a[nother] row of cucumbers—

R. Eliezer permits.

C. And sages prohibit.

M. Kil. 3 : 4 (y. Kil. 3 : 4)

*Comment*: Two rows are regarded as a field by itself and do not fall into the category of 'mixed seeds,' which are prohibited. But one row does not fall into that category as it is not a 'field' by itself. Eliezer regards the second row of cucumbers as showing a fixed pattern—A, B, C, then A—and therefore seeds have not at random been mixed together, so Albeq, *Seder Zera'im*, p. 110.

Eliezer thus introduces a new problem. Six consecutive rows of three types of vegetables will not fall under 'mixed seeds.' Three of three will.

But what of four, as explained? This highlights an ambiguity in the foregoing rule, so Eliezer. The sages see no ambiguity. Both depend upon A, and C obviously depends upon B.

The construction of A1 and A2 is strange. *Prohibited/permitted* do not complete the opening clause, *He who plants*... We should have preferred something like, *It is permitted to*... or *He who*... *has not transgressed*... M. Kil. 3 : 5 supplies a better model: "*A man plants*... *on condition that*..." Likewise here, *A man plants two rows, but not one*... would have been better style, and would have conformed to the language of the context. Why has that construction not been used, or been dropped, in favor of *prohibited/permitted*? Perhaps the construction necessary for B + C has affected A. These too could have followed the style of M. Kil. 3 : 5 "A man plants..., the words of R. Eliezer. And sages prohibit" would appear unchanged. Such a construction is common in the Houses' disputes, but so is this one. So why B + C exhibit their present form I cannot say, but it seems likely that A has been forced to conform to that form, rather than the smoother and more fluent one of the immediately subsequent pericope.

I.i.232.A. And the wine press in a vineyard ten [handbreaths] deep and four wide—

B. R. Eliezer says, "They plant seeds in it."
And sages prohibit.

M. Kil. 5 : 3 (y. Kil. 5 : 3)

*Comment*: Eliezer's case is attached to the following:

> If a ditch that passes through a vineyard is ten deep and four wide, R. Eliezer b. Jacob says, "If it extends (MPWLŠ) from one end of the vineyard to the other, it is regarded as lying between two vineyards and seed may be sown therein; but if not, it is reckoned like to a winepress."

Now Eliezer takes up the case of that winepress introduced in Eliezer b. Jacob's rule. It is in appropriate logical order. Eliezer supplies a different opinion. Eliezer b. Jacob by implication says one may not plant seeds in a winepress, and Eliezer says one may. But this has *not* been rendered as a dispute:

> *A winepress—ten by four—in a vineyard*:
> R. Eliezer [b. Hyrcanus] says, "They sow."
> R. Eliezer b. Jacob says, "They do not sow."

All the requirements of the legal issue are thereby met; M. Kil. 5 : 3B's sages look like Eliezer b. Jacob. But when does Eliezer b. Jacob come? Hyman (I, p. 181) points out that some traditions, e.g. M. Mid. 1 : 2, place him in the Temple, while others have him as ʿAqiba's disciple, among the later disciples at that, along with Meir, Judah, and the like. I am inclined to think the latter traditions are sound, and if so, perhaps the problem for the redactor is having a dispute between ʿAqiba's teacher and ʿAqiba's disciple. This he has glossed over by supplying them with different cases for their opinions.

I.ii.180.A. A ditch (ḤRYṢ) which passes through a vineyard, ten deep and four wide—

B. R. Liezer says, "They sow in it three kinds of seeds, one on this side, one on that, and one in the middle."

C. R. Liezer b. Jacob said, "The words of R. Liezer appear [correct] in respect to a breached ditch (ḤRYṢ MBWRṢ)."

Tos. Kil. 3 : 10, Lieberman, p. 215, ls. 38-40

*Comment*: Eliezer b. Jacob in C is consistent with his position in M. Kil. 5 : 3A: If the ditch extends from end to end, it is permitted to sow seeds therein. Now he agrees with Eliezer in B—on condition that the ditch is in accord with his view to begin with! For chronological reasons we cannot assign this dispute to our Eliezer.

I.i.233.A. A trellised vine that projects from the terrace [of a hillside]—

R. Eliezer b. Jacob says, "If he stands on the ground and gathers all [the grapes], lo, such as this prohibits four handbreadths in the field.

"And if not, it prohibits only what is directly beneath it."

B. R. Eliezer says, "Also, one who plants one [vine] on the ground and one on the terrace—

"If it is ten handbreadths above the ground, it is not joined together with it [the other row, to make up a vineyard].

"And if not, lo, such as this joins with it [to make up a vineyard]."

M. Kil. 6 : 2 (y. Kil. 6 : 2)

*Comment*: Eliezer b. Jacob and Eliezer have juxtaposed rules, but they evidently pertain to different cases. What seems to join the cases is ᵓP, *also*.

Eliezer b. Jacob's case pertains to a vine above the ground, on a terrace; Eliezer's has two vines, one above, the other below. Eliezer b. Jacob measures the space above the ground by reference to the needs of the farmer. If the vine is close enough to the ground so that it can be harvested from there, it is treated as it is on the ground, therefore requires four handbreadths working space, or it will be liable to 'mixed seeds.' Eliezer has two vines, not one, and asks for ten cubits in height; if they are not present, then the single vine requires six cubits.

See Epstein, *Nusaḥ*, p. 1177.

I.ii.181.A. R. Liezer [Lieberman: Leazar] says, "A ditch (ḤRYṢ) which they brought beside the light lattice work (RYPN), lo, the light lattice work (RYPYN) is like a wall.

B. And on condition that there should not be between it and the next [one] as much as its breadth.

Tos. Kil. 4 : 4, Lieberman, p. 218, ls. 6-8

*Comment*: Lieberman (*Tosefta Kifshuṭah Seder Zera'im*, II, p. 638-9) points out that we should have 'RYS, trellised vine. The vine was thus brought up against a light lattice fence. The lattice is regarded as a wall and suffices to separate the vines from the ground, which may then be sown on the other side of the lattice work.

I.ii.182.A "The Heave-offering of the Tithe which has returned to its place renders subject to the laws of Heave-offering (MDM'T), but [if it has returned] to another place, it does not render subject to the laws of Heave-offering"—the words of R. Eliezer.

And sages say, "Whether to its own place or to another place, it renders subject to the laws of Heave-offering (MDM'T)."

R. Simeon says, "In either case, it does not render subject ..."

Tos. Ter. 5 : 12, Lieberman, p. 134,
ls. 70-73 (y. Dem. 4 : 3; M. Dem. 4 : 1)

*Comment*: M. Dem. 4 : 1 says, "If Heave-offering of Tithe from *demai*-produce fell back to where it was, R. Simeon of Shezur says, 'Even on a weekday a man need but inquire of the seller and eat at his word [that it was duly tithed from the first].' " Simeon is consistent with Eliezer here.

Lieberman explains that since that Heave-offering of Tithe which has fallen back to begin with had rendered the sheaf permitted—it indeed *was* Heave-offering—now that it has fallen back, it remains Heave-offering. If it falls elsewhere, it would not have the same effect. But the sages hold that Heave-differing of Tithe of *demai* is not like doubtful Heave-offering. Simeon holds it is neutralized in one hundred and one, as is stated explicitly in M. Orl. 2 : 1.

On M. Dem. 4 : 1, see Epstein, *Nusaḥ*, p. 1078.

I.i.234.A. Fruits [from] which one gave Heave-offering before their work was completed [Danby: "If Heave-offering had been given from produce before the work of storing it was finished"]—

B. R. Eliezer forbids *eating from them in a random [way]* [Danby: "Making a chance meal from it without tithing"].

C. And sages permit, *except from a basket of figs*.

M. Ma. 2 : 4 (y. Ma. 2 : 3)

*Comment*: Eliezer rules that the separation of the Heave-offering forthwith makes the produce liable for the rest of the tithes, even though the completion of work on the produce ("the work of storing"), which normally would signify liability for tithes, has not taken place. Therefore the man must now give the rest of the tithes. The sages' rule is that the tithes are not due until the work is complete, except in the case of a basket of figs (y. Ma. 2 : 3). In that instance the raising up of

Heave-offering establishes the obligation to tithe. These are given out as gifts. If Heave-offering has been given for the basket of figs, it is clear that the man intends to give out as gifts figs from the rest. It therefore is as though the work has been completed, so Albeq, *Seder Zeraʿim*, p. 228.

The pericope bears no relationship to its setting. M. Ma 2 : 1-2 has to do with passing out figs; M. Ma. 2 : 3 deals with bringing produce from Galilee to Judea, an Ushan pericope. Further, the glosses, or additions, in italics, break the expected form, established in M. Ter.

The sages evidently reject Eliezer's rule. They therefore hold that liability for tithes begins only when the produce has been stored. So to them giving Heave-offering by itself does not establish the obligation to give the rest of the required tithes. The issue is whether, having *begun* to give the necessary tithes, one must complete the process forthwith, and in proper order, as discussed in M. Ter. 3 : 6-7, but the issue here is not essential in M. Ter. 3 : 6-7, so one cannot claim that the pericope would find a more appropriate place there.

I.ii.183.A. He who gives Heave-offering from figs and ultimately presses them, or [gives] from dates and ultimately crushes them [for honey]—

B. R. Liezer says, "He should not eat (Y'KL) of them in a random manner."

C. And sages say, "He eats ('WKL) of them in a random manner."

D. R. Liezer agrees with the sages concerning one who gives Heave-offering of sheaves (ŠBLYN) and ultimately threshes them (ʿŚH GWRN), grapes and ultimately makes them into wine, olives and ultimately makes them into oil.

—that he may eat of them in a random [manner].

E. And sages agree with R. Liezer concerning a basket of fruits from which he has given Heave-offering before the(ir) processing was complete, that he should *not* eat from it in a random manner.

Tos. Ma. 2 : 2, Lieberman, p. 231, ls. 7-14 (y. Ma. 2 : 3)

*Comment*: Part A gives in more specific images the case of M. Ma. 2 : 4 A—fruits from which Heave-offering is given before processing is complete. Eliezer's *prohibiting* becomes *he should not eat*. The agreement of the sages in M. Ma. 2 : 4 C is clear. But the Mishnah's *figs* becomes *fruits*—and this then puts the sages into the position of Eliezer in Tos. Ma. 2 : 2B. And Tos. Ma. 2 : 2D has no warrant in the Mishnah.

Clearly, the Tosefta's version is considerably more complex than the Mishnah's. However, as Lieberman observes, Liezer's instances in part D concern processes which greatly change the produce, so much so that giving the Heave-offering does not signifity that these fruits have been fully processed. As to the sages in E: Once the man has given Heave-offering, he cannot add to the basket, lest he mix untithed fruits with fruits whose Heave-offering has been given, so giving the Heave-offering is what completes the processing in respect to tithing.

Lieberman further explains, *Tosefta Kifshuṭah Seder Zera'im* II, p. 677, that the cases specified here are specifically those in which the man's ultimate decision is not clear. In respect to other fruits, the man may or may not complete processing, but in respect to wheat, wine, and oil, there is no doubt as to the end of the process, for in those matters the completion of the work is only in the treshing floor and wine press.

I.i.235.A. These are liable to Dough-offering and exempt from Tithes: Gleanings, and Forgotten Sheaf, and *Pe'ah*, and Ownerless Crops, First Tithe whose Heave-offering has been taken up, and Second Tithe and sanctified property that were redeemed, and the residue of the *'Omer*—

B. And produce that has not reached a third [of its growth].

C. R. Eliezer [Naples: Eleazar; Kaufmann: Eleazar; Parma: Eleazar; Camb.: Leazar] says, "Produce which has not reached a third [of its growth] is free of the liability of Dough-offering."

M. Ḥal. 1 : 3

*Comment*: Albeq explains that Scripture (Num. 15 : 20) compares Dough-offering to Heave-offering: since Heave-offering is not owing from grain which has not yet reached a third of its growth, likewise dough prepared from it is not liable for the Dough-offering.

Eliezer's saying, C, reproduces the language of B, substituting PṬWR for the (understood) ḤYYB. He could not have said simply "free of liability," for the specific item (Dough-offering) in the foregoing list to which reference is made would not have been clear. His saying depends upon, and glosses, the whole antecedent list.

See Epstein, *Nusaḥ*, p. 1177.

I.i.236.A. He who takes [removes] his finger nails with one another or with his teeth, and so his hair, and so his moustache, and so his beard—

B. And so she that dressed [her hair] (GDL), and so painted [her eyes], and so rouged [her cheeks]—

C. R. Eliezer [Naples: Eleazar] declares liable.

D. And sages prohibit, because of *Shevut* [= rabbinically-ordained Sabbath rest].

M. Shab. 10 : 6 (y. Shab. 10 : 6, b. Shab. 94b)

*Comment*: Both authorities prohibit the actions listed in A-B, but differ as to the reason for the prohibition, therefore as to the punishment. Eliezer regards all of these actions as biblically-prohibited work, subsidiaries of the thirty-nine main types of work one must not do. Therefore he declares the violator liable for a Sin-offering. The sages prohibit the actions on the basis of rabbinical rulings concerning Sabbath-rest. They are not to be done, but are not biblically prohibited, therefore do not result in the Sin-offering. The required syzygy is therefore ḤYB *vs.* ʾSR. This preserves the distinction in the origin of prohibitions in respect to Sabbath-work. But PṬR would have served as well, if the issue were merely the Sin-offering; therefore ʾSR is a secondary development, in this setting, of PṬR but ʾSWR. It would seem that the distinction antedates Eliezer, though we have here no evidence that it is credited to "the rabbis" of ancient times. So earlier law on the Sabbath consisted of both biblical rules and later amplifications and extensions of those rules.

See Epstein, *Tan.*, p. 283, n. 67; p. 291.

I.ii.184.A. He that takes out a full scissors' [edge] (MLʾ HZWG) from his hair, lo this one is liable.

B. R. Liezer says, "Even one."

Tos. Shab. 9 : 12, Lieberman, p. 38, ls. 34-5

*Comment*: b. 94b Shab. has the following:

III.ii.86.A. He who plucks out a full scissors' edge [of hair] on the Sabbath is culpable. And how much is a full scissors' edge? Two.

B. R. Eliezer said, "One."

C. But the sages agree with R. Eliezer in the case of one who picks out white hairs from black ones, that he is culpable even for one...

Eliezer's saying here therefore answers an unasked question. M. Shab. 10 : 6 has the sages and Eliezer dispute the case of one who takes out hair by hand. But if he does so with a utensil, even the sages agree he is liable, as in b. Shab. 94b. Here the sages are represented in A, with which Eliezer must agree; he then glosses the ruling.

I.ii.185.A. "He who milks, sets milk (ḤBṢ, for curdling), makes cheese (as much as a fig), sweeps, lays the dust, washes and anoints, and removes the honey-combs [= M. Shev. 10 : 7]—

B. "On the Sabbath, he is liable for a Sin-offering.

C. "And on the festival is flagellated with forty lashes," the words of R. Liezer.

D. And sages say, "Whether on the Sabbath or on the festival, he is free of liability for a Sin-offering and is liable only [on account of rabbinically-ordained rules of] resting (*Shevut*)."

E. R. Simeon b. Leazar says in the name of R. Eliezer, "She who blues [her eyes], arranges [her hair] or rouges—for herself, is free [of liability]; for other women, is liable [b. Shab. 94b: for self, liable; for others, free]."

F. And so would R. Simeon b. Leazar say in the name of R. Liezer,

"A woman should not dry her face with a cloth on which is rouge (SRQ)."

Tos. Shab. 9 : 13, Lieberman, p. 39,
ls. 37-43 (b. Shab. 95a)

*Comment*: The issue is whether the actions listed in A are biblically or rabbinically prohibited. Eliezer holds they are biblical prohibitions, the sages, that they are of rabbinical origin. Here Eliezer distinguishes between doing things for oneself and doing them for others. But as to taking finger-nails off, the law is the opposite, for Eliezer obligates the one who does so for himself to give the sin-offering, but one does so for others is free; see the extended discussion of Lieberman, *Moʿed*, pp. 140-141.

In b. Shab. 95a, Eliezer is given the further distinction, between doing the acts listed in A intentionally or accidentally: Accidentally + Sabbath = liable; intentionally + Festival = flagellated—thus "improving" B-C by adding legal issues and distinctions originally absent.

I know of no evidence that when Simeon b. Leazar quotes an Eliezer, it usually is Eliezer b. Hyrcanus.

I.i.237.A. Honeycombs which he broke on the eve of the Sabbath, and they [the liquids therein contained] exuded of themselves [on the Sabbath]—[the liquids] are forbidden.

B. And R. Eliezer [Kaufmann, Camb., Parma: Leazar] permits.

M. Shab. 22 : 1 (b. Shab. 19b
has Eleazar [b. Shammuʿa])

*Comment*: Eliezer again is in the position of the House of Hillel; what happens by itself, without the man's own participation, is permissible, as in M. Shab. 1 : 4-8. The prohibition of A, Albeq explains (*Seder Zeraʿim*, p. 67), is because, if the honey is permitted, a man may begin to break the honeycombs on the Sabbath. Therefore one prohibits the exuded honey on account of the prohibition of the breaking of honeycombs. Albeq reads Eleazar. But Eliezer's position here is consistent with other lenient rulings attributed to him, so the tradition should likely be Eliezer b. Hyrcanus's, but b. Shab. 19b's Eleazar should be Eleazar (b. Shammuʿa) cited by Eleazar (b. Pedat), and that is decisive.

See Epstein, *Nusaḥ*, pp. 254, 1178; *Tan.*, p. 297.

I.i.238.A. (He placed it [the *ʿeruv*] on a tree, above ten handbreadths, his *ʿeruv* is no *ʿeruv*; below ten handbreadhts, his *ʿeruv* is an *ʿeruv*. He placed it in a pit, even a hundred handbreadths' deep, his *ʿeruv* is an *ʿeruv*. He placed it on the top of a reed or on the top of a stick—if it had been uprooted and stuck [into the ground], even though it is a hundred cubits high, lo, this is an *ʿeruv*.)

B. He placed it in the cupboard and the key was lost, lo, this is an *ʿeruv*.

C. R. Eliezer [Parma, Camb.: Leazar; Kaufmann: Eleazar; b.: Eliezer] says, "*If he does not know that the key is in its place*, it is not an *ʿeruv*."

M. Eruv. 3 : 3 (y. Eruv. 3 : 3; b. Eruv. 34b, 35a)

*Comment*: The principle of B is that since the man can get at the *ʿeruv*, the theoretical use of the *ʿeruv*—as Sabbath food—is still possible. The man can get into the cupboard, if necessary, without a key. Eliezer [Eleazar] rules that if the man does not know where the key is, the key may be lost, and he may not find it. Eliezer [Eleazar] holds one may not open a cupboard except by means of the key. If, however, the man knows the key is in its place, even if he does not know where the place is, the *ʿeruv* is valid—so Albeq, *Seder Moʿed*, p. 92.

It seems to me that the operative clause of B—*the key was lost*—is no different from the operative clause of C—*if he does not know that the key is in its place*. Therefore Eliezer's [Eleazar's] saying does not require the italicized words and is complete with *it is not an ʿeruv*, the normal syzygy, matching B in all respects. Then the opening statement of B serves both B and C; were the order reversed, we would have: Eliezer [Eleazar]: "*It is no ʿeruv*," *and Sages say*, "*It is an ʿeruv*." The gloss is unnecessary and imposes a complicated "explanation" for a simple dispute, unless some substantive difference exists between having lost a key and not knowing whether a key is in its place! I do not understand the necessity for both rearranging the sages' opinion and Eliezer's [Eleazar's] and glossing the latter's. It is not a very good gloss.

Tos. Eruv. 2(3) : 15, p. 97, l. 55 has Leazar, and if so, the Mishnah before us must likewise be Leazar's and not Eliezer's. Lieberman's collection of variants does not include Eliezer, only Leazar vs. Eleazar. See his *Moʿed*, p. 336, n. 78; the Mishnah then should read *Eleazar*.

See Epstein, *Nusaḥ*, p. 1165; *Tan*., pp. 66, 202, 300 n. 7. Epstein assumes, in *Tan*., p. 66, that this is our Eliezer, and observes that various traditions confuse Eliezer's and the sages' opinions. But in *Nusaḥ*, p. 1166, he seems to prefer Eleazar. *Nusaḥ* surely is the better version of Epstein's opinion.

I.i.239.A. "He who slept on the way and did not know that darkness had fallen—he has two thousand cubits in every direction," the words of R. Yoḥanan b. Nuri.

And sages say, "He has only four cubits."

B. R. Eliezer [Kaufmann, Camb., Parma, y.: Eleazar; b. Eruv. 45a-b: Eliezer] says, "And he is in the middle of them [those four cubits]."

C. R. Judah says, "In any direction he wishes, he may go."

D. And R. Judah agrees that if he chose for him [some one direction] he cannot go back."

M. Eruv. 4 : 5 (b. Eruv. 45a-b)

*Comment*: Here, Eliezer [Eleazar] glosses a dispute of Yoḥanan b. Nuri and 'the sages.' Yoḥanan was a Yavnean master, disciple of Ḥalafta father of Yosi b. Ḥalafta. Eliezer [Eleazar] agrees with the sages—or he *is* "the sages"—that the man may go only four cubits, and he is regarded as in the middle of the permitted area; that gives him two cubits. Judah b. Ilai then differs from Eliezer, but does not follow the form of Eliezer's saying. But Judah's saying does repeat the language of Yoḥanan ben Nuri:

| *Yoḥanan* | *Judah* |
|---|---|
| He has | — |
| Two thousand cubits | — (LKL RWḤ ŠYRṢH) |
| in every direction (LKL RWḤ) | In any direction (LKL RWḤ ŠYRṢH) *which he wants, he goes* |

The difference between Yoḥanan's saying and Judah's is that the latter does not specify the number of cubits; we therefore are left with the assumption that he has only four, folllowing the sages + Eliezer, and the difference is with none of the afore-named, for *no one* says he has to go in any one direction to the exclusion of other possibilities. Parts C-D are therefore a pointless supplement to A-C.

The position of Eliezer [Eleazar] and the sages is of interest to us. They hold one does not acquire a place of Sabbath domicile, from which one may proceed in two thousand cubits in any direction, except by knowledge and intent. The man is not in such a status. Therefore he has no right to travel beyond his immediate situation. Eliezer gives the man only two cubits in any one direction. In M. Eruv. 4 : 11, Eliezer [Eleazar] is consistent with his ruling here. Knowing one pericope, one could have stated the position of Eliezer [Eleazar] or the other.

See Epstein, *Nusaḥ*, p. 1168; *Tan*., p. 300, n. 7.

I.i.240.A. He who went forth outside of the Sabbath-limit, even one cubit, may not enter.

B. R. Eliezer says [Camb., Parma, Kaufmann, y. *gemara*: Leazar; b. Eruv. 44a, 52b; Eliezer], "Two—he may enter. Three—he may not enter."

C. He who was overtaken by darkness one cubit outside of the limit may not enter.

D. R. Simeon says, "Even fifteen cubits, he may enter, since the surveyors do not measure exactly, for the sake of those that err."

M. Eruv. 4 : 11 (y. Eruv. 4 : 10; b. Eruv. 52b)

*Comment*: Now the leniency of Eliezer's [Eleazar's] position is clear. He says the man has four cubits of free movement, and he is in the middle of the four; therefore he *may* reenter the Sabbath-boundary. The sages' here rule he has no cubits of free movement at all. If he had four, they would have so specified (*pace* Albeq, p. 101). They would differ not only with Eliezer [Eleazar], the sages, and Judah, of M. Eruv. 4 : 5, but also with Yoḥanan b. Nuri. So the sages here stand far outside the limits of discussion set above.

Eliezer's [Eleazar's] view, Albeq explains, is that if he was standing within two cubits of the border, he is still within the border and may reenter, but if within three, he may not. However, that seems to me to include more than Eliezer is saying, therefore to claim less. Eliezer simply gives four cubits, with the man in the middle.

The saying of A is simply, *He who went forth... may not reenter.* But Eliezer's [Eleazar's] saying about *two/three*, has required the gloss in A: *even one*. Without Eliezer's saying, *even one* would be superfluous. It would have been possible to phrase the two opinions in balance, after a single topic sentence:

> *He who went forth beyond the Sabbath limit*:
> R. Eliezer says, Two cubits—he may return; three, he may not.
> And sages say, *Even one*, he may not [= C].

This is awkward, and leaves no place for C.

See Epstein, *Nusaḥ,* pp. 1044, 1166.

I.i.241.A. A bolt with a knob on its end [to be used to shut a door on the Sabbath, which is not hung or fastened to the door]—

B. R. Eliezer [Camb., y., Parma, Kaufmann, Naples: Leazar] forbids [using such a bolt to close a door on the Sabbath.]

C. And R. Yosi permits.

D. R. Eliezer [Eleazar] said, "MʿŚH B: A synagogue in Tiberias, where they would deem it permitted, until Rabban Gamaliel and the sages came and prohibited it."

E. R. Yosi says, "They deemed it prohibited. Rabban Gamaliel and the sages came and permitted it for them."

M. Eruv. 10 : 10 (y. Eruv. 10 : 10; b. Eruv. 101b)

*Comment*: Eliezer [Eleazar] regards the knob is unnecessary to the bolt. Therefore one cannot use it for locking on the Sabbath. The knob is not part of the object and cannot be carried. Or, Albeq further explains (*Seder Moʿed*, p. 125), that it is like *adding* to the building. Yosi holds it is permitted, for the bolt is unnecessary for the knob; or because the bolt would not appear to be adding to the building, but is merely an utensil. Eliezer's [Eleazar's] story then brings evidence that Gamaliel and the elders agreed with him. Yosi simply turns the details of the story around to support his position. Accordingly, Yosi treats Eliezer's [Eleazar's] tradition as of no consequence.

See Epstein, *Tan*., p. 300, n. 7, and 477.

I.i.242.A. These are removed on Passover: Babylonian porridge,

Median beer, Edomite vinegar, and Egyptian barley-beer; also dyers' pulp, cooks' starch-flour, and writers' paste.

B. R. Eliezer says, "Also women's ornaments (TKŠYṬY) [cosmetics which may contain leaven]."

C. This is the general principle: Whatever is made from any kind of grain must be removed at Passover.

M. Pes. 3 : 1 (y. Pes. 3 : 1; b. Pes. 42a-b, 43a-b, 44a)

*Comment*: Eliezer glosses the antecedent rule; he has no generalization. That comes afterward. His view is that women's cosmetics may contain leaven, therefore fall into the same category as the foregoing examples. Then C obviates the need to specify the items both in A and in B. Eliezer's saying here takes for granted A, but not C.

y. Pes. 3 : 1 and b. Eruv. 42b change *ornaments* (TKŠYṬY NŠYM) to *cosmetics* (ṬYPWLY).

On ʾLW, see Epstein, *Nusaḥ*, p. 427; also pp. 111, 1040; *Tan*., pp. 324, 334, 336, 746.

I.i.243. [M. Pes. 5 : 5-8: The Passover-offering was slaughtered by the people in three groups... An Israelite slaughtered his own [paschal] offering and the priest caught the blood... The priest nearest the altar tossed the blood in one action against the base of the altar... As the rite was performed on a weekday, so was it performed on the Sabbath.]

A. How do they hang up [the Passover, by its back legs] and flay [the hide]?

B. There were iron hooks fixed in the walls and pillars, on which they hang and flay. And whoever had no place to hang and to flay, there were there thin smooth staves and he would place it on his shoulder and on his fellow's shoulder and hang and flay.

C. R. Eliezer [Naples: Eleazar] says, "When the fourteenth falls on the Sabbath, he places his hand on the shoulder of his fellow, and the hand of his fellow on his hand, and hangs and flays [the carcass]."

M. Pes. 5 : 9 (y. Pes. 5 : 9; b. Pes. 64a-b, 65a-b)

*Comment*: Eliezer's problem is to explain how one should make use of the thin smooth staves on the Sabbath. If one made use of them directly, it would represent carrying the staves on the Sabbath. Eliezer therefore supposes that the Passover-sacrifice in this respect will *not* override the Sabbath. But in other respects, he rules that it does, so he contradicts M. Pes. 6 : 2-3.

Eliezer introduces a problem absent in the foregoing, anonymous rule. The rule is phrased in historical language: there *were* such and such. But then it switches to the present, whoever *does not have*... then, staves *were* there, then, be *places*... and *hangs* and *flays*. R. Eliezer's saying is in the descriptive, present-tense participles normal in apodictic laws: He does so-and-so. So the tense-structure does not permit us (theoretically) to assign any element in the pericope to "historical", therefore pre-Yavnean, times.

See Epstein, *Tan*., p. 336.

I.i.244.A. If the Passover-offering was offered [eaten] in uncleanness, men or woman that suffer a flux (ZBYN/ZBWT) and menstrual women (NDWT) and those who have given birth (YWLDWT) should not eat from it, and if they ate, they are free of the liability of cutting off.

B. R. Eliezer [Kaufmann, Parma: Eleazar; Tos.: Leazar] declares exempt even if [in the case, when the Passover is offered in uncleanness] they come to the sanctuary.

M. Pes. 9 : 4 (y. Pes. 9 : 4; b. Pes. 67b, 95b: Eliezer; see Lieberman, *Mo'ed*, p. 626, note to p. 186, l. 35; Sifra Ṣav Pereq 14 : 1, Weiss, p. 37b)

*Comment*: The foregoing rule is known to Eliezer [Eleazar], who adds to its leniency. Even though if they eat other sanctities, they are liable for cutting off, for eating the Passover sacrificed in uncleanness they are not so liable, since it is eaten in uncleanness by those unclean by reason of contact with a corpse. Eliezer then adds that if such as these came into the sanctuary when the Passover was offered in uncleanness, they are free of liability. The prohibition of coming to the sanctuary, as it applies to the person with a flux (ZB), is mentioned in connection with one unclean by reason of contact with a corpse (Num. 5 : 2), which indicates that when those unclean by reason of contact with a corpse are prohibited from coming to the sanctuary, so too are the ones who suffer a flux. But if the one may come without punishment of 'cutting off,' so too the other, even though they do not make the Passover-sacrifice.

See Epstein, *Nusaḥ*, p. 1178.

II.i.8.A. *And the Whole Assembly of the Congregation of Israel Shall Kill It* (Ex. 12 : 6).

B. R. Eliezer says, "Whence can you prove that if all Israel had only one paschal lamb, all of them can fulfill their duty with it? From the passage: *And the whole assembly of the Congregation of Israel shall kill it*."

Mekh. Pisḥa 5 : 106-109, Lauterbach, I, p. 42, (b. Qid. 41b-42a, Pes. 78b, y. Pes. 7 : 5)

II.i.9. *And Ye Shall Eat It in Haste* (Ex. 12 : 11). This refers to the bustle of the Egyptians. You interpret it as referring to the bustle of the Egyptians. Perhaps this is not so, but it refers to the bustle of the Israelites? It says, however: *But against any of the children of Israel shall not a dog whet his tongue* (Ex. 11.7). The bustle of Israel is already referred to there. To what then must I apply: "*And ye shall eat it in haste?*" To the bustle of the Egyptians.

R. Joshua, the son of Qorḥah says, "*And ye shall eat it in haste.*" This refers to the bustle of Israel. You interpret it as referring to the bustle of Israel. Perhaps it is not so, but it refers to the bustle of the Egyptians. But it says: *Because they were thrust out of Egypt and could not tarry* (v. 39). The bustle of the Egyptians is referred to there. Hence, what must Scripture refer to by saying: *And ye shall eat it in haste*? To the bustle of the Israelites."

Abba Ḥanin in the name of R. Eliezer says, "It refers to the haste of *Shekhinah.* And though there is no proof for this, there is a hint of it: *Hark! my beloved! Behold He cometh*, etc. *Behold He standeth behind our wall* (Song 2 : 8-9). One might think that in the future also the deliverance will be in haste. But it says, *For ye shall not go out in haste, neither shall ye go by flight, for the Lord will ge before you* (Is. 52 : 12)."

Mekh. Pisḥa 7 : 5-20, Lauterbach I, pp. 52-3

II.i.10. *And Ye Shall Observe this Thing* (Ex. 12 : 24). "This is to include the passover sacrifice of subsequent generations—it should also be brought only from sheep or from goats"—these are the words of R. Eliezer.

Mekh. Pisḥa 11 : 106-108, Lauterbach I, p. 89.

I.ii.186. R. Eliezer says, "The ark was exiled to Babylonia, as it is said, *Nothing more* (L' YWTR DBR) [will be left] *says the Lord* (II Kings 20 : 17) and *word* (DBR) means only the words (DBRWT) which are in it [the ark]."

Tos. Sheq. 2 : 18, Lieberman, p. 212, ls. 79-80 (y. Sheq. 6 : 1; b. Yoma 53b)

*Comment*; Lieberman explains (*Mo'ed*, p. 697, to l. 79) that the reference is to M. Sheq. 6 : 1, the House of Gamaliel and the House of Ḥananiah Prefect of the Priests had a tradition that the ark was hidden in the Temple. The Toseftan authorities differ. Some hold, as Eliezer here, that the ark was not hidden in the Temple but was exiled to Babylonia. But since Eliezer's saying does not directly allude to Gamaliel's and Ḥananiah's tradition, it cannot supply a firm *terminus ante quem* for M. Sheq. 6 : 1. R. Simeon has the same view, ls. 80-83. Judah b. Laqish differs. b. Yoma has Simeon *b. Yoḥai*, Judah *b. Ilai.*

I.ii.187.A. R. Eliezer says, "The ark was exiled to Babylonia, as it is said, *Behold the days are coming, when all that is in your house and that which your fathers have stored up till this day shall be carried to Babylonia; nothing* (L' YWTR DBR) *shall be left, says the Lord* (II. Kings 20 : 17). DBR is only the Ten Commandments (DYBRWT) which are in it [the ark]."

B. R. Simeon says, "Lo, it says, *In the spring of the year King Nebuchadnezar sent and brought him to Babylonia, with the precious vessels of the house of the Lord* (II Chron. 36 : 10)—This refers to the ark."

C. R. Judah says, "It was hidden in its place, as it says, [*And the cherubim made a covering above the ark and its poles.*] *And the poles were so long that the ends of the poles were seen from the holy place before the inner sanctuary; but they could not be seen from outside; and they are there to this day* (I Kings 8 : 8)."

Tos. Sot. 13 : 1, Zuckermandel, p. 318, ls. 14-18 = Tos. Sheq. 2 : 18, Zuckermandel, p. 177, ls. 14-19

*Comment*: Tos. Sheq. has Judah ben Laqish—certainly not a Yavnean.

I.i.245.A. The Day of Atonement is prohibited in regard to eating, drinking, washing, anointing, fastening the sandal, and sexual relations.

B. "The king and the bride may wash their faces, and the woman after childbirth may fasten the sandal,"—the words of R. Eliezer.

C. And sages prohibit.

M. Yoma 8 : 1 (y. Yoma 8 : 1; b. Yoma 73b)

*Comment*: Eliezer rules leniently in respect to the king and the bride, so that they may not appear ugly, and the woman after childbirth, because she cannot take the cold. His special cases allude to two elements in the general rule, the prohibition of washing and of fastening the sandal, so he had A before him and glossed it.

b. Yoma 78b has Ḥananiah b. Teradion citing Eliezer's sayings.

See Epstein, *Tan.*, pp. 290, 466.

I.i.246.A. R. Eliezer says, "Fourteen meals is a man obligated to eat in the *Sukkah*, one in daytime and one by night."

B. And sages say, "The matter has no limit (QṢBH), except for the nights of the first day of the festival only."

C. And further R. Eliezer said, "He who did not eat on the first night of the festival [in the *Sukkah*] may pay back on the nights of the last days of the festival."

D. And sages say, "The matter has no restitution (TŠLWMYN), as it is said, *That which is crooked cannot be made straight, and that which is wanting cannot be reckoned* (Qoh. 1 : 15)."

M. Suk. 2 : 6 (y. Suk. 2 : 7, b. Suk. 27a-b, 28a; Midrash Tanḥuma Pinḥas 13, ed. Buber, II, p. 78a)

*Comment*: People normally eat two meals a day, therefore on *Sukkot* are obligated to eat fourteen meals in the *Sukkah*. The sages rule there is no limit; whenever one eats a meal, he must do so in the *Sukkah*. This is consistent with the antecedent story:

> MʿŚH B: They brought to Rabban Yoḥanan b. Zakkai to taste the broth, and to Rabban Gamaliel two figs and a pail of water, and they said, "Bring them up to the *Sukkah*." (M. Suk. 2 : 5)

The earlier masters thought even random meals are to be eaten in the *Sukkah*. So the sages are consistent with the older tradition, that one must eat all meals in the *Sukkah*, and Eliezer supplies a more lenient rule, requiring only fourteen meals. The sayings are not matched; A is a full statement of an apodictic rule; B responds to its content, without giving a reason.

C-D is a separate pericope, introduced with the past-tense, *said* because of the joining word, ʿWD. We should have expected, *R. Eliezer says*. Since Eliezer rules one must eat fourteen meals, he is consistent in saying one may make up missed meals. He alludes to the meals due on the first nights of the festival, thus responding to the sages in B. So the two rules are a unity. The sages are equally consistent. While one must eat the first festival meals in the *Sukkah*, since there is no limit as to the total number, there is no way of making up missed meals. They then are given an appropriate proof-text, cited routinely for this purpose.

Behind the opinions of both parties is the rule that one must live in the *Sukkah*, and living there means eating there—the normal number of meals, Eliezer would add (b. Suk. 27a).

As to C, b. Suk. 27a points out that the Sukkah is *not* to be used the last day at all! So that day cannot be used to make up for the missed meals.

See Epstein, *Tan*., pp. 212, n. 79; 302, 350.

I.i.247.A. How was the rite of the Willow-branch (ʿRBH) fulfilled? There was a place below Jerusalem called Moṣa. There they went and cut for themselves young willow-branches. They came and set these up at the sides of the altar so that their tops were bent over the altar. They then blew [on the *Shofar*] a sustained, a quavering, and another sustained blast (TQʿ, HRYʿ, TQʿ). Each day they went in procession a single time around the altar, saying, *Save now, we beseech thee, O Lord. We beseech thee, O Lord, send now prosperity* (Ps. 118 : 25).

R. Judah says, "*Ani waho, save us we pray, ani waho, save us we pray.* But on that day [the seventh] they went in procession seven times around the altar."

B. [Parma, Naples, Camb., Kaufmann omit the following:] When they leave, what do they say? "*Homage to thee O altar, homage to thee, O altar* (YPY LK MZBḤ)."

C. R. Eliezer says, "*To the Lord and to you, O altar, to the Lord and to you, O altar*" (LYH WLK MZBḤ)."

M. Suk. 4 : 6 (y. Suk. 4 : 3, b. Suk. 45a)
[NB: Tos. Suk. 3 : 1, Lieberman,
p. 266, l. 5: *Liezer b. Jacob*]

*Comment*: Eliezer's rule is introduced as an answer to B. Presumably the antecedent rules were known to him. The difference between his 'farewell' saying and that of the anonymous tradent is in the first word alone. It is difficult to know whether or how Eliezer had a different tradition. He cites no authority.

Albeq does not comment on the absence of B-C from several MSS, including all four before us. Nor does he note Tos.'s attribution.

I.i.248.A. If a festival-day of the New Year coincided with the Sabbath, in the Sanctuary they would sound the *shofar* (TQʿ), but not in the provinces. When the Temple was destroyed, Rabban Yoḥanan ben Zakkai ordained that they should sound the *shofar* everywhere in which there is a court.

B. R. Eliezer [Kaufmann, Camb., Parma, Naples: Eleazar] said, "Rabban Yoḥanan b. Zakkai decreed only for Yavneh alone."

M. R.H. 4 : 1 (b. R.H. 29b)

*Comment*: MS evidence varies; b. R.H. 29b has Eliezer; y. R.H. 4 : 1 has R"'.

Eliezer's [Eleazar's] position is that the Yavnean decrees pertained to Yavneh alone; Yoḥanan's authority did not extend beyond. See *Life of Yoḥanan ben Zakkai* (Leiden, 1970²), pp. 196-226, *Development of a Legend: Studies on the Traditions Concerning Yoḥanan ben Zakkai* (Leiden, 1970), pp. 44, 207.

B takes for granted the whole of A and cannot have been formulated without knowledge of the concluding clause, *everywhere in which there is a court*, probably also the whole antecedent ordinance.

See also Epstein, *Nusaḥ*, p. 652; *Tan*., p. 159.

I.i.249. (The story of Reuben is read but not interpreted [in the synagogue]; the story of Tamar is read and interpreted. The first story of the calf is read and interpreted, the second is read but not interpreted. The Blessing of the Priests and the story of David and Amnon are read but not interpreted. They do not use the chapter of the Chariot as a reading from the prophets, but R. Judah permits it.)

A. R. Eliezer [b., Naples: Eleazar] says, "They do not use as a reading from the Prophets (MPṬYRYN) the chapter *Cause Jerusalem to know* (Ezek. 16 : 1)."

M. Meg. 4 : 10 (y. Meg. 4 : 12;
b. Meg. 25a-b, 26a)

*Comment*: The chapter deals with the abominations of Jerusalem, and is not used as a prophetic reading in the synagogue-liturgy on account of the respect for Jerusalem. Eliezer's saying is in the same form as Judah's, and both differ from the foregoing, which are built on *they read... they do/do not interpret* (TRGM). No one differs from Eliezer.

I.ii.188.A. *Cause Jerusalem to know* is read and interpreted.

B. MʿŚH B: One was reading before R. Liezer *Cause Jerusalem to know.* He said to him, "Go and proclaim your mother's abominations." [y. Meg. 4 : 12 adds: "And they investigated him and found he was a *mamzer*."]

Tos. Meg. 4 : 34, Lieberman, p. 363,
ls. 112-114 (y. Meg. 4 : 12; b. Meg. 25b)

*Comment*: Now we have the contradictory, anonymous rule and a story on the basis of which Eliezer's apodictic law has been formulated. But it is *read* rather than MPṬYR.

I.i.250.A. All the vessels which were in the Temple require immersion (ṬBYLH), except for the golden altar and the copper altar—

B. "Because they are like the ground"—the words of R. Eliezer.

C. And sages say, "Because they are plated."

M. Hag. 3 : 8 (y. Hag. 3 : 8, b. Hag. 26b, 27a)

*Comment*: The dispute concerns the reason the altars do not require immersion. Eliezer compares them to the earth, which does not receive uncleanness. The sages say the reason is that they are plated with gold and copper, respectively, and when sources of uncleanness touch them, they touch only the gold or copper plate, and the plate itself does not receive uncleanness. Both parties therefore accept and explain the antecedent, anonymous rule.

See Epstein, *Nusaḥ*, pp. 145, 520.

I.i.251.A. Four brothers—two of them were married to two sisters, and the two that married the two sisters died. Lo these perform *ḥaliṣah* and do not enter Levirate marriage. And if they [the remaining brothers] went and married [them], they put them away.

B. R. Eliezer [Tos. Kaufmann, Camb., Parma: Eleazar] says, "The House of Shammai say, 'They may remain married.'

"And the House of Hillel say, 'They put them away.' "

M. Yev. 3 : 1 (b. Yev. 26a, 28a)

*Comment*: Eliezer's [Eleazar's] tradition glosses the final clause of A. According to him, the anonymous rule, *they put them away*, is the opinion of the House of Hillel in a Houses' dispute.

Both surviving wives, who are sisters, are subject to each of the surviving brothers and are therefore prohibited as 'sisters of the wife'; even after the *ḥaliṣah* of one of the sisters and brothers, the second sister remains prohibited to the second surviving brother, because a woman subject to Levirate marriage prohibited to the Levir at the time she becomes available to him remains prohibited to him for all times. If each of the surviving brothers has taken in Levirate marrriage one of the sisters, he must put the woman away with a *Geṭ* (writ of divorce).

Tos. Yev. 5 : 1 has *Leazar* and Simeon.

See Epstein, *Nusaḥ*, p. 1162; *Tan*., p. 437.

I.i.252.A. One of doubtful sex ('NDRWGYNWS) marries but is not taken in marriage."

B. R. Eliezer [Kaufmann, Parma; Eleazar] says, "One of doubtful sex—they are liable on his account for stoning, like a male."

M. Yev. 8 : 6 (b. Yev. 81a, 82b, 83b, 84a)

*Comment*: Eliezer [Eleazar] does not differ from the rule of A. The *androgynos* cannot be taken in marriage. Eliezer glosses that rule: he is treated as fully male, and one who has intercourse with the *androgynos* is stoned (M. Sanh. 7 : 4). y. Yev. 8 : 6 and Tos. Yev. 10 : 2, Lieberman, p. 31, l. 18, have Eleazar.

See Epstein, *Nusaḥ*, pp. 528, 1163; *Tan*., p. 190.

II.iii.15. R. Eliezer says, "Wherever it says, *Male and female*—the tumtum and the androgynous beast render unfit, but the bird [offering] concerning which *male and female* is not said is not made unfit by an offering of a *tumtum* or an androgynous bird."

Sifra Vayiqra Parashah 6 : 5, Weiss, p. 8a
(b. Yev. 83b; b. Bekh. 47a, b. Zev. 85b)

I.i.253.A. These are the works which the wife must perform for her husband: grinding flour and baking bread and washing clothes and cooking food and suckling her child and making his bed and working in wool.

B. If she brought him in one bondwoman, she need not grind or bake or wash; if two, she need not cook or suckle the child; if three, she need not make his bed or work in wool; if four, she may sit in a chair [all day long.]

C. R. Eliezer [Kaufmann, Eleazar; Camb.: Eliezer b. Jacob] says, "Even though she brought him a hundred bondwomen, he forces her to work in wool, for idleness leads to lewdness."

M. Ket. 5 : 5 (y. Ket. 5 : 6; b. Ket. 59b, 61b)

I.i.254.A. He who prohibits his wife by vow not to have sexual relations—

B. The House of Shammai say, "[They may remain married for] two weeks."

C. And the House of Hillel say, "One week."

D. The disciples go forth to study of the Torah without [the wives'] consent for thirty days. The workers—one week.

E. As to the duty of marriage spoken of in the Torah (Ex. 21 : 10)—

F. "The unemployed (ṬYL), every day; the workers, twice a week; the ass-drivers, once a week; the camel drivers, once in thirty days; the sailors, once in six months"—the words of R. Eliezer [Kaufmann, Parma: Leazar].

M. Ket. 5 : 6 (y. Ket. 5 : 7, b. Ket. 61b, 62b)

*Comment*: Eliezer differs from M. Ket. 5 : 5B. However many servants a woman has, she must be kept busy. The saying of Eliezer takes for granted the foregoing ruling but does not make use of all of its examples, only *wool*. Wool is the last example in the foregoing list; evidently on this account it was selected for Eliezer's saying.

M. Ket. 5 : 6E-F is composed without reference to A-D. Eliezer does not refer either to the case in A or to the example in D. So his saying is an independent logion, attached to the foregoing because of its thematic relevance. But Eliezer differs from D, which has the workers engage in sexual relations at least once in a week. Eliezer would permit the workers only three and a half days away from home. The other items are all new to him. The workers are, Albeq explains (*Seder Nashim*, p. 106), those who go away to work in another city without their wives' permission. They may stay only a week.

Tos. Ket. 5 : 6 (b. Ket. 6a) has: "Workers—twice a week. If they worked in another town—once a week." The rest is as in M. Ket. 5 : 6, but without attribution to Eliezer.

See Epstein, *Nusaḥ*, pp. 1166, 1167, 1181.

I.i.255.A. He that sets his wife up as a store-keeper or appointed her guardian ('PṬRWP'), lo, this one may extract an oath whenever he wants.

B. R. Eliezer [Naples: Leazar] says, "Even [when she is not a shopkeeper] concerning her spindle or her dough."

M. Ket. 9 : 4 (y. Ket. 9 : 4; b. Ket. 86b)

*Comment*: The oath is that the woman has not kept back anything belonging to her husband. Eliezer says such an oath is permitted even from a woman not in charge of her husband's property. b. Ket. 86b asks whether such an oath is only in consequence of her business transactions (A) and concludes that it is not.

See Epstein, *Nusaḥ*, p. 1167.

III.ii.87. (If a Levir married his deceased brother's wife, who was found to have been pregnant, and she gave birth; if the child is viable, he must divorce her ... But if the child is not viable, he may retain her—M. Yev. 4 : 1.)

TNY': In the name of R. Eliezer they said, "He must give her a Geṭ."

b. Yev. 36b

I.i.256. (He that is forbidden by vow to have any benefit from his fellow may still pay the other's *Sheqel*-dues for him, or pay him his debt, or restore to him his lost property; but where a reward is taken for it, the benefit falls to the Temple—M. Ned. 4 : 2).

A. The other [prevented by vow from benefiting his fellow] may set apart for him his Heave-offering and Tithes with his consent; he may offer on the other's behalf the Bird-offerings of a man or woman that has a flux (QNY ZBYN/ZBWT) or of a woman after childbirth, and Sin-offerings and Guilt-offerings, and he may teach him *midrash, halahot*, and *aggadot*, but he may not teach him Scripture; but he teaches Scripture to his sons and daughters. He feeds his wife and children, even though he [who made the vow] is liable for their food.

B. He should not feed his cattle, whether clean or unclean.

C. R. Eliezer says, "He feeds the unclean and does not feed the clean."

D. They said to him, "What is the difference between unclean and clean?"

E. He said to them, "As to the clean [beast], its soul [life] belongs to Heaven, and its body is his, but as to the unclean, its soul [life] *and* body belong to Heaven."

F. They said to him, "Also the unclean's soul [life] belongs to Heaven, but the body belongs to him, for if he wishes, lo, he sells it to gentiles or feeds it to dogs."

M. Ned. 4 : 3 (y. Ned. 4 : 3; b. Ned. 33a, 38a)

*Comment*: The theory of B is that when the beast is fed, its value increases, and therefore the person prevented by vow from giving benefit to his fellow cannot feed the fellow's cattle, without distinction between unclean and clean. That clause implies a distinction was made. Eliezer makes it. He agrees that the clean cattle may not be fed, for the man owns its flesh and wants it to be fat. But the unclean beast's body belongs to heaven, not to the man, who cannot eat it. The sages' reply is that the man indeed may benefit from the unclean as from the clean, for he can sell it or feed it to the dogs.

The form of B-C is standard, with carefully matched opinions, corresponding clause by clause. D introduces the debate; Eliezer ought to have an answer after F, but does not. Therefore the debate is different from the one characteristic of the Houses. Eliezer's distinction fails; the man may benefit from either type of animal. This debate leaves Eliezer with such a poor argument that it looks artificial—that is, wholly composed by the authority behind B.

b. Ned. 33a attributes M. Ned. 4 : 1 to Eliezer, but I do not know why it must be ours.

See Epstein, *Nusaḥ*, pp. 644, 1033.

I.i.257. A sterile woman, an old woman, and a woman who is not fitted to give birth do not drink and do not take the *Ketuvah.*

B. R. Eliezer [y., Kaufmann, Parma: Leazar] says, "He can marry another woman and be fruitful and multiply from her."

C. And other women either drink or do not take the *Ketuvah*.

M. Sot. 4 : 3 (b. Sot. 24a, 26a; y. Sot. 4 : 3)

*Comment*: The rule of A is that women who are not able to give birth are prohibited to their husbands (M. Yev. 6 : 6), therefore they cannot be forced to drink the bitter water but also do not receive the *Ketuvah.* Eliezer says that the marriage is valid, and they are not prohibited to the husband, so they fall into the category of C.

Eliezer does not formulate a contrary saying; he simply alludes to the reason behind A and says it is not correct, and B therefore is a development over what one should have expected.

See Epstein, *Nusaḥ*, p. 1168, *Tan*., p. 410.

I.i.258.A. The woman who said, "Receive my *Geṭ* for me in such-and-such a place," and they received it in another place—it is invalid.

B. R. Eliezer [y., Parma, Kaufmann: Eleazar] declares [it] fit.

C. "Bring me my *Geṭ* from such-and-such a place," and they brought it from another place—it is fit.

M. Git. 6 : 3 (b. Git. 65a)

I.i.259.A. "Bring me my *Geṭ* "—she eats Heave-offering until it the *Geṭ* reaches her hand. "Receive for me my *Geṭ*"—she is prohibited forthwith.

B. "Receive my *Geṭ* for me in such-and-such a place"—she eats Heave-offering until the *Geṭ* reaches that place.

C. R. Eliezer [y., Parma, Kaufmann, Camb.: Eleazar] prohibits forthwith.

M. Git. 6 : 4 (b. Git. 65a-b, y. Dem. 4 : 4; y. Ter. 8 : 1)

*Comment*: The rule of A is that the woman's instructions must be carried out or the agent has not carried out her wishes and cannot receive the *Geṭ* in her behalf. But Eliezer [Eleazar] holds that since a woman may be divorced without her direct knowledge—the husband issues the *Geṭ* without her agreement—she has simply indicated to the agent where the husband might be found and was not setting up a necessary condition for his receiving it. All parties obviously agree that when she says merely, "Bring it from such-and-such a place," the agent is free to bring it from where he finds it. He is not an agent for formally receiving the *Geṭ* in her behalf, merely for delivering it. *Bring* is not language which makes him an agent for receiving the *Geṭ* in her behalf; but merely makes him a delivery-agent—therefore an agent for the husband.

The same difference in language, between *bring* and *receive*, is operative in M. Git. 6 : 4. Here the question is eating Heave-offering. The wife of a priest may do so. When the woman is divorced, she is no longer permitted to eat Heave-offering. If she says merely *bring*, she may continue to eat Heave-offering until the *Geṭ* is in her hand. If she says *receive*, she is prohibited forthwith, because we assume the agent can receive the *Geṭ* in her behalf at any time. But if she then specifies a place in which the *Geṭ* is to be received, the anonymous rule is that she may continue to eat Heave-offering until the *Geṭ* reaches the place which she has specified. One estimates how much time it will take the agent to get there (so Albeq, *Seder Nashim*, p. 291). Eliezer [Eleazar] prohibits forthwith, consistent with his view in 6 : 3 that specifying the place is not a condition, merely an effort to supply the necessary information.

See Epstein, *Nusaḥ*, pp. 637, 1167.

I.260.A. If the scribe wrote a *Geṭ* for the husband and a deed of quittance [receipt for the *Ketuvah*] for the wife, and in error gave the *Geṭ* to the wife and the quittance to the husband, and they [the husband and wife] gave them to one another, and afterward [when she remarried], the *Get* was found in the possession of the man and the quittance in the possession of the woman—

B. She goes forth from this one and from this one. And all the above conditions [Specified in M. Git. 8 : 5] apply to her.

C. R. Eliezer [y., Parma, Kaufmann: Eleazar] says, "If [the *Get*] went forth [was discovered] immediately, it is not a *Get*. If after a time it went forth, lo, this is a *Get*."

D. [For] the first [husband] does not have the power to invalidate the right of the second.

M. Git. 8 : 8 (y. Git. 8 : 7; b. Git. 80a-b)

*Comment*: The supposition of B is that the husband gave the wive the quittance, assuming it was the *Get*, and the wife gave him the *Get*, assuming it was the quittance. Eliezer [Eleazar] says that that is the rule if the exchange took place immediately. But if it took place after a while, when she was already remarried, the *Get* is valid, for, as D explains, the husband has not got the power to reverse the second marriage. We take account of the possibility that the first husband and the wife have conspired and exchanged the documents so as to free her of the second marriage.

See Epstein, *Nusaḥ*, p. 1167.

I.i.261.A. All those forbidden to enter the congregation [Deut. 23 : 1-3] are permitted to marry one another.

B. R. Judah prohibits.

C. R. Eliezer [b., Parma, Kaufmann: Eleazar] says, "They that are of assured stock may intermarry with others that are of assured stock, but they that are of assured stock may not intermarry with them that are of doubtful stock, nor they that are of doubtful stock with others that are of doubtful stock [So Danby, p. 327, for WD'N BWD'N, WD'N BSPQN, etc.]."

D. What are the doubtful stocks? The *Shetuqi*, the Assufi, and the *Kuti* [child of doubtful fatherhood, foundling, Samaritan].

M. Qid. 4 : 3 (y. Qid. 4 : 3, b. Qid. 74a, 75a, 76a)

*Comment*: C alludes directly to A, without reference to the position of Judah. Eliezer qualifies A by saying that A is valid only for those that are surely within the specified forbidden category. But those whose status is doubtful may not marry others whose status is certain. D then glosses C; it has no pertinence to B or A, so serves as a commentary on Eliezer's opinion.

The position of A is that a *Mamzer*, a *Netin*, a *Shetuqi*, and an *Asufi* may intermarry, following M. Qid. 4 : 1:

Ten family stocks came up from Babylonia: Priestly, Levitic, Israelite, impaired priestly stocks, proselyte, freedman, *mamzer*, and *Netin*, and *Shetuqi*, *Assufi*. The Levitic, Israelite, impaired priestly stocks, proselyte, and freedman stocks may intermarry.

The proselyte, freedman, *mamzer*, *Netin*, *Shetuqi*, and *Assufi* stocks may intermarry.

So A repeats the rule of M. Qid. 4 : 1. Eliezer, as noted, qualifies the rule, but does not differ.

See Epstein, *Tan*., p. 99; *Nusaḥ*, p. 1167.

I.ii.189. R. Eliezer said, "All those forbidden to enter the congregation—those that are of assured stock are permitted [to marry] others that are of assured stock...." etc.

Tos. Qid. 5 : 1, Zuckermandel, p. 341, ls. 18-19

I.i.262.A. An unmarried man [who has never been married] may not teach [as] scribes, and a woman may not teach [as] scribes (L' YLMD RWQ SWPRYM).

B. R. Eliezer [Kaufmann: Leazar] says, "Also he who [was married but who now] has no wife may not teach [as] scribes."

M. Qid. 4 : 13 (y. Qid. 4 : 11; b. Qid. 82a)

*Comment*: Eliezer qualifies A by adding that a man whose wife has died or who is divorced is in the same status as the bachelor.

I am not clear on YLMD SWPRYM. Yalon points *yil'mad*. Albeq (*Seder Nashim*, p. 329) says that *soferim* are teachers of Scripture to small children. So the passage means, may not teach *as scribes*.

Danby (p. 329) gives, "An unmarried man may not be a teacher of children," so he evidently took *sopherim* to mean "children," which seems to me impossible.

See Epstein, *Nusaḥ*, p. 1168.

III.i.14. TNY: R. Eleazar says, "Also he who has a wife and children, but they are not with him in that place..."

y. Qid. 4 : 11

*Comment*: Eliezer's logic is extended to a still more extreme case.

I.i.263.A. Five [agents of injury] rank as harmless (TM) and five as an attested danger (MW'D). Cattle do not rank as an attested danger in so far as they butt, push, bite, lie down, or kick.

The tooth [of a beast] is an attested danger in that it consumes whatever is fit for it to consume. The leg is an attested danger in that it breaks down [what it tramples on] as it goes along; so also is an ox which has been declared an attested danger [in that it was used to gore]; and an ox which causes damage in the [private] domain of him that is injured; and man.

B. The wolf, the lion, the bear, the leopard, and the panther and the snake—lo, these are attested dangers (MWʿDYN).

C. R. Eliezer [Kaufmann, Parma, b.: Eleazar] says, "When they are domesticated (BNY TRBWT), they are not an attested danger."

D. And the snake is always an attested danger.

E. What is the difference between a harmless [animal] and an attested danger? But that (ʾLʾ Š) the harmless pays half-damage from its own body, and the attested danger pays full damages from the best property.

M. B.Q. 1 : 4 (y. B.Q. 1 : 5; b. B.Q. 15b, 16b)

*Comment*: Eliezer [Eleazar] glosses a detail of an established list. The specification of the wolf, etc., begins a new clause in the pericope; the "five" introduced at the outset are listed. Then B-C raises a separate, but related issue, namely, the status of normally wild animals, which can be tamed. Perhaps B-C go together; that is, a controversy betwen Eliezer [Eleazar] and the unnamed sages is interpolated into the antecedent, anonymous rule. But if so, B-C take for granted the rules conveyed in, and reasons behind, A. D qualifies C; the snake is never really tamed, therefore not within Eliezer's list.

M. Sanh. 1 : 4 has our Eliezer, so this cannot be *b. Hyrcanus*.

See Epstein, *Nusaḥ*, p. 1179.

I.i.264.A. "If the owner had tied it [the ox] with a halter or shut it in properly, but it nevertheless came out and caused damage, the owner is culpable whether it was an attested danger or accounted harmless," the words of R. Meir.

B. R. Judah says, "If it was accounted harmless, he is liable, but if an attested danger, he is not culpable, for it is written, *And it has been testified to his owner and he has not kept him in* (Ex. 21 : 29). But this one was kept in."

C. R. Eliezer says, "Its only safe-keeping is the knife."

M. B.Q. 4 : 9 (y. B.Q. 4 : 9; b. B.Q. 45b, 46a, 55b; Mekh. Nez. 10:125-130)

*Comment*: Eliezer's saying is given in the position of a comment on a dispute of Meir and Judah. His view is outside the range of argument of A-B; the only good way to keep the ox from doing damage is to slaughter it. Tos. B.Q. 5 : 7, Zuckermandel, p. 353, l. 28, has the same saying, following Meir, Judah, and Eliezer b. Jacob. Perhaps C is to be attributed to Eleazar or Eliezer b. Jacob. See Epstein, *Nusaḥ*, p. 1179.

I.i.265.A. He who moves a jar from place and broke it, whether he is an unpaid bailee or a paid bailee, he is sworn to an oath [that it was not through his neglect, and he is free of liability].

B. R. Eliezer said, "In both cases he is sworn to an oath. [Parma, Kaufmann, Camb., Naples, omit foregoing.] And I am astonished (TMH) that both can be sworn to an oath [to be free of liability]."

M. B.M. 6 : 8 (y. B.M. 6 : 6, b. B.M. 82b)

*Comment*: Eliezer has the identical tradition as A, that both unpaid and paid bailiffs take an oath and are freed of liability. He then expresses surprise that there is no distinction between the two. The paid bailiff is liable to pay for damages caused without his negligence. Why should he be sworn to an oath? The unpaid bailiff cannot be sworn to an oath, for sometimes he causes the damage unknowingly (so Albeq, *Seder Neziqin*, p. 92). M. B.M. 7 : 8 explicitly states that the unpaid bailiff is given an oath for all loss that may occur, swearing that he has guarded the object appropriately, and he then does not have to pay. The paid guardian or a hirer may take an oath if the beast was lamed, driven away, or dead, but makes restitution if it was lost or stolen.

A *baraita* follows: "If a man moved... whether paid or unpaid, he must swear"—the words of R. Meir. R. Judah said, "An unpaid must swear, but a paid trustee is responsible [even when he was not negligent]." So the Mishnah is Meir's, in which case the Eliezer above should not be *b. Hyrcanus*. See Epstein, *Nusaḥ*, p. 1179, *Tan*., p. 99.

I.i.266.A. They do not make a hollow space (ḤLL) under the public road—cisterns, trenches, or vaults.

B. R. Eliezer says, "[If it is] so that a cart may go while bearing stones, [they may make a hole]."

M. B.B. 3 : 8 (y. B.B. 3 : 11; b. B.B. 27b, 60a)

*Comment*: Eliezer glosses A, limiting the rule to hollowed space insufficiently protected so that a heavily laden cart cannot pass over. But one may make a hollow if it is well covered.

See Epstein, *Nusaḥ*, p. 1179.

I.i.267.A. He who sells the courtyard has [also] sold the houses, cisterns, trenches, and vaults but not the movables. When he says to him, "It and all that is in it"—lo, they are all sold.

But in either case (BYN KK WBN KK) he has not sold the bath-house or olive press which are in it.

B. R. Eliezer [Kaufmann, Camb., Parma: Leazar] says, "He who sells the courtyard has sold only the air-space of the courtyard."

M. B.B. 4 : 4 (y. B.B. 4 : 4, b. B.B. 67a)

I.i.268.A. He who sells the olive-press has sold the vat, the grindstone, and the posts, but he has not sold the pressing-boards, the wheel, or the beam; but if he said, "It and all that is in it," all these are sold.

B. R. Eliezer [As above: Leazar] says, "He who sells the olive-press has sold the beam."

M. B.B. 4 : 5 (y. B.B. 4 : 5; b. B.B. 67b, 78b)

*Comment*: Eliezer [Eleazar] rejects the whole of the rule in M. B.B. 4.4A. In his view, the enumerated items do not fall into the category of *courtyard*, so the language of the sale is at issue. But in 4 : 5A, Eliezer [Eleazar] rules that selling the olive-press automatically means one sells the beam, for it is essential to the press. He is therefore consistent in his rulings. b. B.B. 67b adds, "Since it is this which gives the olive-press its name." See Epstein, *Tan*., pp. 239, 479; *Nusaḥ*, p. 1179.

I.ii.190.A. He who sells the house has sold the door, the cross bar (NGR) and the lock and the stationary mortar (MKTŠT ḤQWQH), but he has not sold the oven and not the portable stove (KYRYYM) and not the millstone (RYḤYYM) and not the permanent mortar.

B. R. Eliezer says, "Whatever is attached to the ground, lo, this is sold."

Tos. B.B. 3 : 1, Zuckermandel, p. 401, ls. 25-8 (b. B.B. 65b, 66a-b, 67a-b)

I.i.269.A. If a man made a baldness on his head or rounded the corners of his head, or marred the corners of his beard, or made any cuttings for the dead [Deut. 14 : 21, Ex. 22 : 31, Lev. 11 : 4, Lev. 11 : 42], he is liable to the forty stripes. If he made one cutting for five that were dead, or five cuttings for one that was dead, he is liable on each count.

B. For [cutting off the hair of] the head, [he is liable on] two [counts], once for either side (ʾḤT MKʾN WʾḤT MKʾN); and for [cutting off the hair of] the beard, he is liable on two counts for either side and once for below.

C. R. Eliezer [Camb., Kaufmann: Leazar] says, "If he took it off [all] at once, he is liable only [on] one [count]."

D. He is not liable unless (ʿD Š) he takes it off with a razor.

E. R. Eliezer [Camb.: Leazar] says, "Even if he pulled it out with a pincers (MLQṬ) or with an adze (RHYṬNY), he is culpable."

M. Mak. 3 : 5 (y. Mak. 3 : 5; b. Mak. 20a-b, 21a; b. Ned. 40b-41a)

*Comment*: In C Eliezer holds that cutting the hair counts as a single culpable act, without division of the head into the parts. All depends upon whether it was done at once. Obviously, if it was done in separate actions, Eliezer will agree that the specific actions are punished one by one. In D he rules that one is culpable no matter how he removes the hair.

The larger issue raised by Eliezer in B-C is how one assesses the culpability for transgression, through several acts, of a single law covering a single situation. Eliezer treats the whole as one, the sages treat each separately. See Epstein, *Nusaḥ*, p. 1179. Compare M. Ker., above, p. 256.

III.ii.88.A. TNY' NMY HKY: One who removes [on the Sabbath] a scissors-nip [of hair] is liable to a sin-offering.

B. And how much is a scissors-nip?

C. Two hairs.

D. R. Eliezer says, "One hair."

b. Mak. 20b

I.i.270.A. Five were claiming [against him]. They said to him, "Give us the deposit which we have in your hand." [If he says], "[By] oath there is nothing of yours in my mind," he is liable only on one [count].

[But if he said "By] oath that nothing of yours is in my hand, nor of yours, nor of yours," he is liable for each one.

C. R. Eliezer [b.: Eleazar] says, "Only if (ʿD Š) he says, '[By] oath,' at the end is he liable to each count."

D. R. Simon says, "Unless he will say, '[By] oath' to each one."

M. Shav. 5 : 3 (y. Shav. 5 : 3, b. Shav. 36b)
[Kaufmann omits C-D.; Naples omits D.]

*Comment*: The issue of B–C–D is the liability for an offering if he swears falsely and then confesses (M. Shav. 8 : 3). If he specifies each person, he is liable to each. Eliezer says that he must say, "Nor of yours nor of yours etc. *by oath*," for when he says *oath* at the end, he refers to each, and he therefore is regarded as having sworn to each one of them.

Simeon says this does not suffice; he must say *By oath* to each one before he is liable to each. Both differ from B.

See Epstein, *Nusaḥ*, pp. 552-6.

I.i.271.A. And they do not make ornaments for idolatry—necklaces, ear-rings, or finger-rings.

B. R. Eliezer says, "For a fee (BSKR) it is permitted."

M. A.Z. 1 : 8 (b. A.Z. 19b)

*Comment*: Eliezer qualifies the foregoing; one may not make ornaments for free, but one may do so for a fee. b. supplies an exegesis to back up Eliezer's opinion.

I.i.272.A. [If] he took wood from it (an *asherah*)—it [the wood] is prohibited as to benefit.

He heated the oven with them [the sticks]—if it is new, it must be broken up. If it is old, it must be cooled.

B. [If] he baked the loaf with it [the wood], it is prohibited as to benefit.

C. It [the loaf] was mixed up with other(s) [loaves]—they all are prohibited as to benefit.

D. R. Eliezer says, "Let him bring the benefit [derived from the wood, that is, their value in money] to the Dead Sea [and throw it in, and the bread will be permitted, even when it has not been mixed up with acceptable loaves]."

E. They said to him, "There is no redemption [price] in a matter of idolatry."

F. [If] he took from it [the *asherah*, wood for] a shuttle, it [the shuttle] is prohibited as to benefit. [If] he wove a garment with it, the garment is prohibited as to benefit.

G. If it [the garment] was mixed with others [garments], and others with others—they all are prohibited as to benefit.

H. R. Eliezer says, "Let him bring the [money derived as a] benefit to the Dead Sea."

I. They said to him, "There is no redemption [price] in a matter of idolatry."

M. A.Z. 3 : 9 (y. A.Z. 3 : 12, 3 : 13; b. A.Z. 49a-b; b. Pes. 27a)

*Comment*: Eliezer is consistent in both cases. He holds that one can exchange the object for funds and destroy the funds. The sages rule this is not possible. Similarly above, Eliezer takes a lenient view of making ornaments for idols. One may do so for a fee but not without salary. b. A.Z. 49b explains why two examples of Eliezer's opinion (D, H) are given.

I.i.273.A. "The individual or the ruler (*Nasi*) may become liable to a suspensive guilt-offering, but not so the anointed [high priest] or the court. The individual, the ruler, and the anointed [high priest] may become liable to an unconditional guilt-offering, but not so the court. Through [unwitting transgression of the law touching] him that hears the voice of adjuration or him that swears rashly with his lips or uncleanness in what concerns the Temple and its hallowed things, the court is not liable, but the individual, the ruler, and the anointed [high priest] are liable, except only that the high priest is not liable because of uncleanness in what concerns the Temple and its hallowed things"—the words of R. Simeon [Naples: *R. Eliezer*]

B. And what do they bring [as an offering]?

C. A Rising and Falling offering (Lev. 5 : 6, 7, 11).

D. R. Eliezer [Naples: *Ishmael*] says, "The ruler [*Nasi*] offers a he-goat."

M. Hor. 2 : 7 (y. Hor. 2 : 7, b. Hor. 9a-b, b. Ker. 2b)

*Comment*: Eliezer's gloss alludes to Scripture, Lev. 4 : 23. See Epstein, *Nusaḥ*, p. 483.

II.iii.16. R. Eliezer says, "He that conveys [the blood] to a place where it is necessary to convey it—intention renders it unfit; to a place where it is not necessary to convey it—intention does not render invalid, for intention renders invalid only in a matter which is valid for the cult and in a person who is appropriate for the cult and in a place which is valid for the cult."

Sifra Ṣav Parashah 8 : 5, Weiss, p. 36a (b. Zev. 13a)

*Comment*: The pertinent *gemara* (b. Zev. 13a-15b) contains no hint of a tradition on this subject involving our Eliezer. Tos. Zev. 1 : 5, Zuckermandel, p. 480, ls. 2-10, has Eliezer. M. Zev. 1 : 4 has Eleazar, so Albeq, *Qodashim*, p. 14; also MSS Camb., Kaufmann, and Parma. Naples has Eliezer.

II.iii.17.A. *Before the tent of meeting* (Lev. 3 : 2, 8, 13)—before the tent of meeting [is said] to render valid all directions.

B. R. Eliezer says, "*Before the tent of meeting*—to render valid [slaughter] at the north."

Sifra Vayiqra Pereq 17 : 11, Weiss, p. 13b (b. Zev. 55a)=Sifra Ṣav Parashah 3 : 2, Weiss, p. 32a=Sifra Ṣav Parashah 4 : 3, Weiss, p. 33b

*Comment*: b. Zev. 55a-b has Eliezer, but I have found no evidence that it is ours.

I.i.274.A. He who slaughters for a gentile—his [act of] slaughter is valid.

B. And R. Eliezer declares invalid.

C. R. Eliezer said, "Even if he slaughtered it so that the gentile may eat from the midriff (MḤṢR KBD ŠLH), it is invalid, for—

D. "The normal intention (STM MHŠBT) [Danby, p. 516: An unexpressed intention] of a gentile is [directed] toward idolatry."

E. R. Yosi said, "It is a *qal veḥomer*: If where intention can render a result invalid, as with animal offerings, it depends only on him who does the acts [required in the offering=the priest], how much more, where intention does not render a result invalid [as in slaughtering unconsecrated beasts] does it depend only on him who slaughters them!"

M. Hul. 2 : 7 (b. Hul. 13a, 38b, 39a-b, 116b; b. Git. 45b, y. A.Z. 2 : 3, 7; b. Zev. 47a)

*Comment*: The Jew slaughters a beast belonging to a gentile in behalf of the gentile. A Jew may not make use of the meat according to Eliezer. The *even if* clause of Eliezer's saying in C may simply be a way of making his ruling (D) more extreme. Even though the gentile possesses only the smallest part of the beast, it is still prohibited. The saying means that ordinarily a gentile slaughtering a beast intends it for idolatrous purposes. Therefore Eliezer prohibits the whole.

Yosi then differs. He points out that in slaughtering offerings in the Temple, the intention of the slaughterer, not of the owner of the animal, is decisive. If the priest has the intention of eating the meat after the fixed time, the meat is rendered refuse by the priest's intention (M. Zev. 2 : 2-3), but *not* by that of the owner of the animal. Likewise, the intention of the slaughterer, not of the owner, is decisive in unconsecrated beasts. Therefore the position of A is supported by, and may be attributed to, Yosi.

See Epstein, *Tan*., p. 142.

Note Mekh. Baḥodesh 6 : 39-44, Lauterbach I, p. 240, Eliezer *vs.* Isaac on gentile idolatry.

I.i.275.A. One who is suspected in respect to firstlings [a priest suspected of slaughtering unblemished firstlings which have been given to him]—they do not buy from him the flesh of gazelles or untanned hides.

B. R. Eliezer [Kaufmann, Parma, Camb., Naples: Leazar] says, "They buy from him the hides of females."

C. And they do not buy from him wool that is bleached but still dirty; but they buy from him [what is already] spun [or made into] garments.

M. Bekh. 4 : 7 (b. Bekh. 29b)

*Comment*: The pericope begins a group of laws about how to deal with one suspected of not strictly keeping the law of firstlings, then of Seventh Year produce, then of selling Heave-offering.

A says one may not buy even the meat of gazelles, to which the law of firstlings does not apply, because it is similar to calf-meat. One suspects that the meat may be of a firstling of a calf. But tanned hides certainly are not from firstlings, for the person will quickly sell the hides of firstlings and will not bother to tan them. Eliezer then adds to the rule. One may buy the untanned hides of females, for they are recognizable. C then continues the rule about what one may not buy from the man.

The reasoning behind the items in C is the same as that pertaining to tanned hides.
See Epstein, *Nusaḥ*, p. 1070.

I.i.276. (These same blemishes, whether lasting or passing, likewise render priest unqualified to serve in the Temple.—M. Bekh. 7 : 1.)

A. R. Eliezer [Parma; Camb.: Leazar; Kaufmann: Leazar b. ʿAzariah] says, "Moreover (ʾP), if any have dangling warts, they are unfit among men, and fit among cattle."

M. Bekh. 7 : 6 (b. Bekh. 40b, 45b: Eleazar)

*Comment*: Eliezer's [Eleazar's] saying comes at the end of a long list of disqualifications of priests. He says that a dangling wart will render a priest unfit for the cult, but will not render a beast unfit as a firstling.
See Epstein, *Nusaḥ*, p. 1170; *Tan.*, p. 195.

I.i.277. (The law of the vow of Valuation may sometimes bear leniently and sometimes stringently; the law of the Field of Inheritance [Lev. 27 : 16ff.] may sometimes bear leniently and sometimes stringently.—M. Ar. 3 : 1)

A. In respect to the Field of Inheritance, to bear leniently and to bear stringently, how so?

B. It is all the same whether one sanctified a field or inherited in the desert of Maḥuz or in the orchards of Sebaste—

C. [If he would redeem it] he gives [for every part of a field that suffices for] the sowing of a homer of barley [Lev. 27 : 16]—fifty silver sheqels. And for a field which he has bought he gives its actual value.

D. R. Eliezer [Kaufmann, Camb., Parma: Leazar] says, "A field of Possession and a field which one has bought are one and the same [= he gives the same fifty silver sheqels].

E. "What is the difference between a Field of Possession and a field which he has bought?

"But for the Field of Possession he gives the Added Fifth, and for the field which he has bought he does not give the Added Fifth."

M. Ar. 3 : 2 (b. Ar. 14a-b;
Sifra Beḥuqotai Pereq 11 : 5)

*Comment*: Lev. 27 : 16ff. states *If a man dedicates to the Lord part of the land which is his by inheritance, then your valuation shall be according to the seed for it; a sowing of a homer of barley shall be valued at fifty sheqels of silver... And if he who dedicates the field wishes to redeem it, then he shall add a fifth of the valuation of money to it, and it shall remain his. If he dedicates to the Lord a field which he has bought, which is not a part of his possession by inheritance... and the man shall give the amount of the valuation on that day as a holy thing to the Lord.* According to A-B, what is lenient in the evaluation of the property for redemption by the man who dedicated it is that the actual quality of the land is not taken into account in respect to the field of inheritance. This may lead to a considerable saving. But if it is a field he has bought, he must give its actual value.

Eliezer holds that in respect to the redemption of the field, both kinds are the same; one pays according to the same standard, fifty silver sheqels as specified. They differ in that Scripture has added a Fifth to the value of the field of inheritance, but not to that of the field he has bought. So Eliezer sees the instructions of valuation—*a sowing of a homer of barley shall be valued at fifty sheqels of silver*—as applying also the field which a man has bought ("the amount of the valuation"). The only difference is in what is specified: the Added Fifth. b. Ar. 14b supplies a *baraita* to this effect. M. Ar. 7 : 2 specifies that only the owner does so, but anyone else who redeems a field does not pay the Added Fifth.

See Epstein, *Nusaḥ*, p. 1171.

I.ii.191.A. The substitute of the Passover, the progeny of the substitute of the Passover, and its progeny, and its—in an endless line (ʿD SWP HʿWLM)—should pasture until they are blemished, and be sold, and he brings with their proceeds Peace-offerings.

B. R. Liezer [*sic*] says, "The progeny themselves are offered as Peace-offerings."

C. The substitute of Peace-offerings, the progeny of the substitute of Peace-offerings, and its progeny, and the progeny of its progeny, in an endless line, should pasture until they are blemished, and be sold, and he should bring Peace-offerings with their proceeds.

D. R. Leazar [*sic*] says, "The progeny themselves should be offered as peace-offerings"....

E. He who separates a female for his Passover—it should pasture until blemished and be sold, and its proceeds fall for [purchase of] the Passover.

F. R. Simon b. Judah says in the name of R. Simeon, "It may be sold [even] without blemish."

G. If it bore a male, it [the male] should pasture until blemished and be sold, and he should bring with its proceeds the Passover.

H. R. Leazar says, "It itself should be offered as the Passover."

Tos. Pis. 9 : 18, 20 Lieberman,
pp. 194-5, ls. 70-74, 78-81

*Comment*: B differs from M. Tem. 3 : 1 C, so the whole passage should be assigned to Leazar, as against Eliezer in M. Tem. 3 : 1 and 3 : 3.

I.i.278.A. These vessels save [afford protection for their contents against uncleanness in the 'Tent' wherein there is a corpse] when they have a tightly stopped up cover (Num. 19 : 15—BṢMYD PTYL).

B. Vessels made from cattle dung, stone, unbaked clay, earthenware, and alum-crystal (NTR); fish-bones, fish-skin; the bones of a mammal in the sea, its hide; and vessels made from wood which are not susceptible to uncleanness [because they hold forty *se'ahs* in quantity—M. Kel. 15 : 1].

C. They save whether [the tightly stopped-up cover] is above, or at the side, whether they set on their bottoms or are leaning on their sides.

D. [If] they were turned upside down, they save all that is beneath them to the nethermost deep (THWM).

E. R. Eliezer declares [what is underneath them] unclean.

M. Kel. 10 : 1

*Comment*: Eliezer glosses the foregoing rule. He holds that if they are upside down, they do not protect from uncleanness.

See Epstein, *Tan*., pp. 112, 466; *Nusaḥ*, p. 1053.

I.ii.191.A. A vessel which he firmly closed and whose lips he plastered to the wall saves [from uncleanness] what is in it and what is opposite it in the wall.

B. If he sealed it and plastered its lips to the earth, it saves what is in it and what is opposite it in the earth.

C. R. Eliezer says, "What is turned upside down does not save."

D. And R. Eliezer agrees concerning two stewpots (LPSYN) and two jars which he sealed to one another and plastered with plaster on the sides, that they do not save when tightly stopped up, and if it was a small vessel and does not contain a square handbreadth and it is upside down, it does not save [from uncleanness].

Tos. Kel. B.Q. 7 : 6,
Zuckermandel, p. 577, ls. 16-21

*Comment*: See Lieberman, *Tosefet Rishonim*, III, pp. 26-27.

I.i.279.A. The scorpion-bit of a bridle is unclean, and the cheeks [cheek-pieces] are clean [as mere ornaments].

B. R. Eliezer declares the cheek[pieces] unclean.

C. And sages say, "Only the scorpion-bit is unclean."

D. And when they are joined together, the whole is unclean.

M. Kel. 11 : 5

*Comment*: Eliezer regards the whole as unclean. The sages in C repeat the rule in A. Then D qualifies it; if they are joined together, the whole is unclean, just as Eliezer said.

I.i.280.A. If a necklace has metal beads on a thread of flax or wool, and the thread breaks, the beads are still susceptible to uncleanness, since each one is an article in itself.

If the necklace has a thread of metal, with beads of precious stones, pearls, or glass, and the beads are broken, and the thread alone remains, it is still susceptible to uncleanness.

B. The remnants of a necklace [are unclean] if enough to encompass the neck of a little girl.

C. R. Eliezer says, "Even if one link [remains], it is unclean, for they hang it on the neck."

M. Kel. 11 : 8

*Comment*: Even if only one link remains tied on the thread, it is unclean. Eliezer does not differ in principle from the foregoing rule. B holds that the remnants are unclean if there is enough to use as an ornament. Eliezer says that one link is sufficient for an ornament. So the difference is as to the practical use of one such a link, not as to the principle that what can be used as an ornament remains unclean, however diminished.

See Epstein, *Tan*., p. 288; *Nusaḥ*, p. 1054.

I.ii.192. R. Eliezer says, "Nose-hooklet (ṢYNWR' ŠL NZM) is unclean [when] by itself."

Tos. Kel. B.M. 1 : 9, Zuckermandel, p. 579, l. 13

*Comment*: For the reading, see Lieberman, *Tosefet Rishonim*, III, p. 36. M. Kel. 11 : 8 holds that nose rings (NZMY H'P) are susceptible to uncleanness. But 11 : 9 states that the hooklet (ṢNWR') [of the earring] is not susceptible. Eliezer then rules on another sort of hooklet. He presumably would differ also as to the ear-hooklet.

I.i.281. (These hides are susceptible to *midras*-uncleanness: a hide that is intended for use as a rug, a tanner's apron, the hide used as the lower covering of a bed, a hide used by an ass-driver or flax-worker or porter or physician, a hide used for a cot, or a hide put over a child's heart [against cats], and the hide of a mattress or cushion—all these are susceptible to *midras*-uncleanness.)

A. A hide used to wrap up combed wool and a hide worn by the wool-comber ('WR HSRWQ, 'WR HSWRQ)—

B. R. Eliezer says, "*Midras*."

C. And sages say, "Corpse-uncleanness."

M. Kel. 26 : 5

*Comment*: Eliezer holds that the hide used for holding the combed wool and the one used by the wool-comber on which to comb wool are susceptible to *midras*-uncleanness. The sages say it is subject only to normal corpse-uncleanness. The difference is whether that sort of hide is used for sitting. Eliezer says it is.

See Epstein, *Tan.*, p. 13.

I.i.282.A. A child's shirt—

B. R. Eliezer says, "Of any size [is susceptible to uncleanness]."

C. And sages say, "Only if it is of the prescribed size; and it should be measured double."

M. Kel. 27 : 5

*Comment*: The reference of the sages to 'prescribed size' is M. Kel. 27 : 2:

> Cloth that is three handbreadths square is susceptible to *midras*-uncleanness and to corpse-uncleanness when it is three fingerbreadths square...

The doubled measure alludes to M. Kel. 27 : 6:

> These are measured double [one for the front, one for the back]: socks, long stockings, drawers, caps, and money-belts.

The issue evidently is whether the child's shirt is treated like ordinary cloth, in which case the sages' rule will apply, or whether any size, however small, will be susceptible to receive uncleanness, the position of Eliezer. Eliezer holds that while it is smaller than the given measurements, it serves its own purpose and therefore is like any other cloth.

I.ii.193.A. "They enter between the porch (ʾWLM) and the altar with unwashed hands and feet," the words of R. Meir.

And sages say, "They do not enter."

B. R. Simeon the Modest (HṢNWʿ) said before R. Eliezer, "I entered between the hall and the altar with unwashed hands and feet."

C. He said to him, "Who is more beloved, you or the high priest?"

D. He was silent.

E. He said to him, "You are ashamed to say the dog of the high priest is more beloved than you."

F. He said to him, "Rabbi, you have said so."

G. He said to him, "By the cult! Even the high priest—they break his skull with clubs (GZYRYN)! What will you do that the guardsman (BʿL HPL) not find you!"

Tos. Kel. B.Q. 1 : 6, Zuckermandel, p. 569, ls. 21-26

*Comment*: The pertinent Mishnah is M. Kel. 1 : 9:

> Between the porch and the altar is still more holy, for none that has a blemish or whose hair is unloosed may enter there. The sanctuary is still more holy, for none may enter therein with hands and feet unwashed...

R. Yosi said, "In five things is the space between the porch and the altar equal to the sanctuary, for they may not enter there that have a blemish, or that have drunk wine, or that have hands and feet unwashed..."

I.i.283. (*When a man has on the skin of his body a swelling or an eruption or a spot, and it turns into a leprous disease on the skin of his body, then he shall be brought to Aaron the priest or to one of his sons the priests, and the priest shall examine the diseased spot on the skin of his body; and if the hair in the diseased spot has turned white and the disease appears to be deeper than the skin of his body, it is a leprous disease... (But) when raw flesh appears on him, he shall be unclean. And the priest shall examine the raw flesh and pronounce him unclean; raw flesh is unclean, for it is leprosy.*—Lev. 13 : 2-3, 14-5)

A. Twenty-four tips of members in a man which are not unclean because of raw flesh: The tips of the hands and feet and ears, and the tip of the nose, penis, and nipples in a woman.

R. Judah says, "The nipples in men also."

B. R. Eliezer [Kaufmann, Parma, Naples, Camb.: Leazar] says, "Also the warts and wens are not subject to uncleanness because of raw flesh."

M. Neg. 6 : 7

*Comment*: Eliezer glosses the antecedent rule, without reference to Judah's independent gloss. The tips cannot be seen all at once ("priest shall examine"), so will not become susceptible to uncleanness. Eliezer adds that if there is raw flesh on a wart or a wen, it is not a source of uncleanness, for the same reason as before.

See Epstein, *Nusaḥ*, p. 1173.

I.ii.194.A. R. Eliezer says, "The corn and the wart and the wen do not become unclean on account of raw flesh."

Tos. Neg. 2 : 12, Zuckermandel, p. 620, ls. 21-2

*Comment*: Tos. adds *corns* to the list. On warts, (DLDWL/TLTWL) see Lieberman, *Tosefet Rishonim*, p. 172. Sifra has Eleazar.

I.i.284.A. If he did not have a thumb on his hand or a big toe on his foot, or a right ear, he [the leper] would never have purification.

B. R. Eliezer says, "He [the priest] puts it on their place."

C. R. Simeon says, "If he put it on the left, he has fulfilled his obligation."

M. Neg. 14 : 9 (b. Naz. 46b, b. Sanh. 45b)

*Comment*: Eliezer glosses an antecedent rule about where the priest is to put the blood of purification. The leper was cleansed by a rite described in M. Neg. 14 : 1ff. The blood of the bird-offering was put on the tip of the ear, the hand, and the foot. Then the question is raised, What if he does not have the necessary limbs? The answer is, the rite is then not performed, and the leper remains unclean. Eliezer alters this rule.

See Epstein, *Nusaḥ*, pp. 259, 1173.

I.ii.195. (How did they cleanse the leper? . . . He took cedarwood and hyssop and scarlet wool and bound them together with the ends of the strip [of wool]; and brought near to them the tips of the wings and the tip of the tail of the second bird; and dipped them in the blood of the slaughtered bird, and sprinkled the blood seven times on the back of the leper's hand. . . So likewise they used to sprinkle the lintel of the house from the outside—M. Neg. 14 : 1)

A. Hyssop which is suitable for the sin-rite is suitable for the leprosy-rite. If he sprinkled with it for the sin-rite, it is suitable for the leprosy-rite.

B. R. Eliezer says, "Cedarwood and hyssop and scarlet wool [Lev. 14 : 4] mentioned in the Torah [refer to materials] to which work has not been done [which have not been used]."

Tos. Neg. 8 : 2, Zuckermandel, p. 628, ls. 7-9

*Comment*: The issue raised by Tos. is absent in M. Neg. 14 : 1.

I.ii.196.A. They would make a causeway from the Temple Mount to the Mount of Olives, an archway built over an archway, with an arch directly above each pier [of the arch below], for fear of any grave in the depths below.

B. R. Eliezer says, "There was no causeway there, but pillars of marble were set up, and beams of cedar-wood were on top of them, and the Red Heifer did not have to go out on a causeway."

Tos. Par. 3 : 7, Zuckermandel, p. 632, ls. 14-17

*Comment*: M. Par. 3 : 6 refers to the causeway, exactly as in A. Eliezer's saying is omitted in M. Par. He holds there was no causeway at all.

Presumably someone who had really witnessed the rite would know how it was done. Evidently no one did.

I.ii.197.A. He that comes into drawn water except for his finger-tips—

B. R. Eliezer declares him unclean.

C. And sages say, "Even if only his head and the greater part of him came, he is unclean."

Tos. Miq. 3 : 9, Zuckermandel, p. 655, ls. 32-33

*Comment*: Professor Saul Lieberman (Letter, Sept. 2, 1971), kindly explains as follows: "The law declares that a healthy person who immersed his body in drawn water (i.e., not in a ritually acceptable *miqvah* or a spring) becomes ritually unclean. The same law applies to the case if such water was poured on him, see b. Shab. 13b and parallels. M. Miq. 3 : 4 rules that if such water was poured on a clean, healthy person from four vessels, he remains clean. R. Eliezer in Tos. Miq. 3 : 9 then holds the view that the person does not become unclean unless his whole body (except the tips of his fingers) is immersed in such water, but the sages rule that even if he immersed his head and the greater part of his body, he becomes unclean, provided he immerses his body in the usual way."

I.i.285.A. The Land of Israel is clean and its immersion-pools are clean. The immersion-pools of the gentiles abroad are valid for those that suffer a pollution, even if they are filled with water from a swape-well [so Danby, p. 742, for QYLWN].

B. Those within the Land of Israel which are outside the gate are valid for menstruants; inside the gate [they] are valid for those that have suffered a pollution, and are unfit for all others that are unclean.

C. R. Eliezer [Camb., Naples, Parma, Kaufmann: Eleazar] says, "Those near the town or the road are unclean because of the laundry [done in them], and those distant [from the town or the road] are clean."

M. Miq. 8 : 1

*Comment*: Eliezer glosses the antecedent rule concerning pools outside the gate. Even though they are outside the town they still are unfit because people do laundry in them and there leave the laundry water, which is drawn water. But those farther from the town or the road are not used for laundry and drawn water is not poured into them. So the rule that the immersion pools of Palestine are clean is qualified in two stages: first, the distinction about what is outside and inside the gate, then Eliezer's: those outside the gate near the town or the road and far from the town or the road—a neat progression, leaving Eliezer at the end of the antecedent legislative process.

See Epstein, *Tan.*, p. 107; *Nusaḥ*, p. 1175.

I.i.286.A. These do not interpose [between the water and the body. For immersion to be valid, every part of the body's surface must be touched by the immersion-pool-water]:

B. Matted hair of the head, and of the armpits and of the private parts of a man.

C. R. Eliezer [Camb., Naples, Parma, Kaufmann: Eleazar] says, "It is all the same for a man and a woman. Whatever a person is fastidious about interposes, and whatever a person is not fastidious about does not interpose."

M. Miq. 9 : 3

*Comment*: Eliezer says that the qualification as to the private parts of a man is invalid. The same rule applies to both man and woman. Whatever a person is concerned about will interpose, and this is in accord with M. Miq. 9 : 7, "This is the general rule, whatever a person is concerned about interposes," and *vice versa*, just as above. That is, whatever a person would want to remove from his body will intervene. If a person would remove the matted hair, then its presence will interpose.

See Epstein, *Nusaḥ*, p. 1175; *Tan*., pp. 173, 201.

I.i.287.A. Once one is certified (MŠNZQQ) as a *Zab* (ZYBH), they do not inspect him. [Fluxes that come] inadvertently or in doubt and his semen are unclean, for there is reason for the matter [= to believe he is a *Zab*].

B. If he saw the first appearance [of flux], they examine him. [If he saw] a second [appearance], they examine him.

C. At the third [appearance of flux], they do not examine him.

D. R. Eliezer [Camb., Parma, Kaufmann: Eleazar] says, "Also on the third [appearance of flux] they do examine him, because of the sacrifice [to determine whether he is liable for a sacrifice]."

M. Zab. 2 : 2 (y. Meg. 1 : 8: Leazar; b. Naz. 65b: Eliezer; b. Nid. 35a: Eliezer; b. Nid. 37a)

*Comment*: B-C-D explain the process of certification of the *Zab*. Once he has seen two appearances of flux, they do not examine him. That is, on the occasion of the third flux, he is completely in the status of a *Zab* and brings the offering specified in Lev. 15. Eliezer says even on the third flux one examines him, for if the flux is not on account of his being a *Zab*, he does not bring the offering. According to Eliezer, however, if he saw a fourth during the counting of the seven clean days, he then is certified as a *Zab* and is not examined further.

The examinations referred to are explained in the same place, M. Zab. 2 : 2A, as follows: Along seven lines do they examine a *Zab* if he has not already been certified as a *Zab*. "Concerning what he had eaten, drunk, carried, whether he had jumped, whether he had been sick, what he had seen, or whether he had had impure thoughts. . ." These are factors which may cause flux that will *not* render the man unclean as a *Zab*, for if it was an accidental flux, the man is not a *Zab*. Thus after the first appearance of flux, one investigates its cause, and if the man has had a flux from inadvertence or from the other specified causes, he is not regarded as a *Zab*.

See Epstein, *Nusaḥ*, p. 1176.

I.i.288 R. Eliezer [Kaufmann, Parma, Camb.: Leazar] reports two opinions in which the House of Shammai follow the more lenient and the House of Hillel the more stringent ruling.

According to the House of Shammai the blood of a woman that has not yet immersed herself after childbirth is like to her spittle or her urine.

And the House of Hillel say, "[It conveys uncleanness] whether it is wet or dried up."

But they agree that if a woman gave birth while she had a flux, it renders unclean whether [the blood was] wet or dried up.

I.i.289. If two of four brothers married two sisters, and the two that married the two sisters died, the sisters must perform *ḥaliṣah* and may not contract Levirate marriage; and if the brothers had already married them, they must put them away.

R. Eliezer [Camb., Parma, Kaufmann: Leazar] says, "According to the House of Shammai they may continue the marriage; but according to the House of Hillel they must put them away."

M. Ed. 5 : 4, 5 : 5, trans. Danby, pp. 431-432
[= M. Nid. 4 : 3, M. Yev. 3 : 5]

*Comment*: See *Phar.* II, pp. 336-340. See also Epstein, *Nusaḥ*, pp. 1163, 180; *Tan.*, pp. 436-437.

CHAPTER THREE

# HISTORICAL AND BIOGRAPHICAL TRADITIONS. WISDOM-SAYINGS

Biographical traditions consist of stories and sayings about Eliezer's life. Narratives intended to illustrate his view of the law are given with the legal materials. Historical traditions are stories and sayings about events in Eliezer's own day in which Eliezer plays no important part or no part at all. Wisdom-sayings normally are set in a narrative-biographical framework and therefore come under consideration at this point.

I.I.290. R. Eliezer the Great says, "From the day on which the Temple was destroyed [*what follows is in Aramaic:*] the sages (ḤKYMY') began to be like scribes (SPRY'), and the scribes like synagogue-servants (ḤZNY'), and the synagogue-servants like the ordinary folk (ʿM' D'Rʿ'), and the ordinary folk grow weak, and none seeks [*in Hebrew:*] and on whom is there to rely? On our father in heaven."

M. Sot. 9 : 15

*Comment*: The setting for Eliezer's saying is a long and complex pericope on the decline in the generations. The model is *When X died, Y ceased.* The list of masters is as follows: Meir, Ben ʿAzzai, Ben Zoma, Joshua, Simeon b. Gamaliel, Eleazar b. ʿAzariah, ʿAqiba, Ḥanina b. Dosa, Yosi Kaṭnuta, Yoḥanan b. Zakkai, Gamaliel the Elder, Ishmael b. Phiabi—a mixture of Yavneans and Ushans—and then, Rabbi [Judah the Patriarch]. Eliezer does not occur in this list.

Attached is a saying attributed to Pinḥas b. Ya'ir, "*When the Temple was destroyed* [substituted for *When X died*], the *Ḥaverim* and freemen were ashamed and covered their head, and wonder-workers grew weak, and strong-armed men and gossipers grew strong. None expounds, and none seeks, and none asks. On whom is there to rely? On our father in heaven." All is in Hebrew.

Then comes Eliezer ("the Great"), as above. The saying begins with the same prologue as Pinḥas's *from the day that the Temple was destroyed.* Then instead of active verbs, we have comparisons, *X became like Y*: sages like scribes—who teach Bible, scribes like ḤZN's—who tend synagogues, and so on. The decline ends, however, with an abbreviated form of Pinḥas's *none seeks . . . on whom to depend*, in Hebrew. It would seem likely that Pinḥas's concluding clause has contaminated Eliezer's, rather than *vice versa*. The wording is slightly different, Pinḥas has *On whom [is there] for us to depend*, Eliezer, *On whom is there to depend.* Since the saying of Eliezer is in Aramaic, the inclusion of a Hebrew introductory phrase and conclusion is out of place, and therefore, as suggested, would seem to derive from the foregoing saying. If so, Eliezer's saying is simply an account of the decline in the generation following the destruction of the Temple, so the destruction stands in place of the death of a specific sage, and the Temple is more important than the Torah-masters. This would seem to come before the assignment of the decline to the death of the sage instead of to the Temple. Since *On whom is there to rely* looks like an interpolation, Eliezer's original saying evidently was a melancholy, but commonplace comment that the Temple's destruction marked a significant turning for the worse.

See Epstein, *Tan.*, p. 503; *Nusaḥ*, pp. 949, 976

I.ii.198. When R. Eliezer died, the *Sefer Torah* was annulled (BṬL).

Tos. Sot. 15 : 3, Zuckermandel, p. 321 l. 19
(b. Sot. 49b: was *hidden*)

*Comment*: Eliezer is omitted from the Mishnaic list. Had he been included, his death would have marked the end of the *Sefer Torah.* But ʿAqiba and Gamaliel the Elder come close: "The glory of the Toraẖ" (for *both* of them!). Gamaliel also has purity and separatism (PRYŠWT); perhaps someone has given him *glory of Torah* in addition. Most others in the original list have charismatic gifts: proverb-makers, expositors, goodness, wonder-working, Ḥasidim, splendor of wisdom, splendor of priesthood, modesty, and fear of sin. *Torah* is reserved for ʿAqiba/Gamaliel, and Eliezer is dropped entirely by M. Sot. 9 : 15. Tos. Sot. 14 : 3 continues, "When Joshua died, men of counsel and intention (MḤŠBH) died; ʿAqiba ended the *arms* of Torah (ZRWʿY) and the fountains of wisdom," etc. The *Sefer Torah*-detail seems to be developed into the death-bed saying (below, p. 415) about "arms like Torah-scrolls."

I.i.291.A. Rabban Yoḥanan b. Zakkai received [the Law] from Hillel and from Shammaai.

He used to say: "If thou hast wrought much in the Law, claim not merit for thyself, for to this end wast thou created."

B. Five disciples had Rabban Yoḥanan b. Zakkai, and these are they: R. Eliezer b. Hyrcanus and R. Joshua b. Ḥananiah, and R. Yosi the Priest, and R. Simeon b. Nathaniel, and R. Eleazar b. ʿArakh.

C. Thus used he to recount their praise: Eliezer b. Hyrcanus is a plastered cistern which loses not a drop; Joshua b. Ḥananiah—happy is she that bare him; Yosi the Priest is a saintly man; Simeon b. Nathaniel is fearful of sin; Eleazar b. ʿArakh is an ever-flowing spring.

He used to say, "If all the sages of Israel were in the one scale of the balance and Eliezer b. Hyrcanus in the other, he would outweigh them all."

E. Abba Saul said in his name: "If all the sages of Israel were in the one scale of the balance and with them Eliezer b. Hyrcanus, and Eleazar b. ʿArakh was in the other, he would outweigh them all."

F. He said to them, "Go forth and see which is the good way to which a man should cleave."

G. R. Eliezer said, "A good eye."

R. Joshua said, "A good companion.

R. Yosi said, "A good neighbor."

R. Simeon said, "One that sees what will be."

R. Eleazar said, "A good heart."

He said to them, "I approve the words of Eleazar b. ʿArakh more than your words, for in his words are your words included."

H. He said to them, "Go forth and see which is the evil way which a man should shun."

R. Eliezer said, "An evil eye."

R. Joshua said, "An evil companion."

R. Yosi said, "An evil neighbor."

R. Simeon said, "He that borrows and does not repay. He that borrows from man is as one that borrows from God, for it is written, *The wicked borroweth and payeth not again but the righteous dealeth graciously and giveth.*"

R. Eleazar said, "An evil heart."

He said to them, "I approve the words of Eleazar b. ʿArakh more than your words for in his words are your words included."

I. They [each] said three things.

R. Eliezer said, (1) "Let the honor of thy fellow be dear to thee as thine own, and (2) be not easily provoked, and (3) repent one day before thy death; and (4) warm thyself before the fire of the sages, but be heedful of their glowing coals lest thou be burned.

"For their bite is the bite of a jackal and their sting, the sting of a scorpion and their hiss, the hiss of a serpent, and all their words are like coals of fire."

M. Avot 2 : 8-10, trans. Danby, pp. 448-449

*Comment*: See *Development*, pp. 55ff.

The original list had Yoḥanan praise Eliezer at the end; then Abba Saul has deliberately revised it, naming Eliezer specifically, and substituting Eleazar b. ʿArakh in his place. Eliezer originally stood at the head of the list, as is still the case in the *good-way - evil-way*-sayings.

Eliezer's "three" sayings are: (1) honor; (2) patience; (3) repentence; (4) fire of sages—expanded to jackal, scorpion, serpent, then coals—four in all, with a considerable expansion of the fourth.

The repentence saying is developed in apophthegmatic materials. The others do not recur. The fourth saying possibly relates to, or has generated, the accounts of Eliezer's unhappy relationships with the sages, below, p. 422. The first is an application of Lev. 19 : 18, *Love your neighbor as yourself*, to the sages' interrelationships. The second is a commonplace.

V.i.3.A. Yosi ben Yoʿezer says, "Let thy house be a meeting place for the sages, and sit in the very dust at their feet, and thirstily drink in their words."

B. Another interpretation. "Sit in the very dust at their feet" refers to Rabbi Eliezer, and "thirstily drink in their words" refers to Rabbi ʿAqiba.

ARN, Chap. 6, Goldin, p. 40.

*Comment*: Eliezer and ʿAqiba are glossed into Yosi's saying.

V.i.4. Five disciples did Rabban Yoḥanan ben Zakkai have, for each of whom he had a name.

Eliezer ben Hyrcanus he called "plastered cistern which loses not a drop, pitch-coated flask which keeps its wine."

ARN, Chap. 14, Goldin, p. 74

*Comment*: This is congruent to Eliezer's claim never to have said what he had not heard from his masters. But see *Development*, p. 125.

III.ii.89. R. Eliezer said, "Repent one day before your death." [See Ben Sira 5 : 8.]

His disciples said to him, "Does one know on what day he will die?"

He said to them, "All the more reason that he should repent today, lest he die tomorrow, and thus his whole life is spent in repentence."

b. Shab. 153a (Mid. Ps. 90 : 17)

*Comment*: Eliezer's saying in M. Avot 2 : 10 is now given a narrative setting. The disciples raise the obvious question, and are given the obvious answer. See *Life*, p. 239; *Development*, p. 257.

V.i.5.A. Repent one day before thy death. Rabbi Eliezer was asked by his disciples, "Does, then, a man know on what day he will die, that he should know when to repent?"

"All the more," he replied; "let him repent today lest he die on the morrow; let him repent on the morrow lest he die the day after; and thus all his days will be spent in repentance."

B. Rabbi Yosi bar Judah says in the name of Rabbi Judah son of Rabbi Ilᶜai who said in the name of Rabbi Ilᶜai his father who said it in the name of Rabbi Eliezer the Great, "Repent one day before thy death. Keep warm at the fire of the sages. Beware of their glowing coal lest thou be scorched: for their bite is the bite of a jackal and their sting the sting of a scorpion—moreover all their words are like coals of fire."

ARN, Chap. 15, Goldin, p. 82

*Comment*: Eliezer's saying is supplied in A with a narrative setting, and B has a chain for Eliezer's saying: Ilai, Judah, Yosi. If the chain of tradents is not a later interpolation, then Ilai supplies very early attestation for Eliezer's saying.

V.xii.1. It has been taught: Repent one day before your death. R. Eliezer was asked by his disciples, "Rabbi, does any man know when he will die so that he can repent?"

He answered them, "Should he not all the more repent today lest he die the day after, and then all his days will be lived in repentance."

For that reason it is said, *Let thy garments be always white.* (Qoh. 9 : 8)

Qoh. R. 9 : 8, trans. A. Cohen, p. 236

*Comment*: See *Life*, pp. 122n., 239.

I.i.292.A. R. Eliezer said, "I have heard a tradition that while they were building the Temple, they made curtains for the Temple and curtains for the courtyards, but they built [the walls of] the Temple outside [the curtains], and [the walls of] the courtyards they built within [the curtains]."

B. R. Joshua said, "I have heard a tradition that they may offer sacrifices although there is no Temple, and eat the Most Holy Things although there are no curtains, and the Lesser Holy Things and the Second Tithe although there is no wall; since its first dedication availed both for its own time and for the time to come."

M. Ed. 8 : 6, trans. Danby, p. 436
(b. Shav. 16a, b. Zev. 107b, b. Meg. 10a)

*Comment*: Eliezer's and Joshua's sayings do not correspond. Eliezer's has to do with the building of the sanctuary. He does not specify which building, so we cannot assume it is Herod's, but that would seem most likely, if the tradition is something Eliezer has actually heard from someone who witnessed the process. The builders stood outside of the curtains when constructing the walls of the Temple, and within the curtains when constructing the walls of the courtyard.

Joshua's saying is linked to Eliezer's only by the common form: *I have heard.* He says he has a tradition that it is permissible to make sacrifices even without the Temple—that is, after the destruction; and to eat Most Holy Things even outside the wall of Jerusalem. When the first Temple was sanctified, in the time of Solomon, it was consecrated for its own time and for all time. The holy places remain holy, even without the Temple. It is an astonishing tradition, for, according to Joshua, it was permitted to continue the sacrificial cult in the ruins of Jerusalem.

Eliezer's saying bears no relationship to Joshua's except in form, as noted; perhaps Joshua's allusion to the consecration justifies juxtaposition of Eliezer's to the process of construction, but this seems unlikely. The redactional principle is solely formal.

I.ii.199. R. ʿAqiba said, "Three hundred laws did R. Eliezer expound concerning *Thou shalt not permit the sorceress to live* (Ex. 22 : 17), and I learned (LMD) from him only two things: 'Two gathering cucumbers: one gatherer is liable, and one gatherer is free of liability. [How so?]. He who does a deed [of magic] is liable. He who creates an illusion is free of liability.' "

Tos. Sanh. 11 : 5, Zuckermandel, p. 431, ls. 24-26

*Comment*: The pertinent Mishnah is M. Sanh. 7 : 11:

> The sorcerer [Deut. 18 : 10]: he that performs some act is culpable, and not he that deceives the eyes.
>
> R. ʿAqiba in the name of R. Joshua says, "If two are gathering cucumbers [Danby, p. 393, adds: *by sorcery*], one gatherer may not be culpable, and the other gatherer may be culpable; he that performed the act is culpable, but he that deceived the eyes is not culpable."

III.i.15. R. Joshua b. Ḥananiah said, "Three hundred chapters (PRŠYWT) did R. Liezer expound concerning the chapter of the sorceress, and of all of them, I only heard two things. Two gathering cucumbers—one who gathers is free and one who gathers is liable; he that does a deed is liable and he that deceives the eyes is free."

y. Sanh. 7 : 13, Gilead, p. 81

*Comment*: The traditions are in a confused state. M. Sanh. 7 : 11 has ʿAqiba quoting Joshua, and y. Sanh. explicitly attributes M. Sanh.'s teaching of Joshua *to* Eliezer. Consistently, Tos. Sanh. has ʿAqiba attribute the same tradition to Eliezer. y. Sanh. refers to the chapter of the sorceress, instead of citing the pertinent verse; it removes the implication that what Eliezer taught was not worth learning (ʿAqiba: I only *learned*) by substituting Joshua's *heard*, which leaves the impression that other teachings, also worthwhile, were not heard. Eliezer is thus behind the teachings about the cucumber-gathering for Tos. and y., and Joshua is given the same teaching, in the same words, by ʿAqiba in the Mishnah—a strange state of affairs.

It is difficult to know what lies behind the twisted chain of tradition. Other stories develop the Tos.-y. tradition, below, p. 411. The tradition distinguishes between actual practice of magic and mere deception. As we shall see, that distinction plays no role whatever in the stories generated by the cucumber-teaching.

I.ii.200.A. MʿŚH B: R. Eliezer was seized on account of matters of *Minut*, and they brought him up before the court (BMH) for judgment.

That *hegemon* said to him, "Should an elder like you involve [himself] in these matters?"

He said to him, "The judge (DYYN) is faithful for me (NʾMN ʿLY) [= "I rely upon the Judge."]

That *hegemon* thought that he spoke only of him [himself], but he meant only his Father who is in heaven.

He said to him, "Since you have relied upon me, so have I said, "Is it possible that these white hairs should err (HSYBWT HLLW TWʿYM) in such matters? *Dimissus* [= Pardoned (DYMWS)]. Lo, you are free."

B. And when he had left the court (BMH), he was upset that he was seized on account of matters of *Minut.*

His disciples came in to comfort him and he would not accept [comfort].

R. ʿAqiba entered and said to him, "Rabbi, May I say something before you? Perhaps you will not be distressed."

He said to him, "Speak."

He said to him, "Perhaps one of the *Minim* said something to you of *Minut* and gave you benefit (WHNʾK)."

C. He said, "By heaven! You have reminded me. One time I was walking in the camp (ʾYSṬRTYʾ) of Sepphoris. I found Jacob of Kefar Sikhnin, and he said something of *Minut* in the name of Jesus b. Pantiri [Alt.: PNDYRʾ] and gave me benefit (NHʾNY), and I was seized on account of matters of *Minut*, for I transgressed teachings of Torah: *Keep your way far from her and do not go near the door of her house...* (Prov. 5 : 8)."

D. R. Eliezer would say, "A man should always flee from what is ugly and from what looks like something ugly."

Tos. Hul. 2 : 24, Zuckermandel, p. 503, ls. 18-30

*Comment*: See Lieberman, *Tosefet Rishonim* II, p. 227. The pericope is in three parts. First (A) is the story of the trial. Eliezer outwits the judge by saying something intended for Heaven, which the judge took to be intended for himself. B ties the foregoing to a related, but separate account, (C), of Eliezer and the *Minim*, which is intended to illustrate that one must have no benefit whatever from, or relationships with, *Minim*. D then formulates an appropriate apodictic saying to conclude the second story.

III.ii.90.A. TNW RBNN: When R. Eliezer was arrested because of *Minut*, they brought him up to the tribune (GRDWM) to be judged. Said the *Hegemon* to him, "How can a sage man like you occupy himself with those idle things?"

He replied, "I acknowledge the Judge as right."

The governor thought that he referred to him—though he really referred to his Father in Heaven—and said, "Because you have acknowledged me as right, I pardon (DYMWS). You are acquitted."

B. When he came home, his disciples called on him to console him, but he would accept no consolation.

Said R. ʿAqiba to him, "Master, will you permit me to say one thing of what you have taught me?"

He replied, "Say it."

"Master," said he, "perhaps some of the teaching of the *Minim* came to you, and you did approve of it, and because of that you were arrested?"

C. He exclaimed, "ʿAqiba, you have reminded me. I was once walking in the upper-market of Sepphoris when I came across one [Munich MS adds: *of the disciples of Jesus the Nazarene*] Jacob of Kefar-Sikhnaia by name, who said to me, 'It is written in your Torah, *Thou shalt not bring the hire of a harlot . . . into the house of the Lord thy God* (Deut. 23 : 19). May such money be applied to the erection of a retiring place for the High Priest?' To which I made no reply.

"Said he to me, 'Thus was I taught [Munich MS adds: *by Jesus the Nazarene*], *For of the hire of a harlot hath she gathered them and unto the hire of a harlot shall they return* (Micah 1 : 7), they came from a place of filth, let them go to a place of filth.' Those words pleased me very much, and that is why I was arrested for apostacy; for thereby I transgressed the Scriptural words, *Remove thy way far from her*—which refers to *Minut*—*and come not nigh to the door of her house* (Prov. 5 : 8),—which refers to the ruling power."

b. A.Z. 16b-17a (trans. A. Mishcon, pp. 84-85).

*Comment*: The story closely follows Tos. Hul. 9 : 24 (p. 400) up to C.

Then the teaching of Jacob, which is not preserved in Tos., is spelled out. Prov. 5 : 8 is quoted and expounded; it is merely quoted in Tos. Hul. The teaching about the harlot's hire is in a general way congruent to Eliezer's teaching (above, p. 381), but there is no specific connection. So b. A.Z. expands the crucial point of Tos. Hul.: precisely what Jesus had taught.

V.xii.2.A. Another interpretation of *All things toil to weariness. Words of heresy weary man.*

R. Eliezer was once arrested because of heresy, and the governor took him and made him ascend a dais to be tried.

He said to him, "Rabbi, can a great man like you occupy himself with those idle matters?"

He answered him, "Faithful is the Judge concerning me."

[The governor] thought that he was alluding to him, whereas he said it with reference to God.

He thereupon said to him, "Since I have been acknowledged right by you, I too have been thinking and say, 'Is it possible that these Academies should go astray with such idle matters! You are consequently acquitted and free.' "

B. After R. Eliezer had left the dais, he was sorely grieved at having been arrested because of heresy. His disciples visited him to console him, but he would not accept [their words of comfort].

R. ʿAqiba visited him and said to him, "Rabbi, perhaps one of the *Minim* expounded something in your presence which was acceptable to you."

C. He answered, "By heaven, you have reminded me! Once I was walking up the main street of Sepphoris when there came toward me a man named Jacob of Kefar Sekhaniah who told me something in the name of so-and-so which pleased me: 'It is written in your Torah, *Thou shalt not bring the hire of a harlot, or the price of a dog, into the house of the Lord thy God for any vow* (Deut. 23 : 19). What is to be done with them?' "

"I told him that they were prohibited [for every use]. He said to me, 'They are prohibited as an offering, but is it permissible to destroy them?'

"I retorted, 'In that case, what is to be done with them?'

"He said to me, 'Let bath-houses and privies be made with them.'

"I exclaimed, 'You have said an excellent thing,' and the law [not to listen to the words of a *min*] escaped my memory at the time. When he saw that I acknowledged his words, he added, 'Thus said so-and-so: From filth they came and on filth they should be expended; as it is said, *For the hire of a harlot hath she gathered them and unto the hire of a harlot they shall return* (Micah 1 : 7). Let them be spent on privies for the public,' and the thought pleased me.

"On that account I was arrested for heresy. More than that, I transgressed what is written in the Torah, *Remove thy way far from her, and come not at night to the door of her house* (Prov. 5 : 8)—*Remove thy way far from her*—heresy; *And come not nigh to the door of her house*—immorality. Why? *For she hath cast down many wounded, yea, a mighty host are all her slain* (Prov. 7 : 26)."

Qoh. R. 1 : 8 : 4, trans. A. Cohen, pp. 27-28

*Comment*: On the several stories about Eliezer and the *hegemon*, see David Rokeah, "Ben Stara Is Ben Pantera. Towards the Clarification of a Philological-Historical Problem," (Hebrew) *Tarbiz* 39, 1, 1969, pp. 9-18. Rokeah sees Tos. as the original version. He regards those in Yalqut Micah 551 and Proverbs 937 (not cited) as useless; and Qoh. R. is not much better. Ben Pantera means Jesus was the son of Mary by a soldier, Panthera, an interpretation corroborated by the Gospels [*sic*], Celsus, and the rabbis. The Yavneans sought to combat the idea that Jesus was born of a virgin by claiming he was the son of a soldier. Celsus attributes the story to a Jew. Ben Stara derives from *stauros*, cross. The story about Jesus in Egypt (Tos. Shab., etc.) is turned by the Yavnean rabbis into an accusation that Jesus was a sorcerer.

Of still greater importance is Saul Lieberman, "Roman Legal Institutions in Early Rabbinics and in the Acta Martyrum," *Jewish Quarterly Review* n.s., Vol. 35, 1944, pp. 1-57, in particular, pp. 19-24. Lieberman sees the incident as bearing on Trajan's persecution of the Christians, accepting Herford's view of the matter. He observes that no accuser was present, and so the denunciation was anonymous. We do not know what the judge first asked Eliezer. He "undoubtedly began by asking him for his name, country etc." These details were standard and so omitted from the account. Then the judge began with the reproach—that is, by incriminating questioning. Eliezer should have issued a flat denial: "If the Rabbi had allowed a discussion to develop the judge might have asked him for the reasons of his excommunication. It might have involved an explanation of the intimate internal affairs of the academies. Had R. Eliezer refused to answer this question, once it was asked, the charge would naturally be confirmed." Eliezer could have shown he was not now a Christian by cursing Jesus, but this would not have helped as to his past beliefs. The governor himself was glad to dismiss the case. "The story provides valuable information on the attitude of the Roman governor of Palestine towards the Christians during the persecutions of Trajan," who was probably Q. Pompeius Falco, so Lieberman.

II.i.11.A. Some time ago (WKBR) R. Eliezer was sick and the four elders, R. Ṭarfon, R. Joshua, R. Eleazar b. ʿAzariah, and R. ʿAqiba, went in to visit him.

B. R. Ṭarfon then began, saying, "Master, you are more precious to Israel than the globe of the sun, for the globe of the sun gives light only for this world, while you have given us light both for this world and the world to come."

C. Then R. Joshua began, saying, "Master, you are more precious to Israel than the days of rain, for rain gives life only for this world, while you have given us life for this world and for the world to come."

D. Then R. Eleazar b. ʿAzariah began, saying, "Master, you are more precious to Israel than father and mother. For father and mother bring a man into the life of this world, while you have brought us to the life of the world to come."

E. Then R. ʿAqiba began, saying, "Precious are chastisements."

F. R. Eliezer then said to his disciples, "Help me up."

R. Eliezer then sat up and said to him, "Speak, ʿAqiba."

G. He then said to him, "Behold it says, *Manasseh was twelve years old when he began to reign; and he reigned fifty and five years in Jerusalem. And he did that which was evil in the sight of the Lord* (II Chron. 33 : 1-2). And it also says, *These also are proverbs of Solomon, which the men of Hezekiah king of Judah copied out* (Prov. 25 : 1). And could the thought enter your mind that Hezekiah king of Judah taught the Torah to all Israel, and to his son Manasseh he did not teach the Torah? You must therefore say that all the instruction which he gave him did not affect Manasseh at all. And what *did* have affect upon him? You must say, chastisements. For it is said, *And the Lord spoke to Manasseh and to his people, but they gave no heed. Wherefore the Lord brought upon them the captains of the host of the king of Assyria, who took Manasseh with hooks and bound him with fetters and carried him to Babylonia. And when he was in distress, he besought the Lord his God and humbled himself greatly before the God of his fathers. And he prayed unto him, and he was entreated of him and heard his supplication and brought him back to Jerusalem into his kingdom* (II. Chron. 33 : 10-13). Thus you learn that chastisements are very precious."

Mekh. Baḥodesh 10 : 58-86, Lauterbach II, pp. 280-282

*Comment*: The point of this highly formalized structure is made by ʿAqiba. The others simply praise Eliezer as a master of Torah, but ʿAqiba tells him that his suffering has a good purpose. Eliezer's "praise" of ʿAqiba, unlike Yoḥanan b. Zakkai's of Eleazar b. ʿArakh, comes in the middle, when Eliezer recognizes ʿAqiba by sitting up in order to hear what he has to say.

The story makes Joshua into Eliezer's disciple, who does not even come first in the dialogue and enjoys no recognition as Eliezer's equal in discipleship with Yoḥanan b. Zakkai. He is simply one among several distinguished students of Eliezer, not the best of them. And he speaks to Eliezer as his master, not as "Eliezer, my brother," as is more common among equals. The story tells nothing about Eliezer. It is a story about ʿAqiba, Eliezer's most distinguished student.

IV.ii.18.A. Rabbah b. Bar Ḥana said, "When R. Eliezer fell sick, his disciples entered [his house] to visit him."

He said to them, "There is a fierce wrath in the world."

They broke into tears, but R. ʿAqiba laughed, "Why dost thou laugh?" they inquired of him.

"Why do ye weep?" he retorted.

They answered, "Shall the Scroll of the Torah lie in pain, and we do not weep?"

He replied, "For that very reason I rejoice. As long as I saw that my master's wine did not turn sour, nor was his flax smitten, nor his oil putrefied, nor his honey become rancid, I thought, God forbid, that he may have received all his reward in this world [leaving nothing for the next]; but now that I see him lying in pain, I rejoice [knowing that his reward has been treasured up for him in the next]."

B. He [R. Eliezer] said to him, "ʿAqiba, have I neglected anything of the whole Torah?"

He replied, "Thou, O Master, hast taught us, *For there is not a just man upon earth, that doeth good and sinneth not* (Qoh. 7 : 20)."

C. Our Rabbis taught: When R. Eliezer fell sick, four elders went to visit him, R. Ṭarfon, R. Joshua, R. Eleazar b. ʿAzariah, and R. ʿAqiba.

D. R. Ṭarfon said to him, "Thou art more valuable to Israel than rain [Sifré: the orb of the sun]; for rain is [precious] in this world, whereas thou art [so] for this world and the next."

E. R. Joshua observed, "Thou art more valuable to Israel than the sun's disc [Sifré: rain] for the sun's disc is but for this world, while my master is for this world and the next."

F. R. Eleazar b. ʿAzariah observed, "Thou art better to Israel than a father and a mother; these are for this world, whereas my master is for this world and the next."

G. But R. ʿAqiba observed, "Suffering is precious."

Thereupon he [the sick man] said to them, "Support me, that I may hear the words of ʿAqiba, my disciple, who said, 'Suffering is precious.' "

"'ʿAqiba," queried he, "Whence doest thou know this?" [Sifré: "*Speak ʿAqiba*"]

H. He replied, "I interpret a verse: *Manasseh was twelve years old when he began to reign, and he reigned fifty and five years in Jerusalem etc. and he did that which was evil in the sight of the Lord* (II Kings 21 : 1). Now it is [elsewhere] written, *These are also the proverbs of Solomon, which the men of Hezekiah king of Judah copied out* (Prov. 25 : 1). Now, would Hezekiah king of Judah have taught the Torah to the whole world, yet not to his own son Manasseh? But all the pains he spent upon him, and all the labors he lavished upon him did not bring him back to the right path, save suffering alone, as it is written, *And the Lord spake to Manasseh and to his people but they would not hearken unto him. Wherefore the Lord brought upon them the captains of the host of the king of Assyria, which took Manasseh among the thorns, and bound him with fetters, and carried him to Babylonia* (II Chron. 33 : 10). And it is further written, *And when he was in affliction, he besought the Lord his God, and humbled himself greatly before the God of his fathers. And prayed unto him, and he was entreated of him, and heard his supplication, and brought him again to Jerusalem unto his kingdom, and Manasseh knew that the Lord he was God* (II Chron. 33 : 12). [Sifré omits:] Thus thou learnest how precious is suffering."

b. Sanh. 101a-b, trans. Jacob Shachter, pp. 686-7 (C–H: Sifré Deut. 32, ed. Finkelstein, pp. 57-8, ls. 12-16, 1-12)

*Comment*: Rabbah b. b. Ḥana's story is in two parts, with ʿAqiba the center in both. First, ʿAqiba explains that it is good to suffer in this world so as to enjoy the next. Then he tells Eliezer that he has indeed neglected the Torah!

C is similar to Mekh., but with the embellishments common in the *baraita*-stratum. C-H knows nothing of A-B.

II.iv.23.A. Once (WKBR) R. Eliezer, R. Joshua, and R. Ṣaddoq were reclining at the wedding-banquet of the son of Rabban Gamaliel. Rabban Gamaliel mixed the cup [of wine] for R. Eliezer, but he [Eliezer] did not want to take it.

R. Joshua took it.

B. R. Eliezer said to him, "What is this, Joshua? Is it right that we should recline and Gamaliel *BeRibbi* should stand over and serve us?"

C. R. Joshua said to him, "Let him do service. Abraham, the great one of the world, served the ministering angels, assuming they were Arabs and idolators, as it is said, *And he lifted up his eyes and he saw, and behold, three men* (Gen. 18 : 2). And it is *qal veḥomer*: If Abraham, the great one of the world, served the ministering angels, [even while] assuming they were Arabs and idolators, should not Gamaliel *Beribbi* serve us?

D. R. Ṣaddoq said to them, "You have neglected the honor of the Omnipresent and are occupied with the honor of mortal man. If He who spoke and brought the world into being restores the winds, brings up clouds, brings down rains, raises grain, and sets a table for each and everyone, should not Gamaliel *Beribbi* serve us?"

Sifré Deut. 38, Finkelstein, pp. 74-75
(Mekh. deR. Simeon b. Yoḥai 18 : 12, p. 88;
Mid. Mishlé 21 : 2)

II.vi.1 Once (WKBR) R. Eliezer, R. Joshua, and R. Ṣaddoq were reclining at the wedding party of the son of Rabban Gamaliel.

Rabban Gamaliel mixed the cup for R. Eliezer and he did not want to take it, etc.

Midrash Tannaim to Deut. 11 : 10, Hoffmann, p. 30

*Comment*: Ṣaddoq does not figure in most Eliezer-lists; he will be replaced by ʿAqiba or Eleazer b. ʿAzariah. The story supplies the setting for two homilies about hospitality. Joshua's is built on the hospitality shown by Abraham. Ṣaddoq's ignores Joshua's and teaches that just as *God* supplies hospitality for man, so should men do the same for one another. *Imitatio dei* therefore takes the place of the imitation of the sage. As already observed, the tendency is to supplant the antecedent models of authority or sanctity—the Temple, God—with the sage; in M. Sot. *when the Temple was destroyed* becomes *When Rabbi X died.* Here likewise one should imitate Abraham or God in respect to hospitality. Eliezer has no homily. He merely provides the occasion for Ṣaddoq's and Joshua's homilies.

The pericope is a unity, but D could have been dropped without spoiling the earlier structure; the story could have ended with C, which satisfactorily answers Eliezer's question. Further, the description of the action of Gamaliel in A omits reference to Ṣaddoq; it may be that Ṣaddoq has been glossed into A so that his homily can be added at D, making a Joshua/Eliezer-structure more complex. If so, the story's original exchange was between Eliezer and Joshua.

On the meaning of *beribbi*, Professor Louis Finkelstein kindly informs me (Letter, October 19, 1971):

> The title *Beribbi* was generally used when colleagues were conversing with one another, and one wanted to express a special respect for the other,

> because of his ancestry. *Beribbi*, of course, means only the "son of the master." Rabban Gamaliel's colleagues were talking about him, but in his presence, and they wanted to refer to the fact that he was the son of a great father. They did not call him *Rabban*, even to his face, because they were as old and learned as he and possibly more learned. And yet they did not want to say simply "Gamaliel." The addition of *beribbi*, really a compliment to his father, was incidentally also a compliment to him.

My colleague Dr. David Goodblatt points out, however, that Schwabe and Lipschitz, *Bet She'arim* II, *Greek Inscriptions*, p. 30, *re* no. 89, hold the meaning is BR 'B' (as against S. Klein, *Jüdisch-Palästinisches Corpus Inscriptionum*, 112).

III.ii.91. M'ŚH B: R. Eliezer, R. Joshua and R. Ṣaddoq were reclining at a banquet of Rabban Gamaliel's son, while Rabban Gamaliel was standing over them and serving drink. On his offering a cup to R. Eliezer, he did not accept it; but when he offered it to R. Joshua, he accepted it (QBL).

Said R. Eliezer to him, "What is this, Joshua? We are sitting, while Rabban Gamaliel is standing over us and serving drink!"

"We find that even a greater one than he served," he replied. "Abraham was the greatest man of the generation, yet it is written of him, *And he stood over them* (Gen. 18 : 8). And should you say that they appeared to him as Ministering Angels—they appeared to him only as Arabs. Then shall not R. Gamaliel *Beribbi* stand over us and offer drink!"

Said R. Ṣaddoq to them, "How long will you disregard the honor of the Omnipresent and occupy yourselves with the honor of men! The Holy One, blessed be He, causes the winds to blow, the vapors to ascend, the rain to fall, the earth to yield, and sets a table before every one; and we—shall not R. Gamaliel Beribbi stand over us and offer drink!"

b. Qid. 32b, trans. H. Freedman, p. 158

*Comment*: The *baraita*-version is not materially different from those in the Tannaitic collections.

II.iv.24. *Justice, justice pursue* (Deut. 16 : 20)—Pursue a court whose justice is good—the court of Rabban Yoḥanan b. Zakkai and the court of R. Eliezer.

Sifré Deut. 144, Finkelstein, p. 200

III.ii.92.A. TNW RBNN: *Justice, justice pursue* means, You should seek a good (YPH) court, for example [follow] R. Eliezer [b. Hyrcanus] to Lydda; or R. Yoḥanan b. Zakkai to Beror Ḥēl.

B. TNW RBNN: *Justice, justice pursue*: This means, Follow the scholars to their academies, e.g., R. Eliezer to Lydda, R. Yoḥanan b. Zakkai to Beror Ḥēl, R. Joshua to Peqiʿin, Rabban Gamaliel [II] to Yavneh, R. ʿAqiba to Benai Beraq, R. Mathia to Rome, R. Ḥanania b. Teradion to Siknin, R. Yosi [b. Ḥalafta] to Sepphoris, R. Judah b. Batyra to Nisibis, R. Joshua to the Exile, Rabbi to Bet Sheʾarim, or the Sages to the chamber of hewn stone.

b. Sanh. 32b

*Comment*: The exegesis links Eliezer to Yoḥanan—ignoring all other possible examples. b. Sanh. 32b has other *academies* (YŠYBH), instead of courts, down to the eschaton. See *Development*, pp. 107, 225-227.

II.iv.25. How do we know that one who mixes up the words of R. Eliezer with those of R. Joshua, the words of R. Joshua with those of R. Eliezer, and says about the unclean, 'clean,' and about the clean, 'unclean,' that he transgresses a negative commandment? Scripture says, *You shall not move the boundary stone of your neighbor* (Deut. 19 : 14).

Sifré Deut. 188, Finkelstein, p. 227

*Comment*: Eliezer's and Joshua's names are used as representative: Eliezer/unclean and Joshua/clean—like the House of Shammai/unclean, the House of Hillel/clean—are mnemonic clichés, serving to facilitate the process of memorizing traditions. But we find the two juxtaposed in this way in only a modest proportion of cleanness-pericopae. Again we observe stress on the need accurately to remember precisely what the master has taught. In y. M.Q. 3 : 1 (below, p. 425), Yoḥanan cites a saying of Rabbi [Judah the Patriarch] that the Tannas have a habit of exchanging Eliezer's sayings for those of his opposition (because of his excommunication). The foregoing therefore is a warning to the Tannas to give Eliezer his sayings. This suggests the name of Eliezer is not chosen at random, but because of actual circumstances affecting the transmission of traditions.

III.i.16.A. MʿŠH BY: R. Liezer was dying on the eve of the Sabbath at dusk. And Hyrcanus his son entered to remove his *tefillin*.

B. He said to him, "My son, you have neglected the commandment of the [Sabbath] lamp, which is a matter of Sabbath rest (*Shevut*), and for the neglect of which one is liable for 'cutting off,' and you have come to remove *tefillin*, which are only a matter of *reshut* and are only a *miṣvah*."

C. He went out and was crying, and saying, "Woe is me, that father's mind is deranged."

D. He said to him, "It is *your* mind that is deranged. My mind is not deranged."

E. When his disciples saw that he answered them with a matter of wisdom, they came in to him, and were asking him, and he was saying to them concerning the unclean, 'unclean,' and concerning the clean, 'clean,' and at the end he said, 'Clean,' and his soul went forth.

They said, "It is evident concerning our master that he is clean."

F. R. Joshua entered and removed his *tefillin* and was embracing and kissing him and weeping, and saying, "My master, my master, the vow has been released.

G. *"My master! the chariot of Israel and its horsemen* (II Kings 2 : 12)!"

y. Shab. 2 : 7, Gilead, p. 40

*Comment*: On *reshut*, see S. Lieberman, *HaYerushalmi Kifshuṭo* (Jerusalem, 1935), p. 74.

The story of A-D is out of order. As it stands, after Eliezer instructs his son about the law in B, the son says the father is deranged. But C-D ought to come before B. Eliezer should tell the son not to bother with the *tefillin*; then the son should say C; Eliezer should say D and, finally, B. This is the order in b. Sanh. 68a, below. The legal point of the story is that the Sabbath lamp is more important than the removal of *tefillin.*

E is a separate story. It is linked to the preceding by *when they saw.* E makes the point that to the very end Eliezer was lucid, and at the last he said the word *clean.* This is taken as a sign that Eliezer's excommunication ended at his death, and that his teachings are acceptable.

Finally comes F-G, a third story. Joshua called Eliezer his master and was the chief mourner, evidently the outstanding disciple. Elsewhere ʿAqiba is given that role.

III.ii.93.A. But did R. ʿAqiba learn this from R. Joshua: Surely it has been taught (WHTNY'):

When R. Eliezer fell sick, R. ʿAqiba and his companions went to visit him. He was seated in his canopied four-poster, while they sat in his salon.

B. That day was Sabbath eve, and his son Hyrcanus went in to him to remove his phylacteries. But his father rebuked him, and he retreated crestfallen.

"It seems to me," he said to them, "that my father's mind is deranged."

But R. ʿAqiba said to them, "His mind is clear, but his mother's [of Hyrcanus] is deranged: how can one neglect a prohibition which is punished by death, and turn his attention to something which is merely forbidden as a *shevut*?"

C. The sages, seeing that his mind was clear, entered his chamber and sat down at a distance of four cubits [because he was excommunicated.]

"Why have you come?" said he to them.

"To study the Torah," they replied.

"And why did you not come before now?" he asked.

They answered, "We had no time."

He then said, "I will be surprised if these die a natural death."

D. R. ʿAqiba asked him, "And what will my death be?" He answered, "Yours will be more cruel than theirs."

E. He then put his two arms over his heart, and bewailed them, saying, "Woe to you, two arms of mine, that have been like two Scrolls of the Law that are wrapped up. Much Torah have I studied, and much have I taught. Much Torah have I learned, yet have I but skimmed from the knowledge of my teachers as much as a dog lapping from the sea. Much Torah have I taught, yet my disciples have only drawn from me as much as a painting stick from its tube. Moreover, I have studied three hundred laws on the subject of a deep bright spot, yet no man has ever asked me about them.

F. "Moreover, I have studied three hundred, [or, as others state, three thousand laws] about the planting of cucumbers [by magic] and no man, excepting ʿAqiba b. Joseph, ever questioned me thereon.

G. "For it once happened that he and I were walking together on a road, when he said to me, 'My master, teach me about the planting of cucumbers.'

"I made one statement, and the whole field [about us] was filled with cucumbers.

"Then he said, 'Master, you have taught me how to plant them: now teach me how to pluck them up.'

"I said something, and all the cucumbers gathered in one place."

H. His visitors then asked him, "What is the law of a ball, a shoemaker's last, an amulet, a leather bag containing pearls, and a small weight?"

He replied, "They can become unclean, and if unclean, they are restored to their uncleanliness just as they are."

I. Then they asked him, "What of a shoe that is on the last?"

He replied, "It is clean," and in pronouncing this word his soul departed.

J. Then R. Joshua arose and exclaimed, "The vow is annulled, the vow is annulled!"

K. On the conclusion of the Sabbath R. ʿAqiba met his bier being carried from Caesarea to Lydda. [In his grief] he beat his flesh until the blood flowed down upon the earth.

L. Then R. ʿAqiba commenced his funeral address, the mourners being lined up about the coffin, and said, "*My father, my father, the chariot of Israel and the horsemen thereof* (II Kings 2 : 12). I have many coins, but no money changer to accept them."

M. Thus from this story we see that he learned this [sc. the producing of cucumbers by magic] from R. Eliezer?—He learned it from R. Eliezer, but did not grasp it; then he learned it from R. Joshua, who made it clear to him.

b. Sanh. 68a, trans. H. Freedman, pp. 461-464

*Comment*: A introduces the sages, but they then are ignored in B. B tells the story about Eliezer and the Sabbath light—but the Sabbath light is not mentioned, rather, is merely taken for granted! So b. Sanh. is composed in full knowledge of a story such as appears in y. But ʿAqiba answers, instead of Eliezer. This is a strange 'improvement,' since the point of the story is that Eliezer is fully in control of his senses. He therefore should reply. But since Hyrcanus cannot say to the sages, sitting outside, that his father is deranged, and then have the father reply from within—all this carefully arranged in A—it evidently was necessary for the story-teller to revise matters as he did.

C-D introduces a new 'incident.' The sages are rebuked for not coming to Eliezer while he was under excommunication (b. B.M. 59a-b), but rather than say so, they claim they had no time. Eliezer then curses them. This is heightened in D: ʿAqiba's will be worst of all.

In E Eliezer is given a sad speech. Since no one came to study with him, he was like a Torah-Scroll that no one unrolled to read. This develops Tos. Sot., as noted above, p. 395; or Tos. Sot. is a brief allusion to the saying. Eliezer says, I learned only a small part of what my teachers knew, and taught only a small part of what I knew. This saying is then spelled out in two instances. First, he studied laws about a bright spot which no one ever required. Second, F introduces the separate story about the cucumbers, alluded to elsewhere. Eliezer now reports that in ʿAqiba's presence he had by means of magic created and destroyed a field of cucumbers.

H introduces a still further colloquy. The sages return to the scene. They ask about several leather objects which can become unclean only if they contain a receptacle. These are stuffed with hair or cotton. Is this a receptacle? The sages ruled it is not, since the hollow is made to be filled. Eliezer holds they are unclean. The issue, then, is whether Eliezer maintains his earlier opinions, and the answer of H is that he does. I then introduces the shoe-last, as given earlier, and he gives the ruling cited in M. Kel. 26 : 4; also see above, p. 285. That ends the colloquy, and Eliezer dies.

In J, Joshua announces the ban is ended. Whether this is because he has died or because of the sign that his last word was clean is not stated. This announcement then permits the funeral to be held.

K gives the funeral address of ʿAqiba—so specified, rather than as a record of what ʿAqiba had privately exclaimed; the two are combined. ʿAqiba met the bier, then gave the funeral addres. Elsewhere, when he meets the bier he gives the same saying.

The collection of materials is artfully put together. It is a composite, but everything is given a logical place and made part of a natural sequence.

III.ii.94.A. TNW RBNN: When R. Eliezer fell ill, his disciples came to visit him.

They said too him, "Our master, teach us the way of life that through them we may merit eternal life [the life of the world to come]."

B. He said to them, (1) "Take care for the honor of your colleagues.

(2) "And keep your sons back from speculation (HHGYWN) and set them between the knees of disciples of the sages.

(3) "And when you pray, know before whom you are standing.

"And on this account you will merit the life of the world to come."

And when Rabbi Yoḥanan b. Zakkai fell ill, his disciples...

b. Ber. 28b

*Comment*: B(1) is a reformulation of M. Avot 2 : 10, *Let the honor...* As to prayer, see above, p. 23. But the other sayings are new.

The setting, however, is standard: deathbed sayings of Eliezer. Immediately following is Yoḥanan b. Zakkai's deathbed scene (*Development*, pp. 87, 221-224), in which Yoḥanan says one should fear Heaven as much as he does his fellow-man. The scenes are quite different from one another; Yoḥanan's reactions to death are carefully delineated, while Eliezer is not described, merely cited.

V.i.6.A. When Rabbi Eliezer fell sick his disciples came to visit him, and they sat down before him. "O master," they urged, "teach us [at least] one thing [more]."

He said to them, "Let me teach you this: Go forth and watch over each other's honor. When you pray remember before whom you stand praying, for thereby you shall merit the life of the world to come."

B. Said Rabbi Eleazar ben ʿAzariah, "Five things we learned from

Rabbi Eliezer [on his deathbed] and these gave us more delight [then] than they had given us during his lifetime. These concern: a round cushion, a ball, a shoe last, an amulet, or a phylactery, which was torn. We asked, 'When these objects contract uncleanness what is the status [of that which is within them?] Is it indeed as thou didst teach us?' "

"It is unclean," he replied. "And be careful with such objects and immerse them in an immersion pool as they are—for these are established laws which were transmitted to Moses at Sinai."

ARN, Chap. 20, Goldin, p. 94

*Comment*: ARN unites the two deathbed messages. A has b. Ber., and B summarizes b. Sanh.

V.i.7.A. Of Rabbi Eliezer's [last] illness it is told:

That day was a Sabbath eve, and Rabbi ʿAqiba and his colleagues arrived to visit him. He was sleeping in his room, sitting back on a canopied couch; so they sat down in his hall. Hyrcanus his son entered [his father's room] to remove his *tefillin*, but he would not let him—and he broke into tears. Whereupon Hyrcanus came out and said to the Sages, "Masters, it seems to me that father's mind is deranged."

"My son," Rabbi Eliezer called to him, "it is not my mind that's deranged but thine! For thou hast neglected the kindling of the [Sabbath] lights [at the proper hour]—for which the penalty can well be death, and didst busy thyself with the *tefillin*—for whose use [on the Sabbath] there is only the penalty for transgressing the Sabbath rest."

B. When the Sages saw that his mind was clear, they entered and sat down before him, at a distance of four cubits. "Master," they asked him, "what is the law with regard to a round cushion, a ball, a shoe-last, an amulet, or *tefillin* that were torn? [To wit: if they contract uncleanness, do their contents too] become unclean?"

"They do become unclean," he replied; "the objects are to be immersed in an immersion pool as they are. And be careful with such matters, for these are major laws which were transmitted to Moses at Sinai."

And they kept asking him about the law of cleanness, uncleanness, immersion pools. They would ask him, "Master, what about this?" and he would reply, "It is unclean." "What about that?" And he would reply, "It is clean." And he continued to reply "unclean" for the unclean and "clean" for the clean.

C. Now after that, Rabbi Eliezer said to the Sages, "I fear for the disciples of this generation, that they will be punished by death from Heaven."

"Master," they asked him, "what for?"

"Because," he replied, "they did not come and attend upon me."

D. Then he said to ʿAqiba ben Joseph, "ʿAqiba, why didst thou not come and attend upon me?"

"Master," ʿAqiba replied, "I did not have the time."

Said Rabbi Eliezer to him, "I doubt if thou wilt die a natural death."—And some say that he said naught to him. Rather, when Rabbi Eliezer spoke in this way to his disciples, ʿAqiba's heart suddenly melted within him.—

"Master," Rabbi ʿAqiba asked him, "what manner of death will be mine?"

"ʿAqiba," he replied, "thine will be the hardest of them all!"

D. Rabbi ʿAqiba came forward and sat down before him and said to him, "Master, if so, teach me now."

He began, and taught him 300 laws about the *bright spot.*

E. It was then that Rabbi Eliezer raised his two arms and laid them on his breast and cried, "Woe unto me! For my two arms that are like two Torah scrolls depart from the world!

For if all the seas were ink,
and all the reeds pens,
And all men scribes,
They could not write down
All the Scripture and Mishnah I studied,
Nor what I learned under the Sages in the academy.

Yet I carried away from my teachers no more than does a man who dips his finger in the sea; and I gave away to my disciples no more than a paintbrush takes from the tube.

F. "Moreover, I derived three hundred laws from *Thou shalt not suffer a sorceress to live.*"

And some say that Rabbi Eliezer said, "Three thousand laws"—"but no one ever asked me about them except ʿAqiba ben Joseph.

"For once he said to me, 'Master, teach me how one plants cucumbers [by magic] and how one uproots them.' I pronounced a certain word and the whole field was filled with cucumbers. 'Master,' he said to me, 'thou hast taught me how they are planted; teach me how they are uprooted.' I pronounced a certain word and all the cucumbers were gathered together in one place!'"

G. Said Rabbi Eleazar ben ʿAzariah to him, "Master, what about a shoe [still] on the shoe-last [which comes into contact with something unclean]?"

"It is clean," he replied.

And so he continued to reply "unclean" for the unclean and "clean" for the clean—until his soul went forth pure.

Immediately Rabbi Eleazar ben ʿAzariah rent his clothes and wept.

And he came out and said to the Sages, "Masters, come and look upon Rabbi Eliezer, for he is in a state of purity for the world to come, for his soul has gone forth pure."

After the Sabbath Rabbi ʿAqiba came upon [his remains] being carried on the highway leading from Caesarea to Lydda. Forthwith he rent his clothes and tore at his hair—and his blood ran down to the ground. He kept crying out, weeping and exclaiming, "Woe unto me, my master, because of thee! Woe unto me, my teacher, because of thee! For thou hast left the whole generation fatherless!"

In the mourners' row he delivered the funeral oration and said, "*My father, my father, chariot of Israel and the horsemen thereof*! [Many] coins do I have but no money changer to sort them out!"

ARN Chap. 25, trans. Goldin, pp. 107-110

V.ii.2.A. Everyone should bare an arm at the death of a scholar or a disciple.

For a *Ḥakham* who died, the right arm must be bared.

For an *Ab bet din* who died, the left arm must be bared.

For a *Nasi* who died, both arms must be bared.

B. Now it happened that when Rabbi Eliezer died, Rabbi ʿAqiba bared both arms and beat his breast, drawing blood.

And thus he spoke, "*My master, my master, the chariots of Israel and the horsemen thereof*! (II Kings 2 : 12). A multitude of coins have I, but no money-changer to sort them!"

Mourning 9 : 2, trans. Dov Zlotnick, p. 67

*Comment*: Eliezer is now made into the *Nasi.*

Note also Mekh. deR. Ishmael, Pisḥa 17 : 204-210, Lauterbach, I, pp. 156-7, a ruling consonant with the foregoing story:

> R. Eliezer says, "Since the Sabbath is called a sign and the phylacteries are called a sign, one should not add one sign to another. But perhaps one rather should add one sign to another? You must, however, reason: The Sabbath, for the violation of whose laws one may incur the penalty of extermination or even of death by order of the court, should set aside the phylacteries, for the disregard of whose laws one incurs neither the penalty of extermination nor of death by order of the court."

But the antecedent authority here is R. Isaac, and some MS evidence has Eleazar *b. ʿAzariah.* While the saying is a legal rationale that would stand behind the removal of the *tefillin* in the death-scene, we have no basis either to assign the above to our Eliezer or to suppose he was the original authority for the rule about *tefillin.* For other *tefillin*-sayings assigned to R. Eliezer, see M. Tefillin 63a, and below, p. 471.

IV.i.19.A. When R. Eliezer died, the Scroll of Wisdom was hidden...

B. R. Jacob b. R. ʿIdi in the name of R. Joshua b. Levi [said], "When Rabban Yoḥanan b. Zakkai was dying, he commanded, saying, 'Clear the courtyard on account of the uncleanness, and prepare a throne for Hezekiah the king of Judah.'

"R. Liezer his disciple, when dying, commanded, saying, 'Clear the courtyard on account of the uncleanness and prepare a throne for Rabban Yoḥanan b. Zakkai.' "

C. R. Jacob b. R. ʿIdi in the name of R. Joshua b. Levi [said], "MʿŚH: The elders came into the upper room of the house of Gedya in Jericho, and an echo came and said to them, 'There are among you two who are worthy of the Holy Spirit, and Hillel is one of them, and they set their eyes on Samuel the Small.

"And again the elders came into the upper room in Yavneh and an echo came and said to them, 'There are among you two who are worthy of the Holy Spirit and Samuel the Small is one of them,' and they set their eyes on R. Eliezer b. Hyrcanus. And they were happy that their opinion agreed with the opinion of the Omnipresent."

y. Sot. 9 : 16, Gilead, p. 93

IV.i.20.A. R. Jacob b. R. ʿIdi in the name of R. Joshua b. Levi said, "MʿŚH Š: The elders came into the upper room of the house of Gedya in Jericho. An echo came forth and said to them, 'There are among you two who are worthy of the Holy Spirit, and Hillel the Elder is one of them, and they set their eyes on Samuel the Small.

"Again the elders came into the upper room in Yavneh and an echo came and said to them, 'There are among you two who are worthy of the Holy Spirit and Samuel the Small is one of them,' and they set their eyes on R. Liezer. And they were rejoicing that their opinion agreed with the opinion of the Holy Spirit."

B. R. Jacob b. R. ʿIdi in the name of R. Joshua b. Levi [said], "When Rabban Yoḥanan b. Zakkai was dying, he said, 'Clear out the house on account of the uncleanness and set a throne for Hezekiah King of Judah.'

"R. Liezer his disciple, when he was dying, said, 'Clear out the house on account of uncleanness, and set a throne for Rabban Yoḥanan ben Zakkai.' "

y. A.Z. 3 : 1, Gilead, p. 36 = y. Hor. 3 : 5, Gilead, p. 38

*Comment*: y. Sot. 9 : 16A cites Tos. Sot. on the pertinent Mishnah. B then shows that Eliezer copied his master's deed when he was dying, an example of Eliezer's loyalty to what he had learned. Other death-scenes, to be sure, know nothing of Joshua b. Levi's story. C extends the story of Hillel/Samuel the Small (*Phar.* I, pp. 268-9) to Eliezer, who is favored by the echo. According to Joshua b. Levi Eliezer surely is a Hillelite.

I see no important variations in y. A.Z. 3 : 1, except the order in which the stories are arranged.

V.iv.1. When R. Eliezer was dying, has disciples came and sat down before him and said to him, "Our teacher, teach us a law."

He replied, "What shall I teach you? Go forth and be mindful of each other's honor; and when you pray know before Whom you stand, for through this you will enter into the life of the World to Come."

R. Eleazar b. ʿAzariah said, "Five things did R. Eliezer teach us when he was dying, and gladdened us with them more than with what he taught us during his lifetime, *viz.*, the ball, the shoemaker's last, the amulet, the phylactery, and a round cushion; be mindful of these and immerse them [for purification] just as they are, because they are established laws which were commanded to Moses on Sinai."

Kallah Rabbati 53b, trans. J. Rabbinowitz,
pp. 478-497 = Derekh Ereṣ Rabbah 56b, p. 544

V.iv.2. The Rabbis taught: When R. Eliezer fell sick, all the sages of Israel came to visit him.

That day was the Sabbath-eve and he was wearing his *tefillin.*

His son entered to remove them from him, but he rebuked him and drove him away in anger. [The son] said to the sages, "I believe that my father's mind is deranged."

Whereupon [R. Eliezer] exclaimed, "His mind and that of his mother are deranged, but my mind is not."

As he was dying, he put two of his fingers together and said, "Woe to me because of these two Scrolls of the Torah! Much Torah have I learnt and much Torah have I taught, yet I extracted little from the knowledge of my teachers like a dog lapping from the sea. My disciples have only extracted little from me like a painting-stick from its tube. If all the trees were made into pens and all the seas into ink, they would not suffice to write down all that I expounded. Moreover,

I have studied three hundred laws on the subject of a deep bright spot and three hundred established laws derived from the verse, *Thou shall not suffer a sorceress to live* (Ex. 22 : 17), and no man, excepting ʿAqiba b. Joseph, ever questioned me thereon."

Kallah Rabbati 53b, trans. J. Rabbinowitz, p. 482

V.xii.3.A. R. Eliezer and R. Joshua and R. ʿAqiba made the following observations.

R. Eliezer said, "If all the seas were ink and all the reeds pens and the heaven and earth scrolls, and all mankind scribes, they would not suffice to write the Torah which I have learnt, and I have abstracted no more from it than a man would take by dipping his pen in the sea."

B. R. Joshua said, "If all the seas were ink, and all the reeds pens and the heaven and earth scrolls, and all mankind scribes, they would not suffice to write the Torah which I have learnt, and I have abstracted no more from it than a man would take by dipping the point of his pen in the sea."

C. R. ʿAqiba said, "It is not possible for me to say as my teachers said, for in fact my teachers did take something from it, while I have taken no more than one who smells a citron: he who smells enjoys it, while the citron looses nothing. Or than one who fills his pitcher from a water-course, or one who lights one lamp from another."

D. One day R. ʿAqiba came late to the school-house, so he sat outside.

A question arose, Is such-and-such the law?

They said, "The law is outside." Again a question arose, and they said, ʿAqiba is outside; make way for him."

He came and sat at the feet of R. Eliezer.

E. The school-house of R. Eliezer was shaped like an arena, and there was in it a stone which was reserved for him to sit on.

Once R. Joshua came in and began kissing the stone and saying, "This stone is like Mount Sinai, and he who sat on it is like the Ark of the Covenant."

Song R. 1 : 3,1, trans. Maurice Simon, pp. 36-37

III.i.17. A. MʿŚH B: On a cloudy day, on which sages did not come to the meeting-house, the children came in, and said, "Let us hold an assembly, so that it [the study-time] will not be lost."

B. They said, "What is that, which is written: M M N N Ṣ Ṣ P P K K? From saying (M'MR) to saying, from Faithful (N'MN) to faithful, from Righteous (*Ṣaddiq*) to righteous, from Mouth

(*Peh*) to mouth, from the palm of the hand (*Kaf*) of the Holy One blessed be he to the palm of the hand of Moses."

C. And sages marked (SYM) them, and all of them arose as great men.

D. They say R. Liezer and R. Joshua were among them.

y. Meg. 1 : 9, Gilead, p. 24

*Comment*: The story supplies an explanation for the orthography of the letters M N Ṣ P K in the setting of explanations of R. Mattiah b. Ḥeresh and R. Jeremiah in the name of R. Samuel b. R. Isaac. D adds that among the children were Eliezer and Joshua.

V.vii.1. It once happened on a stormy day that the Sages did not attend the House of Assembly [the Academy].

Some children were there and they said, "Come and let us study [the letters instituted by] the sages. Why are these two forms for *mem*, *nun*, *ṣade*, *peh* and *kaf*?

"It teaches [that the Torah was transmitted] from Utterance to utterance, from Faithful to faithful, from Righteous to righteous, from Mouth to mouth, and from Hand to hand. From Utterance to utterance—from the utterance of the Holy One, blessed be He, to the utterance of Moses. From Faithful to faithful—from the Almighty, who is designated, "God, faithful King," to Moses, who is designated faithful, as it is written, *He* [Moses] *is faithful in all My house* (Num. 12 : 7). From Righteous to righteous—from God, who is designated righteous, as it is written, *The Lord is righteous in all His way* (Ps. 154 : 17), to Moses who is designated righteous, as it is written, *He executed the righteousness of the Lord* (Deut. 33 : 21). From mouth to mouth—from the mouth of the Holy One, blessed be He, to the mouth of Moses. From hand to hand: from the hand of the Holy One, blessed be He, to the hand of Moses."

The scholars noted them, and they grew to be great sages in Israel; some say that they were R. Eliezer, R. Joshua, *and R. ʿAqiba.* They applied to them the verse, *Even a child is known by his doings*, etc. (Prov. 20 : 11).

Gen. R. 1 : 11, trans. H. Freedman, p. 10-11

III.ii.95. TNY᾽: R. Eliezer the Great says, "Whoever has a scrap of bread in his basket and says, 'What shall I eat tomorrow,' is only (᾽YNW ᾽L᾽) among those of little faith."

b. Sot. 48b

*Comment*: Eliezer's saying is taken as illustration of the Mishnaic saying that men of faith died with the destruction of the Temple. Isaac says such are the people who believe in the Holy One blessed be he, and Eliezer's saying is cited. This is followed by a tradition attributed to Eleazar, that Zech. 4 : 10, *For who hath despised the day of small things* signifies the following: "What is the cause that the tables of the righteous are despoiled in the hereafter? The smallness which was in them, that they did not trust in the Holy One."

Eliezer's saying is consistent with Hillel's (*Phar.* I, pp. 324-325), that one should not plan for the Sabbath, as Shammai says, but simply "Bless the Lord day by day," for the blessings of each day as it passes.

II.ii.6. *A day's portion every day* (Ex. 16 : 4).

A. R. Joshua says, "That a man should gather today for tomorrow, and so on Friday for the Sabbath."

B. R. Eliezer says, "That a man should not gather today for tomorrow."

C. And so did R. Eliezer used to say, "He who has something to eat today and asks, What shall I eat tomorrow? lo, such is one of those of little faith, as it says, *A day's portion every day.* He who created the day created its sustenance [food for it]."

Mekhilta deR. Simeon b. Yoḥai, p. 106, ls. 23-26

*Comment*: Eliezer's saying in b. Sot. now has an exegetical foundation.

II.ii.7. *O my dove, in the clefts of the rock, in the covert of the cliff, let me see your face, let me hear your voice, for your voice is sweet and your face is comely* (Song 2 : 14).

A. R. Eliezer says, "This matter is said only concerning the [miracle at] the sea. *Let me see your face* applies to that which is said, *Stand and see the salvation of the Lord* (Ex. 14 : 13). *Let me hear your voice* applies to that which is said, And the children of Israel cried out to the Lord (Ex. 14 : 14). *For your voice is sweet—And their cry came up to God* (Ex. 2 : 23). *And your face is comely—and the people believed* (Ex. 4 : 31)."

B. ʿAqiba says, "This matter refers only to [their standing] before Mount Sinai..." etc.

Mekhilta deR. Simeon b. Yoḥai, p. 143, ls. 3-8

*Comment*: Eliezer praises the faith of Israel at the sea. Compare Shemaʿiah and Abṭalion, *Phar.* I, pp. 142-3.

II.i.12. *Because of the striving of the children of Israel* (Ex. 17 : 7).

A. R. Joshua says, "The Israelites said, 'If He is master over all works as He is master over us, we will serve Him, but if He is not, we will not serve Him.'"

B. R. Eliezer says, "They said, 'If He supplies all our needs we will serve Him, but if He does not, we will not serve Him.' In this sense it is said, *Because of the striving of the children of Israel and because they tried the Lord saying, Is the Lord among us or not?*"

Mekh. Vayassa 7 : 68-74, Lauterbach II, p. 134

*Comment*: Now Eliezer's view is that Israelite faith was based on material considerations. This is congruent to his saying in b. Sot., above, p. 420.

III.ii.96.A. We learnt elsewhere: If he cut it into separate tiles, placing sand between each tile, R. Eliezer declared [it] clean, and the sages declared it unclean; and this was the oven of ʿAkhnai.

B. Why [the oven of] ʿAkhnai? Said Rav Judah in Samuel's name, "[It means] that they encompassed it with arguments as a snake, and proved it unclean."

C. TN': On that day R. Eliezer brought forward all the arguments in the world, but they did not accept them.

D. (1) Said he to them, "If the law agrees with me, let this carob-tree prove it."

The carob-tree was torn a hundred cubits out of its place (others say four hundred cubits).

"No proof can be brought from a carob-tree," they said to him.

(2) Again he said to them, "If the law agrees with me, let the stream of water prove it." The stream of water flowed backwards.

"No proof can be brought from a stream of water," they said to him.

(3) Again he said to them, "If the law agrees with me, let the walls of the schoolhouse prove it." The walls inclined to fall.

R. Joshua rebuked them, saying, "When disciples of sages are engaged in a legal dispute, what have you to interfere?"

Hence they did not fall, in honor of R. Joshua, nor did they resume the upright, in honor of R. Eliezer. (And they are still standing thus inclined).

(4) Again he said to them, "If the law agrees with me, let it be proved from Heaven." An echo went forth and said, "Why do you dispute with R. Eliezer, seeing that in all matters the law agrees with him!"

But R. Joshua arose and exclaimed, "*It is not in heaven* (Deut. 30 : 12)."

D. What did he mean by this? Said R. Jeremiah, "That the Torah had already been given at Mount Sinai; we pay no attention to an echo because Thou has long since written in the Torah at Mount Sinai, *After the majority must one incline* (Ex. 23 : 2)."

E. R. Nathan met Elijah and asked him, "What did the Holy One, blessed be He, do in that hour?"

"He laughed [with joy]," he replied, "saying, 'My sons have defeated Me. My sons have defeated Me.' "

F. It was said: On that day all objects which R. Eliezer had declared clean were brought and burnt in fire. Then they took a vote and excommunicated (BRK) him.

G. Said they, "Who shall go and inform him?"

"I will go," answered R. ʿAqiba, "lest an unsuitable person go and inform him and thus destroy the whole world."

What did R. ʿAqiba do? He donned black garments and wrapped himself in black and sat at a distance of four cubits from him.

"ʿAqiba," said R. Eliezer to him, "why is today [different from] other days?"

"Master," he replied, "it appears to me that the fellows (ḤBRYM) hold aloof from you."

Thereupon he too rent his garments, put off his shoes, removed [his seat] and sat on the earth, while tears streamed from his eyes.

H. The world was then smitten: a third of the olive crop, a third of the wheat, and a third of the barley crop. Some say, the dough in women's hands swelled up.

I. TN': Great was the calamity that befell that day, for everything at which R. Eliezer cast his eyes was burned up.

J. R. Gamaliel too was travelling in a ship, when a huge wave arose to drown him.

"It appears to me," he said, "that this is on account of none other than R. Eliezer b. Hyrcanus."

Thereupon he arose and exclaimed, "Sovereign of the Universe! Thou knowest full well that I have not acted for my honor, nor for the honor of my paternal house, but for Thine, so that strife may not multiply in Israel!"

At that the raging sea subsided.

K. [*What follows is in Aramaic*:] Imma Shalom was R. Eliezer's wife, and sister of R. Gamaliel. From the time of this incident onwards she did not permit him to fall upon his face [in supplication].

Now a certain day happened to be New Moon, but she mistook a full month for a defective one.

Others say, a poor man came and stood at the door, and she took out some bread to him. [On her return] she found him fallen on his face.

"Arise," she cried out to him, "you have slain my brother."

In the meanwhile an announcement (ŠYPWR') was made from the house of Rabban Gamaliel that he had died. "How do you know it?" he questioned her.

"I have this tradition from my father's house: All gates are locked, excepting the gates of wounded feelings."

L. TNW RBNN: He who wounds the feelings of a proselyte transgresses three negative injunctions, and he who oppresses him infringes two. Wherein does wronging differ? Because three negative injunctions are stated: Viz. *Thou shall not wrong a stranger* [i.e., a proselyte] (Ex. 22 : 20). *And if a stranger sojourn with thee in your land, he shall not wrong him* (Lev. 19 : 33). *And ye shall not therefore wrong each his fellowman* (Lev. 25 : 17), a proselyte being included in '*fellowman*.' But for *oppression* also three are written, viz., *and thou shalt not oppress him* (Ex. 22 : 20). *Also thou shalt not oppress a stranger* (Ex. 23 : 9), *and [If thou lend money to any of my people that is poor by thee,] thou shalt not be to him as a usurer* (Ex. 22 : 24) which includes a proselyte! But [say] both [are forbidden] by three [injunctions].

M. TNY': R. Eliezer the Great said, "Why did the Torah warn against [the wronging of] a proselyte in thirty-six (or as others say, in forty-six) places? Because he has a strong inclination to evil."

b. B.M. 59a-b, trans. H. Freedman,
pp. 352-355 (b. Ber. 19a, 52a)

IV.i.21.A. They sought to excommunicate R. Liezer.

They said, "Who will go and inform him?"

R. ʿAqiba said, "I shall go and inform him."

He came to him.

He said to him, "Rabbi, See, your colleagues (ḤBRYK) are excommunicating you (MNDYN LK)."

B. H [Eliezer] took him and went outside. He said, "O carob, carob, if the law is like their words, uproot yourself," and it did not uproot itself.

"If the law is according to my words, uproot yourself," and it uprooted itself.

"If the law is like their words, return [to your place]," and it did not return.

"If the law is like my words, return to your place," and it returned.

C. All such praise and the law is not according to R. Eliezer? R. Ḥanina said, "Once it has been given, it has been given only on condition that one follows the majority, even in error."

And does R. Eliezer not accept the principle that one follows the majority even in error?

He paid no attention until in his very presence they burned the things he had declared clean.

D. There we have learned (TMN TNYNN): If he broke it into rings and put sand between the rings—

R. Liezer declares clean.

And sages declare unclean.

This is the oven of Ḥakhinai.

E. R. Jeremiah said, "A great tribulation (ḤKK) took place [Lit.: was made] on that day. Wherever R. Liezer's eye looked, it was burned, and not only so, but even one grain of wheat—the half [that he looked at] would be burned, and [the other] half not burned."

F. And the columns of the assembly-house were shaking.

R. Joshua said to them, "If the fellows (ḤBRYM) are contending, what business is it of yours?"

F. And an echo came forth and said, "The law follows Eliezer, my son."

R. Joshua said, *"It is not in heaven."*

G. R. Qerispai, R. Yoḥanan in the name of Rabbi, "If a man should say to me, 'Thus did R. Liezer teach,' I should teach according to his words, but (DTNY') the Tannas exchange [the teachings of Eliezer are not attributed to him accurately]."

H. One time he was going through the market and he saw one woman cleaning her house, and she threw out [the dirt], and it fell on his head.

He said, "It would seem that today my colleagues will bring me near, as it is written, *From the dung heap he will raise up the poor* (Ps. 113 : 7)."

y. M.Q. 3 : 1, Gilead, p. 20

*Comment*: The version of y. M.Q. is disjointed and out of order. These are the fragments of a story before they have been put together into a smooth and coherent acccount.

A begins with a reference to the excommunication of Eliezer, but it supplies no reason for that action. This only comes later. The story flows into B. ʿAqiba tells Eliezer he is being excommunicated. Eliezer presumably knows the reason—but the oven of ʿAkhnai is not mentioned—and then calls upon nature to support his opinion. Nature obliges, in the form of the carobs. b. greatly expands this segment of the story. C then gives discussion of the foregoing. Why does Eliezer differ from the majority? C ends with the reference to burning Eliezer's 'purities.' D then brings in the oven of ʿAkhnai; it should have come at the outset, or at least as an introduction to B. b. puts it into its logical place.

Jeremiah's story about Eliezer's magical power is now a fragment, to be developed in b.

F then alludes to the (evidently famous) trembling walls, which supplies the occasion for Joshua's rebuke, and then the second, and similar chria follows. Heaven announces Eliezer is right, and Joshua says the Torah is not in heaven.

Finally we have Yoḥanan's striking citation of Rabbi [Judah the Patriarch] that the law should normally follow Eliezer, but the Tannaitic tradents suppress his name or give his teachings to others. Finally it tells a little story, which shows that Eliezer was disheartened by his experience—to his credit.

These bits and pieces are, as noted, out of proper sequence. They suggest that a *terminus post quem* for the story should be about the time of Rabbi Judah the Patriarch. M. Kel. 5 : 10 alludes to the "famous" oven, so presumably some story (or stories) about the oven of ʿAkhnai circulated before the time of the Mishnah's compilation or the interpolation of "oven—ʿAkhnai". But precisely what they consisted of is difficult to say. The duplicated chria of Joshua's rebuking nature/heaven cannot give evidence of a pre-Mishnaic version, nor does the saying of Ḥanina. A better *terminus* is probably Jeremiah, who tells in his own name a story later on fully articulated by the authority of a Tanna.

b. B.M. shows us what a *baraita*-editor could do with such materials. First of all, everything is set in logical order. The complex pericope begins with an allusion to M. Kel. 5 : 10, then the story, beginning in C, unfolds. Eliezer offers numerous proofs, but none is accepted. Then the carobtree is brought in; it is not merely uprooted, but torn a *hundred cubits* out of place. This is then duplicated: a stream of water flows backward. Then the walls of the school-house are introduced to complete a triad of action. Now comes, as the climax, the heavenly voice. The y. M.Q. allegation that the law follows Eliezer is expanded: now heaven says the law *always* follows him. Joshua cites the appropriate Scripture.

E is introduced quite separately. Why Nathan should be chosen to deliver Elijah's message I cannot say; but Nathan supplies no *terminus* for the story.

F then rejoins the original story. Since Eliezer has been rejected by the sages, what he regards as clean is burned. Only then is Eliezer excommunicated—probably the beginning of the whole assemblage.

Now, in G, comes the problem of informing him. Since Eliezer's mastery of nature is an issue, it is important that he be told such in a way that he will not be moved to destroy the world. So Jeremiah's story in y. M.Q. is not only revised, but expanded and duplicated. But it would seem to me some such consideration lies behind G's story. Now Eliezer's reaction is not to call on nature for proof, as in y. M.Q., but to accept his excommunication. But then H tells us that nature *did* punish the excommunication of Eliezer. This should not have been included, for Eliezer's reaction in b. B.M. G is sufficient: he wept. Then, to make matters worse, b. B.M. I repeats H. Jeremiah is dropped.

I also serves to introduce J, but it is a bad introduction, since Gamaliel's experience has nothing to do with fire. Gamaliel is allowed to say that the issue was keeping the peace, so heaven should forbear. No one evidently is bothered by the problem of how Gamaliel, who supposedly was at the consistory, got out to sea. It is a formulary cliché to have Gamaliel on a boat. I suppose it seemed natural to include the tidal wave, but this is a bad setting for a good saying.

K then develops the theme that Eliezer could have destroyed the world. Imma Shalom kept Eliezer from 'falling on his face,' that is, from offering his individual supplication to God (*Taḥanun*). God would listen and punish Gamaliel her brother. The occasion on which she slipped up is confused. The New Moon case is this: She thought the thirtieth of the month would be the New Moon, on which private prayers are not said, so she relaxed her watch. But the thirtieth was not the New Moon, so he said the supplications. Or, alternatively, a poor man came and she relaxed her watch on her husband; he then said the supplication. At any rate, she miraculously knew that her brother had died. So Eliezer's prayers killed him. This is turned into a case of knowing from a distance that a supernatural event has taken place. But even this supernatural skill is forthwith rationalized. She knew it not because she was confident of her husband's supernatural power, but because of a teaching that the prayers of *anyone*—not only of a holy man—whose feelings had been hurt would be listened to in heaven.

L then goes on to another matter, namely, hurting the feelings of a proselyte; it is included because M has Eliezer's saying that the Scriptures have given strong protection to the proselyte. L-M have nothing to do with the foregoing stories, but are connected by the two themes: *Eliezer* and *hurt feelings.*

II.i.13.A. Beloved are the strangers. For in ever so many passages Scripture warns about them: *And a stranger thou shalt not vex*, etc.; *Love ye therefore the stranger*, etc. (Deut. 10.10); *For ye know the heart of a stranger*, etc. (Ex. 23.9).

R. Eliezer says, "It is because there is a bad streak in the stranger that Scripture warns about him in so many passages."

B. R. Simeon b. Yoḥai says, "Behold, it says: *But they that love Him be as the sun when he goeth forth in his might* (Jud. 5.31). Now, who is the greater, he who loves the king or he whom the king loves?

You must say: It is he whom the king loves. And it is written: *And loveth the stranger*, etc. (Deut. 10.18)."

Mekhilta deR. Ishmael, Neziqin 18 : 9-16, Lauterbach, II, p. 138

*Comment*: Now the saying stands by itself. But Simeon b. Yoḥai has the opposite notion, that proselytes are especially beloved.

III.ii.97. TNW RBNN M'ŚH B: R. Eliezer and R. Joshua were traveling on board a ship. R. Eliezer was sleeping, and R. Joshua was awake. R. Joshua shuddered, and R. Eliezer awoke.

He said to him, "What is the matter, Joshua? What has caused you to tremble?"

He said to him, "I have seen a great light in the sea."

He said to him, "You may have seen the eyes of Leviathan, for it is written, *His eyes are like the eyelids of the morning* (Job 41 : 10)."

b. B.B. 74b, trans. Israel W. Slotki, p. 295

*Comment*: The chriic setting is a ship, because of the vision of Joshua, which had to be at sea.

III.ii.98. TNY': R. Eliezer the Great said, "As soon as the fifteenth of Av arrives, the power of the sun weakened, and they chopped no more wood for the altar."

b. B.B. 121b, trans. I. W. Slotki, pp. 499-500 (*Mishnat R. Eliezer*, ed. H. G. Enelow [N.Y., 1933], p. 144; b. Ta. 31a)

*Comment*: From Nisan to Av (April to August) wood was cut for the year's needs of the altar. After Av, the wood would no longer be sufficiently dried by the sun, so it would produce too much smoke and nurture worms. It was therefore no good for the altar.

IV.i.22. The *tefillin* of Rabban Yoḥanan ben Zakkai did not move from him either in summer or in winter, and so did his disciple R. Eliezer behave after him.

y. Ber. 2 : 3, Gilead, p. 27

*Comment*: The saying, in Aramaic, includes a routine reference to Eliezer's following the practice of Yoḥanan b. Zakkai. Elsewhere it is part of a longer sequence of actions in which Eliezer is said to have imitated the master. See *Development*, pp. 133, 220, 226.

IV.i.23. R. Jeremiah in the name of R. Ḥiyya b. R. Ba: "Aqilas the proselyte translated the Torah before R. Eliezer and R. Joshua, and they praised him and said to him, *You are the fairest of the sons of men. [Grace is poured out on your lips]* (Ps. 45 : 2)."

y. Meg. 1 : 9, Gilead, p. 20

IV.ii.19. R. Jeremiah—or some say R. Ḥiyya b. Abba—also said, "The *Targum* of the Pentateuch was composed by Onqelos the proselyte from the mouth of R. Eliezer and R. Joshua."

b. Meg. 3a, trans. Maurice Simon, p. 9

*Comment*: Jeremiah + Ba's tradition assigns Targum Onqelos to the authority of Eliezer and Joshua, that of the prophets to Jonathan b. Uzziel (*Phar.* I, p. 393).

IV.i.24. [Elisha b. Abbuyah tells as follows:]

Father Abbuyah was one of the great men of Jerusalem.

On the day on which he came to circumcize me, he invited all the great men of Jerusalem and seated them in one house. And R. Eliezer and R. Joshua [he seated] in one house. After they had eaten and drunk, they began to play games (ṬPḤ) and dance.

R. Liezer said to R. Joshua, "While they are busy with theirs, let us occupy ourselves with ours."

They sat and occupied themselves with teachings of Torah, and from the Torah they moved to the prophets, and from the prophets to the writings. And a fire came down from heaven and surrounded them.

Abbuyah said to them, "My masters, have you come to burn down my house?"

They said to him, "God forbid! But we were sitting and reviewing teachings of Torah, and from the Torah [we passed] to the prophets, and from the prophets to the Writings, and the teachings are as joyful as when they were given from Sinai, and the fire licked about them [the words of Torah] as it licked them from Sinai..."

Abbuyah, my father, said to them, "My masters, since such is the power of Torah, if this son lives, I shall set him aside for the Torah."

Because his intention was not for the sake of heaven, therefore it was not fulfilled in that man [Elisha]...

y. Hag. 2 : 1, Gilead, p. 18

V.xii.4. My father, Abbuyah, was one of the notable men of his generation, and at my circumcision he invited all the notables of Jerusalem, including R. Eliezer and R. Joshua. And when they had eaten and drunk, they sang, some ordinary songs and others alphabetical acrostics.

R. Eliezer said to R. Joshua, "They are occupied with their matters, while we neglect ours."

They began therefore with exposition of the Pentateuch, and from the Pentateuch they went on to the Prophets and from the Prophets to the Hagiographa, and the words of the Pentateuch rejoiced as on the day they were given on Sinai, and fire played round them, for were they not originally given on Sinai in fire? as it is said, *And the mountain burned with fire unto the heart of heaven*? (Deut. 4 : 11).

[When my father saw this], he said, "Since so great indeed is the power of the Torah, if my son is granted life, I will dedicate him to the Torah."

And because his intention was not for the glory of God, my Torah did not remain with me.

Ruth R. 6 : 4, trans. L. Rabinowitz, p. 77-78 = Qoh. R. 7 : 8 : 1

*Comment*: The reference to Eliezer and Joshua is part of a speech of Elisha to Meir. Elisha cites a teaching of ʿAqiba, on Qoh. 7 : 8, that something has to start off well to work out well. The story has no Tannaite warrant. The "power" of Torah is supernatural, not magical; one should not seek it, for it comes out of divine grace or recognition of merit.

III.i.18. R. ʿAqiba said, "Thus was the beginning of my service [of study] before sages.

"One time I was walking on the way, and I found a neglected corpse (*met-miṣwah*), and I tended it for about four miles, until I brought it to a burial place and I buried it there.

"And when I came to R. Eliezer and to R. Joshua, I told them about it.

"They said to me, 'Every step which you took is credited to you as if you shed blood.' [You treated the corpse disrespectfully and should have buried him where he lay.]

"I said, 'If, when I intended to acquire merit, I have become liable, when I did *not* intend to acquire merit, how much the more so [am I liable to be punished]!' From that moment I did not budge from serving sages."

y. Naz. 7 : 1, Gilead, pp. 67-8

*Comment*: ʿAqiba's story, like Elisha's, routinely introduces the names of Eliezer and Joshua. But they are not integral to the homily, merely serve to supply the law.

V.v.2. R. ʿAqiba said, "The beginning of my attendance upon the sages was thus:

"I was once on a journey when I came across a neglected corpse (*met miṣvah*) which I carried about four *mil* until I brought it to a cemetery and buried it there.

"When I appeared before R. Eliezer and R. Joshua and told them what had happened, they said to me, 'Every step you took is reckoned against you as if you had shed blood.'

"I said to them, 'If, in a case where I intended to perform a meritorious act, I have made myself liable like a wicked person, how much more [will I deserve punishment] when I have no [meritorious] intention.'

"From that moment I did not let an opportunity pass to minister to the sages."

Derekh Ereṣ Zuṭṭa 59a,
trans. M. Ginsberg, pp. 587-588

IV.i.25. Hyrcanus, the son of R. Joshua b. Ḥananiah, said to R. Joshua. . .

y. Sot. 3 : 4, Gilead, p. 31

*Comment*: Joshua named his son after Eliezer's father, as did Eliezer himself.

IV.i.26. R. Ba said, "At first each one appointed his disciples, for instance Rabbi Yoḥanan b. Zakkai appointed R. Liezer and R. Joshua, R. Joshua [appointed] R. ʿAqiba. . ."

y. Sanh. 1 : 2, Gilead, p. 11

*Comment*: Yoḥanan's line here continues through Joshua, Eliezer appoints no one and is not credited with ʿAqiba.

IV.i.27.A. MʿŚH B: R. Eliezer and R. Joshua and R. ʿAqiba went up to Ḥolat Antokhia to collect funds for the sages (ʿL ʿSQ MGBT ḤKMYM).

B. There was there Abba Judah, who carried out the commandment in a liberal way. One time he lost his goods, saw our rabbis, and despaired [of assisting] them.

He went to his house, and his face was pale.

His wife said to him, "Why is your face pale?"

He said to her, "Our rabbis are here, and I do not know what I shall do."

His wife, who was more righteous than he, said to him, "You have a single field left. Go and sell half of it and give them [the proceeds]."

He went and did so and came to our rabbis and gave them [the proceeds], and our rabbis prayed in his behalf. Our rabbis said to him, "Abba Judah, may the Holy One blessed be he restore what you have lost."

When they departed, he went down to plough in the [remaining] half-field. While he was ploughing in the midst of his half-field, his ox stumbled and broke [a leg]. He went down to raise her up and the Holy One blessed be he enlightened his eyes and he found a treasure (SYM').

He said, "For my benefit did the leg of my ox break."

C. When our rabbis returned, they asked about him, saying, "How is Abba Judah doing?"

They were told, "Who can see the face of Abba Judah—Abba Judah of the oxen, Abba Judah of the camels, Abba Judah of the asses!"

D. Abba Judah returned to his former condition and came to our rabbis, and asked after their welfare.

They said, "How is Abba Judah doing?"

He said to them, "Your prayer produced endless results."

E. They said to him, "Even though others gave more than you at first, you did we write at the top of the list (ṬYMWS)."

They took him and sat him near them and read concerning him this Scripture, *The gift of a man will make room for him and bring him before great men* (Prov. 18 : 16).

y. Hor. 3 : 4, Gilead, pp. 34-35
(Lev. R. 5 : 4; Deut. R. 4 : 8)

*Comment*: The story unfolds smoothly, except that C duplicates D. Eliezer, Joshua, and ʿAqiba are not differentiated and play no individual roles in the story. They are "our rabbis."

IV.ii.20. The daughter of Kalba Shavuʿa betrothed herself to R. ʿAqiba. When her father heard, he vowed she was not to benefit from his property. Then she went and married him in winter...

She counselled him, "Go and become a scholar." So he left her and spent twelve years with R. Eliezer and R. Joshua.

At the end of this period, he was returning home, and from the back of the house heard a wicked man jeering at his wife, "Your father did well to you. Firstly, because he [ʿAqiba] is your inferior, and secondly, he has abandoned you to living widowhood all these years."

She replied, "Yet were he to hear my desires, he would be absent another twelve years."

"Seeing that she has thus given me permission," he said, "I will go back." So he went back and was absent for another twelve years, [at the end of which] he returned with twenty-four thousand disciples...

b. Ned. 50a, trans. H. Freedman, pp. 155-156

*Comment*: The story, in Aramaic, tells another version of how ʿAqiba went to study with Eliezer and Joshua.

IV.ii.21.A. Abba Siqra the head of the *biryoni* in Jerusalem was the son of the sister of Rabban Yoḥanan b. Zakkai. [The latter] sent to him saying, "Come to visit me privately." When he came he said to him, "How long are you going to carry on this way and kill all the people with starvation?"

He replied, "What can I do? If I say a word to them, they will kill me."

He said, "Devise some plan for me to escape. Perhaps I shall be able to save a little."

He said to him, "Pretend to be ill, and let everyone come to inquire about you. Bring something evil-smelling and put it by you so that they will say you are dead. Let then your disciples get under the bed, but no others, so that they shall not notice that you are still light, since they know that a living being is lighter than a corpse."

He did so. R. Eliezer went under the bier from one side and R. Joshua from the other.

B. When they reached the door, some men wanted to put a lance through the bier.

He said to them, "Shall [the Romans] say, 'They have pierced their Master?' "

They wanted to give it a push.

He said to them, "Shall they say that they pushed their Master?" They opened a town gate for him and he got out...

b. Git. 56a, trans. Maurice Simon, p. 257

*Comment*: Eliezer and Joshua are Yoḥanan's chief disciples and take him out of the city. They play no role in the story, apart from carrying the bier. We do not know who *he* is in B. See *Development*, pp. 150, 166, 188, 229-230, 275.

V.i.8. Now, after Rabban Yoḥanan ben Zakkai had spoken to them [the Jerusalemites, urging them to surrender] one day, two and three days, and they still would not attend to him, he sent for his disciples, for Rabbi Eliezer and Rabbi Joshua.

"My sons," he said to them, "arise and take me out of here. Make a coffin for me that I might lie in it."

Rabbi Eliezer took hold of the head end of it, Rabbi Joshua took hold of the foot; and they began carrying him as the sun set, until they reached the gates of Jerusalem.

"Who is this?" the gatekeepers demanded.

"It's a dead man," they replied. "Do you not know that the dead may not be held overnight in Jerusalem?"

"If it's a dead man," the gatekeepers said to them, "take him out," etc.

ARN Chap. 4, Goldin, pp. 35-36

*Comment*: See *Development*, pp. 113ff.

V.xii.5. He said, "Carry me out in the guise of a corpse." R. Eliezer carried him by the head, R. Joshua by the feet, and Ben Baṭṭiaḥ walked in front. When they reached [the city gates, the guards] wanted to stab him. Ben Baṭṭiaḥ said to them, "Do you wish people to say that when our teacher died, his body was stabbed!"...

After Vespasian had conquered the city he asked him, "Have you any friend or relative there? Send and bring him out before the troops enter." He sent R. Eliezer and R. Joshua to bring out R. Ṣaddoq.

Lam. R. 1:5:31,
trans. A. Cohen, pp. 102, 104

IV.ii.22.A. A widow's son asked R. Eliezer, "If my father orders, 'Give me a drink of water,' and my mother does likewise, which takes precedence?"

"Leave your mother's honor, and fulfill the honor due to your father," he replied, "for both you and your mother are bound to honor your father."

B. Then he went before R. Joshua, who answered him the same.

"Rabbi," said he to him, "what if she is divorced?"

"From your eyelids it is obvious that you are a widow's son," he retorted, "pour some water for them into a basin, and screech for them like fowls!"

b. Qid. 31a, trans. H. Freedman, p. 150

*Comment*: Eliezer and Joshua give the same answer, but, when provoked, Joshua further insults the boy. In the Eliezer-Joshua-convert stories, the roles are reversed.

IV.ii.23. What is a man to do in order that he may have a male offspring?

R. Eliezer says, "He should give generously to the poor."

R. Joshua says, "He should make his wife glad to perform the marital office."

b. B.B. 10b, trans. M. Simon, pp. 48-49

V.iv.3. What should a man do in order to have children?

R. Eliezer said, "Let him freely distribute charity to the poor, as it is stated, *He hath scattered abroad, he hath given to the needy... his horn shall be exalted in honor* (Ps. 112 : 9)."

Kallah Rabbati 52b, trans. J. Rabbinowitz, p. 436.

IV.ii.24. They asked Imma Shalom, "Why are your children so beautiful?"

She said to them, "Because he converses with me not at the start nor at the end of the night, but only at midnight, and when he converses, he uncovers a handbreadth and covers a handbreath, and it is as if he is compelled by a demon."

"When I asked him, Why [midnight]," he said to me, "So that I may not think of another woman, lest my children be *mamzerim*."

b. Ned. 20b

V.iv.4. Imma Shalom, the wife of R. Eliezer and sister of Rabban Gamaliel, was asked, "Why are your children beautiful? And during intercourse how does [your husband] conduct himself towards you?"

She replied, "He does not converse with me during the first or last watch of the night, but only during the middle watch; [and when he cohabits] he uncovers a handbreadth and covers a handbreadth, and is as though he were urged on by a demon. And when I questioned him, 'What is the reason for all this?' he replied, 'So that another woman should not come to my mind, and my children consequently come within the category of bastards.'"

Kallah Rabbati 52a, trans. J. Rabbinowitz, pp. 423-424

V.iv.5. Why [are children born] lame, blind, dumb or deaf?

R. Eliezer said, "Because [the husband] claimed marital rights, but she refused."

R. Joshua said, "Because she declared at the time of cohabitation, 'I have been forced.'"

R. ʿAqiba said, "Because they talk in causeless hatred."

Kallah Rabbati 1 : 11, 51b, trans. J. Rabbinowitz, p. 421
(also 50b, Rabbinowitz, pp. 403-4)

V.iv.6.A. R. Judah said, "The bold-face are [destined] to Gehinnom and the shamefaced to the Garden of Eden."

"The bold-faced," R. Eliezer said, "is the bastard."

"The son of a *niddah*," said R. Joshua.

R. ʿAqiba said, "Both a bastard and the son of a *niddah*."

B. The elders were once sitting in the gate when two young lads passed by; one covered his head and the other uncovered his head. Of him who uncovered his head R. Eliezer remarked that he is a bastard. R. Joshua remarked that he is the son of a *niddah*. R. ʿAqiba said that he is both a bastard and the son of a *niddah*.

They said to R. ʿAqiba, "How did your heart induce you to contradict the opinion of your colleagues?"

He replied, "I will prove it concerning him."

He went to the lad's mother and found her sitting in the market selling beans. He said to her, "My daughter, if you will answer the question which I will put to you, I will bring you to the world to come." She said to him, "Swear it to me."

R. ʿAqiba, taking the oath with his lips but annulling it in his heart, said to her, "What is the status of your son?"

She replied, "When I entered the bridal chamber I was *niddah* and my husband kept away from me; but my best man had intercourse with me, and this son was born to me." Consequently the child was both a bastard and the son of a *niddah*.

It was declared, "R. ʿAqiba showed himself a great man when he contradicted his teachers." At the same time they added, "Blessed be the God of Israel, Who revealed His secret to R. ʿAqiba b. Joseph."

Kallah Rabbati 2 : 1 (= 2 : 16), 52a,
trans. J. Rabbinowitz, p. 407, p. 427

IV.ii.25. Rav Judah in the name of Rav said, "A Sanhedrin is not established in a city which does not contain two who can speak [seventy languages] and one who understands them. In Betar were three, and in Yavneh were four: R. Eliezer, R. Joshua, R. ʿAqiba, and Simeon the Temanite, who used to discuss before them sitting on the floor."

b. Sanh. 17b, trans. Jacob Shachter, p. 88

*Comment*: Yavneh's masters are listed.

IV.ii.26. ʾMRW ʿLYW ʿL: Hyrcanus the son of R. Eliezer b. Hyrcanus used to tie his *tefillin* with strips of purple wool, and he [Eliezer] said nothing.

b. Men. 35a

*Comment*: This is taken as evidence that one may do as Hyrcanus did.

V.i.9. A man is duty bound to attend upon *four* scholars, such as Rabbi Eliezer, Rabbi Joshua, Rabbi Ṭarfon, and Rabbi ʿAqiba, as it is said, *Happy is the man that hearkeneth to me, watching daily at my gates, waiting at the posts of my doors* (Prov. 8 : 34): read not *my gates* (*dalṯoṯai*) but *my four gates* (*daleṯ dalṯotai*).

ARN Chap. 3, Goldin, p. 28-29

*Comment*: Now Yavneh's masters drop Simeon and add Ṭarfon.

V.i.10.A. What were the beginnings of Rabbi Eliezer ben Hyrcanus? He was twenty-two years old and had not yet studied Torah. One time he resolved: "I will go and study Torah with Rabban Yoḥanan ben Zakkai." Said his father Hyrcanus to him, "Not a taste of food shalt thou get before thou hast plowed the entire furrow."

He rose early in the morning and plowed the entire furrow (and then departed for Jerusalem).

(B). It is told: That day was the eve of the Sabbath, and he went for the Sabbath meal to his father-in-law's. And some say: He tasted nothing from six hours before the eve of the Sabbath until six hours after the departure of the Sabbath.

(C) As he was walking along the road he saw a stone; he picked it up and put it in his mouth. And some say: It was cattle dung. He went to spend the night at a hostel.

Then he went and appeared before Rabban Yoḥanan ben Zakkai in Jerusalem—until a bad breath rose from his mouth. Said Rabban Yoḥanan ben Zakkai to him, "Eliezer, my son, hast thou eaten at all today?"

Silence.

Rabban Yoḥanan ben Zakkai asked him again.

Again silence.

Rabban Yoḥanan ben Zakkai sent for the owners of his hostel and asked them, "Did Eliezer have anything to eat in your place?"

"We thought," they replied, "he was very likely eating with thee, master."

He said to them, "And I thought he was very likely eating with you! You and I, between us, left Rabbi Eliezer to perish!"

(Thereupon) Rabban Yoḥanan said to him, "Even as a bad breath rose from thy mouth, so shall fame of thee travel for thy mastery of the Torah."

(D). When Hyrcanus his father heard of him, that he was studying

Torah with Rabban Yoḥanan ben Zakkai, he declared, "I shall go and ban my son Eliezer from my possessions."

It is told: That day Rabban Yoḥanan ben Zakkai sat expounding in Jerusalem and all the great ones of Israel sat before him. When he heard that Hyrcanus was coming, he appointed guards and said to them, "If Hyrcanus comes, do not let him sit down."

Hyrcanus arrived and they would not let him sit down. But he pushed on ahead until he reached the place near Ben Hakkeset, Nakdimon ben Gorion, and Ben Kalba Shavuʿa. He sat among them trembling.

E. It is told: On that day Rabban Yoḥanan ben Zakkai fixed his gaze upon Rabbi Eliezer and said to him, "Deliver the exposition."

"I am unable to speak," Rabbi Eliezer pleaded.

Rabban Yoḥanan pressed him to do it, and the disciples pressed him to do it. So he arose and delivered a discourse upon things which no ear had ever before heard. As the words came from his mouth Rabban Yoḥanan ben Zakkai rose to his feet and kissed him upon his head and exclaimed, "Rabbi Eliezer, master, thou hast taught me the truth!"

F. Before the time had come to recess, Hyrcanus, his father, rose to his feet and declared, "My masters, I came here only in order to ban my son Eliezer from my possessions. Now, all my possessions shall be given to Eliezer my son, and all his brothers are herewith disinherited and have naught of them."

ARN, Chap. 6, Goldin, pp. 43-44

V.vii.2.A. *And it came to pass in the days of Amraphel*, etc. (Gen. 14: 1).

R. Joshua commenced his discourse in the name of R. Levi: *The wicked have drawn out the sword*, etc. (Ps. 37 : 14).

B. R. Liezer's brothers were once ploughing in the plain, while he was ploughing on the mountain, when his cow fell and was maimed. It proved fortunate for him that his cow was maimed, for he fled to R. Yoḥanan b. Zakkai.

C. He ate there clods of earth until his mouth emitted an offensive odor, and when they went and told R. Yoḥanan b. Zakkai that the breath from R. Eliezer's mouth smelt foul, he said to him, "As the smell of your mouth became unpleasant for the sake of the Torah, so will the fragrance of your learning be diffused from one end of the world to the other."

D. After some time his father came up to disinherit him, and found him sitting and lecturing with the greatest of the land sitting before him. Ben Ṣiṣit Hakeset, Niqodemon ben Gurion, and Ben Kalba Shavuʿa.

He was expounding this verse: "*The wicked have drawn out the sword, and have bent the bow*; this alludes to Amraphel and his companions; *To cast down the poor and needs*—to Lot; *To slay such as are upright in the way*—to Abraham.

"*Their sword shall enter into their own heart*, as it is written, *And he fought against them by night, he and his servants, and smote them*, etc. (Gen. 14 : 15)."

Said his father to him, "My son, I came up only to disinherit thee; now, however, all my property is given to thee as a gift." "Behold," he replied, "let it be *ḥerem* [accursed] to me; I will take only an equal share with my brothers."

Gen. R. 42 : 1, trans. H. Freedman, p. 340

V.x.2.A. MʿŚH B: R. Eliezer b. Hyrcanus was the son of PYLWṬ [Buber: son of the palace] and his father was close to the government and to matters of the army [So Buber for H'YSṬLṬYWṬYN].

After some days the father of R. Eliezer went to another place. When he felt they [the army? the government officials?] were coming, he said to his sons, "Let us rise and flee before them."

Forthwith he called his slaves and servants. He said, "Bring me the cattle and camels." They put the vessels on the cattle and Hyrcanus and his sons fled.

But R. Eliezer did not go with his father. He rather fled to Jerusalem. And he took in his hand neither a loaf of bread nor money nor any thing, but he entered Jerusalem like a poor man.

B. He saw Rabban Yoḥanan b. Zakkai sitting and teaching Torah, and the disciples were sitting before him [concentrating on] the chapter. When they finished the chapter, he told them lore (HGDH), and afterward, he says [*sic*] a Mishnah.

He [Eliezer] entered and sat by Rabban Yoḥanan b. Zakkai. He worked with him two or three weeks. The matters came against the [other] disciples [they were jealous.] And they smelled the bad breath of his mouth and would stand aside and not speak with him. This happened a second time, and a third. Rabban Yoḥanan b. Zakkai knew that the bad smell was not because of something bad in his mouth, but because of hunger, for he had eaten nothing.

Rabban Yoḥanan b. Zakkai said to the disciples, "By your lives, seek out the matter so you may know the affairs of this disciple, whether he is hungry, and what he is eating."

They went around the whole of Jerusalem asking inn-keepers, "Is there here a *Ḥaver* as a guest," and they were told no. They came to a certain woman, and asked whether a *Ḥaver* was a guest here.

She said to them, "Yes."

"Does he have anything here?"

She said to them, "He has a single sack."

They said to her, "Show it to us."

She brought it to them forthwith. They opened it and found in it dirt, for he would put his head in it and suck as on a wine-bag. They went and told Rabban Yoḥanan b. Zakkai, and he was surprised about it.

And he recognized [this as] righteousness in respect to R. Eliezer, that he had not besought from anyone, saying, "Give me something."

Then he arranged for him a large sum of money, so that he might eat good food, as he was used to in his father's house, for he would eat good food (YŠWTH), until the breath of his mouth was healed.

C. He studied with Rabban Yoḥanan b. Zakkai a year, two, three years, until the father of R. Eliezer returned to his place. When he came back to his place, he waited a month or two, and R. Eliezer, his son, did not come. He was angry, saying, "I have left him [here], and he has gone to Jerusalem."

And the brothers of R. Eliezer said to their father, "See Eliezer your son, what he has done! He has left you and gone off to Jerusalem to eat dainties (PṬWMWT), and you have left your home and gone after him. If it were a bad thing, he would not jump to take an inheritance! And how much is between us and your son! We gave our lives for you and did not leave you, and he did not come to see you in your trouble. Now if he hears that something has happened to you, he will come to us to share our estate with us."

Then he said to them, "By this and that! He will not inherit from me a thing."

They said to him, "After you die, will you disinherit him?"

He said to them, "Call me a notary (PNQS)."

They said to him, "It does no good. A certain *Nasi* is in Jerusalem, and his name is Rabban Yoḥanan b. Zakkai, and he will help him. After you die, certainly he will come, and he will say, 'Who will testify that his father disinherited him?' And we shall bring out the document. And he will say, 'It is a forgery (PLSṬYN). You made it. And I shall not believe it until we shall go to court!' "

He said to them, "Since you have said this to me, let Rabban Yoḥanan b. Zakkai take pride (MTHLL) in him! I shall disinherit him."

D. At that moment his sons put him on a carriage (SṬRNH), and he went to Jerusalem on the eve of the Sabbath. He said, "I shall disinherit him only in the school house, when the whole community will enter."

He went in to sit in the school house, and all Israel entered in their study to hear the teaching which R. Eliezer would give in public, sitting on the throne, with the servant (ḤZN) standing before him. His father saw him enwrapped in his prayer-shawl, with *tefillin* on his head. Forthwith he realized [who it was], for he had thought he had gone forth to bad ways.

E. When he saw him enthroned and expounding, Hyrcanus stood on the bench. He said before the men of Jerusalem, "I came up to Jerusalem only to drive out Eliezer my son, and also to disinherit him. Now lo, I shall give him two portions more than his brothers."

And concerning what matter was R. Eliezer expounding at that time?

Our rabbis said, "It was in this matter: *And it came to pass in the days of Amraphel.*"

R. Eliezer b. Hyrcanus began (etc.)...

Midrash Tanḥuma Lekh Lekha 10,
Buber I, pp. 34b, 35a

*Comment*: ARN's version of the 'beginnings' of Eliezer starts with his resolve to study with Yoḥanan. A gives no reason, but simply says Hyrcanus opposed it. B then tells us that he was married, but gives no name to the wife. If this is Imma Shalom, Gamaliel's sister, then Eliezer came to Jerusalem as the son-in-law of Simeon b. Gamaliel, which is incredible. It seems more likely that the narrator has no knowledge of, or interest in, the question.

C then provides a narrative setting for Yoḥanan's saying about bad breath.

In D Hyrcanus decides to disinherit Eliezer, but there is no clear motivation for his action. The jealous brothers are unknown. All Hyrcanus had earlier demanded was that Eliezer finish ploughing the field, which he had done. Yoḥanan knows Hyrcanus is coming and makes preparations. In E Eliezer gives his exposition, and Yoḥanan blesses him, but ARN knows nothing of what he had actually said. Then comes the conclusion in F: Hyrcanus now disinherits the brothers, who earlier are not mentioned. So it would seem that behind this story and alluded to in it are other stories, which involve the brothers, Eliezer's relationships with Hyrcanus, Eliezer's poverty in Jerusalem, perhaps also what he studied with Yoḥanan, also some account of what he actually said in his speech in E.

Gen. R. supplies a motivation for Eliezer's leaving his family. He was given difficult ground and his cow was injured, so he was distressed and fled. Now we have brothers, but no father. Then comes the chria about bad breath. In D the father comes to disinherit him—we still do not know why. E then tells us the occasion for the exposition: a sermon on Gen. 14 : 1ff. F then has the father offer Eliezer all his property, but Eliezer agrees to accept only his share.

Tanḥuma's version is most elaborate. A now explains in detail the relationships of Eliezer both to the father and to his brothers. The whole family had to flee because of a turn in the father's fortunes. The brothers stay by the father, but Eliezer goes, as a pauper, to Jerusalem. Only then does he discover Yoḥanan b. Zakkai. B *develops* the chria about bad breath—but omits the saying! Instead, the conclusion is that Yoḥanan gives Eliezer sufficient funds.

C returns us to Hyrcanus and the brothers. The brothers incite Hyrcanus to disinherit Eliezer, so a motive is now in hand to explain that element. This is elaborately developed, with the legal problems consequent on disinheritance fully worked out. In D Hyrcanus goes to hear his famous son, but the details of who was present are subsumed under "great men of Jerusalem." Afterward, we have the detail of Eliezer's sermon on Gen. 14 : 1.

V.xii.6. The following befell Rabbi Eliezer, son of Hyrcanus. His father had many ploughmen who were ploughing arable ground, whereas he was ploughing a stony plot; he sat down and wept.

His father said to him, "O my son! Why dost thou weep? Art thou perchance distressed because thou dost plough a stony plot? In the past thou hast ploughed a stony plot, now behold thou shalt plough arable soil with us."

He sat down on the arable ground and wept.

His father said to him, "But why dost thou weep? Art thou perchance distressed because thou art ploughing the arable land?"

He replied to him, "No."

Hyrcanus said to him, "Why dost thou weep?"

He answered him, "I weep only because I desire to learn Torah." Hyrcanus said to him, "Verily thou art twenty-eight years old—yet dost thou desire to learn Torah? Nay, go, take thee a wife and beget sons, and thou wilt take them to the school."

He fasted two weeks not tasting anything, until Elijah—may he be remembered for good—appeared to him and said to him, "Son of Hyrcanus! Why dost thou weep?"

He replied to him, "Because I desire to learn Torah." [Elijah] said to him, "If thou desirest to learn Torah, get thee up to Jerusalem to Rabban Yoḥanan ben Zakkai."

He arose and went up to Jerusalem to R. Yoḥanan ben Zakkai and sat down and wept. [R. Yoḥanan] said to him, "Why dost thou weep?"

He answered him, "Because I wish to learn Torah. [R. Yoḥanan] said to him, "Whose son art thou?" But he did not tell him.

[R. Yoḥanan] asked him, "Hast thou never learnt to read the *Shemaʿ*, or the Prayer, or the Grace after meals?"

He replied to him, "No."

He arose and [R. Yoḥanan] taught him the three [prayers].

[Again] he sat down and wept. [R. Yoḥanan] said to him, "My son, why dost thou weep?"

He replied, "Because I desire to learn Torah."

He [thereupon] taught him two rules [of the Law] every day of the week, and on the Sabbath [Eliezer] repeated them and assimilated them.

He kept a fast for eight days without tasting anything until the odor of his mouth attracted the attention of R. Yoḥanan ben Zakkai, who directed him to withdraw from his presence. He sat down and wept.

[R. Yoḥanan] said to him, "My son, why dost thou weep?"

He rejoined, "Because thou didst make me withdraw from thy presence just as a man makes his fellow withdraw, when the latter is afflicted with leprosy.

[R. Yoḥanan] said to him, "My son, just as the odor of thy mouth has ascended before me, so may the savor of the statutes of the Torah ascend from thy mouth to Heaven."

He said to him, "My son! Whose son art thou?"

He replied, "I am the son of Hyrcanus. Then said [R. Yoḥanan], "Art thou not the son of one of the great men of the world, and thou didst not tell me? By thy life!" he continued, "This day shalt thou eat with me."

[Eliezer] answered, "I have eaten already with my host." [R. Yoḥanan] asked, "Who is thy host?"

He replied, "R. Joshua ben Ḥananiah and R. Yosi the Priest."

[R. Yoḥanan] sent to inquire of his hosts, saying to him, "Did Eliezer eat with you this day? They answered, "No; moreover has he not fasted eight days without tasting any food?"

R. Joshua ben Ḥananiah and R. Yosi the Priest went and said to R. Yoḥanan ben Zakkai, "Verily during the last eight days [Eliezer] has not partaken of any food."

The sons of Hyrcanus said to their father, "Get thee up to Jerusalem and vow that thy son Eliezer should not enjoy any of thy possessions." He went up to Jerusalem to disinherit him, and it happened that a festival was being celebrated there by R. Yoḥanan ben Zakkai. All the magnates of the district were dining with him; [such as] Ben Ṣiṣit Hakkeset, Nicodemus ben Gorion, and Ben Kalba Shavuʿa.

The people said [to R. Yoḥanan], "Behold, the father of R. Eliezer has arrived." He bade them saying, "Prepare a place for him, and seat him next to us."

[R. Yoḥanan] fixed his gaze on R. Eliezer saying to him, "Tell us some words of the Torah." [R. Eliezer] answered him saying, "Rabbi! I will tell thee a parable. To what is the matter like? To this well which cannot yield more water than the amount which it has drawn [from the earth]; likewise am I unable to speak words of the Torah in excess of what I have received from thee."

[R. Yoḥanan] said to him, "I will [also] tell thee a parable. To what is the matter like? To this fountain which is bubbling and sending forth its water, and it is able to effect a discharge more powerful than what it secretes; in like manner art thou able to speak words of the Torah in excess of what Moses received at Sinai." [R. Yoḥanan] continued, "Lest thou shouldst feel ashamed on my account, behold I will arise and go away from thee."

Rabban Yoḥanan ben Zakkai arose and went outside. [Thereupon] R. Eliezer sat down and expounded. His face shone like the light of the sun and his effulgence beamed forth like that of Moses, so that no one knew whether it was day or night.

They went and said to Rabban Yoḥanan ben Zakkai, "Come and see R. Eliezer sitting and expounding, his face shining like the light of the sun and his effulgence beaming like that of Moses, so that no one knows whether it be day or night." He came from [his place] behind him and kissed him on this head, saying to him, "Happy are ye, Abraham, Isaac, and Jacob, because this one has come forth from your loins."

Hyrcanus his father said, "To whom does [R. Yoḥanan] speak thus?"

The people answered, "To Eliezer thy son."

He said to them, "[R. Yoḥanan] should not have spoken in that manner, but [in this wise], 'Happy am I because he has come forth from my loins.' "

Whilst R. Eliezer was sitting and expounding, his father was standing upon his feet. When [Eliezer] saw his father standing upon his feet, he became agitated and said to him, "My father! be seated, for I cannot utter the words of the Torah when thou art standing on thy feet."

Hyrcanus replied to him, "My son, it was not for this reason that I came, but my intention was to disinherit thee. Now that I have come and I have witnessed all this praise, behold thy brothers are disinherited and their portion is given to thee as a gift."

[Eliezer] replied, "Verily I am not equal to one of them. If I had asked the Holy One, blessed be He, for land, it would be possible for Him to give this to me, as it is said, *The earth is the Lord's, and the fulness thereof* (Ps. 24 : 1). Had I asked the Holy One, blessed be He, for silver and gold, He could have given them to me, as it is said, *The silver is mine, and the gold is mine* (Hag. 2 : 8). But I asked the Holy One, blessed be He, that I might be worthy [to learn the] Torah only, as it is said, *Therefore I esteem all precepts concerning all things to be right; and I hate every false way* (Ps. 119 : 128)."

Pirqé de R. Eliezer, Chaps. One and Two, trans. Gerald Friedlander (*Pirke de Rabbi Eliezer* [London, 1916], pp. 1-8).

*Comment*: PRE is closest to ARNB, as summarized in *Development*, pp. 242-247. The compilation comes from the ninth century (Friedlander, p. liv), though some date it as early as 750 A.D.

For an excellent analysis of the several foregoing stories, see Z. Kagan, "Divergent Tendencies and their Literary Moulding in the *Aggadah*," *Scripta Hierosolymitana* XXII. *Studies in Aggadah and Folk-literature* (Jerusalem, 1971), pp. 151-170.

Kagan's analysis stresses the literary aspect of the stories, treating the *Aggadah* primarily as literature. She translates five versions of the story, ARNA, ARNB, Gen. R., Tanh., and PRE (= ARNB). She further compares the main elements of the several stories, though not the exact language of each to the next, according to the subjects. Eliezer's personality as it is revealed in each version is delineated. In ARNA and Gen. R. he is a strong personality. In ARNB=PRE he is passive and hesitant.

Kagan's historical conclusion, however, seems to me entirely unfounded: "We thus have two groups. The first one—ARN I [=A] and Gen. R.—is earlier and more authentic. The Aggadah in Group A was told close to the time when the events took place and for that reason it preserved a more realistic view of the figures, the plot, and numerous details. The Aggadah in Group B,—ARN II [=B] and PRE, was composed at a later time than the historical event. The later editors, who wished to enhance the hero and clothe him in shining armour (legend), were free to introduce changes and additions in the light of this tendency without being tied to the factual and historical yardstick or any need to consider it." Kagan notes (p. 168, n. 11) that the "chronological criterion—the time when the Midrashim were edited—can help us a little, but not decisively. ARN and Gen. R. were finally edited still in the fifth century; PRE in the eighth (or ninth) century. According to our conclusions, the Aggadah in ARN I is early, while that in ARN II is late and many changes were made in it, compared with the original." It need not be denied that the relationships between the two sets of stories are as Kagan claims: ARNA and Gen. R. do come before ARNB and PRE.

But these are relative to one another. Both groups come late in the formation of the traditions about Eliezer. Before Avot, no one has even heard of his discipleship with Yoḥanan b. Zakkai; Eliezer has not a single saying about, story referring to, or law congruent with, Yoḥanan b. Zakkai, attested before the early third century. Eliezer stands wholly outside of the legal framework of Yoḥanan b. Zakkai's materials, and does not rule even on the same issues. Outside of Avot and M. Yad. 4 : 3 Yoḥanan b. Zakkai does not occur before the mid-third-century allusions to Eliezer. So why should we suppose ARNA and Gen. R.'s stories are told "close to the time" of the events they depict. At best, we may say that they stand *closer* to the first century than do ARNB and PRE. But that anyone in the late third, fourth, or fifth centuries knew the difference between a "more realistic view" of the figures he portrayed and a more imaginative view or felt constrained by the requirements of historical inquiry, first established many centuries later, so as not to introduce "changes and additions" and not to "clothe the hero in shining armour"—such a conception is preposterous, and interpretations based upon it are silly. Literary approaches to *aggadah* hardly prepare the way for historical judgments.

V.i.11. When Rabban Yoḥanan ben Zakkai's son died, his disciples came in to comfort him. Rabbi Eliezer entered, sat down before him, and said to him, "Master, by the leave, may I say something to thee?"

"Speak," he replied.

Rabbi Eliezer said, "Adam had a son who died, yet he allowed himself to be comforted concerning him. And how do we know that he allowed himself to be comforted concerning him? For it is said, *And Adam knew his wife again* (Gen. 4 : 25). Thou too, be thou comforted." [= Go have another son!]

Said Rabban Yoḥanan to him, "Is it not enough that I grieve over my own, that thou remindest me of the grief of Adam?"

Rabbi Joshua entered and said to him, "By thy leave, may I say something to thee?"

"Speak," he replied.

Rabbi Joshua said, "Job had sons and daughters, all of whom died in one day, and he allowed himself to be comforted concerning them. Thou too, be thou comforted. And how do we know that Job was comforted? For it is said, *The Lord gave, and the Lord hath taken away; blessed be the name of the Lord* (Job. 1 : 21)."

Said Rabban Yoḥanan to him, "Is it not enough that I grieve over my own, that thou remindest me of the grief of Job?"

Rabbi Yosi entered and sat down before him; he said to him, "Master, by thy leave, may I say something to thee?"

"Speak," he replied.

Rabbi Yosi said, "Aaron had two grown sons, both of whom died in one day, yet he allowed himself to be comforted for them, as it is said, *And Aaron held his peace* (Lev. 10 : 3)—silence is no other than consolation. Thou too, therefore, be thou comforted."

Said Rabban Yoḥanan to him, "Is it not enough that I grieve over my own, that thou remindest me of the grief of Aaron?"

Rabbi Simeon entered and said to him, "Master, by thy leave, may I say something to thee?"

"Speak," he replied.

Rabbi Simeon said, "King David had a son who died, yet he allowed himself to be comforted. Thou too, therefore, be thou comforted. And how do we know that David was comforted? For it is said, *And David comforted Bath-Sheba his wife, and went in unto her, and lay with her; and she bore a son, and called his name Solomon* (II Sam. 12 : 24). Thou too, master, be thou comforted."

Said Rabban Yoḥanan to him, "Is it not enough that I grieve over my own, that thou remindest me of the grief of King David?"

Rabbi Eleazar ben ʿArakh entered. As soon as Rabban Yoḥanan saw him, he said to his servant, "Take my clothing and follow me to the bathhouse, for he is a great man, and I shall be unable to resist him."

Rabbi Eleazar entered, sat down before him, and said to him, "I shall tell thee a parable: to what may this be likened? To a man with whom the king deposited some object. Every single day the man would weep and cry out, saying, 'Woe unto me' when shall I be quit of this trust in peace?' Thou too, master, thou hadst a son; he studied the Torah, the Prophets, the Holy Writings, he studied Mishnah, Halakhah, Aggadah, and he departed from the world without sin. And thou shouldst be comforted when thou hast returned thy trust unimpaired."

Said Rabban Yoḥanan to him, "Rabbi Eleazar, my son, thou has comforted me the way men should give comfort!"

ARN, Chap. fourteen, trans. Goldin, pp. 74-78
(ARNB, ed. Schechter, p. 29a-b, chap. 31, p. 33b)

*Comment*: Eliezer comes first, as in Avot, but is given an unimportant part.

V.vii.3. *And will give me bread to eat, and raiment to put on* (Gen. 28 : 20).

Aqilas the proselyte visited R. Eliezer and said to him, "Does then all the benefit of the proselyte lie in what is said, *And loveth the proselyte in giving him food and raiment* (Deut. 10 : 18)?"

"Is then that a small thing in your eyes," replied he, "for which our ancestor supplicated, praying, *And will give me bread to eat, and raiment to put on*, while He [God] comes and offers it to him [the proselyte] on a reed!"

Then he visited R. Joshua, who began to comfort him with words, "*Bread* refers to the Torah, as it says, *Come, eat of my bread* (Prov. 9 : 5), while '*raiment*' means the [scholar's] cloak: when a man is privileged to [study the] Torah, he is privileged to perform God's precepts.

"Moreover, they [the proselytes] marry their daughters into the priesthood, so that their descendants may offer burnt-offerings on the altar."

Gen. R. 70 : 5, trans. H. Freedman, pp. 638-639

V.xi.4. Aqilas, the proselyte, once went in to R. Eliezer and said to him, "All the glory of the proselyte, then, consists in that He *Loveth the proselyte, in giving him food and raiment* (Deut. 10 : 18)!"

Said the latter to him, "Is this such a trifling matter in your eyes? It is a thing for which that ancestor of ours prostrated himself in prayer, saying, *And will give me bread to eat, and raiment to put on* (Gen. 28 : 20), and now comes this man and He offers it to him on a tray [lit.: 'reed']!"

He [Aqilas] came in to R. Joshua, and the latter began to speak consolingly to him, "*Bread*," he said, "alludes to Torah; as it says, Come, eat of my bread (Prov. 9 : 5). '*Raiment*' alludes to the *tallit*. If a man is worthy of acquiring Torah he is privileged to perform good deeds. Nay, more; they [the pious proselytes] marry their daughters into the priesthood, and their children's children will offer burnt-offerings upon the altar [and so], '*bread*' refers to the shewbread, and '*raiment*' to the robes of High Priesthood. This applies to the Sanctuary. Whence that they have a share in the gifts due to the priest from the land? '*Bread*' refers to the first cake of the dough, and '*raiment*' to the first of the fleece."

For this reason the text, *And every man's hallowed things shall be his* (Num. 8 : 9) is placed in the section dealing with the proselyte.

Num. R. 8 : 9, trans. J. J. Slotki, p. 235

V.xii.7. Furthermore, Aqilas the proselyte asked R. Eliezer, "Is the love which the Holy One, blessed be He, feels towards the proselyte (*ger*) manifested only in the grant of food and clothing, as it is said, *Loveth the stranger in giving him food and raiment* (Deut. 10 : 18)? So numerous are the peacocks and pheasants I possess that even my slaves do not take notice of them!"

He replied to him, "Is, then, a thing trifling in your eyes which our father Jacob begged from the first, as it is said, *And will give me bread to eat and raiment to put on* (Gen. 28 : 20)? Is that something insignificant?"

He went to R. Joshua and put the same question to him. He replied, "[The meaning is that] a proselyte who has become converted for the name of Heaven is worthy that his daughters should marry into the priesthood. *Bread* signifies the shewbread, and *raiment* indicates the priestly vestments."

His disciples criticized his statement and said to him, "Is, then, the thing insignificant in your eyes for which the patriarch begged, as it is said, *And will give me bread to eat*? So why do you put him off with a trifle?"

[R. Joshua] therefore began to speak more persuasively to him, saying, "*Bread* means the Torah, as it is stated, *Come, eat of My bread* (Prov. 9 : 5), and *raiment* signifies glory, as it is stated, *By Me kings reign* (Prov. 8 : 15)."

The text was accordingly applied to him, *The patient in spirit is better than the proud in spirit* (Qoh. 7 : 8).

Qoh. R. 7 : 8 : 1, trans. A. Cohen, pp. 187-8

V.xii.8. A woman once came to R. Eliezer to be made a proselyte, saying to him, "Rabbi, receive me."

He said to her, "Recount your acts to me."

She told him, "My youngest son [was conceived] through my

eldest son." He stormed at her; so she went to R. Joshua, who received her.

His disciples said to him, "R. Eliezer drove her away and you accept her!"

He replied, "When she set her mind on being a proselyte, she no longer lived to the world, as it is written, *None that go unto her return* (Prov. 2 : 19): and if they do return [to their evil ways] *Neither do they attain unto the paths of life.*"

Qoh. R. 1 : 8 : 4, trans. A. Cohen, pp. 28-29

*Comment*: The story about Hillel, Shammai, and the proselyte (b. Shab. 30b-31a) has its counterpart here. Eliezer, like Shammai, puts the prospective proselytes to shame while Joshua treats them in a friendly way.

V.xi.5. *Then it shall come to pass, if she be defiled, and have acted unfaithfully against her husband, that the water... shall enter*, etc. (Num. 5 : 27). When they drank of it, they were tested, and all the sinners died violent deaths.

A Roman lady asked R. Eliezer, "How is it that, though only one sin had been committed in connection with the calf, they died by three kinds of death?"

He said to her, "Woman has no wisdom except at the distaff; for it is written, *And all the women that were wise-hearted did spin with their hands* (Ex. 35 : 25)."

Said Hyrcanus, "Because he did not answer her one thing from the Torah, she deprived him of three hundred *kor* of tithe annually!"

Said the other to him, "Let the words of the Torah be burned rather than be entrusted to women!"

When he [Hyrcanus] departed, his [R. Eliezer's] pupils said to him, "Master! You warded off this woman with a reed, but what answer will you give us?"

R. Berekiah, son of Abba, son of Kahana, in the name of R. Eleazar, said...

Num. R. 9 : 48, trans. J. J. Slotki, pp. 326-327

*Comment*: In this strange pericope, Hyrcanus, Eliezer's son, evidently rebukes the father for not answering the Roman matron's question. Eliezer refused to commit Torah-teachings to a woman—any woman. Then the disciples ask Eliezer why he gave such a poor answer (when he gave none at all). Afterward, R. Berekiah supplies an answer to the question, but this is not integral to the antecedent pericope and is not attributed to Eliezer!

V.xi.6. R. Abbahu said, "R. Eliezer the Great was asked by his disciples, 'Can you give an example of [real] honoring of parents.'

"He replied, 'Go and see what Dama b. Nethina of Askelon did. His mother was mentally afflicted and she used to slap him in the presence of his colleagues, and all that he would say was, Mother, it is enough!' "

Num. R. 1 : 15, trans. J. J. Slotki, p. 16 (y. Pe'ah 1 : 1)

*Comment*: Versions of this story in earlier compilations do not call this Eliezer, "*the Great*," e.g., Pesiqta Rabbati 23/24, Braude, p. 501, Abbahu-Yoḥanan-Eliezer.

V.xi.7. Once our rabbis, R. Eliezer, R. Joshua, and R. Gamaliel, were in Rome when the Senate issued a decree that within thirty days no Jew should be found in the [Roman] world. Now one of the Emperor's senators was a God-fearing man, and he came to R. Gamaliel and disclosed to him the decree...

Deut. R. 2 : 24, trans. J. Rabbinowitz, p. 51-2

*Comment*: Eliezer does not recur in the story. This is the only version of the famous trip to Rome which includes Eliezer, though the Roman-matron-story and the accounts of Eliezer and Joshua on a boat-trip may relate to the same set of traditions. The likelier reading is Eleazar b. ʿAzariah.

V.xii.9.*And at our doors are all manner of precious fruits* (Song 7 : 14).

A. The rabbis compare it to the case of a king who had an orchard, which he handed over to a tenant. What did the tenant do? He filled some buckets with the fruit of the orchard and put them at the entrance of the orchard. When the king passed and saw the goodly show, he said, "All this fine fruit is at the entrance of the orchard; then what must be in the orchard itself!"

B. So in the earlier generations there were the Men of the Great Synagogue, Hillel, Shammai and Rabban Gamaliel the Elder; in the later generations R. Yoḥanan b. Zakkai, R. Eliezer, R. Joshua, R. Meir, and R. ʿAqiba and their disciples; how much the more!

And of these it says, *New and old which I have laid up for thee, O my beloved* (Song 7 : 14).

Song R. 7 : 14 : 1, trans. M. Simon, pp. 301-302

*Comment*: B supplies a gloss for the parable of A. The earlier generations come before 70, the latter ones afterward, down to Meir.

V.xii.10 R. Issi of Caesarea interpreted the verse as applying to heresy. *Whoso pleaseth* (Qoh. 7 : 26); i.e. R. Eleazar, *But the sinner*: i.e. Jacob of Kefar-Nibbuyara.

Another illustration of *Whoso Pleaseth*: i.e. Eleazar b. Dama. *But the sinner*: i.e. Jacob of Kefar-Sama.

Another illustration of *Whoso pleaseth*: i.e. Ḥananiah the nephew of R. Joshua. *But the sinner*: i.e. the inhabitants of Capernaum.

Another illustration of *Whoso pleaseth*: i.e. Judah b. 'Naqosa. *But the sinner*: i.e. the *minim*.

Another illustration of *Whoso pleaseth*: i.e. R. Nathan. *But the sinner*: i.e. his disciple.

Another illustration of *Whoso pleaseth*: i.e. R. Eliezer and R. Joshua. *But the sinner*: i.e. Elisha.

Qoh. R. 7 : 26, trans. A. Cohen, p. 210

*Comment*: The contrast is between the rabbis, on the one side, and heretics, on the other. If the story of Eliezer and the *minim* were known, then presumably Eliezer would have been contrasted with Jacob. Setting Eliezer and Joshua against Elisha b. Abbuyah is pointless; Meir should be here.

CHAPTER FOUR

# EXEGETICAL AND THEOLOGICAL TRADITIONS

The exegetical traditions under consideration explain, or at least pertain to, non-legal Scriptures. Theological traditions may likewise be linked to the exegesis of Scriptures, but their purpose is not limited to Scriptural commentary. Exegeses of Scriptures for legal purposes have been given in Chapter Two. Pericopae in which the explanation of Scriptures is subordinate to the narration or interpretation of biographical and historical events are in Chapter Three.

I.i.293. A. "The generation of the wilderness have no share in the world to come, nor shall they stand in judgment, for it is written, *In this wilderness they shall be consumed and there they shall die* (Num. 14 : 35)"—the words of R. ʿAqiba.

B. And R. Eliezer says, "It says of them [also], *Gather my saints together unto me, those that have made a covenant with me by sacrifice* (Ps. 50 : 5)."

C. "The company of Qoraḥ is not destined to rise, for it is written, *And the earth closed upon them*—in this world. *And they perished from among the assembly*—in the world to come (Num. 16 : 33)"—the words of R. ʿAqiba

D. And R. Eliezer says, "It says of them also. *The Lord killeth and bringeth to life, he brings down to Sheol and brings up* (I Sam. 2 : 6)."

E. "The ten tribes shall not return again, for it is written, *And he cast them into another land like this day* (Deut. 29 : 28). As this day goes and does not return, so do they go and do not return"—the words of R. ʿAqiba.

F. And R. Eliezer says, "As the day grows dark and then grows light, so also the Ten Tribes, as darkness has fallen upon them, light is destined to shine for them."

M. Sanh. 10 : 3

*Comment*: What is striking is that while ʿAqiba cites Scriptures pertinent to the subject, Eliezer does not. In A ʿAqiba has a verse specifically referring to the generation of the wilderness. Eliezer now calls that generation 'saints.' In C ʿAqiba similarly expounds a verse to indicate that the Qoraḥites were eternally damned. Eliezer cites one which says God raises (*all*) the dead—thus including even them. In the third ʿAqiba does not have a Scripture alluding to the Ten Tribes, and Eliezer ignores Scripture altogether, simply reinterpreting the one cited by ʿAqiba.

The form is a contrast of Scriptures, with the noted exception. Instead of *ʿAqiba says*, it is *the words of ʿAqiba*; otherwise the whole is a standard citation of opposed opinions.

I.ii.201. R. Eliezer says, "All gentiles have no portion in world to come, as it is said, *The evil will return to Sheol*, all *gentiles that forget God* (Ps. 9 : 18). *The evil will return to Sheol*—these are evil-doers in Israel."

R. Joshua said to him, "If Scripture had said, *Evil doers will return to Sheol, all gentiles*—and then had stopped, I should say according to your opinion. Now that Scripture says, *Those that forget God*—lo, there are righteous men among the nations of the world, who do have a portion in the world to come."

Tos. Sanh. 13 : 2, Zuckermandel, p. 434, ls. 7-9

*Comment*: Now Joshua is in the "liberal" position. No gentile inherits the world to come, according to Eliezer. Joshua says the righteous gentiles do, for they do not forget God.

I.ii.202. "The generation of the Wilderness has no portion in the world to come and will not live in the world to come, as it is said, *In this wilderness they will perish and there they will die* (Num. 14 : 35). *In this wilderness they will perish*—in this world. *And there they will die*—in the world to come. And it says, *I swore in my anger they will not come to my rest* (Ps. 95 : 11)," the words of R. ʿAqiba.

R. Eliezer says, "They will enter the world to come, and concerning them David said, *Gather to me my saints, those who have made a covenant with me by sacrifice* (Ps. 50 : 5)."

Tos. Sanh. 13 : 10, Zuckermandel, p. 435
ls. 16-29 (= y. Sanh. 10 : 4, Gilead, p. 106)

*Comment*: ʿAqiba's opinion is elaborated. Otherwise Tos. replicates M. Sanh. It is noteworthy that Joshua interprets Ps. 95 : 11 to mean that vows may be released, so he should agree with Eliezer here.

III.ii.99. DTNʾ: R. Eliezer said, "*The wicked shall be turned into hell, and all the nations that forget God* (Ps. 9 : 17). *The wicked shall be turned into hell*—this refers to transgressors among Israel; *and all the nations that forget God*—to transgressors among the heathen." This is R. Eliezer's view.

But R. Joshua said to him, "Is it stated, *and* [those] *among all the nations*? Surely *all the nations that forget God* is written! But [interpret thus:] *The wicked shall be turned into hell*, and who are they? *All the nations that forget God.*

b. Sanh. 105a, trans. H. Freedman, pp. 715-716

III.ii.100.A. Our rabbis taught: "The generation of the wilderness hath no portion in the world to come, as it is written, *In the wilderness they shall be consumed, and there they shall die.* (Num. 14 : 35). *They shall be consumed* refers to this world; *and there they shall die*—to the world to come. And it is also said, *Forty years long was I grieved with his generation* [of the wilderness — . . .] *Unto whom I sware in my wrath that they should not enter into my rest* (Ps. 95 : 10)," the words of R. ʿAqiba.

B. R. Eliezer says, "They will enter the future world, for it is written, *Gather my saints together unto me; those that have made a covenant with me by sacrifice* (Ps. 50 : 5). How then do I interpret *Unto whom I sware in my wrath* [etc.]?—[Only] in my wrath I *sware*, but repented thereof."

C. R. Joshua b. Qorḥa said, "This verse was spoken only in reference to future generations. [Thus:] *Gather my saints together unto me*—this refers to the righteous of every generation; *that have made a covenant with me*—to Ḥananiah, Mishael, and ʿAzariah, who submitted to the fiery furnace; *by sacrifice*—to R. ʿAqiba and his companions, who gave themselves up to immolation for the sake of the Torah."

b. Sanh. 110b, trans. H. Freedman, p. 758

*Comment*: C is a later addition and supplies an Ushan attestation.

V.i.12.A. "The men of Sodom will neither live [in the world to come], nor be brought to judgment, for it is said, *Now the men of Sodom were wicked and sinners against the Lord exceedingly* (Gen. 13 : 13): *were wicked* toward one another; *and sinners* as regards unchastity; *against the Lord* refers to the profaning of the Name; *exceedingly*, in that by their transgressions they had in mind [to rebel against God]," such is the view of Rabbi Eliezer.

B. Rabbi Joshua says, "They shall be brought to judgment, for it is said, *Therefore the wicked shall not stand in the judgment, nor sinners in the congregation of the righteous* (Ps. 1 : 5)—in the congregation of the righteous they do not stand, but they do stand in the congregation of the wicked."

C. Rabbi Nehemiah says, "Even into the congregation of the wicked they do not come, as it is said, *Let sinners cease out of the earth, and let the wicked be no more* (Ps. 104 : 35)."

D. "Young children of the wicked [who died in their minority] will neither live [in the world to come] nor be brought to judgment, as it is said, *For behold, the day cometh; it burneth as a furnace; and all the proud and all that work wickedness shall be stubble; and the day that cometh shall set them ablaze, saith the Lord of hosts, that shall leave them neither root nor branch* (Mal. 3 : 19)." Such is the view of Rabbi Eliezer.

E. Rabbi Joshua says, "They shall enter [into the world to come], and of them Scripture says, *He cried aloud and said thus: Hew down the tree and cut off its branches, shake off its leaves, and scatter its fruit* (Dan. 4 : 11), and continues, *Nevertheless leave the stump of its roots in the earth, even in a band of iron and brass* (Dan. 4 : 12). Here [in Malachi] *roots* are spoken of, and there [in Daniel] *roots* are spoken of: Even as in the Daniel passage, where *roots* are mentioned, Scripture speaks of the tree itself [being hewn down], so in the Malachi passage, where roots are mentioned, Scripture speaks of the [wicked] man himself."

F. "If so," [said Rabbi Eliezer to him,] "how am I to interpret *That shall leave them neither root nor branch*?"

G. "That there will be found no merit for them, on which to base any claims for reward," [he replied] ...

H. "Qoraḥ and his company will neither live [in the world to come] nor be brought to judgment, as it is said, *And the earth closed upon them, and they perished from among the assembly* (Num. 16 : 33)"—such is the view of Rabbi Eliezer.

I. Rabbi Joshua says, "They shall enter [into the world to come], and of them it says, *The Lord killeth, and maketh alive; He bringeth down to the grave, and bringeth up* (I Sam. 2 : 6). [Now] in the Qoraḥ chapter the *grave* is spoken of: *So they, and all that appertained to them, went down alive into the grave* (Num. 16 : 33); and in the Samuel passage, too, the *grave* is spoken of. Even as in the latter passage, where the grave is spoken of, it is said, *He bringeth down and bringeth up*, so in the Qoraḥ passage, where the grave is spoken of, it is implied that [though] they went down, they are destined to come up again."

J. Said Rabbi Eliezer to him, "How then dost thou interpret *And the earth closed upon them, and they perished from among the assembly?*"

K. "From among the assembly they perished," he replied, "but from the world to come they did not perish."

L. "And the generation of the wilderness will neither live [in the world to come] nor be brought to judgment, for it is said, *In the wilderness they shall be consumed, and there they shall die* (Num. 14 : 35); it says also, *Wherefore I swore in My wrath, that they shall not enter into My rest* (Ps. 95 : 11)"—such is the view of Rabbi Eliezer.

M. Rabbi Joshua says, "They shall enter [into the world to come], and of them it says, *Gather My saints together unto Me; those that have made a covenant with Me by sacrifice* (Ps. 50 : 5)."

N. Said Rabbi Eliezer to him, "How dost thou interpret *Wherefore I swore in My wrath*, etc."

O. "That," he replied, "refers to the spies and all the wicked of that generation."

P. Said Rabbi Joshua, "And how dost thou interpret *Gather My saints together unto Me?* "

Q. "That," Rabbi Eliezer replied, "refers to Moses and Aaron and all the saints of that generation of the tribe of Levi."

ARN Chap. 36; Goldin, pp. 147-150

*Comment*: This is an instance in which ARN considerably differs from M. Tos. A-G have no equivalent. H gives ʿAqiba's position to Eliezer, with the same proof-text. Joshua then has Eliezer's position, with the same proof-text as well as an elaboration of the proofs. I similarly reverses Eliezer's and ʿAqiba's positions, but the proof-texts and the wording of the respective opinions remain unchanged. Then M-Q elaborates the argument.

V.xii.11. *The wicked shall be turned into hell, and all the nations that forget God* (Ps. 9 : 18).

A. R. Eliezer taught, "None of the nations has a portion in the world to come."

B. But R. Joshua replied, "If the verse said *The wicked shall be turned into hell, and all the nations*, and said no more, you would have taught well. But what of the words *that forget God*? You must admit that with these qualifying words the verse refers only to the wicked among the nations of the earth."

Midrash on Psalms 9 : 15, trans. W. G. Braude, p. 147

*Comment*: Braude paraphrases extensively in B.

II.i.14.A. *Saying* (Ex. 12 : 1). "This means, go out and tell it to them immediately"—these are the words of R. Ishmael—"As it is said, *And he came out and spoke unto the children of Israel that which he was commanded* (Ex. 34 : 34)."

B. R. Eliezer says, "It means, 'Go out and tell it to them and bring me back word,' as it is said, *And Moses reported the words of the people unto the Lord* (Ex. 19 : 8)."

Mekh. Pisḥa 1 : 114-118, Lauterbach, I, p. 11

*Comment*: Ishmael's saying is interrupted by the attribution. *These are* should follow the Scripture.

II.i.15.A. *To Succoth* (Ex. 12 : 37)—"To the place where they actually put up booths, as it is said, *And Jacob journeyed to Succoth, and built him a house and made booths for his cattle* (Gen. 33 : 17)"—these are the words of R. Eliezer.

B. But the [other] sages say, "Succoth is merely the name of a place, for it is said, *And they journeyed from Succoth, and pitched in Etham* (Num. 33 : 7). Just as Etham is the name of a place, so also is Succoth."

C. R. ʿAqiba says, "Succoth here means only clouds of glory, as it is said, *And the Lord will create over the whole habitation of Mount Zion, and over her assemblies, a cloud and smoke by day, and the shining of a flaming fire by night; for over all the glory shall be a canopy. And there shall be a pavilion for a shadow in the daytime* (Is. 4 : 5-6). So far I know only about the past. How about the future? Scripture says, *And the ransomed of the Lord shall return and come with singing into Zion, and everlasting joy shall be upon their heads* (Is. 35 : 10)."

D. R. Nehemiah says, "To Succoth [*sukkotah*]—Instead of prefixing a *lamed* to indicate 'to,' a *he* is appended at the end of the word."

Mekh. Pisḥa 14 : 11-22, Lauterbach I,
p. 108 (b. Suk. 116)

*Comment*: The three possible opinions about the meaning of *Sukkoth* are, first, it is the plural of *Sukkah*; second, it is the name of a place; third, it means 'clouds of glory.'

Nehemiah, coming later, makes a grammatical observation.

II.iii.18. *That your generations may know that I made the people of Israel dwell in booths when I brought them out of the land of Egypt* (Lev. 23 : 43).

A. R. Eliezer says, "They were real *Sukkot*."
B. R. ʿAqiba says, *In Sukkot* means they were clouds of glory."

Sifra Emor Pereq 17 : 11, Weiss, p. 103a

*Comment*: *Sukkot* as a place-name is dropped.

III.ii.101. TNYʾ: *For I made the children of Israel to dwell in booths* (*Sukkot*) (Lev. 23 : 43).

"These were clouds of glory," the words of R. Eliezer.

R. ʿAqiba says, "They made for themselves real *Sukkot*."

b. Suk. 11b

*Comment*: Now the traditions are reversed. Eliezer sometimes will prefer the plain meaning, ʿAqiba the allegorical interpretation, of Scripture. But overall there is no clear pattern.

II.i.16. R. Eliezer says, "An idol crossed the sea with Israel, as it is said, *And a rival passed through the sea* (Zech. 10 : 11). And which idol was it? The idol of Micah [Judges 17 : 1]."

Mekh. Pisḥa 14 : 95-97, Lauterbach I, p. 114
(= Sifré Num. 84, Friedman, p. 22b, omits Zech. 10 : 11)

*Comment*: Num. R. 16 : 26 drops the attribution to Eliezer. I assign the tradition to our Eliezer because ʿAqiba immediately follows; but ʿAqiba's saying is not closely related to Eliezer's.

III.i.19. TNY in the name of R. Liezer, "An idol passed with Israel in the sea. What is the [Scriptural] reason? (II Sam. 7 : 23) *On account of your people whom you have redeemed from Egypt... nation and its gods*."

R. ʿAqiba said to him, "God forbid! If you say so, you end up making the holy profane. What does Scripture say? *Whom you redeemed for yourself from Egypt* (II Sam. 7 : 23)—as it were, it is as if you redeemed yourself."

y. Suk. 4 : 3, Gilead, p. 37

*Comment*: Here is good evidence for assigning the foregoing to our Eliezer. Now ʿAqiba's saying is a response to him, in which an alternative explanation is given to the same Scripture.

II.i.17.A. *A Night of Watching unto the Lord* (Ex. 12 : 42). "In that night were they redeemed and in that night will they be redeemed in the future"—these are the words of R. Joshua. "As it is said, *This same night is a night of watching unto the Lord*."

B. R. Eliezer says, "In that night they were redeemed; in the future, however, they will not be redeemed in that night, but in the month of Tishri, as it is said, *Blow the horn at the new moon*, etc. Why? *For it is a statute for Israel* (Ps. 81 : 4-5)."

Mekh. Pisḥa 14 : 113-117, Lauterbach I, pp. 115-116

*Comment*: Joshua and Eliezer debate the date of the redemption. Eliezer assigns it to Tishri.

II.ii.8.A. What is the meaning of watching (ŠWMR) [Ex. 12 : 42: *It was a night of watching*]? "This is the Holy One blessed be he, who is called watchman, *Lo, the watchman of Israel does not slumber or sleep* (Ps. 121 : 30)," the words of R. Eliezer.

R. Joshua says, "In Nisan they were redeemed, and in Nisan they are destined to be redeemed, as it is said," etc.

Mekhilta deR. Simeon b. Yoḥai, p. 35, ls. 18-21 (b. R.H. 11b)

*Comment*: The order is reversed. Now Joshua explicitly alludes to Nisan (= "that night"). Eliezer's saying is completely different.

III.ii.102.A. TNY': R. Eliezer says, "In Tishri the world was created; in Tishri the Patriarchs were born; in Tishri the Patriarchs died. On Passover [Nisan] Isaac was born; on New Year Sarah, Rachel and Hannah were visited. On New Year Joseph went forth from prison. On New Year the bondage of our ancestors in Egypt ceased. In Nisan they were redeemed, and in Tishri they will be redeemed in the time to come."

B. R. Joshua says, "In Nisan the world was created; in Nisan the Patriarchs were born; in Nisan the Patriarchs died; on Passover Isaac was born. On New Year Sarah, Rachel and Hannah were visited; on New Year Joseph went forth from prison; on New Year the bondage of our ancestors ceased in Egypt; and in Nisan they will be redeemed in time to come."

C. It has been taught: R. Eliezer says, "Whence do we know that the world was created in Tishri? Because it says, *And God said, Let the earth put forth grass, herb yielding seed, and fruit tree* (Gen. 1 : 11). Which is the month in which the earth puts forth grass and the trees are full of fruit? You must say that this is Tishri. That time was the season of rainfall, and the rain came down and the plants sprouted, as it says, *And a mist went up from the earth* (Gen. 2 : 6)."

D. R. Joshua says, "Whence do we know that the world was created in Nisan? Because it says, *And the earth brought forth grass, herb yielding seed after its kind, and tree bearing fruit* (Gen. 1 : 12). Which is the month in which the earth is full of grass and trees [begin to] produce fruit? You must say that this is Nisan. That time was the period when cattle, beasts and fowls copulate with one another, as it says, *The rams have mounted the sheep,* etc. (Ps. 65 : 14)."

E. R. Eliezer said, "Whence do we know that the Patriarchs were born in Tishri? Because it says, *And all the men of Israel assembled themselves unto King Solomon, at the feast in the month Etanim* (I Kings 8 : 2); that is, the month in which the mighty ones [= patriarchs] [*etanim*] of the world were born.

"How do you know that this word *etan* means 'mighty'? Because it is written, *Thy dwelling place is firm* [*etan*] (Num. 24 : 21), and it also says, *Hear, ye mountains, the Lord's controversy, and ye mighty rocks [etanim] the foundations of the earth* (Mic. 6 : 2). It also says, *The voice of my beloved, behold he cometh, leaping upon the mountains, skipping upon the hills* (Song 2 : 8) [where] *leaping upon the mountains* means, for the merit of the patriarchs, and *skipping upon the hills* means, for the merit of the matriarchs."

F. R. Joshua said, "Whence do we know that the patriarchs were born in Nisan? Because it says, *And it came to pass in the four hundred and eightieth year after the children of Israel were come out of the land of Egypt, in the fourth year in the month of Ziv* (I Kings 6 : 1)—that is, the month in which the brilliant ones [*zewtane*] of the world were born. But how does he explain the expression *month of Etanim*? It means, [the month] which is strong in religious duties."

G. On New Year Sarah, Rachel and Hannah were visited. Whence do we know this?

R. Eliezer said, "We learn it from the two occurrences of the word 'visiting,' and the two occurrences of the word 'remembering.' It is written concerning Rachel, *And God remembered Rachel* (Gen. 30 : 22), and it is written concerning Hannah, *And the Lord remembered her* (I Sam. 1 : 19), and there is an analogous mention of 'remembering' in connection with New Year, as it is written, *A solemn rest, a remembering of the blast of the trumpet* (Lev. 23 : 24). The double mention of visiting [is as follows]: It is written concerning Hannah, *For the Lord had visited Hannah*, and it is written concerning Hannah, *For the Lord had visited Hannah* (I Sam. 2 : 21), and it is written concerning Sarah, *And the Lord visited Sarah* (Gen. 21 : 1)."

H. On New Year Joseph went forth from the prison. Whence do

we know this? Because it is written, *Blow the horn on the new moon, on the covering day for our festival... He appointed it for Joseph for a testimony when he went forth* (Ps. 81 : 4-6).

On New Year the bondage of our ancestors ceased in Egypt. It is written in one place, *And I will bring you out from under the burdens of the Egyptians* (Ex. 6 : 6), and it is written in another place, *I removed his shoulder from the burden* (Ps. 81 : 7).

I. In Nisan they were delivered, as Scripture recounts. In Tishri they will be delivered in time to come. This is learnt from the two occurrences of the word 'horn.' It is written in one place, *Blow the horn on the New Moon* (Ps. 81 : 4), and it is written in another place, *In that day a great horn shall be blown* (Is. 27 : 13).

J. R. Joshua says, "In Nisan they were delivered; in Nisan they will be delivered in the time to come. Whence do we know this? Scripture calls [the Passover] *a night of watchings* (Ex. 12 : 47) [which means], a night which has been continuously watched for from the six days of the creation."

What says the other to this? [He says it means], a night which is under constant protection against evil spirits.

K. R. Joshua and R. Eliezer are herein consistent [with views expressed by them elsewhere], as it has been taught:

*In the sixth hundredth year of Noah's life, in the second month, on the seventeenth day of the month* (Gen. 7 : 11).

R. Joshua said, "That day was the seventeenth day of Iyyar, when the constellation of Pleiades sets at daybreak and the fountains begin to dry up, and because they [mankind] perverted their ways, the Holy One, blessed be He, changed for them the work of creation and made the constellation of Pleiades rise at daybreak and took two stars from the Pleiades and brought a flood on the world."

R. Eliezer said, "That day was the seventeenth of Marheshvan, a day on which the constellation of Pleiades rises at daybreak, and [the season] when the fountains begin to fill, and because they perverted their ways, the Holy One, blessed be He, changed for them the work of creation, and caused the constellation of Pleiades to rise at daybreak and took away two stars [from it] and brought a flood on the world."

L. Our rabbis taught: The wise men of Israel follow R. Eliezer in dating the flood and R. Joshua in dating the annual cycles, while the scholars of other peoples follow R. Joshua in dating the flood also.

b. R.H. 10b-12a, trans. M. Simon, pp. 39-43 (y. R.H. 1 : 1)

*Comment*: The materials in b. R.H. greatly expand the foregoing. The issue of Mekh. is when redemption will take place. Joshua says it will be in Nisan, as in b. R.H.B, and Eliezer says it will be in Tishri. In Mekh. deR. Simeon, Eliezer ignores the problem of the date of redemption.

C and D then produce proof-texts for the first issue in A-B, when creation took place. E-F do the same for the birthdays of the patriarchs. G is limited to Eliezer's position on the remembrance of the mothers, but Joshua agrees with that view. H is anonymous. I likewise pertains to the opinions of both. J then reverts to the issue of redemption.

V.vii.4. *And at the end of days it came to pass* (Gen. 4 : 3).

R. Eliezer and R. Joshua disagree.

R. Eliezer said, "The world was created in Tishri."

R. Joshua said, "In Nisan."

Gen. R. 22 : 4, trans. H. Freedman, pp. 181-182

V.xi.8. *In the seventh month, in the first day of the month shall be a solemn rest* (Num. 23 : 24). This bears on what is written in Scripture, *For ever, O Lord, Thy word standeth fast in heaven* (Ps. 119 : 89).

It was taught in the name of R. Eliezer, "The world was created on the twenty-fifth of Elul."

Num. R. 29 : 1, trans. J. J. Slotki, p. 369 =
Pes. deR. Kahana, ed. Mandelbaum, p. 333, l. 1

*Comment*: This ought not to be our Eliezer.

II.i.18. *But God led the people about, by the way of the wilderness, by the Red Sea* (Ex. 13 : 18).

A. R. Eliezer says, "*By the way*, indicates that it was for the purpose of tiring them, as it is said, *He weakened my strength in the way* (Ps. 102 : 24). *Of the wilderness* indicates that it was for the purpose of refining them, as it is said, *Who led thee through the great and dreadful wilderness* (Deut. 8 : 15). *By the Red Sea* indicates that it was for the purpose of testing them, as it is said, *And they were rebellious at the sea, even at the Red Sea* (Ps. 106 : 7)."

B. R. Joshua says, "*By the way* indicates that it was for the purpose of giving them the Torah, as it is said, *Ye shall walk in all the way which the Lord your God hath commanded you* (Deut. 5 : 30). And it also says, *For the commandment is a lamp, and the teaching (Torah) is light and a way of life* (Prov. 6 : 23); *of the wilderness*, indicates that it was for the purpose of feeding them the *manna*, as it is said, *Who fed thee in the wilderness with manna* (Deut. 8 : 16); *by the Red Sea*, indicates that it was for the purpose performing for them miracles and mighty deeds, as it is said, *Terrible things by the Red Sea* (Ps. 106 : 22), and it also says, *And He rebuked the Red Sea, and it was dried up; and He led them through the depths, as through a wilderness* (Ps. 106 : 9)."

Mekh. Beshallaḥ 1 : 57-69, Lauterbach I, pp. 173-174

*Comment*: Eliezer interprets the trip to the wilderness as a means of tiring, refining, and testing the people. Joshua sees it as the occasion for miracles: revealing the Torah, giving the *manna*, and doing mighty deeds. The sayings are neatly balanced; each treats a segment of Scripture, with the contrary opinions carefully matched.

II.i.19. *That they turn back and encamp before Pi-haḥirot* (Ex. 14 : 2).

A. "What were those Ḥirot? They were not leaning but tapering to the apex. They were not rectilinear but slightly convex. They were not round but square. They were not the work of man but the work of Heaven. They had eyes as openings. They were sort of male and female." These are the words of R. Eliezer.

B. R. Joshua says, "The Ḥirot were on the one side and Migdol on the other, the sea before them and Egypt behind them."

Mekh. Beshallaḥ 2 : 8-15, Lauterbach I, p. 188

II.i.20. *And Israel saw the Great Hand* (Ex. 14 : 31). All sorts of cruel and strange deaths.

R. Yosi the Galilean says, "Whence can you prove that the Egyptians were smitten in Egypt with ten plagues, and at the sea they were smitten with fifty plagues? What does it say about them when in Egypt? *Then the magicians said unto Pharaoh, 'This is the finger of God'* (Ex. 8 : 15). And what does it say about them when at the sea? *And Israel saw the great hand*, etc. Now, with how many plagues were they smitten by the finger? With ten plagues. Hence you must conclude that in Egypt they were smitten with ten plagues and at the sea they were smitten with fifty plagues."

R. Eliezer says, "Whence can you prove that every plague which the Holy One, blessed be He, brought upon the Egyptians in Egypt really consisted of four different plagues? etc."

R. ʿAqiba says, "Whence can you prove that every plague which the Holy One, blessed be He, brought upon the Egyptians in Egypt really consisted of five different plagues? etc."

Mekh. Beshallaḥ 7 : 109-121, Lauterbach I, p. 251

*Comment*: Eliezer's and ʿAqiba's sayings are merely alluded to, not spelled out. Copyists evidently dropped them because of their familiarity in the Passover Haggadah. Ex. R. Spells them out.

V.xi.9.A. Another explanation of *Then sang Moses.* It is written, *The Lord hath made Himself known, He hath executed judgment* (Ps. 9 : 17); this refers to the Egyptians on whom God executed judgment in Egypt and also by the sea.

B. R. Joshua said, "The ten plagues with which the Egyptians were smitten in Egypt were wrought with one finger, for it says, *Then the magicians said unto Pharaoh: This is the finger of God* (Ex. 8 : 15); but at the sea, they were smitten with fifty plagues, for it says, *And Israel saw the great hand* [work] (Ex. 14 : 31). There are five fingers on one hand, and five times ten are fifty. You will likewise find that Job also was smitten with fifty plagues, for it says, *Have pity upon me, have pity upon me, O ye my friends; for the hand of God hath touched me* (Job. 19 : 21)."

C. R. Eliezer said, "The Egyptians were smitten with forty plagues in Egypt, but with two hundred near the sea, for every plague that visited them was accompanied by three others, as it says, *He destroyed their vines with hail* (Ps. 78: 47) and *He sent forth upon them the fierceness of His anger, wrath, and indignation, and trouble, a sending of messengers of evil* (Ps. 49)—'*wrath*' is one, '*indignation*' is two, '*trouble*' is three, and '*A sending of messengers of evil*' is four. If these forty plagues were the work of one finger, then with a whole hand they were smitten with two hundred. This is the meaning of *He hath executed judgment.*"

Ex. R. 23 : 9, trans. S. M. Lehrman, pp. 287-288

V.xii.12. R. Eliezer taught, "Each plague consisted of four plagues, for it is said, *This is the finger of God*, and a finger is four-sided. Accordingly, since the Egyptians were smitten ten times by each side of the finger of God, behold, there were forty plagues. in Egypt. And, on the sea, the Egyptians were smitten with two hundred plagues, for in the verse *He sent forth upon them the fierceness of His anger, wrath, and indignation, and trouble, a sending of messengers of evil* (Ps. 78 : 49), *wrath* refers to one plague, *indignation* refers to a second plague, *trouble* refers to a third plague, and *a sending of messengers of evil* refers to a fourth plague. Behold then! There were two hundred plagues wherewith the Egyptians were smitten at the sea, as can be reckoned from the verse, *And Is-*

*rael saw that great hand which the Lord did upon the Egyptians.*"

Midrash on Psalms 78 : 15, trans. Braude, p. 37

IV.ii.27.A. Wherewith did he [the angel] smite them?

R. Eliezer said, "He smote them with his hand, as it is written, *And Israel saw the great hand* (Ex. 14 : 31), implying the hand that was destined to exact vengeance of Sennacherib."

R. Joshua said, "He smote them with his finger, as it is written, *Then the magicians said unto Pharaoh, This is the finger of God* (Ex. 8 : 14), implying this is the finger destined to punish Sennacherib."

b. Sanh. 95b, trans. H. Freedman

*Comment*: This would seem to relate to the foregoing.

II.i.21. *And the taste of it was like wafers made with honey* (Ex. 16 : 3).

A. R. Joshua says, "Like a stew and a sort of dumpling."

B. R. Eliezer says, "Like very fine flour, which floats above the sieve, kneaded with honey and butter."

Mekh. Vayassa 6 : 47-49,
Lauterbach II, p. 124

II.i.22. *This is my God and I will glorify Him.* (Ex. 15 : 2) R. Eliezer says, "Whence can you say that a maid-servant saw at the sea what Isaiah and Ezekiel and all the prophets never saw? It says about them: *And by the ministry of the prophets have I used similitudes* (Hos. 12 : 11). And it is also written: *The heavens were opened and I saw visions of God* (Ezek. 1 : 1). To give a parable for this, to what is this like? To the following: A king of flesh and blood enters a province surrounded by a circle of guards; his heroes stand to the right of him and to the left of him; his soldiers are before him and behind him. And all the people ask, saying, 'Which one is the king?' Because he is of flesh and blood like those who surround him. But, when the Holy One, blessed be He, revealed Himself at the sea, no one had to ask, 'Which one is the king?' But as soon as they saw Him they recognized Him, and they all opened their mouths and said, 'This is my God and I will glorify Him.' "

Mekh. Shirata 3 : 28-39, Lauterbach II, pp. 24-25 = Mekhilta de R. Simeon b. Yoḥai, p. 154, l. 7, p. 155, ls. 1ff.

*Comment*: See Judah Goldin, *The Song at the Sea* (New Haven, 1971: Yale University Press), pp. 112-113. I do not know why this must be our Eliezer.

II.i.23. *And Moses led Israel onward from the Red Sea* (Ex. 15 : 22).

A. R. Joshua says, "This journey Israel made at the command of Moses. All other journeys they made only at the command of God, as it is said, *At the commandment of the Lord they encamped, and at the commandment of the Lord they journeyed* (Num. 9 : 23). This journey, however, they made merely at the command of Moses. In this sense it is said, *And Moses led Israel onward.*"

B. R. Eliezer says, "They made this journey also at the command of the Almighty, for we find it stated in two or three passages that they journeyed only at the command of the Almighty. Why then does it say here, *And Moses led Israel onward*? To proclaim the excellence of Israel. For when Moses told them, *Arise and journey*, they did not say, 'How can we go out into the desert, without leaving provisions for the journey?' But they believed in Moses and followed him."

Mekh. Vayassa 1 : 1-12, Lauterbach II, p. 84 (see 1 : 28-32)

*Comment*: Eliezer now emphasizes the faith of Israel. See above p. 422.

II.i.24. Another interpretation: *From generation to generation.*

R. Joshua says, "*From generation*, that is from the life of this world; *to generation*, that is from the life of the world to come."

R. Eleazer of Modiʿim says, "From the generation of Moses and from the generation of Samuel."

R. Eliezer says, "From the generation of the Messiah, which really consists of three generations. And whence do we know that the generation of the Messiah consists of three generations? It is said, *They shall fear Thee while the sun endureth and so long as the moon, a generation and two generations* (Ps. 72 : 5)."

Mekh. Amalek 2 : 186-192, Lauterbach II, p. 161

V.ix.2. *From generation to generation* (Ex. 17 : 16).

A. R. Liezer, R. Joshua, and R. Yosi.

B. R. Liezer says, "From the generation of Moses to the generation of Samuel."

C. R. Joshua says, "From the generation of Samuel to the generation of Mordecai and Esther."

D. R. Yosi says, "From the generation of Mordecai and Esther to the generation of King Messiah, which is three generations."

Pesiqta deR. Kahana, ed. Mandelbaum, p. 52, l. 13, p. 53, ls. 1-3 = Midrash Tanḥuma Tēṣē 18, Buber II, pp. 22b-23a

*Comment*: Pesiqta gives the opinion of Eleazar in Mekh. to Eliezer, and now no one refers to the generation of the Messiah.

II.i.25. *With the edge of the sword* (Ex. 17 : 13).

A. R. Joshua says, "He did not disfigure them, but treated them with some degree of mercy."

B. R. Eliezer says, "*With the edge of the sword.* Why is this said? We can learn from this that this war was only by the order of the Almighty."

Mekh. Amalek 1 : 173-175, Lauterbach II, p. 147

*Comment*: Joshua interprets the Scripture to mean the Amalekites were killed in a kindly way. Eliezer has a quite different interpretation, consistent with his view on the journeys (p. 467).

V.xii.13. *The destructions of the enemy shall come to a perpetual end* (Ps. 9 : 7). It is taught in the name of R. Eliezer, "The Holy One, blessed be He, took an oath upon the throne of His glory, that under the whole heaven there should be left neither sprig nor sprout of the seed of Amalek among his people. It is God's command that *Thou shalt blot out the remembrance of Amalek from under heaven* (Deut. 25 : 19), so that it can no longer be said "This tree is Amalek's," "This ewe is Amalek's": *Their cities wilt Thou destroy; their remembrance will perish with them* (Ps. 9 : 7).

Midrash on Psalms 9 : 10, trans. W. G. Braude, p. 14

V.xii.14. *Thou wilt pursue them in anger and destroy them* (3 : 66). Jeremiah said, "Thou wilt pursue them in anger and destroy them." And Moses said, "I will utterly blot out the remembrance of Amalek from under heaven" (Ex. 17 : 14). Samuel said, "Amalek is to be understood literally; *remembrance* alludes to Haman; *blotting out* refers to this world, *I will blot out* to the world to come; *from under heaven*, i.e. him and the whole of that generation to the end of all generations."

R. Joshua said, "[It signifies] that Amalek shall have no descendants; *from under heaven* indicates that nobody will be able to say, 'This tree, or camel, or lamb belongs to Amalek.' "

R. Eliezer says, "Because Amalek sought to destroy Israel from beneath the wings of heaven, Moses spake before the Holy One, blessed be He: 'This wicked one has come to destroy Israel from beneath Thy wings, so who will read in Thy Torah which Thou hast given them?' Another interpretation: Because he sought to destroy the Israelites who are destined to be dispersed from one end of the world to the other, as it is stated, *And the Lord shall scatter thee among all the peoples, from the one end of the earth even unto the other end of the earth* (Deut. 28 : 64) [therefore his fate will be to be destroyed *from under the heavens*]."

R. Eliezer said, "When will the name of these [persecutors of Israel] perish from the world, idolatry and its worshippers be uprooted from the earth, and the Holy One, blessed be He, be [acknowledged] as the one God in the world, according as it is said, *And the Lord shall be King over all the earth; in that day shall the Lord be one, and His name one* (Zech. 19 : 9)? At the time when *Thou wilt pursue them in anger, and destroy them from under the heavens of the Lord.*"

Lam. R. 3 : 66 : 9, trans. A. Cohen, pp. 213-4

II.i.26. R. Eliezer says, "*Then Came Amalek.* He came with defiance. Because all other times that he came, he came secretly, as it is said, 'How he met thee by the way,' etc. This coming, however, was not so, but was with defiance. In this sense it is said: *Then came Amalek*—he came with defiance."

mekh. Amalek 1 : 9-18, Lauterbach II, p. 136.

*Comment*: Yosi b. Ḥalafta follows with a different interpretation. But the other Amalek-teachings of Eliezer suggest this too might be his.

II.i.27. R. Eliezer says, "For what purpose does it say, *Israel prevailed* (Ex. 17 : 11), or what is the purpose of saying, *Amalek prevailed*? Merely to tell that when Moses raised his hands towards heaven, it meant that Israel would be strong in the words of the Torah, to be given through Moses' hands. And when he lowered his hands, it meant that Israel would lower their zeal for the words of the Torah to be given through his hands."

Mekh. Amalek 1 : 131-137, Lauterbach II, p. 144

II.ii.9. *And when Moses raised his hand* (Ex. 17 : 11).

R. Eliezer says, "And did the hands of Moses make Israel strong or break Amalek? But when Israel do the will of the Omnipresent and believe in what the Omnipresent commanded Moses, the Omnipresent does for them miracles and wonders."

Mekhilta deR. Simeon b. Yoḥai, p. 121, ls. 15-17

*Comment*: Eliezer's teaching is that victory in war depends on Torah-teachings. The same opinion is attributed to Yoḥanan b. Zakkai (*Development*, pp. 15-18, 21-22, 24, 27-29). We cannot be certain this is our Eliezer.

III.ii.102.A. TNY': R. Eliezer says, "Rephidim was the name [of a place]."

R. Joshua says, "It means that they relaxed (*rifu*) their hold on the words of the Law. And so Scripture says, *The fathers shall not look back to their children for (rifyon) feebleness of hand* (Gen. 47 : 3)."

B. R. Eliezer says, "Shittim was the name of the place."

R. Joshua says, "It means that they gave themselves up to lust. *And they called to the people unto the sacrifices of their gods* (Num. 25 : 2)."

R. Eliezer says, "This verse means that they [the Israelites] came into contact with naked bodies."

But R. Joshua says, "They all became polluted."

b. Bekh. 5b, trans. L. Miller and M. Simon, pp. 26-27

IV.ii.28.A. *And Israel abode in Shittim* (Num. 25 : 1). R. Eliezer said, "Its name was Shittim."

R. Joshua said, "They engaged in ways of folly [*sheṭut*]."

B. *And they called the people unto the sacrifices of their gods* (Num. 25 : 2).

R. Eliezer said, "They met them naked."

R. Joshua said, "They were all excited to pollution."

C. What is the meaning of Rephidim?

R. Eliezer said, "Rephidim was its name."

R. Joshua said, "[It was so called] because there they slackened in [their loyalty to] the Torah, as it is written, *The fathers shall not look back to their children for feebleness of hands* (Jer. 47 : 3)."

b. Sanh. 106a, trans. H. Freedman, p. 724

II.i.28. *And the name of the other was Eliezer: For the God of my father was my help, and delivered me from the sword of Pharaoh* (Ex. 18 : 4).

A. R. Joshua says, "When did God deliver him? At the time when Dathan said to him, *Who made thee a ruler and a judge... Now when Pharaoh heard this thing* (Ex. 2 : 14-15). They say they seized Moses, brought him to the platform, bound him and put the sword to his throat. But then an angel came down and appeared to them in the likeness of Moses, so that they got hold of the angel and let Moses escape."

B. R. Eliezer says, "God turned the people who set out to capture Moses into different groups. Some of them He made dumb, some He made deaf, and some He made blind. They asked the dumb one, 'Where is Moses?' And they could not answer. They asked the deaf ones, and they could not hear; the blind ones and they could not see, just as it is said, *And the Lord said unto him, Who hath made a man's mouth? or who maketh a man dumb* (Ex. 4 : 11). Referring to this, it is said, *For the God of my father was my help.*"

Mekh. Amalek 3 : 127-140, Lauterbach II, p. 171

*Comment*: The *sword of Pharaoah* is now of *Israel*!

II.i.29. *And How I Bore You on Eagles' wings.* (Ex. 19 : 4) R. Eliezer says, "This refers to the day of Rameses. For they were gathered and brought to Rameses within a little while."

Mekh. Baḥodesh 2 : 18-21, Lauterbach II, p. 202

*Comment*: This is not demonstrably our Eliezer.

II.i.30. *And keep my covenant* (Ex. 19 : 5).

A. R. Eliezer says, "This refers to the covenant of the Sabbath."

B. R. ʿAqiba says, "This refers to the covenant of circumcision and to the covenant against idolatry."

Mekh. Baḥodesh 2 : 43-45, Lauterbach II, p. 204

*Comment*: Elsewhere the positions are reversed.

II.ii.10. *And you will keep the ordinance* (Ex. 13 : 10)—

A. R. Eliezer says, "This is the ordinance of Passover."

B. R. ʿAqiba says, "This is the ordinance of *tefillin*."

Mekhilta deR. Simeon b. Yoḥai, p. 41
ls. 16-17 (b. Men. 36b, y. Ber. 2 : 4)

*Comment*: Now *no one* alludes to circumcision.

V.ix,3. Aqilas the proselyte asked R. Eliezer, "Since circumcision is so beloved of the Holy One, blessed be He, why was its performance not included among the Ten Commandments?"

R. Eliezer replied, "Because it was given before the Ten Commandments, since it is written *And keep my covenant* (Ex. 19 : 5), the reference being not only to the covenant of the Sabbath but also to the covenant of circumcision."

Pesiqta Rabbati 23, trans. Braude, p. 479

*Comment*: Now Sabbath and circumcision are treated as one.

II.ii.11. *And you will keep my covenant* (Ex. 19 : 5).

A. R. Eliezer says, "This is the covenant of circumcision."

B. R. ʿAqiba says, "This is the covenant of the Sabbath."

C. And sages say, "This is the covenant [not to practice] idolatry."

Mekhilta deR. Simeon
b. Yoḥai, p. 139, ls. 3-5

*Comment*: Evidently Aggadat Bereshit 17 : 2 depends upon the above.

V.x.3.A. King Agrippas asked R. Eliezer the Great, saying to him, "If circumcision is beloved before the Holy One, blessed be He, why is it not written in the revelation of the Torah with the Ten Commandments? Lo, he warned concerning idolatry, oath-taking by the divine name, the Sabbath, honor of father and mother, murder, adultery, thievery, false witness, covetousness—concerning all these He warns, but not concerning circumcision!"

B. R. Eliezer said to him, "You have said to me that you know how to read the Torah, but lo, you do not know."

C. He [Eliezer] said to him, "Take [the Torah] and see that before the Holy One, blessed be He, had given the Torah, he had already given them circumcision. And how do we know? As it is said, *In the third month, etc., and Moses went up, etc. You have seen, etc. and Now, if you will hear, etc. and You will keep my covenant* (Ex. 19 : 1, 2, 3, 4, 5). This refers to circumcision."

D. And so R. Eliezer taught, "*And you will keep my covenant*—this is circumcision."

And R. ʿAqiba says, "This is the Sabbath."

Aggadat Bereshit 17 : 2, ed. Buber, p. 16a

*Comment*: Now Eliezer has *covenant* refer only to circumcision. D alludes to the Mekh., preserving the order of the masters and switching their opinions.

II.i.31. *Moses spoke and God answered him by a voice* (Ex. 19 : 19)—

A. R. Eliezer says, "How can you prove that God spoke only after Moses had told Him, 'Speak, for Thy children have already accepted?' It is in this sense that it is said, *Moses spoke*."

B. R. ʿAqiba said, "It surely was so. Why then does it say, *Moses spoke and God answered him by a voice*? It merely teaches that Moses was endowed with strength and force, and that God was helping him with His voice, so that Moses could let Israel hear the same tone which he himself heard. In this sense it is said, *Moses spoke and God answered him by a voice.*"

Mekh. Baḥodesh 4 : 36-44, Lauterbach II, p. 223

II.ii.12.A. R. Eliezer says, "Why did the Holy One blessed be He, revealing Himself from the highest heavens, speak with him from the bush? But just as this bush is the lowest of all the trees in the world, so Israel descended to the lowest stages, and the Holy One blessed be He descended with them and redeemed them, as it is said, *And I went down to save him from the hand of the Egyptians* (Ex. 3 : 8)."

B. R. Joshua says, "Why did the Holy One blessed be He, revealing Himself from the highest heavens, speak with Moses from the bush? But when Israel went down to Egypt, the Divine Presence went down with them, as it is said, *I shall go down with you* (Gen. 46 : 4), and when they went forth, the Divine Presence was revealed with them, as it is said, *And I also shall bring them up...*"

Mekhilta deR. Simeon b. Yoḥai, Epstein-Melamed, p. 1, ls. 12-18 (Ex. R. 2 : 5-15: R. Yosi)

*Comment*: The question attributed to both masters is in exactly the same language, and the point made by both is that God went down with Israel to Egypt (Joshua) or went down in order to redeem them from Egypt (Eliezer).

II.ii.13. *A land flowing with milk and honey* (Ex. 13 : 5).

A. R. Eliezer says, "*Milk*—this is the milk of fruit; *honey*—this is the honey of dates."

B. R. ʿAqiba says, "*Milk*—this is certainly milk ... and *honey* —this is honey of the woods ..."

Mekhilta deR. Simeon b. Yoḥai, p. 38, ls. 22-25

*Comment*: The exegesis is of the plain sense of the Scripture.

II.iii.19. *And they died before the Lord* (Lev. 16 : 1).

A. R. Eliezer says, "They died only outside, in the place where the Levites are permitted to enter as it is said, [*And they offered unholy fire before the Lord ... and fire came forth from the presence of the Lord and devoured them ... And Moses called Mishael and Elzaphan, sons of Uzziel the uncle of Aaron, and said to them, Draw near, carry your brethren from before the sanctuary out of the camp.*] *So they drew near and carried them in their coats out of the camp...* (Lev. 10 : 1-5, *pass.*) If so, why is it said, *And they died before the Lord*? The angel smote them and pushed them and took them out."

B. R. ʿAqiba says, "They died only within, as it is said, *And they died before the Lord.* If so, why is it said, *And they drew near and took them in their coats?* It teaches that they took a spear of iron and dragged them and took them out."

Sifra Mekhilta de Miluʾim 2 : 35, Weiss, p. 45 (b. Sanh. 52)

*Comment*: Eliezer and ʿAqiba debate the place in which the sons of Aaron died.

II.iii.20. *And if in spite of these* (WʾM ʿD ʾLH) (Lev. 26 : 18).

A. R. Eliezer says, "The Omnipresent brings punishment on Israel only after he first testifies against them, as it is said, *And in spite of these.*"

B. R. Joshua says, "That Israel should not say, 'The punishments have ended and he has no other to bring on us,' Scripture says, *And if in spite of these*—moreover I have others besides these and like these to bring."

Sifra Beḥuqotai Pereq 5 : 1, Weiss, p. 11b

*Comment*: Punishment is preceded by warning—so Eliezer. Joshua interprets the passage in a different way.

V.xii.15. R. Phinehas opened his discourse with the text, *And if ye will not yet for these things hearken unto Me*, etc. (Lev. 26 : 18).

R. Eliezer and R. Joshua [make comments].

R. Eliezer says, "The Holy One, blessed be He, does not bring punishments upon Israel without first warning them. That is the meaning of what is written, *And if ye will not yet for these things.*"

R. Joshua says, "So that Israel shall not declare, 'The afflictions are exhausted; He has no others to bring upon me,' therefore Scripture states, *And if ye will not yet for these things* [which may be read as] if further (ʿōd) these things, i.e. He has other and similar afflictions to bring."

Lam. R. Proem 27, trans. A. Cohen, p. 53.

II.iv.26. *But the Lord was angry at me on your account and did not listen to me* (Deut. 3 : 26).

R. Eliezer says, "He was filled with anger against me."

R. Joshua says, "Like a woman who cannot bend (ŠWḤ) because of the embryo."

Sifré Deut. 29, Finkelstein, p. 45

(Sifré Num. 135; Tanḥuma: Judah *vs.* Nehemiah)

*Comment*: ʿAqiba seems to gloss Eliezer's saying: God was filled with anger *like...* But see Finkelstein, *ad loc.*

II.vi.2. *And the Lord was angry with me on your account*:

A. R. Eliezer says, "He was filled with anger against me."

B. R. Joshua says, "Like a woman who cannot bend because of the embryo."

Midrash Tannaim to Deut. 3 : 26, Hoffmann, p. 17

*Comment*: Mid. Tan. copies Sifré Deut.

II.iv.27. R. Eliezer says, If *with all your soul* (Deut. 4 : 6) is said, why is *with all your might* said, and if *with all your might* is said, why is *with all your soul* said? You have a man whose body is more beloved to him than his money. Therefore *with all your soul* is said. And you have a man whose money is more beloved to him than his body. Therefore *with all your might* is said."

R. ʿAqiba says...

Sifré Deut. 32, Finkelstein, p. 55 (b. Pes. 25a, b. Yoma 82a, b. Sanh. 7a; Mid. Tan. to Deut. 6 : 5, ed. Hoffmann, p. 25)

III.ii.103. *And thou shalt love the Lord thy God with all your heart, with all your soul, and with all your might* (Deut. 6 : 5).

TNYʾ: R. Eliezer says, "If *with all your soul* is said, why is *with all your might* said, and if *with all your might* is said, why is *with all your soul* said?

"But if you have a man whose body is more precious to him than his money, for that purpose it is said *with all your soul*, and if you have a man whose money is more valuable to him than his body, for that one is said *with all your might*."

R. ʿAqiba says, "*With all your soul*—even if he takes your soul."

b. Ber. 61b

*Comment*: ʿAqiba takes the Scripture to refer to martyrdom. Eliezer supplies a more commonplace interpretation.

II.iv.28. *And the Lord said to him, This is the land* (Deut. 34 : 1).

A. R. ʿAqiba says, "This Scripture tells that the Omnipresent showed Moses all the corners of the land of Israel like a table fully set, as it is said, *And the Lord showed him the land*."

B. R. Eliezer says, "He gave strength to the eyes of Moses, and he saw from one end of the world to the other, and so you find that righteous men see from one end of the world to the other..."

Sifré Num. 136, Friedman, p. 51a

*Comment*: The normal order is reversed. ʿAqiba gives the plain-sense. Eliezer derives the lesson that righteous men see a great distance.

II.iv.29. *And he saw the whole of the land of Canaan* (Deut. 32 : 49).

R. Eliezer says, "The finger of the Holy One, blessed be He, was the Meṭaṭron for Moses, and it showed him all the cities (QRYY) of the land of Israel: 'To here is the border of Ephraim [Mid. Tan.: Judah], to here is the border of Manasseh [Mid. Tan.: Benjamin, Ephraim].' "

R. Joshua says, "Moses himself saw it. How so? He gave strength to the eyes of Moses and he saw from one end of the world to another."

Sifré Deut. 338, Finkelstein, p. 388
(Midrash Tannaim to Deut. 32 : 49)

*Comment*: Joshua differs from the opinion of ʿAqiba in Sifré Num. 136. Eliezer's view now is that God showed the land, ʿAqiba's above. The real dispute is between ʿAqiba and Joshua on whether Moses saw with his own strength or with God's help. Eliezer's dispute with ʿAqiba concerns what Moses is supposed to have seen.

II.vi.3.A. *So that you may learn to fear the Lord* (Deut. 14 : 22)—tells that tithes bring a man to fear sin.

B. R. Eliezer says, "When a man brings vows and free-will offerings to the chosen House, his heart moves him to the study of Torah."

C. R. Ishmael says, "When a man brings Second Tithe to the chosen House, he enters the hewn-stone room and sees sages and their disciples sitting and busy in the study of Torah, and his heart moves him to study of Torah."

Midrash Tannaim to Deut. 14 : 22, Hoffmann, pp. 77-8

*Comment*: Eliezer and Ishmael relate priestly offerings and tithing to study of Torah.

II.v.6.A. R. ʿAqiba says, "How do we know that a man's agent is like himself? As it is said, *And you will offer a fire-offering to the Lord* (Lev. 23 : 8). And did not the priests [and not all Israel] make the offering? But this proves that a man's agent is like himself."

B. R. Joshua says, "How do we know that a man's agent is like himself? As it is said, *And the whole congregation of the community of Israel will slaughter it* (Ex. 12 : 6). And does the whole congregation slaughter? And does not only one man slaughter? But from here it is shown that a man's agent is like himself."

C. R. Eliezer says, "How do we know that a man's agent is like himself? As it is said, *And the word of the Lord came to Jeremiah after the king burned the scroll, 'Again take for yourself another scroll and write on it'* [Jer. 36 : 27-28). What did Jeremiah do? He took another scroll and gave it to Baruch ben Neriah, and *he* wrote it. And did not the Holy One blessed be He say to him, 'Write!'? But from here we see that a man's agent is like himself."

Sifré Zuṭṭa 13 : 34, Horovitz, p. 279

*Comment*: Shammai takes the same position (*Phar.* I, pp. 201, 204).

III.i.20.A. TNY: R. Eliezer says, "*If your sins are as red* (ŠNYM) etc. (Is. 1 : 18). Like the years which are between heaven and earth. *They will be white like snow*—more than this, they will be like wool (ṢMR)."

B. R. Joshua says, "*If your sins are as red* (ŠNYM)—like the years of the Fathers. *They will be like snow*—more than this, they will be like wool."

y. Shab. 9 : 3, Gilead, p. 119, y. Yoma 6 : 5

*Comment*: The masters differ on ŠNYM, which they interpret to mean years. The years of the fathers are of Abraham, Isaac, and Jacob. Both take for granted that long-standing sins will be forgiven.

III.i.21.A. R. Eliezer says, "If Israel does not repent, they will never be redeemed, as it is said, *In returning and rest, you shall be saved* (Is. 30 : 15)."

R. Joshua said to him, "If Israel stands and does not repent, do you say they will never be saved? "

B. R. Eliezer said to him, "The Holy One blessed be he will raise up over them a king as harsh as Haman, and forthwith they will repent and be redeemed. What is the [Scriptural] reason? *It is a time of distress for Jacob, yet he shall be saved out of it* (Jer. 30 : 7)."

R. Joshua said to him, "And lo it is written, *For nothing were you sold, and not with money will you be redeemed* (Is. 52 : 3) [And not by repentence]? "

C. How does R. Liezer interpret that Scripture?

It refers to repentence, as Scripture says, *He took a bag of money with him* (Prov. 7 : 20).

D. R. Joshua said to him, "And lo, it is written, *I the Lord in its time will hasten it* (Is. 60 : 22)."

E. How does R. Liezer interpret that Scripture?

[It refers to] repentence, as it says, *And now, Israel, what does the*

*Lord your God ask of you, but to fear the Lord your God, to walk in all his ways, to love him, to serve the Lord your God with all your heart and with all your soul* (Deut. 10 : 12).

F. R. Aḥa in the name of R. Joshua b. Levi, "If you have merit, *I shall hasten it*, and if not, *in its time*."

G. When R. Joshua said to him, "*And he raised up his right hand and his left to heaven and swore by him who lives forever that it shall be for a time, times and a half, and when he shall have accomplished to scatter the power of the holy people, all these things shall be finished* (Dan. 12 : 7), R. Liezer departed (ʾYSTLQ).

y. Ta. 1 : 1, Gilead, p. 5

III.ii.104.A. TNYʾ: R. Eliezer said, "If Israel repent, they will be redeemed; if not, they will not be redeemed."

R. Joshua said to him, "If they do not repent, will they not be redeemed? But the Holy One, blessed be He, will set up a king over them, whose decrees shall be as cruel as Haman's, whereby Israel shall engage in repentance, and he will thus bring them back to the right path."

B. Another [*baraita*] taught: R. Eliezer said, "If Israel repent, they will be redeemed, as it is written, *Return, ye backsliding children, and I will heal your backslidings* (Jer. 3 : 22)."

R. Joshua said to him, "But is it not written, *You have sold yourselves for nought; and you shall be redeemed without money? You have sold yourselves for nought*, for idolatry; *and you shall be redeemed without money*—without repentance and good deeds (Is. 52 : 3)."

R. Eliezer retorted to R. Joshua, "But is it not written, *Return unto me, and I will return unto you* (Mal. 3 : 7)?"

R. Joshua rejoined, "But is it not written, *For I am master over you: and I will take you one of a city, and two of a family, and I will bring you to Zion* (Jer. 3 : 14)?"

R. Eliezer replied, "But it is written, *In returning and rest shall ye be saved* (Is. 30 : 15)."

R. Joshua replied, "But is it not written, *Thus saith the Lord, Redeemer of Israel, and his Holy One, to him whom man despiseth, to him whom the nations abhorreth, to a servant of rulers, kings shall see and arise, princes also shall worship* (Is. 49 : 7)."

R. Eliezer countered, "But is it not written, *If thou wilt return, O Israel, saith the Lord, return unto me* (Jer. 4 : 1)?"

R. Joshua answered, "But it is elsewhere written, *And I heard the man clothed in linen, which was upon the waters of the river, when he held up his right hand and his left hand unto heaven, and swore by him that liveth for ever that it shall be for a time, times and a half; and when he shall have accomplished to scatter the power of the holy people, all these things shall be finished* (Dan. 7 : 12)."

At this R. Eliezer remained silent.

b. Sanh. 97b-98a, trans. H. Freedman, p. 660-661

V.x.4.A. R. Eliezer says, "If Israel repents, they will be redeemed."

B. R. Joshua says, "Whether or not they repent, when the end comes, they will forthwith be redeemed, as it is said, *I the Lord in its time will hasten it* (Is. 60 : 22)."

Midrash Tanḥuma Beḥuqotai 5, Buber II, p. 56a

*Comment*: The issue is best phrased in Tanḥuma. y. Ta. has Joshua ask Eliezer whether he says what he has just said. Then in B Eliezer answers that he does, but it is inevitable that Israel will repent. This puts the two close together. Then Joshua cites a Scripture to prove Israel will be redeemed for nothing. Eliezer says the Scripture refers to repentance. Then in D Joshua cites the proof-text used in Tanḥuma: when the time comes, God will hasten matters. Finally, Joshua cites Dan. 12 : 7, which is treated in y. and b. as unambiguous evidence that redemption does not depend upon anything Israel will do.

b. Sanh. greatly expands the debate and assigns it to Tannaitic authority, although it is clear in y. Ta. that Palestinian Amoraim participate in the formation of the pericope. Now Eliezer's answer in y. Ta. becomes Joshua's. The king as cruel as Haman will produce a penitential spirit—but this is pretty much in accord with Eliezer's position on the need for repentance, so b. must be wrong. Then b. Sanh. cites a full repertoire of Scriptures, most of them unknown to y., ending with Dan. 7 : 12 and the same conclusion.

III.ii.105. *And all the peoples of the earth shall see that the name of the Lord is called upon thee and they shall fear thee* (Deut. 28 : 10)—

And it has been taught: R. Eliezer the Great says, "This refers to the *tefillin* of the head."

b. Ber. 6a, 57a (b. Hul. 89a, b. Sot. 17a: Eliezer the *Elder*; b. Men. 35b, b. Meg. 16b)

*Comment*: Eliezer says Jews are feared when they wear *tefillin* on their head.

III.ii.106.A. TNY': *Unstable* (PaḤaZ) *as water, thou shalt not excel* (Gen. 49 : 4).

R. Eliezer interpreted, "Thou wast hasty (*Paztah*), thou wast guilty (*Ḥabtah*), thou didst disgrace (*Zaltah*)."

B. R. Joshua interpreted, "Thou didst overstep (*Pasatah*) the law, thou didst sin (*Ḥatatha*), thou didst fornicate (*Zunitha*)."

C. R. Gamaliel interpreted, "Thou didst meditate (*Pillaltah*), thou didst supplicate (*Ḥaltah*), thy prayer shone forth (*Zarḥah*)."

D. Said R. Gamaliel, "We still need [the interpretation of] the Modiite."

E. R. Eleazar the Modiite said, "Reverse the word and interpret it: Thou didst tremble (*Ziᶜazᶜata*), thou didst recoil (*Hirtᶜatah*), thy sin fled (*Parḥah*) from thee."

b. Shab. 55b, trans. H. Freedman, p. 257

V.vii.5.A. R. Eliezer and R. Joshua [interpret it differently].

R. Eliezer interpreted it, "*Paḥazta* (thou didst hasten), *Ḥaṭatha* (thou hast sinned), *Zanitah* (thou didst commit adultery)."

B. R. Joshua interpreted, "*Parakta* (thou didst throw off) the yoke, *Ḥilalta* (thou didst defile) my bed, thy passion did stir (*Zaᶜ*) within thee."

C. R. Eliezer b. Jacob interpreted, "*Pasaᶜta* (thou didst trample upon) the law; *Ḥabta* (thou didst forfeit) thy birthright; *Zar* (a stranger) didst thou become to thy gifts."

D. The rabbis said, "We still need the Modiite."

E. For R. Eleazar of Modiᶜim came and interpreted it, "*Zaᶜta* (thou didst recoil), *Ḥaradta* (thou didst tremble), *Paraḥ ḥet* (the sin has flown) from thy head."

Gen. R. 98 : 64, trans. H. Freedman, p. 949

*Comment*: Eliezer and Joshua both interpret the saying as criticism of Reuben. Gamaliel and Eleazar say it is praise of Reuben. Gen. R. is consistent in general, but gives different specific interpretations to the two masters, then adds Eliezer b. Jacob, drops Gamaliel, and supplies a slightly different saying to Eleazar.

IV.ii.29. *Give a portion unto seven, yea, even unto eight* (Qoh. 11 : 2).

R. Eliezer says, "*Seven*—the seven days of creation and *eight*—the eight days of circumcision."

R. Joshua says, "*Seven*—the seven days of Passover, and *eight*—the eight days of *Sukkot*."

b. Eruv. 40b (Compare Pesiqta Rabbati 52 : 4, trans. W. G. Braude, pp. 877-8: Joshua, *Eleazar*, Nehemiah, and considerable expansion)

*Comment*: Eliezer and Joshua explain the meaning of the two numbers. In Pes. R. Eleazar says *seven* refers to the Sabbath; Joshua says *eight* applies to Sukkot and other holidays. Both then are given various proof texts. Eliezer again stresses circumcision.

V.ix.4. *Give a portion to seven and also to eight* (Qoh. 11 : 2).

A. R. Liezer and R. Joshua.

B. R. Liezer says, "*Give a portion to seven*—these are the seven days of the week. *And also to eight*—these are the eight days of circumcision."

C. And R. Joshua says, "*Give a portion to seven*—these are the seven days of Passover. *And also to eight*—eight days of the Festival."

Pesiqta deR. Kahana, ed. Mandelbaum,
p. 419, ls. 10-13 (= p. 427, ls. 10ff.)

V.xii.16. *Divide a portion into seven, yea, even into eight* (Qoh. 11 : 2).

R. Eliezer and R. Joshua comment.

R. Eliezer says, "*Divide a portion into seven* alludes to the seven days of the week, as the word is used in *And it came to pass on the seventh* [day] (I Kings 18 : 44), i.e. the Sabbath day. *Yea, even into eight* alludes to the eight days of circumcision, for it is written, *And put his face between his knees.* Why *between his knees*? He spoke before the Holy One, blessed be He, 'Lord of the universe, even if there be in the possession of Thy children only these two commandments, Sabbath and circumcision, it is right that Thou shouldst have mercy upon them.' "

R. Joshua says, "*Divide a portion into seven* alludes to the seven days of Passover; *Yea, even into eight* alludes to the eight days of the Festival [of Tabernacles]. And whence do we know that Pentecost, the New Year, and the Day of Atonement are to be included? The text states *even* and this word denotes inclusion."

Qoh. R. 1 : 1, trans. A. Cohen, p. 289

*Comment*: Qoh. R. expands the earlier versions, as is normal in the medieval compilations.

III.ii.107. TNW RBNN: As for all the songs and praises which David said in the book of Psalms—

R. Eliezer says, "He spoke them with reference to himself."

R. Joshua says, "He spoke them with reference to the [Jewish] community."

And sages say, "Some of them refer to the community, others to himself."

b. Pes. 117a

*Comment*: We have the three possible positions.

III.ii.108. TNY': R. Eliezer said, "The whole world draws its water supply from the waters of the ocean, as it is said, *But there went up a mist from the earth and watered the whole of the ground* (Gen. 2 : 6)."

Thereupon R. Joshua said to him, "But are not the waters of the ocean salty?"

He replied, "They are sweetened by the clouds."

R. Joshua said, "The whole world drinks from the upper waters, as it is said, *And drinketh water as the rain of heaven cometh down* (Deut. 11 : 11)."

C. If so, what is the force of the verse, *But there went up a mist from the earth*? This teaches that the clouds grow in strength as they rise towards the firmament and then open their mouth as a flask and catch the rain water, as it is said, *Which distil rain from His vapor* (Job. 36 : 27), they are perforated like a sieve and they slowly distil (*meḥashrot*) waters on the ground, as it is said, *Distilling (ḥashrot) of waters, thick clouds of the skies* (II Sam. 22 : 12).

b. Ta. 9b, trans. J. Rabbinowitz, pp. 40-41

*Comment*: The issue is the source of rain-water. Eliezer says it comes from the ocean. Joshua says it comes from the upper waters. C then defends Joshua's position.

V.vii.6.A. *But there went up a mist from the earth*, etc. (Gen. 2 : 6). *All the rivers run into the sea, yet the sea is not full* (Qoh. 1 : 7).

R. Eliezer and R. Joshua were once travelling on the great sea, when their ship entered a non-flowing stretch of water.

Said R. Eliezer to R. Joshua, "We have come here simply for a test."

Thereupon they filled a barrel of water from there.

When they arrived in Rome, Hadrian asked them, "What is the nature of the water of the ocean [i.e., the Mediterranean]?"

"It is water that absorbs other water," replied they.

"Show it to me," he demanded.

[They filled] a flaskful of that and poured more [ordinary] water therein, and the former absorbed it. In the opinion of R. Eliezer, *thither they return* [is the essential meaning of the verse]; in the opinion of R. Joshua, it is, *thither they return to go on.*

B. And whence does the earth drink? R. Eliezer and R. Joshua disagree.

R. Eliezer said, "From the waters of the ocean, for it is written, *But there went up a mist from the earth and watered.*"

Said R. Joshua to him, "But surely the waters of the Ocean are salty!"

"They are sweetened in the clouds," replied he, "for it is written, *Which the skies distil* (Qoh. 36 : 28): where are they distilled [i.e. sweetened]? In the skies [clouds]."

R. Joshua said, "[The earth drinks] from the upper waters, for it is written, *And drinketh water as the rain of heaven cometh down* (Deut. 11 : 11); the clouds, however, mount up to heaven and receive them [the waters] as from the mouth of a bottle, for it is written, *They gather up (yazoqqu) water into its cloud.* They distil it as from a sieve, not one drop touches another, for it is written, *Distilling waters from the thick clouds* (II Sam. 22 : 12)."

Gen. R. 13 : 9, 13 : 10,
trans. H. Freedman, pp. 103-104, 105

V.xii.17. *His pavilion round about Him were dark waters, and thick clouds of the skies* (Ps. 18 : 12).

R. Eliezer said, "The earth drinks only from the waters of the Great Sea."

R. Joshua asked, "But the waters of the Great Sea, are they not salty?"

R. Eliezer replied, "The waters of the sea are made sweet in the clouds, as is said *The clouds . . . distill* (Job 36 : 28). Where are the waters of the sea distilled? In the clouds!"

But R. Joshua maintained, "The earth drinks from the upper waters, as is said *The earth . . . drinketh water of the rain of heaven* (Deut. 11 : 11). The clouds, rising up from earth to heaven, take water as from a gourd's mouth, for is it written *As from a gourd they gather water out of His vapor* (Job. 36 : 27). They distill drops as through a sieve, so that not one drop touches another, as is said, *Distilling waters from the thick clouds* (II Sam. 22 : 12)."

Midrash on Psalms 18 : 16,
trans. W. G. Braude, p. 245

V.xii.18. *All the rivers run into the sea* (Qoh. 1 : 7). From whence does the earth drink?

R. Eliezer and R. Joshua offer answers.

R. Eliezer says, "It drinks from the waters of the ocean, because it is written, *But there went up a mist from the earth, and watered the whole face of the ground* (Gen. 2 : 6)."

R. Joshua said to him, "But are not the waters of the ocean salty?"

He answered, "They are sweetened by the clouds; as it is written, *Which the skies pour down* (Job. 35 : 28). Where are the waters distilled? In the skies."

R. Joshua, on the other hand, says, "The earth drinks from the upper waters, because it is written, *Drinketh water as the rain of heaven cometh down* (Deut. 11 : 11). The clouds raise themselves from earth to heaven and receive the waters as from the mouth of a bottle; as it is written, *Which distil rain from His vapor* (Job 36 : 27). And [the clouds] distil it as through a sieve and one drop does not touch another; as it is written, *Darkness of waters, thick clouds of the skies* (Ps. 18 : 12)."

Another interpretation of *All the rivers run into the sea*: i.e. the ocean; *Yet the sea is not full* refers to the ocean, which is never filled.

Once R. Eliezer and R. Joshua were travelling on the great sea. The ship entered a place where the water did not flow.

R. Eliezer said to R. Joshua, "We have only come here so as to be able to make a test."

They filled a cask with water from that place.

When they arrived at Rome, Hadrian asked them, "What are the waters of the ocean?"

They replied, "It consists of water which absorbs water."

He said to them, "Is it possible that the river should run into it without it becoming full?"

They answered, "It absorbs all the water in the world."

He said to them, "I will not believe you until you prove it to me."

They took the water which they had drawn from the ocean, filled a flask with it and then poured further water into it which was absorbed by the ocean-water.

According to the opinion of R. Joshua [all water] returns there.

Qoh. R.1.6.1, trans. A. Cohen, pp. 19-21

*Comment*: Normally, the rabbis in Rome do not include Eliezer, but Eleazar b. ʿAzariah, and that would seem a more likely reading here as well. But Hadrian is surely the wrong emperor!

III.ii.109.A. TNY': R. Eliezer said, "The dead whom Ezekiel resurrected stood up, uttered song, and [immediately] died. What song did they utter? *The Lord slayeth in righteousness and reviveth in mercy* (I Sam. 2 : 6)."

R. Joshua said, "They sang thus, *The Lord killeth and maketh alive: he bringeth down to the grave, and bringeth up* (I Sam. 2 : 6)."

b. Sanh. 92b, trans. H. Freedman, pp. 618-619

III.ii.110.A. It has been taught: R. Eliezer says, "The world is like an *exedra*, and the north side is not enclosed, and so when the sun reaches the northwest corner, it bends back and returns [to the east] above the firmament."

R. Joshua, however, says, "The world is like a tent [completely enclosed by the firmament], and the north side is enclosed, and when the sun reaches the north-west corner it goes round at the back of the tent [till it reaches the east], as it says, *It goeth toward the south and turneth again toward the north*, etc. (Qoh. 1 : 6). *It goes toward the south*—by day, and *turneth again toward the north*—by night. *It turneth about continually in its course and the wind returneth again to its circuits*: this refers to the eastern and western sides of the heaven, which the sun sometimes traverses and sometimes goes round."

He [R. Joshua] used to say, "We have come round to the view of R. Eliezer, [since we have learned], *Out of the chamber cometh the storm* (Job 37 : 9): this is the south wind; and *from the scatterers cold*: this is the north wind. *By the breath of God ice is given*: (Job 37 : 10): this is the west wind: *and the abundance of waters in the downpouring*: this is the east wind."

b. B.B. 25a-b, trans. M. Simon, p. 126

III.ii.111.A. For it was taught. R. Eliezer says, "The world was created from its center, as it is said, *When the dust cometh unto a mass, and the clods keep fast together* (Job 38 : 38)."

R. Joshua says, "*For He saith to the snow: 'Fall thou on the earth'; likewise to the shower of rain, and to the showers of His mighty rain* (Ps. 50 : 1)."

R. Isaac the Smith said, "The Holy One, blessed be He, cast a stone into the ocean, from which the world then was founded as it is said: *Whereupon were the foundations thereof fastened, or who laid the corner-stone thereof?* (Job 38 : 6)."

But the sages say, "The world was [started] created from Zion as it is said: *A Psalm of Asaph, God, God, the Lord [hath spoken]* (Ps. 50 : 1), whereupon it reads on *Out of Zion, the perfection of the world*

(Ps. 50 : 2), that means from Zion was the beauty of the world perfected."

B. It was taught: R. Eliezer the Great said, "*These are the generations of the heavens and of the earth in the day that the Lord God made earth and heaven* (Gen. 2 : 4). The generations [the creations] of heaven were made from the heaven and the generations of the earth were made from the earth."

But the sages said, "Both were created from Zion, as it is said, *A Psalm of Asaph: God, God, the Lord, hath spoken, and called the earth from the rising of the sun to the going down thereof.* And Scripture further says, *Out of Zion, the perfection of beauty, God hath shined forth*, that means from it the beauty of the world was perfected."

b. Yoma 54b, trans. Leo Jung, pp. 257-8

*Comment*: B drops Joshua and Isaac; the sages' saying is not pertinent to Eliezer's. The original stratum should have had Eliezer and Joshua.

V.vii.7.A. R. Eliezer and R. Joshua differed.

R. Eliezer said, "All that is in heaven was created out of heaven, and all that is on earth was created out of the earth."

He proves this from the following, *Praise ye the Lord* [ye that were created] *from the heavens; Praise ye Him, all His angels... hosts... sun... moon...* etc. (Ps. 148 : 1); *Praise the Lord* [ye that were created] *from the earth, ye sea-monsters... fire and hail... mountains... hills... beasts... cattle* (Ps. 148 : 7).

R. Joshua maintained, "All that is in heaven and on earth was created from nought but heaven."

He proves it from the following, *For He saith to the snow: Be thou on the earth*, etc. (Job 37 : 6). Just as the snow is created out of heaven, though its existence is on the earth; so everything that is in heaven and on earth was created from nought but heaven.

Gen. R. 12 : 11, trans. H. Freedman, p. 97

V.xii.19.A. *All go unto one place; all are of the dust, and all return to dust* (Qoh. 3 : 20). R. Eliezer and R. Joshua [make statements].

R. Eliezer says, "All that the Holy One, blessed be He, created in heaven has its origin in heaven, and all that he created on earth has its origin in the earth. On what is this statement based? *Praise ye the Lord from the heavens, praise Him in the heights. Praise ye Him, all*

*His angels... Praise the Lord from the earth, ye sea-monsters, and all deeps; fire and hail, snow and vapor,* etc. (Ps. 148 : 1)."

R. Joshua says, "All that the Holy One, blessed be He, created in heaven and on earth has its origin in heaven. Although it is written concerning snow, *For He saith to the snow: Be of the earth* (Job 37 : 6), nevertheless its origin is only from heaven, as it is stated, *For as the rain cometh down and the snow from heaven* (Is. 55 : 10)."

Qoh. R. 3 : 18 : 1, trans. A. Cohen, pp. 107f.

III.ii.112. TNY': *The earth is given into the hand of the wicked* (Job 9 : 24). R. Eliezer said, "Job sought to turn the dish upside down."

R. Joshua said to him, "Job was only referring to the Satan."

b. B.B. 16a, trans. M. Simon, p. 79

*Comment*: My colleague, Professor David Pingree, Brown University Department of the History of Mathematics, comments on the foregoing pericopae:

"R. Eliezer consistently attempts to interpret natural phenomena in accordance with the theories of Greek, and especially Aristotelian, science, though he discovers a biblical passage to support these interpretations (cf. the Christian Hexaëmera). He believes that the element out of which the heavenly spheres are constituted, aether, is radically different from the four elements of the sub-lunar sphere (b. Yoma 54b, Gen. R. 12 : 1). One attribute of the celestial objects that distinguishes them from sublunar objects is the eternity of their circular motions about the earth; R. Eliezer insists on the eternity of the motion of the planets (Gen. R. 25 : 2), and that the sun, at night, travels on a circular orbit, compared to an *exedra* or a semicircular bench, in the heavens (b. B.B. 25a-b). In making this latter point he opposes those who believe in a flat earth surrounded by a rectangular tent and in the nocturnal motion of the sun behind the northern tent-wall. R. Eliezer's final scientific statement is that the natural process of the evaporation of sea-water to form clouds, and their subsequent condensation into rain are analogous to the process of distillation (b. Ta. 9b, Gen. R. 13 : 9). One argument in favor of an oceanic origin of rain-water is that, if the oceans were not emptied by continual evaporation, they would soon be filled to overflowing by the inflowing rivers.

"The story of R. Eliezer's and R. Joshua's collecting water from a place in the sea from which all currents and tides were absent and demonstrating to Hadrian that, as more water is poured in, the volume does not increase, is surely spurious, as its intent is to refute the argument that sea-water must evaporate or else the seas would overflow, by a pseudo-experiment proving that seawater 'absorbs' river-water without expanding in volume. The other stories present a consistent Aristotelian outlook; whether that is R. Eliezer's or not cannot be determined. Possible clues to the age of the collection are the analogy of the *exedra* and that of the distillation of sea-water; both *may* point to the first or second century A.D., though further investigation is needed to confirm this. The Hadrian-story does not belong to this original collection, but, in fact, contradicts it."

III.ii.113. TNY': R. Eliezer the Great said, "If the Holy One, blessed be He, wished to enter in judgment with Abraham, Isaac or Jacob, not [even] they could stand before His reproof. As it is said, *Now therefore stand still, that I may plead with you before the Lord concerning all the righteous acts of the Lord, which He did to you and to your fathers* (I Sam. 7 : 12). [It is written] *Such is the generation of them that seek after Him, that seek Thy face, even Jacob, Selah* (Ps. 24 : 6)."

b. Arakh. 17a, trans. Leo Jung, p. 97

III.ii.114.A. How far shall reproof be administered?

Rav said, "Until he [the reprover] be beaten."

Samuel said, "Until he be cursed."

R. Yoḥanan said, "Until he be rebuked."

This is a point at issue between Tannaim.

B. R. Eliezer said, "Until he be beaten."

R. Joshua said, "Until he be cursed.

Ben ʿAzzai said, "Until he be rebuked."

C. Said R. Naḥman b. Isaac, "All the three expounded one Scriptural verse; [It is written], *Then Saul's anger was kindled against Jonathan and he said unto him: Thou son of perverse rebellion, do not I know that thou hast chosen the son of Jesse to thine own shame, and unto the shame of thy mother's nakedness* (I Sam. 20 : 30). And it is written, *And Saul cast his spear at him to smite him* (I Sam. 20 : 33). The one who said [above], Until he be beaten [said so] because it is written: *to smite him*; the other, who said, Until he be cursed [said so] because it is written: *to thine own shame and to the shame of thy mother's nakedness*; the other, who said, Until he be rebuked [said so] because it is written: *Then Saul's anger was kindled.*"

b. Arakh. 16b, trans. Leo Jung, p. 95

*Comment*: It is curious that the Amoraim in A give the same opinions, in the same words, as the Tannaim in B.

III.ii.115.A. TNY': R. Eliezer says, "The *vine* is the world, the *three branches* are [the patriarchs] Abraham, Isaac and Jacob—*And as it was budding its blossoms shot forth* (Gen. 40 : 10). *And the clusters thereof brought forth ripe grapes* (Gen. 40 : 10).—These are the tribes."

B. Thereupon R. Joshua said to him, "Is a man shown [in a dream] what has happened? Surely he is only shown what is to happen! Therefore, I say, The *vine* is the Torah, the *three branches* are Moses, Aaron and Miraim. *And as it was budding its blossoms shot forth*—these are [the members of] the Sanhedrin. *And the clusters thereof brought forth ripe grapes*, are the righteous people of every generation."

C. R. Gamaliel said, "We still stand in need of the Modiite, for he explains the verse as referring to one place."

For R. Eleazar the Modiite says, "The *vine* is Jerusalem, the *three branches* are the Temple, the King and the High priest, *As it was budding its blossoms shot forth*—these are the young priests; *and the clusters thereof brought forth ripe grapes*—these are the drink-offering."

D. R. Joshua b. Levi interprets it in regard to the gifts [bestowed by God upon Israel].

For R. Joshua b. Levi said, "The *vine* is the Torah, the *three branches* are the well, the pillar of smoke, and the manna; *and as it was budding its blossoms shot forth*, these are the first fruits; *and the clusters thereof brought forth ripe grapes*, these are the drink-offerings."

b. Hul. 92a, trans. Eli Cashdan, p. 515

*Comment*: Eliezer interprets the Scripture in terms of the patriarchs. Joshua applies it to Moses, that is, what is about to happen. That completes the matter. Then, in C, Gamaliel-Eleazar apply it to the Temple. And the pericope continues with Joshua b. Levi and Jeremiah b. Abba (not cited). So it would seem to have been supplemented.

IV.ii.30.A. Rabban Yoḥanan b. Zakkai said to his disciples, "My sons, what is the meaning of the verse, *Righteousness exalteth a nation, but the kindness of the peoples is sin* (Prov. 14 : 34)."

B. R. Eliezer answered and said, "*Righteousness exalteth a nation*: this refers to Israel, of whom it is written, *Who is like thy people Israel one nation in the earth*? (II Sam. 7 : 23). But the kindness of the peoples is sin: all the charity and kindness done by the heathen are counted to them as sin, because they only do it to magnify themselves, as it says, *That they may offer sacrifices of sweet savor unto the God of heaven, and pray for the life of the king and of his sons* (Ezra 6 : 10)."

C. R. Joshua answered and said, "*Righteousness exalteth a nation*: this refers to Israel, of whom it is written, *Who is like thy people*

*Israel, one nation in the earth? The kindness of peoples is sin*: all the charity and kindness that the heathen do are counted sin to them, because they only do it in order that their dominion may be prolonged, as it says, *Wherefore O king, let my counsel be acceptable to thee, and break off thy sins by righteousness, and thy iniquities by showing mercy to the poor, if there may be a lengthening of thy tranquillity* (Dan. 4 : 27)."

D. Rabban Gamaliel answered saying, "*Righteousness exalteth a nation*: this refers to Israel of whom it is written, *Who is like thy people Israel*, etc. *And the kindness of the peoples is sin*: all the charity and kindness that the heathen do are counted as sin to them, because they only do it to display haughtiness, and whoever displays haughtiness is cast into Gehinnom, as it says, *The proud and haughty man, scorner in his name, he worketh in the wrath* ['ebrah] *of pride* (Prov. 21 : 24), and wrath connotes Gehinnom, as it is written, *A day of wrath is that day* (Zeph. 1 : 15)."

E. Said Rabban Gamaliel, "We have still to hear the opinion of the Modiite."

R. Eliezer the Modiite says, "*Righteousness exalteth a nation*: this refers to Israel, of whom it is written, *Who is like thy people Israel, one nation in the earth. The kindness of the peoples is sin*: all the charity and kindness of the heathen are counted to them as sin, since they do it only to reproach us, as it says, *The Lord hath brought it and done according as he spake, because he has sinned against the Lord and has not obeyed his voice, therefore this thing is come upon you* (Jer. 40 : 3)."

F. R. Neḥuniah b. HaQanah answered saying, "Righteousness exalteth a nation, and there is kindness for Israel and a sin-offering for the peoples."

Said R. Yoḥanan b. Zakkai to his disciples, "The answer of R. Nehuniah b. HaQanah is superior to my answer and to yours, because he assigns charity and kindness to Israel and sin to the heathen."

G. This seems to show that he also gave an answer: what was it? As it has been taught: R. Yoḥanan b. Zakkai said to them, "Just as the sin-offering makes atonement for Israel, so charity makes atonement for the heathen."

b. B.B. 10b, trans. M. Simon, pp. 50-51

V.ix.5. *Righteousness will exalt a nation, and mercy is a sin for the nations* (Prov. 14 : 34).

A. R. Liezer, and R. Joshua, and the rabbis.

B. R. Liezer says, "*Righteousness exalts a nation*—this is Israel. *And the mercy is a sin to the nations*—the mercies are sins for the nations, for they take pride in them."

C. R. Joshua says, "*Righteousness exalts a people*—this is Israel. *And mercy is a sin for the nations*—it is a pleasure for the nations of the world when Israel sins, for they [then] go and subjugate them."

D. And Rabban Gamaliel says, "*Righteousness exalts a nation*—this is Israel. *And mercy is a sin for the nations*—the mercy which the nations of the world do is a sin for them, for so says Daniel to Nebuchadnezzar, *And your sin with righteousness is wiped away* (Dan. 4 : 24)."

E. R. Leazar b. ʿArakh says, "*Righteousness exalts a nation and mercy*—this is Israel. But *sins* belong to the nations of the world."

F. Rabban Yoḥanan b. Zakkai said, "I prefer the words of R. Leazar b. ʿArakh to your words, for he assigns righteousness and mercy to Israel, and sins to the nations of the world."

Pesiqta de R. Kahana, ed. Mandelbaum,
p. 20, ls. 6-11, p. 21, ls. 1-3

*Comment*: See *Life*, pp. 183-4, 246-249, and *Development*, p. 103, 240.

IV.ii.31.A. All the names mentioned in connection with Naboth (I Kings 21 : 10, 13) are sacred; in connection with Micah (Judges 17-18) they are secular.

R. Eliezer said, "In connection with Naboth [all are] sacred, in connection with Micah, some are secular, and some sacred: [the name beginning] *alef lamed* is secular (Judges 17 : 50); *yod he* (Judges 17 : 2 etc.) is sacred; except this which is *alef lamed* and is sacred: *all the time that the house of God was in Shiloh* (Judges 18 : 31).

B. All the names mentioned in connection with Gibeah of Benjamin (Judges 20 : 18-28)—

R. Eliezer said, "They are secular."

R. Joshua said, "They are sacred."

R. Eliezer said to him, "Does He then promise, and not fulfill?"

R. Joshua replied to him, "What He promised, He fulfilled; but they did not inquire whether [the result would be] victory or defeat; later when they did inquire [of the Urim and Tummim], they approved their action, as it is said, *And Phineas, the son of Eleazar, the son of Aaron, stood before it in those days—saying, 'Shall I yet again go out to battle against the children of Benjamin my brother, or shall I cease?'* [*And the Lord said, 'Go up; for tomorrow I will deliver them into thy hand.'*] (Judges 20 : 28)."

b. Shav. 35b, trans. A. E. Silverstone, p. 206

*Comment*: I take it that A is our Eliezer because of B.

V.iii.2. With regard to the benediction of mourners on the Sabbath, when mourning is suspended, it is said after the statutory service in the presence of the worshippers over a cup of wine.

For R. Eliezer b. Hyrcanus said, "Solomon saw the greatness of those who bestow lovingkindness, and built two gates for Israel, one for bridegrooms and the other for mourners and excommunicated persons. On the Sabbath the inhabitants of Jerusalem used to congregate, ascend the Temple Mount, and take their seats between these two gates to show kindness to these persons. Since the Temple was destroyed, it was enacted that bridegrooms and mourners should go to the Synagogue, so that kindness could be shown to them"

Soferim 42b, trans. Israel W. Slotki, p. 309

V.vii.8. R. Levi said, "The waters said to each other, 'Let us go and obey the fiat of the Holy One, blessed be He'; thus it is written, *The floods have lifted up their voice*, etc. (Psalms 93 : 3). 'But whither shall we go,' asked they? '*Let the floods take up* (*dokyam*),' asked they? '*Let the floods take up* (*dokyam*),' replied He.

R. Levi said, "[*Dokyam*] means, *derek yam* (to the way of the sea)."

R. Abba b. Kahana interpreted it, "To such and such a place (*dok*), to such and such a corner."

R. Huna explained, "To this sea (*ha-dak yama*)."

R. Joshua b. Ḥananiah said, "To the receptacle (*diksa*) of the sea."

R. Eliezer said, "The sea absorbed them, as you read, *Hast thou entered into the springs of the sea* (Job 38 : 16)? Which means, into the waters absorbed by the sea."

Gen. R. 5 : 3, trans. H. Freedman,
pp. 35-6 (see b. Ta. 9b, above, p. 482)

*Comment*: It is difficult to explain the juxtaposition of Joshua and Eliezer with the later Amoraim.

V.vii.9. R. Yoḥanan said, "The planets did not function the entire twelve months [of the flood]."

Said R. Jonathan to him, "They did function, but their mark was imperceptible."

R. Liezer said, "*They shall not cease* (Gen. 8 : 22) implies that they never ceased."

R. Joshua deduced, "*They shall not cease*: hence it followed that they had ceased."

Gen. R. 25 : 2, trans. H. Freedman, p. 207 =
Gen. R. 33 : 3, trans. p. 263 =
Gen. R. 34 : 11, trans. H. Freedman, p. 277

*Comment*: Yohanan is the same as Joshua, Jonathan is similar to Eliezer.

V.vii.10. *In the morning sow thy seed, and in the evening withhold not thy hand* (Qoh. 1 : 6). R. Eliezer and R. Joshua discussed this.

R. Eliezer said, "If you have sown in the early season, sow in the late season, for you do not know which will be successful, whether the early sowing or the late sowing, as Scripture continues, *For thou knowest not which shall prosper, whether this or that, or whether they both shall be alike good.*"

R. Joshua said, "If a poor man comes to you in the morning, relieve him; if in the evening, relieve him too, because you do not know which of them the Holy One, blessed be He, has allotted to you, *Whether this or that or whether they both shall be alike good.*"

Gen. R. 61 : 3, trans. H. Freedman, pp. 541-542

V.xii.20. *In the morning sow thy seed* (Qoh. 1 : 5). R. Eliezer and R. Joshua comment.

R. Eliezer says, "If you have sown in the early season, sow also in the late season, because you do not know which will succeed for you, whether the early or late sowing, *For thou knowest not which shall prosper, whether this or that.*"

R. Joshua says, "If you are married in your youth and your wife died, marry again in your old age. If you had children in your youth, have them also in your old age, as it is said, *In the morning sow thy seed, and in the evening withhold not thy hand; for you knowest not which shall prosper, whether this or that.*"

Qoh. R. 11 : 5.1, trans. A. Cohen, p. 294

*Comment*: Eliezer gives the plain meaning. In Gen. R. Joshua alludes to the poor, in Qoh. R. to marriage.

V.vii.11.A. *Have not thou the excellency* (Gen. 49 : 3).

R. Eliezer and R. Joshua both interpreted it, "So hast thou not left aught for thyself."

R. Eleazar of Modiim explained it, "Nought of thy sin shall be left to thee."

B. *Because thou wentest up.* R. Eliezer and R. Joshua maintain that *Because thou wentest up* is meant literally.

R. Eleazar of Modiim interpreted it, "*Because thou wentest up*: where? In the incident of the mandrakes [Gen. 30 : 14]."

C. *Then defiledst thou it.* R. Eliezer and R. Joshua both maintain that *Then defiledst thou it* is meant literally.

R. Leazar of Modiim said, "This..."

D. *He went up.* R. Eliezer and R. Joshua both explain, "It [my couch] went up through thy sin."

R. Eleazar of Modiim explained it, "It [my couch] became exalted through thy gift."

Gen. R. 98 : 4, trans. H. Freedman, pp. 949-951

V.viii.1.A. *If anyone shall sin through error, in any of the things which the Lord hath commanded not to be done,* etc. (Lev. 4 : 2).

Thus Scripture says, *And moreover I saw under the sun, in the place of justice, that wickedness was there; and in the place of righteousness, that wickedness was there* (Qoh. 3 : 16).

R. Eliezer said, "The place where the Great Sanhedrin had sat and decided the lawsuits of Israel, *There was the wickedness,* there *All the princes of the king of Babylon came in and sat in the middle gate* (Jer. 39 : 3)., i.e. in the place where they used to decide the law. And the Holy Spirit exclaims, saying, *In the place of righteousness, there was wickedness committed*: i.e. in the place of which it is written, *Righteousness lodged in her* (Is. 1 : 21), *But now murderers,* i.e. they perpetrate murders; there they slew Zechariah and Uriah."

B. R. Joshua said, "*In the place of justice there was the condemnation*: In the place where the divine Attribute of Justice displayed itself in the episode of the Golden Calf, of which it is said, *Go to and fro, from gate to gate* (Ex. 32 : 27), *There was punishment executed,* there *The Lord smote the people, because they had made the calf.* And the Holy Spirit exclaims, saying, *In the place of righteousness, there was the wickedness,* the place where I attributed to them righteousness, and called them god-like, even as it is said, *I said: Ye are godlike beings, and all of you children of the Most High* (Ps. 82 : 6), *There was wickedness*: there they acted wickedly by making the Golden Calf, and prostrating themselves to it."

Lev. R. 4 : 1, trans. J. Israelstam, pp. 47-8

V.viii.2.A. *If a woman produce offspring* (Lev. 12 : 2). This is alluded to in what is written, *Who shut up the sea with doors, when it broke forth, and issued out of the womb* (Job 38 : 8)?

R. Eliezer and R. Joshua and R. ʿAqiba gave explanations.

R. Eliezer said, "Just as a house has doors, so a woman, too, has doors, as it is written, *Because it shut not up the doors of my* [mother's] *womb* (Job 3 : 10)."

R. Joshua said, "Just as for a house there are keys (*mafteaḥ*), so, likewise, for a woman, as it is written, *And God hearkened to her, and opened (pataḥ) her womb* (Gen. 30 : 22)."

R. ʿAqiba said, "Just as a house has hinges (*ṣirim*), even so has a woman birthpangs (*ṣirim*), as it is written, *She knelt and gave birth, for her pains (ṣirim) came suddenly upon her* (I Sam. 4 : 19). *When it broke forth, and issued out of the womb*, by raising itself to issue forth."

Lev. R. 14 : 4, trans. J. Israelstam, p. 183

V.viii.3. *His locks are as curls* (Song 5 : 11) alludes to the ruled lines [to guide the writing in Torah-scrolls]; *His locks (qewuṣṣah) are . . . as black (shaḥor) as ravens (ʿoreb)* alludes to the pointed stroke (*koṣah*) of the letters [of the Hebrew alphabet].

R. Eliezer and R. Joshua said, "*Curls* (*taltalim*)," (as if it were written, *tillé tillim*, i.e. piles upon piles [of legal teachings]).

With whom are these preserved? With such as occupy themselves with them early at dawn (*shaḥar*) and late in the evening (*ʿerev*)."

Lev. R. 19 : 1, trans. J. Israelstam, p. 234-5

V.ix.6. *And Reuben returned to the pit*, etc. (Gen. 37 : 29).

A. R. Liezer and R. Joshua and the Rabbis.

B. R. Liezer says, "In his sack-cloth and fasting he was occupied on account of that incident which happened [Tamar], and he did not have leisure (NPNH). When he had leisure from his sack cloth and ashes, he came and looked into the pit, *And lo, Joseph was not in the pit*."

C. R. Joshua says, "The burden of the household was cast upon him, and he did not have leisure. When he had leisure from the burden of the household and came and looked into the pit, *Lo, Joseph was not in the pit*."

D. And rabbis say, "The Holy One, blessed be He, said to him, 'You sought to restore the beloved son to his father. By your life, the son of your son will restore Israel to their father in heaven, and who is this? This is Hosea.' "

Pesiqta deR. Kahana, ed. Mandelbaum,
p. 356, ls. 6-11, p. 357, ls. 1-2 (= Gen. R. 84 : 19)

V.ix.7. As to the interpretation of the concluding words of the verse, namely, *Even the days that were ordained*, etc. (Ps. 139 : 16).

R. Eliezer and R. Joshua differed.

R. Eliezer read *And not one of them failed to come as God had ordained it*, each on its particular day, as, for example, the day of Sisera, of Sennacherib.

B. R. Joshua read *And yet one of the days was already His*: of the three hundred sixty-five days in the solar year, the Only One of the universe already had designated one of them as His very own.

And what day was that? R. Levi and R. Isaac differed.

R. Levi said that it was the Day of Atonement: *Is such the fast that I have chosen, the day for a man to afflict his soul?* (Is. 58 : 5).

R. Isaac said, however, that it was the Sabbath day.

Pesiqta Rabbati, 23 : 1, trans. W. G. Braude, p. 473

V.x.5.A. *In thy book were written every one of them, the days that were formed for me, when as yet there was none of them* (Ps. 139 : 16).

And what is the meaning of *Not one among them* (Lʾ ʾḤD BHM)?

R. Eliezer and R. Joshua.

B. R. Eliezer says, "The days were created and not one among them [failed.]

"The Holy One blessed be He said, 'This day I shall redeem my sons from Egypt; this day I shall divide the sea and cast down their enemies; this day I shall give the Torah; and not one day was altered or changed.' That is what Scripture says, *And not one among them*."

C. R. Joshua says, "And to him (LW) [belongs] one among them. "From the days that the Holy One created, He chose for Himself one of them. And which is this? It is the Day of Atonement."

Midrash Tanḥuma Bereshit 28, ed. Buber, I, p. 12

*Comment*: Eliezer's saying is similar to his lemma in Pes. R., but the examples are different. In C, Joshua designates the Day of Atonement—Levi's opinion in Pes. R.!

V.xi.10.A. *And if the woman be not defiled* (Num. 5 : 28) in the past, *But be clean* (Num. 5 : 28) in the future, *Then she shall be cleared* (Num. 5 : 28) immediately from the curses and the oath, *And shall conceive seed.*

B. R. Eliezer observed, "The suffering was sufficiently great to entitle her to be given children as some recompense, and so if she was barren, she is remembered with a child."

C. R. Joshua objected, "If that be the case, all the barren women will go and act in a suspicious manner in order that they may be remembered, while the woman who remains at home will be the loser! In fact, however, what is meant by *She shall be cleared, and shall conceive seed* is that if she has hitherto suffered in childbirth she will henceforth be delivered with ease; if she gave birth to females she will now give birth to males; if she had dark children she will now have fair; if undersized ones she will have well-grown ones; if she had a child once in two years she will now have one every year; if she gave birth to one, she will now give birth two."

Num. R. 9 : 25, trans. J. J. Slotki, p. 292

V.xi.11. *And the Lord put a word in Balaam's mouth* (Num. 23 : 5).

R. Eliezer says, "An angel was speaking."

R. Joshua says, "It was the Holy One, blessed be He."

Num. R. 20 : 18, trans. J. J. Slotki, pp. 806-807

V.xii.21. *Now Boaz went up to the gate, and sat him down there; and, behold, the near kinsman of whom Boaz spoke came by* (Ruth 4 : 1). R. Berekiah said, "Thus did these great men, R. Eliezer and R. Joshua, expound:

"R. Eliezer said, 'Boaz played his part, and Ruth played hers, and Naomi played hers, whereupon the Holy One, blessed be He, said, 'I too must play Mine.' And He said: Ho, Peloni Almoni! *Turn aside, sit down here* (Ruth 4 : 1).'

"R. Joshua said, 'His name was Peloni Almoni.' "

Ruth R. 7 : 7, trans. L. Rabinowitz, p. 85

V.xii.22. Commenting on *terrible as troops with banners* (Song 6 : 10), R. Eliezer and R. Joshua differed.

R. Eliezer said, "[To the nations] Israel resembled the ministering angels who stand arrayed like troops with banners."

R. Joshua said, "Israel looked as when going out of Egypt they stood drawn up in their places like troops under banners."

Midrash on Psalms 22 : 12, trans. W. G. Braude, p. 308

V.xii.23. In a different exposition the verse is read, *Make us glad according to the days of the Messiah* (Cf. Ps. 90 : 15).

And how long is the "day" of the Messiah?

R. Eliezer said, "A thousand years, as it is said, *For a thousand years in Thy sight are but as yesterday when it is past* (Ps. 90 : 4)."

R. Joshua said, "Two thousand years, for the plural *days* in *According to the days wherein Thou hast afflicted us* implies two days, one day of the Holy One, blessed be He, being a thousand years, as is said, *For a thousand years in Thy sight are but as yesterday when it is past.*"

Midrash on Psalms 90 : 4, trans. Braude, p. 97

## ADDENDUM

My student, William Scott Green, has analyzed M. Ter. 4 : 11 in a way different from the explanation given above, pp. 49-53. His interpretation follows.

A. A *se'ah* of Heave-offering which fell into the mouth of a storage-bin (MGWRH) and stayed on the top (WQP'H)—

B. R. Eliezer says, "If there are one hundred *se'ahs* in the top layer [of the bin] (BQPWY), it will neutralize in one hundred and one."

C. And R. Joshua says, "It will not neutralize."

D. A *se'ah* of Heave-offering which fell into the mouth of a storage-bin: he should skim it off (YQP'NH).

E. And if so, why did they say, "Heave-offering is neutralized in one hundred and one?"

F. If it is not known if they are mixed up or where it fell.

M. Ter. 4 : 11 (y. Ter. 4 : 8)

*Comment*: A *se'ah* of Heave-offering fell into a storage-bin filled with unconsecrated produce and remained on the top. So this case differs from the previous one in that here there can be no doubt that the top and bottom layers of the bin do *not* come into contact. This is because the entire *se'ah* of Heave-offering is visible (see Lieberman, *Tosefta Kifshuṭah*, *Seder Zera'im* I, p. 370). Thus Eliezer rules only with respect to the top layer of the produce. If it contained one hundred *se'ahs*, then the *se'ah* of Heave-offering, which is the hundred and first, is neutralized, as per his ruling in 4 : 7 above. Joshua says that it is not neutralized. Part D provides the justification for his ruling. Heave-offering which fell into the mouth of a storage-bin should be removed, and therefore it is not neutralized. The question of E is therefore directed at Eliezer (and/or the law of M. 'Orlah 2 : 1). Since the Heave-offering should be removed, why say it is neutralized in one hundred and one? F, which follows the pattern of 'Aqiba's statement in C of 4 : 8 and thus may be the product of 'Aqiban tradents, explains that Eliezer's rule applies only when the fallen Heave-offering cannot be identified. So it upholds Joshua's principle. When we know where the Heave-offering has fallen, it will not neutralize; when we do not know, it will.

The above five pericopae may be regarded as one large composite designed to present Eliezer's and Joshua's opinions on two issues of the general topic of mixing Heave-offering with unconsecrated produce. The first is the size of the mixture which will neutralize the Heave-offering. Eliezer says one hundred and one; Joshua one hundred and more. The second is the factors which disqualify the unconsecrated produce from neutralizing the Heave-offering. Eliezer says the physical characteristics of the produce disqualify, and Joshua says the location of the Heave-offering in the unconsecrated produce disqualifies. Each is consistent throughout. But, as Neusner has already noted (pp. 49ff.) ʿAqiba's "compromise" in C of M. Ter. 4 : 8 and now G of M. Ter. 4 : 11 make the entire controversy unnecessary and in fact, impossible.

In translating WQPʾH in A of 4 : 11 I have followed Albeck's reading and Yalon's pointing and read it as a *qal* perfect, third person feminine singular. Likewise, I have read QPWY of B as a *qal* past participle. The pointing in Kaufmann and Parma MSS. treat both words likewise. However, most commentators seem to regard WQPʾH as a *piʿel* perfect third person masculine singular with a feminine singular objective suffix. Thus they read, "A *seʾah* of Heave-offering which fell into the mouth of a storage bin and *he skimmed it off*" in place of "and it stayed on the top." In either rendering, "it" can only have the fallen *seʾah* of Heave-offering as its antecedent. A rendering of WQPʾH as a *piʿel* is, however, problematic, for it makes Eliezer's ruling in B virtually meaningless. If the *seʾah* of Heave-offering has already been removed, how can it possibly be combined with the top layer?

If one follows a traditional interpretation and reads WQPʾH as "and he skimmed it off," then to make sense of the pericope the last half of A and the first half of B must be eliminated, yielding the following:

> A *seʾah* of Heave-offering which fell into the mouth
> of a storage-bin:
> Eliezer: It is neutralized [in a hundred and one parts]
> Joshua: It is not neutralized.

This is simply a repeat of the M. Ter. 4 : 7 controversy since the specific example is irrelevant to the disagreement. By following Albeck's suggestion here, no alteration of the passage is required to explain it.